SIXTH EDITION

CANADIAN CRIMINOLOGY TODAY

THEORIES AND APPLICATIONS

FRANK SCHMALLEGER

Distinguished Professor Emeritus
The University of North Carolina at Pembroke

REBECCA VOLK

Algonquin College

Pearson

Editorial Director: Claudine O'Donnell
Acquisitions Editor: Keriann McGoogan
Marketing Manager: Euan White
Program Manager: Madhu Ranadive
Project Manager: Jessica Mifsud
Manager of Content Development: Suzanne Schaan
Developmental Editor: Joanne Sutherland
Permissions Project Manager: Kathryn O'Handley

Photo Permissions Research: iEnergizer Aptara®, Ltd.
Text Permissions Research: iEnergizer Aptara®, Ltd.
Interior Designer: iEnergizer Aptara®, Ltd.
Cover Designer: Anthony Leung
Cover Image: Juergen Faelchle/Shutterstock
Vice-President, Cross Media and Publishing Services:
 Gary Bennett

Pearson Canada Inc., 26 Prince Andrew Place, Don Mills, Ontario M3C 2T8.

ISBN 13: 978-0-13-430446-5

2 2019

Library and Archives Canada Cataloguing in Publication

Schmalleger, Frank, author
 Canadian criminology today: theories and applications/Frank Schmalleger
 (Distinguished Professor Emeritus, The University of North Carolina at Pembroke),
 Rebecca Volk (Algonquin College).—Sixth edition.

Includes bibliographical references and index.
ISBN 978-0-13-430446-5 (softcover)

 1. Criminology—Textbooks. 2. Criminology—Canada—Textbooks.
3. Textbooks. I. Volk, Rebecca, author II. Title.

HV6025.S34 2017   364   C2017-901135-9

NEW AND UPDATED CONTENT IN THE SIXTH EDITION

- expanded discussion of the use of technology in the fight against crime
- expanded discussion of crimes against the public order to include new laws addressing terrorism
- expanded examination of victims of crime to include theories of victimization
- updated analysis of various legislation, including the Canadian *Victims Bill of Rights*, the *Anti-Terrorism Act*, and the *Safe Streets and Communities Act*
- updated chapters examining biological and psychological explanations of criminal behaviour to reflect advances in this focus of criminology
- updated case studies and *Who's Responsible—The Individual or Society?* stories

INSTRUCTOR SUPPLEMENTS

These instructor supplements are available for download from a password-protected section of Pearson Canada's online catalogue (www.pearsoncanada.ca/highered). Navigate to your book's catalogue page to view a list of available supplements. Speak to your local Pearson sales representative for details and access.

Instructor's Resource Manual. For each chapter of the text, this manual provides learning objectives, a brief chapter outline, and detailed lecture outlines with teaching tips.

The Test Item File is a comprehensive test bank featuring multiple-choice, true–false, and essay questions with references to text page numbers, level of difficulty, and skill level.

PowerPoint Presentations. This instructor resource contains key points to accompany each chapter in the text.

ACKNOWLEDGMENTS

The sixth edition of *Canadian Criminology Today: Theories and Applications* would not have been possible without the support from the team at Pearson Canada. It has been a pleasure to work with Carolin Sweig, Madhu Ranadive, and Joanne Sutherland once again. My sincere gratitude to all—Joanne for her patient guidance and sage advice, and to Carolin and Madhu for their vision and leadership. Thanks also to Jessica Mifsud, Sadika Rehman, and Melissa Churchill (with whom I share an unexpected connection), whose editorial talents and feedback have ensured that this edition is accessible and easy to read.

Reviews and insights from colleagues have helped to make this book relevant and up-to-date. Special recognition and thanks are due to colleagues Oliver Stoetzer of Fanshawe College and Lisa Roots of Algonquin College for their ongoing support. Thanks also to Cindy Gervais of Fleming College her feedback.

My strength and resolve come from Martin, Monica, and Aaron—you continue to be my guides. In memoriam Gail Allan, whose wisdom, friendship, and wit I miss very much.

The future of criminology lies in the minds and hearts of those students in whom the passion for the discipline has been ignited. I salute them and encourage them to take on the challenges presented by the realities of crime and criminality in our ever-changing world, always with the goal of bettering the lives of all those affected.

Rebecca Volk

About the Authors

Frank Schmalleger, Ph.D., is professor emeritus at the University of North Carolina at Pembroke, where he also was recognized as Distinguished Professor. Dr. Schmalleger holds degrees from the University of Notre Dame and Ohio State University; he earned both a master's (1970) and a doctorate (1974) in sociology, with a special emphasis in criminology, from Ohio State University. From 1976 to 1994, he taught criminology and criminal justice courses at the University of North Carolina at Pembroke, and for the last 16 of those years, he chaired the university's Department of Sociology, Social Work, and Criminal Justice. As an adjunct professor with Webster University in St. Louis, Missouri, Schmalleger helped develop the university's graduate program in security administration and loss prevention and taught courses in that curriculum for more than a decade. Schmalleger has also taught in the New School for Social Research's online graduate program, helping build the world's first electronic classrooms in support of distance learning through computer telecommunications.

Schmalleger is the author of numerous articles as well as many books: *Criminal Justice Today: An Introductory Text for the 21st Century* (Pearson, 2016), now in its 14th edition; *Juvenile Delinquency*, 9th edition (with Clemmens Bartollas; Pearson, 2014); *Criminal Justice: A Brief Introduction*, 11th edition (Pearson, 2016); *Criminal Law Today*, 6th edition (Pearson, 2016); *Corrections in the Twenty-First Century* (with John Smykla; McGraw-Hill, 2015); *Crime and the Justice System in America: An Encyclopedia* (Greenwood Publishing Group, 1997); *Trial of the Century: People of the State of California vs. Orenthal James Simpson* (Prentice Hall, 1996); *Career Paths: A Guide to Jobs in Federal Law Enforcement* (Regents/Prentice Hall, 1994); *Computers in Criminal Justice* (Wyndham Hall Press, 1991); *Criminal Justice Ethics* (Greenwood Press, 1991); *Finding Criminal Justice in the Library* (Wyndham Hall Press, 1991); *Ethics in Criminal Justice* (Wyndham Hall Press, 1990); *A History of Corrections* (Foundations Press of Notre Dame, 1983); and *The Social Basis of Criminal Justice* (University Press of America, 1981). He is also the founding editor of the journal *Criminal Justice Studies* (formerly *The Justice Professional*).

Schmalleger's philosophy of both teaching and writing can be summed up in these words: "In order to communicate knowledge we must first catch, then hold, a person's interest—be it student, colleague, or policy maker. Our writing, our speaking, and our teaching must be relevant to the problems facing people today, and they must—in some way—help solve those problems."

Rebecca Volk currently oversees the Centre for Organizational Learning at Algonquin College in Ottawa, Ontario, after many years as a coordinator and professor in the Police Foundations Program at the college. She holds a bachelor's degree in political science from Queen's University in Kingston, Ontario, and an applied master's degree in criminology from the University of Ottawa. She is also co-author of *Police Ethics: A Matter of Character*.

Volk's professional experience has included involvement with a variety of offender aftercare and advocacy agencies, federal and provincial correctional institutions and residential centres, legal aid services, and various police agencies. She serves on the boards of several organizations devoted to promoting social justice for the most vulnerable among us.

Chapter 1
What Is Criminology?

AF archive/Alamy Stock Photo

Rather than attributing crime and all that is evil to a relatively small group of people, I am saying that crime and socially harmful behaviour is widely (although not evenly) dispersed in society.

—*Thomas Gabor*[1]

LEARNING OBJECTIVES

After reading this chapter, you should be able to

1.1 Understand what crime is and how it is defined in this text.

1.2 Recognize the difference between criminal and deviant acts and the complexity of this distinction.

1.3 Discuss who decides what should be criminal and how such decisions are made.

1.4 Define what criminology is and the role of theoretical criminology.

1.5 Explain what criminologists do.

1.6 Appreciate the role of research and experimentation in theory building in criminology.

1.7 Explain how social policy in the area of crime control is determined.

1.8 Discuss the theme of this text and explain the distinction between the social problems and social responsibility perspectives of crime causation.

1.9 Understand what it means to say that "criminal activity is diversely created and variously interpreted."

1.10 Discuss the discipline that has contributed the most to the theoretical understandings of crime causation over the past century.

INTRODUCTION

According to social commentators, people are simultaneously attracted to and repulsed by crime—especially gruesome crimes involving extreme personal violence. The popularity of today's TV crime shows, crime movies, true-crime books and magazines, and websites devoted exclusively to the coverage of crime supports that observation. The hit series *Person of Interest* was recognized as one of the most popular scripted TV shows in 2016 and was nominated as the "Favorite TV Crime Drama" in the People's Choice Awards that year. Earlier, *CSI: Miami*, which ran for 10 seasons before going off the air in 2012, garnered 50 million regular viewers in more than 55 countries. By its eighth season it had become the most popular television show in the world.[2] The popularity of prime-time television crime shows is not limited to *Person of Interest* or *CSI*. Other widely followed series include the Canadian police shows *Rookie Blue*, *Murdock Mysteries*, and *Flashpoint* and the popular American hits *Criminal Minds*, *The Wire*, *Cold Case*, and *Law and Order*—along with the *Law and Order* spin-offs, *Law and Order: Criminal Intent* and *Law and Order: Special Victims Unit*—and the Scandinavian series *The Bridge*. Documentary miniseries such as *Making a Murderer* and *OJ: Made in America* have also attracted millions of viewers. Social commentators note that the plethora of crime shows bombarding the airwaves today reveals a penchant among North American TV viewers for crime-related entertainment and a fascination with criminal motivation and detective work.

A poster for the movie *Training Day*. The public's interest in crime-related entertainment and fascination with criminal motivation and detective work has given birth to many movies, TV dramas, and documentaries. What is crime? What definition of crime does this text use? How might crimes vary between jurisdictions?

Everett Collection, Inc./Alamy Stock Photo

discrimination, and the breakdown of traditional social institutions. On the other, it contrasts the social problems approach with a social responsibility perspective, which claims that individuals are fundamentally responsible for their own behaviour and maintains that they choose crime over other, more law-abiding courses of action. The thematic contrast is an important one, for it provides students with a useful framework for integrating the large amount of material contained within the field of criminology. Contrasting the two perspectives, as this book does, provides fertile ground for discussion and debate, allowing students to better understand the central issues defining contemporary criminology and to reach their own conclusions about the value of criminology theory.

AN APPLIED FOCUS

Canadian Criminology Today meets the needs of students preparing for careers in the Canadian criminal justice system. Its applied focus on the explanations of crime and deviance and their application to real-life examples of criminal behaviour reflects the learning outcomes of introductory criminology courses. The text addresses the latest social issues and discusses innovative criminological perspectives in an interesting and accessible manner; it makes use of current events, news briefs, images, charts, and graphs. Study tools, such as learning objectives, margin definitions, and end-of-chapter review and multiple-choice questions, serve to reinforce student learning.

The goal is that today's students will find *Canadian Criminology Today* relevant, interesting, informative, and useful. It is designed to assist them in understanding the reasons and motivations behind criminal and deviant behaviour, to allow them to draw their own conclusions about the most effective ways to address such behaviour, and, ultimately, to prepare them for their future careers within the criminal justice system. After all, only by understanding the reality of crime and criminal behaviour can we ever hope to come close to solving and preventing it.

FEATURES IN THE SIXTH EDITION

Learning features in the sixth edition of *Canadian Criminology Today* build on those found in the fifth edition. They include the following:

- Numbered *Learning Objectives* align with each of the major sections within the chapter.
- Current crime stories opening each chapter pique interest and alert students to key topics.
- Updated *Crime in the News* boxes provide students with reality-based studies.
- Updated *Who's Responsible—The Individual or Society?* boxes provide case studies and critical-thinking questions to help students focus on the book's overall theme of social problems versus social responsibility.
- *Social Structure Theories Applied* graphic features appear at the end of Chapters 5 to 10, putting complex theories into context for students. These features present questions about the chapter-opening case study, encouraging students to apply each of the theories presented in the chapter.
- An increased use of visuals in the form of additional graphics, boxed information, and photos enhance reader focus and support comprehension.
- Margin definitions provide students with immediate comprehension and application of key terms.
- The end-of-chapter *Summary of Learning Objectives* is numbered, and each point relates directly to start-of-chapter learning objectives in order to help students focus on the important material covered in each section.
- End-of-chapter *Multiple-Choice Questions* allow students another opportunity to test their understanding of chapter material and reinforce their learning.

Preface

Almost half a century ago, the noted criminologist Austin Turk began the preface to his book *Criminality and Legal Order* with these words:

> Embarrassment provided much of the initial push that led to the writing of this book. I was embarrassed at my lack of good answers when confronted by students who wondered, somewhat irreverently, why criminology is "such a confused mish-mash." . . . Some of these students were especially bothered by the "unreality" of criminological studies, by which they meant the lack of sustained attention to connections between the theories and statistics about crime and what they heard every day about relations among social conflicts, political manoeuvers, and law violation and enforcement.[*]

Much has changed since Turk's time, yet much remains the same. Crime is still with us in the 21st century and is becoming more complex and difficult to understand. Issues of national security and how to ensure it have left pundits questioning just how much freedom people should be willing to sacrifice to enhance security. In addition to the realities of everyday conventional crime, we are now faced with transnational and international activities. Computers and cyberspace mean that criminal actors and activities can more easily cross national and international boundaries. Worldwide recessions, corporate scandals, and stock market losses have all challenged our faith in the integrity of big business and those who control it. Added to the mix by the beginning of 2016 were shocking acts of criminality that emanated from all corners of the world, including terror attacks in France and Belgium; depravities of sex tourism involving human trafficking; mass shootings at schools and public venues; the theft of hundreds of thousands of personal identities; and websites selling drugs, hits for hire, sexual services, weapons, and just about anything else.

Criminologists find themselves wondering what new laws might be enacted to add additional control to the globalization of crime and the misuse of technology as policy-makers and criminal justice personnel strive to remain one step ahead of these emerging trends in crime and criminality. For the student of crime and criminal behaviour, the crucial question that still remains to be answered is *why?*—why, despite all the theorizing and studies, can we not "solve" the crime puzzle? Do some people commit acts of mass shootings because they are "born violent"? Or, is it their exposure to violence in childhood that is the cause? Why does the affluent chief executive officer of a corporate conglomerate engage in financial fraud while the young person living in a high-crime neighbourhood remains crime-free? What is it that motivates one person and not another to violate social norms? And does this motivation vary according to the type of law broken?

THEME OF SOCIAL PROBLEMS VERSUS SOCIAL RESPONSIBILITY

This sixth edition of *Canadian Criminology Today: Theories and Applications* continues to examine these questions, offering students a clear, contemporary, and comprehensive introduction to criminology that encourages critical thinking about the causes of crime and crime-prevention strategies. The thematic approach of *Canadian Criminology Today* is dualistic: On the one hand, it presents a social problems framework, which holds that crime may be a manifestation of underlying cultural issues, such as poverty,

---

[*]Austin Turk, *Criminality and Legal Order* (Chicago: Rand McNally, 1969), p. vii.

Part II Crime Causation   121

Contents

Brief Contents

Some crimes cry out for explanation. Yet one of the things that fascinates people about crime—especially violent crime—is that it seems inexplicable. Some crimes are especially difficult to understand, but our natural tendency is to seek out some reason for the unreasonable. We search for explanations for the seemingly unexplainable. How, for example, can the behaviour of child killers be understood, anticipated, and even prevented? Why don't terrorists acknowledge the emotional and personal suffering they inflict? Why do some robbers or rapists kill and even torture, utterly disregarding human life and feelings?

People also wonder about "everyday" crimes such as theft, assault, vandalism, and computer intrusion. Why, for example, do people fight? Does it matter to a thief that he may face prison time? How can people sacrifice love, money, careers, and even their lives for access to illegal drugs? What motivates terrorists to give up their own lives to take the lives of others? Why do gifted techno-savvy teens and preteens hack sites on the internet thought to be secure? While this text may not answer each of these questions, we will examine the causative factors in effect when a crime is committed and encourage an appreciation of the challenges of crafting effective crime-prevention and crime-control policy.

WHAT IS CRIME?

1.1 | LEARNING OBJECTIVE

As the word implies, CRIMINOLOGY is clearly concerned with CRIME. As we begin our discussion of criminology, we need to consider just what the term *crime* means. Like anything else, crime can be defined in several ways, and some scholars have suggested that at least four definitional perspectives can be found in contemporary criminology. These diverse perspectives see crime from (1) legalistic, (2) political, (3) sociological, and (4) psychological viewpoints. How we see any phenomenon is crucial because it determines the assumptions that we make about how that phenomenon should be studied. The perspective that we choose to employ when viewing crime determines the kinds of questions we ask, the nature of the research we conduct, and the type of answers that we expect to receive. Those answers, in turn, influence our conclusions about the kinds of crime-prevention and crime-control policies that might be effective.

Legalistic Perspective

Seen from a legalistic perspective, **crime** is human conduct in violation of the criminal laws of a state, the federal government, or a provincial or local jurisdiction that has the power to make such laws. Without a law that circumscribes a particular form of behaviour there can be no crime, no matter how deviant or socially repugnant the behaviour in question may be.

The notion of crime as behaviour[3] that violates the law derives from the work of criminologists who defined crime as "an intentional act in violation of the criminal law . . . committed without defense or excuse, and penalized by the state as a felony or misdemeanor."[4] Edwin Sutherland, one of the best-known criminologists of the last century, said of crime that its "essential characteristic . . . is that it is behavior which is prohibited by the State as an injury to the State and against which the State may react . . . by punishment."[5]

A serious shortcoming of the legalistic approach to crime is that it yields the moral high ground to powerful individuals who are able to influence the making of laws and the imposition of criminal definitions on lawbreakers. By making their own laws, powerful but immoral individuals can escape the label "criminal." While we have chosen to adopt the legalistic approach to crime in this book, it is important to realize that laws are social products, so crime is socially relative in the sense that it is created by legislative activity. Hence, sociologists define crime as "whatever society says it is." In Chapter 10,

Crime Human conduct in violation of the criminal laws of the federal government or a provincial or local jurisdiction that has the power to make such laws.

Criminalize   To make illegal.

we will explore this issue further and focus on the process of criminalization, which is the method used to **criminalize** some forms of behaviour—or make them illegal—while other forms remain legitimate.

Another problem with the legalistic perspective is its insistence that the nature of crime cannot be separated from the nature of law, as the one explicitly defines the other. Not always recognized by legalistic definitions of crime, however, is the social, ethical, and individual significance of fundamentally immoral forms of behaviour. Simply put, some activities not yet contravened by **statute** still call out for a societal response, sometimes leading commentators to proclaim, "That ought to be a crime!" or "There should be a law against that!"

Statute   A formal written enactment of a legislative body.

The legalistic definition of crime also suffers from its seeming lack of recognition that formalized laws have not always existed. Undoubtedly, much immoral behaviour occurred in past historical epochs, and contemporary laws probably now regulate most such behaviour. English common law, for example, upon which much of Canadian **statutory law** is based, judged behaviour in terms of traditional practice and customs and did not make use of written statutes. Although Canada has enacted a comprehensive legal code, it still adheres to a common-law tradition. (The exception to this is Quebec provincial law, which operates under the civil-law system used in many continental European countries. Dating back to the law of the Romans, the modern civil-law system is based on the Napoleonic Code of the early 19th century.) In such "common-law states," individuals may be prosecuted for violating traditional notions of right and wrong, even though no violation of written law took place. Common law is discussed in more detail in Chapter 5. (See Box 1.1 for the distinction between three primary forms of law.)

Statutory law   Law in the form of statutes or formal written strictures made by a legislature or governing body with the power to make law.

Changes in the laws will undoubtedly continue to occur, perhaps even legitimizing former so-called crimes where fundamentally moral or socially beneficial forms of behaviour have been criminalized. Recently, for example, the federal government, along with members of the general public, has debated the pros and cons of euthanasia/assisted suicide and certain forms of biomedical research, especially those involving human cloning and the use of human stem cells.

In what continues to be seen as a landmark case in the assisted suicide debate, in 1993, Sue Rodriguez, a 42-year-old British Columbia woman, challenged before the Supreme

Box 1.1 PRIMARY FORMS OF LAW

Criminal law

Regulates actions that have the potential to harm interests of the state. Categories of criminal law include

- *indictable offences:* serious crimes, including murder, robbery, sexual assault, hostage taking, perjury, and passing counterfeit money, among others. Carry a sentence of incarceration of 14 years or longer.

- *summary conviction offences:* less serious crimes, including making indecent telephone calls, material benefit from sexual services, causing a disturbance in or near a public place, and loitering on private property at night. Carry a maximum sentence of six months of incarceration.

- *hybrid offences (dual procedure):* may be tried either as indictable or summary conviction offences. The decision on how to treat a hybrid offence is made by the Crown

and is based on the circumstances surrounding the offence and the accused. They include pointing a firearm, driving while disqualified, and uttering death threats.

Civil law

Exists primarily for the purpose of enforcing private rights and deals with arrangements between individuals, such as contracts and claims to property.

Administrative law

Regulates many daily business activities. Violation of such regulations generally results in warnings or fines, depending on their adjudged severity. For example, decisions of the British Columbia Crime Victim Assistance Program or the Ontario Workplace Safety and Insurance Board constitute part of administrative case law.

Court of Canada the statute that criminalizes the act of assisted suicide. Suffering a slow and painful death from amyotrophic lateral sclerosis (ALS), also known as Lou Gehrig's disease, Ms. Rodriguez felt that the law forbidding a third party to assist in her death violated her rights under the *Canadian Charter of Rights and Freedoms*. "If I cannot give consent to my own death, whose body is this? Who owns my life?" asked the Victoria woman.[6] The Supreme Court ruled against Rodriguez, and she committed suicide two years later. (Note that assisted suicide and euthanasia are different. Assisted suicide is providing another with the knowledge or means to intentionally end his or her own life; euthanasia is deliberate action undertaken by one person with the intention of ending the life of another person to relieve that person's suffering where that act is the cause of death.)

The debate continued for decades, and several cases went to the Supreme Court. It wasn't until 2014, in the case of *Carter v. Canada*, that the Supreme Court unanimously found that the prohibition on assisted suicide (then s. 241) violates section 7 of the *Canadian Charter of Rights and Freedoms*. The federal, provincial, and territorial governments were directed to revise existing or craft new laws. In April 2016, the federal minister of justice introduced Bill C-14, an act to amend the *Criminal Code*. In June 2016, the bill received royal assent, lifting the legal ban on physician-assisted dying and ensuring that Canadians may now legally access assisted dying under the guidelines put forth by the Supreme Court's *Carter* decision.

Until a national framework is passed, eligibility for physician-assisted dying will be determined based on the Supreme Court's guidelines, which decriminalized physician-assisted death for Canadians with a "grievous and irremediable" medical condition (an illness, disease, or disability) that causes enduring suffering that is intolerable to the individual. The Court did not define "grievous and irremediable," but it is clearly not limited to terminal illness. Only competent, consenting adults will be allowed to access physician-assisted death. The Supreme Court decision does not compel physicians to assist a patient in dying and leaves the decision as to whether hospices, hospitals, and other health care institutions must provide physician-assisted death to the lawmakers and health care regulators. Despite the amendments to the *Criminal Code*, debate continues and includes concerns about striking the right balance between personal autonomy for those seeking access to medically assisted dying and protecting the vulnerable.

Political Perspective

A second perspective on crime is the political one, where crime is the result of criteria that have been built into the law by powerful groups and are then used to label selected

The debate over assisted suicide highlights the changing nature of criminal activity. The 2014 Supreme Court case of *Carter v. Canada* found that the prohibition on assisted suicide violated section 7 of the *Canadian Charter of Rights and Freedoms*. Kay Carter was suffering from spinal stenosis, or the abnormal narrowing of the spinal canal. Do you agree that Canadians should be able to legally access assisted dying?

Sean Kilpatrick/The Canadian Press

undesirable forms of behaviour as illegal. Those who adhere to this point of view say that crime is a definition of human conduct created by authorized agents in a politically organized society. Seen this way, laws serve the interests of the politically powerful, and crimes are merely forms of behaviour that are perceived by those in power as direct or indirect threats to their interests. Thus, the political perspective defines crime in terms of the power structures that exist in society and asserts that criminal laws do not necessarily bear any inherent relationship to popular notions of right and wrong. Even though political processes that create criminal definitions are sometimes easier to comprehend in totalitarian societies, the political perspective can also be meaningfully applied to Canadian society. John F. Galliher, a contemporary criminologist, pointed out that, because legal definitions of criminality are arrived at through a political process, the subject matter of criminality will be artificially limited if we insist on seeing crime solely as a violation of the criminal law.[7]

Some criminologists insist that the field of criminology must include behaviours that go beyond those defined as crimes through the political process; not doing so, they say, restricts rather than encourages inquiry into relevant forms of human behaviour.[8]

Sociological Perspective

Adherents of the third perspective, the sociological viewpoint, would likely agree with this statement by Canadian criminologist Ezzat Fattah, who saw crime as "an antisocial act of such a nature that its repression is necessary or is supposed to be necessary to the preservation of the existing system of society."[9] Some criminologists have gone so far as to claim that any definition of crime must include all forms of anti-social behaviour.[10] Ron Claassen, a modern-day champion of restorative justice (discussed more fully in Chapter 10), suggested, for example, that "crime is primarily an offense against human relationships, and secondarily a violation of a law—since laws are written to protect safety and fairness in human relationships."[11]

A more comprehensive sociological definition of crime was offered by Herman Schwendinger and Julia Schwendinger in 1975: crime encompasses "any harmful acts," including violations of "the fundamental prerequisites for well-being, [such as] food, shelter, clothing, medical services, challenging work and recreational experiences, as well as security from predatory individuals or repressive and imperialistic elites."[12] The Schwendingers have challenged criminologists to be less constrained in what they see as the subject matter of their field, saying that violations of human rights may be more relevant to criminological inquiry than many acts that have been politically or legally defined as crime. "Isn't it time to raise serious questions about the assumptions underlying the definitions of the field of criminology," asked the Schwendingers, "when a man who steals a paltry sum can be called a criminal while agents of the State can, with impunity, legally reward men who destroy food so that price levels can be maintained whilst a sizable portion of the population suffers from malnutrition?"[13]

Jeffrey H. Reiman, another contemporary criminologist, asked similar questions. "The fact is that the label 'crime' is not used in America to name all or the worst of the actions that cause misery and suffering to Americans," said Reiman. "It is primarily reserved for the dangerous actions of the poor." Writing about unhealthy and unsafe workplaces, Reiman asked, "Doesn't a crime by any other name still cause misery and suffering? What's in a name?"[14] While a sociological approach to understanding crime is attractive to many, others claim that it suffers from wanting to criminalize activities that cause only indirect harm—that is, it is easier for most people to appreciate the criminality involved in a robbery or a sexual assault than in the cost-cutting efforts made by a businessperson.

Psychological Perspective

Finally, a psychological perspective states that "crime is a form of social maladjustment which can be designated as a more or less pronounced difficulty that the individual has in reacting to the stimuli of his environment in such a way as to remain in harmony with that environment."[15] Seen this way, crime is problem behaviour, especially human activity that contravenes the criminal law and results in difficulties in living within a framework of generally acceptable social arrangements. According to Matthew B. Robinson, "The maladaptive view of crime does not require any of the [traditional] elements . . . in order for an act to be a crime: no actual harm to others; no prohibition by law before the act is committed; no arrest; and no conviction in a court of law. Any behavior which is maladaptive . . . would be considered crime. If criminologists adopted this view of crime," said Robinson, "the scope of criminology would be greatly expanded beyond its current state. All actually or even potentially harmful behaviors could be examined, analyzed, and documented for the purpose of gaining knowledge about potentially harmful behaviors and developing strategies to protect people from all harmful acts, not just those that are called 'crime' today."[16]*

As this discussion shows, a unified or simple definition of crime is difficult to achieve. The four points of view that we have discussed here form a kind of continuum, bound on one end by strict legalistic interpretations of crime and on the other by much more fluid behavioural and moralistic definitions.

CRIME AND DEVIANCE

SOCIOLOGICALLY SPEAKING, MOST CRIMES CAN BE REGARDED AS DEVIANT FORMS OF behaviour—that is, as behaviours that are in some way abnormal. Piers Beirne and James Messerschmidt, two contemporary criminologists, defined *deviance* as "any social behavior or social characteristic that departs from the conventional norms and standards of a community or society and for which the deviant is sanctioned."[17] Their definition, however, does not count as deviant any sanctionable behaviour that is not punished or punishable. Hence, the definition of **deviant behaviour** that we will use in this text is as follows: deviant behaviour is human activity that violates social norms.

Abnormality, deviance, and crime are concepts that do not always easily mesh. Some forms of deviance are not criminal, and the reverse is equally true (see Figure 1.1). Deviant styles of dress, for example, although perhaps outlandish to the majority, are not circumscribed by criminal law, unless (perhaps) decency statutes are violated by a lack of clothing. Even in such cases, laws are subject to interpretation and may be

Deviant behaviour Human activity that violates social norms.

Figure 1.1 The Overlap between Deviance and Crime

*From Matthew B. Robinson, "Defining 'Crime,'" by Matthew B. Robinson, published by Appalachian State University. © 2006.

modified as social norms change over time. Some years ago, the Court of Appeal in Ontario overturned the conviction of Gwen Jacob, who had been charged with committing an indecent act after she walked topless down a city street on a hot summer's day. The three judges on the panel ruled that there had to be a sexual connotation for the act to be considered indecent, and they found that Jacob had no such motivation. The Topfree Equal Rights movement that has emerged across Canada and the United States highlights the role that societal interpretation plays in defining a criminal offence.

Some types of behaviour, although quite common, are still against the law even if those who engage in them do not think of them as deviant. Speeding on provincial highways, for example, although probably something that most motorists engage in occasionally, is illegal. Complicating matters further is the fact that some forms of behaviour are either illegal or defined differently in various jurisdictions. For example, every province in Canada has some form of distracted-driving law banning the use of cell phones to call or text-message while driving, but this legislation varies widely.[18]

WHAT SHOULD BE CRIMINAL?

BY NOW, YOU HAVE PROBABLY REALIZED THAT THE QUESTION "WHAT IS CRIME?" DIFFERS from the question "What should be criminal?" Although most people agree that certain forms of behaviour, such as murder, sexual assault, burglary, and theft, should be against the law, there is far less agreement about the appropriate legal status of things like drug use, gambling, and "deviant" forms of consensual adult sexual behaviour. Recall the earlier discussion about the legalization of doctor-assisted death in Canada.

While the question "What should be criminal?" can be answered in many different ways, the social and intellectual processes by which an answer is reached can be found in three contrasting points of view: (1) the consensus perspective, (2) the pluralist perspective, and (3) the conflict perspective. Each sees the relationship between the law and the social order somewhat differently; indeed, a criminologist's choice of perspective can influence his or her approach in explaining the causes of crime and criminal behaviour and, in turn, his or her suggestions for their prevention or control.

Deviance is relevant to the social context within which it occurs. "Creepshots" are photos taken of women in public, without their consent, and then posted to social media. Should women have a reasonable expectation to privacy when in public? Should this activity be illegal?

Hoi Tung Wong/Alamy Stock Photo

Consensus Perspective

The **consensus perspective** is built around the notion that most members of society agree on what is right and wrong and that the various elements of society—including institutions such as churches, schools, government agencies, and businesses—work together toward a common vision of the greater good. The consensus viewpoint holds that laws should be enacted to criminalize given forms of behaviour when members of society generally agree that such laws are necessary. According to Raymond J. Michalowski, whose excellent analytical work is used to describe each of the three major approaches discussed in this section, the consensus perspective is characterized by four principles:[19]

Consensus perspective An analytical perspective on social organization that holds that laws should be enacted to criminalize given forms of behaviour when members of society generally agree that such laws are necessary.

- Most members of a society believe in the existence of core values. The consensus perspective holds that shared notions of right and wrong characterize the majority of society's members.

- Laws reflect the collective will of the people. Law is seen as the result of a consensus achieved through legislative action and represents a kind of social conscience.

- Law serves all people equally. From the consensus point of view, the law not only embodies a shared view of justice but also is perceived to be just in its application.

- Law violators represent a unique subgroup with distinguishing features. The consensus approach holds that law violators must somehow be improperly socialized, be psychologically defective, or suffer from some other lapse that leaves them unable to participate in what is otherwise widespread agreement on values and behaviour.

The consensus perspective is most applicable to homogeneous societies or those characterized by shared values, norms, and belief systems. In a multicultural and diverse society like Canada, however, a shared consensus may be difficult to achieve. In such a society, even relatively minor matters may lead to complex debates over the issues involved, and consensus is difficult to find. Modern debates centre on issues such as recreational drug use, assisted suicide, the death penalty, the purpose of criminal justice agencies in a diverse society, social justice, the rights and responsibilities of minorities and other underrepresented groups, women's issues, the proper role of education, economic policy, social welfare, the function of the military in a changing world, environmental concerns, and appropriate uses of technology. As many contemporary public forums would indicate, there exists within Canada today a great diversity of social groups, each with its own point of view regarding what is right and what is wrong. (See the discussion about polygamy in the Who's Responsible? box.)

Pluralist Perspective

The second perspective, the **pluralist perspective** of crime, mirrors the thought that a multiplicity of values and beliefs exists in any complex society and that different social groups will have their own respective sets of beliefs, interests, and values. A crucial element of this perspective is the assumption that although different viewpoints exist, most individuals agree on the usefulness of law as a formal means of dispute resolution. From the pluralist perspective, the law exists as a peacekeeping tool that allows officials and agencies within the government to settle disputes effectively between individuals and among groups; whatever settlement is reached will be acceptable to all parties because of their agreement on the fundamental role of law in dispute settlement. The basic principles of the pluralistic perspective include the following:[20]

Pluralist perspective An analytical approach to social organization that holds that a multiplicity of values and beliefs exists in any complex society but that most social actors agree on the usefulness of law as a formal means of dispute resolution.

- Society consists of many diverse social groups. Differences in age, gender, sexual preference, ethnicity, and the like often provide the basis for much naturally occurring diversity.

Should Polygamy Be a Protected Religious Practice?

Winston Blackmore with six of his daughters and some of his grandchildren.

Jonathan Hayward/The Canadian Press

The rural town of Bountiful in the southeastern interior of British Columbia is a community of about 1000 residents, all of whom are members of the Fundamentalist Church of Jesus Christ of Latter Day Saints (FLDS). The community is openly polygamous, in accordance with the most well-known tenet of the religion.

In January 2009, the Royal Canadian Mounted Police (RCMP) arrested Winston Blackmore, 52, and James Oler, 44, of Bountiful, charging them each with one count of practising polygamy under section 293 of the *Criminal Code of Canada*. The charges against Blackmore were linked to his marriages to 19 women, dating back to May 2005. The charges against Oler were linked to his marriages to three women, dating back to November 2004. It was alleged that Mr. Blackmore had as many as 26 wives, including one who was under the age of 16, and more than 100 children.

The RCMP investigated the case starting in 2005, interviewing almost 100 people in British Columbia and the United States. After the investigation, British Columbia's Crown prosecutors remained reluctant to lay polygamy charges for fear they would be declared unconstitutional on the basis of religious freedom, recommending that the government get a court ruling on the constitutionality of Canada's anti-polygamy laws. The then attorney general of British Columbia, Wally Oppal, finally appointed a third special prosecutor and charges were laid.

In September 2009, the Supreme Court of British Columbia dismissed the charges against Blackmore and Oler, ruling that the attorney general did not have the authority to appoint a new special prosecutor to consider the cases given that prosecutors had recommended against charges. The province appealed the ruling to the British Columbia Supreme Court and, in November 2011, that court upheld Canada's polygamy laws, ruling that while the law does infringe on religious freedom, it is justified given the harm that polygamy causes to children, women, society, and the institution of monogamous marriage. In 2015, Winston Blackmore's latest effort to have the criminal charge against him dismissed failed when the Supreme Court of British Columbia dismissed his petition.

Think about it:

1. What rights should members of minority faiths have when they advocate or engage in behaviour that goes beyond social norms or violates the law? Give some examples.

2. Would the rights you identified above extend to the practice of polygamy? Why or why not?

3. What is the legal history of the practice of polygamy in Canada? When did it become illegal? Why?

Source: Based on CBC News, "Canada's polygamy laws upheld by BC Supreme Court," November 23, 2011, www.cbc.ca/news/canada/british-columbia/story/2011/11/23/bc-polygamy-ruling-supreme-court.html; CBC News, "Polygamy charges in Bountiful B.C. thrown out," September 23, 2009, www.cbc.ca/news/canada/british-columbia/story/2009/09/23/bc-polygamy-charges-blackmore-oler-bountiful.html; CTV News, "Polygamy charges laid against Bountiful, B.C. leaders," January 9, 2010, www.ctvnews.ca/polygamy-charges-laid-against-bountiful-b-c-leaders-1.358027; The Fifth Estate, "Bust-up in Bountiful," April 12, 2008, www.cbc.ca/fifth/bustupinbountiful/, Geordon Omand, "B.C. gets go-ahead to pursue polygamy charge against religious leader", *Globe and Mail*, June 25, 2015, http://www.theglobeandmail.com/news/british-columbia/bc-gets-go-ahead-to-pursue-polygamy-charge-against-bountiful-bc-leader/article25113882/.

- Each group has its own characteristic set of values, beliefs, and interests. Variety in gender, sexual orientation, economic status, ethnicity, and other forms of diversity produces interests that may unite like-minded individuals but that may also place them in natural opposition to other social groups.

- A general agreement exists on the usefulness of formalized laws as a mechanism for dispute resolution. People and groups accept the role of law in the settlement of disputes and accord decisions reached within the legal framework at least a modicum of respect.

- The legal system is value-neutral, that is, free of petty disputes or above the level of general contentiousness that may characterize relationships between groups.

- The legal system is concerned with the best interests of society. Legislators, judges, prosecutors, attorneys, police officers, and correctional officials are assumed to perform idealized functions that are beyond the reach of self-serving groups, so official functionaries can be trusted to act in accordance with the greater good, to remain unbiased, and to maintain a value-free system for the enforcement of laws.

Conflict Perspective

The third perspective, the **conflict perspective**, maintains that conflict is a fundamental aspect of social life itself that can never be fully resolved. Formal agencies of social control merely coerce the disempowered or the disenfranchised to comply with the rules established by those in power. Laws are a tool of the powerful, useful in keeping others from wresting control over important social institutions. Rather than being the result of any consensus or process of dispute resolution, social order rests upon the exercise of power through law. Those in power must work ceaselessly to remain there, although the structures they impose on society—including patterns of wealth building that they define as acceptable and circumstances under which they authorize the exercise of legal power and military might—give them all the advantages they are likely to need. The conflict perspective can be described in terms of the following key elements:[21]

> **Conflict perspective** An analytical approach to social organization that holds that conflict is a fundamental aspect of social life and can never be fully resolved.

- Society is made up of diverse social groups, and diversity is based on distinctions that people hold to be significant, such as gender, sexual orientation, and social class.

- Each group holds to differing definitions of right and wrong, so moralistic conceptions and behavioural standards vary from group to group.

- Conflict between groups is both socially significant and unavoidable because groups defined by such characteristics as ethnicity, gender, and social class compete for power, wealth, and other forms of power.

- The fundamental nature of group conflict centres on the exercise of political power, which is the key to the accumulation of wealth and to other forms of power.

- Law is a tool of power and furthers the interests of those powerful enough to make it. Laws allow those in control to gain what they define as legitimate access to scarce resources and to deny such access to the politically disenfranchised.

- Those in power are inevitably interested in maintaining their power against those who would usurp it.

WHAT IS CRIMINOLOGY?

1.4 LEARNING OBJECTIVE

THE ATTEMPT TO UNDERSTAND CRIME PREDATES WRITTEN HISTORY. PREHISTORIC evidence, including skeletal remains showing signs of primitive cranial surgery, seems to indicate that preliterate people explained deviant behaviour in terms of spirit possession. Primitive surgery was an attempt to release unwanted spiritual influences. In the thousands of years since, many other theoretical perspectives on crime have been advanced. This text describes various criminological theories and covers some of the more popular ones in detail.

Defining Criminology

Before beginning any earnest discussion, however, it is necessary to define the term *criminology*. As our earlier discussion of the nature of crime and deviance indicates, not only must criminologists deal with a complex subject matter—consisting of a broad range of illegal behaviours committed by frequently unknown or uncooperative individuals—they must also manage their work under changing conditions mandated by ongoing revisions of the law and fluctuating **social policy**. In addition, as we have already seen, a wide variety of perspectives on the nature of crime abound. All this leads to considerable difficulties in defining the subject matter under study.

Social policy A government initiative, program, or plan intended to address problems in society.

There is some evidence that the term *criminology* was coined by a Frenchman, Paul Topinard, in 1889;[22] he used it to differentiate the study of criminal body types within the field of anthropology from other biometric pursuits.[23] While he may have coined the term, Topinard did little to define it. As with the concept of crime, various definitions of criminology can be found in the literature today. About two decades ago, criminologist Joseph F. Sheley wrote, "There seem to be nearly as many definitions of *contemporary criminology* as there are criminologists."[24]

One straightforward definition can be had from a linguistic analysis of the word *criminology*. As most people know, *-ology* means "the study of something," and the word *crimen* comes from Latin, meaning "accusation," "charge," or "guilt." Hence, linguistically speaking, the term *criminology* literally means "the study of crime." In addition to this fundamental kind of linguistic definition, three other important types of definitions can be found in the literature: (1) disciplinary, (2) causative, and (3) scientific. Each type of definition is distinguished by its focus.

Disciplinary definitions are those that, as the name implies, focus on criminology as a discipline. Seen from this viewpoint, criminology is a field of study or a body of knowledge. Some of the earliest criminologists of the past century, including Edwin H. Sutherland, who is often referred to as the "dean of criminology," offered definitions of their field that emphasized its importance as a discipline of study. Sutherland, for example, wrote in the first edition of his textbook *Criminology* in 1924, "Criminology is the body of knowledge regarding the social problem of crime."[25] Sutherland's text was to set the stage for much of North American criminology throughout the rest of the 20th century. Reprinted in 1934 with the title *Principles of Criminology*,[26] it was to become one of the most influential textbooks ever written in the field of criminology.

Although Sutherland died in 1950, his revered text was revised for many years by Donald R. Cressey and later by David F. Luckenbill. By 1974, Sutherland's classic definition of criminology had been modified by Cressey: "Criminology is the body of knowledge regarding delinquency and crime as a social phenomenon. It includes within its scope the processes of making laws, of breaking laws, and of reacting toward the breaking of laws."[27]

Causative definitions emphasize criminology's role in uncovering the underlying causes of crime. In keeping with such an emphasis, contemporary criminologists Gennaro F. Vito and Ronald M. Holmes stated, "Criminology is the study of the causes of crime."[28]

Finally, some point to the scientific nature of contemporary criminology as its distinguishing characteristic. According to Clemens Bartollas and Simon Dinitz, for example, "Criminology is the scientific study of crime."[29] Writing in 1989, Bartollas and Dinitz seemed to be echoing an earlier definition of criminology offered by Marvin E. Wolfgang and Franco Ferracuti, who wrote in 1967, "Criminology is the scientific study of crime, criminals, and criminal behavior."[30]

One of the most comprehensive definitions of the term *criminology* that is available today comes from the European Society of Criminology (ESC), which in its constitution defined criminology as "all scholarly, scientific and professional knowledge concerning the explanation, prevention, control and treatment of crime and delinquency, offenders and victims, including the measurement and detection of crime, legislation, and the practice of criminal law, and law enforcement, judicial, and correctional systems."[31] ESC's emphasis is on "knowledge"; even though it mentions the "practice" of what many would call criminal justice (that is, policing, courts, and corrections), it is the study and knowledge of such practice that form the crux of the ESC perspective.

For our purposes, we will use a definition somewhat simpler than that of the ESC, one that brings together the works of previous writers but also recognizes the increasingly professional status of the criminological enterprise. Throughout this text, then, we will say that **criminology** is an interdisciplinary profession built around the scientific study of crime and criminal behaviour, including their manifestations, causes, legal aspects, prevention, and control. As this definition indicates, criminology includes consideration of possible solutions to the problem of crime. Hence, this text (in later chapters) describes prevention and treatment strategies and social policy initiatives that have grown out of the existing array of theoretical explanations for crime.

Our definition is in keeping with the work of J.P. Gibbs, a notable 20th-century criminologist who wrote that the purpose of criminology is to offer well-researched and objective answers to four basic questions: (1) "Why do crime rates vary?" (2) "Why do individuals differ as to criminality?" (3) "Why is there variation in reactions to crime?" and (4) "What are the possible means of controlling criminality?"[32] It is important to note that our definition and Gibbs's guiding queries encompass a number of different terms that are sometimes easily confused. Criminology, **criminality**, crime, deviance, and **criminal behaviour** are five concepts used in this chapter and throughout this text, and learning the definition of each provides a good start for anyone studying in this field.

As a field of study, criminology in its present form is primarily a social scientific discipline. Contemporary criminologists generally recognize, however, that their field is *interdisciplinary*—that is, it draws upon other disciplines to provide an integrated approach to understanding the problem of crime in contemporary society and to advancing solutions to the problems crime creates. Hence, anthropology (especially cultural anthropology or ethnology), biology, sociology, political science, psychology, economics, ethology (the study of character), medicine, psychiatry, law, philosophy, ethics, and numerous other fields all have something to offer the student of criminology, as do the tools provided by statistics, computer science, and other forms of scientific and data analysis.

It is important, however, to note that although criminology may be interdisciplinary as well as cross-professional, few existing explanations for criminal behaviour have been successfully or fully integrated. Just as physicists today are seeking a unified field theory to explain the wide variety of observable forms of matter and energy, criminologists have yet to develop a generally accepted, integrated approach to crime and criminal behaviour that can explain the many diverse forms of criminality while also leading to effective social policies in the area of crime prevention and control. The attempt to construct criminological theories that are relevant to the problems of today is made all the more difficult because, as discussed earlier, the phenomenon under study—crime—is very wide-ranging and is subject to arbitrary and sometimes unpredictable legalistic and definitional changes.

Criminology An interdisciplinary profession built around the scientific study of crime and criminal behaviour, including their forms, causes, legal aspects, prevention, and control.

Criminality A behavioural predisposition that disproportionately favours criminal activity.

Criminal behaviour Human behaviour, both intentional and negligent, that violates criminal law. It may include a failure to act when there is a legal obligation to do so.

Criminology examines the causes of crime and seeks ways to prevent or control it. Criminal justice examines the criminal justice system, including police, courts, and corrections. How do the two disciplines complement one another?

Richard Lautens/Toronto Star/ZUMApress. com/Alamy Stock Photo

A successfully integrated criminology must bring together the contributions of various theoretical perspectives and disciplines, but it must also—if it is to have any relevance—blend the practical requirements of our nation's judicial system with emotional and rational calls for morality and justice. Should capital punishment, for example, be reinstated? If so, on what basis? Is it because it is a type of vengeance and therefore deserved? Or can we continue to say that it is unjustified because many sociological studies have shown that it does little to reduce the rate of serious crime, such as murder? Just what do we mean by *justice*, and what can criminological studies tell us—if anything—about what is just and what is unjust?

The editors of the journal *Theoretical Criminology*, which began publication over a decade ago, wrote in the inaugural issue that "criminology has always been somewhat of a haphazardly assembled, umbrella-like structure which nevertheless usefully shelters a variety of theoretical interests that are espoused and employed by different disciplinary, methodological, and political traditions."[33] In other words, while the field of criminology can benefit from the wide variety of ideas available via a multiplicity of perspectives, all of which seek to understand the phenomenon we call "crime," cross-discipline collaboration can be quite difficult.

As our earlier definition of criminology indicates, however, it is more than a field of study or a collection of theories; it is also a discipline and a profession.[34] Notably, criminology also contributes to the discipline of **criminal justice**, which emphasizes application of the criminal law and study of the components of the justice system, especially the police, courts, and corrections. As one author stated, "Criminology gives prominence to questions about the *causes of criminality*, while the *control of law-breaking* is at the heart of criminal justice."[35]

Theoretical Criminology

Theoretical criminology, a subfield of general criminology, is the type of criminology most often found in community colleges and universities. Theoretical criminology, rather than simply describing crime and its occurrence, posits explanations for criminal behaviour. As Sutherland stated, "The problem in criminology is to explain the criminality of behavior . . . However, an explanation of criminal behavior should be a specific part of [a] general theory of behavior and its task should be to differentiate criminal from non-criminal behavior."[36]

To explain and understand crime, criminologists have developed many theories. As we will see later in this chapter, a **theory**, at least in its ideal form, is made up of

Criminal justice The scientific study of crime, the criminal law, and components of the criminal justice system, including the police, courts, and corrections.

Theory A series of interrelated propositions that attempt to describe, explain, predict, and ultimately control some class of events. A theory gains explanatory power from inherent logical consistency and is "tested" by how well it describes and predicts reality.

clearly stated propositions that posit relationships, often of a causal sort, between events and things under study. An old Roman theory, for example, proposed that insanity is caused by the influence of the moon and may even follow its cycles—hence the term *lunacy*.

Theories attempt to provide us with explanatory power and help us to understand a phenomenon under study. The more applicable a theory is found to be, the more generalizable it is from one specific instance to others—in other words, the more it can be applied to other situations. A **general theory** of crime is one that attempts to explain all (or at least most) forms of criminal conduct through a single overarching approach. Unfortunately, as Don Gottfredson observed, "theories in criminology tend to be unclear and lacking in justifiable generality."[37] When we consider the wide range of behaviours regarded as criminal—from murder, to drug use, to white-collar and computer crime—it seems difficult to imagine one theory that can explain them all or even the same type of behaviour under varying circumstances. Still, many past theoretical approaches to crime causation were unicausal while attempting to be all-inclusive. In other words, the approaches posited a single, identifiable source for all serious deviant and criminal behaviour.

An **integrated theory**, in contrast to a general theory, does not necessarily attempt to explain all criminality but is distinguishable by the fact that it merges (or attempts to merge) concepts drawn from different sources. Put another way, "an integrative criminology . . . seeks to bring together the diverse bodies of knowledge that represent the full array of disciplines that study crime."[38] Hence, integrated theories provide potentially wider explanatory power than narrower formulations. Recognizing that no one theory can explain all criminal behaviour, Don G. Gibbons noted, "The basic idea of theoretical integration is straightforward; it concerns the combinations of single theories or elements of those theories into a more comprehensive argument. At the same time, it would be well to note that in practice, integration is a matter of degree: some theorists have combined or integrated more concepts or theoretical elements than have others."[39]

Both the general applicability and the theoretical integration of criminological theories to a wide variety of law-violating behaviours are intuitively appealing concepts. Even far more limited attempts at criminological theorizing, however, often face daunting challenges. To date, "criminologists have not managed to articulate a large collection of relatively formalized arguments in a general or integrated form."[40] Hence, although we will use the word *theory* in describing the many explanations for crime covered by this text, it should be recognized that the word is only loosely applicable to some of the perspectives we will discuss.

As we shall learn later in this chapter, many social scientists insist that to be considered theories, explanations must consist of sets of clearly stated, logically interrelated, and measurable propositions. The fact that only a few of the theories described in this text rise above the level of organized conjecture—and those offer only limited generalizability and have rarely been integrated—is one of the greatest challenges facing criminology today.

General theory A theory that attempts to explain all (or at least most) forms of criminal conduct through a single overarching approach.

Integrated theory An explanatory perspective that merges (or attempts to merge) concepts drawn from different sources.

WHAT DO CRIMINOLOGISTS DO?

1.5 | LEARNING OBJECTIVE

A TYPICAL DICTIONARY DEFINITION OF A **CRIMINOLOGIST** IS "ONE WHO STUDIES CRIME, criminals, and criminal behaviour."[41] Occasionally, the term *criminologist* is used broadly to describe almost anyone who works in the criminal justice field, regardless of formal training. There is a growing tendency, however, to reserve application of the term *criminologist* to academics, researchers, and policy analysts with advanced degrees who are involved in the study of crime and crime trends and in the analysis

Criminologist One who is trained in the field of criminology; also, one who studies crime, criminals, and criminal behaviour.

of societal reactions to crime. Hence, it is more appropriate today to describe specially skilled investigators, crime-laboratory technicians, fingerprint experts, crime-scene photographers, ballistics experts, and others who work to solve particular crimes as *criminalists*. A **criminalist** is "a specialist in the collection and examination of the physical evidence of crime."[42] Police officers, corrections professionals, probation and parole officers, judges, Crown attorneys, defence counsel, and others who do the day-to-day work of the criminal justice system are often referred to as *criminal justice professionals*.

Academic criminologists and research criminologists generally hold doctoral or master's degrees in the field of criminology or criminal justice from an accredited university. Some criminologists hold degrees in related fields, such as sociology and political science, and have specialized in the study and control of crime and deviance. Many academic criminologists teach either criminology or criminology-related subjects in institutions of higher learning, including universities and community colleges. Nearly all criminology professors are involved in research or writing projects by which they strive to advance criminological knowledge. Other criminologists are strictly researchers and work for federal agencies, such as the Department of Justice Canada, Public Safety Canada, or the Canadian Centre for Justice Statistics.

The results of criminological research in Canada and the United States are generally published in journals such as the *Canadian Journal of Criminology and Criminal Justice* (the official publication of the Canadian Criminal Justice Association), the *Canadian Journal of Law and Society*, the *Canadian Journal of Women and the Law*, *Criminology* (the official publication of the American Society of Criminology), *Theoretical Criminology*, *Crime and Delinquency*, and *Social Problems*. International English-language journals are numerous and include the *International Review of Victimology*, the *Australian and New Zealand Journal of Criminology*, and the *British Journal of Criminology*.[43]

People who have earned undergraduate degrees in the field of criminology often find access to police investigative or support work, probation and parole agencies, court-support activities, and correctional (prison) work. Criminologists also work for government agencies interested in developing effective social policies to deter or prevent crime.

Private security provides another career track for individuals interested in criminology and criminal justice. The number of personnel employed by private security agencies today is one-third greater than that by public law enforcement agencies, and the gap is widening.[44] Many upper- and midlevel managers working for private security firms hold criminology or criminal justice degrees. A similar trend is emerging in the field of public policing. While most Canadian police services require applicants to have a high school diploma as a minimum, a majority of recent new recruits to the profession have attained higher levels of education.

With the expanded use of technology in the field of criminology and the increased reality of cybersecurity issues, those with a criminology background may also combine it with computer science, information technology (IT) systems, or software development to find employment in the IT security sector or the growing field of geographic information systems (GIS).

Anyone trained in criminology has various alternatives (see Table 1.1). Some people with undergraduate degrees in criminology or criminal justice go on to law school. Some teach high school, while others become private investigators. Many criminologists provide civic organizations (such as victims' assistance and justice advocacy groups) with much-needed expertise, a few work for politicians and legislative bodies, and some appear on talk shows to debate the pros and cons of various kinds of social policies designed to fight crime. Some criminologists even write books such as this one!

Criminalist A specialist in the collection and examination of the physical evidence of crime.

Table 1.1 What Do Criminologists Do?

The term *criminologist* is usually applied to credentialed individuals, such as those holding advanced degrees in the field, who engage in the study of crime, criminal behaviour, and crime trends. The word *criminalist* is used to describe people who specialize in collecting and examining the physical evidence associated with specific crimes. Others working in the criminal justice system are called *criminal justice professionals*. This table lists some of the activities and jobs open to individuals working in the three areas.

Activities of Criminologists

Data gathering	Public service
Data analysis	Analysis of crime patterns and trends
Theory construction	Scholarly presentations and publications
Hypothesis testing	Education and training
Social policy creation	Threat assessment and risk analysis
Public advocacy	Teaching
	Service as expert witness in court proceedings

Jobs in the Field of Criminalistics

Forensics examiner	Crime-scene photographer
Crime-laboratory technician	Polygraph operator
Ballistics expert	Fingerprint examiner
Crime-scene investigator	

Jobs in the Field of Criminal Justice

Law enforcement officer	Judge
Probation or parole officer	Defence attorney
Corrections officer	Crown attorney
Prison administrator	Cybercrime investigator
Private security officer	Young offender worker
Private cybersecurity analyst	Court support worker
Private geographic information system (GIS) analyst	Victims' advocate

THE EVOLVING SCIENCE OF CRIMINOLOGY

THE THEORETICAL PERSPECTIVES ADOPTED BY CRIMINOLOGISTS PROVIDE THE underpinning for the direction of their research and the development of their theories. Indeed, over the past century, criminologists have undertaken the task of building a scientific or **evidence-based criminology,** (also referred to as knowledge-based criminology), as distinguished from what had been the "armchair criminology" of earlier times. Armchair criminologists offered their ideas to one another as conjecture. The ruminations of armchair criminologists may have achieved a considerable degree of popular acclaim through the involvement of distinguished lecturers, the association of such ideas with celebrated bastions of higher learning, and their publication in prestigious forums, but they were rarely founded on anything other than mere speculation. By contrast, evidence-based criminology is an increasingly popular form of contemporary criminology that is founded upon the experimental method. The method utilizes the techniques of the social sciences (especially randomized, controlled experiments) in theory testing. When used in this context, the word *evidence* refers to scientific findings, not to the kind of evidence gathered by the police or used in criminal trials.

Evidence-based criminology A form of contemporary criminology that uses rigorous social scientific techniques, especially randomized, controlled experiments and the systematic review of research results.

Although it is easy to dispense with armchair criminology as the relaxed musings of carefree intellectuals undertaken almost as sport, it is far more difficult to agree on the criteria necessary to move any undertaking into the realm of serious scientific endeavour. Present-day criminology is decidedly more scientific, however, than its intellectual predecessor—which means that it is amenable to objective scrutiny and systematic testing. A variety of criteria has been advanced for declaring any endeavour "scientific." Among them are these:[45]

- the systematic collection of related facts (as in the building of a database)
- an emphasis on the availability and application of the scientific method
- "the existence of general laws, a field for experiment or observation, and control of academic discourse by practical application"
- "the fact that it has been accepted into the scientific tradition"
- an "emphasis on a worthwhile subject in need of independent study even if adequate techniques of study are not yet available" (as in the investigation of paranormal phenomena)

Probably all the foregoing could be said of criminology. For one thing, criminologists do gather facts. The mere gathering of facts, however, although it may lead to a descriptive criminology, falls short of offering satisfactory explanations for crime. Hence, most contemporary criminologists are concerned with identifying relationships among the facts they observe and attempting to understand the many and diverse causes of crime. This emphasis on unveiling causality moves criminology beyond the merely descriptive into the realm of conjecture and theory building. A further emphasis on measurement and objectivity gives contemporary criminology its scientific flavour.

Theory Building

A few years ago, Inspector Andy Parr of the Sussex Police Department in England reviewed crime statistics for the town of Brighton and found that violent crime was higher on nights when the moon was full.[46] "I compared a graph of full moons and a graph of last year's violent crimes and there is a trend," Parr told the United Kingdom's *Telegraph* newspaper. "People tend to be more aggressive" when the moon is full, Parr concluded. His findings were supported, he said, by his patrol experience. "When you try to reason with people on a full moon they become more aggressive and less rational," he told reporters. "When you try to reason with them on a full moon they become more argumentative."

Ultimately, the goal of research within criminology is the construction of theories or models that allow for a better understanding of criminal behaviour and that permit the development of strategies intended to address the problem of crime. Simply put, a theory consists of a set of interrelated propositions that provide a relatively complete form of understanding (see Figure 1.2). Hence, even if we find that crime is higher when the moon is full, we must still ask why. Is it because the light from full moons makes it possible for those interested in committing crime to see better at night? If so, then we would expect crime to be higher in areas where there is no cloud cover than in areas with clouds. Likewise, lighted cities should show less of a rise in crime during full moons than rural areas and small towns. In any event, a complete lunar theory of crime causation would contain specific propositions about the causal nature of the phenomena involved.

There are many ways to define the word theory. One cogent definition comes from Don M. Gottfredson, a well-known criminologist of modern times: "Theories consist of postulates [assumptions], theoretical constructs, logically derived hypotheses, and definitions. Theories can be improved steadily through hypothesis testing, examination of evidence from observations, revisions of the theory, and repetitions of the

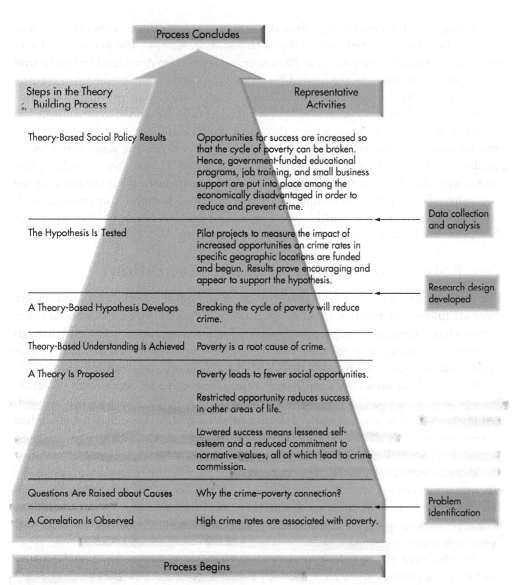

Figure 1.2 The Theory-Building Process

cycle, repeatedly modifying the theory in light of the evidence."[47] (A hypothesis is an explanation that accounts for a set of facts and that can be tested by further investigation.) Another well-known methodologist describes theories this way: "A theory is a set of related propositions that suggest why events occur in the manner that they do. The propositions that make up theories are of the same form as hypotheses: they consist of concepts and the linkages or relationships between them."[48]

These definitions both have something to offer. For our purposes, a theory is a series of interrelated propositions that attempts to describe, explain, predict, and ultimately control some class of events. Theories gain explanatory power from inherent logical consistency and are "tested" by how well they describe and predict reality. In other words, a good theory provides relatively complete understanding, is supported by observations, and stands up to continued scrutiny.

Theories serve a number of purposes. For one thing, they give meaning to observations, explaining what we see in a particular setting by relating those observations to other things already understood. Hence, a theory of physics can explain the behaviour of light by saying that light has the properties of both waves and particles. Such a theory is immediately useful because we can easily grasp ideas like waves and particles even if we have trouble conceptualizing light's essence.

Theories within criminology serve the same purpose as those within the physical sciences, but they are often more difficult to test. For example, few people can intuitively understand the motivation of "lust murderers" (a term developed by the Federal Bureau of Investigation in the United States and popularized by the media to refer to men who sexually abuse and kill women, often sadistically). Some psychiatric theories (discussed in Chapter 7) suggest that lust murderers kill because of a deep-seated hatred of women. Hate is something that most minds can grasp, and a vision of lust murder as an extreme example of the age-old battle between the sexes provides an intellectual "handle" that at least some can comprehend. Hence, theory building dispenses with the old adage that "it takes one to know one," instead bringing at least the possibility of understanding within the reach of all. Note, however, that although such limited explanations as the one discussed here may provide a degree of understanding, they must still be tested to determine whether they are true.

The Role of Research and Experimentation

More important than the claims made by theories and by the theorists who create them are findings of fact that either support those claims or leave them without foundation. Hence, theories, once proposed, need to be tested against the real world through a variety of research strategies, including experimentation and case studies. This is equally true whether the proposed theory is relatively simple or dauntingly complex.

Reliable determinations of program effectiveness are made through research. **Research** can be defined as the use of standardized, systematic procedures in the search for knowledge.[49] Some researchers distinguish between applied research and non-applied or pure research. **Applied research** "consists of scientific inquiry that is designed and carried out with practical application in mind."[50] In applied research, the researcher is working toward some more or less practical goal. It may be the reduction of crime, the efficient compensation of victims of crime, or an evaluation of the effectiveness of policies implemented to solve some specific aspect of the crime problem. **Pure research**, on the other hand, is undertaken simply for the sake of advancing scientific knowledge and "does not carry the promise or expectations of immediate, direct relevance."[51]

Another type of research, secondary research or secondary analysis, can be distinguished from primary research.[52] **Primary research** is "characterized by original and direct investigation,"[53] whereas **secondary research** consists of new evaluations of existing information collected by other researchers.

Scientific research generally proceeds in stages, which can be divided conceptually among (1) problem identification, (2) the development of a research design, (3) a choice

Research The use of standardized, systematic procedures in the search for knowledge.

Applied research Research based on scientific inquiry that is designed and carried out with practical application in mind.

Pure research Research undertaken simply for the sake of advancing scientific knowledge.

Primary research Research characterized by original and direct investigation.

Secondary research Research based on new evaluations of existing information collected by other researchers.

The full moon over New York City. It is the job of researchers to determine the validity of claimed relationships—and of theorists to explain why such relationships hold. Are phases of the moon correlated with changes in the rate of occurrence of certain crimes? If so, why?

Gary718/Shutterstock

Former Vancouver Police Service detective Kim Rossmo (centre) used the hypothesis that humans—offenders included—are creatures of habit as the basis for his geographic profiling tool. How do hypotheses presented by researchers gain credibility?

Nick Wass/AP/The Canadian Press

of data-gathering techniques, and (4) a review of findings (which often includes statistical analysis).

Problem Identification Problem identification, the first step in any research, consists of the naming of a problem or choice of an issue to be studied. Topics may be selected for a variety of reasons. Perhaps the researcher has a personal interest in a particular issue and wants to learn more, or maybe a professor or teacher has assigned a research project as part of the requirements for a class. Whatever the reason for beginning research, however, the way in which a research problem is stated and conceptualized will help narrow the research focus and will serve as a guide to the formulation of data-gathering strategies.

Although some criminological research undertaken today is purely descriptive, the bulk of such research is intended to explore issues of causality, especially the claims made by theories purporting to explain criminal behaviour. As such, much contemporary research in criminology is involved with the testing of hypotheses.

Within the modern scientific tradition, a hypothesis serves two purposes: (1) it is an explanation that accounts for a set of facts and that can be tested by further investigation, and (2) it is something that is taken to be true for the purpose of argument or investigation. Some criminologists, as mentioned earlier, have observed what appears to be a correlation, or relationship, between phases of the moon and the rate of crime commission. Such observers may propose the following hypothesis: the moon causes crime. Although this is a useful starting hypothesis, it needs to be further refined before it can be tested. Specifically, the concepts contained within the hypothesis must be translated into measurable variables. A **variable** is simply a concept that can undergo measurable changes.

Variable A concept that can undergo measurable changes.

Scientific precedent holds that only measurable items can be satisfactorily tested. We might, for example, move a step closer to both measurability and specificity in our hypothesis about the relationship between the moon and crime by restating it as follows: rates of murder, rape, robbery, and assault rise when the moon's fullness increases and are highest when the moon is fullest. Once the concepts within our hypothesis are measurable, we can test the hypothesis itself; that is to say, we can observe what happens to crime rates as the moon approaches fullness, as well as what happens when the moon is full, and see whether our observations support our hypothesis.

Development of a Research Design Research designs structure the research process. They provide a kind of road map to the logic inherent in one's approach to a research problem, and they also serve as guides to the systematic collection of data.

Research design consists of the logic and structure inherent in any particular approach to data gathering. A simple study, for example, might be designed to test the assertion that the consumption of refined white sugar promotes aggressive or violent tendencies. One could imagine researchers approaching prison officials with the proposal that inmate diets should be altered to exclude all refined sugar. Likewise, the prison canteen would be prohibited from selling items containing sugar for the duration of the experiment.

To determine whether the forced reduction in sugar consumption actually affected inmates' behaviour, researchers might look at the recorded frequency of aggressive incidents occurring within the confines of the prison before the experiment was initiated and compare such data with similar information on such incidents following the introduction of dietary changes. Researchers employing a strategy of this type would likely examine differences between the two sets of observations, one made before introduction of the experimental intervention and the other after. The difference, they may assume, would show changes in behaviour resulting from changes in diet—in this case, the exclusion of refined white sugar. Although this basic research design illustrates well the logic behind naïve experiments, it does not lend good structure to a research undertaking because it does not eliminate other possible explanations of behavioural change. For example, during the time between the first and second observations, inmates may have been exposed to some other influence that reduced their level of aggression. Television cable service to the prison may have been disrupted, lowering the exposure inmates received to violent programming; a new warden may have taken control of the facility, relaxing prison rules and reducing tensions; or a transfer or release of especially troublesome inmates may have occurred. The possibilities for rival explanations (that is, those that rival the explanatory power of the hypothesis under study) are nearly limitless. Rival explanations such as these, called *competing hypotheses* by some researchers and **confounding effects** by others, make the results of any single series of observations uncertain.

To have the confidence that the changes intentionally introduced into a situation are the real cause of observed variations, it is necessary to achieve some degree of control over factors that threaten the certainty that experimental interventions did indeed cause the changes observed in the study group. **Controlled experiments** are those that attempt to hold conditions (other than the intentionally introduced experimental intervention) constant. In fact, some researchers have defined the word *experiment* simply as "controlled observation."

Hence, although criminologists sometimes employ true experimental designs in the conduct of their research, they are more likely to find it necessary to use **quasi-experimental designs**. These designs are especially valuable when aspects of the social setting are beyond the control of the researcher. The crucial defining feature of quasi-experimental designs is that they give researchers control over the "when and to whom" of measurement, even though others decide the "when and to whom" of exposure to the experimental intervention.

Sometimes, for example, legislators enact new laws intended to address some aspect of the crime problem, specifying the kinds of crime-preventative measures to be employed and what segment of the population is to receive them. Midnight basketball, intended to keep youth off the streets at night, is an example of such legislatively sponsored intervention. The question, of course, is whether money spent in support of such an activity would actually reduce the incidence of street crime committed by youth. Unfortunately, good research data that could answer the question ahead of time are often unavailable. However, once the programs are in place, researchers can study

Research design The logic and structure inherent in an approach to data gathering.

Confounding effect A rival explanation, or competing hypothesis, that is a threat to the internal or external validity of a research design.

Controlled experiment An experiment that attempts to hold conditions (other than the intentionally introduced experimental intervention) constant.

Quasi-experimental design An approach to research that, although less powerful than an experimental design, is deemed worthy of use when better designs are not feasible.

them. Hence, although criminologists are not politically situated so as to be able to enact midnight basketball legislation, they are able to study the effects of such legislation after it has been enacted.[54]

Choice of Data-Collection Techniques

Once a research problem has been identified, concepts have been made measurable, and a design for the conduct of the research has been selected, investigators must decide on the type of data to be gathered and the techniques of data gathering they wish to employ. Ultimately, all research depends on the use of techniques to gather information, or data, for eventual analysis. Many first-time researchers select data-gathering techniques on the basis of ease or simplicity, and some choose according to the cost or the amount of time the techniques require. The most important question to consider when beginning to gather information, however, is whether the data-gathering strategy selected will produce information in a usable form. The kind of information needed depends on the questions to be answered. Surveys of public opinion as to the desirability of the death penalty, for example, cannot address issues of the punishment's effectiveness as a crime-control strategy.

Five major data-gathering strategies typify research in the field of criminology: surveys, case studies, participant observations, self-reporting, and secondary analysis.

Surveys: **Survey research** typically involves the use of questionnaires or surveys. Respondents may be interviewed in person or over the telephone, or queried via email or fax. Mail surveys are common, although they tend to have a lower response rate than other types of social surveys. The information produced through the use of questionnaires is referred to as *survey data*. Statistics Canada data, for example, are gathered by survey-takers who are trained periodically for that purpose. Survey data also inform the Canadian Urban Victimization Survey and other Statistics Canada–related reports produced by the Canadian Centre for Justice Statistics. Surveys have also been used in criminology to assess fear of crime and attitudes toward the police and to discover the extent of unreported crime.

Survey research Research using a social science data-gathering technique that involves the use of questionnaires.

Case studies: **Case studies** are built around in-depth investigations into individual cases. The study of one (perhaps notorious) offender, scrutiny of a particular criminal organization, and analysis of a prison boot camp all may qualify as case studies. Case studies are useful for what they can tell us to expect about other similar cases. If a study of a street gang, for example, reveals the central role of a few leaders, we would expect to find a similar organizational style among other gangs of the same kind. Although they may suffer from high levels of subjectivity in which feelings cannot be easily separated from fact, case studies provide the opportunity to investigate individual cases—an element lacking in both surveys and participant observations.

Case study An investigation into an individual case.

Participant observation: **Participant observation** "involves a variety of strategies in data gathering in which the researcher observes a group by participating, to varying degrees, in the activities of the group."[55] Some participant researchers operate undercover, whereas others make their identity and purpose known from the outset. It is possible to distinguish between at least two additional kinds of participant observation: (1) the participant as observer and (2) the observer as complete participant. When researchers make their presence known to those whom they are observing without attempting to influence the outcome of their observations or the activities of the group, they fit the category of participants who are observers. But researchers who make their presence known may inadvertently influence outcomes because people tend to act differently when they know they are being watched. When researchers become complete participants in the group they are observing, however, they run the risk of influencing the group's direction.

Participant observation A strategy in data gathering in which the researcher observes a group by participating, to varying degrees, in the activities of the group.

Self-reporting: Another subjective data-gathering technique is the **self-report**, which investigates aspects of a problem not otherwise amenable to study. When

Self-report A research investigation of subjects in order to record and report their behaviours.

official records are lacking, research subjects may be asked to record and report rates of otherwise secretive behaviour. Self-reports may prove especially valuable in providing checks on official reports consisting of statistical tabulations gathered through channels such as police departments, hospitals, and social services agencies.

Many self-reporting techniques require the maintenance of a diary or personal journal and request vigilant and ongoing observations of the study subject's own behaviour. Hence, sex researchers may ask subjects to maintain an ongoing record of their frequency of intercourse, the variety of sexual techniques employed, and their preference in partners—items of information that are not easy to come by through other means or that cannot be accurately reconstructed from memory.

Secondary analysis The reanalysis of existing data.

Secondary analysis: Not all data-gathering techniques generate new data. **Secondary analysis** purposely culls preexisting information from data that have already been gathered (possibly for another purpose) and examines it in new ways. The secondary analysis of existing data and the use of previously acquired information for new avenues of inquiry are strategies that can save researchers a considerable amount of time and expense.

One important source of data for secondary analysis is the Canadian Centre for Justice Statistics (CCJS), created through the National Justice Statistics Initiative (NJSI) of the federal government. The mandate of the NJSI is "to provide information to the justice community and the public on the nature and extent of crime and the administration of criminal justice in Canada."[56] Through the CCJS, the NJSI is meant to ensure the production of useful information to support legislative, policy, management, and research agendas and to inform the public. Access to CCJS data is open to the public, and data sets are available for sale to individual researchers. (A more detailed look at the CCJS is found in Chapter 2.)

Review of Findings

Some data, once collected, are simply archived or stored, but most data are subject to some form of analysis. Data analysis generally involves the use of mathematical techniques intended to uncover correlations between variables and to assess the likelihood that research findings can be generalized to other settings. These are statistical techniques, and their use in analyzing data is called *statistical analysis*. Statistical techniques provide tools for summarizing data and also provide quantitative means for identifying patterns within the data and for determining the degree of **correlation** that exists between variables.

Correlation A causal, complementary, or reciprocal relationship between two measurable variables.

Quantitative method A research technique that produces measurable results.

Quantitative versus Qualitative Methods

There are some who feel that there has been a tendency in criminology research over the past half century to overemphasize **quantitative methods** or techniques—that is, those that produce measurable results that can be analyzed statistically. To be sure, as such critics would be quick to admit, a considerable degree of intellectual comfort must be achieved in feeling that one is able to reduce complex forms of behaviour and interaction to something countable (as, say, the frequency of an offence). Intellectual comfort of this sort derives from the notion that anything expressible in numbers must somehow be more meaningful than that which is not.

It is crucial to realize, however, that numerical expression is mostly a result of how researchers structure their approach to the subject matter and is rarely inherent in the subject matter itself. Such is especially true in the social sciences, where attitudes, feelings, behaviours, and perceptions of all sorts are subject to quantification by researchers, who impose upon such subjective phenomena artificial techniques for their quantification.

Qualitative method A research technique that produces subjective results, or results that are difficult to quantify.

Qualitative methods, in contrast to quantitative methods, produce subjective results, or results that are difficult to quantify. Even though their findings are not expressed numerically, qualitative methods provide yet another set of potentially useful criminological research tools. Qualitative methods are important for the insight they provide into the subjective workings of the criminal mind and the processes by which meaning is accorded to human experience. Introspection, life histories, case studies, and participant observation all contain the potential to yield highly qualitative data.[57]

Consider, for example, how the following personal account of the motivation needed to rob banks provides subjective insights into the life of a young offender that would otherwise be difficult to express:[58]*

> I rob banks for the money. I like the excitement and thrills, but I do it for the money. The danger is exciting, but I don't do it for that. I spend my money on drugs—a lot on coke. It really does fly. I don't know where half of it goes. I had an apartment when I was sixteen and I was really proud of it. I bought a bed, a T.V., a four-metre-long couch worth $1600. I was proud of myself. I was doing well. I was living with a chick who was 18, but she was just a friend. I'd also spend a lot of money on my family. I'd give some to my sisters. I'd spend a lot on taxis. I'd take them everywhere. On movies and amusement parks. Money is important to me. I never have enough, I always want more. If I was to get a big score, I would want another big score. After a while you start getting bigger ideas. I've thought about doing an armoured vehicle and I've watched them make deliveries.
>
> It's only a fluke or a set-up that gets you caught. You either get caught cold-cock or you don't get caught at all. If they don't catch us in the first couple of hours, then forget it. They don't have a very good chance. This was the first time I got caught, but I think I learned a lot. Next time it will not be so easy. Once you get caught, everyone goes through a process where they don't want to do it anymore. Then after a couple of months, you're willing to do it again. I'm supposed to have a job when I hit the street, but if I have no job and no money I would do a bank for sure. It's your only means of survival. If I have no job and nowhere to stay, of course I'm going to do a bank. It's what I know. I've been trained to do that.

This passage is taken from an interview with Jules, aged 17. From a French-Canadian family of eight brothers and eight sisters, Jules started robbing banks at 15. His five older brothers have all been convicted of robbing banks and armoured vehicles.

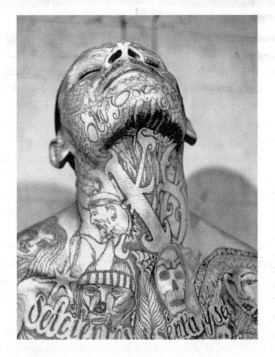

A gang member who identifies himself as "criminal." Some researchers doubt that quantitative methods can adequately assess the real-life, subjective experiences of offenders. What are some of these real-life, subjective experiences?

Rodrigo Abd/AP Images

---

* Patrick J. Desroches, *Behind the Bars—Experiences in Crime* (Toronto: Canadian Scholars' Press Inc./ Women's Press, 1996), pp. 27–28. Reprinted by permission of Canadian Scholars' Press Inc. and/or Women's Press.

Although the preceding is a purely personal account and may hold questions of generalizability for researchers, imagine the difficulties inherent in acquiring this kind of data through the use of survey instruments or other traditional research techniques. Autobiographical accounts, introspection, and many forms of participant observation amount to a kind of phenomenological reporting, in which description leads to understanding and intuition is a better guide to theory building than are volumes of quantifiable data. A growing number of criminologists believe that qualitative data-gathering strategies represent the future of criminological research.

Values and Ethics in the Conduct of Research

Research, especially research conducted within the social sciences, does not occur in a vacuum. Values enter into all stages of the research process, from the selection of the problem to be studied to the choice of strategies to address it. In short, research is never entirely free from preconceptions and biases, although much can be done to limit their impact.

The most effective way of controlling the effects of biases is to be aware of them at the outset of the research. If, for example, researchers know that the project they are working on elicits strong personal feelings but necessitates the use of interviewers, it would be beneficial to strive to hire interviewers who are relatively free of biases or can control the expression of their feelings. Data gatherers who are prejudiced against subgroups of potential respondents can represent a threat to the validity of the research results, and they may turn off some respondents, perhaps through racial innuendo, personal style, mannerisms, and so forth.

Of similar importance are ethical issues. Although they may not affect the validity of research results, these issues can have a significant impact on the lives of both researchers and research subjects. The protection of human subjects, privacy, and **data confidentiality**—which embraces the principle of protecting the confidentiality of individual research participants while preserving justified research access to needed information provided by them—are all critical ethical issues.

Informed consent, a strategy used by researchers to overcome many of the ethical issues inherent in criminological research, means that research subjects are informed as to the nature of the research about to be conducted, their anticipated role in it, and the uses that will be made of the data they provide. Ethics may also require that data derived from personal interviews or the testing of research subjects be anonymous (not associated with the names of individual subjects) and that raw (unanalyzed) data be destroyed after a specified interval (often at the completion of the research project).

Federal regulations require a plan for the protection of sensitive information as part of grant proposals submitted to federal agencies. In Canada, the *Tri-Council Policy Statement: Ethical Conduct for Research Involving Humans* has been adopted as a common research ethics policy for those conducting, participating in, or reviewing human research. Some universities, research organizations, and government agencies have established institutional review boards tasked with examining research proposals to determine whether expectations of ethical conduct have been met before these proposals are submitted to funding organizations. Institutional review boards often consist of other researchers with special knowledge of the kinds of ethical issues involved in criminological research.

Participant observation sometimes entails an especially thorny ethical issue: should researchers themselves violate the law if their research participation appears to require it? Those researching gang activity, for example, have sometimes been asked to transmit potentially incriminating information to other gang members, to act as drug couriers, and even to commit crimes of violence to help establish territorial claims

Data confidentiality The ethical requirement of social scientific research to protect the confidentiality of individual research participants while preserving justified research access to the information participants provide.

Informed consent The ethical requirement of social scientific research that research subjects be informed as to the nature of the research about to be conducted, their anticipated role in it, and the uses to which the data they provide will be put.

important to members of the gang. Researchers who refuse may endanger not only their research but also themselves. Compliance with the expectations of criminal groups, of course, evokes other kinds of dangers, including the danger of apprehension and prosecution for violations of the criminal law.

Although the dilemma of a participant observer, especially one secretly engaged in research, is a difficult one, some of the best advice on the subject was offered by Frank E. Hagan: "In self-mediating the potential conflicting roles of the criminal justice researcher, it is incumbent on the investigator to enter the setting with eyes wide open. A decision must be made beforehand on the level of commitment to the research endeavor and the analyst's ability to negotiate the likely role conflicts. Although there are no hard and fast rules *the researcher's primary role is that of a scientist*."[59]

Hagan also suggested that a code of ethics should guide all professional criminologists in their research undertakings, requiring each researcher to do the following:[60]

- Avoid procedures that may harm respondents.
- Honour commitments to respondents and respect reciprocity.
- Exercise objectivity and professional integrity in performing and reporting research.
- Protect confidentiality and privacy of respondents.

SOCIAL POLICY AND CRIMINOLOGICAL RESEARCH

1.7 | LEARNING OBJECTIVE

IDEALLY, RESEARCH RESULTS IN THE FIELD OF CRIMINOLOGY SHOULD HAVE BOTH PRACTICAL implications that can guide daily practice in relevant areas and a significant impact on those who formulate public crime-control policy. It is understood that "the normative educative model assumes that a rational use of data by policy-makers, practitioners, and scientists will be of value to the field."[61] For example, studies have shown that arrests (rather than mere warnings) of domestic violence perpetrators prove effective in reducing the likelihood of reoffending, resulting in some police departments advising their officers to make such arrests and some legislators advocating passage of mandatory arrest laws.[62]

Unfortunately, publicly elected officials are often either ignorant of current criminological research or do not heed the advice of professional criminologists, seeking instead to create politically expedient policies, which has led some to proclaim the "irrelevance" of criminology. Kevin Haggerty, from the University of Alberta, argued that

> the long-standing relationship between criminal justice policy and the advice of
> criminologists has been ruptured in the past two decades. Three interrelated factors
> help to account for this displacement of criminological thought: (1) the rise of neo-
> liberal forms of governance which have made traditional forms of criminological
> knowledge and preferred sites of intervention increasingly superfluous to the prac-
> tice of governance; (2) the ascendancy of a highly symbolic public discourse about
> crime; and (3) the transformation of the criminal justice system by new technolo-
> gies of detection, capture and monitoring.[63]

So, while the work of criminologists continues to influence the development of specific criminal justice policies, these three realities pose additional hurdles.

Similarly, in a recent examination of the state of evaluation research in Canada, Scot Wortley and Rosemary Gartner contend that "although support for evaluation research may be strong, the actual Canadian evaluation record is not that impressive." They identify five major obstacles to evaluation research: (1) ideology and intuition, (2) lack of resources, (3) resistance from funders, (4) resistance from funding recipients, and (5) the nature of academic discourse.[64]

A look at the three-strikes laws of our American neighbours illustrates Wortley and Gartner's contention that "the consequences of impeding evidence-based research or dismissing unpopular evaluation results can be profound."[65] Three-strikes laws, which became popular near the end of the 20th century, require that convicted offenders receive lengthy prison sentences (often life without possibility of parole) following their third conviction. Such laws are built on the seemingly commonsense notion that "getting tough" on repeat offenders by putting them in prison for long periods should reduce the crime rate; logic seems to say that lengthy prison sentences for recidivists will reduce crime by removing the most dangerous offenders from society.

Many studies of the three-strikes laws have concluded that such legislation typically results in clogged court systems and crowded correctional facilities and encourages three-time offenders to take dramatic risks to avoid capture.[66] One particular study, dubbed "the most comprehensive study ever of crime prevention,"[67] found that "much of the research on prisons was inadequate or flawed, making it impossible to measure how much crime was actually prevented or deterred by locking up more criminals."[68] Despite this evidence suggesting otherwise, the U.S. laws that support the lock-up of more offenders remain popular with the voting public, and lawmakers have been quick to seize upon "get-tough" crime-prevention policies in the interest of getting votes.

In an even more puzzling development, recently Canadian policy-makers appear to be following suit. In 2012, the introduction of Bill C-10, the *Safe Streets and Communities Act*, instituted increased use of incarceration as a response to crime—including increased use of mandatory minimum prison sentences, more frequent pretrial detention, and harsher penalties of incarceration for young offenders. Detractors to this approach point to the U.S. experience, stressing that if treating offenders more harshly resulted in less crime, the United States would lead the world in crime reduction. Yet, despite a prison population that has more than doubled in the past 20 years, the U.S. crime rate has not significantly decreased. Japan, on the other hand, is an industrialized nation that has seen its crime rates decrease in recent years. It also has one of the lowest per capita incarceration rates in the world, relying on a system of "retributive shaming" or "confession, repentance and absolution."[69] (See Chapter 11 for a more in-depth look at the *Safe Streets and Communities Act*.)

Another case in point is the area of Aboriginal justice initiatives in Canada. In an article entitled "The Impact of Aboriginal Justice Research on Policy: A Marginal Past and an Even More Uncertain Future," Carol La Prairie wrote:

> The benefits of research for Aboriginal criminal justice in Canada have scarcely been tapped. There have been some issue-specific activities over the past 25 years but research has not systematically been designed and integrated into policy, practice, and project development. Because research is often negatively perceived by Aboriginal people and is of sporadic interest to government, its history of shaping justice projects and influencing policy decision-making has been marginal at best.[70]

La Prairie concluded that this apparent lack of research impact and integration results from the fact that government legislators equate Aboriginal justice issues with the self-government movement, which has largely served to portray Aboriginal justice problems (such as the over-representation of Aboriginals as offenders in the criminal justice system) as conflicts over race and culture rooted in a colonial history of conflict and discrimination. She claimed that the emphasis of research on the race/cultural issue has failed to consider other possible explanations for problems faced by Aboriginal people, such as "community marginalization, inequity of distribution of community resources, and family breakdown and dysfunction."[71]

Professional criminologists are acutely aware of the need to link sound social policy to the objective findings of well-conducted criminological research, and they continue to work to forge this link. "We can be fairly certain that the public, when provided with adequate information to respond to questions about crime and justice matters, favours approaches that are meaningful and those which use justice resources sensibly."[72]

Social Policy and Public Crime Concerns

"If it bleeds, it leads" is a phrase often used by the media to determine how much attention and coverage is given to a news story. Indeed, the news media, the internet, and social media seem to be preoccupied with delivering stories about war, disease, and incidents of violent crime. Many argue that the media are simply giving the public what it wants; others argue that the public's perception about threats to its safety and protection is skewed. A seminal report by Julian Roberts identified a number of ways that the mass media influence public attitudes and beliefs about crime: (1) the media tend not to report or to emphasize declining crime rates, (2) national crime figures (which for the past decade have been reporting declining crime rates) are published only once a year, allowing the media the remainder of each year to concentrate on extreme, violent cases, and (3) crime stories reported by the media are rarely put in a statistical context, and the electronic and print news outlets neglect to comment on trends in crime rates over time.[73]

Although Canadian crime rates have been declining for more than a decade, concern over personal and national security, and increasingly terrorism, remains pervasive. A recent Canadian public opinion poll indicated that the majority of Canadians endorse the Canadian government's anti-crime proposals. For example, 91 percent support a mandatory two-year jail term for anyone selling drugs at or near a school, 82 percent would include all sex offenders in a national registry, and 61 percent think mandatory minimum sentences are a good idea.[74]

Fear of crime is not necessarily related to the actual incidence of crime. A 2012 public opinion telephone survey asked almost 2000 Canadians whether they thought violent crime was increasing. Of those asked, 54 percent agreed, 33 percent disagreed, and the remainder responded that they were unsure.[75] A Department of Justice report concluded that "despite an increasing concern for crime, the public's fears remain unrelated to actual crime rates and potential for victimization, as perceptions of criminal activity and violence are not in tune with reality."[76] Even though crime rates have declined, concern over crime remains an important determinant of public policy. Hence, political agendas that promise to lower crime rates or to keep them low, as well as those that call for changes in the conditions that produce crime, can be quite successful for candidates or incumbents who promote them in an environment where concern

According to pollsters, fear of crime is a persistent concern among Canadians. Given recent statistics showing falling crime rates, is such fear realistic? What role does the media play in the perception of crime among Canadians?

Cultura Creative/Alamy Stock Photo

over crime remains high.[77] In his book entitled *Risk: The Science and Politics of Fear*, Dan Gardner contended that we are all becoming more susceptible to irrational fear, and this irrationality is caused in part by those politicians, activists, and media that promote fear for their own gain. Why is it that we find ourselves worrying about what statistics tell us are unlikely threats—terrorism, child abduction, cancer caused by chemical pollution—while we largely ignore serious risks like obesity and smoking?[78]

1.8 LEARNING OBJECTIVE

THE THEME OF THIS TEXT

AT THE CORE OF TODAY'S THINKING ABOUT CRIME EXISTS A CRUCIAL DISTINCTION BETWEEN those who believe that crime is a *manifestation of underlying social problems* beyond the control of individuals (the social problems perspective) and those who emphasize that crime is a matter of *individual responsibility* (the social responsibility perspective). Building upon this distinction, this text contrasts these two perspectives (see Figure 1.3).

One point of view, termed the **social problems perspective**, holds that crime is a manifestation of underlying social problems such as poverty, discrimination, the breakdown of traditional social institutions, the low level of formal education among some disadvantaged groups, pervasive family violence experienced during the formative years, and inadequate socialization practices that leave too many young people without the fundamental values necessary to contribute meaningfully to the society in which they live. Advocates of the social problems perspective, while generally agreeing that crime and violence are serious social problems, advance solutions based on what is, in effect, a public health model. Adherents of that model say that crime must be addressed in much the same way as public health concerns like AIDS, cancer, or the avian flu.

Proponents of the social problems perspective typically foresee solutions to the crime problem as coming in the form of government intervention in support of social programs designed to address the issues that lie at the root of crime. Government-funded initiatives, designed to enhance social, educational, occupational, and other opportunities, are perceived as offering programmatic solutions to ameliorate most causes of crime. The social problems approach to crime is characteristic of what social scientists term a *macro approach* because it portrays instances of individual behaviour (crimes) as arising out of widespread and contributory social conditions that enmesh unwitting individuals in a causal nexus of uncontrollable social forces.

Within the Canadian setting, the social problems perspective has generally influenced crime-prevention policy. In 1993, the Solicitor General and the Parliamentary Standing Committee on Justice produced a report entitled *Crime Prevention in Canada: Toward a National Strategy*. The report recommended the implementation of a "National Strategy on Community Safety and Crime Prevention" (now known as the

Social problems perspective The belief that crime is a manifestation of underlying social problems such as poverty, discrimination, pervasive family violence, inadequate socialization practices, and the breakdown of traditional social institutions.

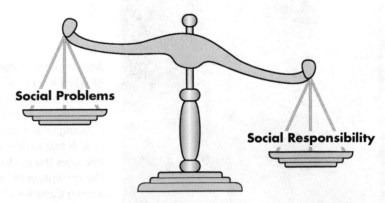

Figure 1.3 The Theme of This Text: Social Problems versus Social Responsibility

30   Part 1 The Crime Picture

National Crime Prevention Strategy) focused on developing new plans to look at the causes of crime and to develop partnerships with communities across the country to carry out crime-prevention activities. Phase I of the National Strategy (1994–1998) saw the creation of the National Crime Prevention Council (NCPC), whose mandate was the promotion of crime prevention through social development, with particular emphasis on early-prevention programs targeting children and youth. The NCPC identified a number of factors that place children and youth at risk of engaging in criminal behaviour. These included child poverty, inadequate living conditions, inconsistent and uncaring parenting, childhood traumas such as physical and sexual abuse, family breakdown, racism and other forms of discrimination, difficulties in school, delinquent friends, and living situations where there is alcohol, drug, and other kinds of substance abuse. Since 1998, Phase II has been building on the work done by the NCPC and focusing on helping communities develop programs and partnerships to reduce crime and victimization. The NCPC is moving toward a results- and evidence-based approach to crime prevention. Its funding programs and activities are focused on addressing known risk factors associated with crime and violence in high-risk populations and places. With this evolution, the approaches to crime prevention have become more evidence based. In addition to focusing on children and youth, this phase places priority on Aboriginal people and women's personal safety.[79] (A detailed examination of the National Crime Prevention Strategy can be found in Chapter 11.)

A contrasting perspective looks to individual perpetrators as an explanation for crime. This point of view holds that individuals are fundamentally responsible for their own behaviour and maintains that they choose crime over other, more law-abiding courses of action. Perpetrators may choose crime, advocates of this perspective say, because it is exciting, it offers illicit pleasures and the companionship of like-minded thrill-seekers, or it is simply less demanding than conformity. This viewpoint, which we shall call the **social responsibility perspective**, has a close affiliation with rational choice theory (discussed in Chapter 5) and is associated with a belief in the importance of free will. Although the social responsibility perspective might also be termed the *individual responsibility perspective*, because it stresses individual responsibility above all else, we've chosen to use the term *social responsibility perspective* instead, as it holds that individuals must be ultimately responsible to the social group of which they are a part and that they should be held accountable by group standards if they are not. In short, this perspective is characterized by societal demands for the exercise of individual responsibility.

Advocates of the social responsibility perspective, with their emphasis on individual choice, tend to believe that social programs are limited in their ability to solve the problem of crime because, they say, a certain number of crime-prone individuals, for a variety of personalized reasons, will always make irresponsible choices. Hence, advocates of the social responsibility approach suggest highly personalized crime-prevention and -reduction strategies based on firm punishments, imprisonment, individualized rehabilitation, and increased security, as well as a wider use of police powers. The social responsibility perspective characteristically emphasizes a *micro approach* that tends to focus on individual offenders and their unique biology, psychology, background, and immediate life experiences.

The social responsibility perspective is most evident in the approach to crime prevention and control adopted by our neighbours to the south. *The Violent Crime Control and Law Enforcement Act* of 1994, for example, expanded the number of capital crimes under federal law from a handful of offences to 52.[80] The law also made billions of dollars available to municipalities to put tens of thousands of new police officers on the streets and allocated billions for states to build and operate prisons and incarceration alternatives like "boot camps." Prison funding was intended to ensure that additional

Social responsibility perspective The belief that individuals are fundamentally responsible for their own behaviour and that they choose crime over other, more law-abiding, courses of action.

prison cells would be available to put—and keep—violent offenders behind bars. A subchapter of the 1994 *Violent Crime Control and Law Enforcement Act* created a federal "three strikes and you're out" law, mandating life imprisonment for criminals convicted of three violent federal felonies or drug offences. Similarly, the law increased or created new penalties for over 70 federal criminal offences, primarily covering violent crimes, drug trafficking, and gun crimes. Since the 1994 federal legislation was passed, many states have moved to toughen their own laws against violent criminals; violent juveniles and repeat offenders have been especially targeted. The *USA PATRIOT Act*—enacted in 2001 and renewed with modifications in 2006—targets terrorism and crimes committed in support of terrorist activity. The *PATRIOT Act* has been criticized by many for going too far in limiting individual freedoms and restricting personal choice, although its supporters argue that its provisions are needed to effectively fight the "war on terrorism."

1.9   LEARNING OBJECTIVE

THE SOCIAL CONTEXT OF CRIME

CRIME DOES NOT OCCUR IN A VACUUM. EVERY CRIME HAS A UNIQUE SET OF CAUSES, consequences, and participants. Crime affects some people more than others, having a special impact on those who are direct participants in the act itself—offenders, victims, police officers, witnesses, and so on. Crime, in general, provokes reactions from its victims, from concerned groups of citizens, from the criminal justice system, and sometimes from society as a whole, which manifests its concerns through the creation of new social policy. Reactions to crime, from the everyday to the precedent setting, may colour the course of future criminal events.[81]

In this text, we shall attempt to identify and examine some of the many social, psychological, economic, biological, and other causes of crime while expounding on the many differing perspectives that have been advanced to explain both crime and criminality. Popular conceptions of criminal motivation are typically shaped by media portrayals of offender motivation, which often fail to take into consideration the felt experiences of the law violators. By identifying and studying this diversity of perspectives on criminality, we will discover the characteristic disjuncture among victims, offenders, the justice system, and society as to the significance that each assigns to the behaviour in question—and often to its motivation.

Making Sense of Crime: The Causes and Consequences of the Criminal Event

This text recognizes that criminal activity is diversely created and variously interpreted. In other words, it depicts crime not as an isolated individual activity but as a *social event*.[82] Like other social events, crime is fundamentally a social construction.[83] To say that crime is a social construction is not to lessen the impact of the victimization experiences that all too many people undergo in our society every day, nor does such a statement trivialize the significance of crime-prevention efforts or the activities of members of the criminal justice system. Likewise, it does not underplay the costs of crime to individual victims and to society as a whole. It does, however, recognize that although a given instance of criminal behaviour may have many causes, it also carries with it many different kinds of meanings—at least one for offenders, another (generally quite different one, of course) for victims, and still another for agents of the criminal justice system. Similarly, a wide range of social interest groups, from victims' advocates to prisoner rights and gun-control organizations, all interpret the significance of law-breaking behaviour from unique points of view, and each arrives at different conclusions as to what should be done about the so-called crime problem.

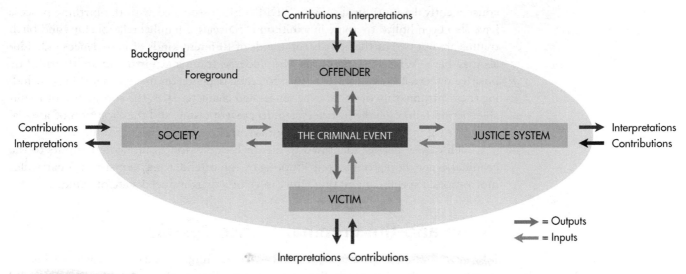

Figure 1.4 The Causes and Consequences of Crime

For these reasons, it is important to apply the concept of social relativity to the study of criminality.[84] **Social relativity** means that social events are interpreted differently according to the cultural experiences and personal interests of the initiator, the observer, or the recipient of that behaviour. Hence, as a social phenomenon, crime means different things to the offender, to the criminologist who studies it, to the police officer who investigates it, and to the victim who experiences it first-hand.

Figure 1.4 illustrates the causes and consequences of crime in rudimentary diagrammatic form. In keeping with the theme of this text, it depicts crime as a social event. The figure consists of a foreground, describing those features that immediately determine the nature of the criminal event (including responses to the event as it is transpiring), and a background, in which generic contributions to crime can be seen with interpretations of the event after it has taken place. We call the background causes of crime *contributions* and use the word *inputs* to signify the more immediate propensities and predispositions of the actors involved in the situation. Inputs also include the physical features of the setting in which a specific crime takes place. Both background contributions and immediate inputs contribute to and shape the criminal event. The more or less immediate results or consequences of crime are termed *outputs*, while the term *interpretations* appears in the diagram to indicate that any crime has a lasting impact both on surviving participants and on society. As Figure 1.4 shows, although the criminal event may occur at a particular point in time and within a given setting, it is ultimately a result of the coming together of inputs provided by (1) the offender, (2) the criminal justice system, (3) the victim, and (4) society (including other individuals who do not fit in any of the first three categories).

Crime and the Offender

Offenders bring with them certain background features, such as personal life experiences, a peculiar biology (insofar as they are unique organisms), a distinct personality, personal values and beliefs, and various kinds of skills and knowledge (some of which may be useful in the commission of crime). Background contributions to crime can be vitally important. Recent research, for example, tends to cement the existence of a link between child-rearing practices and criminality in later life. Joan McCord, reporting on a 30-year study of family relationships and crime, found that self-confident, non-punitive, and affectionate mothers tend to insulate their male children from delinquency and,

Social relativity The notion that social events are differently interpreted according to the cultural experiences and personal interests of the initiator, the observer, or the recipient of that behaviour.

consequently, later criminal activity.[85] Difficulties associated with the birthing process have also been linked to crime in adulthood.[86] Negative familial relationships and birth trauma are but two of the literally thousands of different kinds of experiences individuals may have. Whether individuals who undergo trauma at birth and are deprived of positive maternal experiences will turn to crime depends on many other things, including their own mixture of other experiences and characteristics, the appearance of a suitable victim, failure of the justice system to prevent crime, and the evolution of a social environment in which criminal behaviour is somehow encouraged or valued.

Each of the parties identified in Figure 1.4 contributes immediate inputs to the criminal event. Foreground contributions by the offender may consist of a particular motivation, a specific intent (in many cases), or a drug-induced state of mind.

Crime and the Criminal Justice System

Like the offender, the **criminal justice system** (meaning the various agencies of justice, such as the lawmakers, the police, the courts, and corrections) also contributes to the criminal event, albeit unwillingly, through its failure to (1) prevent criminal activity, (2) adequately identify specific offenders prior to their involvement in crime, and (3) prevent the early release of convicted criminals who later become repeat offenders. Such background contributions can be seen in prisons that serve as "schools for crime," fostering anger against society and building a propensity for continued criminality in those released. Similarly, the failure of system-sponsored crime-prevention programs—ranging from the patrol activities of local police departments to educational and diversionary programs intended to redirect potential offenders—helps to set the stage for the criminal event.

On the other hand, proper system response may reduce crime. One study found that police response (especially arrest) can, under certain demographic conditions, dramatically reduce the incidence of criminal behaviour.[87] Additionally, the study found that arrest "constitutes communication to criminals in general," further supporting the notion that inputs provided by the justice system have the power to either enhance or reduce the likelihood of criminal occurrences. Immediate inputs provided by the justice system typically consist of features of the situation such as the presence or absence of police officers, the ready availability (or lack thereof) of official assistance, the willingness of police officers to intervene in pre-crime situations, and the response time required for officers to arrive at a crime scene.

Crime and the Victim

Few crimes can occur without a victim. Sometimes the victim is a passive participant in the crime, such as an innocent person killed by an impaired driver. In such cases, the victim is simply in the "wrong place at the wrong time." Even then, however, merely by being present, the victim contributes his or her person to the event, thereby increasing the severity of the incident (i.e., the impaired driver who injures no one may still be breaking the law but is committing a far less serious crime than a similar incident in which somebody is killed). Sometimes, however, victims more actively contribute to their own victimization by appearing defenceless (having characteristics such as old age, drunkenness, or disability), by failing to take appropriate defensive measures (leaving doors unlocked or forgetting to remove the key from a car's ignition), by unwisely displaying wealth (flashing large-denomination bills in a public place), or simply by making other unwise choices (walking down a dark alley in a dangerous section of the city at 3:00 a.m.). In a study of Canadian victimization, Leslie W. Kennedy and David R. Forde found that violent personal victimization "is contingent on the exposure that comes

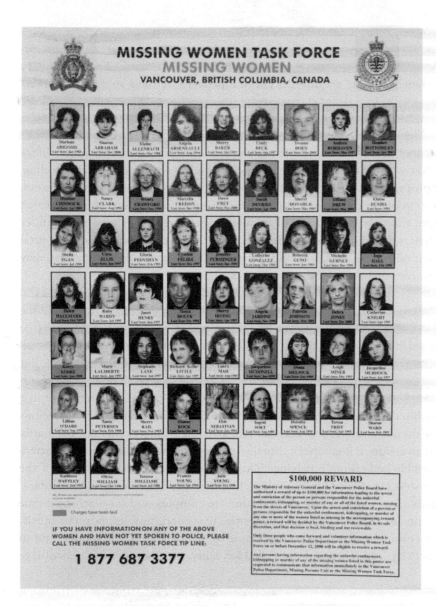

In 2007, Robert Pickton was convicted of the murders of six women and charged in the deaths of an additional 20 women (stayed in 2010), many of them prostitutes and drug users. The Missing Women Commission of Inquiry, established in 2010 by the B.C. Lieutenant-Governor, released a report that identified blatant police failure triggered by systemic bias against poor, vulnerable women of Vancouver's Downtown Eastside as the reason that Pickton was able to evade arrest for so many years.

Darryl Dyck/The Canadian Press

from following certain lifestyles," which is especially true "for certain demographic groups, particularly young males."[88]

Although lifestyles may provide the background that fosters victimization, a more active form of victimization characterizes "victims" who initiate criminal activity, such as the barroom brawler who picks a fight but ends up on the receiving end of the ensuing physical violence. Victim-precipitated offences are those that involve active victim participation in the initial stages of a criminal event and that take place when the soon-to-be victim instigates the chain of events that ultimately results in the victimization. (See Chapter 4 for a further discussion on victims of crime.)

Crime and Society

Finally, the general public (termed *society* in Figure 1.4) contributes to the criminal event both formally and informally. Society's formal contributions sometimes take the form of legislation, whereby crime itself is defined. Hence, as we shall discuss in considerable detail in Chapter 11, society structures the criminal event in a most fundamental way by delineating (through legislation and statute) what forms of activity are to be thought of as criminal.

Society's less formal contributions to crime arise out of generic social practices and conditions such as poverty, poor and informal education, various forms of discrimination by which pathways to success are blocked, and the **socialization** process (the process whereby people acquire the cultural patterns of their society). Socialization has an especially important impact on crime causation because it provides the interpretative foundation used to define and understand the significance of particular situations in which we find ourselves, and it is upon those interpretations that we may (or may not) decide to act. Date rape, for example, can occur when a man concludes that his date "owes" him something for the money he has spent on her. That feeling, however inappropriate from the point of view of the victim and the justice system, probably has its roots in early-learned experiences—including values communicated from television, the movies, and popular music—about gender-related roles under such circumstances. In other words, society, through the divergent values and expectations it places upon people, property, and behaviour under particular conditions, may provide the motivational basis for many offences.

The contributions society makes to the backgrounds of both offender and victim and to the structure of the justice system, and the influences each in turn have upon the general social order, provide for a kind of "feedback loop" in our vision of crime (the loop is not shown in Figure 1.4 for fear of unnecessarily complicating it). Through socialization, for example, individuals learn about the dangers of criminal victimization, but when victimization occurs and is publicized, it reinforces the socialization process, leading to an increased wariness of others, and so on. An example can be seen in the fact that children throughout Canada are routinely taught to avoid strangers and to be suspicious of people they do not know. A few decades ago, avoiding strangers was not ordinarily communicated to children; it entered cultural awareness following a number of horrendous and well-publicized crimes involving child victims and is now a shared part of the socialization process experienced by countless children every day throughout Canada.

The contributions made by society to crime are complex and far-reaching. Some say that the content of the mass media (websites, television, movies, popular music, etc.) can lead to crime by exposing young people to inappropriate role models and to the kinds of activity—violence and unbridled sexuality, for example—that encourage criminality.

Society's foreground contributions to crime largely emanate from the distribution of resources and the accessibility of services, which are often the direct result of economic conditions. In a study of the availability of medical resources (especially quality hospital emergency services), William G. Doerner found that serious assaults may "become" homicides when such resources are lacking but that homicides can be prevented through the effective use of capable medical technology.[89] Hence, societal decisions leading to the distribution and placement of advanced medical support equipment and personnel can effectively lower homicide rates in selected geographic areas. Of course, homicide rates will be higher in areas where such equipment is not readily available. In Doerner's words, "the causes of homicide transcend the mere social world of the combatants."[90]

The moments immediately preceding any crime are ripe with possibilities. When all the inputs brought to the situation by all those present coalesce into activity that violates the criminal law, a crime occurs. Together, the elements, experiences, and propensities brought to the situation by the offender and the victim, and those contributed to the pending event by society and the justice system, precipitate and decide the nature, course, and eventual outcome of the criminal event. While certain circumstances contribute to the criminal event as it unfolds, it is also important to note that some of the inputs brought to the situation may be inhibiting—that is, they may tend to reduce the likelihood or severity of criminal behaviour.

The Consequences of Crime

As mentioned earlier, the causes of crime, however well documented, tell only half the criminological story. Each and every crime has consequences. Although the immediate consequences of crime may be relatively obvious for those parties directly involved (for example, the offender and the victim), crime also has an indirect impact on society and the justice system. Figure 1.4 terms the immediate effects of crime *outputs*. As with the causes of crime, however, the real impact of such outputs is mediated by perceptual filters, resulting in what the figure terms *interpretations*. After a crime has taken place, each party to the event must make sense of what has transpired. Such interpretations consist of cognitive, emotional, and (ultimately) behavioural reactions to the criminal event.

Interpretations are ongoing. They happen before, during, and after the criminal event and are undertaken by all those associated with it. An interesting and detailed study of the interpretive activity of personnel in the criminal justice system documents what happens when callers reach the 911 dispatcher on police emergency lines.[91] Because prank calls and calls for information are made to 911 operators, the operators must judge the seriousness of every call that comes through. What the caller says was found to be only a small part of the informational cues that the dispatcher seeks to interpret prior to assigning the call to a particular response (or non-response) category. Honest calls for help may go unanswered if the operator misinterprets the call. Hence, quite early on in the criminal event, the potential exists for a crucial representative of the justice system to misinterpret important cues and conclude that no crime is taking place.

Other interpretative activities may occur long after the crime has transpired, but they are at least as significant. The justice system, taken as a whole, must decide guilt or innocence and attempt to deal effectively with convicted offenders. Victims must attempt to make sense of their victimizations in such a way as to allow them to testify in court (if need be) and to pick up the pieces of their crime-shattered lives. Offenders must come to terms with themselves and decide whether to avoid prosecution (if escape, for example, is possible), accept blame, or deny responsibility. Whatever the outcome of these more narrowly focused interpretative activities, society—because of the cumulative impact of individual instances of criminal behaviour—will also face tough decisions through its courts and lawmaking agencies. Society-level decision making may revolve around the implementation of policies designed to stem future instances of criminal behaviour, the revision of criminal codes, or the elimination of unpopular laws.

Our perspective takes a three-dimensional integrative view of the social event called *crime*. We will (1) attempt to identify and understand the multiple causes giving rise to criminal behaviour, (2) highlight the processes involved in the criminal event as it unfolds, and (3) analyze the interpretation of the crime phenomenon, including societal responses to it. From this perspective, crime can be viewed along a temporal continuum as an emergent activity that (1) arises out of past complex causes; (2) assumes a course that builds upon immediate relationships between victim, offender, and the social order that exists at the time of the offence; and (3) elicits a formal response from the justice system, shapes public perceptions, and (possibly) gives rise to changes in social policy after it has occurred.

The advantages of an integrative perspective can be found in the completeness of the picture that it provides. The integrative point of view results in a comprehensive and inclusive view of crime because it emphasizes the personal and social underpinnings as well as the consequences of the crime. The chapters that follow employ the integrative perspective advocated here to analyze criminal events and to show how various theoretical approaches can be woven into a consistent perspective on crime.

THE PRIMACY OF SOCIOLOGY

THIS TEXT RECOGNIZES THE CONTRIBUTIONS MADE BY NUMEROUS DISCIPLINES, INCLUDING biology, economics, psychology, psychiatry, physiology, and political science, to the study of crime and crime causation. It is important to recognize, however, that the primary perspective from which most contemporary criminologists operate is a sociological one. Hence, a large number of today's dominant theoretical understandings of criminal behaviour are routinely couched in the language of social science and fall within the framework of sociological theory. The social problems versus social responsibility theme, around which this text is built, is in keeping with such a tradition.

Some, however, would disagree with those who claim that the sociological perspective should be accorded heightened importance in today's criminological enterprise. Those who argue for the primacy of the sociological perspective emphasize the fact that crime, as a subject of study, is a social phenomenon. Central to any study of crime must be the social context of the criminal event, which brings victims and criminals together.[92] Moreover, much of contemporary criminology rests upon a sound tradition of social scientific investigation into the nature of crime and criminal behaviour that is rooted in European and North American sociological traditions that are now well over 200 years old.[93]

One of the challenges of the sociological perspective has been its apparent reluctance to accept the significance of findings from other fields as well as its frequent inability to integrate such findings into existing sociological understandings of crime. Another has been its seeming difficulty in conclusively demonstrating effective means of controlling violent (as well as other forms of) crime. In the words of one prominent criminologist, "Sociological factors play a role. But they have not been able to explain why one person becomes violent and another doesn't."[94]

While sociological theories continue to develop, new and emerging perspectives ask to be recognized. The role of biology in explaining criminal tendencies, for example, appears to be gaining strength as investigations into the mapping of human DNA continue. Nonetheless, whatever new insights may develop over the coming years, it is likely that the sociological perspective will continue to dominate the field of criminology for some time to come. Such dominance is rooted in the fact that crime, regardless of all the causative nuances that may be identified in its development, occurs within the context of the social world. As such, the primary significance of crime and of criminal behaviour is fundamentally social in nature, and any control over crime must stem from effective social policy.

SUMMARY OF LEARNING OBJECTIVES

1.1 In this chapter, the term *crime* was defined as a violation of the criminal law. Near the end of this chapter, we recognized the complexity of crime, calling it an *emergent activity*. In the process, crime was redefined as a law-breaking event whose significance arises out of an intricate social nexus involving a wide variety of participants.

1.2 Deviance, or deviant behaviour, refers to a violation of social norms. Some forms of behaviour (such as murder, sexual assault, and most serious crimes) are both criminal and deviant. Others may be deviant but not criminal (for example, nudity under certain circumstances), or may be criminal but not regarded as deviant by many members of society (for example, the recreational use of marijuana).

1.3 Decisions as to what should be criminal are generally made by legislatures at both the provincial and federal levels. Such decisions are arrived at through a political process that involves input from social interest groups, including those in favour of criminalizing certain behaviours and those opposed to criminalizing them.

1.4 *Criminology* is an interdisciplinary profession built around the scientific study of crime and criminal behaviour, including their forms, causes, legal aspects, and control. It is a social science that endeavours to develop theories based on applied techniques of data collection and hypothesis testing. Theoretical criminology, in turn, contributes to a more complete understanding of the nature of crime and crime causation.

1.5 The term *criminologist* is applied to credentialed individuals who engage in the study of crime, criminal behaviour, and crime trends. *Criminalist* is used to describe people who specialize in the collection and examination of the physical evidence associated with specific crimes. *Criminal justice professionals* include law enforcement officers, judges, criminal defence attorneys, prosecutors, cybercrime investigators, victims' advocates, jailers, corrections officers, and so on.

1.6 Research refers to the use of standardized, systematic procedures in the search for knowledge. Determinations of program effectiveness are made through research. Experimentation uses data collection and hypothesis testing to validate theory. Quantitative methods tend to produce results that are easy to measure, whereas qualitative methods produce subjective results that are difficult or impossible to quantify. Values and ethics enter into all stages of the research process. Protection of human subjects from harm, need for privacy, disclosure of research methods, and data confidentiality are all critical ethical issues.

1.7 Ideally, research results in the field of criminology should have a significant impact on public crime-prevention policy. Unfortunately, publicly elected officials often either are ignorant of current criminological research or do not heed the advice of professional criminologists, seeking instead to create politically expedient policies.

1.8 This text builds on a social policy theme by asking what the sources of crime and criminality are and what we can do to prevent and control crime. The theme contrasts two perspectives: the *social responsibility perspective* holds that crime is a matter of individual responsibility; the *social problems perspective* holds that crime is a manifestation of underlying social problems beyond the control of individuals.

1.9 This text sees crime as a social event, not an isolated individual activity. A given instance of criminal behaviour may have many causes and many different kinds of meanings. Social relativity holds that social events are interpreted differently according to the cultural experiences and personal interests of the initiator, the observer, and the recipient of that behaviour.

1.10 The discipline of sociology has had the most impact on theoretical understandings of crime and crime causation, so a large number of today's theoretical explanations of criminal behaviour are routinely couched in the language of social science and fall within the framework of sociological theory. Nonetheless, it is important to recognize the contributions made by numerous other disciplines (biology, economics, psychology, psychiatry, physiology, political science), making the study of crime and crime causation interdisciplinary.

Questions for Review

1. What is crime? How might the notion of crime change over time?

2. What is deviance? How are crime and deviance similar? How do they differ?

3. Who decides what should be criminal? How do the three perspectives of theoretical criminology differ in how they might determine what should be criminal?

4. What is criminology? In what ways is contemporary criminology interdisciplinary?

5. What are some of the employment opportunities available in the field of criminology? Do you think you might want to become a criminologist? Why or why not?

6. What is a theory? What purposes do theories serve? What role do research and experimentation play in theory building in criminology? Why are values and ethics important in research?

7. How is social policy in the area of crime control determined?

8. What is the theme of this text? Upon which two contrasting viewpoints does it build?

9. How would you describe the various participants in a criminal event? How does each contribute to an understanding of the event?

10. In what ways has the discipline of sociology contributed the most to theoretical understandings of crime causation over the past century?

Multiple-Choice Questions

1. Evidence-based criminology is a form of contemporary criminology that does not rely on

   _____.

   a. rigorous social scientific techniques

   b. conjecture and speculation

   c. controlled experiments

   d. systematic review of research results

   e. randomized experiments

2. The legalistic perspective defines crime as

   a. "an antisocial act of such a nature that its repression is necessary or is supposed to be necessary to the preservation of the existing system of society."

   b. a definition of human conduct created by authorized agents in a politically organized society.

   c. human conduct in violation of the criminal laws of a state, the federal government, or a provincial or local jurisdiction that has the power to make such laws.

   d. "a form of social maladjustment which can be designated as a more or less pronounced difficulty that the individual has in reacting to the stimuli of his environment in such a way as to remain in harmony with that environment."

   e. human conduct in violation of the criminal laws of a state, the federal government, or a provincial or local jurisdiction.

3. _____ is research based on scientific inquiry that is designed and carried out with practical application in mind.

   a. Pure research

   b. Theory building

   c. Applied research

   d. Hypothesis development

   e. Problem identification

4. Which of the following statements about the social responsibility perspective is false?

    a. It contends that individuals are fundamentally responsible for their own behaviour.

    b. It emphasizes the development of social and educational opportunities as a way of dealing with crime.

    c. It emphasizes crime-prevention efforts such as harsher sentences.

    d. It suggests that perpetrators may choose crime because it is exciting or simply less demanding than conformity.

    e. It suggests that solutions to crime need to come in the form of highly personalized crime prevention based on firm punishments, imprisonment, and individualized rehabilitation.

5. _____ is a strategy used by researchers to overcome many of the ethical issues inherent in criminological research.

    a. Informed consent

    b. Personal bias

    c. The quantitative method

    d. Case study

    e. Quasi-experimental design

Multiple Choice Answers: 1b, 2d, 3c, 4b, 5a

Chapter 2
Crime Statistics

Colin Mcconnell/The Toronto Star/ZUMAPRESS.com/Newscom

Who does what? When? How often? These are the perennial questions about crime. There is no scarcity of answers. Indeed, there is a surplus. The problem is that the answers seldom satisfy. Dissatisfaction follows from the fact that our measures of crime are of doubtful accuracy.

—John Hagen[1]

LEARNING OBJECTIVES

After reading this chapter, you should be able to

2.1 Describe how the collection and study of crime statistics has developed through history.

2.2 Explain the usefulness and limitations of crime statistics.

2.3 Recognize various methods used to collect and disseminate crime data.

2.4 Assess the correlations that exist between the predominant social dimensions of crime and criminal behaviour.

INTRODUCTION

Seventy-seven-year-old Melissa Shepard knows little about statistics, but she is familiar with crime. Shepard, also known as Melissa Stewart, Melissa Weeks, and Melissa Friedrich, lives in Nova Scotia and has been arrested and convicted on numerous occasions for crimes including grand theft forgery, fraud, misrepresentation, theft, manslaughter, and most recently in October 2012, attempted murder for trying to poison her husband. She is alleged to have administered the tranquilizer benzodiazepine to him two days after their marriage.

Shepard's most recent run-in with the law has earned her the nickname the "Internet Black Widow" for her ability to persuade grieving widowers to marry her; she then steals their money and kills them. In 1991, she killed her husband Gordon Stewart, of Prince Edward Island, on a deserted road near Halifax. He had been heavily drugged when she ran him over twice with a car. She was sentenced to six years in jail for manslaughter and was released after serving two.

Shortly after being released from jail, Melissa Stewart, as she was known at the time, travelled to Florida, where she met Robert Friedrich at a Christian retreat. They married in Nova Scotia in 2000, but a year later the Friedrich family noticed that Robert's health was faltering; he was suffering from mysterious fainting spells, slurred his speech, and was in and out of hospital. They also said his money had started to disappear. In 2002, Friedrich died of cardiac arrest, and no one was charged in his death.

In 2005, Shepard was sentenced to five years in prison on seven counts of theft from Alexander Strategos, a Florida man she had met online. On the day they moved in together, he was taken to hospital after hitting his head. Strategos wound up being hospitalized eight times over a two-month period, and eventually a drug was found in his system. Investigators reported that Shepard syphoned about $20 000 U.S. out of his bank account. For that incident, Shepard was sentenced to five years in a Florida prison. Upon her release in 2009, she was deported to Canada and moved to New Glasgow, Nova Scotia.

In 2012, Shepard, aged 78, was charged in Cape Breton with attempted murder and administering a noxious thing to her then husband, Fred Weeks, whom she had married just two weeks earlier. In 2013, Shepard pled guilty to charges of administering a noxious thing and failing to provide the necessities of life and received a three-and-a-half-year sentence of incarceration. In 2016, Shepard was arrested in Halifax for accessing the internet in the public library, a violation of the conditions of her release. Her case has yet to come to court.[2]

A HISTORY OF CRIME STATISTICS

2.1 LEARNING OBJECTIVE

MELISSA SHEPARD IS A STATISTICAL ANOMALY. FEW PEOPLE ARE INVOLVED IN CRIME PAST middle age. Fewer still are involved in crime at Shepard's age. And even fewer are female. Data from the Canadian Centre for Justice Statistics showed that the likelihood of someone committing a crime declines with age. People 65 years of age and older, for example, commit fewer than 1 percent of all crimes, and the proportion of crimes committed by women, especially violent crimes, is so small that it cannot be meaningfully expressed as a percentage of total crime.

Although the gathering of crime statistics is a relatively new phenomenon, population statistics have been collected periodically since pre-Roman times. Old Testament accounts of enumerations of the Hebrews, for example, provided evidence of Middle Eastern census taking thousands of years ago. In like manner, the New Testament described how the family of Jesus had to return home to be counted during an official census—providing evidence of routine census taking during the time of Christ. The *lustrum*, which was a ceremonial purification of the entire ancient Roman population after census taking, has led historians to conclude that Roman population counts were made every five years. Centuries later, the *Domesday Book*, created by the order of William the Conqueror in 1085–1086, provided a written survey of English landowners and their property. Other evidence shows that primitive societies around the world also took periodic counts of their members. The Incas, for example, a pre-Columbian indigenous empire in western South America, required successive census reports to be recorded on knotted strings called *quipas*.

Although census taking has occurred throughout history, inferences based on statistical **demographics** appear to be a product of the last 200 years. In 1798, the English economist Thomas Robert Malthus (1766–1834) published his *Essay on the Principle of Population as It Affects the Future Improvement of Society*, in which he described a worldwide future of warfare, crime, and starvation. The human population, Malthus predicted, would grow exponentially over the following decades or centuries, leading to a shortage of needed resources, especially food. Conflict on both interpersonal and international levels would be the result, Malthus claimed, as individuals and groups competed for survival.

Demographics The characteristics of population groups, usually expressed in statistical form.

André-Michel Guerry and Adolphe Quételet

As a direct result of Malthusian thought, investigators throughout Europe began to gather "moral statistics," or social enumerations, which they thought might prove useful in measuring the degree to which crime and conflict existed in societies of the period. Such statistics were scrutinized in hopes of gauging "the moral health of nations"—a phrase commonly used throughout the period. One of the first such investigators was André-Michel Guerry (1802–1866), who calculated per capita crime rates throughout various French provinces in the early 19th century.

In 1835, the Belgian astronomer and mathematician Adolphe Quételet (1796–1864) published a statistical analysis of crime in a number of European countries, including Belgium, France, and Holland. Quételet set for himself the goal of assessing the degree to which crime rates varied according to climate and people's sex and age. He noticed what is still obvious to criminal statisticians today—that crime changes with the seasons, with many violent crimes showing an increase during the hot summer months and property crimes increasing in frequency during colder times of the year. As a consequence of these observations, Quételet proposed what he called the "thermic law." According to thermic law, Quételet claimed, morality undergoes seasonal variation—a proposal that stimulated widespread debate in its day.[3]

The first officially published crime statistics appeared in London's *Gazette* beginning in 1828 and France's 1825 *Compte generale*. Soon, comparisons (or what contemporary statisticians call *correlations*) began to be calculated between economic conditions and the rates of various types of crime. From a study of English statistical data covering the years 1810 to 1847, Joseph Fletcher concluded that prison commitments increased as the price of wheat rose. Similarly, the German writer Georg von Mayr, whose data covered the years 1836 to 1861, discovered that the rate of theft increased with the price of rye in Bavaria.

The work of statisticians such as Guerry and Quételet formed the historical basis for what has been called the **statistical school** of criminology. The statistical school anticipated the development of both sociological criminology and the ecological school, perspectives that are discussed in considerable detail later in this book.

Statistical school A criminological perspective with roots in the early 19th century that seeks to uncover correlations between crime rates and other types of demographic data.

USEFULNESS OF CRIME STATISTICS

HOW MANY ASSAULTS WERE COMMITTED LAST YEAR IN CANADA? WHO COMMITTED THEM? Who were the most likely to be victims? What part of the country had the highest rate of assault? Why?

These are the types of questions frequently asked not only by those with a particular interest in the study of crime and offenders but also by members of the general public. Crime statistics help provide answers to these and other questions and paint a picture of the reality of crime in this country. Often the first step toward solving a problem is understanding it, and this certainly applies to the problem of crime. Criminologists, students of criminology, and interested members of the public must understand the crime problem before any serious attempts at controlling or preventing it can be made. Crime statistics and data can be useful toward this end in a number of ways.

Crime data assist in describing the nature and extent of crime, which is necessary to develop effective crime-prevention policies. These policies, in turn, are usually responses to public pressure. Since it is the public that is the major player in reporting crime, the types of crime it reports reflect those issues most concerning it. By providing descriptive information about criminal activity, crime data serve as a gauge of the community's well-being.

Chapter 1 provides a brief discussion of the usefulness of theory development in the study of crime and criminals. Crime data provide the empirical support for the hypotheses developed by criminologists, who attempt to explain the phenomenon of crime and criminals. Crime data ultimately provide the test for theoretical assertions.

Just as crime statistics are used as a basis for developing social policy, they are also crucial in evaluating that policy. Whether or not a get-tough approach with young offenders will reduce the amount of youth crime or the introduction of increased penalties and mandatory sentences of incarceration will reduce the amount of violent crime will ultimately be assessed through an analysis of the data (see Chapter 11 for an in-depth look at specific crime-prevention initiatives). Program evaluation is often difficult to do well, and many such evaluations fall prey to the cost factor. Some programs are introduced largely because they are more cost-effective than conventional approaches, yet they may not achieve the desired result of reducing crime. Likewise, some programs that successfully reduce crime are shelved because they are seen as too expensive.

Most criminologists agree that the prevention of crime is generally considered preferable to its punishment and prevention is largely based on prediction. What types of people are most likely to commit what types of crime and why? Where will they commit them? Criminologists and others use crime data to help provide answers to these questions. The Canadian Crime Prevention Through Environmental Design model (CPTED) is based on the theory that the proper design and effective use of a physical space can help reduce the incidence of crime in that area. This theory, in turn, is based on crime data showing that crime occurs more often in areas where the opportunities for criminal activity are greatest (see Chapters 8 and 11 for a further description of the CPTED model) .

It is important to note that predicting criminal activity and behaviour is an inexact science open to numerous pitfalls. In the early part of the 20th century, for example, Cesare Lombroso believed he could predict future criminal behaviour based on an individual's physical characteristics, such as the size of his ears or the shape of her nose. In the search for a quick fix to the crime problem, some people subscribed to such predictors. For others, prediction models for crime and criminal behaviour seem about as accurate as flipping a coin.[4]

Finally, crime data are useful in providing a picture of risk. Public perceptions of the amount and types of crime are often inconsistent with reality. Crime statistics are useful in assessing the risk to various segments of the population. For example, does one's sex, age, or social class have any bearing on his or her risk of becoming a victim of crime or of becoming involved in criminal behaviour? The study of risk assessment, with crime data used as its basis, is a growing area of interest within criminology.

Canadians are fearful of violent crime. Here police investigate a fatal shooting. Is the public's perception of the amounts and types of crime borne out by official statistics?

Jon Santa Cruz/Alamy Stock Photo

2.3 LEARNING OBJECTIVE

SOURCES OF CRIME STATISTICS

COMPILATION OF CRIME STATISTICS HAS CONTINUED APACE EVER SINCE CRIME-RELATED DATA began to be gathered over a century ago. Crime statistics in Canada are reported in two major surveys: the **Uniform Crime Reporting Survey (UCR)** and the **Victimization Survey**, conducted through the General Social Surveys (GSS). Both fall under the auspices of Canada's national statistics department, Statistics Canada. In 1981, the Canadian Centre for Justice Statistics (CCJS) was created as a satellite of Statistics Canada, through the cooperation of the federal and provincial governments. See Box 2.1 for an overview of the CCJS.

It is important to realize at the outset that these two types of data differ. Because of the differences in methodology and crime coverage, the two approaches examine the nation's crime reality from unique perspectives, and results are not strictly comparable. Nevertheless, the two surveys can complement each other, and each is certainly useful in providing an overall picture of criminal activity. The two surveys are compared in detail later in the chapter.

Uniform Crime Report Survey (UCR) A summation of crime statistics tallied annually by the Canadian Centre for Justice Statistics (CCJS) and consisting primarily of data on crimes reported to the police.

Victimization Survey First conducted as the Canadian Urban Victimization Survey in 1981 by Statistics Canada and then every five years since 1988 as part of the General Social Survey. It provides data on surveyed households reporting that they had been affected by crime.

Box 2.1 THE CANADIAN CENTRE FOR JUSTICE STATISTICS

As the collection of crime data became more formalized through the introduction of uniform crime reports in the 1960s and victimization and self-report surveys in the 1970s, it became apparent that Canada needed a national centre for the collection, collation, and dissemination of these data. The creation of the Canadian Centre for Justice Statistics (CCJS) in 1981 was a result of a decade of numerous task forces and ongoing federal–provincial negotiations around this issue. By 1985, the CCJS had evolved as the administrative arm of Canada's National Justice Statistics Initiative (NJSI), whose mandate is to "provide information to the justice community and the public on the nature and extent of crime and the administration of justice in Canada."[5] It is through the CCJS that the NJSI produces statistical information to be used to support the legislative, policy, management, and research agenda of the Canadian government and also to inform the public.

The work of the CCJS is subdivided into subtopics, including crime and justice (general), crimes and offences, law enforcement, correctional services, criminal courts, civil courts and family law, family violence, justice system spending,

legal aid, victims and victimization, and youth justice. The work of the CCJS also includes collecting and collating data to examine the incidence of crime and criminal activity in Canada as well as compiling information on other aspects of the criminal justice system, including justice-system expenditures, prisons and corrections data, probation and parole populations, inmate profiles, and public perceptions and fear of crime. This information is made available to the public through a service bulletin known as *Juristat*, which is published periodically throughout the year. *Juristat* and other CCJS reports are made available online or in person through the CCJS in Ottawa or through a number of Statistics Canada Regional Reference Centres throughout the country. Most public, community college, and university libraries also carry this information in reference departments. Publications of the CCJS and statistical information are available through the Statistics Canada website at www.statcan.gc.ca. Information can also be obtained by telephone at 1-800-263-1136 or by online request form at http://www.statcan.gc.ca/eng/reference/refcentre/index.

The Uniform Crime Reporting Survey

The Uniform Crime Reporting Survey (UCR) was initiated in 1961 through the efforts of Statistics Canada and the Canadian Association of Chiefs of Police. It provides a standardized procedure by which police departments across the country can collect information about crimes that come to their attention and then report this information to Statistics Canada, specifically to the CCJS. The CCJS then collates the raw data and makes them available to the public.

Between 1962 and 1988, the official crime statistics generated from the UCR were based on summarized monthly police reports from police departments across the country. Known as the Aggregate Uniform Crime Reporting Survey, these police reports included the number of incidents and offences reported to police, the number of actual offences, the number of offences cleared, the number of adults charged, the number of youths charged, and the sex of those charged.

Changes in the UCR after 1988 shifted the emphasis of data collection away from summary or aggregate collection to include incident-based collection. The new system, known as the Revised UCR2 Survey or Incident-Based UCR, included data collection in the following areas:

- *information on victims*: age, sex, victim/accused relationship, level of injury, type of weapon causing injury, drug and/or alcohol use;

- *information on the accused*: age, sex, type of charges laid or recommended, drug and/or alcohol use; and

- *information on the circumstances of the incident*: type of violation (or crime), target of violation, types of property stolen, dollar value of property affected, dollar value of drugs confiscated, type of weapon present, time, and type of location of the incident.[6]

A revised version of the UCR2 known as the UCR2.1 was introduced in 1998. This survey was designed to provide certain efficiencies in reporting for police services. In 2004, another version named UCR2.2 was introduced to take into account new violations and variables, such as organized crime, cybercrime, hate crime, and geocode information. In 2008, a police-reported **Crime Severity Index (CSI)** was introduced to measure changes in the severity of crime from year to year. This index assigns a weight to each offence that is derived from actual sentences handed down by courts in all provinces and territories. Weights are calculated using the five most recent years of available sentencing data. More serious crimes are assigned higher weights, less serious offences lower weights. As a result, when all crimes are included, more serious offences have a higher impact on changes in the index.

Police services are required to respond to the survey. On average, more than 1200 separate police detachments comprising 204 different police forces from across the

Arson causes millions of dollars' worth of property damage yearly. Are UCR statistics on arson accurate?

Condor 36/Shutterstock

Crime Severity Index (CSI) Used in measuring the volume of crime across Canada, this tool accounts for the varying degrees of severity that exist between offence types by weighting each according to a scale of seriousness and thereby allowing crime trends to be analyzed and compared according to the gravity of the offences.

country supplied data for the complete year to the UCR2 Survey.[7] The UCR records offences cleared by charge or otherwise and rates of crime. The phrase *offence cleared by charge* refers to an offence that is closed when police have formally charged a person or when there is sufficient evidence to lay a charge against an identified person, even if that person has not been apprehended by police. *Offence cleared otherwise* refers to a case in which police cannot or do not charge a person even if they have identified a suspect and have enough evidence to support the laying of a charge. Examples include cases of diplomatic immunity, instances in which the complainant declines to proceed with charges against the accused, cases in which police have opted not to lay a charge (e.g., the uses of extrajudicial measures for youth), or cases where the alleged offender dies before being formally charged.[8] The *clearance rate* indicates the proportion of incidents that are cleared by charge or otherwise for different types of offences compared to the total number of actual incidents.

Crime rate Crime per capita based on the number of recorded crimes calculated per 100 000 population.

The **crime rate** used in the UCR is calculated by summing all *Criminal Code* incidents reported by the police and calculating the rate per 100 000 population. The crime rate excludes *Criminal Code* traffic violations as well as other federal statute violations, such as drug offences. In addition to the overall crime rate, total rates are calculated for violent crime, property crime, and other *Criminal Code* offences. For example, in 2014, the total number of recorded crimes was 1 793 534. The rate of crime was 5046 based on a Canadian total population of 35 540 400. This crime rate was calculated as follows:

$$\frac{\# \ of \ reported \ crimes}{total \ population} \times 100\ 000$$

$$\frac{1\ 793\ 534 \ crimes \ reported}{35\ 540\ 400 \ total \ population} \times 100\ 000 = 5046$$

Thus, we see that there were 5046 crime incidents per 100 000 population in Canada in 2014. If we consider a specific type of crime, such as homicide, and apply the same procedure, the equation looks like this:

$$\frac{516 \ homicides \ reported}{35\ 540\ 400 \ total \ population} \times 100\ 000 = 1.4$$

This tells us that there was just more than one homicide for every 100 000 Canadians in 2014.[9]

To calculate the traditional police-reported crime rate, all offences are counted equally, regardless of their seriousness. For example, one incident of homicide is counted as equivalent to one incident of theft. In 2008, a police-reported Crime Severity Index was developed to address the limitation of the crime rate being driven by high numbers of less-serious offences. The CSI not only takes into account the volume of crime but also the seriousness of crime.

For the purposes of the CSI, each violation is assigned a weight. CSI weights are based on the violation's incarceration rate as well as the average length of prison sentence handed down by criminal courts. The more serious the average sentence, the higher the weight assigned to the offence, meaning that the more serious offences have a greater impact on the index. Unlike the traditional crime rate, all offences, including *Criminal Code* traffic violations and other federal statute violations, such as drug offences, are included in the CSI.

To calculate the CSI, the weighted offences are totaled and then divided by the population. To allow for ease of comparison, the CSI is then standardized to a base year of "100" (for the CSI, the base year is 2006). In other words, all CSI values are relative to the Canada-level CSI for 2006.

In addition to the overall CSI, both a violent Crime Severity Index and a non-violent Crime Severity Index have been created, which like the CSI are both available

- The Crime Severity Index (CSI) measures the volume and severity of police-reported crime in Canada, and has a base index value of 100 for 2006. Between 2013 and 2014, the CSI decreased 3% from 68.8 in 2013 to 66.7 in 2014. This decrease was driven primarily by a decline in breaking and entering, and robbery. The decline in the CSI in 2014 represented the eleventh consecutive decrease.

- The police-reported crime rate, which measures the volume of police-reported crime, also declined in 2014, decreasing 3% from the previous year to 5,046 incidents per 100,000 population. This represented the eleventh consecutive decrease in the police-reported crime rate, and the lowest rate recorded since 1969.

- There were just under 1.8 million *Criminal Code* incidents (excluding traffic) reported by police in 2014, approximately 33,000 fewer incidents than in 2013.

- Despite a decrease in the majority of *Criminal Code* violations (excluding traffic) between 2013 and 2014, the rate of police-reported violations increased for child pornography (+41%), terrorism (+39%), extortion (+16%), identity fraud (+8%), sexual violations against children (+6%), abduction (+4%), fraud (+2%), and motor vehicle theft (+1%).

- Almost all provinces and territories recorded a decline in their police-reported CSI and crime rate in 2014. The only exceptions were Yukon, where the CSI was up 11% from 2013 and the crime rate remained stable, as well as British Columbia, where the CSI was up 3% from the previous year and the crime rate increased 2%. In addition, Alberta's CSI increased slightly between 2013 and 2014, up 1%, while the police-reported crime rate remained stable.

- Several of Canada's census metropolitan areas (CMAs) reported an increase in their CSI values in 2014. With a 10% increase between 2013 and 2014, Saskatoon (109.7) had the highest CSI among CMAs for the first time, followed by Regina (102.8), Vancouver (96.7) and Thunder Bay (89.9). In contrast, Barrie (43.6), with a 2% increase in its CSI from the previous year, recorded the lowest CSI among CMAs in 2014.

- The overall volume and severity of violent crime, as measured by the violent CSI, declined 5% between 2013 and 2014 to 70.2, and was driven largely by a decrease in robbery. This drop marked the eighth consecutive decline in the violent CSI.

- In 2014, police reported 516 homicides, four more than the previous year. While the number of homicides increased slightly between 2013 and 2014, the homicide rate (1.45 homicides per 100,000 population) remained virtually unchanged from the previous year.

- The overall volume and severity of non-violent crime, as measured by the non-violent CSI, was down 2% in 2014 from the previous year to 65.2. The decrease was largely the result of fewer reported incidents of breaking and entering.

- The overall rate of *Controlled Drugs and Substances Act* (*CDSA*) violations decreased in 2014, down 6% from the previous year. This decrease was primarily the result of fewer drug offences involving cannabis and cocaine

- Police-reported youth crime also decreased in 2014, with both the youth Crime Severity Index and the youth crime rate declining 9% from the previous year. The rate of youth accused of some of the most serious violations also decreased, including a drop in the rate of youth accused of homicide (−38%).

Source: Jillian Boyce, "Police-reported crime statistics in Canada, 2014," *Juristat*, vol. 34, no. 1 (Ottawa: Minister of Industry, 2015). Reproduced and distributed on an "as is" basis with the permission of Statistics Canada.

Note: Changes in public attitudes about certain types of crime, such as child pornography, have resulted in the public's inclination to report these crimes more readily. Does an increase in the number of reported child pornography cases mean that there are more incidents of child pornography occurring or simply that more cases are being reported?

back to 1998. The violent CSI is comprised of all police-reported violent violations, and the non-violent CSI is comprised of all police-reported property violations, other *Criminal Code* violations, *Criminal Code* traffic violations, and other federal statute violations. In 2014, the total Crime Severity Index was 66.7.[10] A summary of the UCR findings for 2014 is reproduced in Box 2.2.

Shortcomings of the UCR   The most significant methodological feature of the Uniform Crime Reporting Survey is indicated by its name. It is a "reporting" system. In other words, only crimes that are reported to the police (or discovered by them or by someone else who then reports them) are included in the statistics compiled by the system. Unless someone complains to the police about a criminal incident, it will go unreported and will not appear in the UCR. Most complaints are made by victims.

Because UCR data are based on *reported* crime, the system has been criticized for underestimating the true incidence of criminal activity within Canada—a measurement that would also include unreported crimes. Unreported and under-reported criminal activity has been called the **dark figure of crime**. Some experts say that sexual assault is the most under-reported crime in the UCR. Reasons for not reporting a crime such as sexual assault are numerous and include (1) the victim's fear of the perpetrator; (2) the victim's shame, which may carry over from traditional attitudes about sexual behaviour and a woman's role in sexual encounters; (3) the victim's fear of not being believed; and (4) the victim's fear of further participation in the justice system (such as the possibility of the victim being required to go to court and testify against the offender, thereby exposing herself to potentially embarrassing cross-examination and public scrutiny). Other general reasons cited by victims for failure to report a crime include "fear of revenge," "nothing can be done," "the crime was too minor," or the incident was a "private matter."

Many other crimes are under-reported as well. Although sexual assault is indeed seriously under-reported (a conclusion drawn from a comparison of UCR and Victimization Survey sexual assault statistics), the most seriously under-reported crime may in fact be theft $5000 and under, because the theft of small items may never make it into official police reports and may even be forgotten by victims during interviews with victimization surveyors.

Another concern raised about the accuracy of UCR numbers lies with the way in which police services record and report the criminal activity that is detected. The UCR receives crime data from municipal police departments across Canada as well as from the RCMP, the Ontario Provincial Police, and the Sûreté du Québec—Quebec's provincial police force. To expect that all these police services record their crime statistics in a uniform manner is unrealistic, although the CCJS does work with police agencies on an ongoing basis to detect and resolve any difficulties in the reporting or transmission of data. Nevertheless, for a number of reasons, there are variations in how the police count crime. Changes in the number of police services and police officers will most certainly affect the number of detected crimes. Enforcement practices or mandates often vary from one police department to another. For example, if commercial break and enters are a problem in one community, local police will be more vigilant toward this type of criminal activity, which will be reflected in the crime report.

Related to police recording and reporting are methodological concerns with the way the UCR "counts" crime, especially in an incident involving multiple offences. The UCR counts only the most serious offence (MSO) in the incident. For example, if someone breaks into a store, severely assaults the security personnel, and steals a laptop, only the assault is recorded. The MSO is determined by the maximum sentence length; in the scenario just mentioned, although the break and enter and assault both carry a maximum life sentence, the crime against the person is considered more serious and takes precedence over the crime against property. As a result, less serious offences tend to be under-represented by the UCR Survey. The introduction of the police-reported Crime Severity Index is an attempt to address this shortcoming. For the purposes of counting, even though crimes against the person take precedence over crimes against property, this is not the case when the crime rate is calculated. Recall that the crime rate is the total number of reported crimes in a given year per 100 000 population. This total encompasses all categories of crime, including federal and provincial statute violations. For example, the number of reported motor vehicle thefts might skyrocket in a given year, while the number of assaults might fall. The resulting overall crime rate for that year would be higher than for the year before because both classifications of crime are assigned the same weight.

Dark figure of crime The portion of criminal activity that goes unreported and/or undetected by official sources.

For violent crime, the UCR records the number of incidents in terms of number of victims. If one person assaults two people, two incidents are recorded. But if two people assault one person, only one incident is recorded. The exception to this scoring rule for violent crime is robbery: one occurrence of robbery is counted as one incident regardless of the number of victims. Since robbery can involve many people who could be considered victims (for example, in the case of a bank robbery), counting each one would seriously overstate the occurrence of robbery. Thus, the total number of incidents recorded in the UCR is actually equal to the number of victims of violent crimes (other than robbery) plus the number of individual occurrences of non-violent crimes and robbery.

A final concern about the accuracy of the UCR centres on the legal definition of crime. A case in point: the renaming and redefinition of rape to sexual assault in 1983 means that the types of behaviour constituting sexual assault have been more clearly defined to include those behaviours from unwanted sexual touching to aggravated sexual assault that endangers the life of the victim. Similarly, amendments to the definition of arson in 1990 now include mischief fires as arson, and in 2013, seven new terrorism violations were added to the *Criminal Code*. These redefinitions and inclusions have broadened the scope of these criminal activities and have resulted in a corresponding increase in the statistical incidence of these crimes and crime overall.

The consistency of definition is also a concern. Part of the difficulty in measuring child abuse, for example, arises from the fact that there is no apparent consensus as to the legal age of a "child" at the provincial and territorial level, where child-welfare services are organized and delivered. For example, the maximum age of the child to be protected—under 16 in Newfoundland and Labrador to under 19 in British Columbia—and the policies underlying child protection vary across the country. It is estimated that cases of child abuse would double if threats and acts of indecent exposure were added to the definition. As well, the distinction between corporal punishment and physical abuse is not clear, which further thwarts the accurate accounting of child abuse. For the purposes of recording, the CCJS defines child abuse as incidents of physical and sexual assault and homicide in cases in which the victim is under 18 years of age.[11]

Victimization Surveys

Victimization Surveys differ from the UCR in one especially significant way: rather than depending on reports of crimes to the police, the data contained in Victimization Surveys consist of information elicited through interviews with members of randomly selected households throughout the country. Hence, these surveys uncover a large number of crimes that may not have been reported and are therefore regarded by many researchers as a more accurate measure of the actual incidence of crime in Canada than is the UCR.

A number of significant Victimization Surveys have been undertaken in Canada. The first, and perhaps the most comprehensive, was the Canadian Urban Victimization Survey (CUVS) conducted in 1981 under the auspices of the Solicitor General of Canada. It randomly sampled roughly 60 000 Canadians over the age of 16 in seven major cities. In telephone interviews, respondents were asked to describe any victimization experiences they had suffered in the preceding calendar year. Eight categories of crime were included in the survey: sexual assault, robbery, assault, break and enter, motor vehicle theft, theft of household property, theft of personal property, and vandalism. The survey uncovered over 700 000 personal victimizations and almost 900 000 household victimizations for the calendar year of 1981. It also revealed that fewer than 42 percent of these victimizations had been reported to the police or had otherwise come to police attention.[12]

Beginning in 1988, Statistics Canada has conducted a Victimization Survey every five years as part of the General Social Survey (GSS). The 2014 GSS (the latest one from which victimization data are available) sampled a national target population of roughly 33 000 Canadians aged 15 and over in the provinces and territories, excluding full-time residents of institutions. Interviews were conducted by telephone from February to December 2014, using random-digit dialling techniques. (It is interesting to note that the 2014 GSS used a slightly different sample design than previous GSS cycles. In the past, only those households with a landline telephone could have been selected for the survey. Given Canadians' increased use of cell phones, as well as the increase of households with no landline, it was necessary to include cell phones in the sample frame to ensure the sample was as representative of the Canadian population as possible.) In an interview lasting 30 minutes on average, respondents were asked about their experiences with the criminal justice system in the previous 12 months and specifically about eight types of criminal victimization: sexual assault, robbery (and attempted robbery), physical assault, theft of personal property, break and enter (and attempted break and enter), motor vehicle/parts theft (and attempts), attempts at and theft of household property, and vandalism; respondents were not asked about crimes targeting businesses or institutions.

Respondents who had been victims of a crime were asked for detailed information about each incident, including when and where it occurred, whether the incident had been reported to the police, and how they had been affected by the experience. Respondents were also questioned about their perceptions and fear of crime and their knowledge and perceptions of the criminal justice system. Demographic information about the respondents was also gathered, including age, sex, and marital status, as well as educational, occupational, and income levels. Highlights of the findings of the survey are presented in Table 2.1 and Figure 2.1. In 2014, just fewer than 20 percent of Canadians aged 15 years and older (approximately 5.6 million people) reported that they or their household had been the victim of at least one of the eight crimes measured by the GSS in the 12 months preceding the survey. This proportion is down from the previous survey in 2009, when roughly 28 percent of Canadians reported having been a victim of a crime.

Canadians reported a total of 6.4 million criminal incidents in 2014. The majority (65 percent) of those incidents were non-violent. Theft of personal property was the crime most frequently reported by Canadians to the GSS, representing one-third (34 percent) of all victimization incidents. Physical assault, the most frequent violent

Table 2.1 Victimization Incidents Reported by Canadians, by Type of Offence, 2014

Type of Offence	2014 Number (thousands)	Rate
Sexual Assault	633	22
Robbery	190	6
Physical Assault	1422	48
Total violent victimization	2245	76
Break and Enter	441	31
Motor vehicle/parts theft	261	18
Theft of household property	766	54
Vandalism	561	40
Total household victimization	2029	143
Theft of personal property	2154	73

Source: Statistics Canada, General Social Survey, 2014. Reproduced and distributed on an "as is" basis with the permission of Statistics Canada.

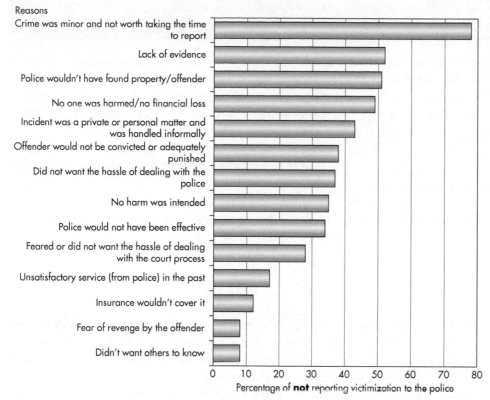

Reasons

- Crime was minor and not worth taking the time to report
- Lack of evidence
- Police wouldn't have found property/offender
- No one was harmed/no financial loss
- Incident was a private or personal matter and was handled informally
- Offender would not be convicted or adequately punished
- Did not want the hassle of dealing with the police
- No harm was intended
- Police would not have been effective
- Feared or did not want the hassle of dealing with the court process
- Unsatisfactory service (from police) in the past
- Insurance wouldn't cover it
- Fear of revenge by the offender
- Didn't want others to know

Percentage of **not** reporting victimization to the police

Figure 2.1 Reasons for Not Reporting Victimization Incidents to the Police, by Type of Offence, 2014

Source: Adapted from Statistics Canada, General Social Survey, 2014. This does not constitute an endorsement by Statistics Canada of this product.

crime, followed at 22 percent. This was followed by theft of household property (12 percent), sexual assault (10 percent), vandalism (9 percent), break and enter (7 percent), theft of motor vehicle or parts (4 percent), and robbery (3 percent).

Most Canadians who had been victimized reported only a single incident. However, more than one-third (37 percent) of victims reported having been the target of at least two victimization incidents in the preceding 12 months. It is interesting to compare these rates of victimization with the concerns about fear of crime among Canadians, discussed in Chapter 1.

While the CUVS and subsequent GSS have helped to provide a picture of the amounts and types of crime generally in Canada, other surveys have been conducted to look at specific types of crime victims. Most notable among these is the national Violence Against Women Survey (VAWS), only undertaken once, by Statistics Canada in 1993. Over 12 000 women 18 years of age and older were interviewed by telephone about their experiences of physical and sexual violence since the age of 16 and their perceptions of their personal safety. The findings of the survey indicated significantly more incidents of violence against women than had ever been previously indicated in official UCR numbers. One-half of all Canadian women reported having experienced at least one incident of violence since age 16, and almost one-half reported that this violence had been perpetrated by men known to them. A summary of the findings from the VAWS is outlined in Box 2.3.

A number of initiatives have been undertaken at the international level to compare victimization rates from country to country. The International Crime Victimization Survey (ICVS) is one such initiative, first implemented in 1989. The last and most recent survey (2004/2005) was coordinated with the European Survey on Crime and

Box 2.3 HIGHLIGHTS OF THE VIOLENCE AGAINST WOMEN SURVEY (VAWS)

- About 50% of all Canadian women have experienced at least one incident of violence since the age of 16.

- Almost 50% of women reported violence by men known to them, and 25% reported violence by a stranger.

- Approximately 25% of all women have experienced violence at the hands of a current or past marital partner (includes common-law unions).

- Roughly 15% of currently married women reported violence by their spouses; 50% of women with previous marriages reported violence by a previous spouse.

- More than 10% of women who reported violence in a current marriage have at some point felt their lives were in danger.

- About 60% of Canadian women who walk alone in their own area after dark feel "very" or "somewhat" worried doing so.

- Women with violent fathers-in-law are at three times the risk of assault by their partners than are women with non-violent fathers-in-law.

Source: Statistics Canada, "*The Daily* 11-001-XPE," Released 11/18/1993. Reproduced and distributed on an "as is" basis with the permission of Statistics Canada.

Safety (EU ICS). Canada was one of 30 countries participating in this survey that set out to provide comparable information on the incidence of victimization around the world. People aged 16 years and older were asked through random telephone sampling for information on 10 offences (robbery/attempted robbery, sexual offences, physical assaults/threats, theft of personal property, burglary of residence, attempted burglary of residence, theft of car/van/truck, theft from car, theft of motorcycle, theft of bicycle). Respondents were asked when, where, and how often offences had occurred during the previous year and the previous five years; whether offences were reported to police; and whether victimization experiences were considered serious. Respondents were also asked for their opinion on public safety, policing, and sentencing. An average of 1000 to 5000 individuals per country were interviewed. Despite some recognized methodological shortcomings, such as the likelihood of fairly large sampling errors, the findings of the survey are interesting. Seventeen percent of Canadians reported having been victimized within the previous year, which was slightly above the average of 16 percent when compared to the 29 other countries participating in the survey. A summary of the highlights of this survey can be found in Box 2.4.

Box 2.4 HIGHLIGHTS OF THE INTERNATIONAL CRIME VICTIMIZATION SURVEY (ICVS)

- According to the results of the International Crime Victimization Survey (ICVS), in 2004 17% of Canadians aged 16 and over had been victims of at least one of the 10 crimes measured by the survey. The overall international victimization rate was 16%.

- Canada's highest victimization rate was for theft from a vehicle. For almost all countries participating in the ICVS, the offences with the highest victimization rates were theft of personal property, theft from a car, and theft of a bicycle.

- Canada, along with Finland and Luxembourg, ranked relatively low with respect to the proportion of incidents (theft from a car, theft of a bicycle, burglary, attempted

burglary, and theft of personal property) reported to the police. At 48%, the proportion of Canadian victims of these crimes who reported the incident to the police in 2004 was below the international average (53%).

- In 2004, 86% of Canadians aged 16 and over believed that the police were doing a good or excellent job at controlling crime in their area. Canada, along with Finland and the United States, was among the countries whose populations were the most satisfied with the job done by the police.

Source: Statistics Canada, *Juristat*, 85-002-XIE2008010 vol. 28 no. 10. Released December 15, 2008. Reproduced and distributed on an "as is" basis with the permission of Statistics Canada.

Shortcomings of Victimization Surveys   Just as the UCR has been criticized for under-representing the actual incidence of criminal activity in Canada, Victimization Surveys in general, and the GSS in particular, can be criticized for possible over-reporting of some crimes. It is beyond the purview of a Victimization Survey to verify the actual occurrence of any of the crimes reported to the interviewers; therefore, no measure exists to determine the number of crimes that might be over-reported. Victimization Surveys are dependent on the ability of the respondent to not only recall incidents and their details but also to accurately place them in time. Some respondents provide more detailed and accurate accounts of their victimization experiences, which may skew the data. As well, by their nature, Victimization Surveys exclude data on homicide, kidnapping, so-called victimless crimes (public intoxication, prostitution, and gambling), impaired driving, drug offences, crimes such as vandalism and theft committed against commercial or public property, and crimes committed against children under the age of 15.

Comparing Uniform Crime Reporting Surveys and Victimization Surveys   Even though the data generated by the UCR and Victimization Surveys are based on the same categories of crime, they reveal very different pictures. Findings from the UCR are the reports of crimes recorded by the police, who are generally alerted to the crime as a result of a call from a victim. The type and frequency of calls to police change over time and vary according to location. For example, as the community tolerance for sexual assault and family violence declines, victims or witnesses of these crimes may be more willing to report them to authorities, and authorities will be more likely to treat them as crimes.

Victimization Surveys, on the other hand, were developed to provide a way of looking at crime from the perspective of individual victims. They describe what has happened to individual Canadians and the way in which these individuals respond to their victimization experiences. Without a doubt, these surveys reveal that many Canadians do not report personal victimizations and suggest the reasons for this.

Despite their divergent focuses, UCR and Victimization Surveys can complement one another. Victimization data can help place UCR findings in context. For instance, how much change in official crime data for family violence can be attributed to changes in reporting patterns or police practices? (Police in Ontario and some other provinces are mandated to lay charges against the perpetrator in a domestic assault situation if sufficient evidence exists, regardless of the victim's willingness to concur.) How are crime trends a reflection of people's attitudes toward crime and the criminal justice system? While neither UCR nor victimization data can provide comprehensive information about crime, when considered together they are useful in providing a picture of crime and criminal activity in Canada. See Table 2.1 for a comparison of the UCR and GSS.

Three recent reports produced by Statistics Canada, in collaboration with the federal, provincial, and territorial ministers responsible for the status of women, have contributed to the body of evidence on, and provided a broader understanding of, violence against women in all its forms. Assessing Violence Against Women: A Statistical Profile was released in 2002, followed by Measuring Violence Against Women: Statistical Trends 2006, and most recently Measuring Violence Against Women: Statistical Trends 2013. The information in the most current report is based on data gathered using both UCR and Victimization Surveys. It includes information on dating violence, violence against girls, and violence that occurs outside of the intimate partner/family context. It also shows trends over time and provides data at national, provincial/territorial, and census metropolitan area levels. It also includes a study of the economic impacts of one form of violence against women—spousal violence. A summary of the highlights of the report can be found in Box 2.5.

Prevalence and severity of violence against women

- According to police-reported data, about 173 600 women aged 15 years and older were victims of violent crime in 2011. This translates to a rate of 1207 female victims for every 100 000 women in the population, slightly higher than the rate for men (1151).

- In 2011, the five most common violent offences committed against women were common assault (49%), uttering threats (13%), serious assault (10%), sexual assault level I (7%), and criminal harassment (7%). Women were 11 times more likely than men to be victims of sexual offences and three times as likely to be victims of criminal harassment (stalking).

- Overall, men were responsible for 83% of police-reported violence committed against women. Most commonly, the accused was the woman's intimate partner (includes both spouses and dates) (45%), followed by acquaintances or friends (27%), strangers (16%), and non-spousal family members (12%). This contrasts with violent crimes against men, where intimate partners were among the least common perpetrators (12%).

Self-reported violence against women

- According to victimization data, rates of self-reported violent victimization against women were stable between 1999 and 2009. Among the three types of violent victimization against women measured by the General Social Survey (GSS) on victimization, robbery was the only type to have increased since 1999.

- While women and men self-report similar rates of spousal violence, women's experiences are different from men's.

Women are more likely than men to experience the most severe forms of self-reported spousal victimization, such as multiple victimizations and incidents with physical injuries.

Risk factors of violence against women

- Based on both police-reported and self-reported victimization data, being young was a consistent risk factor for violence against women. According to these data, risk of violence decreases with increasing age.

- Women most at risk of non-spousal violence included those who were young, participated in many evening activities, were single, used drugs, identified as an Aboriginal person, and lived in a community with social disorder, such as vandalism, noisy neighbours, and people using or dealing drugs.

Responses to violence against women

- According to victimization data, less than one-third (30%) of female victims of spousal violence stated that the incident came to the attention of police, down from 36% in 2004. No change was recorded in the levels of reporting to police for non-spousal violence against women (28%).

- Certain types of spousal violence were more likely to come to the attention of police, including incidents where the woman was sexually assaulted (53%) or beaten, choked, or had a weapon used against her (60%). By contrast, sexual assaults perpetrated by someone other than a spouse were least likely to come to the attention of police. Nine in 10 non-spousal sexual assaults were never reported to police.

Source: Adapted from Maire Sinha (ed.), "Measuring violence against women: Statistical trends", *Juristat*, vol. 33, no. 1 (Ottawa: Minister of Industry, 2013). This does not constitute an endorsement by Statistics Canada of this product.

Self-Report Studies

Self-report study A data collection method requiring subjects to reveal their own participation in criminal behaviour.

Another approach to the production of data on the amount and types of crime is the **self-report study**. Within the field of criminology, there is a widely held belief that to understand crime, it is important to ask people about their involvement with it. There have been countless self-report studies conducted with various groups of individuals, most notably with youth. The results of the groundbreaking work by Short and Nye[13] led many to believe that traditional police data have the potential to be biased toward certain segments of society, in particular the lower socio-economic classes. Other gaps between official sources of data and self-report data have been found in the age, sex, and race of the offender. A recent Canadian study for the Department of Justice conducted by Latimer, Kleinknecht, Hung, and Gabor identifies correlates of self-reported delinquency of Canadian youth between the ages of 12 and 15.[14] The statistical information used in the study was based on data supplied by the National Longitudinal Survey of Children and Youth (NLSCY). The NLSCY is a long-term

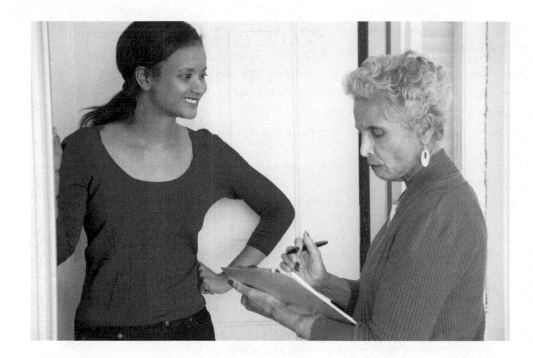

The self-report study allows criminologists to understand crime from the perspective of the perpetrator. What is a drawback of this approach to data collection?

Edbockstock/Fotolia

study of Canadian children that follows their development and well-being from birth to early adulthood. Begun in 1994 and jointly conducted by Statistics Canada and Human Resources and Skills Development Canada (HRSDC), the study is designed to collect information about factors influencing a child's social, emotional, and behavioural development and to monitor the impact of these factors on the child's development over time. The survey covers a comprehensive range of topics, including the health of children; information on their physical development, learning, and behaviour; as well as data on their social environment (family, friends, schools, and communities). Self-report surveys are used for all ages and aspects of the study. Fourteen questions are used to address the topic of criminal behaviour and are reproduced in Table 2.2.

In general, self-report studies are recognized within the field of criminology as one means of counting crime and criminals. When considered in conjunction with other methods of information gathering, self-report studies help provide a clearer and more complete picture of crime and who commits it. They are considered to be particularly useful in highlighting the relationship between social class and crime and in uncovering much crime that goes undetected.[15]

Shortcomings of Self-Report Studies   Since their acceptance as a legitimate means of examining the reality of crime and criminals, self-report studies have consistently become more sound. Nevertheless, a number of methodological shortcomings continue to exist. For example, the accuracy of this research approach is largely predicated on the honesty and forthrightness of the respondent. Inaccurate answers may result from a number of factors, including the respondent's failure to disclose behaviour, the tendency to exaggerate behaviour, or the respondent's failure to remember. Often respondents are concerned about confidentiality and anonymity, which is understandable given the information they are being asked to reveal. This may affect the way they answer or indeed whether they even participate in the survey. Analyses of self-report studies indicate that the more offences a respondent has committed, the fewer he or she is likely to admit to. Conversely, a respondent who has committed a lesser number of offences is more likely to admit to them in a self-report survey.

Table 2.2 Self-Report Questions Regarding Criminal Behaviour from the National Longitudinal Survey of Children and Youth

In the past 12 months, about how many times have you tried to force someone into having sex with you?

In the past 12 months, about how many times have you threatened someone in order to get their money or things?

In the past 12 months, about how many times have you sold any drugs?

In the past 12 months, about how many times have you set fire on purpose to a building, a car, or something else not belonging to you?

In the past 12 months, about how many times have you attempted to touch the private parts of another person's body (while knowing that they would probably object to this)?

In the past 12 months, about how many times have you broken into, or snuck into, a house or building with the idea of stealing something?

In the past 12 months, about how many times have you fought with someone to the point where they needed care for their injuries (for example, because they were bleeding, or had broken bones)?

In the past 12 months, about how many times have you been in a fight where you hit someone with something other than your hands (for example, a stick, club, knife, or rock)?

In the past 12 months, about how many times have you carried a gun other than for hunting or target shooting?

In the past 12 months, about how many times have you used or bought or tried to sell something you knew was stolen?

In the past 12 months, about how many times have you stolen something from a store or school?

In the past 12 months, about how many times have you taken a car, motorbike, or motorboat without permission?

In the past 12 months, about how many times have you damaged or destroyed anything that didn't belong to you (for example, damaged a bicycle, car, school furniture, broken windows or written graffiti)?

In the past 12 months, about how many times have you taken money from your parents without their permission?

Source: *The Correlates of Self-Reported Delinquency: An Analysis of the National Longitudinal Survey of Children and Youth.* 2003. http://www.justice.gc.ca/eng/rp-pr/fl-lf/famil/rr03_yj2-rr03_jj2/rr03_yj2.pdf, page 21. Department of Justice Canada, 2003. Reproduced with the permission of the Department of Justice Canada, 2016.

Other methodological limitations include a lack of standardized data collection methods, such as comparable questions, time frames, or geographic areas. Nevertheless, there seems to be agreement that self-report studies are useful in providing a more rounded picture of the criminal, especially when compared with the picture that is often captured in official statistics based on police reports. While the official statistics provide information on tangibles such as the age and sex of an offender, self-report studies serve to reveal characteristics such as education levels, home life, peer group, and general socio-economic realities of the offender. It has been suggested that this approach could be used to include an examination of those biological and psychological factors that contribute to criminal behaviour, thereby complementing the environmental realities they already help to illuminate. Whether the findings of these self-report studies that target a specific group in a specific time and place can be used to deduce general assumptions about criminals and the crimes they commit is still open to debate.

2.4 | LEARNING OBJECTIVE

THE SOCIAL DIMENSIONS OF CRIME

CRIME DOES NOT OCCUR IN A VACUUM. IT INVOLVES REAL PEOPLE—HUMAN PERPETRATORS and victims. Because society defines certain personal characteristics as especially important, it is possible to speak of the "social dimensions of crime"—that is, aspects of crime and victimization as they relate to socially significant attributes by which groups are defined and according to which individuals are assigned group membership. Socially significant attributes include sex and gender, ethnicity or race, age, income or wealth, profession, and social class or standing within society. Such personal characteristics provide criteria by which individuals can be assigned to groups such as "the rich," "the poor," "male," "female," "young," "old," "black," "white," "white-collar worker," "manual labourer," and so on.[16]

We have already alluded briefly to the fact that the UCR, GSS or Victimization Surveys, and self-report studies structure the data they gather in ways that reflect socially significant characteristics. The UCR, for example, provides information on reported crimes, which reveals the sex and age of perpetrators. Victimization statistics document the age and sex of crime victims and the educational, occupational, and income levels of households reporting victimizations. Self-report studies provide some insight into the age, sex, ethnic background, education levels, social habits, and socio-economic status of those engaged in delinquent or criminal behaviour.

The social dimensions of crime are said by statisticians to reveal relationships or correlations. A **correlation** is simply a connection or association observed to exist between two measurable variables. Correlations are of two types: positive and negative. If one measurement increases when its correlate does the same, then a positive correlation or positive relationship is said to exist between the two. When one measurement decreases in value as another rises, a negative or inverse correlation has been discovered. Victimization data, for example, show a negative relationship between age and victimization—as people age, victimization rates decline. So, although some elderly people do become crime victims, older people as a group tend to be less victimized than younger people. Uniform Crime Report data, on the other hand, show a positive relationship between youth and likelihood of arrest—specifically, between young adulthood and arrest. Young adults, it appears, commit most crimes. Hence, as people age, they tend to be both less likely to be victimized and less likely to become involved in criminal activity.

A word of caution is in order. Correlation does not necessarily imply causation. Because two variables appear to be correlated does not mean that they have any influence on one another or that one causes another either to increase or to decrease. Correlations that involve no causal relationship are said to be *spurious*. A study of crime rates, for example, shows that many crimes seem to occur with greater frequency in the summer. Similarly, industry groups tell us that food retailers sell more ice cream in the summer than at any other time. Are we to conclude, then, from the observed correlation between crime rates and ice cream sales that one in some way causes the other? To do so on the basis of an observed correlation alone would obviously be foolish.

Some observed correlations do appear to shed at least some light on either the root causes of crime or the nature of criminal activity, often referred to as **correlates of crime**. When considering these correlates, a further distinction needs to be considered. Correlates of crime are often grouped into static factors and dynamic factors. Static factors are not amendable to change through direct interventions; included in this category are age, gender, and ethnicity. Dynamic factors, on the other hand, are amendable to change through direct interventions and include parenting, education and attachment to school, peer groups, geography and neighbourhoods, and some psychological factors, such as aggression and conduct disorders. This distinction is useful when developing interventions designed to reduce criminal behaviour, since it is the dynamic factors that can be targeted for change in an effort to prevent further criminal behaviour.[17] In the discussion that follows, we will consider the static correlates of crime—age, sex, ethnicity, and social class. The dynamic correlates are discussed in conjunction with the theories of criminal behaviour that are found in Chapters 5, 6, 7, 8, 9, and 10.

Correlation A causal, complementary, or reciprocal relationship between two measurable variables.

Correlates of crime Those variables observed to be related to criminal activity, such as age, sex and gender, ethnicity, and social class. Often classified into static and dynamic factors.

Age and Criminal Behaviour

If records of persons accused are any guide, criminal activity is associated more with youth than any other stage of life. Year after year, Uniform Crime Reports consistently

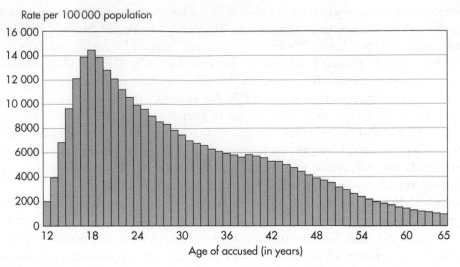

Rate per 100 000 population

Figure 2.2 Persons Accused of Crime, Age 12 to 65 Years, Canada

Source: Statistics Canada, Canadian Centre for Justice Statistics, Uniform Crime Reporting Survey. Reproduced and distributed on an "as is" basis with the permission of Statistics Canada.

show that younger people, from their mid- to late teens to their early and mid-20s, account for the bulk of the crime reported in this country. Indeed, age is one of the strongest correlates of criminal behaviour.

A Statistics Canada report indicated that persons aged 15 to 24 represented 14 percent of the total population but accounted for 45 percent of those charged with property crimes and 32 percent of those charged with violent crimes.[18] See Figure 2.2 for a graphical depiction.

Canadian statistics tell us that crime rates in Canada have followed population shifts, with somewhat of a time lag. According to Statistics Canada, most of the baby boomers were 15 years of age between 1960 and 1980, a time that witnessed steady increases in violent and property crime rates. Property crime rates levelled out in the 1980s as the percentage of 15- to 24-year-olds began to drop and increased slightly in the early 1990s before declining sharply (as the percentage of 25- to 34-year-olds began to decline). It is interesting to note that violent crimes do not parallel as closely the demographic shift; the violent crime rate continued to increase steadily until 1993. The decline in the violent crime rate began several years after the start of the decline in the 15–24 age group.[19] Other studies suggest that our crime rates have steadily declined due to positive changes in economic and employment opportunities for youth today as compared to the realities of the recession years of the 1980s, which negatively affected the cohort of those born in the 1960s.[20] Further questions about the explanations for the correlation between youth and crime are raised in Box 2.6.

When considering the correlation between age and victimization, the most recent statistics show that Canadians between the ages of 15 and 24 years experienced personal victimization at rates greater than the rates for other groups. The risk of violent victimization steadily declined as age increased. For example, those 15 to 24 years of age had a rate of 163 per 1000 compared to a rate of 68 per 1000 for the group aged 35 to 44. Rates of violent victimization were lowest among those aged 65 and older. These Canadians had a rate of 13 violent incidents per 1000 population.[21] Statistics show that children are over-represented as victims of certain types of crimes. While Victimization Surveys only poll Canadians over 15 years of age, UCR statistics indicate that overall, youth aged 12 to 17 reported higher rates of sexual violence than younger children and young adults (aged 18 to 24). Youth aged 12 to 14 (348 per 100 000) and aged 15 to 17 (300 per 100 000) experienced rates of sexual violence that were more than double that of young adults

Why is there such a strong correlation between age and crime? Explanations range from the biological, which look at hormonal variables, such as higher levels of testosterone in males, to an examination of the social and personal realities existing at various stages of life.

Do offenders "grow out of crime" as they mature?

Do they develop significant attachments to people, such as spouses and children, or to jobs that they do not want to risk losing through continued involvement in crime?

Do offenders settle down and no longer see criminal or deviant behaviour as fun or as a means to attain immediate gratification or peer approval?

Does the age at which a youth becomes involved in criminal behaviour and is labelled by the criminal justice system as an offender have any bearing on how long his or her criminal career will last?

Do some offenders simply grow too tired and physically unable to continue in a criminal lifestyle?

There is no simple explanation as to why age and crime are correlated. Keep these questions in mind as you consider the theories of criminal behaviour presented in Chapters 5, 6, 7, 8, 9, and 10. Can the age of the offender be factored into any or all of these theories?

(130 per 100 000). The rate of sexual victimization of female victims under the age of 18 is highest through the teenage years, peaking at ages 13 through 15 (almost 700 per 100 000).[22]

Sex and Criminal Behaviour

Sex appears so closely linked to most forms of criminal activity that it has been called "the best single predictor of criminality."[23] The most recent data available indicate that males account for 77 percent of those adults accused of a criminal offence. This is particularly true when considering violent crimes; adult males make up 90 percent of all charges for homicide and 98 percent of all charges for sexual assault, child pornography, and sexual violations against children. With property crimes, adult males constitute 73 percent of overall charges related to property offences. The offences with the highest representation of females include abduction (49 percent), prostitution (45 percent), and theft under $5000 (37 percent). The most common offences for which females are accused are theft under $5000, assault level 1, and administration of justice violations (e.g., failure to appear in court, breach of probation, etc.).[24]

The continued lower rate of female criminality has been explained by some as primarily due to cultural factors, including early socialization, role expectations, and a reluctance among criminal justice officials to arrest and prosecute women. Women who are struggling with poverty, homelessness, and addiction may turn to illegal activities to support themselves and their families. Others have assumed a biological propensity toward crime and aggression among men that may be lacking in women. These and other issues are addressed in Chapters 5, 6, 7, 8, 9, and 10.

Worthy of note is that, while the rate of adult males charged with a criminal offence has been declining over the past 20 years, the proportion of women charged with criminal activity has increased by as much as 15 percent over the past three decades. This difference in trends is even more pronounced for violent crime. Since 1991, the rate of males charged with violent crime has declined 32 percent, while the rate for females has increased 34 percent. However, males still accounted for more than four in five people accused of violent crime in 2011.[25]

Some criminologists cite *role convergence*, or the adaptation of the role of women to more closely resemble that of men, as an explanation for this. Others see the significant increases in female involvement in offences such as shoplifting, credit card fraud, and passing bad cheques as a manifestation of the *feminization of poverty* rather than the convergence of male and female roles.[26] As the number of poor female single parents grows, their marginalization may be reflected in increases in certain types of female property crimes.

When women commit crime, they are more often followers than leaders. One study of women Tin correctional settings, for example, found that women are far more likely to assume "secondary follower roles during criminal events" than "dominant leadership roles." Only 14 percent of women surveyed played primary roles, but those who did "felt that men had little influence in initiating or leading them into crime."[27]

However, trends that focus on the relative proportion of female offenders should be interpreted with caution. Whether the rise in adult female rates of police-reported crime reflects an actual increase in female offending or a change in enforcement practices cannot be determined simply by an examination of statistical data. Changes to how police approach certain offences may affect the number of women charged.[28]

Concerning victimization, there is very little difference in the overall risk of personal victimization for women and men. The General Social Survey (GSS) indicates that the rate of personal violent victimization in 2014 was 85 incidents per 1000 population for women as compared to 67 per 1000 for men. While men reported higher rates for physical assault (54 per 1000 population for men, 43 for women) and for robbery (8 for men, 5 for women), women were still much more likely to be victims of sexual assault at a rate of 37 per 1000 population as compared to 5 per 1000 for men. When all other risk factors were taken into account, women maintained a risk of violent victimization that was about 20 percent higher than for men.[29] Table 2.3 looks at adult victims of violent crime based on sex and age for selected categories of crime. The Violence Against Women Survey (VAWS) indicates that up to one-half of all Canadian women have experienced at least one incident of violence since the age of 16. Specifically, the VAWS findings indicate that 34 percent of women surveyed reported having experienced a physical assault, 39 percent reported having been sexually assaulted, and 15 percent had experienced unwanted sexual touching. Almost one-half of the women surveyed experienced violence by men known to them (boyfriends, dates, marital partners, friends, family, neighbours).[30] A more detailed examination of some of the current Canadian legislation aimed at assisting victims of crime, and female victims in particular, can be found in Chapter 4.

Although much female criminality has long been overlooked, criminologists are now increasingly aware of gender issues. How does the criminality of men and women appear to differ?

Stroheim Gerda/WoodyStock/Alamy Stock Photo

Table 2.3 Personal Victimization Incidents Reported by Canadians, by Type of Offence and Selected Demographic and Socio-economic Characteristics, 2014

Characteristics	Sexual Assault	Robbery	Physical Assault	Total Violent Victimization	Theft of Personal Property
Sex					
Male	12%	59%	55%	44%	50%
Female	88%	41%	45%	56%	50%
Age Groups					
15–24	52%	55%	23%	33%	23%
25–34	26%	25%	27%	26%	22%
35–44	8%	-	18%	11%	21%
45–54	11%	20%	18%	16%	18%
55–64	3%	-	10%	8%	11%
65 and over	-	-	3%	3%	6%

Source: Adapted from Samuel Perreault, *Criminal Victimization in Canada, 2014*, Juristat, 85-002-X, vol. 35, no. 1, 2015. This does not constitute an endorsement by Statistics Canada of this product.

Ethnicity and Criminal Behaviour

Unlike data from the United States, Canadian crime statistics do not routinely report on the racial and ethnic makeup of offenders. The only official Canadian statistics that report on the correlation between ethnicity and crime derive from studies that consider incarcerated offender or inmate profiles. The number of inmates, while accurate, is not representative of the actual number of offenders and offences detected by police. Nevertheless, correctional statistics can be useful in shedding light on the reality of ethnicity and crime in Canada, especially with respect to the representation of Aboriginal Canadians. Figure 2.3 shows the representation of the adult offender population in federal custody (serving a custody sentence of two years or more) by race.

The reality of Aboriginal over-representation in the Canadian criminal justice system has been studied for some time. Correctional Service Canada statistics indicate that in 2015, Aboriginals represented approximately 21.9 percent of the federal adult inmate population (35.5 percent of the female inmate population, 24.1 percent of the male inmate population) while representing 3.8 percent of the total Canadian adult population.[31]

A number of reasons have been cited for the disproportionate number of Aboriginals in the Canadian criminal justice system. Some maintain that this reality is a result of the discriminatory treatment of Aboriginals by the criminal justice system. A number of studies have concluded that "biased discretion,"" or selective enforcement by criminal justice officials, translates into the over-represented numbers of Aboriginals in the system.[32] While there may be instances when discrimination has played a role in a police officer's decision to arrest an Aboriginal person or in the decision of a justice of the peace to deny bail to an Aboriginal offender, there is limited research evidence to support the claim of active, systemic discrimination against Aboriginals by the Canadian criminal justice system. The most recent report by the federal correctional investigator provided a profile of the Aboriginal offender that included the correctional realities for this group of inmates. See the Who's Responsible? box for an overview of this part of the correctional investigator's report. In a 2016 investigative article in *Maclean's* magazine entitled "Canada's Prisons Are the New Residential Schools," the assertion is made that "at every step, discriminatory practices and a biased system work against an Indigenous accused, from the moment

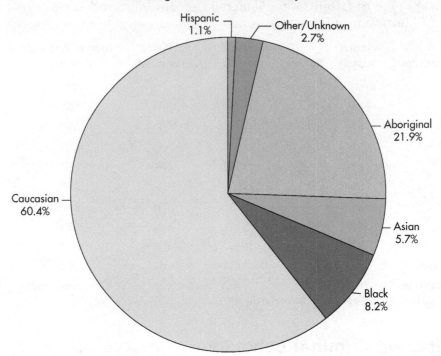

Percentage of Total Offender Population

Hispanic 1.1%
Other/Unknown 2.7%
Aboriginal 21.9%
Asian 5.7%
Black 8.2%
Caucasian 60.4%

Figure 2.3 Percentage of Total Federal Offender Population (by Race, Canada)

- The federal offender population is becoming more diverse, as evidenced by the decrease in the proportion of Caucasian offenders (from 64.4% in 2010–11 to 60.4% in 2014–15).
- Between 2010–11 and 2014–15, the Aboriginal population has increased by 17.1% (from 4,285 to 5,016).

Source: Corrections and Conditional Release Statistical Overview: Annual Report, page 42, Public Safety Canada, 2011, Reproduced with the permission of the Minister of Public Works and Government Services Canada, 2013.

a person is first identified by police, to their appearance before a judge, to their hearing before a parole board. The evidence is unambiguous: If you happen to be Indigenous, justice in Canada is not blind."[33]

Other explanations look to the socio-economic realities of many Aboriginal Canadians. The role of social and economic inequality and the realities of past and current living conditions for many Aboriginals are more often cited as causes contributing to criminality among Native peoples.[34]

Research by Carol La Prairie explored the contribution that certain large Canadian cities may make to the over-representation of Aboriginal peoples in the system. She concluded that a disproportionate number of Aboriginals living in urban centres (most notably Thunder Bay, Winnipeg, Regina, and Saskatoon) experience the social realities of low income, unemployment, lack of education, unstable housing, and single-parent families. For La Prairie, what explains an Aboriginal person's likelihood of involvement in the criminal justice system is "the concentration of poor, single-parent, and poorly educated Aboriginal people in the inner core of their large cities."[35] In addition to the social realities identified by La Prairie, the role of alcohol and substance abuse in the offences committed by Aboriginals cannot be overlooked. A review of a number of Canadian studies concluded that alcohol is a major contributor to the crimes committed by Native peoples.[36] Furthermore, a significant number of Aboriginals serving provincial terms of incarceration are doing so for default of an original fine sentence. Some studies indicated that almost two-thirds of the Aboriginals in some provincial institutions are serving sentences for such defaults.[37] It is most likely that socio-economic conditions have more to do with the inability to meet fine payments than a wilful refusal to pay.

As victims of crime, 28 percent of Aboriginal Canadians report having been victimized as compared to 18 percent of non-Aboriginal Canadians. In particular, Aboriginals experience violent victimization at a rate of 163 incidents per 1000 population as compared to 74 incidents, a rate more than double. The sexual assault rate for Aboriginal people (58 incidents per 1000) was almost three times that of non-Aboriginal people (20 per 1000), while Aboriginal peoples' rate of physical assault (90 per 1000) was close to double that of non-Aboriginal people (47 per 1000). Aboriginal females (220 incidents per 1000) had an overall rate of violent victimization that was close to triple that of non-Aboriginal females (81 per 1000) and more than triple that of non-Aboriginal males (66 per 1000), while for Aboriginal males, the pattern is different, with a rate of violent victimization that is similar (218 for Aboriginal males versus 239 incidents for non-Aboriginal males per 1000 males).[38]

WHO'S RESPONSIBLE—THE INDIVIDUAL OR SOCIETY?

Aboriginal Offender Profile Compared to Non-Aboriginal Offenders

Aboriginal Offender Profile

Compared to non-Aboriginal offenders, Aboriginal inmates are:

- younger (median age is 27);
- less formally educated;
- more likely to present a history of substance abuse, addictions, and mental health concerns;
- more likely to be incarcerated for a violent offence;
- more likely to have served previous youth and/or adult sentences;
- disproportionately from backgrounds of domestic or physical abuse; and
- more likely to be gang affiliated.

Regional Distribution

- Aboriginal inmates account for 47.21% of all inmates in the Prairie Region. The Prairie Region has led population growth and is now the largest region both in geography and population.
- Several institutions in the Prairie Region have Aboriginal inmate populations exceeding 50% of their total population:
  - Edmonton Institution for Women (60.26%)
  - Saskatchewan Penitentiary (60.19%)
  - Stony Mountain Institution (57.32%)
  - Regional Psychiatric Centre (56.36%)

Correctional Outcomes

Aboriginal inmates are:

- classified as higher risk and higher need in categories such as employment, community reintegration, substance abuse, and family supports;
- over-represented in segregation and maximum-security populations;
- disproportionately involved in use-of-force interventions and prison self-injury;
- released later in their sentence; and
- more likely to return to custody (either for a new offence or revocation of parole).

Think about it:

1. Are Aboriginal offenders victimized by the Canadian correctional system? What is the correctional system's responsibility to these offenders?

2. Does the over-representation of Aboriginals in the criminal justice system indicate systemic discrimination toward Aboriginals? Defend your opinion.

3. Why do you think Aboriginal inmates are "disproportionately involved in the use-of-force interventions and prison self-injury" and "released later in their sentences"?

Source: Based on *Annual Report of the Office of the Correctional Investigator, 2014–2015*. Government of Canada, © 2015

Socio-economic Status and Criminal Behaviour

Prior to 1960, criminologists generally assumed that a correlation existed between socio-economic status and crime. They believed that members of lower social classes were more prone to commit crime, and they thought that this propensity applied to all types of criminal activity. In the early 1960s, studies of the relationship between social class and crime, which made use of offender self-reports, seemed to show that the relationship between social class and criminality was an artefact of discretionary practices within the criminal justice system.[39] Such studies of teenagers found that rates of self-reported delinquency and criminality were fairly consistent across various social classes within North American society. Similar studies of white-collar criminality seemed to show that, although the nature of criminal activity may vary between classes, members of all social classes had nearly equal tendencies toward criminality. The apparent penchant for crime among members of the lower social classes was explained partially by the fact that the types of crime traditionally committed by these groups were those most likely to come to the attention of law enforcement officials and be fully prosecuted by the criminal justice system. While there is no doubt that people from all social classes commit crimes, a number of studies have pointed to a significant correlation between lower socio-economic status and criminal activity, as we shall see below.

In 1978, a comprehensive re-evaluation of 35 earlier studies of the relationship between socio-economic status and crime concluded that previously claimed links were non-existent.[40] Publication of the report fuelled further study of the relationship between social class and crime, and in 1981 a seminal article by Australian criminologist John Braithwaite, which summarized the results of 224 previous studies on the subject, concluded convincingly that members of lower social classes were indeed more prone to commit crime.[41] In contrast to earlier studies, Braithwaite found that "socio-economic status is one of the very few correlates of criminality which can be taken, on balance, as persuasively supported by a large body of empirical evidence."

Many of the difficulties surrounding research into the relationship between social class and crime appear to stem from a lack of definitional clarity. In the many different studies evaluated by Braithwaite, for example, neither *crime* nor *class* was uniformly defined. Some researchers have similarly suggested that earlier studies may have been seriously flawed by their near-exclusive focus on young people and by their conceptualization of crime in terms of relatively minor offences (truancy, vandalism, etc.).[42] Hence, a lack of concise definitions of the subject matter, combined with inadequate measurement techniques, may have led to misleading results.

Canadian studies of street youth in Toronto and Edmonton found that many came from lower-class families and were on the street because of poor relationships at home and at school. The struggle for survival often resulted in involvement in delinquency and crime.[43] A Canadian study surveyed over 3200 students in grades 7 to 9 in 177 classes in Toronto. The survey collected information on topics including family background and family bonds, attachment to school and neighbourhood, commitment to school, use of alcohol and drugs, and time devoted to paid and voluntary work. The results of the self-report survey concluded that delinquent behaviour was significantly more prevalent among students who reported consuming alcohol and drugs, those who indicated having little parental supervision, and those living in a step-family or blended family at the time of the survey.[44] The study by Latimer, Kleinknecht, Hung, and Gabor identifies five primary correlates of general delinquency: (1) negative school attachment, (2) anti-social peers, (3) victimization, (4) aggression, and (5) negative parenting. The findings are encouraging in that these are primarily dynamic factors amenable to change through targeted interventions with youth and their families.[45]

Unemployment, poverty, and income inequality are often cited as risk factors for criminal activity. Inasmuch as these factors can be used as indicators of socio-economic status, statistical trends indicate that unemployment rates in Canada were relatively high in the 1980s

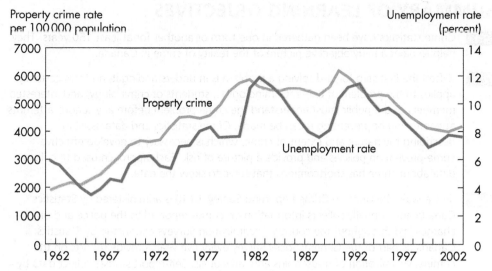

Figure 2.4a Comparison over Time in Rates of Property Crime and Unemployment, 1962 to 2003

Source: Statistics Canada, "Exploring Crime Patterns in Canada," 85-561-MIE2005005 no. 5. Released June 29, 2005. Reproduced and distributed on an "as is" basis with the permission of Statistics Canada.

and 1990s. Similarly, overall trends in property crime were also high in the same time periods. Interestingly, rates of violent crime do not seem to follow these patterns.[46] A comparison of unemployment and crime rates is found in Figures 2.4a and 2.4b. Overall, however, the relationship between social class and criminal behaviour is far from conclusive. While some studies do indicate that youth from lower-status families are at a higher risk for delinquency than those from higher-status families,[47] this finding is not consistent across studies.[48]

Are those from the lowest socio-economic classes also most likely to be victims of crime? Victimization Survey data from the GSS indicate that those households with incomes below $20 000 had the highest violent victimization rate at 79 per 1000 population, significantly higher than the rate of those in other income categories. People with household incomes of more than $140 000 had the highest rate of theft of personal property at 84 incidents per 1000 population.[49]

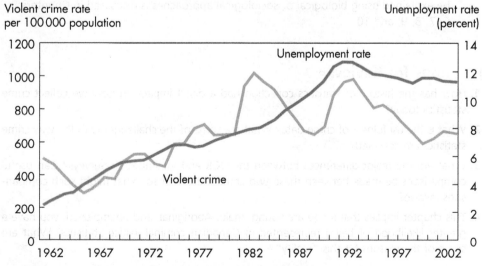

Figure 2.4b Comparison over Time in Rates of Violent Crime and Unemployment, 1962 to 2003

Source: Statistics Canada, "Exploring Crime Patterns in Canada," 85-561-MIE2005005 no. 5. Released June 29, 2005. Reproduced and distributed on an "as is" basis with the permission of Statistics Canada.

SUMMARY OF LEARNING OBJECTIVES

2.1 Crime statistics have been gathered in one form or another for at least 150 years. They help to paint a fairly objective picture of the reality of crime in Canada.

2.2 Often the first step toward solving a problem is in understanding it, and this certainly applies to the problem of crime. Criminologists, students of criminology, and interested members of the public must understand the crime problem before any serious attempts at controlling or preventing it can be made. Crime statistics and data assist in describing the nature and extent of crime, which is necessary to develop effective crime-prevention policies and provide a picture of risk. Each approach used to collect data about crime has shortcomings that serve to skew the data.

2.3 In Canada, the Uniform Crime Reporting Survey (UCR) is administered by Statistics Canada and annually collects information on crimes reported to the police and on charges laid throughout the country. Victimization Surveys conducted by Statistics Canada as part of the General Social Survey every five years provide reports on the criminal victimization of households and individuals. Self-report studies collect data by requiring subjects to reveal their own participation in criminal activity.

2.4 Social dimensions of crime are aspects of crime and victimization as they relate to socially significant attributes by which groups are defined and according to which individuals are assigned group memberships. Also referred to as *correlates of crime*, these aspects are often grouped into static factors and dynamic factors. Static factors are not amendable to change through direct interventions; included in this category are age, gender, and ethnicity. Dynamic factors, on the other hand, are amendable to change through direct interventions and include parenting, education and attachment to school, peer groups, geography and neighbourhoods, and some psychological factors, such as aggression and conduct disorders. A consideration of the strongest static social dimensions of crime includes age, sex, ethnicity, and socio-economic status. Canadian crime statistics tell us that young men are especially over-represented in the criminal justice system, and among these men, Aboriginals account for a proportion that is vastly over-representative of their numbers in our population. Socio-economic status is a less significant indicator of criminal behaviour, yet some studies do show a correlation between crime and social class as measured by employment, levels of education, and so on. Whether the strong correlations between crime and age, sex, ethnicity, and social class can be explained using biological or sociological approaches is discussed in Chapters 5, 6, 7, 8, 9, and 10.

Questions for Review

1. How has the history of statistics collection had a direct impact on how we collect crime statistics today?

2. What is the usefulness of crime data? What are some of the challenges with the way crime statistics are collected?

3. What are the major differences between the UCR and Victimization Surveys? Can useful comparisons be made between these two crime indices? If so, what might such comparisons involve?

4. This chapter implies that if you are young, male, Aboriginal, and unemployed, you have a greater likelihood of being represented in Canadian criminal justice statistics. What are some of the reasons for this "reality"?

Multiple-Choice Questions

1. Which one of the following statements is false?
   a. The revised UCR provides information on the number and types of offences reported to police.
   b. The revised UCR provides information on nearly 100 crime categories.
   c. The revised UCR was introduced in 1998.
   d. The revised UCR is administered by the Department of Justice.
   e. The revised UCR provides information on the accused, such as age, sex, and types of charges laid.

2. Data gathering using victimization surveys usually relies on _____.
   a. self-report surveys
   b. uniform crime reporting surveys
   c. a correlation of crime analysis
   d. geographic information studies
   e. telephone surveys

3. Based on 20 924 incidents of reported robbery and a total population of 35 540 400, what would the rate of crime be for robbery?
   a. 58.87
   b. 85.87
   c. 588.70
   d. 88.57
   e. 5.88

4. In Canada, those at the lowest risk of personal victimization are between the ages of _____.
   a. 50 and 65
   b. 35 and 50
   c. 24 and 35
   d. 12 and 18
   e. 18 and 24

5. The socially significant attributes by which groups are defined and according to which individuals are assigned group membership in reference to crime and victimization are known as _____.
   a. common characteristics
   b. social dimensions of crime
   c. socio-economic traits
   d. commonalities
   e. cultural traits

Multiple Choice Answers: 1d, 2e, 3a, 4a, 5b

Chapter 3
Patterns of Crime

Deepa Designs/Shutterstock

The one thing we know with any kind of certainty is that a falling crime rate doesn't have much to do with policies related to punishment. Sending more people to prison may reduce the likelihood that they're committing offences while they're in prison but, if anything, it increases the likelihood that they'll commit offences after they've been released.

—Anthony Doob[1]

LEARNING OBJECTIVES

After reading this chapter, you should be able to

3.1 Understand how crimes are classified and identify the major categories of crime classified by the Uniform Crime Report Surveys and the major crime rate trends in Canada.

3.2 Describe the offences classified as violent crime and apply various theories that explain why people commit acts of violence.

3.3 Describe the offences classified as property crime and apply various theories that suggest motivating factors in cases of property crime.

3.4 Describe the offences classified as crimes against the public order and apply various theories that propose explanations for public order crimes.

INTRODUCTION

The former wife of a Vancouver-area man accused of criminally harassing her says she hopes the legal process he's about to go through will give her enough time to change her identity and hide. Since 2014, Patrick Fox, also known as Richard Riess, has maintained and promoted a website in his ex-wife's name dedicated to ruining her reputation. The website is full of vulgar content, demeaning images, and private photos and lists her address and phone number. On it, Fox describes his ex-wife as a white supremacist, child abuser, and drug addict. Fox has been doing this in revenge for his ex-wife taking their son and moving to Arizona.

Desiree Capuano, who lives near Tucson, Arizona, with the couple's son, was first alerted to the site by a co-worker after the URL was emailed to all of her contacts on LinkedIn. Capuano, who has had trouble finding work and lives in fear, has fought to get the site shut down, appealing to U.S. and Canadian police and the internet provider to help. "There has got to be a way to take that down," Capuano said. "He told me once that his ultimate goal was to make me commit suicide. I won't let him win."

In December 2015, an Arizona judge issued a protective order that stopped Fox from sending Capuano emails but did not order the website taken down. Fox's site and the couple's email exchanges were also investigated by Burnaby RCMP. In July 2015, Fox was arrested and the RCMP recommended a charge of criminal harassment. The Crown did not approve the charge and Fox was released. Throughout it all, Fox has remained defiant, claiming that nothing short of Capuano's death or "when she is destitute and homeless" will prompt him to take down the site. "She ruined both of our lives," said Fox, who blames Capuano for taking his son and having him deported to Canada.

In June 2016, Fox was charged in a Vancouver provincial court with criminal harassment and possession of firearms in an unauthorized location after being turned over to the RCMP by American authorities. Fox had attempted to enter the United States; he was forbidden from doing so after being arrested and deported several times before. He is currently being held without bail awaiting a court appearance.

Criminal harassment is usually the charge laid when someone is physically stalked. The fact that this case involves allegations of online and email harassment has many in the legal community watching closely. According to Kevin Westell, a lawyer and prosecutor in Vancouver, "This case may be a sign that police are recognizing and taking very seriously the harm that can be done by way of a website as opposed to direct communication like a text message or email. The publication of false information meant to harass and humiliate is now being treated as potentially criminal as opposed to merely libellous or slanderous."[2]

CLASSIFICATIONS OF CRIME

3.1 | LEARNING OBJECTIVE

A SIGNIFICANT PORTION OF THIS TEXT IS DEVOTED TO EXAMINING A VARIETY OF explanations for why people commit crime. Chapter 2 provides an overview of the ways in which crime statistics are collected so that a picture of the incidence of crime and the number and types of criminals in a given period will emerge.

But what *types* of crime are committed in Canada? How many of each type occur annually? Typically, crimes are organized into categories, or **typologies of crime**. The Uniform Crime Report Surveys (UCR) classifies crimes into the following categories: violent crime, property crime, other *Criminal Code* crime, *Criminal Code* traffic violations, drug offences, and other federal statute violations (including violations of the *Youth Criminal Justice Act*). Categorization helps to identify patterns within these groupings and to focus discussion concerning the offender's motivation. For example, does the person who commits murder do it for reasons distinct from those of the person who breaks into someone's home and robs it?

Typologies of crime Classifications of crime are useful in identifying patterns of criminal activity and motivations for criminal behaviour.

This chapter examines three categories of crime: violent crime, property crime, and crimes against the public order, such as counterfeiting and drug abuse. In addition to providing a snapshot of the incidence of crime committed in Canada for each of these categories, this chapter makes the link to theoretical explanations discussed in later chapters that might be used to explain why these crimes are committed. Unless otherwise noted, all the 2014 statistics cited in this chapter are taken from 2014 UCR crime statistics, which indicate that approximately 2 million *Criminal Code* offences were reported in 2014, or 3 percent fewer than in 2013. The decrease in the police-reported crime rate in 2014 represented the continuation of a downward trend that began in the early 1990s; the crime rate in 2014 was the lowest recorded since 1969 and was 34 percent lower than the previous decade.[3] Table 3.1 provides a statistical snapshot of the crime picture in Canada in 2014.

Table 3.1 Police-Reported Crime for Selected Offences, Canada, 2013 and 2014

Type of offence	2013[r]		2014		Percentage change in rate 2013 to 2014	Percentage change in rate 2004 to 2014
	Number	Rate	Number	Rate	Percent	
Total *Criminal Code* (excluding traffic)— "crime rate"	1 826 431	5195	1 793 534	5046	−3	−34
Violent crime						
Homicide	512	1	516	1	0	−26
Other violations causing death[1,2]	141	0	90	0	−37	−41
Attempted murder	636	2	617	2	−4	−17
Sexual assault level 3—aggravated	133	0	105	0	−22	−50
Sexual assault level 2—weapon or bodily harm	368	1	319	1	−14	−28
Sexual assault level 1	20 695	59	20 311	57	−3	−19
Sexual violations against children[3,4,5]	4174	12	4452	13	6	. . .
Assault level 3—aggravated	3241	9	3242	9	−1	7
Assault level 2—weapon or bodily harm	46 019	131	44 788	126	−4	−14
Assault level 1	158 259	450	153 352	431	−4	−25
Assault peace officer	9826	28	9450	27	−5	−7
Other assaults[6]	2639	8	2091	6	−22	−49
Firearms—use of, discharge, pointing	1892	5	1828	5	−4	−26
Robbery	23 249	66	20 924	59	−11	−39
Forcible confinement or kidnapping	3231	9	3266	9	0	−15
Abduction	375	1	393	1	4	−45
Extortion	2310	7	2716	8	16	43
Criminal harassment	21 546	61	19 653	55	−10	−27
Uttering threats	63 984	182	62 387	176	−4	−34
Threatening or harassing phone calls	16 506	47	14 375	40	−14	−49
Other violent *Criminal Code* violations	4649	13	4484	13	−5	−1
Total	**384 385**	**1093**	**369 359**	**1039**	**−5**	**−26**
Property crime						
Breaking and entering	156 470	445	151 921	427	−4	−51
Possess stolen property[7,8]	16 983	48	17 143	48	0	−57

Table 3.1 Police-Reported Crime for Selected Offences, Canada, 2013 and 2014 (Continued)

Theft of motor vehicle	72 512	206	73 964	208	1	−61
Theft over $5000 (non-motor vehicle)	14 336	41	14 258	40	−2	−24
Theft of $5000 or under (non-motor vehicle)	472 226	1 343	474 879	1 336	−1	−37
Fraud (excluding identity fraud)[9]	79 744	227	82 049	231	2	−24
Identity fraud[9,10]	11 635	33	12 729	36	8	. . .
Mischief[11]	273 688	779	264 976	746	−4	−33
Arson	8915	25	8484	24	−6	−41
Total	**1 106 509**	**3 148**	**1 100 403**	**3 096**	**−2**	**−40**
Other *Criminal Code* offences						
Counterfeiting	630	2	572	2	−10	−76
Weapons violations	13 733	39	13 898	39	0	−19
Child pornography[12,13]	2818	8	4020	11	41	264
Prostitution[14]	2046	6	1073	3	−48	−85
Terrorism[15]	71	0	100	0	39	. . .
Disturbing the peace	109 307	311	103 266	291	−7	−21
Administration of justice violations	177 552	505	171 897	484	−4	−7
Other violations	29 380	84	28 946	81	−3	−24
Total	**335 537**	**954**	**323 772**	**911**	**−5**	**−15**
***Criminal Code* traffic violations**						
Impaired driving[16]	77 558	221	74 781	210	−5	−16
Other *Criminal Code* traffic violations	58 050	165	54 724	154	−7	20
Total	**135 608**	**386**	**129 505**	**364**	**−6**	**−4**
Drug offences						
Possession—cannabis	59 354	169	57 314	161	−4	7
Possession—cocaine	7729	22	7596	21	−3	−17
Possession—methamphetamines[17,18]	3387	10	4720	13	38	. . .
Possession—heroin	919	3	1242	3	34	140
Possession—methylenedioxyamphetamine[18,19]	284	1	368	1	28	. . .
Possession—other drugs[18,20]	6521	19	6660	19	1	. . .
Trafficking, production, or distribution—cannabis	14 185	40	10 696	30	−25	−52
Trafficking, production, or distribution—cocaine	9523	27	8502	24	−12	−13
Trafficking, production, or distribution—methamphetamines[17,18]	1288	4	1528	4	17	. . .
Trafficking, production, or distribution—heroin	631	2	714	2	12	93
Trafficking, production, or distribution—methylenedioxyamphetamine[18,19]	161	0	160	0	−2	. . .
Trafficking, production, or distribution—other drugs[18]	5109	15	4257	12	−18	. . .
Total	**109 091**	**310**	**103 757**	**292**	**−6**	**−4**
Other federal statute violations						
Youth Criminal Justice Act	9428	27	7969	22	−16	−60

(Continued)

Other federal statutes	18 218	52	17 426	49	−5	−2
Total	**27 646**	**79**	**25 395**	**71**	**−9**	**−33**
Total—all violations	**2 098 776**	**5970**	**2 052 191**	**5774**	**−3**	**−31**

. . . not applicable

ʳ revised

1. Includes, for example, criminal negligence causing death.

2. The decrease in "Other Violations Causing Death" between 2013 and 2014 is partly attributable to fewer incidents of criminal negligence, which were specific to the Lac-Mégantic rail disaster in 2013.

3. Excludes sexual assaults against children and youth, which are reported as level 1, 2, or 3 sexual assault.

4. Sexual violations against children is a relatively new crime category with only partial data available prior to 2010, therefore the percentage change from 2004 to 2014 is not shown.

5. Includes sexual interference, invitation to sexual touching, sexual exploitation, luring a child via a computer/agreement or arrangement, and making sexually explicit material available to a child for the purpose of facilitating sexual offences against children/youth.

6. A notable portion of the decrease in "Other Assaults" in 2014 is attributable to a change in Toronto Police Service's records management system whereby incidents previously reported as other assaults are now being reported as common assaults.

7. Includes trafficking and the intent to traffic stolen goods.

8. In 2011, the Uniform Crime Reporting Survey was modified to create separate categories for possession of stolen property of $5000 or under, and possession of stolen property over $5000. As a result, incidents of possession of $5000 or under may now be reported as secondary offences when occurring in conjunction with more serious offences, leading to a decrease in the number of possession of stolen property incidents reported since 2011.

9. In January 2010, the Uniform Crime Reporting Survey was modified to create new violation codes for identity fraud and identity theft. Prior to 2010, those offences would have been coded as fraud. Therefore, the percentage change from 2004 to 2014 for fraud includes identity fraud and identity theft.

10. Includes identity theft.

11. Includes altering/removing/destroying a vehicle identification number.

12. Due to the complexity of these cyber incidents, the data likely reflect the number of active or closed investigations for the year rather than the total number of incidents reported to police. Data are based on police-reported incidents that are recorded in police services' records management systems.

13. The offence of "Child Pornography" includes offences under section 163.1 of the *Criminal Code* which makes it illegal to access, possess, make, print, or distribute child pornography. When the actual victim is not identified, this offence is reported to the Uniform Crime Reporting Survey with the most serious offence being "Child Pornography" which falls under the larger crime category of "Other *Criminal Code*". In cases where an actual victim is identified, police will report the most serious offence as sexual assault, sexual exploitation or other sexual violations against children, which falls under the category of "Violent Violations," and child pornography may be reported as a secondary violation.

14. On December 20, 2013 the Supreme Court of Canada found laws surrounding prostitution to be unconstitutional, and gave parliament 12 months to review and rewrite legislation. As a result of this, a large number of incidents of prostitution were no longer being reported, leading to a large decrease in the number of prostitution incidents in 2014. New legislation came into force December 6, 2014, therefore comparisons to previous years should be made with caution.

15. Includes seven new terrorism violations which were introduced mid-year 2013, as a result of the enactment of Bill S-7 (An *Act* to amend the *Criminal Code*, the *Canada Evidence Act* and the *Security of Information Act*). Therefore, comparisons to previous years should be made with caution. Terrorism is a relatively new crime category with only partial data available prior to 2010; therefore, the percentage change from 2004 to 2014 is not shown.

16. Includes alcohol and/or drug impaired operation of a vehicle, alcohol and/or drug impaired operation of a vehicle causing death or bodily harm, failure or refusal to comply with testing for the presence of alcohol or drugs, and failure or refusal to provide a breath or blood sample. In some jurisdictions, including British Columbia, impaired driving incidents that meet the elements of the *Criminal Code* may be handled using a provincial statute. Collection of these incidents is within the scope of the Uniform Crime Reporting Survey.

17. Includes substances such as crystal meth, speed, etc.

18. In April 2008, the Uniform Crime Reporting Survey began counting violations involving methamphetamines (e.g., crystal meth) and methylenedioxyamphetamine (MDA) (e.g., ecstasy) under their own unique violation codes. Prior to this, violations involving methamphetamines and MDA were counted within the category of "Other Drugs". Therefore, the percentage change from 2004 to 2014 for violations involving methamphetamines, MDA or "Other Drugs" are not shown.

19. Referred to as MDA for short, and commonly known as ecstasy.

20. Includes all other drugs listed under the *Controlled Drugs and Substances Act*, as well as possession of precursors and equipment.

Note: Additional data are available on CANSIM (Table 252-0051). Police-reported statistics may be affected by differences in the way police services deal with offences. In some instances, police or municipalities might choose to deal with some offences using municipal bylaws or provincial provisions rather than *Criminal Code* provisions. Counts are based on the most serious violation in the incident. One incident may involve multiple violations. Data for specific types of crime are available, in most cases, from 1977. Rates are calculated on the basis of 100 000 population. Percentage changes are based on unrounded rates. Populations are based upon July 1st estimates from Statistics Canada, Demography Division.

Source: Jillian Boyce, "Police-reported crime statistics in Canada, 2014", *Juristat*, vol. 34, no. 1 (Ottawa: Minister of Industry, 2015). Reproduced and distributed on an "as is" basis with the permission of Statistics Canada.

VIOLENT CRIME

VIOLENT CRIME INCIDENTS INCLUDE HOMICIDE, ATTEMPTED MURDER, ASSAULT, SEXUAL assault, robbery, use of firearms, forcible confinement or kidnapping, abduction, extortion, criminal harassment and uttering threats, and threatening or harassing telephone calls. In 2014, violent crimes continued to account for about one-fifth (21 percent) of all police-reported *Criminal Code* offences (excluding traffic). There were approximately 369 500 violent police-reported incidents in 2014, about 15 000 fewer than the previous year; common assault accounted for 42 percent of the total number. While almost all forms of violent crime decreased between 2013 and 2014, rates increased for the violent violations of extortion (+16 percent), sexual violations against children (+6 percent), and abduction (+4 percent). In 2014, the violent crime rate in Canada was 1039 violent incidents per 100 000 population, which was 5 percent lower than in 2013 and 26 percent lower than a decade ago. Across the regions of the country, violent crime rates decreased or remained stable from the previous year in all provinces and territories, with the most notable declines in Prince Edward Island (−13 percent), Newfoundland and Labrador (−8 percent), and Manitoba (−7 percent). Nunavut, Northwest Territories, and Yukon posted the highest violent crime rates in the country (7935, 6911, and 4547 per 100 000, respectively), while the province reporting the highest violent crime rate was Saskatchewan, at 1963 per 100 000. Ontario recorded the lowest rate of violent crime at 787 per 100 000.

Homicide

Rene Michaud was found guilty of first-degree murder in the deaths of two Ottawa schoolteachers, Bob and Bonnie Dagenais. In a case that made national news, Michaud, with a 16-year-old accomplice, broke into the Dagenaises' cottage in the middle of the night and then shot the couple with a shotgun when they confronted him. The Dagenaises had recently retired after successful careers as teachers in the Ottawa School Board. Bob Dagenais was well known and so popular that when he was transferred from one high school to another, the students walked out to protest the move. Rene Michaud was convicted of first-degree murder and received a life sentence with no chance of parole for 25 years.[4]

The terms *homicide* and *murder* are often used interchangeably, but they are not synonymous. **Homicide** occurs when a person, directly or indirectly, by any means, causes the death of a human being. Homicide, therefore, can be either culpable or non-culpable. *Culpable homicide* is considered an offence under the *Criminal Code of Canada* and includes murder, manslaughter, and infanticide. *Non-culpable homicide* consists of justifiable and/or excusable homicide. Justifiable homicide includes legally authorized acts such as a police officer killing someone in the course of duty, while excusable homicide includes acts of self-defence, defence of others, or defence of property.

Murder (s. 229 of the *Criminal Code of Canada*) occurs when a person intentionally causes the death of another human being or intends to cause bodily harm likely to result in death. Murder is further classified into first-degree murder and second-degree murder. **First-degree murder** (defined in s. 231) describes culpable homicide that is planned and deliberate; or involves the killing of a peace officer such as a police officer or correctional worker; or occurs during the commission of another serious offence, such as sexual assault, kidnapping, or hijacking. **Second-degree murder** (defined in s. 231) includes all murder that is not first degree—in other words, murders that are intentional and unlawful but not planned. **Manslaughter** (s. 234) is considered to be a non-intentional homicide committed in response to sudden provocation, as a result of impaired judgment due to alcohol or drug consumption, or as a result of recklessness or carelessness. **Infanticide** (s. 233) occurs when a female causes the death of her

Homicide When a person, directly or indirectly, by any means, causes the death of a human being. Homicide can be culpable or non-culpable.

Murder When a person intentionally causes the death of another human being or intends to cause bodily harm likely to result in death.

First-degree murder Culpable homicide that is planned and deliberate.

Second-degree murder All murder that is not first-degree murder.

Manslaughter All non-intentional homicide.

Infanticide When a female considered disturbed from the effects of giving birth causes the death of her newborn child (under one year old).).

newborn child (under one year old) if her mind is considered disturbed from the effects of giving birth.

Serial murder and mass murder are two varieties of what is usually termed first-degree murder. Although most murderers kill only once in their lives, serial and mass murderers kill more than one person. **Serial murder** has been defined as culpable homicide that "involves the killing of several victims in three or more separate events."[5] These separate events are sometimes spread out over years. Infamous Canadian serial killers include Clifford Olson, who killed at least 11 young people aged 9 to 18 over a nine-month period in 1980–1981 in British Columbia. Between 1987 and 1990, Paul Bernardo committed at least 18 violent sexual assaults in Toronto and later went on to abduct, sexually assault, and strangle two teenaged girls in 1991 and 1992 in St. Catharines, Ontario. He was assisted in these murders by his wife, Karla Homolka, who subsequently testified against her husband. Allan Legère killed a grocery store owner in 1987 and went on to kill four other people in Miramichi, New Brunswick, terrorizing the rural community between 1987 and 1989 and earning for himself the nickname "The Monster of the Miramichi." Robert Pickton was found guilty on six counts of second-degree murder for the deaths of sex-trade workers who went missing between 1995 and 2002. Other notorious American serial killers include Jeffrey Dahmer, who killed and dismembered 15 young men in the 1980s; David Berkowitz, better known as "Son of Sam," who killed young men and women in New York City in the 1970s; Charles Manson, who ordered his followers to kill seven people in California; Ted Bundy, who killed many college-aged women; and the female serial killer Aileen Carol Wuornos, who killed six men who had picked her up as she hitchhiked through Florida.[6] Internationally infamous killers include Dr. Harold Shipman of Britain, who was convicted of killing 15 female patients and suspected in the deaths of 23 more, and Javed Iqbal, convicted of sexually assaulting and killing 100 street children in Pakistan and sentenced to die in the same way his victims died—by strangulation.

Mass murder is different from serial murder in that it entails "the killing of four or more victims at one location, within one event."[7] On December 6, 1989, in what has become known as the "Montreal Massacre," Marc Lepine shot and killed 14 female students at Montreal's École Polytechnique. Other mass murderers in Canada include Victor Hoffman, who, at age 19, killed nine members of a family as they slept in their Saskatchewan farmhouse in 1967; Mark Chahal, a Vancouver accountant who shot dead his ex-wife and eight other members of her family at a home in Vernon, British Columbia, in 1996; James Roszko, who ambushed and then killed four RCMP officers on his Alberta farm in 2005; and Phu Lam, who killed his wife and seven other family members in Edmonton, and Matthew de Grood, who stabbed five young people to death at a house party in Calgary, both in 2014 . Other infamous mass murders include the 12 people killed in a movie theatre in Colorado in 2012; 77 people, many of them youth, gunned down at a summer camp in Norway in 2011; 12 high school students and a teacher killed by two fellow students who marched through the halls of Columbine High School in Colorado targeting specific individuals in 1999; and 16 school-aged children and their teacher killed in Dunblane, Scotland, in 1996. Politically motivated mass murders, often referred to as *terrorist attacks*, occur around the world; some are perpetrated by a lone individual, others by an organized group of two or more.

Homicide continues to be a relatively rare event in Canada. In 2014, homicides (516) and attempted murders (617) accounted for approximately 0.1 percent (less than half of 1 percent) of all police-reported violent crimes committed in Canada. Even though there were four more homicides committed in 2014 than in the previous year, the homicide rate has generally been decreasing, with the 2014 rate of 1.45 per 100 000 being the lowest since 1966. The rates of attempted murder remained the same as the

Serial murder Culpable homicide that involves the killing of several victims in three or more separate events.

Mass murder The illegal killing of four or more victims at one location, within one event.

Robert Pickton, a former multi-millionaire pig farmer, was convicted and sentenced to life in prison in 2007 for the second-degree murder of six women. He was also charged in the deaths of an additional 20 women; these charges were stayed by the Crown in 2010.

Andy Clark/REUTERS

previous year at 2 percent per 100 000. Geographically, during the same time period, homicide rates increased from east to west in Canada.[8] The lowest rates were reported in Newfoundland and Labrador (0.4), Nova Scotia (0.6), and Quebec (0.9). The highest homicide rates per 100 000 were found in Manitoba (3.4), followed by Alberta (2.5) and Saskatchewan (2.1). In absolute numbers, Ontario and Alberta led the country in 2014, with 155 and 104 homicides respectively, although Ontario's rate, at 1.1 per 100 000, is below the national average of 1.5. With 83 homicides in 2014 (1.4 per 100 000), Toronto reported the most homicides of any metropolitan area, an increase of 3 homicides from the previous year. However, when population differences were taken into account, rates were higher in Thunder Bay (9.0), Winnipeg (3.3), Edmonton (3.0), and Saskatoon (2.6). Police reports indicate the majority of homicides were committed by males (87 percent), with the highest number among males aged 25 to 44 (130) in 2014. A decrease of 36 percent in the rate of youth aged 12 to 17 accused of homicide was the lowest since 1969. In 2014, 84 homicides were considered by police to be gang related, one less than the previous year, accounting for 16 percent of all homicides reported to police and representing the lowest number since 2005.

Among solved homicides in 2014, most victims (71 percent) knew their killer. Acquaintances made up the majority of accused persons (37 percent), followed by family members (34 percent), strangers (17 percent), and criminal relationships (6 percent). In recent years, the number of intimate partner homicides has been relatively stable. (*Intimate partners* are defined as married, common-law, or dating partners.) In 2014, there were 83 victims of homicide by an intimate partner, 11 more than the previous year. Women continue to be about four times more likely to be victims of intimate partner homicide than men.

Since the 1980s, the most common method used to commit homicide has fluctuated between shootings and stabbings. In 2014, both the number and rate of firearm-related homicides increased. Police reported 156 firearm-related homicides, 21 more than the previous year. As such, the rate of firearm-related homicides grew from 0.38 to 0.44 per 100 000 population (+1 percent). Despite that increase, the 2014 rate of firearm-related homicides was the second lowest recorded since homicide tracking began in 1974.

By comparison, U.S. statistics indicate that of the 14 249 homicides committed in 2014, almost 68 percent involved the use of a firearm, and 68 percent of these involved a handgun.[9] Although there have been some annual fluctuations, by some reports, the rate of homicides by firearm has decreased from 7.0 in 1993 to 3.4 in 2014.[10]

Statistics Canada also collects information related to the occupation of homicide victims. In 2014, there were 81 homicides that were directly related to the victim's profession. The majority of these homicides were linked to illegal activities, including drug trafficking and prostitution (83 percent). Fourteen homicide victims' deaths were related to their legal profession. This was up from 4 the previous year. Of these victims, police officers made up the largest proportion (21 percent). There were 3 police officers killed in 2014, an increase of 2 from the year before. The highest number of police officers killed in a given year was 5 in 2005.

Sexual Assault

The *Criminal Code of Canada* distinguishes between three levels of sexual assault, according to the seriousness of the incident. These levels reflect amendments made to the *Criminal Code* in 1983. Prior to that year, section 143 of the *Criminal Code* defined rape to have occurred when "a male person has sexual intercourse with a female person who is not his wife (a) without her consent, or (b) with her consent if the consent (i) is extorted by threats or fear of bodily harm, (ii) is obtained by impersonating her husband, or (iii) is obtained by false or fraudulent representations as to the nature and quality of the act." Under this definition, the act was largely defined as one of sexual penetration, and the offender was presumed to be a male and the victim female. As well, under the old legislation, husbands could not be charged with raping their wives.

Currently, sexual assault legislation focuses on the violent nature of the act, rather than its sexual nature. **Sexual assault** is considered to be an assault committed in circumstances of a sexual nature such that the sexual integrity of the victim is violated. The current laws allow for the accused (including legally married spouses) to be charged with sexual assault regardless of whether or not penetration occurred. As well, the offence has been "degenderized" such that perpetrators can be either male or female, as can victims. Critics charge, however, that it is overwhelmingly men who sexually assault women and that it has now been left to the discretion of the courts to determine what constitutes sexual assault, as opposed to common assault.[11] *Level 1 sexual assault* (s. 271) is assault that violates the sexual integrity of a person and can include unwanted sexual touching; *level 2 sexual assault* (s. 272) is sexual assault that involves a weapon, bodily harm, or threats to cause bodily harm to a person; *level 3 sexual assault* (s. 273) is sexual assault that wounds, maims, disfigures, or endangers the life of another person.[12]

Statistics on sexual assault collected by the UCR are delineated according to the three levels of sexual assault. In 2014, 20 735 sexual assaults were reported nationwide—99 percent of those were classified as level 1. Following a general trend seen over the past decade, the overall rate of police-reported sexual assaults continued to decrease in 2014, down 3 percent from the previous year, amounting to 58 sexual assaults per 100 000 population. While the rate of sexual assault decreased for all three categories between 2013 and 2014, aggravated sexual assault (level 3) saw the greatest decline (−22 percent). The overall rate of sexual assault at 62 per 100 000 population was over 25 percent lower than a decade earlier but still significantly higher than the rate in 1983, when the new definition of the offence was introduced (41 per 100 000). (Refer to Chapter 2 for a discussion of the impact of crime definitions on crime rates.) It is interesting to note that the sexual assault rate for females is effectively twice that indicated by the official figures, since any realistic tally of such crimes should compare the number of female victims assaulted with the number of females in the overall population (rather than to a count of the entire population, which includes males).

Sexual assault An assault committed in circumstances of a sexual nature such that the sexual integrity of the victim is violated. The categories of sexual assault include level 1—assault that violates the sexual integrity of a person; level 2—sexual assault that involves a weapon, bodily harm, or threats to cause bodily harm to a person; and level 3—sexual assault that wounds, maims, disfigures, or endangers the life of another person.

Data from the most recent statistics indicate that over 80 percent of victims of sexual assault were female, compared to 56 percent of victims of all other violent crimes.[13] Most had been victimized by a friend or acquaintance and the remainder by a family member or stranger. Fifty-two percent of all sexual assault victims reported to the police were between the ages of 15 and 24.

Also important to note is that that the number of sexual assaults reported by police is likely an underestimate of the true extent of sexual assault in Canada, as these types of offences are likely to go unreported to police. For instance, self-reported victimization data suggest that the majority (88 percent) of sexual assaults experienced by Canadians aged 15 years and older are not brought to the attention of police.[14] The reasons for victims' hesitancy vary: some feel they are responsible for some aspect of their social relationship that led to the sexual assault, some are ashamed or embarrassed, some believe that the incident wasn't important enough, and some feel that it's a private matter.

The ability to capture the extent of sexual violence against women remains hampered by socio-cultural factors that contribute to under-reporting. **Rape myths** are false assumptions about sexual assault that continue to characterize much of the discourse surrounding sexual violence: that women bring false sexual assault charges to get even with men, that women bring rape upon themselves by wearing provocative clothing, that women are "asking for it" by going to bars alone, and that women say no when they really mean yes. In 1980, Martha R. Burt first began researching rape myth ideology;[15] since then, numerous other studies have supported widespread acceptance of these myths.[16] Rape myths serve to undermine the traumatic nature of this offence and to discount the experiences of women by placing stereotypical parameters around who can and who cannot be sexually assaulted. Rape myths inhibit the reporting of sexual assault and normalize sexual assault as a crime of violence.[17] Largely as a result of such myths, women continue to report that the criminal justice system does not respond with sensitivity and compassion toward their victimization. Social media such as Facebook and Twitter are increasingly being used by sexual assault victims to "go public" about their abuse, in the hopes of raising awareness and encouraging other victims to come forward (see Box 3.1).

Rape myth A false assumption about sexual assault, such as "When a woman says no, she really means yes."

The sexual assault laws are applicable to all victims regardless of age. The UCR also collects information on sexual violations specific to children, a category that includes sexual interference, invitation to sexual touching, sexual exploitation, luring a child via a computer agreement or arrangement, and making sexually explicit material available to a child for the purpose of facilitating sexual offences against children/youth.

Police reported over 4452 incidents of sexual violations against children in 2014. The rate of sexual violations against children rose 3 percent between 2013 and 2014, making it one of the few categories of violent offences to increase in 2014. The UCR also captures data on incidents of child pornography, which includes offences under section 163.1 of the *Criminal Code*, which makes it illegal to access, possess, make, print, or distribute child pornography. Police reported more than 4020 incidents of child pornography in 2014, 1202 more than in 2013. The rate of child pornography incidents increased 41 percent. Fluctuations in the rate of child pornography are most likely reflective of police-based programs and initiatives targeting this particular offence, in particular a proactive project initiated by the British Columbia Integrated Child Exploitation Unit that recorded Internet Protocol (IP) addresses that were in possession of, and possibly sharing, child pornography.[18]

Related to the offence of sexual assault is the offence of criminal harassment, often referred to as *stalking*. Legislation regarding this offence was first enacted in Canada in 1993 as a response to violence against women. The goal of the legislation is

Box 3.1 WHY SEX ASSAULT VICTIMS GO PUBLIC

The stigma surrounding victims of sexual assault means that many never come forward with their stories or begin criminal proceedings. The recent 2016 criminal case involving CBC Radio host Jian Ghomeshi and the controversial verdict, reinforced for many women that even when they do speak out, the outcome does not often support them.

Many victims of sexual assault look to other means to report their experiences. Facebook groups such as "I Am a Survivor of Sexual Abuse" and "Sexual Assault Survivors" have helped women bond and connect victims to support and advocacy services. Some women, such as Alice Moran, are going online even more broadly to share their journeys and in some cases, to shame perpetrators.

Amanda Dale, executive director of the Barbra Schlifer Commemorative Clinic, which serves women experiencing violence in Toronto, reinforces the cathartic healing that can occur for women once they have "come out" online. According to Ms. Dale, "We don't want to reinforce the message of shame and keep these things so private that we never shift the conversation. That's why young women like [Alice Moran] are taking the step to go bold and go public, because they feel like they're warriors on the edge of a social taboo."

In March 2016, the Ontario provincial government announced a $2.8 million dollar project that would ensure survivors of sexual assault access to four hours of free legal advice. Piloted in Toronto, Ottawa and Thunder Bay, this initiative is meant to assist these victims in making informed choices about how to proceed, which may or may not include a legal option.

"At this stage what we're really looking for is to level the playing field a little bit, for the claimant to understand the process in a clear-eyed way . . . to give women somewhat

Some victims of sexual assault go public in order to gain control over their stories and in some cases to "out" and shame their perpetrators.

Rick Madonik/ZUMA Press/Newscom

adequate support and (awareness of the) realities of the criminal system," says Amanda Dale.

Sources: Zosia Bielski, "Why Sex Victims Are Going Public," Globe and Mail, September 6, 2012. http://www.theglobeandmail.com/life/why-sex-assault-victims-are-going-public/article4524879/; Ashley Csanady, "In a Canadian first, survivors of sexual violence will get free legal advice in Ontario pilot program", National Post, March 11, 2016. http://news.nationalpost.com/news/canada/canadian-politics/in-a-canadian-first-survivors-of-sexual-violence-will-get-free-legal-advice-in-ontario-pilot-program [Accessed November 13, 2016]

Criminal harassment Also known as *stalking*, the repeated following, watching, or communicating with a person or someone known to the person in a way that causes that person to fear for his or her safety or for the safety of someone known to him or her.

to identify and respond to criminal harassment before it escalates into serious physical harm to victims and to prohibit deliberate conduct that is psychologically harmful to others in causing them to fear for their safety. **Criminal harassment** (s. 264) is generally defined as "repeated following, watching or communicating with a person or someone known to them in a way that causes them to fear for their safety or for the safety of someone known to them" and applies equally to all victims.[19]

Canadians' increased use of the internet has also led to an increase in the incidence of *cyberstalking*, or online harassment. Closely related to real-life stalking, individuals use chat rooms, message boards, and emails to threaten or post obscene messages about the victim. It is possible for cyberstalking to extend to real life as the stalker may use the internet or obtain information about the target and then use it in a conventional stalking incident. While online stalkers can be charged under the criminal harassment provision of the *Criminal Code*, the nature of the activity makes it difficult to identify stalkers. There are rarely any witnesses, and jurisdictional problems arise if the stalker is located in a city or country different from that of the victim. The limited

evidence that does exist about cyberstalking indicates that the majority of victims are women.[20] See Chapter 12 for a more in-depth look at cybercrimes.

Statistics from the UCR on criminal harassment show 19 653 reported incidents, a rate of 55 per 100 000 population. Females accounted for 76 percent of all victims of criminal harassment, compared to about half (51 percent) of victims of overall violent crime.[21]

In most cases, the offender is known to the victim; 45 percent of all female victims are stalked by a former partner, 22 percent by a casual acquaintance, and 6 percent by a current partner. Other offenders include strangers (12 percent), business relations (5 percent), and other family members (5 percent). Male victims of criminal harassment are most commonly stalked by casual acquaintances (37 percent), ex-partners (22 percent), business acquaintances (12 percent), strangers (11 percent), other family members (5 percent), and current partners (2 percent).[22]

Robbery

The crime of **robbery** (s. 343) is regarded as a violent personal crime because it is committed in the presence of a victim and involves threatened or actual use of force or violence in the commission of a theft or attempted theft from another person. Although some individuals mistakenly use the terms *robbery* and *break and enter* interchangeably (as in the phrase "my house was robbed"), it should be remembered that robbery is a personal crime and that individuals, not houses, are robbed.

The 2014 UCR reported that 20 924 robberies came to the attention of the authorities across the nation that year, meaning that the robbery rate was 59 for every 100 000 people in Canada. This was a decrease of 11 percent (or 2325 incidents) from the previous year and 39 percent lower than in 2004. The involvement of weapons, such as firearms or knives, to commit robbery has gradually declined while the use of physical force or threats (but no weapon) was higher than a decade earlier. Statistics for robbery indicate that robberies without a weapon accounted for more than half (57 percent) of all incidents.

Robbery The unlawful taking or attempted taking of property that is in the immediate possession of another by threatened or actual use of force or violence.

Most robberies occurred in an outdoor public location, such as the street or a parking lot (50 percent). Forty percent occurred in a commercial location, such as a convenience store, bank or financial institution, gas station, or school, while residential settings accounted for 10 percent.[23]

Assault

Assault The intentional or threatened application of force on another person without consent. The categories of assault include level 1—assault or common assault; level 2—assault that involves the use of a weapon or that causes bodily harm; and level 3—assault that results in wounding or endangering the life of the victim.

Assault (defined in s. 265) involves the intentional or threatened application of force on another person without consent. As with sexual assault, the *Criminal Code of Canada* includes several categories of assault: *level 1 assault* (s. 266), or common assault, which is the least serious type of assault and includes behaviours such as punching, pushing, slapping, shoving, or threats by act or gesture; *level 2 assault* (s. 267), which involves the use of a weapon or results in bodily harm; *level 3 assault* (s. 268), which includes assaults that wound, maim, disfigure, or endanger the life of the victim; and *other assaults*, which involve use of force against a peace officer, unlawfully causing bodily harm, and discharge of a firearm with intent.

Of the 203 473 incidents of recorded assaults in 2014, common assault (level 1) accounted for 75 percent of all assaults and 42 percent of all reported violent incidents. Overall, the rate of common assault for 2014 (431 per 100 000 population) decreased by 4 percent from the previous year. The majority of assaults continue to be perpetrated by adult males, yet, among youth aged 12 to 17, about a third of assaults are committed by females. Unlike sexual assaults, victims of assault are as likely to be male as female.

Hate Crime

Hate crime A criminal act directed toward a person or group because of race, national or ethnic origin, religion, language, colour, sex, age, sexual orientation, or mental or physical disability. Also referred to as *hate-motivated crime*, or *bias crime*.

The definition of **hate crime** has evolved out of the sections of the *Criminal Code* that address hate propaganda and the *Purpose and Principles of Sentencing*. Sections 318 and 319 of the *Criminal Code* refer to "advocating genocide, public incitement of hatred, or the wilful promotion of hatred against an identifiable group, including those distinguished by colour, race, religion, ethnic origin, or sexual orientation." Section 718.2 of the *Criminal Code*, which addresses sentencing principles, allows the courts to take into consideration whether an offence was "motivated by bias, prejudice, or hate based on race, national or ethnic origin, language, colour, religion, sex, age, mental or physical disability, sexual orientation, or any other similar factor."[24] In other words, courts now consider hate motivation as an aggravating circumstance.

In 2013, police services reported 1176 incidents that had been motivated by hate, representing a rate of 3.3 per 100 000 population, 17 percent lower than the previous year. The most common type of hate crime was mischief in relation to religious property motivated by hate (4 percent), and 45 percent were other types of mischief, including acts of graffiti or vandalism of public property, the commission of which were deemed by police as motivated by hate. Minor assaults (21 percent) and uttering threats (11 percent) were the most common types of violent hate-crime offences.

There are three primary motivations for hate crimes: race or ethnicity, religion, and sexual orientation. In 2007, among incidents where the motivation was known to police, the most common was race or ethnicity, accounting for 51 percent of the incidents in that year. Religious motivations accounted for another 28 percent of hate crimes, and sexual orientation for 16 percent. The remaining 5 percent were motivated by factors such as the victim's language, disability, sex, occupation, or political beliefs.[25] See Box 3.2 for a summary of the police-reported hate crime in 2008.

Box 3.2 POLICE-REPORTED HATE CRIME IN CANADA, 2013: HIGHLIGHTS

Canadian police services reported 1167 hate-motivated crimes in 2013, down from 1414 in 2012. This represented a decrease of 17 percent. The vast majority of hate crimes have stemmed from one of three motivations: race/ethnicity, religion, or sexual orientation (see Figure 3.1). Non-violent offences, usually mischief, were the most common type of offences in 2013. Almost 5 in 10 persons accused of hate crime were between 12 and 24 years of age, over 80 percent of whom were male.

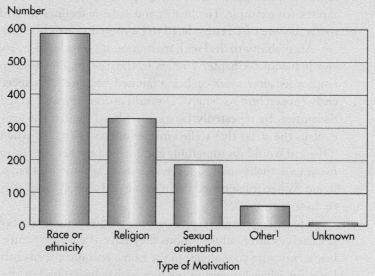

Number

1. Includes mental or physical disability, language, sex and other similar factors (e.g. occupation or political beliefs).
Note: Information in this chart raflects data reported by police services covering 99% of the populaion of Canada.

Figure 3.1 Police-Reported Hate Crimes, by Type of Motivation, Canada, 2013

Incidents against blacks represented the largest category of racially motivated hate crimes (44 percent). The majority (56 percent) of religion-motivated hate crimes in 2013 involved crimes against the Jewish faith.

Source: Adapted from Mary Allen, "Police-Reported Hate Crime in Canada, 2013," *Juristat*, vol. 35, no. 1 (Ottawa: Ministry of Industry, June 2015). This does not constitute an endorsement by Statistics Canada of this product.

Theoretical Explanations of Violent Crime

Why do people commit acts of violence? What compels a man to sexually assault a woman or a youth to pick up a knife and force a convenience store clerk to hand over the money in the till? While there are no easy answers to these questions, there are certainly a number of theoretical explanations commonly accepted within the field of criminology that might provide answers.

Cases of mass or serial murder, such as the 14 women killed by Marc Lepine in Montreal on December 6, 1989, or the six women Robert Pickton was convicted of confining, assaulting, and murdering between 2005 and 2007, often tempt us to examine the individual offender for clues. Surely people who kill others must have "something wrong with them" that compels them to commit these heinous acts. Chapters 6 and 7 examine a number of biological and psychological/psychiatric explanations of crime that can be applied to violent offenders. The biological theories found in Chapter 6 question whether certain individuals are predisposed to violence. Is the male sex drive, which has been developed through evolution to perpetuate the species, an explanation for men's sexual aggression toward women? Can naturally-occurring levels of the male hormone testosterone be seen as a reason why males commit close to 90 percent of all violent crime in Canada? Chapter 7 outlines a number of psychological considerations, including moral development, frustration-aggression, as well as psychotic symptoms, such as hallucinations, paranoia, and distorted views of reality, that may account for criminal behaviour. Various personality disorders, including antisocial personality disorder and psychopathy in particular—are considered as possible causes for deviant sexual behaviour. Psychological theories emphasizing personality types look to Freudian analysis and contend that it is the *id*, or that aspect of personality from which drives, wishes, urges, and desires emanate, that causes the behaviour of rapists, for example. The hostile and sadistic feelings toward women many rapists tend to display are often considered to be rooted in psychotic or personality disorders.

An inability to deal with frustration is considered by some to contribute to aggressive behaviour. Chapter 7 refers to the case of Pierre Lebrun, who killed four fellow employees after years of being taunted because of a speech impediment; this apparently caused him to "snap." Donald Lauzon, 19, who killed his two-year-old daughter, Samantha, by repeatedly banging her head against the arm of a sofa, was at a loss to explain the anger that welled inside him and surfaced whenever he became frustrated. "The kid would do something and I would hit her," he is quoted as saying. "I wouldn't mean to actually use full force, but that's what would happen. I hit her. Kid would go flying. When it happened I'd freak out, I'd go 'Oh God. What did I do? I'm never going to do this again.'"[26]

Social learning theories assume that people learn how to behave by modelling themselves after others whom they have the opportunity to observe. Does a young boy's exposure to violence in the home account for his future violent behaviour? Violence on television and in the movies has been cited as the cause of violence in some instances, most notably in the tragic case of James Bulger, aged two, of Liverpool, England, who was abducted from a shopping mall, beaten to death, and dumped on a railway track by two 10-year-old boys, who claimed they got the idea after watching the

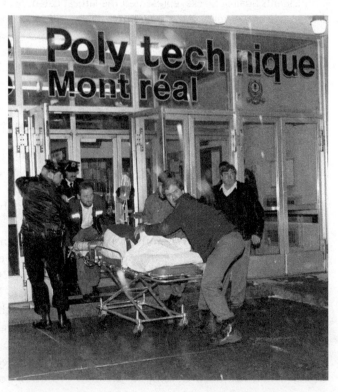

Mass murderer Marc Lepine killed 14 female students at L'École Polytechnique in Montreal. Which theories do you think work best to explain such violent criminal behaviour: those from the social responsibility perspective or those from the social problems perspective?

Shaney Komulainen/The Canadian Press

same violent video several times the previous day. The individual responsibility perspective contends that it is the psychological makeup of each person that determines the way in which observed behaviour is absorbed, processed, and acted upon. Some individuals may be exposed to violence in the home and never become violent themselves, while others are compelled to model their behaviour on the actions, and even deviant actions, of others.

The same issues can be examined in the debate over whether or not those children who are physically or sexually abused in the home later go on to inflict harm on others. The link between family violence and future criminality is not a direct one, and there appear to be numerous other factors that need to be taken into consideration. Polyvictimization, a concept that entered the criminological literature only a few years ago, recognizes the ripple effects of victimization.[27] A notable characteristic of polyvictimization is the far greater level of additional lifetime adversities and levels of distress that polyvictimized children suffer. Polyvictims are more likely to have other kinds of lifetime adversities, such as illnesses, accidents, family unemployment, parental substance abuse, and mental illness. Moreover, they are at a disadvantage when it comes to future life experiences and suffer from greater rates of poverty, incarceration, drug use, and mental illness later in life than do people who were not victims of multiple crimes or of multiple offenders when they were children. Some criminologists argue that, while being victimized as a child may increase the risk of future violence or criminality, many people who are victims of childhood violence do not become violent adult offenders.[28]

In contrast to the individual responsibility perspective are those theories that fall under the social problems perspective. Discussed in Chapters 8, 9, and 10, these theories look to socialization and cultural factors as explanations for acts of violence. Are males raised to behave more aggressively? Are our cultural values responsible for sending a message to young males that the way to deal with stress and frustration is through the use of aggression? Well-known accounts of drivers who assault others as a result of

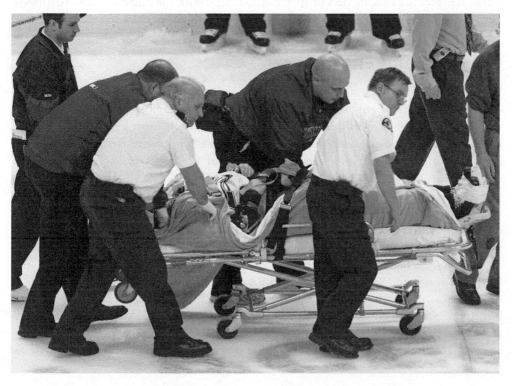

Professional hockey player Steve Moore is wheeled to an ambulance after being hit from behind by Vancouver Canucks hockey star Todd Bertuzzi during a 2004 game. Moore suffered broken neck vertebrae, a concussion, and nerve damage in the incident, ending his hockey career. Bertuzzi was suspended by the National Hockey League and prevented from finishing the season. In a controversial decision, he was also charged and pled guilty to assault causing bodily harm and served a year on probation and 80 hours of community service. In 2014, Moore won a civil suit after seeking $68 million in damages. Do you think Bertuzzi should have been criminally charged for his actions?

Chuck Stoody/The Canadian Press

what is known as *road rage* suggest that perhaps societal tolerance for the use of violence to solve disputes has increased.

The subculture of violence theory in Chapter 8 is frequently cited as an explanation for acts of violence perpetrated by individuals from a certain subculture that promotes particular values or codes of conduct. For example, the expectation that young males defend their honour and reputation at all costs naturally leads to the use of violence if that is what is necessary to achieve this end. Therefore, it is conformity to this set of values that leads to violence; violence is not seen in these subcultural settings as the result of deviant behaviour. This argument is further used to explain why victims of violence in these groups are usually members of the group and not outsiders. The account of the murder of Sylvain Leduc in Chapter 8 helps to illustrate this point.

The feminist criminology perspective discussed in Chapter 10 would explain violence against women as resulting from societal inequalities due primarily to gender. The physical and sexual assault of women is a means by which males are able to maintain their dominance over women. Thus, the sexual victimization of girls is a behaviour learned by young males in a patriarchal society.

3.3 | LEARNING OBJECTIVE

PROPERTY CRIME

PROPERTY CRIMES COMPRISE UNLAWFUL ACTS PERPETRATED WITH THE INTENT OF GAINING property but without the use or threat of violence. Included in this category are breaking and entering, possession of stolen property, theft of a motor vehicle, theft over $5000, theft under $5000, fraud, identity fraud, mischief, and arson.

The 2014 UCR reported 1 100 403 incidents of property crime, or a rate of 3096 per 100 000 population in that year, which represents a 5 percent drop from the previous year. The rates of property crime declined in almost every province, with the most significant drops recorded in Prince Edward Island (–23 percent), Quebec (–10 percent), and Newfoundland and Labrador (–7 percent). Quebec recorded the lowest rate in the country at 2101 per 100 000 population. Overall, the western provinces and the territories recorded the highest property crime rates, with the highest in the Northwest Territories (23 171 per 100 000), the Yukon (9354), and Saskatchewan (5628).

Breaking and Entering

Breaking and entering The unlawful entry of a place to commit an indictable offence.

Breaking and entering (s. 348) is one of the most common and serious of property offences. This crime constitutes an invasion of personal territory or a workspace and often results in the theft or destruction of property. While most break and enters are property crimes, the potential for personal violence is inherent. Breaking and entering a dwelling house carries a maximum penalty of life imprisonment (as compared with 10 years for breaking and entering a place other than a dwelling house, such as a place of business), reflecting the possibility of violent confrontation between the offender and the homeowner. In the UCR, police-reported breaking and entering is categorized into three different types: (1) residential—the breaking and entering of a private residence, including single homes as well as attached garages, garden homes, apartments, cottages, mobile homes, rooming houses, and so on; (2) business—the breaking and entering of a facility used for commercial or public affairs, including financial institutions, stores, and non-commercial enterprises, such as government buildings, schools, churches, and non-profit agencies; and (3) other—the breaking and entering of private property structures, such as sheds, detached garages, or storage and transportation facilities. The UCR statistics include attempted as well as completed break and enters.

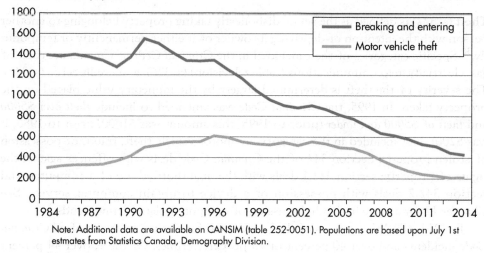

Rate per 100 000 population

Note: Additional data are available on CANSIM (table 252-0051). Populations are based upon July 1st estmates from Statistics Canada, Demography Division.

Figure 3.2 Breaking and Entering and Motor Vehicle Theft, Police-Reported Rates, Canada, 1984 to 2014

Source: Jillian Boyce, "Police-reported crime statistics in Canada, 2014", *Juristat*, vol. 34, no. 1 (Ottawa: Minister of Industry, 2015). Reproduced and distributed on an "as is" basis with the permission of Statistics Canada.

Police-reported incidents of breaking and entering in 2014 totalled 151 921 break-ins, representing a rate of 427 per 100 000 population and accounting for 14 percent of all property-related offences. This is a decrease of 4 percent from the previous year, in keeping with the consistent decreases in the last four decades. Since peaking in the early 1990s, breaking and entering has steadily been declining in Canada, a trend that continued in 2014. Between 2004 and 2014, the rate of breaking and entering dropped by 51 percent. (See Figure 3.2 for a representation of this trend.) Part of the decline in breaking and entering, however, may be a result of fewer Canadians choosing to report this offence.

The type of property stolen from residences is quite different from that stolen from businesses. Audio/video equipment, jewellery, money, cheques or bonds, personal accessories, machinery and tools, photographic equipment, office equipment, and bicycles typify the property stolen from residences. Thefts from break and enters into businesses include money, cheques or bonds, office equipment, consumable goods (alcohol, cigarettes), audio/video equipment, machinery and tools, and personal accessories. Firearms were more frequently stolen from homes during break and enters than from businesses. The majority of these were rifles and shotguns, while the minority consisted of restricted weapons. Data from the most recent breaking and entering statistics suggest that break and enters involving violence occur in fewer than 5 percent of cases. Of these, the majority involve an assault, while others involve robbery, sexual assault, abduction, and criminal harassment. Almost all violent break and enters occur at a place of residence.[29]

In 2014, there was a decrease in the rate of police-reported breaking and entering in almost all provinces and territories, with the exception of the three westernmost provinces. Saskatchewan (+10 percent), British Columbia (+4 percent), and Alberta (+1 percent) all recorded increases in the rate of police-reported breaking and entering. Among the provinces, Saskatchewan continued to record the highest rate of breaking and entering (756 per 100 000 population), while Ontario continued to record the lowest rate (291 per 100 000 population).

Theft

Theft (s. 322) is defined as the act of dishonestly taking property belonging to another person with the intention of depriving its owner of it either permanently or temporarily.[30] Specific categories of theft included in the *Criminal Code of Canada* are theft of gas, electricity, telecommunications (cable television) (s. 326), and credit cards (s. 342). The severity of the theft is determined largely by the monetary value placed on the property taken. In 1995, the *Criminal Code* was amended to include *theft over $5000* and *theft of $5000 and under* (prior to 1995, this amount was $1000; prior to 1986, it was $200). Not included in the category are motor vehicle theft, fraud, or possession of stolen property. Section 342 of the *Criminal Code* deals with offences against the rights of property; section 342.1 deals with the unauthorized use of a computer; and section 342.2 deals with possession of a device to obtain computer service. See Chapter 12 for a more in-depth discussion of computer-related crime trends.

In 2014, 489 137 incidents of theft accounted for about 24 percent of all *Criminal Code* incidents and over 40 percent of all property crimes. Of these, over 44 percent were classified as theft $5000 and under. This figure most likely under-represents the amount of theft that occurs, since theft under $5000 remains one of the crimes most under-reported by victims. Official statistics indicate that it constitutes a rate of 1336 incidents per 100 000 population, while the rate for theft over $5000 stood at 40 per 100 000 for 2014. The overall theft rate was about 2 percent lower than for the previous year and has been declining over the past decade.

Compared with other types of offences, the number of females charged with theft $5000 and under is quite high—females constitute about a third of both adults and youth aged 12 to 17 charged. The majority of these females were charged with shoplifting (see Chapter 2 for a discussion of the correlation between females and criminal behaviour and the feminization of poverty).

Motor Vehicle Theft

Motor vehicle theft is defined as the taking of a vehicle without the owner's authorization. A motor vehicle is defined as a car, truck, van, bus, recreational vehicle, semi-trailer truck, motorcycle, construction machinery, agricultural machinery, or other land-based motor vehicle (such as a go-kart, snowmobile, all-terrain vehicle, or dune buggy).[31] Excluded from the category of motor vehicle theft is theft of airplanes, boats, trains, and spacecraft, which are counted as thefts over $5000.

Motor vehicle theft was one of the few property offences—and offences in general—that did not decline in 2014. With about 74 000 police-reported motor vehicle thefts in 2014, the rate increased slightly (+1 percent, to 208 per 100 000) from the previous year, ending the consecutive annual decline seen over the past 10 years. Despite the slight increase in the rate of motor vehicle theft between 2013 and 2014, the 2014 rate was still 61 percent lower than 10 years earlier.[32] Cars continue to be the most commonly stolen vehicles, followed by trucks, minivans, and sport-utility vehicles. Motor vehicle theft is one of the least likely crimes to be solved by police; the clearance rate continues to be lower than other property-related offences. It is also a crime often associated with youth. Statistics show that over 30 percent of people charged with motor vehicle theft were youth aged 15 to 17. Of these, the vast majority were male.[33]

The national increase in motor vehicle thefts in 2014 was reflective of more police-reported motor vehicle thefts in British Columbia, the Northwest Territories, Manitoba, and Alberta. With about 3 500 more motor vehicle thefts in 2014 than the previous year, British Columbia recorded the largest increase in this rate, up 29 percent. Among the provinces, rates of police-reported motor vehicle thefts were highest in Alberta (402 per 100 000 population) and Saskatchewan (386 per 100 000 population) and lowest in Prince Edward Island (52 per 100 000 population) and Newfoundland and Labrador (91 per 100 000 population).

Identity Fraud

In 2010, the *Criminal Code of Canada* was amended to include several new offences specifically targeting those aspects of identity theft that were not already covered by existing provisions. **Identity fraud** (s. 403) is defined as fraudulently personating another person, living or dead, with intent to gain advantage for themselves or another person, to obtain any property or an interest in any property, to cause disadvantage to the person being personated or another person, or to avoid arrest or prosecution or to obstruct, pervert, or defeat the course of justice. **Identity theft** (s. 402.2) is defined as knowingly obtaining or possessing another person's identity information with the intent of using the information to commit an indictable offence that includes fraud, deceit, or falsehood as an element of the offence. Identity theft also extends to transmitting, making available, distributing, selling, or offering for sale another person's identity information for the purposes of committing an offence. Prior to 2010, these offences were coded as fraud. The penalties for these activities range from a maximum penalty of 10 years' imprisonment for identity fraud and 5 years for identity theft.

The 2014 UCR indicated that there were 12 729 police-reported incidences of identity fraud, or 36 per 100 000 population, an increase of 8 percent from the previous year. According to the RCMP, the unprecedented rise in crimes associated with personal identity information over the past decade has made this type of crime a primary concern for Canadians. Identity-related crime is considered to be one of the fastest-growing crimes in the world.[34]

While identity crime has always existed, previous iterations included offences based on impersonation and the theft, forgery, or misuse of personal documents using relatively labour-intensive methods, such as telephone scams, accessing information found on discarded receipts, or stealing letters from mailboxes. The use of technology such as automated banking services and the internet has opened up a vast array of new methods for committing identity crime as well as a global market for stolen identity information. Schemes including online phishing for personal and/or financial data, skimming, and computer hacking are all used to illegally obtain identity information, which can then be trafficked online and used by others. According to the Canadian Association of Chiefs of Police, "Identity thieves use the information they have stolen in countless ways. It is important for law enforcement officers to understand that identity crime is often used to facilitate other crimes, such as credit card fraud, loan and mortgage fraud, mail theft and mail fraud, narcotics violations, money laundering, weapons trafficking, computer crimes, wire fraud, and terrorism."[35]

Theoretical Explanations for Property Crime

The realities surrounding property crime are complex and belie the ability to pinpoint a simple explanation. Does the person who breaks into someone's home and steals the television and laptop do this for the same reason that someone else breaks into a car and rides around in it at high speeds?

The most obvious motivating factor in many cases of property crime appears to be greed, and many criminological theories have used this notion as a starting point.

Identity fraud Fraudulently personating another person, living or dead, with intent to gain advantage for themselves or another person, to obtain any property or an interest in any property, to cause disadvantage to the person being personated or another person, to avoid arrest or prosecution, or to obstruct, pervert, or defeat the course of justice.

Identity theft Knowingly obtaining or possessing another person's identity information with the intent of using the information to commit an indictable offence that includes fraud, deceit, or falsehood as an element of the offence.

These theories fall under the social problems perspective heading, because they largely assume that property crime is the manifestation of a variety of underlying social problems, not the least of which is poverty. Theories such as the strain theory (discussed in Chapter 8) and the routine activities theory (Chapter 5) suggest that there is a desire to achieve a universal goal, which is defined in terms of money and the goods, services, privileges, and prestige it can buy. The opportunity to achieve this goal through legitimate means such as schooling and employment is restricted for some people, who then turn to illegitimate or criminal opportunities to do so. If the illegitimate opportunities become more accessible (as with the use of technology) and outnumber the legitimate ones, the temptation for some to seek this "easy route" may become too great to resist. The increase in the amount of fraud being committed using credit cards over cheques may be explained using this theory, for example.

Still other theories contend that the commission of property crimes, including motor vehicle theft, breaking and entering, and shoplifting, all satisfy a need for excitement. The subcultural theories discussed in Chapter 8 maintain that material needs are often insufficient to explain the fascination with theft some people have. These theories suggest that crime is fun and is done to achieve a sense of status and belonging within a peer group.

The social process theories outlined in Chapter 9 look to the interaction between individuals as an explanation for criminal behaviour. What influence, for example, do peer pressure and group behaviour have on the behaviour of some individuals? Can association with delinquent peers promote the learning of crimes such as theft and joyriding in stolen cars? The differential association theory suggests this is so. The social control theory outlined in Chapter 9 looks to the individual's attachment to positive role models, commitment to realistic goals, involvement in recreational and school activities, and belief in conventional values as a means of decreasing the likelihood of criminal behaviour. This theory suggests that those people, especially youth, who are bored and have no positive direction in life run a much greater risk of being attracted to crimes such as theft, shoplifting, arson, and vandalism.

When youth engage in property crimes such as vandalism to public property, are they behaving in response to peer pressure and simply looking to have some excitement?

Nic Cleave Photography/Alamy Stock Photo

CRIMES AGAINST THE PUBLIC ORDER

OFFICIAL POLICE-REPORTED CRIME STATISTICS THAT ARE CLASSIFIED BY THE UCR AS neither violent nor property-related are reflected in a catch-all category of crimes known as "Other *Criminal Code* Offences." Offences in this grouping include counterfeiting, weapons violations, child pornography, prostitution, disturbing the peace, administration of justice violations (bail violations), and in 2013, seven new offences classified as terrorism. The UCR also includes a "*Criminal Code* Traffic Violations" category that tracks impaired driving and a "Drug Offences" category that reports on incidences of possession, trafficking, production, or distribution of a variety of illegal drugs.

A number of these activities are often referred to in criminological terms as *public order crimes* or *victimless crimes*. While it is debatable whether these activities do or do not victimize, it is generally agreed that though they violate prevailing morality, social policy, and public opinion, it is open to debate whether they should be classified as criminal. Such crimes against the public order traditionally refer to activities and behaviours involving sex, such as commercial sex, pornography, and erotic materials; activities involving the use, abuse, and sale of drugs and alcohol; and behaviours involving individual lifestyle choices, such as gambling and assisted suicide.

Counterfeiting

Counterfeiting (s. 448) is considered to include any unauthorized reproduction of a thing with the intention that it be accepted as genuine. Counterfeiting can thus refer to anything that is capable of reproduction, including things that are subjects of rights of private property, such as art, or things that are subject to protection as intellectual property. It most commonly refers to the reproduction of currency (s. 449); forging of credit cards or debit cards (s. 342); documents for identification, such as passports (s. 57); or any paper that represents value (e.g., stamps, travellers' cheques, or negotiable instruments (ss. 370, 376). The penalties for these activities range from a maximum of 14 years' imprisonment for counterfeiting currency and forging a passport to 10 years for fraudulent credit cards.

Counterfeiting is somewhat unique in that, for a relatively high-volume offence, police-reported statistics show large year-to-year fluctuations. For example, between 2002 and 2004, the rate increased by 147 percent, but it has declined by 76 percent since then. Police-reported statistics for 2014 indicate that 572 incidences of counterfeiting were detected that year, a 10 percent drop from the previous year.

The National Anti-Counterfeiting Bureau of the RCMP is another source of information on trends in counterfeiting. The RCMP identifies *counterfeit currency* as banknotes (bills) that have been successfully passed without detection and seized notes that have been intercepted by law enforcement officials. Access to sophisticated computer devices and software and high-quality colour photocopiers has been among the reasons for the prevalence of counterfeiting currency. The RCMP also indicates that organized crime groups have become increasingly involved in the production and distribution of counterfeit banknotes and documents. Chapter 12 takes another look at the extent of the involvement of organized crime groups in a number of criminal activities.

A number of organizations are involved in prevention, detection, and awareness-raising around the growing activity of counterfeiting, including the Bank of Canada and coalitions such as the Anti-Counterfeiting Network. The Bank of Canada, for example, continues to issue banknotes with added security features (see Box 3.3). The introduction of the polymer $20, $50, and $100 banknotes in 2011 is

Counterfeiting Any unauthorized reproduction of a thing with the intention that it be accepted as genuine. It can thus refer to anything that is capable of reproduction, including things that are subjects of rights of private property. It also includes the reproduction of documents for identification, such as passports, or any paper that represents value (e.g., stamps, travellers' cheques, or negotiable instruments).

The introduction of the *Polymer* series by the Bank of Canada features new security features as well as an educational approach (Feel.Look.Flip.) to assist the public in remembering how to check bills.

Feel the raised ink on the large number, the shoulders of the large portrait, and the words *Bank of Canada* and *Banque du Canada*. (1)

Look

- for transparency through the large window containing a metallic portrait and building (2)

- at the details in the metallic portrait in the large window. It matches the large portrait (3)

- at the details in the metallic building in the large window. Tilt the note to see sharp colour changes in the building (4)

- at the numbers in and around the large window that match the value of the note. Some of the numbers appear in reverse (5)

- at the word *Canada*. It is transparent and feels slightly raised (6)

- at the maple leaves that border the large window. Some of the leaves cross into the window (7)

- at the frosted maple leaf window to see that it has a transparent outline (8)

- at the hidden numbers by using a small light like an incandescent bulb or a pot light (added security feature) (9)

Flip the note to see the features repeated in the same colours and detail on the other side.

Source: *From* Courtesy of The Bank of Canada, published by Bank of Canada. © 2016.

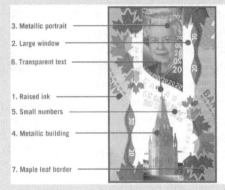 

Feel.Look.Flip

Used with the permission of the Bank of Canada

likely to result in the reduction of illegal activity involving these denominations. Thirty-two countries around the world have successfully used this polypropylene material since it was pioneered by the Reserve Bank of Australia beginning in 1988.[36] Increased education and awareness by merchants and retailers in detecting counterfeit bills and enhanced law enforcement efforts have also contributed to the recorded drops.

Recent reports from the National Anti-Counterfeiting Bureau of the RCMP indicate that the production of counterfeit money is dwindling largely due to the effectiveness of the polymer bills. While current counterfeiting attempts are quite crude (using strips of glittery wrapping paper taped to transparent plastic strips in a crude attempt to simulate security holograms), forgers aligned with organized crime groups are becoming more sophisticated, even buying holographic sheets from shops in China. The RCMP reports the emergence of more sophisticated polymer counterfeits in Australia where they are being produced. "It takes a while for the counterfeiter to experiment. And we are seeing the experiments. The Bank of Canada is aware of that and the Bank of Canada is currently looking at the next series," said Robert Moyes, who has been working at the RCMP National Anti-Counterfeiting Bureau for 31 years.[37]

Prostitution

Prostitution, or the exchange of money for sex, is not illegal in Canada. Prior to 2014, what *was* illegal was the associated activities, such as publicly communicating with another person for the purposes of buying or selling sexual services (s. 213), running a bawdy house (s. 210), or living on the avails of the prostitution of another person (s. 212). In December 2014, the Supreme Court of Canada struck down all these prostitution-related prohibitions as violations of the *Charter of Rights and Freedoms'* constitutional guarantee to life, liberty, and security of the person. The court gave the government a year to bring in new legislation.

Bill C-36, the *Protection of Communities and Exploited Persons Act*, was brought into force in December 2015. Critics argued that the changes to the former prostitution laws were minimal and did little to ensure the safety and security of those engaged in the sex trade. Section 213 of the *Criminal Code* remained (with a minor amendment), ensuring that publicly communicating with another person for the purposes of buying or selling sexual services remains illegal. Section 212 was repealed and replaced by provision 286.2—material benefit from sexual services. The new provision continues to criminalize those who gain material benefits from sex work. This version of the law applies to exploitative and abusive relationships and to those in which a person supplies drugs or alcohol. A completely new provision (286.4) bans advertising of

Prostitution Most commonly used to refer to the illegal activities of publicly communicating with another person for the purposes of buying or selling sexual services, material benefit from sexual services, or advertising sexual services.

Sex-trade workers and their supporters gather on the front steps of the Supreme Court of Canada in Ottawa. In 2014, the Court struck down the existing prostitution laws as violations of the *Charter of Rights and Freedoms'* constitutional guarantee to life, liberty, and security of the person, and new legislation was enacted in December 2014. Critics continue to argue that the new laws do little to protect sex-trade workers. Why do you think the laws regarding prostitution are so controversial?

John Mayor/QMI Agency/Sun Media Corporation

sexual services, thereby making illegal any advertising in newspapers, online, or other forms of media by sex workers.

Prostitution is a controversial issue, and there seems to be little consensus as to the best means of dealing with it. While it is generally considered to be a voluntary activity and is therefore often classified as a victimless crime, there are serious safety, health, social, legal, and community issues associated with it. Other forms of activity, such as drug trafficking and use, are often linked to it. Those neighbourhoods in which prostitutes ply their trade constantly struggle with the health and safety risks associated with discarded needles and condoms. Health concerns, such as the spread of sexually transmitted diseases, affect the prostitutes, their customers, and the families of customers.

Official statistics on prostitution are very closely tied to the law enforcement practices of any given police service and therefore vary across provinces and municipalities. In 2014, the rate of prostitution incidents reported to the police decreased by 48 percent from the previous year. This decrease is most probably a reflection of the Supreme Court ruling and the fact that a large number of incidents of prostitution were no longer being reported.

Public concerns continue about the ever-decreasing age of prostitutes. Incidents of children being recruited and sold into a life of prostitution in countries such as Thailand, Brazil, India, and the Philippines are well documented.[38] The alarming increase in the trafficking of persons for sexual exploitation is discussed in detail in Chapter 12. Of equal concern to law enforcement officials is the increased practice of what is known as "sex tourism," which involves the promotion to Canadians of travel packages designed for the purpose of illegal sexual encounters, often with minors. Box 3.4 outlines the amended sections of the *Criminal Code of Canada* that target this illegal activity.

Box 3.4 CANADA'S "SEX TOURISM" LAW

Donald Bakker's was the first case involving charges under Canada's sex tourism law. In 2005, Bakker was charged with 22 counts of assault involving adult prostitutes and 16 counts related to children in a foreign country. His case did not proceed to trial when he subsequently pled guilty to 10 counts of sexual assault, three of which involved attacks on women in British Columbia and the rest involving children in Asian countries. A 1997 amendment to the *Criminal Code* introduced section 7.4(1)*, or what has become known as the sex tourism law. Section 7.4(1) reads:

Notwithstanding anything in this Act or any other Act, everyone who, outside Canada, commits an act or omission that if committed in Canada would be an offence against section 151, 152, 153, 155, or 159, subsection 160(2) or (3), section 163.1, 170, 171 or 173 or subsection 212(4) shall be deemed to commit that act or omission in Canada if the person who commits the act or omission is a Canadian citizen or permanent resident within the meaning of subsection 2(1) of the *Immigration and Refugee Protection Act* who is ordinarily resident in Canada.

*The offences listed in section 7.4(1) are

- **s.151** sexual interference
- **s.152** invitation to sexual touching
- **s.153** sexual exploitation
- **s.155** incest
- **s.159** anal intercourse
- **s.160(2)** compelling the commission of bestiality
- **s.160(3)** bestiality in the presence of a child under 14/ inciting child under 14 to commit
- **s.163(1)** making, distributing, selling, or possessing child pornography
- **s.170** parent or guardian procuring sexual activity
- **s.171** householder permitting sexual activity
- **s.173** indecent acts/exposure
- **s.212(4)** prostitution of a person under 18

Do you agree that Canadian citizens should be subject to prosecution if they sexually abuse children, including engaging in child prostitution, while outside Canada?

Illicit Drugs

There is a correlation between illicit drug use and criminal activity, albeit a complex one. Research has linked illicit drug use to crime in a number of ways, including the involvement of organized crime in the supply and distribution of illegal substances, the social disorganization that can be associated with drug abuse, and individuals who commit crime while under the influence of illegal drugs or for the purposes of acquiring illegal drugs. The relationship between drugs and crime is also reflected in Canada's National Anti-Drug Strategy, which includes a law enforcement component along with goals of prevention and treatment.[39]

This examination of illicit drugs considers those related criminal activities contained in the *Controlled Drugs and Substances Act* (CDSA). Essentially, the drug law is made up of two categories of offences: *supply offences*, which include the growing and distribution (trafficking and importing) of illegal and prohibited drugs, and *possession offences*, which include the purchase and use of illegal and prohibited drugs. The official number of recorded offences is obviously sensitive to enforcement and detection practices. An increase in the number of arrests and seizures does not necessarily indicate an increase in the population's use of illicit drugs but rather may indicate an increased circulation of drugs or stepped-up enforcement at national or international levels. Canadian government estimates indicate that the illegal drug market in Canada generates billions of dollars annually.[40]

In 2014, police reported more than 103 757 drug crimes, of which more than two-thirds (66 percent) were related to cannabis, primarily cannabis possession. The overall rate of CDSA offences decreased 6 percent from the previous year, due largely to the result of fewer drug offences involving cannabis and cocaine. While the rates of possession of cannabis (−4 percent) and possession of cocaine (−3 percent) decreased between 2013 and 2014, the rates of possession of methamphetamines (e.g., crystal meth) (+38 percent), heroin (+34 percent), methylenedioxyamphetamine (e.g., MDMA or ecstasy) (+28 percent), and other substances banned under the CDSA (+1 percent) increased during this period. Similarly, while rates of trafficking, production, or distribution of cannabis (−25 percent) and cocaine (−12 percent) showed large decreases between 2013 and 2014, increases were recorded in the rates of trafficking, production, or distribution of methamphetamines (+17 percent) and heroin (+12 percent).

While decreases in almost all provinces and territories contributed to the national decline in cannabis-related offences in 2014, the national decrease in cocaine-related offences was primarily the result of fewer incidents in Saskatchewan (−45 percent), British Columbia (−14 percent), and Ontario (−8 percent). Similarly, the rise in the rate of "other" drug-related offences (including heroin, crystal meth, and ecstasy) was partly explained by increases in Alberta (+44 percent) and British Columbia (+18 percent). The general upward trend in police-reported drug offences in Canada may be related to varying policies, practices, and resources available across different police services and over time. A police service's decision to target particular offences or offenders may result in the identification of more incidents of drug-related crime rather than representing an increase in the number of incidents that are actually occurring. Also, in instances when other types of crime are declining, police may be able to focus more resources and efforts on crime involving drugs.[41]

The recent legalization or decriminalization of cannabis in other countries, including some U.S. states, has contributed to ongoing debates around this issue in Canada. Self-reported surveys indicate that Canadians, both adult and youth, have some of the higher rates of cannabis use in the world. Public opinion polls suggest that the majority of Canadians support the legalization or decriminalization of cannabis, and Canadian youth tend to view cannabis as less harmful than other illegal

Cannabis advocates, activists, and users openly smoke the drug in front of the Parliament Buildings in Ottawa on April 20. *420* is code-term that refers to the consumption of cannabis, especially smoking cannabis around the time 4:20 p.m. and smoking and celebrating cannabis on the date April 20 (4/20). Do you think cannabis use will ever be legalized in Canada? Do you think it should be?

Source: PA Images/Alamy Stock Photo

substances.[42] On April 20, 2016 (or *420*, as it is known to cannabis activists and advocates), the Canadian government announced its plans to legalize and regulate cannabis, designed to restrict access to children and organized crime groups. "We know it is impossible to arrest our way out of this problem," Health Minister Jane Philpott said. "Our approach to drugs must be comprehensive, collaborative and compassionate. It must respect human rights while promoting shared responsibility and it must have a firm scientific foundation."[43]

Terrorism

Terrorism An act committed in whole or in part for a political, religious, or ideological purpose, objective, or cause with the intention of intimidating the public with regard to its security, including its economic security, or compelling a person, a government, or a domestic or an international organization to do or to refrain from doing any act.

Section 83.01 of the *Criminal Code* defines **terrorism** as an act committed "in whole or in part for a political, religious or ideological purpose, objective or cause" with the intention of intimidating the public "with regard to its security, including its economic security, or compelling a person, a government or a domestic or an international organization to do or to refrain from doing any act." Other applicable violations include participation in the activity of a terrorist group (s. 83.18), facilitating terrorist activity (s. 83.19), commission of an offence for a terrorist group (s. 83.2), instructing to carry out activity for a terrorist group (s. 83.21), instructing to carry out terrorist activity (s. 83.22), and advocating or promoting commission of terrorism offences (s. 83.221). Activities recognized as criminal within this context include death and bodily harm with the use of violence, endangering a person's life, risks posed to the health and safety of the public, significant property damage, and interference or disruption of essential services, facilities, or systems.[44]

In 2014, the number of police-reported acts of terrorism was 100, an increase of 29 (or 39 percent) from the previous year. In 2013, new terrorism violations were introduced into the *Criminal Code of Canada* and new violations added in 2013 as a result of the enactment of Bill S-7, an act to amend the *Criminal Code*, the *Canadian Evidence Act*, and the *Security of Information Act*, which may account for some of the increase.

Theoretical Explanations of Crimes against the Public Order

The radical criminology perspectives outlined in Chapter 10 contend that behaviours are deemed to be deviant or criminal by definition. Crimes against the public order are seen by many as examples of *conflict crimes*, or those behaviours around which there is much controversy within society as to their acceptance. Social conflict criminology would contend that laws against behaviours such as prostitution and substance abuse are made by the powerful segment of society to ensure the subordination of those who engage in these activities. Feminist criminology, for example, would propose that, in the case of prostitution, women are conditioned to be subservient to men and are transformed into commodities to be bought and sold.

Many of the other social problem theories are useful to explain public order crimes. Refer to the differential association theory in Chapter 9; how can the crimes of prostitution and drug use be explained in terms of learned behaviour brought on through peer pressure? Similarly, social control theory, with its emphasis on strong bonds between the individual and the social order, might be applicable when explaining the criminal behaviour of bored and unfocused youth. Weak attachments to the family early on in life because of dysfunction within the home can compel many youth to flee and find refuge in the street, where prostitution and drug abuse are available options.

Individual responsibility theories can be seen to apply to public order crimes as well. For example, is it possible that dependency on alcohol and drugs has a genetic basis? Are addictive personality types passed on from generation to generation? Chapter 6 looks at some genetic roots of crime, while Chapter 7 examines theories of personality and asks whether there are certain personality types that are predisposed to certain types of criminal behaviour. For example, does low self-esteem, poor self-image, and anxiety result in a personality that is prone to addiction?

SUMMARY OF LEARNING OBJECTIVES

3.1 The Uniform Crime Report Surveys (UCR) classify crimes into the following categories: violent crime, property crime, other crime, traffic offences, federal drug legislation offences, and other federal statute violations. Canada's overall police-reported crime rate dropped 3 percent in 2014, continuing the downward trend that began in the early 1990s; the crime rate in 2014 was the lowest rate recorded since 1969 and was 34 percent lower than a decade earlier. This drop in crime was seen in most parts of the country and for virtually all offences. Of the 1.8 million *Criminal Code* incidents reported, violent crime constituted 21 percent, property crimes 61 percent, and other offences, such as counterfeiting, prostitution, bail violations, and mischief, 18 percent.

3.2 Violent crime incidents include homicide, attempted murder, assault, sexual assault, robbery, use of firearms, kidnapping and abduction, criminal harassment, and uttering threats. Social problems theories look to socialization and cultural factors as explanations for acts of violence, while social learning theories assume that people learn how to behave by modelling themselves after others they have observed. However, the individual responsibility perspective contends that it is the psychological makeup of each person that determines the way in which observed behaviour is absorbed, processed, and acted upon. Biological theories question whether certain individuals are predisposed to violence.

3.3 Property crimes comprise those unlawful acts perpetrated with the intent of gaining property but do not involve the use or threat of violence. Included in this category are breaking and entering, theft, fraud, crime involving motor vehicles, arson, mischief, and possession of stolen property. The social problems perspective largely assumes that the motivating factor in many cases of property crime is greed, while social process theories emphasize the role of peer pressure and group behaviour.

3.4 Crimes against the public order traditionally refer to activities and behaviours involving sex; activities involving the use, abuse, and sale of drugs and alcohol; and behaviours involving individual lifestyle choices, such as gambling and assisted suicide. Crimes against the public order are seen by many as examples of conflict crimes, or those behaviours around which there is much controversy within society as to their acceptance.

Questions for Review

1. How are typologies of crime useful in understanding patterns of crime? What are the categories used by the Canadian Uniform Crime Reporting Survey (UCR)?

2. Which of the categories of crime discussed in this chapter do you think has the most accurate crime count? Why?

3. How does the definition of a crime affect the counting of it? How do police enforcement activities affect the count?

4. This text emphasizes a social problems versus social responsibility theme. Which perspective best explains the reality of crime in this country? Is one perspective more appropriate when considering violent crime? Property crime? Crime against the public order?

Multiple-Choice Questions

1. Classifications of crime useful in identifying patterns of criminal activity are known as _____.
   a. textures of crime
   b. typologies of crime
   c. subtexts of crime
   d. classifications of crime
   e. layers of crime

2. The largest number of hate crimes in 2013 stemmed from which motivation?

   a. religion

   b. race/ethnicity

   c. age

   d. physical/mental disability

   e. sexual orientation

3. Which of the following offences is classified as a violent offence?

   a. robbery

   b. breaking and entering

   c. theft of a motor vehicle

   d. arson

   e. possession of stolen property

4. In December 2015, the Canadian government introduced changes to prostitution laws with the _____ Act.

   a. *Royal Canadian Mounted Police*

   b. *Identification of Criminals*

   c. *Safe Streets and Communities*

   d. *Protection of Communities and Exploited Persons*

   e. *Canadian Crime Victims*

5. The highest incidence of property crime involves _____.

   a. theft over $5000

   b. mischief

   c. breaking and entering

   d. theft of a motor vehicle

   e. theft under $5000

Chapter 4
Victimology: The Study of the Victim

Dennis McColeman/Getty Images

To strengthen the Bill, the rights of victims must be enhanced throughout the criminal justice process, starting at time of crime, through the courts and through to post-conviction and conditional release.

—Sue O'Sullivan, Federal Ombudsman for Victims of Crime[1]

LEARNING OBJECTIVES

After reading this chapter, you should be able to

4.1 Discuss the development of the field of victimology, the differences between a number of theories of victimization, and the realities of being a victim of crime.

4.2 Describe the emergence of victims' rights.

4.3 Identify current directions in victimology and the services available to victims of crime.

4.4 Understand the concept of victim restitution and describe how the process works in Canada.

4.5 Assess emerging directions in the field of victimology.

INTRODUCTION

In March 2003, the grief-stricken family of Andy Moffitt left an Ottawa courtroom unable to believe or understand the five-year prison sentence just handed down to the man who had killed their son.

Several years earlier, Moffitt, a computer engineering student at the University of Ottawa, was celebrating the end of his exams with some friends at a neighbourhood bar. Just after midnight, Moffitt and his friends witnessed a scuffle between a man and the bar manager. One of Moffitt's companions ran to the aid of the manager but was immediately attacked. Moffitt rushed to help his friend and was stabbed once in the chest by the assailant. Moffitt was pronounced dead later at the hospital. "This guy was a great kid and he was trying to be a Good Samaritan by smoothing out the fight," Detective Dale Hayes said. "For trying to help, he got shanked."[2]

Several hours later, a man telephoned 911, asking police to come and pick him up. Henry Danninger, a 26-year-old student also attending the University of Ottawa, was apprehended and charged with second-degree murder. Danninger had gone to the restaurant that evening looking for a roommate whom he believed had taken some drugs belonging to him. The bar manager was trying to remove Danninger from the establishment when Moffitt stepped in to help. Danninger and Moffitt had never met before. Moffitt was simply in the wrong place at the wrong time.

The five-year sentence of incarceration was a shock to Moffitt's family. They had hoped for a much stiffer penalty, but a plea-bargain arrangement reduced the charge from second-degree murder to manslaughter. That, in conjunction with the time Danninger had spent in pretrial custody and the fact that he had no prior criminal record, compelled Justice Roydon Kealey to impose the sentence. "I'm speechless," said the victim's mother, Paulette Moffitt of Brockville, who'd been hoping for a sentence twice as long. "I will never forget having to phone Andy's older brother to tell him his brother was dead," said Ms. Moffitt. "I was the one [who] broke his heart, telling him the most dreadful news imaginable. To witness the pain that Andy's two brothers and my husband have endured because of Henry Danninger is like his knife is slowly piercing my heart."[3]

"I hope for the remainder of his life that he thinks about what he did to Andy," she railed before walking away from the courthouse one final time.[4]

In 2003, the governor general of Canada honoured Andy Moffitt with a Medal of Bravery for the heroic deed that cost him his life. In 2005, a private member's bill, Bill C-393, was introduced into the House of Commons, proposing the introduction of mandatory minimum sentences for carrying a concealed weapon and for manslaughter of an unarmed person inflicted with a knife that was previously concealed. It has yet to be passed into law. The Andrew Moffitt Memorial Scholarship has awarded thousands of dollars to engineering students at the University of Ottawa since it was established, and in 2010, an Ottawa park was renamed Andy Moffitt Trail to honour him.

VICTIMOLOGY

4.1 | LEARNING OBJECTIVE

NO STUDY OF CRIME WOULD BE COMPLETE WITHOUT A CONSIDERATION OF THE ROLE that victims play in the criminal event. **Victimology**, or the study of the victim, includes more than just theories and extends to all aspects of the scientific study of criminal victimization, including the process of victimization, the criminal, the victim, the justice system, and society. As such, **victimologists** study particularly vulnerable groups of people and attempt to understand the victimization process.[5] Victimologists can be members of various academic or professional organizations. One of the largest

Victimology The scientific study of crime victims and the victimization process.

Victimologist One who studies victims and the process of criminal victimization.

is the World Society of Victimology. The International Victimology Institute at Tilburg University (INTERVICT) in the Netherlands promotes interdisciplinary research that contributes to a comprehensive, evidence-based body of knowledge on the status of victims. In Canada, non-profit organizations such as the Canadian Resource Centre for Victims of Crime and the Victim Justice Network advocate and provide information about services and supports for victims and survivors of crime.

Theories of Victimization

Victimogenesis The contribution to victimization made by the background of a victim.

While theories of crime causation frequently focus on the offender, some consider the role of the victim in setting the stage leading up to the criminal event. See Table 4.1 for an overview of the theories of victimization. Theories that emphasize the role of the victim in crime causation were some of the earliest contributions to the study of victimology. **Victimogenesis** is a term that refers to the origin or cause of victimization and includes a cluster of variables that ultimately lead to victimization. Some victims actively contribute to their own victimization by appearing defenseless (i.e., being old and frail, being intoxicated, or displaying a physical disability), by failing to take appropriate defensive measures (leaving doors unlocked or forgetting to remove the key from a vehicle), by displaying wealth (flashing large amounts of cash or other valuables in a public place), or simply by making other unwise choices (like walking down a dark alley in a high-risk neighbourhood at three o'clock in the morning).

Victim precipitation Any contribution made by the victim to the criminal event, especially one that led to its initiation.

Victim Precipitation Victim–offender relationships were the focus of first-generation victimologists, who classified victims according to the degree to which they contributed to their own victimization. These early victimologists developed the important notion of **victim precipitation**. This concept examines the characteristics of victims, the nature of their surroundings, or the quality of their relationships, insofar as they play a role in precipitating victimization. So, for example, individuals who live in inner-city high-crime areas are, generally speaking, more likely to become crime victims than those who reside in gated suburban communities. Similarly, those who work in certain occupations (i.e., late-night convenience store clerks) are more likely to become victims of crime than those in certain other occupations (i.e., college teachers).

Other first-generation victimologists include Benjamin Mendelsohn and Hans von Hentig; each developed a typology of victims. Mendelsohn, a Romanian lawyer who is often referred to as the *father of victimology*, coined the term *victimology* in 1947 and proposed the creation of a victimological research institute, a journal of victimology, and the establishment of a society for the study of victims.[6] He is best remembered for the creation of a six-part victimology typology based on degree of victim culpability.

Table 4.1 Theories of Victimization

Theory	Victim Precipitation	Lifestyle Exposure	Routine Activities	Deviant Places
Period	1940s–1970s	1970s–present	1970s–present	1980s–present
Theorists	Benjamin Mendelsohn and others	Michael Hindelang and others	Lawrence Cohen and others	Rodney Stark
Concepts	Victim precipitation, victim proneness	Lifestyles	Motivated offenders, suitable targets, capable guardians	Stigmatized neighbourhoods

For the most part, Mendelsohn believed that victims had an unconscious aptitude for victimization. Mendelsohn's six types of victims ranged from the completely innocent victim (i.e., a completely unconscious person or an infant) to the imaginary or simulated victim (i.e., individuals who, as a result of a psychological disorder, believe that they have been victimized when in fact they have not). In between were victims with minor guilt, victims as guilty as the offender, and victims with more guilt than the offender. Of his six types, only the completely innocent victim was truly blameless in Mendelsohn's scheme. Hans von Hentig, who wrote in the late 1940s, published an important book, *The Criminal and His Victim*, in which he created a taxonomy describing how victims might be responsible for the harms that befell them.[7] Von Hentig classified victims into 13 categories depending on psychological, social, and biological factors, which he believed correlated with victimization risk.

Lifestyle Exposure Theory

Michael J. Hindelang, Michael R. Gottfredson, and James Garofalo developed the *lifestyle exposure theory* (aka **lifestyle theory**) of victimization in 1978.[8] The theory originally attempted to explain crimes against persons, but it has since been expanded to include property crimes. *Lifestyle* refers to a style of life, or the way a person lives. Lifestyles are composed of repetitive, patterned, regular, and recurrent events that people engage in on an everyday basis. Because lifestyles are associated with exposure to people, places, and times with varying risk of victimization, they determine a person's vulnerability to criminal victimization.[9] Simply put, certain lifestyles favour victimization because they offer more opportunities for it.[10]

> **Lifestyle theory** A perspective that holds that an individual's lifestyle contributes significantly to the likelihood of his or her criminal victimization.

Lifestyle theory proposes that demographic variables, including things such as age, gender, race/ethnicity, and socio-economic status, influence lifestyles and hence determine victimization risk through their effect on lifestyle. Someone working a late-night shift in a crime-prone area, for example, is likely at higher risk of victimization than someone who is asleep at home. Similarly, a person who routinely withdraws large sums of cash from the same ATM machine on a regular basis is more likely to be victimized than one who conducts transactions at a teller's window in a bank or who varies his or her routine—especially if he or she frequently visits ATMs in poorly lit areas late at night.

Routine Activities Theory

Routine activities theory was proposed by Lawrence Cohen and Marcus Felson in 1979.[11] Writing shortly after the introduction of lifestyle theory, Cohen and Felson noted that "routine activities deliver easy crime opportunities to the offender." They stated that "the risk of criminal victimization varies dramatically among the circumstances and locations in which people place themselves and their property."[12] In other words, the nature or pattern of routine social interaction contributes significantly to both the volume and the type of crime found in society. Cohen and Felson assume that there will always be a substantial number of **motivated offenders** but that **suitable targets** (either vulnerable people or unattended valuables) and **capable guardians** (watchful friends and neighbours, the police, and security personnel) vary with the place and over time. Social activities engaged in by potential victims who are suitable targets for robbery contribute substantially to criminal opportunities when they are undertaken in the absence of a capable guardian—as when someone wearing valuable jewellery fails to consider the potential threat of being out in public unaccompanied by others.[13]

> **Routine activities theory** A theory that examines the interaction of motivated offenders, capable guardians, and suitable targets as an explanation for crime, and which suggests that an individual's everyday activities contribute significantly to the likelihood of his or her criminal victimization.
>
> **Motivated offender** The population of potential criminal offenders in a given area.
>
> **Suitable target** Something or someone of value to offenders in a criminal offence.
>
> **Capable guardian** One who effectively discourages crime; effective deterrents to criminal activity.

Ezzat Fattah, a Canadian criminologist recognized as one of the leading thinkers in the field of victimology, attempted to integrate the various lifestyle/opportunity theories into a comprehensive scheme. He contended that this scheme comprised 10 components,[14] which he identified as

1. *Opportunities*, which are closely linked to the characteristics of potential targets and to the activities and behaviour of these targets

2. *Risk factors*, particularly those related to socio-demographic realities such as age, sex, area of residence, and so on

3. *Motivated offenders* who do not choose their victims/targets at random but select them according to specific criteria

4. *Exposure* of the victim to potential offenders and to high-risk situations that increase the risk of criminal victimization

5. *Associations* between offenders and victims so that those who are in close personal, professional, or social contact with offenders run a greater risk of being victimized

6. *Dangerous times and dangerous places*, which include evenings, weekends, and places of public entertainment

7. *Dangerous behaviours*, such as provocation, which increases the risk especially of violent victimization, and other behaviours, such as negligence and carelessness, which enhance chances of property victimization

8. *High-risk activities*, which increase the potential for victimization and can include deviant and illegal activities

9. *Defensive/avoidance behaviours*, which tend to contribute to a reduction in the risk of victimization; those who take precautions are less likely to be victimized than those who are risk-takers

10. *Structural/cultural proneness* of people, which means that those who are powerless and culturally stigmatized and marginalized are more likely to be criminally victimized

It is interesting to note that the findings of the most recent General Social Survey in Canada indicate that the risk of victimization, and in particular violent victimization, is greatest for women, those aged 20 to 24, those involved in binge drinking, those with a mental health–related disability, those with a history of homelessness, and those living in a neighbourhood with low social cohesion.[15]

Deviant places theory A spatially oriented theory of victimization that suggests that victimization occurs most frequently in socially disorganized, high-crime areas and that people become victims as a result of their exposure to such areas.

Stigmatized neighbourhoods Residential areas with bad reputations that hold little attraction for those who can afford to live elsewhere.

Deviant Places Theory

Deviant places theory suggests that victimization occurs most frequently in socially disorganized areas and that people become victims as a result of their exposure to such areas—by living in them, transiting through them, or visiting them. The theory focuses primarily on the geographically determined risk of coming into contact with an offender, irrespective of lifestyle, behaviour, or personal characteristics. Sociologist Rodney Stark proposed deviant places theory in 1987 and called it "a theory of the ecology of crime."[16] Stark had observed that certain locations had high and unchanging victimization rates even after an almost complete turnover of the population—during which previous residents moved away and new ones moved in. He concluded that victimologists needed a "kinds of places" theory to supplement other theories, which he called "kinds of people" theories. Stark examined more than a century of ecological research on crime and integrated his findings into a set of propositions. Those propositions focused on neighbourhood conditions and, taken together, they form the crux of deviant places theory. Certain neighbourhood conditions produce what Stark called **stigmatized neighbourhoods**—that is, neighbourhoods with bad reputations that hold little attraction for those who can afford to live elsewhere. Stigmatized neighbourhoods are characterized by crowded homes, transience, dilapidation, and the lack of successful role models.

Stark recognized that while stigmatized neighbourhoods increase the likelihood of victimization for those living in or visiting them, most neighbourhood residents do not become criminal. He noted that his theory of deviant places depends entirely upon ecological features associated with a given location and not upon racial, ethnic, or other personal characteristics of the people who live there.

Realities of Being a Victim

Some authors have identified a number of procedural models that can be applied to a study of the victimization process, the experience the victim undergoes during and following victimization.[17] The "victims of crime model" developed by Morton Bard and Dawn Sangrey postulated that three stages are involved in any victimization: (1) the stage of impact and disorganization, during and immediately following the criminal event; (2) recoil, during which the victim formulates psychological defences and deals with conflicting emotions of guilt, anger, acceptance, and desire for revenge (the state of recoil is said to last from three to eight months); and (3) the reorganizational stage, during which the victim puts his or her life back together and gets on with daily living in a more-or-less normal fashion.[18] Some victims do not successfully adapt to the victimization experience, and a maladaptive reorganizational stage may last for many years.

The model developed by Elizabeth Kübler-Ross to describe the stages that dying persons go through has some applicability to the victimization process. Kübler-Ross described a five-part transitional process of denial, anger, bargaining, depression, and acceptance.[19] Victims often either deny the likelihood of their own victimization or believe that "this can't be happening to me." After the victimizing event, many victims feel anger, and some express rage toward their victimizers. Bargaining occurs when victims negotiate with themselves as well as with family members, representatives of the criminal justice community, and social service providers over how the victimization experience should be personally interpreted and officially handled. Acceptance occurs when the victim finally acknowledges that victimization has occurred, and the victim makes the adjustments necessary to go on with life. Of course, as in the case of other models, the Kübler-Ross model allows for maladjustment in the final phase as some victims never successfully integrate the victimization experience into their psyches in a way that avoids reduction in the quality of their lives.

Countless studies examining the psychological well-being of victims[20] have concluded that criminal victimization

- can leave psychological scars that last as long as or longer than any physical or financial loss
- can result in anxiety disorders, depression, drug and alcohol abuse, fear, flashbacks, lowered self-esteem, sexual dysfunction, thoughts of suicide, suspiciousness, and a feeling of social isolation
- can result in the development of post-traumatic stress disorder (PTSD)
- can result in feelings of guilt, with victims of violence experiencing the greatest level of guilt
- can result in a decreased sense of satisfaction with life and a perception that the world is less caring

In addition to the literature examining the psychological realities of criminal victimization, there has been much discussion about **secondary victimization**, which sometimes blurs the line between victim and offender. This refers to social injuries that occur not as a direct result of the criminal act but through the response of social institutions and individuals to the victim. A significant form of secondary victimization happens when the justice system imposes requirements on the victim that are difficult to meet or that interfere with his or her ability to recover from the initial victimization. In some instances, members of the public may be unsympathetic to the victim, communicating messages via social media or in other ways that say "she got what she deserved." Likewise, members of the press and media photographers can intrude on the victim's privacy and file inaccurate reports of what actually took place. Finally, the

Secondary victimization Social injuries that occur not as a direct result of a criminal act but through the response of social institutions and individuals to the victim.

victim may come to feel frustrated with the justice system and believe that he or she has been extended fewer considerations than the victimizer or is accorded fewer "rights" as the criminal justice process wends its way to conclusion. Cases that are plea-bargained are most likely to leave the victim feeling that justice has not been served and that additional victimization has occurred at the hands of the justice system. Secondary victimization should be distinguished from secondary victims, who are persons not directly affected by a criminal event but who suffer unintended consequences of the victimization of others whom they are close to, like family members, friends, co-workers, and neighbours.[21]

In an often-cited article, Dean Kilpatrick and Randy Otto contend that "promising victims' rights that are not delivered may involve a certain danger: providing rights without remedies would result in the worst of consequences, such as feelings of helplessness, lack of control and further victimization. Ultimately, with the victims' best interests in mind, it is better to confer no rights than 'rights' without remedies."[22]

4.2 | LEARNING OBJECTIVE

VICTIMS' RIGHTS

FUELLED LARGELY BY THE EXPANSION OF THEORETICAL STUDY WITHIN THE FIELD OF criminology of the victim as a participant in the criminal event, a focus on the victim's role in the formal criminal justice process took hold in Canada in the late 1980s and early 1990s. The emergence of victims' advocacy and support organizations served to further highlight the need to critically examine the role and rights of victims within the criminal justice system.

A History of the Victim

In early times, victims took the law into their own hands. If they were able to apprehend their victimizers, they enacted their own form of revenge and imposed some form of personal retaliation. One of the earliest known legal codes, the Code of Hammurabi (circa 1750 BCE) required that many offenders make restitution; if the offender could not be found, the victim's family was duty bound to care for the needs of the victim.

Eventually crimes came to be understood as offences against society, and the victim was forgotten. By the late Middle Ages, the concept of "King's Peace" had emerged, wherein all offences were seen as violations of imperial law. The notion of private injury became one of public wrong, and the law of wrongdoing became the law of crime. It became the duty of local governments to apprehend, try, and punish offenders, effectively removing the victim from any direct involvement in judicial decision making. Society's moral responsibility toward making victims "whole again" was forgotten, and victims as a class were moved to the periphery of the justice process. Justice for the victim was forgotten, translated instead into the notion of justice for the state.

By the 14th century, the victim was no longer the focus of the criminal process, and the notion of an active role for the victim did not re-emerge until the 19th century. It wasn't until the 20th century, however, that a renewed interest in the plight of victims led to a resurgence of positive sentiments around the world. Discussion of the role of the victim in the formal criminal justice process ensued, with supporters and detractors of the victim's right to participate in the process lining up on opposite sides of the argument. Much of the current academic debate continues to centre on the discussion of whether or not increased protection for victims can be achieved only at the expense of the rights of the accused. For example, some victims' rights advocates recommend that victims be allowed to express an opinion or recommendation as to a

Commemorative vigils like this one have been held every year on December 6 since the Montreal Massacre in 1989 when 14 women died at the hands of gunman Marc Lepine. Do you think that this type of public memorial helps to raise the awareness of victims' rights?

Ryan Remiorz/The Canadian Press

convicted offender's sentence at the sentencing portion of the formal court process. Those who caution against the increased participation of victims in the court process argue that this will only serve to whittle away at the accused's right to due process and turn the sentencing into an opportunity for victims to seek revenge.[23]

Within the emerging discipline of victimology, academic discussion focused on the development of a pedagogical basis for the growing victims' rights movement. This discussion centred largely on the two models of criminal justice put forth by Herbert Packer in 1968. In *The Limits of the Criminal Sanction*, Packer presented the *crime control model* and the *due process model*.[24] The former model describes an assembly-line approach to justice, focusing on the efficient repression of crime and the safety of the community. The latter model discusses an approach to criminal justice that emphasizes civil liberties and the importance of the verdict rather than the efficiency of the process. In the late 1990s, Kent Roach, then dean of law at the University of Saskatchewan, proposed a third model as a theoretical base for victims' rights, referring to it as the *victims' rights model* and calling for more laws and prosecutions, a greater role for the victim in the trial, and more services and support for victims.[25]

Roach developed his model by distinguishing between what he identified as the *punitive* victims' rights model and the *non-punitive* victims' rights model. He described the punitive approach as one resembling the crime control model because it focuses on the enactment of criminal law, prosecution, and punishment as ways to control crime.

His non-punitive model of victims' rights, on the other hand, looked away from the reliance on criminal sanction and punishment and toward the prevention of crime and restorative justice. Roach went on to advocate that the non-punitive approach would seek to shift the focus of importance away from traditional crime control strategies and agents, such as the police, prosecutors, defence lawyers, and judges, and toward the victim, the offender, families, and supporters. Victims, in turn, would play the most significant role in determining how the offender should be dealt with.

CURRENT DIRECTIONS IN VICTIMOLOGY AND VICTIMS' RIGHTS LEGISLATION

Against this backdrop of increasing recognition for victims, a number of laws and legislation have been developed, the earliest of which were intended to provide compensation primarily to victims of violent crimes.

The first modern victim compensation statute was adopted by New Zealand in 1963. Known as the *Criminal Injuries Compensation Act*, it provided an avenue for claims to be filed by victims of certain specified violent crimes. One year later, partially in response to a movement led by the social reformer Margaret Fry, Great Britain established a similar board. In 1965, California passed the first piece of U.S. legislation intended to assist victims of crime, and today all 50 states have passed similar legislation.

The first Canadian criminal injuries compensation plan was created in Saskatchewan in 1967. By 1988, a compensation program was available in every province and territory, providing financial compensation for injuries or death resulting from a crime of violence committed by another person. Each provincial compensation program is unique, but all include time limits on the filing of an application and set maximum award amounts per applicant, varying from $5000 to $30 000. In addition, most plans allow surviving relatives of murder victims and those injured while preventing a crime to qualify for compensation. In all plans, payments for lost wages, medical expenses, and prescription drugs are commonly made. Some provincial plans compensate victims for general damages, including pain and suffering caused by the offence. Victims who are responsible in some significant way for their own victimization may receive a lower reward or be disqualified completely. Factors such as intoxication, prior knowledge of the offender's criminalistic tendencies, and provocation of the offender can result in reduced awards. Payments are not generally awarded for victims with injuries caused by motor vehicle accidents.

Although many tout the benefits of victim compensation programs, some studies of the effectiveness of government-sponsored compensation programs have found that most crime victims are reluctant to seek compensation and that those who do are generally from households with higher incomes. Frustrations with delays, poor information about the programs, and unmet expectations regarding assistance with psychological and support needs as well as financial needs were also cited as limitations.[26]

A 2007 report by the ombudsman of Ontario, entitled *Adding Insult to Injury*, strongly criticized that province's Criminal Injuries Compensation Board, calling it a "colossal failure that needlessly revictimizes people." In his report, the ombudsman claimed that the board has become mired in bureaucratic red tape that serves only to delay or deny compensation to victims. He detailed the cases of several victims, including one who was forced to choose between buying food and burying his murdered daughter and another who had his claim returned because he had failed to dot an *i* on his form.[27] At the 1979 Federal–Provincial Conference of Ministers Responsible for Criminal Justice, the issue of victims' rights was raised by provincial ministers and subsequently formally brought to the attention of the federal government. A loose coalition of Canadian feminist organizations, Canadian victim assistance programs, and the strengthening U.S. victims' rights movement came together to move the issue to the forefront. In 1983, a Federal–Provincial Task Force on Justice for the Victims of Crime made 79 recommendations addressing the needs of victims and the requirements for effective victim services, many of which are in place today. Among these are provisions for improvements in emotional and practical assistance for victims as well as provisions within the *Criminal Code of Canada* that ensure criminal injuries compensation, the increased use of restitution, and the introduction of the idea of a victim impact statement in the pre-sentence report.

International attention to the issue saw a number of nations sign on to the 1985 United Nations Declaration of Basic Principles of Justice for Victims of Crime and

Abuses of Power, which is essentially a declaration of general principles. In adopting the declaration, the General Assembly of the United Nations stated that it was "cognizant that millions of people throughout the world suffer harm as a result of crime and abuse of power, and that the rights of these victims have not been adequately recognized."[28] Despite the lack of concrete details regarding implementation of these rights for victims, the document served as a catalyst for similar documents around the world, not the least of which was the Canadian Statement of Basic Principles of Justice for Victims of Crime, endorsed by the provincial and territorial ministers of justice in 1988 and amended in 2003. These principles served to guide the development of policy and legislation for the victims of crime at both the federal and the provincial levels. A 1998 report from the House of Commons Standing Committee on Justice and Human Rights entitled *Victims' Rights—A Voice, Not a Veto* made a number of recommendations regarding further amendments to the *Criminal Code* to strengthen the voice of victims of crime. Most provinces and territories in Canada have enacted legislation to promote and protect the interests of victims.

Almost all of the provincial governments have also enacted legislation to recognize the rights of victims. In 1986, Manitoba was the first province to incorporate principles from the UN declaration into its own law.[29] Many of these provincial bills emphasize the notion of empowerment for the victim and provide rights of participation and notification. Ontario's legislation, known as *An Act Respecting Victims of Crime—Victims' Bill of Rights*, is emblematic of the rights enshrined in most provincial and territorial legislation.

In 2005, a National Office for Victims was established under the auspices of Public Safety Canada. As a central resource for victims of offenders under federal responsibility, the office provides general information for victims and the public and makes referrals on behalf of victims to Correctional Service Canada and the National Parole Board, when required.[30] Two years later, the independent Office of the Federal Ombudsman for Victims of Crime was created. By facilitating access of victims to existing programs, addressing complaints of victims about legislative compliance, enhancing awareness of criminal justice personnel and policy-makers about the needs of victims, and identifying emerging trends that may adversely affect victims, the Office of the Ombudsman works to ensure that the federal government meets its responsibilities to victims of crime.[31] The Policy Centre for Victim Issues within the Department of Justice engages in legislative reform, consultation, policy development, research, and project funding.[32] The Federal Victims Strategy was created in 2011 within the Department of Justice and was designed to bring together federal efforts to give victims of crime a more effective voice in the criminal justice system. Working with other federal institutions as well as victims, victim advocates, and provincial and territorial governments, the Department of Justice develops policy and criminal law and explores best practices to address victims' needs. Within the Federal Victims Strategy, the Victims Fund provides financial resources to provinces, territories, and non-governmental organizations, whose activities and operations support the Victims Strategy.

On July 23, 2015, Bill C-32, the *Victims Bill of Rights Act* came into force. This legislation created the **Canadian Victims Bill of Rights** to provide clear statutory rights at the federal level for victims of crime for the first time in Canada's history.

The *Canadian Victims Bill of Rights* establishes statutory rights to information, protection, participation, and to seek restitution, and it ensures that a complaint process is in place for breaches of these rights by a federal department or agency. The quasi-constitutional status of the *Bill of Rights* affords a number of remedies for victims who believe their rights have been violated. Time will tell how and if these rights are ensured at both the federal and provincial levels of government. Box 4.1 provides an overview of the *Canadian Victims Bill of Rights*.

Canadian Victims Bill of Rights Federal legislation establishing statutory rights to information, protection, participation, and to seek restitution for victims of crime.

Box 4.1   CANADIAN VICTIMS BILL OF RIGHTS

The *Canadian Victims Bill of Rights* enshrines the following rights for victims:

Information

General information:

Every victim has the right, on request, to information about

(a) the criminal justice system and the role of victims in it;

(b) the services and programs available to them as a victim, including restorative justice programs; and

(c) their right to file a complaint for an infringement or denial of any of their rights under this Act.

Investigation and proceedings:

Every victim has the right, on request, to information about

(a) the status and outcome of the investigation into the offence; and

(b) the location of proceedings in relation to the offence, when they will take place and their progress and outcome.

Information about offender or accused:

Every victim has the right, on request, to information about

(a) reviews under the *Corrections and Conditional Release Act* relating to the offender's conditional release and the timing and conditions of that release; and

(b) hearings held for the purpose of making dispositions, as defined in subsection 672.1(1) of the *Criminal Code*, in relation to the accused, if the accused is found not criminally responsible on account of mental disorder or unfit to stand trial, and the dispositions made at those hearings.

Protection

Security:

Every victim has the right to have their security considered by the appropriate authorities in the criminal justice system.

Protection from intimidation and retaliation:

Every victim has the right to have reasonable and necessary measures taken by the appropriate authorities in the criminal justice system to protect the victim from intimidation and retaliation.

Privacy:

Every victim has the right to have their privacy considered by the appropriate authorities in the criminal justice system.

Identity protection:

Every victim has the right to request that their identity be protected if they are a complainant to the offence or a witness in proceedings relating to the offence.

Testimonial aids:

Every victim has the right to request testimonial aids when appearing as a witness in proceedings relating to the offence.

Participation

Views to be considered:

Every victim has the right to convey their views about decisions to be made by appropriate authorities in the criminal justice system that affect the victim's rights under this Act and to have those views considered.

Victim impact statement:

Every victim has the right to present a victim impact statement to the appropriate authorities in the criminal justice system and to have it considered.

Restitution

Restitution order:

Every victim has the right to have the court consider making a restitution order against the offender.

Enforcement:

Every victim in whose favour a restitution order is made has the right, if they are not paid, to have the order entered as a civil court judgment that is enforceable against the offender.

Remedies

Under the *Canadian Victims Bill of Rights*, when a victim believes that his or her rights have been breached, the victim first files a complaint with the appropriate federal department or agency. The legislation includes a requirement for all federal departments and agencies that have responsibilities under the *Canadian Victims Bill of Rights* to have internal complaint mechanisms accessible to victims to review complaints, make recommendations to correct any infringement, and notify victims about the results of the review. Complaints regarding a provincial or territorial agency, including police, prosecutors, and victim services, will be addressed in accordance with the applicable provincial or territorial legislation.

Canadian Victims Bill of Rights. 2015. http://laws-lois.justice.gc.ca/ PDF/C-23.7.pdf, pages 3–9. Department of Justice Canada, 2015. Reproduced with the permission of the Department of Justice Canada, 2016.

Box 4.2 PROVINCIAL/TERRITORIAL VICTIM SERVICES

Alberta

Victim Services Alberta
http://victimservicesalberta.com
The largest, exclusively police-based victims' services association in Canada, this non-profit association promotes and advocates the rights of victims of crimes through information, support, and community referrals.

British Columbia

Ministry of Justice (Youth Services)—Court Prep
http://www.courtprep.ca
This interactive information site provides an overview of criminal court procedures for youth, including the roles of victims and witnesses of crime.

Newfoundland and Labrador

Department of Justice and Public Safety—Services for Victims
http://www.justice.gov.nl.ca/just/victim_services
Eleven regional offices throughout the province provide support to victims through information about the justice system, their court cases, pre-court preparation, assistance with victim impact statements, referrals to specialized community resources, and short-term emotional support and counselling.

Ontario

Ontario Network of Victim Service Providers—SupportLink
http://www.victimservicesontario.ca
Located in 20 communities across the province, this service provides safety planning, follow-up contact, and, where appropriate, wireless phones pre-programmed to 911 to people at high risk of sexual assault, domestic violence, and stalking.

Quebec

Justice Québec—Crime Victims Assistance Centre (CAVAC)
http://www.cavac.qc.ca/english/index.html
Located in most urban centres throughout Quebec, CAVACs provide free and confidential services, including post-traumatic shock counselling and support to victims through the court process.

Yukon

Department of Justice—Domestic Violence Treatment Option Court (DVTO Court)
http://www.yukoncourts.ca/courts/territorial/dvtoc.html
Specially assigned judiciary, Crown attorneys, and defence council deal with domestic assault cases only in this court, which sits one afternoon a week. Probation officers, counsellors, and victim services personnel provide assistance to the process as well as the victim. Disposition in this court often involves the offender's participation in the Spousal Assault Program.

Services for Victims

In addition to the development of and changes to legislation and laws, and the creation of national and provincial government advocacy offices, the movement to recognize the needs and rights of victims has led to the development of a variety of services and programs across the country. According to the most recent victim services review, of the 760 victim services identified across the country, the majority address issues of protection, support in crisis situations, information about the criminal justice system, and assistance with participation in the criminal justice system and have provided assistance to about 460 000 primary and secondary victims, the majority of whom were female.[33] Most of these services were not available as recently as 30 years ago. A number of these services are highlighted in Box 4.2.

Police-Based Services   Thirty-six percent of all victim services are police-based.[34] Usually located in police departments, these types of programs are designed to help victims as soon as possible after their contact with the criminal justice system begins. These types of services typically include death notification, information about the investigation, assistance with various applications for compensation, and referrals. In

An annual National Victims of Crime Awareness Week has been sponsored by the Canadian government since 2004. How do such events engage all Canadians to assist victims of crime?

Source: Jonathan Hayward/The Canadian Press

order to provide this support to victims, many police services across Canada now have in-house victim services units.[35] Usually staffed by civilians and volunteers, these services are available 24 hours a day for immediate victim support. For example, in the case of a fatal car accident, responding police officers can call upon their department's victim services unit to provide crisis intervention at the scene of the accident. Such services not only allow police officers to resume their duties but also ensure that the victim is supported by a trained professional. Many victim services units also use volunteers who represent various cultural, ethnic, and linguistic groups to help meet the specific needs of victims.

Some provinces have also established and funded independent crisis intervention services that provide victim support through referrals from police. In Ontario, the Victim Crisis Assistance Ontario (VCAO) is found in numerous centres across the province. A full-time coordinator and a group of trained volunteers, who are available as support to police at the scene of a crime, staff most VCAO programs. Available 24 hours a day and 7 days a week, VCAO personnel help victims cope with the impact of the crime or tragic circumstance. This may mean helping an elderly woman clean up after her home has been burglarized or spending time with survivors of a fatal car accident. Follow-up is often provided in the form of referrals for ongoing counselling if required.

Court-Based Services   Most court-based victims' programs are located within the courthouses and work closely with the Crown's office. Most assist those victims whose cases have resulted in prosecution. They emphasize court preparation and are designed to assist the victim through the trial process. One such program is the **Victim/Witness Assistance Program** located throughout Ontario. It provides services such as notification of court dates and adjournments, guided tours through the courtroom, explanations of court proceedings, and emotional support throughout the trial, especially on the day(s) of victim testimony.[36] Many provinces also provide specialized court-based support programs for child victims and witnesses.

The recognition of the victim's involvement and the need for support throughout the court process has resulted in a number of provisions outlined in the *Criminal Code of Canada* with special attention to victims of violence. For example, section 722

Victim/Witness Assistance Program   A program in Ontario that counsels victims, orients them to the justice process, and provides a variety of other services, such as transportation to court, child care during court appearances, and referrals to social service agencies.

allows victims to record a statement describing the emotional suffering, trauma, and/ or financial hardship experienced as a result of their victimization. Known as a **victim impact statement**, these accounts are introduced into court after conviction and prior to sentencing. They are most common in cases of interpersonal victimization, and judges are expected to consider these statements in arriving at an appropriate sanction for the offender. The extent to which victim impact statements affect a judge's sentencing determination is debatable, and most victims do not submit one. Proponents of victim impact statements contend that they allow victims to have their say and feel involved in the criminal justice process, providing, for many, a cathartic emotional outlet.[37] Box 4.3 presents a number of testimonials from Canadian victims.

> **Victim impact statement** A written document that describes the losses, suffering, and trauma experienced by the crime victim or by the victim's survivors. Judges are expected to consider these effects in arriving at an appropriate sentence for the offender.

A number of other *Criminal Code* provisions are aimed at reducing the secondary victimization often experienced by people who appear as witnesses at trials. In order to protect the identity of victims, a trial judge may override the fundamental principle of justice that trials be public and issue an order to "exclude all or any members of the public from the courtroom for all or part of the proceedings" (s. 486(1)). Rarely done, this action is meant to allow for the "proper administration of justice" by allowing a victim or witness to testify free from stress or fear. These public-exclusion orders are most often used in cases involving child witnesses.

Additionally, section 486(3) states that judges can order "the identity of the complainant or of a witness and any information that could disclose the identity of the complainant or of a witness shall not be published in any document or broadcast in any way." These publication bans can be imposed in specific types of cases only, such as those involving sexual assault, incest, extortion, or a sexual offence involving children. Contravention of a publication ban is a summary conviction offence. Subsections 276.2 and 276.3 restrict the publication of proceedings to determine the admissibility of evidence regarding a sexual assault complainant's sexual history.

Other provisions intended to facilitate the participation of witnesses include subsection 486(1.2), which permits a support person to be present in court with a witness under the age of 14 in sexual-offence proceedings, and subsection 486(2.1), which permits a sexual offence complainant who is under the age of 18 to provide his or her testimony from behind a screen or by closed-circuit television. This provision has recently been expanded to include victims and witnesses in prostitution and assault cases. Subsection 715.1 permits, as evidence, a videotaped version of a witness's testimony in proceedings relating to sexual offences where the victim or witness was under the age of 18 at the time of the offence.

Victims and Corrections Victim involvement with the criminal justice system often continues after the offender is convicted and sentenced. The federal *Corrections and Conditional Release Act* (CCRA), for example, outlines the role of the victim in the parole process. In addition to those victims' rights highlighted in Box 4.4, the victim and/or any other interested party may attend a parole hearing, provided a written request has been made in advance of the hearing. Victims must travel to the location of the hearing and absorb any associated costs. Written transcripts of the hearing are made available upon request to those victims who cannot attend a hearing. In addition, some provinces have adopted legislation and procedures allowing the victim to remain informed of changes in the status of incarcerated offenders. Amendments made to the CCRA in 2007 ensure that victims can receive advance notice and reasons for offender transfers to minimum-security facilities or temporary absences from institutions, as well as information about offender program participation and any convictions for any serious disciplinary offences.

Box 4.4 VICTIMS' RIGHTS AND THE CORRECTIONAL PROCESS

How does a victim receive information about the offenders who harmed them?

If you are a victim of crime and you want to receive information about an offender, you must request it in writing from Correctional Services Canada (CSC) or Parole Board of Canada (PBC). In order to complete your registration, you must submit a written request or complete and sign an Application to Receive Information as a Victim and send it to CSC or PBC. You can register as a victim or authorize someone else in writing to act as your representative.

Is the offender notified when a victim registers?

No. Offenders do not have the right to be notified if you register to receive information from CSC or PBC.

Does a victim's registration ever expire?

Registration for victims to receive information does not expire. The file may be inactivated if any of the following situations occur:

■ The offender's sentence expires. However, if the offender receives a subsequent federal sentence, you will be notified and asked if you want to receive ongoing information again.

■ You advise CSC or PBC, in writing, that you no longer want to receive information about the offender.

■ The offender dies while incarcerated or under CSC supervision in the community.

Keep in mind that if you change your address or telephone number(s), be sure to update your contact information with CSC.

Can victims request no contact from an offender?

Yes. Victims can request that an offender have no contact with them at various times during the criminal justice process.

Can victims share the impact of the crime with CSC or NPB?

Yes. You are encouraged to provide a Victim Statement describing how a crime has affected you—emotionally, physically, and financially. It is given to the judge and used in sentencing if the accused is found guilty or pleads guilty. If one was submitted prior to sentencing, a victim impact statement may be on CSC's offender's file and may be considered prior to temporary absences or parole.

CSC considers this information through the course of the offender's sentence in

■ Decisions related to the offender's institutional security level;

>

- Decisions about whether the offender should be released on a temporary absence or a work release;
- Evaluations of the offender's programming needs and overall risk of re-offending; and
- Recommendations to PBC about whether the offender should be granted conditional release and what special conditions, if any, should be placed on the offender.

PBC uses victim information in

- Decisions with respect to community releases (unescorted temporary absences, day parole, full parole, statutory release) that may or may not have special conditions imposed.

Can a victim find out about the institution where the offender is placed?

Yes. Victims can find out more about CSC institutions on the Regions and Facilities page of CSC's website.

How is an offender released into the community?

Law and policy determine if and when CSC can release eligible federal offenders into the community under various types of conditional release: temporary absence, day parole, full parole, statutory release, or accelerated parole review. In each case offenders are subject to strict monitoring and control. Conditions may include regular meetings with a parole officer, curfews, or drug testing.

Public safety is the number one consideration in all decisions related to an offender's release. If an offender's risk becomes unmanageable in the community, his or her release will be suspended, and in many cases, revoked by PBC or conditions will be imposed.

By law, CSC must release offenders who have reached the warrant expiry date of their sentence.

Source: *Correctional Service Canada*, an agency of the Government of Canada. Victims Services at CSC, Frequently Asked Questions (www.csc-scc.gc.ca/victims/003006-1000-eng.shtml), July 2015. Reproduced with the permission of the Minister of Public Services and Procurement Canada, 2016.

In British Columbia, the Victim Safety Unit of the Ministry of Justice operates an automated Victim Notification System. Victims can register to be notified of changes in the custody status of an offender. The notification system provides victims with a personal identification number to access such information about their cases.

System-Based Services   This approach to the provision of assistance to victims emphasizes a system-based approach instead of one that is police- or court-based. It allows victims to receive all their services from one location and assists victims throughout their contact with the criminal justice system. This may include, but is not limited to, providing information, support and referrals, short-term counselling, court preparation and accompaniment, Victim Impact Statements preparation, and liaising with police, courts, Crown, and Corrections.

VICTIM RESTITUTION

4.4 | LEARNING OBJECTIVE

THE VICTIMS' MOVEMENT HAS ALSO SPAWNED A REBIRTH OF THE CONCEPT OF RESTITUTION. **Restitution** is punishment through imposed responsibility—in particular, the payment of compensation to the victim. Restitution encompasses the notion that criminal offenders should shoulder at least a portion of the financial obligations required to make the victim whole again and places responsibility for the process back upon the offender who caused the loss of wholeness initially. Restitution, which works through court-imposed fines and garnishments, has many advocates who claim that it benefits society by leading to an increased sense of social and individual responsibility on the part of convicted offenders.

Restitution   A criminal sanction, in particular the payment of compensation by the offender to the victim.

At one time in Canada, the responsibility for requesting restitution lay with the victim. Many who were not aware of this option failed to petition the court, and restitution was not ordered. Currently, a judge can unilaterally order restitution or do so at the request of the Crown; it can be so ordered as a standalone sentence or as part of another, such as a probation order or a conditional sentence. These types of sentences help ensure that beneficiaries of the restitution order receive payment. Failure to pay

Thirteen-Year-Old Boy an Offender or a Victim?

In Ottawa in the mid-summer of 2009, a 13-year-old boy was arrested with four friends as they fled the third bank they had robbed that day. Not only was he charged with robbery; he was also the only one in the group who faced weapons and obstructing police charges as well. How had he found himself in this place?

Not long after the boy was born, his mother moved in with a man who was violent. The boy was frequently beaten, tied to a pole in the basement, and left in the dark for hours. The boy's mother was often whipped with a skipping rope, and his 15-year-old sister was frequently woken at night by her stepfather's belt lashing her thighs. The boy's mother feared for her life and told no one of the abuse.

Forbidden to even speak at home, the boy took to stealing. He shoplifted toys from a department store before he was 10 years old, he stole an MP3 player from his doctor's office, and then he escalated to stealing a car from a construction site. The boy's sister describes him as "addicted to stealing." "He thinks stealing is going to make it better," she says.

When he began to disappear for days at a time, his mother placed her son in a group home from which he constantly ran away. In fact, he was missing from a group home in the days before the bank robberies.

His sister blames their stepfather for her brother's problems. While she is finishing high school and intending to go to university for nursing, her stepfather's treatment has left her timid and shy. "My brother listens to me," she says. "If he's out with me he doesn't get into trouble . . . He's got a lot of things in there different from everybody else. He needs someone to figure him out and get inside his head."

Think about it:

1. Is this young boy an offender or a victim? Why?

2. How should our criminal justice system treat youth like this young boy?

Source: Based on *Ottawa Citizen*: Only 13, but in trouble once again by Tony Spears, Published by Vlad Tepes, © 2009

---

in either instance can lead to a breach of the sentence and incarceration. Beneficiaries can also use civil courts to enforce a restitution order.

A relatively recent addition to the *Criminal Code of Canada* has extended the use of restitution to criminal cases involving criminal injury. Subsection 738(1) allows a judge to impose a sentence of restitution to cover expenses to the victim relating to things such as loss of income or support, costly dental work, or physiotherapy expenses. In addition, in the case of an offence causing bodily harm to the offender's spouse or child in instances of family violence, this subsection allows restitution to be ordered for readily ascertainable expenses incurred by the victim as a result of moving out of the offender's household, for temporary housing, child care, food, and transportation.

> **Victim surcharge** A mandatory, judicial imposition of a monetary fine administered in addition to a criminal sentence and used to finance victim services.

Section 737 of the *Criminal Code of Canada* requires a **victim surcharge** to be automatically imposed in addition to any other sanction handed down to an offender convicted of an offence in the *Criminal Code* or the *Controlled Drugs and Substances Act*. The revenue raised by this surcharge remains in the province or territory where it is imposed and is to be used specifically to fund programs and initiatives providing assistance to victims of crime. In 2013, the federal government passed the *Offenders Accountability for Victims Act*, which doubled the surcharges, making them at minimum 30 percent of any fine levied or $100 for summary conviction offences and $200 for indictable offences and also removed a judge's discretion to waive the surcharge. When the increased surcharges first came into effect, some judges refused to impose it, others gave offenders years to pay, some issued nominal fines that reduced the surcharge to virtually nothing, while still others found offenders in default of the surcharge immediately after their guilty plea and sentenced them to jail time concurrent to sentences they were already receiving. In 2014, an Ontario Court Justice wrote a decision declaring the surcharge as unconstitutional. The case is likely to proceed to the Supreme

Court; until that time, judges remain divided and victims' rights groups continue to appeal for additional resources to support services to victims. This provision further stipulates that the maximum victim fine surcharge is 15 percent of any fine imposed or, where no fine is imposed, is not to exceed $50 for an offence punishable by summary conviction and $100 in the case of an offence punishable by indictment. The sentencing judge may waive the victim fine surcharge where the imposition of the surcharge would cause undue hardship. Most provinces and territories have also enacted legislation imposing a surcharge on provincial offences such as highway traffic violations. This revenue is also used to fund victim programs and services.

FUTURE DIRECTIONS IN VICTIMOLOGY

4.5 | LEARNING OBJECTIVE

INITIATIVES TAKEN BY THE FEDERAL AND PROVINCIAL GOVERNMENTS IN CANADA IN recent years have done much to emphasize and highlight the rights and role of victims within our criminal justice system. However, despite this recognition, there is still concern that the needs of victims are not being fully met.

An internal Justice Department report from 2014 says that Canadians have little confidence in the courts and the prison system. The report uses data from many years of opinion polls and research, some of it unpublished, to emphasize that while public confidence in the police remains high, Canadians believe the courts are slow, sentences are lenient, and offenders are not rehabilitated through the correctional system. In addition, some of the research indicates that the public believes that victims are often ignored in criminal justice proceedings.[38]

Indeed, some assert that the victims' movement has been adopted by governments to boost ratings and opinion polls and justify a platform of increased penalties for offenders as the primary way of recognizing victims' rights. Ezzat Fattah asserted, "Crime victims are not the first group whose cause is exploited by unpopular

The reality of violence against women brings victims and their supporters together in Take Back the Night marches like this one. Do you think that there are currently sufficient services for victims of crime?

ZUMA Press Inc/Alamy Stock Photo

governments seeking a higher rating in public opinion polls, by opportunistic politicians seeking electoral votes, or by incompetent public officials trying to detract attention from their failure to control crime or reduce its incidence."[39] Others, such as Kent Roach, believe that there needs to be a fundamental structural change away from an adversarial approach to our criminal justice system and toward a restorative, victims-centred approach before victims' rights can be truly respected. Until that time, any recognition of victims' rights and roles in the criminal process cannot be considered as anything more than "window dressing," and the modern crime victim can be seen only as a participant who is "all dressed up with nowhere to go."[40]

Irvin Waller, a leading Canadian academic, advocate in the field of victimology, and president of the International Organization for Victims' Assistance, suggested that much of what is needed to support victims of crime has already been agreed upon through the international recognition of the Declaration on Basic Principles of Justice for Victims of Crime and Abuse of Power, adopted by the General Assembly of the United Nations in 1985. Waller stated that "there is much rhetoric on doing justice and support for victims. Indeed, there are often laws and a patchwork of services to implement those laws. But much needs to be done to make support services universal, to get restitution paid, and to provide equitable compensation."[41]

The recently enacted *Canadian Victims Bill of Rights* establishes statutory rights to information, protection, and participation, and to seek restitution for victims of crime. The question now is how these rights will be ensured and upheld. Victims' rights and advocacy groups still have questions. Sue O'Sullivan, federal ombudsman for the victims of crime, believes that

> the tabling of this legislation provides not only some immediate benefit to victims, but has also helped to spur important public discourse and dialogue around victims' issues which is, in itself, valuable. On the whole, the majority of public discussions about victims' issues have focused on either the offender and his/her treatment, or the length and severity of sentencing. Neither of these points help Canadians to truly understand and become sensitive to the day-to-day practical and emotional challenges victims face and their frustration with a system they often feel does not meet their needs or hear their voice. Whether specific stakeholders find themselves in favour of, or criticizing the Bill, what is important is the marking of a cultural shift to more fully consider and integrate victims in Canada's criminal justice system and, jointly, the opportunity for important discourse about victims' needs and how to better address them.[42]

The struggle to recognize crime victims' needs and rights continues. There is no doubt that victims have been left out of the criminal process for too long. Governments at all levels have formally acknowledged this. In addition to resources for the development and provision of services for victims, attention is also being paid to research the realities and needs of crime victims. In 2016, the Social Sciences and Humanities Research Council (SSHRC), a federal research funding agency, awarded $200 000 to Algonquin College in Ottawa to support new and applied research. Dr. Benjamin Roebuck, coordinator of the victimology program at the college, contends that "through this applied research project, we aim to create innovative training materials, contribute a Canadian perspective to international literature on the subject, and examine how the strengths of victims of crime contribute to their resilience."[43]

SUMMARY OF LEARNING OBJECTIVES

4.1 Victimology extends to all aspects of the scientific study of criminal victimization, including the process of victimization, the criminal, the victim, the justice system, and society. While early theories of victimology tended to blame the victim for his or her own victimization, more recent victimological approaches examine lifestyles, routine activities, and features of deviant places as factors that contribute to criminal victimization. Victimization brings with it significant psychological and in some cases physical challenges.

4.2 The Code of Hammurabi (circa 1750 BCE) required that many offenders make restitution. By the late Middle Ages, the concept of "King's Peace" had emerged, wherein all offences were seen as violations of imperial law. The situation remained largely unchanged until the 20th century. The emerging discipline of victimology is focused on the strengthening of the victims' rights movement. A focus on the role of the victim in the formal criminal justice process took hold in Canada in the late 1980s and early 1990s.

4.3 Provincial and federal governments in Canada have enacted legislation to recognize and support victims' rights, services, and programs. The *Canadian Victims Bill of Rights* is federal legislation establishing statutory rights to information, protection, and participation, and to seek restitution for victims of crime. Current services for victims of crime are made available in conjunction with police, the Crown, the courts, and correctional services across the country.

4.4 Restitution is a criminal sanction, in particular the payment of compensation by the offender to the victim. Restitution works through court-imposed fines and garnishments. A judge can unilaterally order restitution or do so at the request of the Crown; restitution can be so ordered as a standalone sentence or as part of another, such as a probation order or a conditional sentence.

4.5 Questions continue to be asked about the needs of victims, the impact of the criminal justice process on the well-being of victims, the role of the victim in the justice process, and whether our current criminal justice structure ensures the true participation of victims.

Questions for Review

1. What are some of the realities of victimization? What is meant by *secondary victimization*?

2. What is the difference between the *punitive* victims' rights model and the *nonpunitive* victims' rights model as described by Kent Roach?

3. What are some of the existing services for victims of crime? Do you think they adequately address the concerns of victims?

4. What is the purpose of victim restitution? Does restitution benefit society? Why or why not?

5. Should the role of victims in the criminal process be changed from its current status? Do you think the newly enacted *Canadian Victims Bill of Rights* will have an impact on this role? Explain your position.

Multiple-Choice Questions

1. Which of the following rights for victims is *not* enshrined in the *Canadian Victims Bill of Rights*?

    a. the right to protection

    b. the right to restitution

    c. the right to information

    d. the right to legal defence

    e. the right to participation

2. The perspective that holds that an individual's lifestyle contributes significantly to the likelihood of his or her criminal victimization is known as the _____ theory.

    a. routine activities

    b. lifestyle

    c. victimogenesis

    d. victim precipitation

    e. deviant places

3. The most recent General Social Survey in Canada indicates that the risk of victimization, and in particular violent victimization, is greatest for _____.

    a. women

    b. those involved in binge drinking

    c. those living in a neighbourhood with low social cohesion

    d. those with a history of homelessness

    e. all of the above

4. Deviant places theory, developed by _____, is a theory of victimization that suggests that victimization occurs most frequently in socially disorganized high-crime areas and that people become victims as a result of their exposure to such areas.

    a. Ezzat Fattah

    b. Margaret Fry

    c. Benjamin Mendelsohn

    d. Lawrence Cohen

    e. Rodney Stark

5. According to the Code of Hammurabi, victims could _____.

    a. receive restitution from the offender

    b. seek revenge from the offender

    c. impose personal retaliation on the offender

    d. meet with the offender

    e. seek protection from the offender

Multiple Choice Answers: 1d, 2b, 3e, 4e, 5a

Chapter 5
Classical and Neoclassical Thought

David Levenson/Alamy Stock Photo

The more promptly and the more closely punishment follows upon the commission of a crime, the more just and useful will it be.

—Cesare Beccaria[1]

LEARNING OBJECTIVES

After reading this chapter, you should be able to

5.1 Discuss the major principles of the classical school of criminology.

5.2 Name some of the forerunners of classical thought in criminology and explain the relevance of the history of criminology and its early thinkers to current views of crime and criminality.

5.3 List some important thinkers of the classical school of criminology and understand their legacy.

5.4 Define neoclassical criminology and describe how it differs from the classical perspective.

5.5 Explain the role of punishment in neoclassical criminology.

5.6 Discuss the policy implications of the classical school.

5.7 Assess the shortcomings of the classical and neoclassical perspectives on crime.

INTRODUCTION

On December 2, 2015, Syed Rizwan Farook and Tashfeen Malik entered a banquet room rented for a holiday party for employees of the Department of Public Health in San Bernardino, California, and opened fire, killing 14 people and seriously injuring 22. After the shooting, the couple fled; four hours later they were killed by police in a shootout. The Federal Bureau of Investigation (FBI) opened a counter-terrorism investigation the following day and on December 6, in an address to the nation, U.S. president Barack Obama defined the shooting as an act of terrorism. FBI director James Comey told a Senate judiciary committee that the FBI investigation had shown that the shooters were "homegrown violent extremists" who were "inspired by foreign terrorist organizations." Farook was an American-born, U.S. citizen of Pakistani descent, and Malik was a Pakistani-born lawful permanent resident of the United States. The two had reportedly spent at least a year preparing for the attack, and Comey reported that, although the investigation showed that the killers were radicalized and possibly inspired by foreign terrorist organizations, there was no indication that the couple was directed by such a group or part of a broader terrorist network.[2]

Because of alleged "telephonic connections" between the couple and other people of interest, the FBI obtained a warrant to retrieve information on the iPhone belonging to one of the killers. However, the encryption software built into the phone meant that they could not access the information, and so the FBI approached Apple Inc. to devise a way to disable the security features on the phone. Apple declined, claiming that compliance would undermine the security features of its products, one of the major selling features of its brand. The FBI responded by successfully applying to a federal judge to issue a court order, citing the *All Writs Act of 1789*. This act gives federal judges the power to issue orders to compel people to do things within the limits of the law and has been used most recently only in extraordinary instances where there is no other law that applies to the situation at hand.

In an open letter to its customers on February 16, 2016, Apple CEO Tim Cook clearly stated Apple's condemnation of terrorists and terrorist acts; however, he opposed the order, citing the threat to the security of Apple iPhone users. "The passcode lock and requirement for manual entry of the passcode are at the heart of the safeguards we have built in to iOS. It would be wrong to intentionally weaken our products with a government-ordered backdoor. If we lose control of our data, we put both our privacy and our safety at risk," Cook wrote. In addition, he argued that compliance with the order would set a dangerous precedent in expanding the powers of the government, powers that could ostensibly be extended to recording conversations, surveillance, or location tracking.[3] The Justice Department retorted that Apple is not acting out of principle but is opposing the government as a public relations ploy to protect its brand.

Adding complexity, in a parallel case, Justice James Orenstein denied the Justice Department's application for an order to compel Apple to unlock the cell phone of convicted drug dealer Jun Feng. "Not only has Apple done nothing wrong in marketing devices with such strong data security features, it has exercised a freedom that Congress explicitly deemed appropriate in balancing the needs of law enforcement against the interests of private industry," the judge wrote. "The fact that the government or a judge might disapprove Apple's preference to safeguard data security and customer privacy over the stated needs of a law enforcement agency is of no moment: In the absence of any other legal constraint, that choice is Apple's to make." In short, Judge Orenstein argued the powers of the *All Writs Act* are not binding; it is Congress that is required to decide how much cooperation companies like Apple must provide. He criticized the government for making "the considered decision that it is better off securing such crypto-legislative authority from the courts rather than taking the chance that open legislative debate might produce a result less to its liking." If courts continue to grant orders to the Justice Department in these cases, he said, the result will be "a virtually limitless expansion of the government's legal authority to surreptitiously intrude on personal privacy."[4]

The FBI dropped its legal battle against Apple when the FBI was able to bypass the security on the iPhone and extract the contents. Even though the San Bernardino cases were resolved, the controversy sparked by the Apple iPhone case is an excellent example of the debate between individual rights versus the powers of the government and the collective rights of citizens. Some argue that an overemphasis on individual rights comes at the expense of the rights of the group. Others fear that the erosion of individual rights may make the state too powerful. This debate has roots in the Enlightenment and the emergence of the classical school of criminology, both of which are discussed in this chapter.

MAJOR PRINCIPLES OF THE CLASSICAL SCHOOL

THIS BRIEF SECTION SUMMARIZES THE CENTRAL FEATURES OF THE CLASSICAL SCHOOL OF criminological thought. Each of the points listed in this discussion can be found elsewhere in this chapter; this overview is intended to provide a summation and to be a guide to the rest of this chapter (see Table 5.1).

Most classical theories of crime causation make the following basic assumptions:

- Human beings are fundamentally rational, and most human behaviour is the result of free will coupled with rational choice.

- Pain and pleasure are the two central determining factors of human behaviour.

- Punishment serves to deter law violators and serves as an example to others who might contemplate violating the law.

- The principles of right and wrong are inherent in our nature and cannot be denied.

- Society exists to provide benefits to individuals that they would not receive in isolation.

- When people band together for the protection offered by society, they forfeit some of their personal freedoms in order to enjoy the benefits of living among others cooperatively.

- Certain key rights of the individual are necessary in the enjoyment of life, and governments that restrict and prohibit the exercise of those rights should be disbanded.

- Crime lessens the quality of the contractual bond that exists between individuals and their society. Therefore, criminal acts cannot be tolerated by any members if everyone wants to receive the most benefit from living in a cooperative society.

Table 5.1 The Classical School and Neoclassical Thinkers

Theory	Classical Criminology	Neoclassical Criminology
Period	1700s–1880s	1970s–present
Theorists	Cesare Becarria, Jeremy Bentham, and others	Lawrence Cohen, Marcus Felson, Ronald V. Clarke, Derek B. Cornish, and others
Concepts	Free will, deterrence through punishment, social contract, natural law, due process, Panopticon	Rational choice, routine activities, capable guardians, situational crime prevention, just deserts, determinate sentencing, specific deterrence, general deterrence

FORERUNNERS OF CLASSICAL THOUGHT

THE NOTION OF CRIME AS A VIOLATION OF ESTABLISHED LAW DID NOT EXIST IN MOST primitive societies. Lack of lawmaking bodies, absence of formal written laws, and loose social bonds precluded the concept of crime as law violation, but all human societies from the simplest to the most advanced did evidence their own widely held notions of right and wrong. Sociologists term such fundamental concepts of morality and propriety as *mores* and *folkways*. Mores, folkways, and *law* were terms used by William Graham Sumner to describe the three basic forms of behavioural strictures imposed by social groups upon their members.[5] Mores and folkways govern behaviour in relatively small primitive societies, whereas in large complex societies, they are reinforced and formalized through written laws.

Mores consist of proscriptions covering potentially serious violations of a group's values (for example, murder, sexual assault, and robbery). **Folkways** are time-honoured customs; although they carry the force of tradition, their violation is less likely to threaten the survival of the social group. The fact that Canadian men have traditionally worn little jewellery illustrates a folkway that has given way in recent years to various types of male adornment, including earrings, gold chains, and make-up. Although they may be powerful determinants of behaviour, mores and folkways are nonetheless informal, because only laws have been codified into formal strictures wielded by institutions and created specifically for enforcement purposes.

Another method of categorizing socially proscriptive rules is provided by some criminologists who divide crimes into the dual categories of *mala in se* and *mala prohibita*. Acts that are **mala in se** are said to be fundamentally wrong, regardless of the time or place in which they occur (for example, forcing someone to have sex against his or her will and the intentional killing of children). Those who argue for the existence of *mala in se* offences usually point to some fundamental rule, such as religious teachings (the Bible's Ten Commandments, the Koran, etc.), to support their belief that some acts are inherently wrong.

Offences termed **mala prohibita** are said to be wrong in areas where they are prohibited (for example, prostitution, gambling, drug use, and premarital sexual behaviour). The status of such behaviours as *mala prohibita* is supported by the fact that they are not necessarily crimes in every jurisdiction; gambling, for example, is legal in parts of Canada, mainly because of the huge revenue potential it holds.

Mores Behavioural proscriptions covering potentially serious violations of a group's values. Examples might include strictures against murder, sexual assault, and robbery.

Folkways Time-honoured customs. Although folkways carry the force of tradition, their violation is unlikely to threaten the survival of the group.

Mala in se An act that is thought to be wrong in and of itself.

Mala prohibita An act that is wrong only because it is prohibited.

The Demonic Era

Since time began, humankind has been preoccupied with what appears to be an ongoing war between good and evil. Evil has often appeared in impersonal guise, as when the great bubonic plague (the "black death") ravaged Europe and Asia in the 14th century, leaving as much as three-quarters of the population dead in a span of 20 years. At other times, evil has seemed to wear a human face, as when the Nazi Holocaust claimed millions of Jewish lives during World War II.

Whatever its manifestation, the very presence of evil in the world has begged for interpretation, and sage minds throughout human history have advanced many explanations for the evil conditions that individuals and social groups have at times been forced to endure. Some forms of evil, such as the plague and the Holocaust, appear cosmically based, whereas others—including personal victimization, criminality, and singular instances of deviance—are the undeniable result of individual behaviour. Cosmic-level evil has been explained by ideas as diverse as divine punishment, karma, fate, and the vengeful activities of offended gods. Early explanations of personal deviance ranged from demonic possession to spiritual influences to temptation by fallen angels.

Early Sources of the Criminal Law

The Code of Hammurabi   Modern criminal law is the result of a long evolution of legal principles. The Code of Hammurabi is one of the first known bodies of law to survive for study today. King Hammurabi ruled the ancient city of Babylon from 1792 to 1750 BCE and created a legal code consisting of strictures that were originally intended to establish property and other rights and that were crucial to the continued growth of Babylon as a significant commercial centre. Hammurabi's law spoke to issues of theft, property ownership, sexual relationships, and interpersonal violence. Well-known criminologist Marvin Wolfgang observed, "In its day, 1700 BCE, the Hammurabi Code, with its emphasis on retribution, amounted to a brilliant advance in penal philosophy mainly because it represented an attempt to keep cruelty within bounds."[6] Prior to the code, captured offenders often faced the most barbarous **retribution**, frequently at the hands of revenge-seeking victims, no matter how minor their transgressions had been.

Retribution   The act of taking revenge upon a criminal perpetrator.

Early Roman Law   Of considerable significance for our own legal tradition is early Roman law. Roman legions under Emperor Claudius I (10 BCE–54 CE) conquered England in the middle of the first century, and Roman customs, law, and language were forced upon the English population during the succeeding three centuries under the Pax Romana—a peace imposed by the military might of Rome.[7]

Early Roman law derived from the **Twelve Tables**, a collection of basic rules regulating family, religious, and economic life written around 450 BCE They appear to have been based on common and fair practices generally accepted among early tribes that existed prior to the establishment of the Roman Republic; only fragments of the tables survive today.

Twelve Tables   Early Roman laws written circa 450 BCE that regulated family, religious, and economic life.

The best-known legal period in Roman history occurred during the reign of Emperor Justinian I (527–565 CE). By the end of the sixth century, the Roman Empire had declined substantially in size and influence and was near the end of its life. Possibly to preserve Roman values and traditions, Justinian undertook the laborious process of distilling Roman laws into a set of writings. The Justinian Code, as these writings came to be known, actually consisted of three lengthy legal documents—the Institutes, the Digest, and the Code itself—and distinguished between two major legal categories: public and private laws. Public laws dealt with the organization of the Roman state, its Senate, and governmental offices. Private law concerned itself with contracts, personal possessions, the legal status of various types of persons (citizens, free people, slaves, freedmen, guardians, husbands and wives), and injuries to citizens. It contained elements of our modern civil and criminal law and influenced Western legal thought through the Middle Ages.

Common Law   **Common law** refers to a traditional body of unwritten legal precedents created through everyday practice in English society. It was based on shared traditions and standards and was supported by court decisions during the Middle Ages. As novel situations arose and were handled by British justices, their declarations became the start for any similar future deliberation.

Common law   Law originating from usage and custom rather than from written statutes. The term refers to non-statutory customs, traditions, and precedents that help guide judicial decision making.

Common law was given considerable legitimacy in the 11th century with the official declaration by the English king Edward the Confessor (1042–1066 CE) that it was the law of the land. The authority of common law was further reinforced by the decision of William the Conqueror to use popular customs as the basis for judicial action following his subjugation of Britain in 1066 CE.

Eventually, court decisions were recorded and made available to barristers (English trial lawyers) and judges. As criminologist Howard Abadinsky wrote, "Common law involved the transformation of community rules into a national legal system. The

The Magna Carta, an important source of modern Western laws and legal procedure. What are some other important sources of modern criminal law?

Chris Maddaloni/Newscom

controlling element [was] precedent."[8] Today, common law forms the basis for much of our statutory and case law and has been called *the* major source of modern criminal law in English-speaking countries around the world.

The Magna Carta The Magna Carta (literally, "great charter"), another important source of modern laws and legal procedure, was signed on June 15, 1215, by King John of England at Runnymede, under pressure from British barons who took advantage of his military defeats to demand a pledge to respect their traditional rights and to be bound by law. At the time of its signing, the Magna Carta (63 chapters in length) was little more than a feudal document listing specific royal concessions.[9] Its original purposes were to ensure feudal rights, to guarantee that the king would not encroach on the landowning barons' privileges, and to ensure respect for the customs of towns.

Its wording, however, was later interpreted, during a judicial revolt in 1613, to support individual rights and jury trials. Sir Edward Coke, chief justice under James I, held that the Magna Carta guaranteed basic liberties for all British citizens and ruled that any acts of Parliament that contravened common law would be void.[10] Section 7 of the *Canadian Charter of Rights and Freedoms* assures this fundamental right for Canadians today. Similarly, a specific provision of the Magna Carta, designed originally to prohibit the king from prosecuting the barons without just cause, was expanded into the concept of due process of law, a cornerstone of modern legal procedure. Because of these later interpretations, the Magna Carta has been called "the foundation stone of our present liberties."[11]

The Enlightenment

The Enlightenment A social movement that arose during the 17th and 18th centuries and built upon ideas such as empiricism, rationality, free will, humanism, and natural law.

Social contract The Enlightenment-era concept that human beings abandon their natural state of individual freedom to join together and form society. In the process of forming a social contract, individuals surrender some freedoms to society as a whole, and government, once formed, is obligated to assume responsibilities toward its citizens and to provide for their protection and welfare.

The Enlightenment (or the Age of Reason), a highly significant social movement occurring during the late 17th and 18th centuries, was built upon ideas developed by many important thinkers. Because of their indirect contributions to classical criminological thought, it is worthwhile to briefly discuss the writings of a few of these historical figures.

Thomas Hobbes The English philosopher Thomas Hobbes (1588–1679) developed what many writers regard as an extremely negative view of human nature and social life, which he described in his momentous work, *Leviathan* (1651). Fear of violent death, he said, forces human beings into a **social contract** with one another to create a state that demands the surrender of certain natural rights and submission to the absolute authority of a sovereign while offering protection and succour to its citizens. The social contract concept significantly influenced many of Hobbes's contemporaries, but much of his writing was condemned for assuming an overly pessimistic view of both human nature and existing governments.

John Locke In 1690, the English philosopher John Locke (1632–1704) published his *Essay Concerning Human Understanding*, in which he put forth the idea that the natural human condition at birth is akin to that of a blank slate upon which interpersonal encounters and other experiences indelibly inscribe the traits of personality. In contrast to earlier thinkers, who assumed that people are born with certain innate propensities and even rudimentary intellectual concepts and ideas, Locke ascribed the bulk of adult human qualities to life experiences.

In the area of social and political thought, Locke further developed the Hobbesian notion of the social contract and contended that human beings, through a social contract, abandon their natural state of individual freedom and lack of interpersonal responsibility to join together and form society. Although individuals surrender some freedoms to society, government, once formed, is obligated to assume responsibilities toward its citizens, to provide for their protection and welfare, and to guarantee them certain inalienable rights, such as the right to life, health, liberty, and possessions. A product of his times (the dictatorial nature of monarchies and the Roman church were being much disparaged), Locke stressed the duties that governments have toward their citizens while paying very little attention to the responsibilities of individuals to the societies of which they are a part, and he argued that political revolutions, under some circumstances, might become an obligation incumbent upon citizens.

Locke also developed the notion of checks and balances between divisions of government, a doctrine elaborated on by French jurist and political philosopher Charles Louis de Secondat Montesquieu (1689–1755). In *The Spirit of Laws* (1748), Montesquieu wove Locke's notions into the concept of a separation of powers between divisions of government. The Canadian parliamentary system is based on these very principles.

Jean-Jacques Rousseau Swiss-French philosopher and political theorist Jean-Jacques Rousseau (1712–1778) further advanced the notion of the social contract in his treatise of that name (*Social Contract*, 1762), stating that human beings are basically good and fair in their natural state but historically were corrupted by the introduction of shared concepts and joint activities, such as property, agriculture, science, and commerce. As a result, the social contract emerged when civilized people agreed to establish governments and systems of education to correct the problems and inequalities brought on by the rise of civilization.

Rousseau also contributed to the notion of **natural law**, a concept originally formulated by St. Thomas Aquinas (1225–1274), Baruch Spinoza (1632–1677), and others to provide an intuitive basis for the defence of ethical principles and morality. Natural law was used by early Christian church leaders as a powerful argument in support of their interests. Submissive to the authority of the church, secular rulers were pressed to reinforce church doctrine in any laws they decreed. Aquinas wrote in his *Summa Theologica* that any human-made law that contradicts natural law is corrupt in the eyes of God. Hence, natural law was incorporated into English common law throughout the Middle Ages.

Rousseau agreed with earlier writers that certain immutable laws are fundamental to human nature and can be readily ascertained through reason. Human-made law (or "positive law"), in contrast, derives from human experience and history, both of which are subject to continual change, and thus changes from time to time and from

Natural law The philosophical perspective that certain immutable laws are fundamental to human nature and can be readily ascertained through reason. Human-made laws, in contrast, are said to derive from human experience and history—both of which are subject to continual change.

epoch to epoch. Rousseau expanded the concept of natural law to support emerging democratic principles.

Natural rights Rights that, according to natural law theorists, individuals retain in the face of government action and interests.

Thomas Paine   Thomas Paine (1737–1809), an English-American political theorist and author of *The Rights of Man* (1791 and 1792), defended the French Revolution, arguing that only democratic institutions could guarantee individuals' **natural rights**. For example, commentators have cited the "crimes against humanity" committed by Nazis during World War II as indicative of natural law principles. The chilling testimony of Rudolf Hess,[12] Hitler's deputy, during the 1945 war crimes trial in Nuremberg, Germany, as he recalled the "Fuehrer's" order to exterminate millions of Jews indicates the extent of the planned "final solution":

> In the summer of 1941 I was summoned to Berlin to Reichsfuehrer SS Himmler to receive personal orders. He told me something to the effect—I do not remember the exact words—that the Fuehrer had given the order for a final solution of the Jewish question. We, the SS, must carry out that order. If it is not carried out now then the Jews will later on destroy the German people. He had chosen Auschwitz on account of its easy access by rail and also because the extensive site offered space for measures ensuring isolation.[13]

Although Hitler's Nazi Party made the law in Germany at the time, natural law supporters (largely in other countries) argued that Hitler's final solution to the Jewish "question" was inherently wrong and that any laws passed in furtherance of it were immoral and should have been struck down.

Although the concept of natural law has waned somewhat in influence over the past half century, many people today still maintain that the basis for various existing criminal laws can be found in immutable moral principles or some other identifiable aspect of the natural order. Modern-day advocates of natural law claim that it comes from outside the social group and that it is knowable through some form of revelation, intuition, or prophecy.

The debate over abortion is an example of modern-day use of natural law arguments to support both sides in the dispute. Those who oppose abortion (frequently called "pro-lifers" or "right-to-lifers") claim that an unborn fetus is a person, that he or she is entitled to all the protection we would give to any other living human being, and that such protection is basic and humane and lies in the natural relationship of one human being to another and within the relationship of a society to its children. Abortion advocates (also called "pro-choice") maintain that abortion is a right of any pregnant woman, because she is the only one who should be in control of her body, and claim that the legal system must address the abortion question by offering protection for this natural right.

5.3   **LEARNING OBJECTIVE**

THE CLASSICAL SCHOOL

THE ENLIGHTENMENT FUELLED THE FIRES OF SOCIAL CHANGE, LEADING EVENTUALLY TO the French and American revolutions. It also inspired other social movements and freed innovative thinkers from the chains of convention. As a direct consequence of Enlightenment thinking, superstitious beliefs were discarded and men and women began to be perceived, for the first time, as self-determining entities possessing a fundamental freedom of choice; free will and rational thought came to be recognized as the linchpins of all significant human activity. In effect, the Enlightenment inspired the re-examination of existing doctrines of human behaviour from the point of view of rationalism.

Within criminology, the Enlightenment led to the development of the **classical school** of criminological thought. Crime and deviance, which had been previously explained by reference to mythological influences and spiritual shortcomings, took their place in Enlightenment thought alongside other forms of human activity as products of the exercise of free will. Once people were seen as having control over their lives, crime came to be explained as a particularly individualized form of evil—that is, as a moral wrongdoing fed by personal choice.

Classical school A criminological perspective of the late 18th and early 19th centuries that had its roots in the Enlightenment and held that men and women are rational beings, that crime is the result of the exercise of free will, and that punishment can be effective in reducing the incidence of crime to the degree that it negates the pleasure to be derived from crime commission.

Cesare Beccaria

Cesare Beccaria (1738–1794) was born in Milan, Italy, the eldest of four children; he was trained at Catholic schools and earned a doctor of law degree by the time he was 20. In 1764, Beccaria published his *Essay on Crimes and Punishments*, which consisted of 42 short chapters covering a few major themes to communicate his observations on the laws and justice system of his time. In the *Essay*, Beccaria distilled the notion of the social contract into the idea that "laws are the conditions under which independent and isolated men united to form a society."[14] More than anything else, his writings consisted of a philosophy of punishment. Beccaria claimed that the purpose of punishment should be deterrence rather than retribution, and punishment should be imposed to prevent offenders from committing additional crimes. Beccaria saw punishment as a means to an end and not an end in itself, and crime prevention was more important to him than revenge.

To help prevent crimes, Beccaria argued, adjudication and punishment should be both swift and, once punishment is decreed, certain: "The more promptly and the more closely punishment follows upon the commission of a crime, the more just and useful it will be." Punishment that is imposed immediately following crime commission, according to Beccaria, is connected with the wrongfulness of the offence, both in the mind of the offender and in the minds of others who might see the punishment imposed and thereby learn of the consequences of involvement in criminal activity.

Beccaria concluded that punishment should be only severe enough to outweigh the personal benefits to be derived from crime commission and that any additional punishment would be superfluous. "In order," he said, "for punishment not to be, in every instance, an act of violence of one or of many against a private citizen, it must be essentially public, prompt, necessary, the least possible in the given circumstances, proportionate to the crimes, [and] dictated by the laws."

Beccaria distinguished among three types of crimes: those that threatened the security of the state, those that injured citizens or their property, and those that ran contrary to the social order. Punishment should fit the crime—theft should be punished through fines, personal injury through corporal punishment, and serious crimes against the state (such as inciting revolution) via application of the death penalty. (Beccaria was opposed to the death penalty in most other circumstances, seeing it as a kind of warfare waged by society against its citizens.)

Beccaria condemned the torture of suspects, a practice still used in the 18th century, saying that it was a device that ensured that weak suspects would incriminate themselves, whereas strong ones would be found innocent. Torture was also unjust because it punished individuals before they had been found guilty in a court of law. In Beccaria's words,

> No man can be called guilty before a judge has sentenced him, nor can society deprive him of public protection before it has been decided that he has in fact violated the conditions under which such protection was accorded him. What right is it then, if not simply that of might, which empowers a judge to inflict punishment on a citizen while doubt still remains as to his guilt or innocence?

Beccaria's *Essay* touched upon a variety of other topics. He distinguished, for example, between two types of proof: "perfect proof," where there was no possibility of innocence, and "imperfect proof," where some possibility of innocence remained. Beccaria also believed in the efficacy of a jury of one's peers, recommending that half of any jury panel consist of the victim's peers and half consist of the accused's peers.

Beccaria's ideas were widely recognized as progressive by his contemporaries. His principles were incorporated into the French penal code of 1791 and significantly influenced the justice-related activities of European leaders such as Catherine the Great of Russia, Frederick the Great of Prussia, Emperor Joseph II of Austria, and the framers of the American Constitution. Perhaps more than anyone else, Beccaria is responsible for the contemporary belief that criminals have control over their behaviour, that they choose to commit crimes, and that they can be deterred by the threat of punishment.

Jeremy Bentham

Jeremy Bentham (1748–1832), another founder of the classical school, wrote in his *Introduction to the Principles of Morals and Legislation* (1789) that "nature has placed mankind under the governance of two sovereign masters, pain and pleasure."[15] To reduce crime, or, as Bentham put it, "to prevent the happening of mischief," the pain of crime commission must outweigh the pleasure to be derived from criminal activity. Bentham's claim rested upon his belief, spawned by Enlightenment thought, that human beings are fundamentally rational and that criminals will weigh in their minds the pain of punishment against any pleasures thought likely to be derived from crime commission.

Bentham advocated neither extreme nor cruel punishment—only punishment sufficiently distasteful to the offender that the discomfort experienced would outweigh the pleasure to be derived from criminal activity. The more serious the offence is, the more reward it holds for its perpetrator and therefore the more weighty the official response must be. "Pain and pleasure," said Bentham, "are the instruments the legislator has to work with" in controlling anti-social and criminal behaviour.

Hedonistic calculus or utilitarianism The belief, first proposed by Jeremy Bentham, that behaviour holds value to any individual undertaking according to the amount of pleasure or pain that it can be expected to produce for that person.

Bentham's approach has been termed **hedonistic calculus or utilitarianism** because of its emphasis on the worth any action holds for an individual undertaking it. Bentham stated, "By the principle of utility is meant that principle which approves or disapproves of every action whatsoever, according to the tendency which it appears to have to augment or diminish the happiness of the party whose interest is in question; or, what is the same thing . . . to promote or to oppose that happiness." In other words, Bentham believed that individuals could be expected to weigh the consequences of their behaviour before acting to maximize their pleasure and minimize their pain, based on intensity, duration, certainty, and immediacy (or remoteness) in time.

Like Beccaria, Bentham focused on the potential held by punishment to prevent crime and to act as a deterrent for those considering criminal activity. Regarding criminal legislation, he wrote that "the evils of punishment must be made to exceed the advantage of the offence."

Utilitarianism is a practical philosophy, and Bentham was quite practical in his suggestions about crime prevention. He recommended the creation of a centralized police force focused on crime prevention and control—a recommendation that found life in the English *Metropolitan Police Act* of 1829, which established London's New Police under the direction of Sir Robert Peel. This model of policing was adopted in the creation of Canada's first national police force in 1867, the Dominion Police Force.

Bentham's other major contribution to criminology was his suggestion that prisons be designed along the lines of what he called a "Panopticon House." The

Jeremy Bentham (1748–1832), whose work is closely associated with the classical school of criminology. What are the key features of the classical school?

Georgios Kollidas/Fotolia

Panopticon was to be a circular building with cells along the circumference, each clearly visible from a central location staffed by guards. Panopticons were to be constructed near or within cities so that they might serve as an example to citizens of what would happen to them should they commit crimes. Bentham also wrote that prisons should be managed by contractors who could profit from the labour of prisoners and that the contractor should "be bound to insure the lives and safe custody of those entrusted to him." Although a Panopticon was never built in Bentham's England, French officials funded a modified version of such a prison, which was eventually built at Lyon, and three prisons modelled after the Panopticon concept were constructed in the United States.

Bentham's critics have been quick to point out that punishment often does not seem to work and that even punishment as severe as death appears not to have any effect on the incidence of crimes such as murder (discussed in greater detail later in this chapter). Such critics forget Bentham's second tenet: For punishment to be effective, "it must be swift and certain."

Panopticon A prison designed by Jeremy Bentham that was to be a circular building with cells along the circumference, each clearly visible from a central location staffed by guards.

Heritage of the Classical School

The classical school was to influence criminological thinking for a long time and has been instrumental in moulding the way in which thinkers on the subject of crime have viewed the topic for more than 200 years. The heritage left by the classical school is still operative today in the following five principles:

1. *Rationality:* Human beings have free will and the actions they undertake are the result of choice.
2. *Hedonism:* Pleasure and pain, or reward and punishment, are the major determinants of choice.
3. *Punishment:* Criminal punishment is a deterrent to unlawful behaviour, and deterrence is the best justification for punishment.

4. *Human rights:* Society is made possible by individuals cooperating together. Hence, society owes to its citizens respect for their rights in the face of government action and for their autonomy insofar as such autonomy can be secured without endangering others or menacing the greater good.

5. *Due process:* An accused should be presumed innocent until proven otherwise, and an accused should not be subject to punishment before guilt is lawfully established.

Some of these concepts are easily recognizable in the *Canadian Charter of Rights and Freedoms*, the *Criminal Code of Canada*, and the *Youth Criminal Justice Act*.

5.4 | LEARNING OBJECTIVE

NEOCLASSICAL CRIMINOLOGY

Positivism The application of scientific techniques to the study of crime and criminals.

Hard determinism The belief that crime results from forces beyond the control of the individual.

Neoclassical criminology A contemporary version of classical criminology that emphasizes deterrence and retribution, with reduced emphasis on rehabilitation.

BY THE END OF THE 19TH CENTURY, CLASSICAL CRIMINOLOGY, WITH ITS EMPHASIS ON FREE will and individual choice as the root causes of crime, had given way to another approach known as *positivism*. **Positivism** (discussed in greater detail in Chapter 6) made use of the scientific method in studying criminality and was based on an acceptance of **hard determinism**, the belief that crime results from forces beyond the control of the individual. The original positivists completely rejected the notion of free will and turned their attention to the impact of socialization, genetics, economic conditions, peer group influences, and other factors that might determine criminality. Acceptance of the notion of hard determinism implied that offenders were not entirely (if at all) responsible for their crimes and suggested that crime could be prevented by changing the conditions that produced criminality.

While positivism remains an important component of contemporary criminology, many of its assumptions were undermined in the 1970s by (1) studies that seemed to show that offenders could not be rehabilitated no matter what was tried, (2) a growing and widespread public fear of crime that led to "get tough on crime" policies, and (3) a cultural reaffirmation of the belief that human beings had a rational nature. The resulting resurgence of classical ideals, called **neoclassical criminology**, focused on the importance of character (a kind of middle ground between total free will and hard determinism) and the dynamics of character development, as well as the rational choices that people make when faced with opportunities for crime.

The neoclassical movement appears to have had its start with a number of publications produced in the 1970s, such as Robert Martinson's national survey of rehabilitation programs.[16] In an often-quoted article entitled "What Works?" Martinson found that, when it came to the rehabilitation of offenders, nothing seemed to work, as most resumed their criminal careers after release from prison. "Nothing works!" became a rallying cry of conservative policy-makers, and the nothing-works doctrine received much public attention. Many conservative politicians and some criminologists began calling existing notions of crime prevention and rehabilitation into question and claimed that enhanced job skills, increased opportunities for employment, and lessened punishment did nothing to stem what was a rising tide of crime.

In 1975, political scientist James Q. Wilson wrote *Thinking about Crime*, suggesting that crime is not a result of poverty or social conditions and cannot be affected by social programs.[17] He argued for the lengthy incarceration of offenders and for the elimination of criminal opportunity. Also in 1975, David Fogel published a book called *We Are the Living Proof: The Justice Model of Corrections*.[18] His justice model was predicated on the growing belief that prisons do not rehabilitate or cure and that criminal offenders *deserve* punishment because of the choices they make. Fogel argued that, for the criminal justice process to work, offenders must be treated "as responsible as well as accountable, that is, volitional."[19] The American "three-strikes legislation," which mandates life imprisonment for criminals convicted of three violent felonies or serious drug offences, is a reflection of the justice model.

Rational Choice Theory

Rational choice theory, a product of the 1980s, mirrors many of the principles found in classical criminology. The theory, as described by Ronald V. Clarke and Derek B. Cornish,[20] rests upon the belief that individuals make a conscious, rational, and at least partially informed choice to commit crime and employs cost-benefit analysis (as in the field of economics), viewing human behaviour as the result of personal choices made after weighing both the costs and the benefits of available alternatives. "[Rational choice] predicts that individuals choose to commit crime when the benefits outweigh the costs of disobeying the law. Crime will decrease when opportunities are limited, benefits are reduced, and costs are increased."[21]

Two varieties of rational choice theory can be identified. One builds on an emerging emphasis on victimization and is called **routine activities theory or lifestyle theory**; the second, largely an extension of the rational choice perspective, is called **situational choice theory**.

Routine activities theory was proposed by Lawrence E. Cohen and Marcus Felson in 1979.[22] Cohen and Felson stated that lifestyles contribute significantly to both the volume and the type of crime found in any society and suggested that changes in American society during the 1960s and 1970s (specifically increased personal affluence and greater involvement in social activities outside the home) brought about increased rates of household theft and personal victimization by strangers. Central to the routine activities approach is the claim that crime is likely to occur when a motivated offender and a suitable victim come together in the absence of a "capable guardian," meaning one who effectively discourages crime, and that a person who has taken crime-prevention steps is less likely to be victimized. According to Cohen and Felson, "The risk of criminal victimization varies dramatically among the circumstances and locations in which people place themselves and their property."[23] For example, a person who routinely uses an automated teller machine late at night in an isolated location is far more likely to be preyed upon by robbers than is someone who stays home after dark. Lifestyles that contribute to criminal opportunities are likely to result in crime because they increase the risk of potential victimization.[24]

Although a non-criminal lifestyle at certain points of one's lifetime are in part due to unavoidable social roles and assigned social positions, those who participate in a given lifestyle generally make rational decisions about specific behaviours (such as going to a particular automated teller machine at a certain time). The same is true of criminal lifestyles. Hence, the meshing of choices made by both victims and criminals contributes significantly to both the frequency and the type of criminal activity observed in society. See the Crime in the News box for an examination of a Canadian geographic profiling system used to track down criminals that is based on this notion of routine activities.

In a later work, Felson suggested that a number of "situational insights" might combine to elicit a criminal response from individual actors enmeshed in a highly varied social world, pointing out that "individuals vary greatly in their behaviour from one situation to another" and that criminality might flow from temptation, bad company, idleness, or provocation.[25] Convenience stores, for example, create temptations toward theft when they display their merchandise within easy reach of customers. Other authors have defined the term *situation* to mean "the perceptive field of the

Rational choice theory A perspective holding that criminality is the result of conscious choice and predicting that individuals choose to commit crime when the benefits outweigh the costs of disobeying the law.

Routine activities theory or lifestyle theory A brand of rational choice theory posited by Lawrence Cohen and Marcus Felson that suggests that lifestyles contribute significantly to both the volume and the type of crime found in any society.

Mapping Out Sex Crimes Arrest

An alleged sexual predator on the loose for a year was snared by geo-profiling.

Sex Crimes Unit investigators called upon D/Const Manny San Pedro, a geographic profiling analyst at Corporate Planning, to put his knowledge to work on a long series of occurrences involving a man exposing himself to children.

Over the course of a year, there had been 20 similar occurrences in North York and Scarborough, in which a man drove up to early-teen and preteen girls and exposed himself while in his vehicle.

"It had become an issue," said lead investigator Sex Crimes Unit Det. Kim Hancock, noting the man had been targeting young girls quite often. Area schools sent out notices to parents while police issued news releases.

"Escalation of his behaviour was a community concern." There was a partial licence plate, a description of the vehicle and a composite picture of the suspect but all efforts to identify and find him had yielded nothing.

The mapping system shows hot spots where the suspect allegedly exposed himself to children.

The Badge, Newspaper of the Toronto Police Service

After putting together his profile of coloured maps and graphs using the Rigel Analyst software, San Pedro was left with a 292 square-kilometre area, crisscrossed by highways 404 and 401, to find a place where the man would strike again. Two distinct areas where occurrences had occurred stood out. He identified a peak area of seven square kilometres.

Adding the schools in the area and a five-minute walking buffer around them for children walking home, he was left with a good target area for investigators.

"You identify the routine activity space for potential victims," he said, of looking for a future occurrence.

"By the offender's behaviour so far, he's likely to return to that area," said San Pedro, who also looked for times the offender struck when children were en route to and from school.

Because the case qualified as a sex crime and was more complex, San Pedro consulted with Ontario Provincial Police geoprofiler D/Sgt Brad Moore who offered his advice on the case.

San Pedro prescribed a one-month project, targeting the areas on specific days of the week at certain times of day, briefing officers from 33 and 41 Divisions where the crimes had taken place and handing them a geo-profile package.

"You could see the pattern, certain days and school hours," Hancock said. "Manny inputted all the information, got rid of the peripheral stuff and gave us an area to focus on."

Teams of officers were then dispatched to the roads San Pedro had highlighted as potential offender trolling areas.

Within 33 minutes of setting up on a driveway at a street, Consts. Jessica McInnis and Colleen Sweetnam, 41 Division's school liaison officers, saw a van matching the description pass them. They followed the van and eventually pulled it over after the man is alleged to have driven for several blocks.

Hancock said the profile helped focus the search.

"It was wonderful," Hancock said, of the profile. "It helped focus us. We had officers driving around a bigger catchment area the week before."

The man is charged with invitation to sexual touching, criminal harassment and dangerous operation of a motor vehicle, four counts of exposure to person under 14 years, and 10 counts of indecent act.

"It's great to see we can net some good results," San Pedro said. "The analysts don't solve crimes, we provide investigative leads—it's all about the strategic deployment of resources so you're not wasting our efforts."

He said gathering more eyewitness accounts and other evidence makes the geo-mapping process more powerful because it thrives off information. He said the open lines of communication between himself and Sex Crimes investigators helped a great deal.

(Continued)

individual at a given point in time" and have suggested that it "can be described in terms of who is there, what is going on, and where it is taking place."[26]

Situational choice theory provides an example of **soft determinism**, which views criminal behaviour "as a function of choices and decisions made within a context of situational constraints and opportunities."[27] The theory suggests that the probability of criminal activity can be reduced by changing the features of a given social situation or of the surrounding environment. Clarke and Cornish, collaborators in the development of the situational choice perspective, analyzed the choice-structuring properties of a potentially criminal situation, defining them as "the constellation of opportunities, costs, and benefits attaching to particular kinds of crime."[28] Clarke and Cornish suggested the use of situational strategies to lower the likelihood of criminal victimization in given instances. They also recognized that the rationality of criminal offenders is inevitably bounded or limited, as it is for all of us, by the amount and accuracy of information available to them at the time they are weighing the costs and consequences of future actions.[29]

In brief, rational choice theorists concentrate on "the decision-making process of offenders confronted with specific contexts . . . [shifting] the focus of the effort to prevent crime from broad social programs to target hardening, environmental design or any impediment that would [dissuade] a motivated offender from offending."[30]

Earlier approaches focused largely on the balance between pleasure and pain as the primary determinant or preventative of criminal behaviour, whereas rational choice theory tends to place less emphasis on pleasure and emotionality and more on rationality and cognition. Some rational choice theorists distinguish among the types of choices offenders make as they move toward criminal involvement. One type of choice, known as *involvement decisions*, has been described as "multi-stage" and is said to "include the initial decision to engage in criminal activity as well as subsequent decisions to continue one's involvement or to desist."[31] Another type of choice, event decisions, relates to particular instances of criminal opportunity (such as the decision to rob a particular person or to let him or her pass); in contrast to involvement decisions, which may take months or even years to reach, event decisions are usually made quickly.

Situational Crime-Control Policy Building on the work of rational and situational choice theorists, Israeli criminologist David Weisburd described the advantages of a situational approach to crime prevention:

Crime prevention research and policy have traditionally been concerned with offenders or potential offenders. Researchers have looked to define strategies that would deter individuals from involvement in crime or rehabilitate them so they

Situational choice theory A brand of rational choice theory that views criminal behaviour "as a function of choices and decisions made within a context of situational constraints and opportunities."

Soft determinism The belief that human behaviour is the result of choices and decisions made within a context of situational constraints and opportunities.

would no longer want to commit criminal acts. In recent years crime prevention efforts have often focused on the incapacitation of high-rate or dangerous offenders so they are not free to victimize law-abiding citizens. In the public debate over crime prevention policies, these strategies are usually defined as competing approaches.[32]

However, Weisburd pointed out that "they have in common a central assumption about crime prevention research and policy: that efforts to understand and control crime must begin with the offender. In all of these approaches, the focus of crime prevention is on people and their involvement in criminality."

A new approach developed in large part as a response to the failures of traditional theories and programs. "Although this assumption [the focus on people] continues to dominate crime prevention research and policy," said Weisburd, "it has begun to be challenged by a very different approach that seeks to shift the focus of crime prevention efforts." For many scholars and policy-makers, this meant having to rethink assumptions about criminality and how offenders might be prevented from participating in crime, with some suggesting that a more radical reorientation of crime-prevention efforts was warranted. They argued that the shift must come not in terms of the specific strategies or theories that are used, but in terms of the unit of analysis that forms the basis of crime-prevention efforts. Rather than focusing on people who commit crime, they called for an emphasis on the context in which crime occurs.

Situational crime prevention A social policy approach that looks to develop greater understanding of crime and more effective crime-prevention strategies through concern with the physical, organizational, and social environments that make crime possible.

This approach, which is called **situational crime prevention**, looks to develop greater understanding of crime and more effective crime-prevention strategies through concern with the physical, organizational, and social environments that make crime possible.[33] The situational approach does not ignore offenders; it merely places them as one part of a broader crime-prevention equation that is centred on the context of crime. It demands a shift in the approach to crime prevention from one concerned primarily with why people commit crime to one that looks primarily at why crime occurs in specific settings. It moves the context of crime into central focus and sees the offender as only one of a number of factors that affect it. Situational crime prevention is closely associated with the idea of a "criminology of place," discussed in Chapter 8.

Weisburd suggested that a "reorientation of crime prevention research and policy from the causes of criminality to the context of crime provides much promise. . . . At the core of situational prevention is the concept of opportunity."[34] In contrast to offender-based approaches to crime prevention, which usually focus on the dispositions of criminals, situational crime prevention begins with the opportunity structure of the crime situation, meaning the immediate situational and environmental components of the context of crime. This approach to crime prevention tries to reduce the opportunities for crime in specific situations through efforts as simple and straightforward as **target hardening** or access control.

Target hardening The reduction in criminal opportunity for a particular location, generally through the use of physical barriers, architectural design, and enhanced security measures.

The value of a situational approach lies in the fact that criminologists have found it difficult to identify who is likely to become a serious offender or to predict the timing and types of future offences that repeat offenders are likely to commit. Weisburd explained that "legal and ethical dilemmas make it difficult to base criminal justice policies on models that still include a substantial degree of statistical error." He added that "if traditional approaches worked well, of course, there would be little pressure to find new forms of crime prevention. If traditional approaches worked well, few people would possess criminal motivation and fewer still would actually commit crimes."

Situational prevention advocates argue that the context of crime provides a promising alternative to traditional offender-based crime-prevention policies.[35] They assume that situations provide a more stable and predictable focus for crime-prevention efforts than do persons. In part, this assumption develops from common-sense notions of the relationship between opportunities and crime. Shoplifting, for example, is by definition clustered in stores and not residences, and family disputes are unlikely to be a problem outside of the home. High-crime places, in contrast to high-crime people, cannot flee to avoid criminal justice intervention, and crime that develops from the specific characteristics of certain places cannot be easily transferred to other contexts.

In short, situational crime control works by removing or reducing criminal opportunity. If we accept that opportunity is a cause of crime equal in importance to the personal and social characteristics that other researchers point to as causes, then much of the crime-prevention work that is already being done by police agencies, private security, and businesses aimed at reducing criminal opportunity directly affects the basic causes. The Crime Prevention Through Environmental Design (CPTED) approach is one used by police services across Canada; it is discussed in more detail in Chapter 11.

Critique of Rational Choice Theory   Rational and situational choice theories (as well as routine activities theory) can be criticized for an overemphasis on individual choice and a relative disregard for the role of social factors in crime causation, such as poverty, poor home environment, and inadequate socialization. According to one study, rational choice theory does not adequately consider the impact of emotional states on cognitive ability and the role of psychopharmacological agents in decision making.[36] The study examined the effects of alcohol and anger on aggression and found that "alcohol diminishes individuals' perceptions of the costs associated with aggression and, in some instances, actually increases the perceived benefits." Similarly, high arousal levels, such as those associated with anger and other emotions, appear to impair judgment. So, when acting under the influence of alcohol or when experiencing strong emotions, "the individual's capacity to anticipate gratification and aversion, success and failure, and cost is diminished."[37] The authors note that other studies show that approximately 40 percent of offenders are under the influence of alcohol when committing the crimes for which they are arrested and suggest that future research involving the rational choice perspective should include the role of emotions and the potential impact of psychopharmacological agents such as drugs or alcohol on the decisions made by people who commit crimes.

One 2005 study that explored the deterrent effect of punishment offers insight into the potential that rational choice theory holds for social policy. In that study, researchers examined how juvenile offenders respond to the likelihood of significantly higher sanctions associated with criminality when they reach adulthood.[38] They found that a 230 percent increase in expected sentence length was associated with only a 1.8 percent reduction in the likelihood of arrest, so they reasoned that even enormous increases in sentence length seem to do little to reduce the probability of repeat offending: "The small behavioral responses that we estimate suggest that potential offenders are extremely impatient, myopic, or both."[39]

Rational choice theory seems to assume that everyone is equally capable of making rational decisions when such is probably not the case. Some individuals are more logical by virtue of temperament, personality, or socialization, whereas others are emotional, hotheaded, and unthinking. Empirical studies of rational choice theory have added scant support for the perspective's underlying assumptions, tending to show instead that criminal offenders are often unrealistic in their appraisals of the relative risks and rewards facing them.[40] Similarly, rational and situational choice theories seem to disregard individual psychology and morality with their emphasis on external situations; moral individuals, when faced with easy criminal opportunities, may rein in their desires and turn their backs on temptation, say critics.

Finally, the emphasis of rational and situational choice theories upon changing aspects of the immediate situation to reduce crime has been criticized for resulting in the **displacement** of crime from one area to another.[41] Target hardening,[42] a key crime-prevention strategy advocated by such theorists, has sometimes caused criminals to find new targets of opportunity in other areas.[43]

Displacement   A shift of criminal activity from one spatial location to another.

PUNISHMENT AND NEOCLASSICAL THOUGHT

PUNISHMENT IS A CENTRAL FEATURE OF BOTH CLASSICAL AND NEOCLASSICAL THOUGHT. Whereas punishment served the ends of deterrence in classical thought, its role in neoclassical thinking has been expanded to support the ancient concept of retribution. Those advocating retribution see the primary utility of punishment as revenge.

Modern neoclassical thinkers argue that, if a person is attracted to crime and chooses to violate the law, then he or she *deserves* to be punished because the consequences of the crime were known to the offender before the crime was committed. Moreover, the criminal *must* be punished so that future criminal behaviour can be curtailed.

Notions of revenge and retribution are morally based on a sense of indignation at criminal behaviour and on the sense of righteousness inherent in Judeo-Christian notions of morality and propriety. Both philosophies of punishment turn a blind eye to the mundane and practical consequences of any particular form of punishment. Hence, advocates of retributive philosophies of punishment easily dismiss critics of the death penalty, who frequently challenge the efficacy of court-ordered capital punishment on the basis that such sentences do little to deter others. Wider issues, including general deterrence, become irrelevant when a person focuses narrowly on the emotions that crime and victimization engender in a given instance. From the neoclassical perspective, some crimes cry out for vengeance while others demand little more than a slap on the wrist or an apology from the offender.

Just Deserts

Just deserts model The notion that criminal offenders deserve the punishment they receive at the hands of the law and that punishments should be appropriate to the type and severity of the crime committed.

The old adage "he got what was coming to him" well summarizes the thinking behind the **just deserts model** of criminal sentencing, which refers to the concept that criminal offenders deserve the punishment they receive at the hands of the law and that any punishment that is imposed should be appropriate to the type and severity of crime committed. The idea of just deserts has long been a part of Western thought, dating back at least to Old Testament times. The Old Testament dictum of "an eye for an eye, and a tooth for a tooth" has been cited by many as divine justification for strict punishments, although some scholars believe that in reality the notion of "an eye for an eye" was intended to *reduce* the barbarism of existing penalties, whereby an aggrieved party might exact the severest of punishments for only minor offences (even petty offences were often punished by whipping, torture, and sometimes death).

According to the neoclassical perspective, doing justice ultimately comes down to an official meting out of what is deserved. Justice for an individual is nothing more or less than what that individual deserves when all the circumstances surrounding that person's situation and behaviour are taken into account.

Deterrence

Deterrence The prevention of crime.

Specific deterrence A goal of criminal sentencing that seeks to prevent a particular offender from engaging in repeat criminality.

General deterrence A goal of criminal sentencing that seeks to prevent others from committing crimes similar to the one for which a particular offender is being sentenced.

True to its historical roots, **deterrence** is a hallmark of modern neoclassical thought. In contrast to early thinkers, however, today's neoclassical writers distinguish between specific deterrence and general deterrence. **Specific deterrence** is a goal of criminal sentencing that seeks to prevent a particular offender from engaging in repeat criminality. **General deterrence** works by way of example, seeking to prevent others from committing crimes similar to the one for which a particular offender is being sentenced.

Following their classical counterparts, modern-day advocates of general deterrence frequently stress that for punishment to be an effective impediment to crime, it must be swift, certain, and severe enough to outweigh the rewards flowing from criminal activity. Those who advocate punishment as a deterrent are often frustrated by the complexity of today's criminal justice system and the slow and circuitous manner in which cases are handled and punishments are meted out. Punishments today, even when imposed by a court, are rarely swift in their imposition; the wheels of modern criminal justice are relatively slow to grind to a conclusion, given the many delays inherent in judicial proceedings and the numerous opportunities for postponement and appeal. Certainty of punishment is also anything but a reality. Certain punishments are those that cannot be easily avoided, but even when punishments are ordered, they are frequently not carried out—at least not fully.

If the neoclassicists are correct, ideally, criminal punishments should prevent a repetition of crime or **recidivism**—the repetition of criminal behaviour by those already involved in crime. The definition of recidivism becomes more complicated when the question of what constitutes this repeat criminal behaviour is considered. Does recidivism refer to the perpetration of a new offence? To a return to the criminal justice system? Or to a return to the correctional system? Does it include any breach of release conditions or only a breach of the most serious conditions?[44] Despite the definitional challenges, recidivism can also be used to measure the success of a given approach to the problem of crime. When so employed, it is referred to as a **recidivism rate**, expressed as the percentage of convicted offenders who have been released from a correctional facility and who are later rearrested for a new crime or a violation of the conditions of their release (known as a *technical violation*). While the public perception is that recidivism rates in Canada are high, the reality is somewhat different. In the last comprehensive study issued by the Canadian federal government, offenders were tracked for up to two years after their release into the community. The study found that the reconviction rate for offenders released from federal institutions was 43 percent. Non-violent offences accounted for the majority of reconvictions. The violent reconviction rate was 13 percent, while the sexual reconviction rate was very low, at 0.7–1.7 percent. The study also indicated that more than half of the reconvictions occurred after the sentence was completed when the offender was no longer under supervision.[45]

Recidivism The repetition of criminal behaviour.

Recidivism rate The percentage of convicted offenders who have been released from prison and who are later rearrested for a new crime.

The Death Penalty

Notions of deterrence, retribution, and just deserts all come together in **capital punishment**, the legal imposition of a death sentence. The many different understandings of crime and crime control, along with arguments over free will and social determinism, combine with varying philosophies of punishment to produce considerable disagreement over the efficacy of death as a form of criminal sanction.

Capital punishment The legal imposition of a sentence of death upon a convicted offender.

Opponents of capital punishment make 10 claims:

1. Capital punishment does not deter crime.
2. The death penalty has been imposed on innocent people, and no workable system is currently in place to prevent the accidental execution of innocents (see the Crime in the News box for cases of wrongful imprisonment).
3. Human life, even the life of a murderer, is sacred.
4. State-imposed death lowers society to the same moral (or amoral) level as the murderer.
5. The death penalty has been (and may still be) imposed in haphazard and seemingly random fashion.
6. The death penalty is imposed disproportionately upon ethnic minorities.
7. Capital punishment goes against the most fundamental precepts of almost every organized religion.
8. The death penalty is more expensive than imprisonment.
9. Capital punishment is internationally viewed as inhumane and barbaric.
10. There is a better alternative (usually said to be life in prison without possibility of parole).

Advocates of capital punishment generally discount each of these claims, countering with the notion that death is *deserved* by those who commit especially heinous acts and that anything short of capital punishment under certain circumstances is an injustice in itself; some people deserve to die for what they have done. Such arguments have evolved from a natural law perspective, are sometimes supported on religious grounds, and are based on the notion of just deserts (discussed earlier).

Strong feelings on both sides of the issue have generated a plethora of studies of the efficacy and fairness of capital punishment as a criminal sanction. The extent to which the death penalty acts as a general deterrent has been widely examined. Some researchers have compared murder rates between U.S. states that have eliminated the death penalty and those that have retained it, finding little variation in the rate at which murders are committed.[46] Others have looked at variations in murder rates over time in jurisdictions that have eliminated capital punishment, with similar results.[47] In an important recent study of the deterrent effect of capital punishment, researchers found "no empirical support for the argument that the existence or application of the death penalty deters offenders from committing homicide."[48] The study made use of homicide data from all 50 U.S. states and the District of Columbia between the years 1977 and 2006, and the study's design allowed researchers both to assess the impact of changes in capital punishment laws and to compare murder rates in death-penalty jurisdictions with those without capital punishment laws. Regardless of studies to the contrary, many death-penalty advocates remain unconvinced that the sanction cannot be an effective deterrent, saying that a death penalty that is swift and certain is likely to deter others.

While capital punishment has not been legal in Canada since 1976, there are some Canadians who would like to see its reinstatement. It is practised in many states in the United States and in other countries, including Japan, India, and China.

Canada's Wrongful Convictions: Cases Where the Courts Got It Wrong

Code of Canada, enable the justice minister to use his or her discretion to respond to persons who believe they have been wrongfully convicted.

Groups such as the Association in Defence of the Wrongfully Convicted have also advocated on behalf of those they say have been jailed unfairly.

Here are some of the major cases in recent Canadian history:

Donald Marshall Jr.

In 1971, Marshall was wrongfully convicted of murdering his friend, Sandy Seale, in a Sydney, N.S., park. Marshall was just 17 years old when he received a life sentence.

He was released in 1982 after RCMP reviewed his case. He was cleared by the Nova Scotia Court of Appeal the following year. Though the Appeal Court declared him not guilty, Marshall was told he had contributed to his own conviction and that any miscarriage of justice was more apparent than real.

Marshall, a Mi'kmaq, was exonerated by a royal commission in 1990 that determined systemic racism had contributed to his wrongful imprisonment. The seven-volume report pointed the finger at police, judges, Marshall's original defence lawyers, Crown lawyers and bureaucrats.

Roy Ebsary, an eccentric who bragged about being skilled with knives, was eventually convicted of manslaughter in Seale's death and spent a year in jail.

Marshall died in a Sydney hospital in August 2009 after a lengthy illness. He was 55.

David Milgaard

Milgaard was charged with the 1969 murder of Saskatoon nursing aide Gail Miller and in January 1970 was sentenced to life in prison. Appeals to the Saskatchewan Court of Appeal and Supreme Court of Canada in the two years after his conviction were unsuccessful.

Milgaard's mother, Joyce, believed from the day he was arrested that her son was innocent. She kept his case alive, talking to whoever would listen—and many who didn't—while he spent more than two decades in prison.

In 1991, Justice Minister Kim Campbell directed the Supreme Court of Canada to review the conviction. The Supreme Court of Canada set it aside in 1992, and Milgaard was subsequently cleared by DNA evidence five years later.

The Saskatchewan government awarded Milgaard $10 million for his wrongful conviction in 1999. That same year, Larry Fisher was found guilty of the rape and stabbing death of Gail Miller.

A provincial judicial inquiry, which released a comprehensive 815-page report in September 2008, concluded that "the criminal justice system failed David Milgaard." The inquiry also found that Milgaard might have been released from jail years sooner if police had followed up on a lead they received in 1980.

Guy Paul Morin

Christine Jessop, a nine-year-old girl, disappeared from her Queensville, Ont., home in October 1984. Her body was found in a farmer's field two months later. Guy Paul Morin, the Jessops' next-door neighbour in the community about 60 km north of Toronto, was later charged with her murder.

Morin was acquitted in 1986, but a new trial was ordered by the Ontario Court of Appeal. At this second trial, Morin was convicted and sentenced to life in prison. He appealed and in 1995 was exonerated by DNA testing.

A public inquiry into the case was called, and its report was tabled in 1998. It concluded that mistakes by the police, prosecutors and forensic scientists combined to send an innocent man to jail.

Steven Truscott

In 1959, Truscott was sentenced to be hanged at age 14 for a schoolmate's murder, becoming Canada's youngest death-row inmate. After the original conviction, he spent four months in the shadow of the gallows until his death sentence was commuted to life imprisonment. Paroled in 1969, Truscott disappeared into an anonymous existence in a southern Ontario city.

On August 28, 2007—48 years later—the Ontario Court of Appeal unanimously overturned Truscott's conviction and acquitted him, declaring the case "a miscarriage of justice" that "must be quashed." The judges went on to say, however, that "the court is not satisfied that the appellant has been able to demonstrate his factual innocence." In July 2008, the Ontario government announced it would pay Truscott $6.5 million in compensation for his ordeal.

Discussion Questions

1. Canada abolished capital punishment in 1976. If this criminal sanction had still been an option, what might have happened to these men?

2. How do cases of exoneration, like the ones described in this box, influence public opinion about capital punishment?

3. What are your feelings about capital punishment? Explain.

Source: Based on Canada's Wrongful Convictions: Cases Where The Courts Got It Wrong, Published by CBC News, © 2016

POLICY IMPLICATIONS OF THE CLASSICAL SCHOOL

DURING THE PAST SEVERAL DECADES, NORTH AMERICAN JUSTICE PHILOSOPHY HAS BEEN strongly influenced by the punishment practices of determinate sentencing and truth in sentencing. Because both determinate sentencing and truth in sentencing are rational forms of justice, most criminologists see them as natural consequences of a classical view of crime and punishment.

Determinate sentencing is a strategy that attempts to address the issue of sentencing certainty. This approach mandates a specific and fixed amount of time to be served for every offence category. Under determinate sentencing schemes, for example, judges might be required to impose seven-year sentences on offenders convicted of armed robbery but only one-year sentences on those convicted robbers who used no weapon. Determinate sentencing schemes build upon the two notions of classical thought: (1) the pleasure of a given crime can be somewhat accurately assessed, and (2) a fixed amount of punishment necessary for deterrence can be calculated and specified. Proponents contend that determinate sentences may also reduce sentencing bias since disparity based on race or social status would be eliminated. Canadian judges have voiced the concern that determinate sentencing models limit the amount of discretion or personal judgment they can exercise when meting out a sentence. It is unlikely that determinate sentencing models will be fully adopted in Canada, although increasing numbers of *Criminal Code* offences carry a mandatory minimum sentence from which Canadian judges cannot vary. Official statistics indicate that there were about 22 895 adults incarcerated in 2013–2014 (54 per 100 000), an increase of 3 percent since 2012–2013.[49] By comparison, in 2013 the state and federal prison population in the United States stood at 1 574 700 inmates, or approximately 570 per 100 000 in 2013.[50] See Chapter 11 for a further discussion of this "getting tough on crime" approach.

Truth in sentencing is a collection of different but related public policy stances on sentencing of those convicted of crimes in the justice system. In Canada, the *Truth in Sentencing Act* (Bill C-25) came into force in 2010. It amends s.719 of the *Criminal Code of Canada* by limiting the discretion of sentencing judges to give credit to individuals who have spent time incarcerated prior to conviction. Prior to this bill being implemented, credit for pre-sentencing custody (commonly referred to as "dead time") was frequently granted a two-for-one credit: for every day of incarceration prior to conviction, judges would credit two days on the sentence. As a result of Bill C-25, this credit is assessed at 1:1 and in some exceptional instances at 1.5:1. In the United States, truth in sentencing requires judges to assess and make public the actual time an offender is likely to serve, once sentenced to prison, and many recently enacted truth-in-sentencing laws require that offenders serve a large portion of their sentence (often 80 percent) before they can be released.

Imprisonment is one component of a strategy of **incapacitation** (the use of imprisonment or other means to reduce the likelihood that an offender will be capable of committing future offences). Proponents of modern-day incapacitation often distinguish between the terms *selective incapacitation*, in which crime is controlled via the imprisonment of specific individuals, and *collective incapacitation*, whereby changes in legislation and/or sentencing patterns lead to the removal from society of entire groups of individuals judged to be dangerous. Advocates of selective incapacitation as a crime-prevention strategy point to studies that show the majority of crimes are perpetrated by a small number of hard-core repeat offenders. The most famous of those studies, conducted by University of Pennsylvania professor Marvin Wolfgang, focused on 9000 men born in Philadelphia in 1945.[51] By the time this cohort of men had reached age 18, Wolfgang was able to determine that 627 "chronic recidivists" were responsible

Determinate sentencing A criminal punishment strategy that mandates a specified and fixed amount of time to be served for every offence category. Under the strategy, for example, all offenders convicted of the same degree of robbery would be sentenced to the same length of time behind bars.

Truth in sentencing A collection of different but related public policy stances on sentencing of those convicted of crimes in the justice system.

Incapacitation The use of imprisonment or other means to reduce the likelihood that an offender will be capable of committing future offences.

Criminal Behaviour: Rational Choice or Adrenalin Rush?

Following his arrest for the theft of a police car, Moonbeam Kittaro met with one of his friends in the visiting area of the local jail. Here's what he said:

> I stole a cop car and s***, was it exciting!
>
> I mean, the thing was just sitting there running in the parking lot with the keys in it. Who wouldn't take it?
>
> I've never been so high on pure adrenaline. It was an adrenaline rush being behind the wheel of that f***ing car.
>
> It turned my girlfriend on too.
>
> I drove over to her place with the lights and siren on, and as soon as she saw the car she wanted to go for a ride.
>
> We must have hit 140 on the Interstate!
>
> Then we pulled into a rest stop and made love in the back seat.
>
> It was the whole illegal thing that got her so excited.
>
> But that's when we got arrested.

The cops surrounded the car, guns drawn and all that s***.

We didn't even hear them coming.

Think about it:

1. Why did Kittaro steal the car? Do you think that he knew, before he stole it, that the theft would lead to so much excitement?

2. Can the desire for excitement explain crimes like Kittaro's? Can the same desire explain other kinds of crimes? If so, what might they be?

3. If excitement explains crime commission, then why doesn't everyone commit crime for the excitement that it brings?

4. What kinds of crime-prevention programs might be based on the principles illustrated here?

Note: This example is a fictionalized one intended to encourage critical thinking.

for the large majority of all serious violent crimes committed by the group. Other more recent studies have similarly shown that a small core of criminal perpetrators may be responsible for most criminal activity.

Such thinking has led to the development of incapacitation as a modern-day treatment philosophy and to the creation of innovative forms of incapacitation that do not require imprisonment, such as house arrest, use of halfway houses, or provision of career-training centres for convicted offenders. Similarly, such thinkers argue, the decriminalization of many offences and the enhancement of social programs designed to combat what they see as the root causes of crime—including poverty, low educational levels, general lack of skills, and inherent or active discrimination—will lead to a much reduced incidence of crime in the future, making high rates of imprisonment unnecessary.

CRITIQUE OF CLASSICAL THEORIES

5.7 | LEARNING OBJECTIVE

CLASSICAL AND NEOCLASSICAL THOUGHT REPRESENTS MORE A PHILOSOPHY OF JUSTICE than it does a theory of crime causation. As some writers have observed, however, "the true test of Beccaria's essay can be judged by the influence it has had over time on our justice system."[52] The influence of Beccaria, the Enlightenment, and classical thinkers remains today in the *Canadian Charter of Rights and Freedoms*, in "get-tough" approaches to crime, and in a continuing emphasis on individual rights. The classical school "has left behind a legacy that we see in almost every aspect of our present-day justice system."[53] Not surprisingly, advocates of today's neoclassical approaches to crime control take much of the credit for the recent drop-off in crime rates. After all, following the implementation of "get tough on crime" policies like the determinate sentencing schemes called for by the just deserts model, official rates of crime have shown substantial declines.

Critics charge, however, that the classical school lacks explanatory power over criminal motivation, other than to advance the simple claim that crime is the result of free will and individual choice. Such critics point out that classical theory is largely bereft of meaningful explanations about how a choice for or against criminal activity is made. Similarly, classical theory lacks any appreciation for the deeper fonts of personal motivation, including those represented by human biology, psychology, and the social environment. The classical school, as originally detailed in the writings of Beccaria and Bentham, lacked any scientific basis for the claims it made. Although neoclassical writers have advanced the scientific foundation of classical claims (via studies such as those showing the effectiveness of particular forms of deterrence), many still defend their way of thinking by reference to philosophical ideals, such as just deserts.

CLASSICAL AND NEOCLASSICAL THEORIES APPLIED

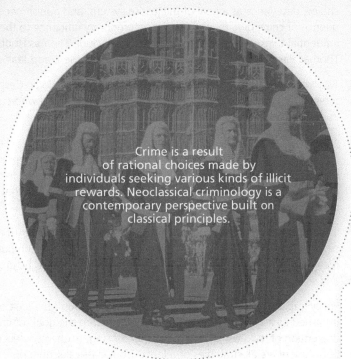

Crime is a result of rational choices made by individuals seeking various kinds of illicit rewards. Neoclassical criminology is a contemporary perspective built on classical principles.

NEOCLASSICAL CRIMINOLOGY holds that it is character and character development, as well as the choices people make when faced with opportunities for crime, that determine criminal behaviour.
Is the case involving the FBI and Apple Inc. one that can be explained using the notions of rational choice and opportunity?

CLASSICAL CRIMINOLOGY holds that human beings are fundamentally rational, pain and pleasure are the two central determinants of human behaviour, and punishment is necessary to deter law violators and to serve as an example to others.
How do the classical tenets of individual rights versus the rights of society apply to the case involving the FBI and Apple Inc.?

SUMMARY OF LEARNING OBJECTIVES

5.1 The classical school in criminology posits that at least some illegal activity is the result of rational choices made by individuals seeking various kinds of illicit rewards. The classical perspective sees human beings as fundamentally rational, portrays pain and pleasure as the two central determinants of human behaviour, and sees punishment as necessary to deter law violators and to serve as an example.

5.2 The classical school grew out of the Enlightenment. Notions of free will, individual choice, deterrence as a goal of the justice system, and punishment as a natural consequence of crime owe much of their contemporary influence to the classical school. Influential thinkers of the Enlightenment era include Thomas Hobbes, John Locke, Thomas Paine, Charles Louis de Secondat Montesquieu, and Jean-Jacques Rousseau.

5.3 Two important thinkers of the classical school of criminology, Cesare Beccaria and Jeremy Bentham, saw crime as providing pleasure to those who commit it and believed in punishment as the way to prevent it.

5.4 Neoclassical criminology is a contemporary perspective built on classical principles emphasizing the importance of character and character development, as well as the choices people make when faced with opportunities for crime. Rational choice theory recognizes the opportunities for crime and the important role that capable guardians play in preventing it.

5.5 In neoclassical criminology, punishment is seen as providing both a deterrent and just deserts. Just deserts implies that criminal offenders deserve the punishment they receive and that any criminal punishment meted out should be appropriate to the type and severity of the crime committed.

5.6 Policy implications of the classical school revolve around the idea of a rational offender punished by a system working purposefully toward the goals of crime reduction and prevention of recidivism. Determinate sentencing, truth in sentencing, and capital punishment are all strategies developed from classical school principles.

5.7 Classical perspectives can be criticized for their lack of comprehensive explanatory power over criminal motivation and for their lack of both meaningful explanations as to how a choice for or against criminal activity is made and any appreciation for the deeper fonts of personal motivation.

Questions for Review

1. What are the central concepts that define the classical school of criminological thought? Which of those concepts are still alive? Where do you see evidence for the survival of those concepts?

2. Name the various pre-classical thinkers identified in this chapter. What ideas did each contribute to Enlightenment philosophy? What form did those ideas take in classical criminological thought?

3. Who were the important thinkers of the classical school of criminology, and what heritage did their way of thinking provide?

4. This text emphasizes a theme of social problems versus social responsibility. Which perspective is more clearly supported by classical and neoclassical thought? Why?

5. How would you define recidivism? What is a recidivism rate? Why are recidivism rates so high today? What can be done to lower them?

6. What are the policy implications of the classical school? What kinds of crime-prevention and crime-control programs might be based on classical principles?

7. What are the shortcomings of the classical school and neoclassical thinking about crime and punishment?

Multiple-Choice Questions

1. The _____ was an important source of modern Western laws and legal procedure, supporting individual rights and jury trials.

   a. Code of Hammurabi

   b. classical school

   c. Enlightenment

   d. social contract

   e. Magna Carta

2. The purpose of punishment should be deterrence rather than retribution, according to _____.

   a. Jeremy Bentham

   b. Thomas Paine

   c. Thomas Hobbes

   d. Cesare Beccaria

   e. Jean-Jacques Rousseau

3. Which of the following is an example of a *mala prohibita* offence?

   a. assault

   b. murder

   c. drug use

   d. break and enter

   e. theft

4. The heritage left by the classical school is still operative today in which of the following principles?

   a. human rights

   b. hedonism

   c. punishment

   d. due process

   e. all of the above

5. _____ seeks to prevent others from committing crimes similar to the one for which a particular offender is being sentenced.

   a. General deterrence

   b. Retribution

   c. Specific deterrence

   d. Recidivism

   e. Rehabilitation

Multiple Choice Answers: 1e, 2d, 3c, 4e, 5a

Chapter 6
Biological Roots of Criminal Behaviour

Steve Baccon/Photodisc/Thinkstock/Getty Images

Biological theories are theories of criminality, not crime. Criminality is a property of individuals, a continuous trait that is itself an amalgam of other continuous traits, and thus belongs to a more inclusive kind of criminology.

—*Anthony Walsh*[1]

LEARNING OBJECTIVES

After reading this chapter, you should be able to

6.1 Identify the basic principles that characterize biological theories of crime causation.

6.2 Be aware of the early and emerging research linking genetics, heritability, and criminal behaviour.

6.3 Identify the theories of body chemistry that are used to explain criminal behaviour and crime.

6.4 Consider the contribution of sociobiology to the study of criminality.

6.5 Explain how criminality can be explained from a biosocial perspective.

6.6 Identify modern-day social policy that reflects the biological approach to crime causation.

6.7 Assess the shortcomings of biological theories of criminal behaviour.

INTRODUCTION

A few years ago, the Dutch Ministry of Justice implemented a program of nutritional supplements in 14 prisons across the Netherlands. Under the program, nearly 500 inmates were provided with healthy diets, devoid of added sugar and supplemented with vitamins and important micronutrients.[2] According to Ap Zaalberg, the project's director, the link between good nutrition and lower levels of anti-social behaviour had already been clearly established by studies published in England only a few years earlier, and the Dutch wanted to see if good eating habits could lower levels of violence in their prisons. Zaalberg's interest came from reading an article published in the *British Journal of Psychiatry* in 2002 by Oxford University professor C. Bernard Gesch.[3] Gesch reported on the results of work he had done in recruiting 231 young British prisoners. He assigned half of them to receive carefully selected dietary supplements while the other half received a placebo. Before Gesch's nutritional program was implemented, the placebo and active-treatment groups had been matched according to the number of disciplinary incidents in which each had been involved. There were no significant individual or psychological differences between the two groups in terms of IQ, verbal ability, anger, anxiety, or depression. After Gesch's experimental subjects took specially formulated vitamins, minerals, and essential fatty acids for 142 days, he found that prisoners taking the supplements committed an average of 26.3 percent fewer offences compared with the placebo group. He also observed a 35.1 percent reduction in overall offences in the group receiving the supplements and a 37 percent drop in violent incidents. According to Gesch, "evidence is mounting that putting poor fuel into the brain significantly affects social behavior. We need to know more about the composition of the right nutrients. It could be the recipe for peace."[4]

The field of criminology has been cautious about giving credence to biological theories of human behaviour. One reason for this, as noted in Chapter 1, is that contemporary criminology's academic roots are firmly grounded in the social sciences. As the well-known biocriminologist C. Ray Jeffery, commenting on the historical development of the field, observed,

> The term *criminology* was given to a social science approach to crime as developed in sociology. Sutherland's (1924) text *Criminology* was pure sociology without any biology or psychology; beginning with publication of that text, criminology was offered in sociology departments as a part of sociology separate from biology, psychology, psychiatry, and law. Many of the academicians who call themselves criminologists are sociologists.[5]

Another traditional challenge with biological explanations for criminality and disordered behaviour is the concern with concepts such as genetic determinism, which have come to be seen as synonymous with inevitability since the physical makeup of a person is hard to change.

For those studying criminology today, the field is interdisciplinary, recognizing contributions from many different disciplines. Open inquiry requires objective consideration of all points of view and an unbiased examination of each for its ability to shed light upon the subject under study. The influence of biology on behaviour of any kind is more often the result of an interaction among genetic, hormonal, and other biological features of an individual and his or her social and physical environments. This chapter considers four broad categories of biological theories: (1) those that look at genetic factors and focus on physical features, the evolution of the gene pool, and heredity (both early and emerging); (2) those that consider the ways in which external factors, such as diet, hormones, and environmental contaminants, affect body chemistry; (3) the new direction offered by sociobiology emphasizing the biological basis of all social behaviour; and (4) the emergence and coming of age of biosocial criminology, with its emphasis on the interactions between biology and the physical environment in explaining human behaviour. Each category considers both the historical and contemporary biological perspectives on crime. As we will see, many early biological theories were relatively simplistic in their approaches to explaining human behaviour and crime while more recent biosocial perspectives hold that genes and related biological features are more likely to be facilitators rather than determinants of behaviour.

6.1 LEARNING OBJECTIVE

Biological theory A theory that maintains that the basic determinants of human behaviour, including criminality, are constitutionally or physiologically based and often inherited.

MAJOR PRINCIPLES OF BIOLOGICAL THEORIES

THIS BRIEF SECTION SERVES TO SUMMARIZE THE CENTRAL FEATURES OF **BIOLOGICAL theories** of crime causation. Each of these points can be found elsewhere in this chapter, so this section is meant to be a guide (see Table 6.1).

Biological theories of crime causation make certain fundamental assumptions:

■ The brain is the organ of the mind and the locus of personality.

■ The basic determinants of human behaviour, including criminal tendencies, are, to a considerable degree, constitutionally or genetically based.

■ Observed gender and racial differences in rates and types of criminality may be, at least partially, the result of biological differences between the sexes and between racially distinct groups.

■ The basic determinants of human behaviour, including criminality, may be passed on from generation to generation; that is, a tendency toward crime may be inherited.

■ Much of human conduct is fundamentally rooted in instinctive behavioural responses that are characteristic of biological organisms everywhere. Territoriality and acquisitiveness are examples of human behaviour that may be instinctual to human beings.

■ The biological roots of human conduct have become increasingly disguised because modern forms of indirect expressive behaviour have replaced more primitive and direct ones.

■ At least some human behaviour is the result of biological propensities inherited from more primitive developmental stages in the evolutionary process. In other

Table 6.1 Biological Theories

Theory	Genetics	Body Chemistry	Sociobiology	Biosocial Criminology
Period	1890s–1930, 1930s–1940s, 1960s–present	1940s–present	1975–present	1987–present
Theorists	Franz Joseph Gall, Cesare Lombroso, Ernst Kretschmer, and others	Ingrid Helland, Roger Masters, and others	Konrad Lorenz, Edwin O. Wilson	James Q. Wilson, Richard J. Herrnstein
Concepts	Phrenology, atavism, born criminals, criminaloids, somatotyping, twin studies, human genome project	Food additives, hypoglycemia, vitamins, lead, serotonin, testosterone	Altruism, tribalism, survival of the gene pool	Constitutional factors, genetic inheritance

words, some human beings may be further along the evolutionary ladder than others, and their behaviour may reflect that fact.

- The interplay among heredity, biology, and the social environment provides the nexus for any realistic consideration of crime causation.

GENETICS AND CRIME

6.2 | LEARNING OBJECTIVE

MOST BIOLOGICAL THEORIES THAT CONSIDER GENETICS, PHYSICAL FEATURES, AND heredity are among the earliest inquiries into the connection between biology and criminal behaviour. These early biological theories of crime, while not as sophisticated as their modern counterparts, are significant because they built on the scientific tradition of positivism. **Positivism**, as mentioned in Chapter 5, is associated with the belief that all valid knowledge is acquired only through observation and not through the mere exercise of reason or blind adherence to belief. Early positivism was built on two important principles: (1) an unflagging acceptance of social determinism, or the belief that human behaviour is determined not by the exercise of free choice but by causative factors beyond the control of the individual, and (2) the application of scientific techniques to the study of crime and criminology. The term *positivism* had its roots in the writings of Auguste Comte (1798–1857), who proposed use of the scientific method in the study of society in his 1851 work A *System of Positive Polity*.[6] Comte, who later became known as the father of sociology, believed that social phenomena could be observed, explained, and measured in objective and quantitative terms. For a strict positivist, reality consists of a world of clearly defined facts that can be scientifically measured and—some would hope—controlled.[7] As a framework for thought and analysis, positivism was a giant leap forward because it established a scientific basis for the burgeoning field of criminology.

Positivism The application of scientific techniques to the study of crime and criminals.

Physical Features and Crime

Some of the earliest studies in the field of criminology used data from the fields of biology and anthropology to identify physical abnormalities that early criminologists thought could be used to distinguish criminal offenders from other people. One of the earliest attempts to use bodily features to identify criminals was proposed by European anatomist Franz Joseph Gall (1758–1828) in his theory of **phrenology** (also called craniology). Gall believed that the shape of the human skull was related to personality and could be used to distinguish criminals from normal men and women. Gall's approach built on four themes:

Phrenology The study of the shape of the head to determine anatomical correlates of human behaviour.

1. The brain is the organ of the mind.
2. Particular aspects of personality are associated with specific locations in the brain.
3. Portions of the brain that are well developed will cause personality characteristics associated with them to be more prominent in the individual under study, whereas poorly developed brain areas lead to a lack of associated personality characteristics.
4. The shape of a person's skull corresponds to the shape of the underlying brain and is therefore indicative of the personality.

Gall was one of the first Western writers to firmly locate the roots of personality in the brain. Prior to his time, it was thought that aspects of personality resided in various organs throughout the body—a fact reflected in linguistic anachronisms surviving

Early criminologists believed the shape of the skull reflected the brain's ability. Here is a phrenological map of the skull. Do you think biology plays a role in crime?

Frank Schmalleger

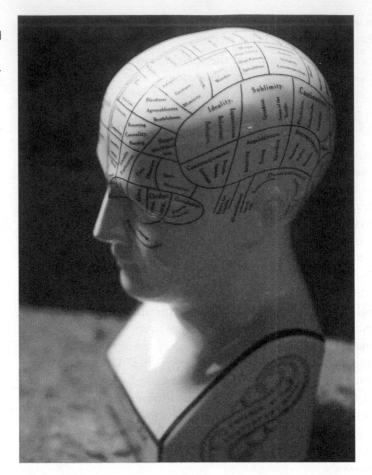

into the present day (for example, when someone is described as being "hard-hearted" or as having "a lot of gall"). Greek philosopher Aristotle was said to believe that the brain served no function other than to radiate excess heat from the body, so Gall's perspective, although relatively primitive by today's standards, did much to advance physiological understandings of the mind–body connection in Western thought.

Although Gall never tested his theory, it was widely accepted by many of his contemporaries because it represented something of a shift away from theological perspectives prevalent at the time and a move toward scientific understanding—a trend that was well underway by the time of his writings. Phrenology also provided for systematic evaluation of suspected offenders and was intriguing for its ease of use. One of Gall's students, Johann Gaspar Spurzheim (1776–1853), brought phrenological theory to North America and helped to spread its influence through a series of lectures and publications on the subject. Phrenology's prestige in North America extended into the 20th century, finding a place in classification schemes used to evaluate newly admitted prisoners. Even Arthur Conan Doyle's fictional character Sherlock Holmes was described as using phrenology to solve a number of crimes.

The Italian School

One of the best-known early scientific biological theorists—19th-century Italian army prison physician Cesare Lombroso (1836–1909)—coined the term **atavism** to suggest that criminality was the result of primitive urges that survived the evolutionary process in modern-day human throwbacks. Lombroso, whose work had consisted mostly of postmortem studies of the bodies of executed offenders and deceased criminals,

Atavism A term used by Cesare Lombroso to suggest that criminals are physiological throwbacks to earlier stages of human evolution.

measured the bodies in many different ways.[8] He claimed that, using his system, not only could criminal offenders be separated from the general population but even specific types of criminals could be identified.

Discussing murderers, for example, Lombroso wrote, "He has a cold concentrated look; sometimes the eye appears injected with blood; the nose is often aquiline or hooked, always large; the ears are long; the jaws powerful; the cheek-bones widely separated; the hair is crisp and abundant; the canine teeth well developed, and the lips thin; often a nervous tic or contraction, upon one side of the face only, uncovers the canine teeth, producing the effect of a threatening look or a sardonic laugh."[9]

Lombroso believed that thieves could be recognized because they have "less cranial capacity" and "a remarkable mobility of countenance, the eye small and restless, the eye-brows thick and meeting, the nose flat, and the forehead always low and retreating." Lombroso called physical features that he thought to be indicative of criminality *stigmata of degeneration* and suggested that they could be used to predict later criminal behaviour among individuals who possessed them. He described "the nature of the criminal" as "an atavistic being who reproduces in his person the ferocious instincts of primitive humanity and the inferior animals."[10]

Lombroso's ideas gave rise to the **Italian school of criminology**, also referred to today as criminal anthropology. **Criminal anthropology** is the scientific study of the relationship between human physical characteristics (in particular bodily measurements) and criminality. Criminal anthropology probably derives from earlier subjective feelings, prominent for millennia, that unattractiveness, deformity, and disfigurement are somehow associated with evil, spiritual malaise, and general uncleanliness. Although the earlier works of Gall and others might be subsumed under the umbrella of criminal anthropology, the term is usually reserved in today's criminological literature for the work of Lombroso and other members of the Italian school of criminology, especially Enrico Ferri and Raffaele Garofalo.

At about the time that Lombroso's ideas were becoming popular, Charles Darwin was making a substantial impact on the scientific world with his theory of biological evolution. Darwin proposed that human beings and other contemporary living organisms were the end products of a long evolutionary process governed by rules such as natural selection and survival of the fittest. Lombroso adapted elements of Darwin's theory to suggest that primitive traits survived in present-day human populations and led to heightened criminal tendencies among individuals who harboured them. Darwin himself had proposed this idea when he wrote, "With mankind some of the worst dispositions, which occasionally without any assignable cause make their appearance in families, may perhaps be reversions to a savage state, from which we are not removed by very many generations."[11]

Lombroso has been called "the father of modern criminology" because he was the first criminologist of note to employ the scientific method—particularly measurement, observation, and generalization—in his work. Other writers have preferred to limit his influence, referring to him simply as the father of the Italian school of criminology in recognition of the fact that 19th-century positivism began in Italy under his tutelage.

Lombroso's most famous term, *atavism*, implies that criminals are born that way. He continually reassessed his estimates of the proportion of all offenders who were **born criminals**. At one point, he asserted that fully 90 percent of offenders committed crimes because of atavistic influences; he later revised the figure downward to 70 percent, admitting that normal individuals might be pulled into lives of crime. In addition to the category of born criminal, Lombroso described other categories of offenders, including the insane, "criminaloids," and criminals incited by passion. The insane were said to include mental and moral degenerates, alcoholics, drug addicts, and so forth.

Italian school of criminology A perspective on criminology developed in the late 1800s that held that criminals can be identified by physical features and are throwbacks to earlier stages of human evolution.

Criminal anthropology The scientific study of the relationship between human physical characteristics and criminality.

Born criminal An individual who is born with a genetic predilection toward criminality.

Criminaloid   A term used by Cesare Lombroso to describe occasional criminals who were pulled into criminality primarily by environmental influences.

Criminaloids, also called "occasional criminals," were described as people who were enticed into breaking the law by virtue of environmental influences. Nevertheless, most criminaloids were seen by Lombroso as exhibiting some degree of atavism and hence were said to "differ from born criminals in degree, not in kind." Those who became criminals by virtue of passion were said to have surrendered to intense emotions, including love, jealousy, hatred, or an injured sense of honour.

In 1893, Lombroso published *The Female Offender*.[12] In that book, he expressed his belief that women exhibited far less anatomical variation than do men, but he insisted that criminal behaviour among women, as among men, derived from atavistic foundations. Lombroso saw the quintessential female offender, however, as a prostitute, who was "the genuine typical representative of criminality" among women.[13] Prostitutes, he claimed, act out atavistic yearnings and, in doing so, return to a form of behaviour characteristic of humankind's primitive past.

Evaluations of Atavism

Following in Lombroso's positivistic footsteps around the turn of the 20th century, the English physician Charles Buckman Goring (1870–1919) conducted a well-controlled statistical study of Lombroso's thesis of atavism. Using newly developed but advanced mathematical techniques to measure the degree of correlation between physiological features and criminal history, Goring examined nearly 3000 inmates at Turin prison beginning in 1901. Enlisting the aid of London's Biometric Laboratory, he concluded that "the whole fabric of Lombrosian doctrine, judged by the standards of science, is fundamentally unsound."[14] Goring compared the prisoners with students at Oxford and Cambridge universities, British soldiers, and non-criminal hospital patients, and published his findings in 1913 in his lengthy treatise *The English Convict: A Statistical Study*.[15]

A similar study was conducted between 1927 and 1939 by Earnest A. Hooton, a professor of anthropology at Harvard University. In 1939, Hooton published *Crime and the Man*, in which he reported having evaluated 13 873 inmates from 10 states, comparing them along 107 physiological dimensions with 3203 non-incarcerated individuals who formed a control group.[16] His sample consisted of 10 953 prison inmates, 2004 county jail prisoners, 743 criminally insane, 173 "defective delinquents," 1227 "insane civilians," and 1976 "sane civilians." Hooton concluded that criminals showed an overall physiological inferiority to the general population and that crime was the result of "the impact of the environment upon low grade human organisms."[17]

Today the ideas of the Italian school, which linked observable physical abnormalities to crime, are no longer a factor in criminological thinking. However, as Nichole Hahn Rafter says, "Because criminal anthropologists' doctrine of the criminal as a physically anomalous human has long been discredited, we tend to ignore their work, at the same time overlooking the legacy of professional issues that they, as the first criminologists, bequeathed to us."[18]

Even though mainstream criminology is no longer concerned with claims that physical abnormalities may be linked to crime, some contemporary researchers have examined the link between criminality and minor physical abnormalities, including neuro-deficits, fetal alcohol syndrome, and hormone deficits. In a study of teenage boys reported in 2000, for example, Canadian researchers L. Arseneault and R.E. Tremblay conducted hormonal, anthropometric, psychophysiological, neuropsychological, and psychiatric evaluations of 1037 boys who had attended kindergarten in 1984 in a socially and economically disadvantaged area of Montreal.[19] Using evaluations provided years later by parents, teachers, classmates, and the children themselves, Arseneault and Tremblay concluded that subtle physical abnormalities, including minor abnormalities in the shape of the ears, tongue, and teeth, were associated with an increased risk of behavioural and psychiatric problems in later years. The researchers suggested that such minor physical abnormalities might have resulted from genetic problems or prenatal insults associated with exposure to toxins, concluding that "both the total count of minor physical anomalies and the total count of minor physical anomalies of the mouth were significantly associated with an increased risk of violent delinquency in adolescence, beyond the effects of childhood physical aggression and family adversity." Arseneault and Tremblay recognized, however, that abnormalities of the type they identified might be associated with neurological deficits and that abnormalities of the mouth could lead to feeding problems in the first months after birth, which might somehow cause problems in development or socialization.

Constitutional Theories

Constitutional theories explain criminality by reference to offenders' body types, genetics, or external observable physical characteristics. A constitutional, or physiological, orientation that found its way into the criminological mainstream during the early and mid-20th century was that of **somatotyping** (classifying according to body types), primarily associated with the work of Ernst Kretschmer and William H. Sheldon. Kretschmer, a professor of psychiatry at the German University of Tubingen, proposed a relationship between body build and personality type and created a rather detailed "biopsychological constitutional typology."

Influenced by Kretschmer, Sheldon used measurement techniques to connect body type with personality.[20] Sheldon felt that Kretschmer had erred in including too large an age range in his work, so he limited his study to 200 boys between the ages of 15 and 21 at the Hayden Goodwill Institute in Boston. Sheldon concluded that four basic body types characterized the entire group (see Figure 6.1):

1. The **endomorph** is soft and round, with "digestive viscera [that] are massive and highly developed" (the person is overweight and has a large stomach).

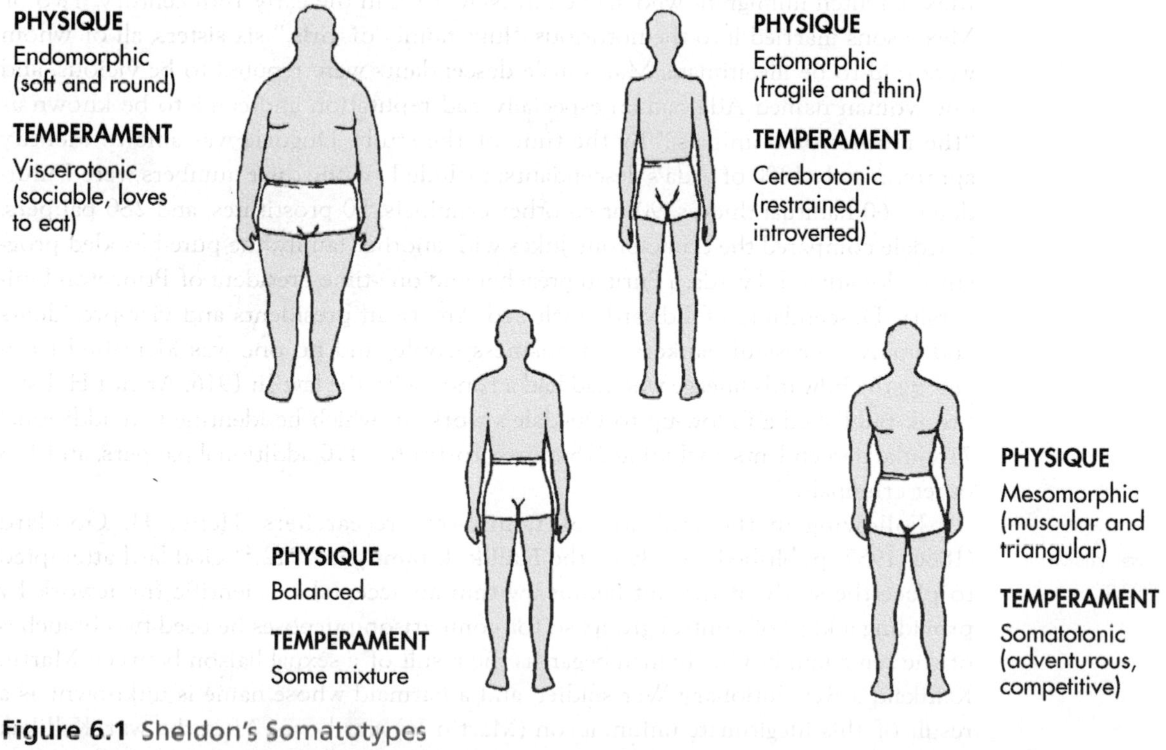

> **Constitutional theories** Theories that explain criminality by reference to offenders' body types, inheritance, genetics, or external observable physical characteristics.
>
> **Somatotyping** The classification of human beings into types according to body build and other physical characteristics.
>
> **Endomorph** A body type described as soft and round or overweight.

PHYSIQUE
Endomorphic
(soft and round)

TEMPERAMENT
Viscerotonic
(sociable, loves
to eat)

PHYSIQUE
Ectomorphic
(fragile and thin)

TEMPERAMENT
Cerebrotonic
(restrained,
introverted)

PHYSIQUE
Balanced

TEMPERAMENT
Some mixture

PHYSIQUE
Mesomorphic
(muscular and
triangular)

TEMPERAMENT
Somatotonic
(adventurous,
competitive)

Figure 6.1 Sheldon's Somatotypes

Source: Bartol, Criminal Behaviour A psychological approach., 1st Ed., ©1980, p. 23. Reprinted and Electronically reproduced by permission of Pearson Education, Inc., Upper Saddle River, New Jersey.

Mesomorph A body type described as athletic and muscular.

Ectomorph A body type described as thin and fragile, with long, slender, poorly muscled extremities and delicate bones.

2. The **mesomorph** is athletic and muscular, with "somatic structures [that] are in the ascendancy" (the person has larger bones and considerable muscle mass).

3. The **ectomorph** is thin and fragile and has "long, slender, poorly muscled extremities, with delicate, pipestem bones."

4. The balanced type is a person of average build, not overweight, thin, or exceedingly muscular.[21]

Individuals (excluding the balanced type) were ranked along each of the three major dimensions using a seven-point scale. Sheldon claimed that varying types of temperament and personalities were closely associated with each of the body types he identified: Ectomorphs were said to be "cerebrotonic," or restrained, shy, and inhibited; endomorphs were "viscerotonic," or relaxed and sociable. Mesomorphs, or muscular body types, were most likely to be associated with delinquency or "somatotonia," which he described as "a predominance of muscular activity and vigorous bodily assertiveness."

Early biological theorists like Gall, Lombroso, and Sheldon provide an interesting footnote to the history of criminological thought. Today, however, their work is mostly relegated to the dustbins of academic theorizing.

Criminal Families

Some scholars have suggested that a penchant for crime may be inherited and that criminal tendencies are genetically based. Beginning in the late 1880s, and supported by growing notions of heredity, researchers in the field of criminal anthropology focused on criminal families or families that appeared to exhibit criminal tendencies through generations.

Juke family A well-known "criminal family" studied by Richard L. Dugdale.

In 1877, Richard L. Dugdale (1841–1883) published a study of one such family—the **Juke family**.[22] Dugdale traced the Juke lineage back to a notorious character named Max, a Dutch immigrant who arrived in New York in the early 18th century. Two of Max's sons married into the notorious "Juke family of girls," six sisters, all of whom were said to be illegitimate. Max's male descendants were reputed to be vicious, and one woman named Ada had an especially bad reputation and came to be known as "the mother of criminals." By the time of the study, Dugdale was able to identify approximately 1200 of Ada's descendants; included among their numbers were 7 murderers, 60 habitual thieves, 90 or so other criminals, 50 prostitutes, and 280 paupers. Dugdale compared the crime-prone Jukes with another family, the pure-blooded progeny of Jonathan Edwards, a Puritan preacher and one-time president of Princeton University. Descendants of Edwards included American presidents and vice-presidents and many successful bankers and businesspeople, and no one was identified from among the Edwards lineage who had had a run-in with the law. In 1916, Arthur H. Estabrook published a follow-up to Dugdale's work, in which he identified an additional 715 Juke descendants, including 378 more prostitutes, 170 additional paupers, and 118 other criminals.[23]

Kallikak family A well-known "criminal family" studied by Henry H. Goddard.

Following in the tradition of family-tree researchers, Henry H. Goddard (1866–1957) published a study of the **Kallikak family** in 1912.[24] Goddard attempted to place the study of deviant families within an acceptable scientific framework by providing a kind of control group, so for comparison purposes he used two branches of the same family. One branch began as the result of a sexual liaison between Martin Kallikak, a Revolutionary War soldier, and a barmaid whose name is unknown; as a result of this illegitimate union, a son (Martin Jr.) was born. After the war, Kallikak returned home and married a righteous Quaker girl, and a second line of descent began. The legitimate branch produced only a few minor deviants, but the illegitimate line resulted in 262 feeble-minded births and various other epileptic, alcoholic, and criminal descendants. (The term *feeble-minded*, which was much in vogue at the time of Goddard's study, was later recast as *mentally retarded*, and today people exhibiting similar characteristics might be referred to as *mentally handicapped* or *mentally challenged*.) Because feeble-mindedness appeared to occur with some predictability in Goddard's study but criminal activity seemed to be only randomly represented among the descendants of both Kallikak lines, Goddard concluded that a tendency toward feeble-mindedness was inherited but that criminality was not.

Like the ideas of the Italian school, constitutional theories and studies of criminal families have largely been discarded today as biosocial researchers develop more sophisticated perspectives on criminology. Early biological theories, because they tended to encourage the **eugenics** movement of the late 1880s and early 1900s, were vigorously opposed by many in the criminological community throughout the latter part of the 20th century. The eugenics movement proposed selective human breeding as a way to improve the species, and **eugenic criminology**, an offshoot of the movement,[25] held that the root causes of criminality were largely passed from generation to generation in the form of "bad genes." Eugenic criminology, which accepted the idea of **genetic determinism**, or the belief that genes are the major determining factor in human behaviour, replaced the idea of the "feeble-minded criminal" with the "defective delinquent," and social policies developed during the eugenics movement called for the sterilization of mentally handicapped women to prevent their bearing additional offspring. In Canada, sexual sterilization laws in Alberta and British Columbia resulted in the sterilization of almost 3000 citizens between 1928 and 1972. During this period, the legislation targeted not only those with mental illness but also the poor, Aboriginal people, unwed mothers, and non-English-speaking immigrants.[26]

The eugenics movement, as it existed before World War II, was largely discredited by intense condemnation of Nazi genetic research, mass sterilization, and eugenics programs, including those that led to the Holocaust.

Eugenics The study of hereditary improvement by genetic control.

Eugenic criminology A perspective that holds that the root causes of criminality are passed from generation to generation in the form of "bad genes."

Genetic determinism The belief that genes are the major determining factor in human behaviour.

The XYY Supermale

The first well-known study of the modern era on genetic differences as an explanation for criminality was undertaken by British researcher Patricia A. Jacobs.[27] Jacobs and her colleagues examined 197 Scottish prisoners in 1965 for chromosomal abnormalities through a relatively simple blood test known as karyotyping.[28] Twelve members of the group displayed chromosomes that were unusual, and seven were found to have an XYY chromosome. Normal male individuals possess an XY chromosome structure; normal female individuals are XX. Some other unusual combinations might be XXX, wherein a woman's genetic makeup contains an extra X chromosome, or XXY (also called Klinefelter's syndrome), in which a man might carry an extra X, or female, chromosome. Klinefelter's men often have male genitalia but are frequently sterile and evidence breast enlargement and intellectual retardation.[29] The XYY man, however, whose incidence in the prison population Jacobs placed at around 3.5 percent, was quickly identified as potentially violent and termed a **supermale**.

Following the introduction of the supermale notion into popular consciousness, a number of offenders attempted to offer a chromosome-based defence. In 1969, for example, Lawrence E. Hannell, who was adjudged a supermale, was acquitted of murder in Australia on the grounds of insanity.[30] Such a defence, however, did not work for Richard Speck, who also claimed to be an XYY man but was convicted of killing eight Chicago nursing students in 1966; it was later learned that Speck did not carry the extra Y chromosome.

Supermale A male individual displaying the XYY chromosome structure.

The supermale phenomenon (also called the XYY syndrome) appears to have been based more on sensationalism than fact. Today, little evidence suggests that XYY men actually commit crimes of greater violence than do other men, although they may commit somewhat more crimes overall. A 1976 Danish study of 4000 men born in Copenhagen between 1944 and 1947 may have helped put the issue to rest with its finding that the incidence of XYY men was less than 1 percent in the general male population.[31] More recent research has similarly concluded that "studies done thus far are largely in agreement and demonstrate rather conclusively that males of the XYY type are not predictably aggressive."[32]

Twin Studies

Studies of the criminal tendencies of fraternal and identical twins have provided a methodologically sophisticated technique for ferreting out the role of inheritance in crime causation. Fraternal twins, or **dizygotic (DZ) twins**, develop from different fertilized eggs and share only that genetic material common among siblings. Identical twins, or **monozygotic (MZ) twins**, develop from the same egg and carry virtually the same genetic material. Hence, if human behaviour had a substantial heritable component, twins would display similar behavioural characteristics despite variations in their social environment, with any observed relationship being stronger among MZ twins than among DZ twins.

One of the first studies to link MZ twins to criminality was published in the 1920s by German physician Johannes Lange.[33] Examining 13 pairs of MZ twins and 17 pairs of DZ twins, he found that in 10 of the 13 MZ pairs both twins were criminal, whereas only 2 of the 17 DZ twins exhibited such similarity. Lange's findings drew considerable attention, even though his sample was small and he was unable to adequately separate environmental influences from genetic ones. A much larger twin study was begun in 1968 by the European researchers Karl O. Christiansen and Sarnoff Mednick, who analyzed all twins (3586 pairs) born on a selected group of Danish islands between 1881 and 1910.[34] Christiansen and Mednick found significant statistical support for the notion that criminal tendencies are inherited: 52 percent of identical twins and 22 percent of fraternal siblings displayed the same degree of criminality within the twin pair. Such similarities remained apparent even among twins separated at birth and raised in substantially different environments. Mednick noted, however, that genetic influences appeared to be stronger in the commission of petty, non-violent offences than in more violent types of crime. He and Christiansen also found that the genetic risk for criminal behaviour was enhanced by the environment in cases where one of the twins was raised in a family with at least one criminal adoptive parent.

The study of twins is still a common practice in criminology. In 1996, for example, British researchers studying 43 MZ and 38 DZ same-sex twins through the use of self-report questionnaires stated that "common bad behaviors of the sort admitted to by the majority of adolescents have a substantially heritable component. Additive genetic effects account for most of the variation, with no evidence of a contribution from shared environment."[35] The researchers also determined that genetic effects on behaviour appear to increase with age. The British research was supported by the findings of a joint U.S.–Australian examination of 2682 adult twin pairs; in that study, researchers found "a substantial genetic influence on risk for conduct disorder" (defined to include chronic stealing, lying, bullying, arson, property destruction, weapons use, cruelty to animals or people, fighting, aggression, truancy, and running away from home).[36]

In 2003, researchers examined the behaviour of 1116 pairs of five-year-old twins participating in a longitudinal study and asked mothers, teachers, study examiners, and the children themselves to evaluate the degree of the children's level of anti-social

Dizygotic (DZ) twin A twin who develops from a separate ovum and who carries the genetic material shared by siblings.

Monozygotic (MZ) twin A twin who develops from the same egg and who carries virtually the same genetic material.

behaviour.[37] Findings showed that anti-social children can be identified early in life, that their behaviour can be nearly impossible to control by the time they reach kindergarten, and that heredity plays a far greater role in determining such behaviour than does home life or parenting. Because of similar behaviour among twin pairs, the researchers concluded that genetic influences were extremely powerful determinants of anti-social behaviour across diverse social settings, writing that "research and theory on the etiology of childhood antisocial behavior must look beyond the current focus on socioeconomic contexts and parenting processes, to incorporate genetic explanations and develop new theories of nature-nurture interplay."[38]

The Human Genome Project, Genetics, and Crime

One of the most important recent efforts in understanding human nature is the Human Genome Project (HGP), an international research program designed to construct detailed maps of the **human genome**. The HGP began in the United States in 1990 through a joint effort of the Department of Energy and the National Institutes of Health. It had as its goal the determination of the complete chemical sequence of human DNA. Researchers participating in the project worked together to localize the nearly 100 000 genes within the human genome and to determine the sequences of the 3 billion chemical base pairs that make up human DNA. The human genome refers to a complete copy of the entire set of human gene instructions.[39] Genes are made of DNA and carry coded instructions for making everything the body needs. Chromosomes are bundles of genes.[40]

Human genome A complete copy of the entire set of human gene instructions.

The HGP was officially declared completed on April 14, 2003—almost exactly 50 years after James Watson and Francis Crick published their historic findings on the double-helix, three-dimensional structure of DNA.[41] After completion of the HGP, which resulted in the sequencing of the entire genome sequence of a "reference human genome," the focus of genomics research turned to finding individual differences or variants from that reference sequence.[42] Ongoing research projects include the Hap-Map Project and the Encyclopedia of DNA Elements (ENCODE), which became operational in 2007. The second phase of ENCODE, the 1000 Genomes Project, has only recently begun.

The HGP marked the beginning of a new era of research into human biology and recast understandings of human nature, disease, cognition, and behaviour. The use of

Dr. Francis Collins, former director of the Human Genome Project and current director of the National Institutes of Health. The international Human Genome Project was a research program that determined the complete nucleotide sequence of human DNA. What ethical, legal, and social implications are inherent in such a project?

Michael Ventura/Alamy Stock Photo

genetic knowledge developed by the HGP may have significant implications for both individuals and society. Many of the questions criminologists have raised about the role of genetics in criminal behaviour may be answered by the results of research begun by the HGP.[43] In the area of crime control policy, HGP-related information is expected to support the development of public policy options related to crime prevention and the treatment of offenders.

In 1993, only three years after the launch of the HGP, Dutch criminologists caught worldwide attention with their claim that they had uncovered a specific gene with links to criminal behaviour. Researcher H. Hilger Ropers, geneticist Han G. Brunner, and collaborators studied what media sources called "the Netherlands' most dysfunctional family."[44] Although members of the unnamed family displayed IQs in the near-normal range, they seemed unable to control their impulses and often ended up being arrested for violations of the criminal law; the arrests, however, were always of men. Tracing the family back five generations, Brunner found 14 men whom he classified as genetically given to criminality. None of the women in the family displayed criminal tendencies, although they were often victimized by their crime-prone male siblings.

According to Ropers and Brunner, because men have only one X chromosome, they are especially vulnerable to any defective gene, whereas women, with two X chromosomes, have a kind of backup system in which one defective gene may be compensated for by another wholesome and correctly functioning gene carried in the second X chromosome. After a decade of study, Ropers and Brunner announced that they had isolated the specific mutation that caused the family's criminality.[45] The gene, they said, is one that is responsible for production of an enzyme called monoamine oxidase A (MAO-A), which is crucially involved in the process by which signals are transmitted within the brain. MAO-A breaks down the chemicals serotonin (a hormone that plays the role of a neurotransmitter) and noradrenaline (another neurotransmitter). Neurotransmitters are the chemicals that facilitate the flow of electrical impulses from one neuron to the next across nerve synapses, and the presence or absence of both serotonin and noradrenaline has been linked to aggressive behaviour in human beings. Because men with the mutated gene do not produce the enzyme necessary to break down chemical transmitters, the researchers surmised, their brains are overwhelmed with stimuli, resulting in uncontrollable urges and, ultimately, criminal behaviour.

In 2002, Avshalom Caspi and Terrie Moffitt and their colleagues offered a model of *gene-environment interaction* that recognized that childhood maltreatment appears to be a "universal risk factor for antisocial behavior" in adulthood. Previous research had demonstrated that children who experience abuse—especially those exposed to erratic, coercive, and punitive parenting—frequently develop conduct disorders and display anti-social personality symptoms, and they are known to be at greater risk of becoming violent adult offenders than are children who do not experience such maltreatment.[46] Using data from the Dunedin Multidisciplinary Health and Development Study—a longitudinal study of 1037 children born in the maternity hospital in Dunedin, New Zealand, between April 1, 1972, and March 31, 1973—Caspi and Moffitt noted that not all maltreated children grow up to become criminal,[47] but they hypothesized that the development of anti-social behaviour is mediated by an interaction between a gene responsible for the production of the enzyme MAO-A and an environment variable (maltreatment). The researchers demonstrated a significant biosocial interaction between MAO-A and early child abuse, leading to violence later in life.[48] Their findings showed that maltreatment "has lasting neurochemical correlates in human children" and that deficient MAO-A activity may cause "neural hyperreactivity" in children in response to threats. The researchers concluded that "childhood maltreatment predisposes most strongly to adult violence among children whose MAO-A is insufficient to constrain maltreatment-induced changes to neurotransmitter systems."[49] Maltreated children with high MAO-A activity did not develop anti-social behaviour. The finding was supported by two separate Swedish studies published in 2007.[50]

Research into the contribution of the relationship between genetic predispositions and interaction with surrounding social and physical environments to delinquency have continued apace. In 2008, researchers with the National Institute on Drug Abuse in the Unites States announced that "as much as half of an individual's risk of becoming addicted to nicotine, alcohol, or other drugs depends on his or her genes."[51] The researchers stated, "Pinning down the biological basis for this risk is an important avenue of research for scientists trying to solve the problem of drug abuse."

In 2011, making a genetic argument for at least some forms of callous, unemotional behaviour, Nathalie Fontaine and her colleagues reported that heritability (which is a statistical construct that estimates the amount of variation in the traits of a population that is attributable to genetic factors) leads to persistently high levels of such behaviour among twin boys.[52] The data on which Fontaine reported were derived from the United Kingdom's ongoing Twin Early Development Study (TEDS), which uses information gathered from over 15 000 families to explore how people change through childhood and adolescence.[53] A similar study, conducted at about the same time, examined differences in self-control between male and female twins. The study authors concluded that "there are genetic differences in self-control that are operating across the sexes in adolescence and adulthood."[54] The results of the study showed that "the same genetic factors influence levels of self-control in males and females," meaning that the "genetic influences on self-control are not gender-specific." Some of the studies discussed here may appear to point to criminal genes that, once inherited, inevitably produce anti-social behaviour. Such a conclusion, however, is not warranted. As we shall see later in this chapter, genes may simply influence the way in which people respond to their surroundings. As one researcher puts it, "genes and environments operating in tandem [are] required to produce significant antisocial behavior."[55] Hence, so-called criminal genes may be nothing more than genetic predispositions to respond in certain ways to a criminogenic environment. In other words, neither genes nor the environment is sufficient by itself to explain anti-social behaviour; rather, it is the interaction between the two that determines what happens in most circumstances.

BODY CHEMISTRY AND CRIMINALITY

6.3 | LEARNING OBJECTIVE

TODAY'S BIOLOGICAL THEORISTS HAVE MADE SIGNIFICANT STUDIES IN LINKING VIOLENT OR disruptive behaviour to body chemistry. Body chemistry is influenced by factors such as eating habits, vitamin deficiencies, environmental contaminants, and the endocrine system. Hence, the old maxim "you are what you eat" may contain more than a grain of truth.

Ingested Substances and Nutrition

One of the first studies to focus on chemical imbalances in the body as a cause of crime was reported in the British medical journal *Lancet* in 1943.[56] The authors of the study linked murder to **hypoglycemia**, or low blood sugar. Low blood sugar, produced by too much insulin in the blood or by near-starvation diets, was said to reduce the mind's capacity to effectively reason or to judge the long-term consequences of behaviour. More recent studies have linked excess consumption of refined white sugar to hyperactivity, excitability, and impairment of the ability to make reasoned decisions. Popular books such as *Sugar Blues* provide guides for individuals seeking to free themselves from the negative effects of excess sugar consumption.[57]

Hypoglycemia A medical condition characterized by low blood sugar.

To some degree, even courts have accepted the notion that excess sugar consumption may be linked to crime. In the early 1980s, for example, Dan White, a former San Francisco police officer, was given a reduced sentence after his lawyers used what came to be known as the "Twinkie Defence." They argued that White's night-long binge on large numbers of Coca-Colas and Twinkies before he murdered San Francisco mayor George Moscone and City Councillor Harvey Milk was evidence of White's unbalanced mental state; the consumption of junk food was presented as evidence of depression since White was normally very health conscious. More than 10 years later, however, a well-conducted 1994 study reported in the *New England Journal of Medicine* seemed to contradict the notion that sugar may lead to hyperactivity;[58] neither sugar nor artificial sweeteners were shown to have any link to an increase in learning disabilities. In the study, researchers at Vanderbilt University and the University of Iowa varied the diets of supposedly sugar-sensitive youngsters from a diet that was high in sugar to a diet that was low in sugar but contained the artificial sweetener aspartame, and a third experimental diet contained very little sugar but had added saccharin. After surveying parents, teachers, and babysitters and testing the study group for changes in memory, concentration, and math skills, the researchers concluded, "We couldn't find any difference in terms of their behavior or their learning on any of the three diets."[59] Hence, to date, the evidence concerning sugar's impact on behaviour is unclear.

Some studies have implicated food additives, such as the flavour enhancer monosodium glutamate (MSG), dyes, and artificial flavourings in producing criminal violence.[60] Other research has found that coffee and sugar may trigger anti-social behaviour;[61] researchers were led to these conclusions through finding that inmates consumed considerably greater amounts of coffee, sugar, and processed foods than others.[62] It is unclear, however, whether inmates drink more coffee because of boredom, or whether "excitable" personalities feel a need for the kind of stimulation available through coffee consumption. On the other hand, habitual coffee drinkers in non-prison populations have not been linked to crime, and other studies show no link between the amount of sugar consumed by inmates and hyperactivity.[63] Nonetheless, some prison programs have been designed to limit intake of dietary stimulants through nutritional management and the substitution of artificial sweeteners for refined sugar.

Vitamins have also been examined for their impact on delinquency. At least one researcher found that disruptive children consumed far less than optimal levels of vitamins B_3 and B_6 than did non-problem youths.[64] Some researchers have suggested that the addition of these vitamins to the diets of children who were deficient in them could control unruly behaviour and improve school performance. In a recent study, schoolchildren receiving vitamin supplements showed a 47 percent lower rate of anti-social behaviour than children who received placebos.[65] More important, the drop in disciplinary infractions among children taking the supplements was due mostly to a decrease in infractions by those who had been identified as habitual offenders before entering the study.

Other nutrients have been studied to assess their possible behavioural impact. In 2003, for example, Ingrid B. Helland reported that maternal diet during pregnancy can strongly affect IQ and early infant behaviour and concluded that it might also determine the risk of delinquency and criminality in later life.[66] Helland and her colleagues supplemented the diets of pregnant and lactating women with either omega-3 (DHA) or omega-6 fatty acids and followed the development of their offspring for years after the supplementation program had ended. They found that children receiving dietary omega-3 supplementation had significantly higher IQ levels by age four and performed better on problem-solving tests than those receiving omega-6 fatty acids.

A year later, a study of the relationship between omega-3 intake levels and chronic hostility among 3600 urban young adults concluded that higher consumption of omega-3 fatty acids was related to significantly lower levels of hostility. Researchers concluded that "high dietary intake of DHA and consumption of fish rich in omega-3 fatty acids may be related to lower likelihood of high hostility in young adulthood."[67] A 2007 study conducted in the United Kingdom found that anti-social behaviour could be reduced in children through dietary supplementation with poly-unsaturated fatty acids.[68]

Environmental Pollution

Various substances found in our environment are thought to be linked to criminal behaviour. In 1997, British researchers Roger D. Masters, Brian Hone, and Anil Doshi published a study purporting to show that industrial and other forms of environmental pollution cause people to commit violent crimes.[69] The study used statistics from the FBI's Uniform Crime Reporting Program and data from the U.S. Environmental Protection Agency's Toxic Release Inventory. A comparison between the two data sets showed a significant correlation between juvenile crime and high environmental levels of both lead and manganese. Masters and his colleagues suggested an explanation based on a *neurotoxicity hypothesis*. Another author stated,

> According to this approach, toxic pollutants—specifically the toxic metals lead and manganese—cause learning disabilities, an increase in aggressive behavior, and—most importantly—loss of control over impulsive behavior. These traits combine with poverty, social stress, alcohol and drug abuse, individual character, and other social and psychological factors to produce individuals who commit violent crimes.[70]

The largest study of lead contamination and its effects on behaviour was an examination of 1000 African-American children in Philadelphia. It showed that the level of exposure to lead was a reliable predictor of the number of juvenile offences among the exposed male population, the seriousness of juvenile offences, and the number of adult offences. More recent studies seem to support this thesis.[71] The researchers reasoned that toxic metals affect individuals in complex ways. Because lead diminishes a person's normal ability to detoxify poisons, it may heighten the effects of alcohol and drugs. Industrial pollution, automobile emissions, lead-based paints, and aging water-delivery systems are all possible sources of lead contamination. In a recent interview, Masters noted, "The presence of pollution is as big a factor [in crime causation] as poverty. It's the breakdown of the inhibition mechanism that's the key to violent behavior."[72] When brain chemistry is altered by exposure to heavy metals and other toxins, people lose the natural restraint that holds their violent tendencies in check.

More recent studies have focused on prenatal exposure to substances like cannabis, tobacco smoke, and alcohol. In 2000, for example, results of a 10-year study that monitored the development of the children of more than 600 low-income women found that prenatal cannabis use was significantly related to increased hyperactivity, impulsivity, inattention symptoms, increased delinquency, and externalizing problems.[73] The findings remained significant even when researchers controlled for other lifestyle features.

Similarly, a study of 1022 New Zealand children who had been followed for 18 years found that "children whose mothers smoked one pack of cigarettes or more per day during their pregnancy had mean rates of conduct disorder symptoms that were twice as high as those found among children born to mothers who did not smoke during their pregnancy."[74] The observed relationship was twice as strong among male teens as among females. Similar relationships between prenatal smoking and aggression and hyperactivity in later life have been reported by Dutch researchers.[75] A similar 2006 meta-analysis by researchers at Washington State University also found that smoking by pregnant mothers contributed slightly to their children's subsequent anti-social behaviour.[76]

Prenatal alcohol exposure also seems to be linked to delinquency and psychiatric problems later in life. A 1999 study of 32 children found that alcohol-exposed children exhibited greater delinquency and less intelligence than a control group of children who had not suffered from alcohol exposure while in the womb. The researchers concluded that their findings, which are consistent with the work of other researchers,[77] showed that "alcohol-exposed children, although less impaired intellectually, are more likely than children with mental retardation to exhibit antisocial behaviours, lack of consideration for the rights and feelings of others, and resistance to limits and requests of authority figures."[78]

Hormones and Criminality

Testosterone The primary male sex hormone. It is produced in the testes, and its function is to control secondary sex characteristics and sexual drive.

A hormone is a chemical substance produced by the body that regulates and controls activity of certain cells or organs. Hormones have come under scrutiny as potential behavioural determinants. The male sex hormone **testosterone**, for example, has been linked to aggression (see the following Who's Responsible? box). Most studies on the subject have consistently shown an apparent relationship between high blood testosterone levels and increased aggressiveness in men, and focused studies have unveiled a direct relationship between the amount of the chemical present and the degree of violence used by sex offenders.[79] Other researchers have linked steroid abuse among bodybuilders to destructive urges and psychosis.[80] Anabolic steroids are human-made drugs that have similar effects to testosterone in the body.

Some contemporary investigations have demonstrated a link between testosterone levels and aggression in teenagers,[81] and others have shown that adolescent problem behaviour and teenage violence rise in proportion to the amount of testosterone levels in the blood of young men.[82] In 1987, for example, Swedish researcher Dan Olweus reported that boys aged 15 to 17 showed levels of both verbal and physical aggression that correlated with the level of testosterone present in their blood, stating that boys with higher levels of testosterone "tended to be habitually more impatient and irritable than boys with lower testosterone levels."[83] He concluded that high levels of the hormone led to increased frustration and habitual impatience and irritability.

In what may be the definitive work to date on the subject, Alan Booth and D. Wayne Osgood concluded that there is a "moderately strong relationship between testosterone and adult deviance" but suggested that the relationship "is largely mediated by the influence of testosterone on social integration and on prior involvement in juvenile delinquency."[84] In other words, measurably high levels of testosterone in the blood of young men may have some effect on behaviour, but those effects are likely to be moderated by the social environment.

A few limited studies have attempted to measure the effects of testosterone on women. Although women's bodies manufacture roughly one-tenth the amount of the hormone secreted by men, subtle changes in testosterone levels in women have been linked to changes in personality and sexual behaviour.[85] One such study showed that relatively high blood levels of testosterone in female inmates were associated with "aggressively dominant behaviour" in prison.[86] Another study whose results were reported in 2003 attempted to measure the impact of high levels of androgens (male hormones, including testosterone) on both males and females.[87] The study examined the "externalizing behaviour" of 87 14-year-olds (51 females and 36 males); other data on externalizing behaviour, including aggression, were available from information

Hormones and Criminal Behaviour

Lamont Ridgeway, 22, was arrested and charged with sexual assault after 21-year-old Nicole Bachman called police to her home at 2:00 a.m. Ridgeway and Bachman had met in an evening class at the local community college, and Bachman invited Ridgeway to her apartment for a beer after the class was over. Officers couldn't help but notice that Bachman was an unusually attractive young woman whose clothes were in disarray and that she was visibly intoxicated and slurred her words as she spoke; Ridgeway was passed out on her couch, apparently after having had far too much to drink.

"He raped me!" Bachman told the two officers who responded to her call for help. "I told him to stop, and he wouldn't," she said.

Ridgeway was roused from sleep, arrested, searched, handcuffed, and taken to jail, where he was booked and charged with sexual assault. After being advised of his rights not to speak and to have a lawyer represent him, he decided to tell the officers who were questioning him that it wasn't really sexual assault. "She came on to me," he said. "She took her blouse off, then her pants. And she gave me a lot to drink. Yeah, she said 'No,' but by then we were already there. I couldn't stop. Why would she want to, anyway?"

When Ridgeway's lawyer arrived, he advised Ridgeway not to say anything more. The lawyer, hired by Ridgeway's wealthy parents, read the statement that he had given to the police and then hired a psychiatrist to help in building a defence that might stand up in court.

When the case went to trial two months later, the psychiatrist testified as an expert witness for the defence. He told the jury that blood tests showed that Ridgeway had abnormally large amounts of testosterone naturally occurring in his blood, that testosterone was the chemical messenger responsible for the male sex drive (which, he said, differed substantially from that of women), and that Ridgeway had consequently been unable to control his behaviour on the night of the alleged assault. "The young man was simply doing what his hormones made him do," the psychiatrist testified. "It's my professional opinion," he concluded, "that with that amount of testosterone affecting his judgment, he really didn't have much choice in his behavioural responses once he was offered alcohol and was then visually stimulated by the young woman's removal of her clothes. If this was my patient," the psychiatrist added, "I'd treat him with the testosterone antagonist Depo-Provera, and we would see the strength of his sex drive substantially diminished. You could be sure that this kind of thing wouldn't happen again."

In response, the prosecution called its own expert, a noted biochemist who, citing various studies, said that there was no clearly established link between blood levels of testosterone and aggressive sexual behaviour in human beings. "Even if there were," he said, "people are not mindless animals. We have free choice. We are not so driven by our blood chemistry that we cannot decide what we are going to do in any given situation."

Think about it:

1. With which expert witness do you agree more—the psychiatrist or the biochemist? Why?

2. Do you believe that blood chemistry can ever be an explanation for behaviour? For crime?

3. How do our understandings of criminal motivation and crime causality influence our policies on the treatment, punishment, and reformation of those who violate the law?

Note: This example is a fictionalized one, intended to encourage critical thinking.

---

gathered when the children were 8, 11, and 14 years old. Findings showed that boys with the highest blood plasma levels of androgens exhibited the most persistent aggression, but no association was found between aggression and androgen levels in females.

Serotonin   A 1997 study by Paul C. Bernhardt found that testosterone might not act alone in promoting aggression.[88] Bernhardt discovered that aggressive behaviour in men may be influenced by high testosterone levels combined with low brain levels of the neurotransmitter **serotonin**. Serotonin is a hormone that is commonly found in the pineal gland, the digestive tract and intestines, the central nervous system, and the blood platelets. Serotonin plays an important role in the regulation of learning, mood, and sleep and in the constriction of blood vessels.

Serotonin   A neurotransmitter that is commonly found in the pineal gland, the digestive tract and intestines, the central nervous system, and the blood platelets.

Bernhardt postulated that testosterone's true role is to produce dominance-seeking behaviour but not necessarily overt aggression. According to Bernhardt, when individuals are frustrated by their inability to achieve dominance, serotonin acts to reduce the negative psychological impact of frustration, producing calmer responses. Men whose brains are lacking in serotonin, however, feel the effects of frustration more acutely and therefore tend to respond to frustrating circumstances more aggressively, especially when testosterone levels are high.

Serotonin has been called a "behaviour-regulating chemical," and animal studies have demonstrated a link between low levels of the neurotransmitter present in the brain and aggressive behaviour. For example, monkeys with low serotonin levels have been found more likely to bite, slap, and chase others of their kind. Studies at the National Institute on Alcohol Abuse and Alcoholism in Bethesda, Maryland, have linked low serotonin levels in humans to impulsive crimes. Men convicted of premeditated murder, for example, have been found to have normal serotonin levels, whereas those convicted of crimes of passion have lower levels.[89]

One 1998 study of 781 men and women age 21 found a clear relationship between elevated *blood* levels of serotonin (which correspond to lower *brain* levels of the chemical) and violence in men.[90] The study controlled for a host of possible intervening factors, including gender, diet, psychiatric medications, illicit drug use, season of the year (during which the blood test was done), plasma levels of tryptophan (the dietary precursor of serotonin), alcohol and tobacco use, psychiatric diagnoses, platelet count, body mass, socio-economic status, IQ, and history of suicide attempts. The relationship held true when both court records and self-reports of violence were assessed. No relationship between serotonin levels and aggression was seen in female subjects.

Similar research by Swedish neuropsychiatrists in 2003 found that a "dysregulation of serotonin" in the brain and central nervous system could lead to increased impulsivity, irresponsibility, aggression, and need for stimulation.[91] The researchers examined the cerebrospinal fluid (CSF) of 28 violent and sexual offenders and noted that an imbalance between levels of serotonin and dopamine was highly associated with psychopathic traits.

Canadian UFC welterweight champion Georges St-Pierre pins Nick Diaz. Sex hormones such as testosterone have been linked to aggressive behaviour. Testosterone also enhances secondary sexual characteristics, such as body hair and muscle mass in males. What kinds of crimes might be hormonally influenced?

Ryan Remiorz/The Canadian Press

Hormones, such as testosterone and the thyroid hormone T_3, have also been implicated in delinquency and poor impulse control. A few years ago, two separate Swedish studies found evidence suggesting that elevated levels of the thyroid hormone T_3 were related to alcoholism, psychopathy, and criminality.[92] Blood serum levels of the thyroid hormone T_4 (thyroxine), on the other hand, were negatively related to anti-social behaviour. The researchers concluded that the results of their studies indicate an intimate relationship between T_3 and T_4 and abuse and anti-social behaviour. They emphasized the importance of further studies on T_3 as a biological marker for abuse, social deviance, and repeated violent behaviour.[93]

As the criminologist Leah E. Daigle points out, however, "changes in hormone levels alone do not account for aggressive behavior. Instead, these hormonal changes may affect a third, unspecified variable (such as self-control or social bonds) that lead to aggressive responses."[94] In other words, says Daigle, "rather than directly affecting behavior, hormones may instead interact with social factors to produce criminal behavior."

SOCIOBIOLOGY

6.4 | **LEARNING OBJECTIVE**

Sociobiology The systematic study of the biological basis of all social behaviour.

Paradigm An example, model, or theory.

IN THE INTRODUCTION TO HIS ARTICLE SUMMARIZING **SOCIOBIOLOGY**, ARTHUR FISHER wrote, "Every so often, in the long course of scientific progress, a new set of ideas appears, illuminating and redefining what has gone before like a flare bursting over a darkened landscape."[95] To some, sociobiology—which appeared upon the social science scene in 1975—held the promise of just such a new **paradigm**, or model.[96] The development of this new paradigm, however, was preceded by the work of ethnologists, including John H. Cook, Sir Julian Huxley, and Austrian Konrad Lorenz, who studied the social behaviour of both people and animals and laid the groundwork for later sociobiological perspectives.

The Biological Roots of Aggression

In 1966, Austrian animal expert Konrad Lorenz published his now famous work *On Aggression*.[97] In it, Lorenz described how aggression permeates the animal kingdom and asked, "What is the value of all this fighting?" "In nature," he said, "fighting is such an ever-present process, its behavior mechanisms and weapons are so highly developed and have so obviously arisen under the pressure of a species-preserving function, that it is our duty to ask this question."[98]

Lorenz accepted the evolutionary thesis of the 19th-century biologist Charles Darwin that aggression within a species favoured the strongest and best animals in the reproductive process, but he concluded that aggression served a variety of other purposes as well. Aggression, said Lorenz, ensures an "even distribution of animals of a particular species over an inhabitable area" and provides for a defence of the species from predators.[99] Human aggression, he claimed, meets many of the same purposes but can take on covert forms. The drive to acquire wealth and power that was so characteristic of Western men at the time of his writing is part of the human mating ritual, whereby a man might "win" a prized woman through displays of more civilized forms of what could otherwise be understood as intraspecies aggression.

Two male wolves prepare to fight for pack dominance. Sociobiologists tell us that certain traits, such as territoriality, are common to both animals and humans. How might territoriality lead to crime?

Kane513/Shutterstock

Lorenz's greatest contribution to the study of human behaviour may have been his claim that all human behaviour is, at least to some degree, "adapted instinctive behaviour"; in other words, much of human conduct is fundamentally rooted in instinctive behavioural responses characteristic of biological organisms everywhere and present within each of us in the form of a biological inheritance from more primitive times. Even rational human thought derives its motivation and direction from instinctual aspects of human biology, and the highest human virtues, such as the value placed on human life, "could not have been achieved," said Lorenz, "without an instinctive appreciation of life and death."[100]

Building upon the root functions of aggression, Lorenz concluded that much of what we today call "crime" is the result of overcrowded living conditions combined with a lack of legitimate opportunity for the effective expression of aggression. Crowding increases the likelihood of aggression, while contemporary socialization works to inhibit it. In the words of Lorenz, "In one sense we are all psychopaths, for each of us suffers from the necessity of self-imposed control for the good of the community."[101] When people break down, said Lorenz, they become neurotic or delinquent, and crime may be the result of stresses that have been found to typically produce aggression throughout the animal kingdom.

Lorenz's explanations, like many of the biological-based theories we will encounter in this chapter, appear more applicable to violent crime than to other forms of criminal offence. But it is important to recognize that modern frustrations and concomitant manifestations of aggression may be symbolically, rather than directly, expressed. Hence, a stockbroker who embezzles a client's money, spurred on by the need to provide material goods for an overly acquisitive family, may be just as criminal as the robber who beats his victim and steals her purse to have money to buy liquor.

The New Synthesis

Evolutionist Edward O. Wilson is credited with coining the term *sociobiology*. In his groundbreaking book, *Sociobiology: The New Synthesis*, Wilson defined sociobiology as "the systematic study of the biological basis of all social behavior [that is] a branch of evolutionary biology and particularly of modern population biology."[102] Through his entomological study of social insects (especially ants), Wilson provided examples of altruism (selfless, helping behaviour) in multiple species and, contrary to the beliefs of some evolutionary biologists, he found that helping behaviour facilitated the continuity of the gene pool found among altruistic individuals. The primary determinant of behaviour, including human behaviour, said Wilson, was the need to ensure the survival and continuity of genetic material from one generation to the next—and altruism played a role in survival.

Territoriality, according to Wilson's writings, explains many of the conflicts— including homicide, warfare, and other forms of aggression—between and among human beings. In Wilson's words, "Part of man's problem is that his intergroup responses are still crude and primitive, and inadequate for the extended extraterritorial relationships that civilization has thrust upon him." The "unhappy result," as Wilson termed it, may be "**tribalism**," expressed through the contemporary increase of street gangs, racial tension, and hardened encampments of survivalist and separatist groups.

Sociobiological theory not only tells us that the violence and aggressiveness associated with territoriality are often reserved for strangers but also explains intragroup aggression (violence occurring within groups). Wilson's theory suggests that within the group "a particularly severe form of aggressiveness should be reserved for actual or suspected adultery. In many human societies where sexual bonding is close and personal knowledge of the behavior of others detailed, adulterers are harshly treated. The sin is regarded to be

Tribalism The attitudes and behaviour that results from strong feelings of identification with one's own social group.

even worse when offspring are produced." Hence, territoriality and acquisitiveness extend to location, possessions, and even other people. Human laws, explained Wilson, are designed to protect genetic relationships people have with one another as well as their material possessions and their claimed locations in space; thus, violations of these intuitive relationships result in crime and in official reactions by the legal system.

Wilson's writing propelled researchers into a flurry of studies intended to test the validity of his assertions. A Canadian study by Martin Daly and Margo Wilson of violence in the homes of adoptive children found that stepchildren run a risk 70 times greater of being killed by their adoptive parents than do children living with their natural parents.[103] Some writers have concluded that "murderous behavior, warfare, and even genocide were unavoidable correlates of genetic evolution, controlled by the same genes for territorial behavior that had been selected in primate evolution."[104] Others have suggested that biological predispositions developed during earlier stages of human evolution colour contemporary criminal activity. Male criminals, for example, tend toward robbery and burglary—crimes in which they can continue to enact their "hunter" instincts developed long ago—whereas the criminality of women often involves shoplifting and simple theft, more typical of "gatherer" instincts.

Human behavioural predilections can be studied in a variety of ways. In the 1989 book *Evolutionary Jurisprudence*, John H. Beckstrom reported on his examination of over 400 legal documents as well as legal claims and court decisions spanning over 300 years of judicial activity that showed support for Wilson's contentions that humans tend to act to preserve territorial claims, their likelihood of successful reproduction, and the continuation of their own particular genetic material.[105] Other theorists have gone so far as to imply that, among humans, there may be a genetic tendency to experience guilt and to develop a conscience and that notions of right and wrong, whether embodied in laws or in social convention, may flow from such a naturalistic origin.

As sociobiology began to receive expanded recognition from investigators (most of whom are American), some social scientists began to treat it as "criminology's anti-discipline."[106] Criticisms included the following charges:

- Sociobiology fails to convey the overwhelming significance of culture, social learning, and individual experiences in shaping the behaviour of individuals and groups.

- Sociobiology is fundamentally wrong in its depiction of the basic nature of human beings; there is no credible evidence of genetic or determined tendencies to act in certain ways.

- Sociobiology is just another empirically unsupported rationale for the authoritative labelling and stigmatization of despised, threatening, and powerless minorities.

- Human beings are so thoroughly different from other animal species, even other primates, that there is no rational basis for the application to humans of findings from animal studies.

Today, many scholars are beginning to sense the growing need for a new synthesis, a way to consider the impact of biological theories like sociobiology and insights drawn from studies of twins and other long-accepted perspectives like sociology and psychology in explaining human behaviour. Gail Anderson, internationally renowned Canadian professor of forensic entomology (the use of insect evidence at crime scenes), provided an integrative approach to considering criminal behaviour by examining the role of biology in criminal behaviour and how biology interacts with sociological forces to lead to crime.[107] Recent studies examining the relationship between genetics and criminality and body chemistry and criminality, many of which have already been discussed in this chapter, indicate that the field of criminology appears ready to consider a new multi-causal approach.

BIOSOCIAL CRIMINOLOGY

IN THE MID-1980S, CRIMINOLOGIST JAMES Q. WILSON AND PSYCHOLOGIST RICHARD J. Herrnstein teamed up to write *Crime and Human Nature*, a book-length treatise that reiterates many of the arguments proposed by biological criminologists over the previous century.[108] Part of their purpose was to reopen discussion of biological causes of crime. "We want to show," Herrnstein said, "that the pendulum is beginning to swing away from a totally sociological explanation of crime."[109] Their avowed goal was "not to state a case just for genetic factors, but to state a comprehensive theory of crime that draws together all the different factors that cause criminal behavior."[110]

Wilson and Herrnstein cited several constitutional factors that they believed made important and undeniable contributions to criminal behavour:[111]

- *Gender:* "Crime has been predominantly male behavior."
- *Age:* "In general, the tendency to break the law declines throughout life."
- *Body type:* "A disproportionate number of criminals have a mesomorphic build."
- *Intelligence:* Criminality is said to be clearly and consistently associated with low intelligence.
- *Personality:* Criminals are typically aggressive, impulsive, and cruel.

Although personality, behavioural problems, and intelligence may be related to environment, the authors said that "each involves some genetic inheritance." Wilson and Herrnstein recognized social factors in the development of personality but suggested that constitutional factors predispose a person to specific types of behaviour and that societal *reactions* to such predispositions may determine, to a large degree, the form of continued behaviour.

In the 1990s, Anthony Walsh of Boise State University, who is one of today's best-known proponents of **biosocial criminology**, continued the movement toward recognizing biology's contributions to understanding criminal behaviour. Walsh emphasized the importance of the *interaction* between biology and the environment in the formation of behavioural responses to given situations. "Biological factors do not operate in an environmental vacuum," said Walsh, "nor do environmental factors operate in a biological vacuum, and we must cease formulating our theories as if they do."[112]

Walsh became one of the founders of contemporary biosocial criminology—a scientific endeavour that attempts to take all that is known about the biological underpinnings of human behaviour and to use that knowledge to assess how human biology interacts with the surrounding physical, cultural, and social environments in producing a criminal event. Biosocial criminology is not so much a theory about crime as it is a perspective on criminality that recognizes the importance of the interaction between biology and the surrounding physical and social environments.

Walsh observes that biosocial perspectives are theories of criminality, not crime.[113] He goes on to explain that crime is a "legal label" that is placed on specific behaviours that violate the criminal law. Criminality, on the other hand, says Walsh, "is a property of individuals, a continuous trait that is itself an amalgam of other continuous traits, and thus belongs to a more inclusive kind of criminology."[114] According to Walsh, criminality can be seen as the willingness to violate individual rights and social norms, whether or not such behaviour is against the law. Criminality, says Walsh, consists of "a relative lack of empathy, conscience, self-control, and fear, as well as self-centeredness, and a penchant for risky behavior."[115] Seen this way, biosocial explanations of criminality are more likely to be couched in terms of a propensity for violence, aggression, deceit, recklessness, fearlessness, and so on, and features of the surrounding environment determine how such propensities are expressed.

Biosocial criminology A theoretical perspective that sees the interaction between biology and the physical and social environments as key to understanding human behaviour, including criminality.

Echoing Walsh, behavioural science expert Diana Fishbein notes that "biological differences do not function in a vacuum to increase risk." Instead, she writes that biological factors interact dynamically with many social and environmental conditions "to contribute to or protect from social dysfunction."[116] It is this emphasis on *interaction* between biology and the environment—especially culture and the social environment—that differentiates biosocial criminology from other biological perspectives on crime.

Researchers are beginning to understand just how complex the relationship between biology, behaviour, and the social environment can be. Biosocial criminology attempts to recognize this complexity by embracing the role of a multitude of factors leading to criminality and including the interaction of those factors with the surrounding environment.

Gender Differences in Criminality

A number of contemporary writers propose that criminologists must recognize that "the male is much more criminalistic than the female."[117] With the exception of crimes such as prostitution and shoplifting, the number of crimes committed by men routinely exceeds the number of crimes committed by women in almost all categories. Biosocial researcher Kevin Beaver explains it this way: "In virtually every study ever conducted, males are much more likely than females to engage in violence, aggression, and serious crimes. As the seriousness of the offence/behavior increases, the gender gap also tends to increase, such that the most violent criminal acts are almost exclusively a male phenomenon." Beaver calls the differences between female and male rates of offending the *gender gap*. He and other writers also refer to it as the *gender ratio problem* and call for its explanation.[118]

The data on the extent of male–female criminality in Canada show regularity over time: for example, the proportion of homicides committed by men versus women has remained more or less constant—with about 87 percent of all murders committed by men on average since 1966.[119] Similarly, the proportion of men murdered by men versus the proportion of women murdered by women has been consistent, indicating a much greater propensity for men to murder one another.

If culture exercises the major role in determining criminality, then we would expect to see recognizable increases in the degree and nature of female criminality over time, especially as changes in socialization practices, cultural roles, and other ethnographic patterns increase the opportunity for women to commit what had previously been regarded as traditionally male offences. Although women comprise 51 percent of the Canadian population, they commit 17 percent of all *Criminal Code* offences, less than 20 percent of all violent crimes, 30 percent of frauds, and 38 percent of minor thefts.[120] These gender differences can also be seen in cross-cultural studies. (See Figure 6.2).

Such findings contrast with the suggestions of authors like Freda Adler, who, in her classic 1975 book *Sisters in Crime*, proposed that as women entered non-traditional occupations and roles, there "would be a movement toward parity with men in the commission of crime in terms of both incidence and type."[121] Criminologist Thomas Bernard and colleagues Jeffrey Snipes and Alexander Gerould have advanced the proposition that "the issue of why always and everywhere males commit more criminal acts than females is the 'single most important fact that criminology theories must be able to explain.'"[122] Biosocial criminologists suggest that the organic correlates of gender provide the needed explanation. Walsh, for example, says that the gender ratio problem is only a problem "if we are constrained to operate under sociology's strict environmentalist paradigm, which is suspicious of psychological or biological factors that differentiate among individuals and categories of individuals."[123] If we admit, Walsh

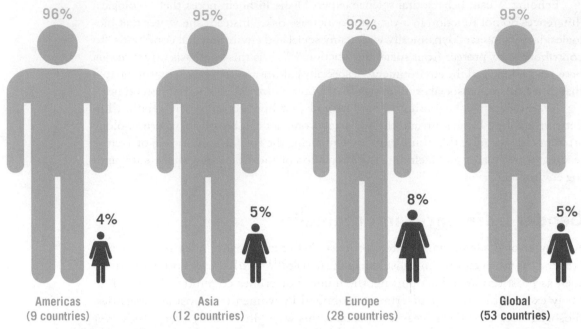

Figure 6.2 Percentage Distribution of Persons Convicted of Homicide, by Sex, and by Region, 2012

Source: United Nations Office on Drugs and Crime. Global Study on Homicide 2013 (Vienna: UNODC 2014) p. 94. Used by permission of United Nations Office on Drugs and Crime (UNODC).

writes, that "there is something about gender per se" that is responsible for the observed differences, the problem is resolved.[124]

One of the primary contemporary paradigms useful in understanding gender differences in criminality is the concept of sexual selection. Sexual selection, which is a form of natural selection that influences an individual's ability to find or choose a mate, derives from Charles Darwin's theory of evolution.[125] While Darwin was most concerned with explaining how the process of natural selection (survival of the fittest) determines trait differences between species, the concept of sexual selection seeks to explain male–female differences within species. Contemporary writers, for example, claim that the important roles of child bearing, child protection, and child rearing created evolutionary pressures for females to become sensitive to immediate environmental stimuli—or what is happening in their immediate vicinity. Such awareness, they claim, provided the ability to identify threats and to shield their offspring from danger. Consequently, because of evolutionary forces, females today may be more sensitive than men to many environmental stimuli, are more easily aroused, are quicker to respond to what is going on around them, and tend to avoid dangerous or threatening situations. Some researchers have found support for such an argument in discoveries that the reticular activating system, which accounts for sensitivity and response, is more finely tuned in women than in men.[126] To compensate for lower levels of arousal, men tend to be more sensation-seeking than women, these researchers say, and their desire for increased arousal and environmental stimulation are closely linked to risk-taking and crime.[127]

None of this, of course, denies the fact that genetic behavioural differences between men and women are moderated by aspects of the social environment, including socialization, the learning of culturally prescribed roles, and the expectations of others. Walsh concludes, however, that "we must realize that gender socialization rests on the solid bedrock of sex differentiated biology forged by countless thousands of years of contrasting sexual selection pressures."[128]

POLICY IMPLICATIONS OF BIOLOGICAL THEORIES

IN 1992, THE TERM *STANDARD SOCIAL SCIENCE MODEL* (SSSM) WAS INTRODUCED TO THE general public by Jerome H. Barkow and his colleagues in the edited volume *The Adapted Mind*.[129] The SSSM—which assumes that human beings come into this world like blank slates and acquire almost all of their values, behavioural patterns, and modes of thought through socialization into their surrounding cultures—was identified as the perspective that had characterized much social scientific thought during the 20th century. According to Barkow, the SSSM provided the underpinnings for the work of many famous sociologists, social psychologists, and social anthropologists of the 1900s, including anthropologists Margaret Mead and Leslie White and sociologist Ellsworth Faris.

Only in the last decade or two has the SSSM largely given way to broader perspectives that include an examination of the role of biology and genetic influences on human behaviour. In a more recent book, *The Blank Slate: The Modern Denial of Human Nature*,[130] Steven Pinker, a scientist at the Massachusetts Institute of Technology, told readers that today's social scientists still continue to unjustly ignore the biological basis of human behaviour, and it is only when the impact of biology on human behaviour is fully recognized that effective social policies—including those aimed at controlling crime—can be developed.

Although biological theories of crime have problems, some criminologists believe that to ignore the potential contributions of biological theorists does a disservice to the science of criminology and denies the opportunity for compassionate and objective researchers to realistically assist in the process of crime prevention and reduction. In 1997, in an attempt to bring biological theorizing into the criminological mainstream, Lee Ellis and Anthony Walsh expanded on the theme of genetic predispositions, noting that

> in the case of behavior, nearly all of the effects of genes are quite indirect because they are mediated through complex chains of events occurring in the brain. This means that there are almost certainly no genes for something as complex as criminal behavior. Nevertheless, many genes may affect brain functioning in ways that either increase or reduce the chances of individuals learning various complex behavior patterns, including behavior patterns that happen to be so offensive to others that criminal sanctions have been instituted to minimize their recurrence.[131]

CRITIQUE OF BIOLOGICAL THEORIES

A CENTRAL CONCERN WITH ALL EARLY BIOLOGICAL THEORIES OF CRIMINAL BEHAVIOUR has to do with the fact that they seemed to relegate the role of free will in human behaviour to a kind of philosophical dustbin. If a person's behaviour is largely determined, for example, by inherent and unchangeable atavistic features, then he or she may be condemned to a life of crime, and efforts at reformation can be expected to have little positive effect on future behaviour. Consequently, some people continue to shy away from biological explanations for criminality and disordered behaviour because phrases like "genetic determinism," have come to be synonymous with inevitability.

Given the difficulty in sorting out this kind of complex relationship, it may be impossible to identify any biological features shared solely by criminals. As today's theorists understand, the influence of biology on behaviour of any kind is more often the result of an interaction among genetic, hormonal, and other biological features of an individual and his or her social and physical environments. Biological and biosocial approaches to explaining crime, including those related to genetics and body chemistry, have been criticized because they fail to predict criminality accurately while purporting to understand its causes. For example, if a genetic attribute or a certain body chemistry is associated with a greater tendency toward law violation, then why would such theories fail to predict which individuals with those biological realities will offend and which will obey the law? Many of the critiques identified in regard to chemical precursors can be applied to perspectives involving hormones and criminal behaviour. Hormones, after all, are chemicals that are made by the body (or are sometimes injected into the bloodstream). As is the case with chemical precursors, hormones apparently don't affect everyone the same way. Not all men with high testosterone levels, for example, are violent or aggressive.

Biosocial theories, for their part, can be criticized in a number of ways.[132] Some critics claim, for example, that biosocial research is fraught with methodological problems because studies in the area have often been based on small, non-representative samples.[133] Also, most research in the area of biosocial theory has been done on offenders who have been placed in clinical treatment settings, making it impossible to tell if study findings are relevant only to convicted criminals in correctional facilities or to the criminal population as a whole. Findings from such studies are difficult to generalize to other settings, and it may be difficult to draw definitive conclusions from small samples that have been studied under unique conditions.

Other critics note that biosocial theories fail to explain regional and temporal variations in crime rates. Biosocial theories, for example, do not seem to explain adequately why one country has higher rates of violent crime than others, or why one region of a city has different rates of property crime. Similarly, biosocial theories cannot totally account for changes in crime rates over time or among different age groups within the same population.

Biological theories that focus on environmental and chemical precursors to crime cannot explain why certain kinds of crime are more likely to occur in certain parts of the country, in particular types of communities, and among members of specific subcultures rather than in others. Such differences imply that much more is at work than chemicals themselves and suggest that cultural differences play a significant role in criminality. Critics also claim that theories involving chemical precursors cannot account for changes in crime rates over time. Crime rates have trended substantially downward over the past couple of decades, during the same time period that exposure to chemical substances of all types throughout the general population has expanded.

Some biosocial criminologists have been accused of racial and class bias for failing to explain why a disproportionate number of certain kinds of crime are committed by poor people and by racial and ethnic minorities.[134] Critics say that it would be more useful to focus on social settings rather than on biological variables to explain such differences and that characteristics of the social environment—including racism, oppression, discrimination, and economic strain—are more effective at explaining differences in criminality between racial and ethnic groups and social classes. These critics also note that some people may try to use biosocial perspectives to support their own biases and to justify continued social inequality.

The dangers of too great a dependence on biological approaches to crime have been raised by Canadian criminologists Julian Roberts and Thomas Gabor, who observed, "People who accept the view that variations in crime rates reflect genetic factors may also embrace an underlying message about crime prevention. Social programs aim to eradicate educational, social, and economic inequities. These efforts can only be undermined by statements stressing the importance of genetic factors in determining criminality."[135] Ronald Walters, a political scientist at Howard University, similarly observed that "seeking the biological and genetic aspects of violence is dangerous to African-American youth. When you consider the perception that black people have always been the violent people in this society, it is a short step from this stereotype to using this kind of research for social control."[136]

BIOLOGICAL THEORIES APPLIED

GENETICS
holds that criminality can be explained by physical features, body type, inheritance, or external observable physical characteristics.
How do the tenets of the genetic explanations of crime align with the studies equating proper nutritional diet with a reduction in aggressive behaviour described in the introduction?

SOCIOBIOLOGY
holds that there is a biological basis to all social behaviour, and hence criminal behaviour is linked to an individual's biological makeup and the interaction between biology and the environment.
Can the ingestion of good food and vitamins impact an individual's biological makeup?

Crime is a result of many behavioural predispositions that are genetically determined and focus on physical features and heredity or are predetermined by internal and external factors that affect body chemistry. New directions in biological theory emphasize the biological basis of all social behaviour and the interaction between biology and the physical environments.

How are the scientific studies outlined in the introduction that measured the impact of proper diet and aggressive behaviour supported by biological theories of crime?

BODY CHEMISTRY
holds that criminal behaviour is a result of chemical influences, including hormones, food additives, allergies, vitamins, and other chemical substances.
What is the evidence that ingested substances and nutrition have an impact on aggressive behaviour as presented in the introduction?

BIOSOCIAL CRIMINOLOGY
holds that the interaction between biology and the physical and social environments is key to understanding human behaviour, including criminality.
How can the crime-control approach advocated by biosocial criminology be supported by the findings of the research studies outlined in the introduction?

SUMMARY OF LEARNING OBJECTIVES

6.1 Biological theories hold that crime is a result of many behavioural predispositions that are genetically determined and focus on physical features and heredity or are predetermined by internal and external factors that affect body chemistry. New directions in biological theory emphasize the biological basis of all social behaviour and the interaction between biology and the physical environments.

6.2 Some scholars have suggested that a penchant for crime may be inherited and that genetic characteristics and variations in human chromosomes play an important role in crime causation. Although contemporary criminologists do not believe that there is one single and identifiable "criminal gene," they do believe that individuals who are genetically predisposed to certain types of behaviour may become aggressive or criminal through their interactions with the surrounding physical and social environments.

6.3 Body chemistry theories say that violent or disruptive behaviour can sometimes be linked to poor nutrition, vitamin deficiencies, and other conditions that affect the body. Studies of eating habits, environmental contaminants, and hormonal influences have all contributed to advances in understanding such behaviour.

6.4 Sociobiology is a theoretical perspective developed by Edward O. Wilson that can be described as "the systematic study of the biological basis of all social behaviour." Wilson believed that the primary determinant of human behaviour was the need to ensure the survival and continuity of genetic material from one generation to the next. Sociobiologists often focus on explaining the violence and aggression associated with territoriality. Sociobiology has been employed to explain intergroup and intragroup aggression.

6.5 Biosocial criminology sees the interaction between biology and the physical and social environments as key to understanding human behaviour, including criminality. It holds that genetic predispositions and their interaction with the surrounding social and physical environments may combine to produce criminality.

6.6 In the past, biology was often seen as deterministic. A contemporary approach to crime control needs now to be based on modern understandings of the link between biology and crime.

6.7 Few biological studies adequately conceptualize criminality, methodological problems have been found in many studies attempting to evaluate the role of genetics in crime, and results obtained outside North America may not be applicable within this country. Many criminologists have concluded that while biology provides a context for human behaviour, biological predispositions are overshadowed by the role of volition, mechanisms of human thought, and undeniable influences of socialization and acculturation.

Questions for Review

1. What are the central assumptions of biological theories of crime? How do such theories differ from other perspectives that attempt to explain the same phenomena?

2. What have research studies in the field of genetics had to say about possible causes of crime?

3. What role might diet, vitamin deficiencies, or hormonal influences have on criminal behaviour?

4. What is sociobiology? How do sociobiologists explain criminality?

5. How is criminality explained from a biosocial perspective?

6. What are the policy implications of biological theories of crime? What Canadian example discussed in this chapter might presage a type of policy based on such theories?

7. Why have biological approaches to crime causation encountered stiff criticism? Do you agree or disagree with those who are critical of such perspectives? Why?

Multiple-Choice Questions

1. The use of genetic knowledge developed by the Human Genome Project may have implications for understanding criminal behaviour by _____.

   a. identifying body types

   b. identifying diet deficiencies

   c. contributing to the relationship between genetic predispositions and interaction with surrounding social and physical environments

   d. better explaining the similarities between twins

   e. identifying males with the XYY chromosome

2. Cesare Lombroso called physical features that he thought to be indicative of criminality _____.

   a. atavisms

   b. ectomorphs

   c. stigmata of degeneration

   d. diplastics

   e. cyloids

3. Constitutional theories that explain criminality by reference to offenders' body types are primarily associated with _____.

   a. Richard J. Herrnstein and William H. Sheldon

   b. Cesare Lombroso

   c. Sheldon and Eleanor Glueck

   d. Ray Jeffrey

   e. Frank Joseph Gall

4. Studies considering the relationship between body chemistry and criminality consider _____.

   a. shape of nose and size of teeth

   b. emotional intelligence

   c. body shape

   d. chromosomes and genetic makeup

   e. hypoglycemia and pollution

5. Biosocial criminology contends it is the _____ that explains criminal behaviour.

   a. interaction between biology and the environment

   b. individual's genetic makeup

   c. social environment

   d. environmental pollution

   e. peer group

Multiple Choice Answers: 1c, 2a, 3a, 4e, 5a

Chapter 7
Psychological and Psychiatric Foundations of Criminal Behaviour

Regina Leader-Post/Bryan Schlosser/The Canadian Press

The major sources of theoretical development in criminology have been—and continue to be—psychological. A theory of criminal conduct is weak indeed if uninformed by a general psychology of human behaviour.

—*Donald Andrews and James Bonta*[1]

LEARNING OBJECTIVES

After reading this chapter, you should be able to

7.1 Recognize the major principles of psychological and psychiatric perspectives on criminal behaviour.

7.2 Discuss the ways in which personality can be used to explain criminality.

7.3 Explain cognitive theories and their contribution to the understanding of criminal behaviour.

7.4 Discuss psychopathy and its relationship to anti-social personality disorder and criminal behaviour.

7.5 Explain the roles of social cognition and role modelling in activating aggressive patterns of behaviour.

7.6 Understand the insights into criminal behaviour offered by the psychoanalytic perspective.

7.7 Identify current policy and treatment implications of the psychological and psychiatric approaches to criminal behaviour.

7.8 Identify some of the shortcomings of the psychological and psychiatric approaches to criminality.

7.9 List some assumptions underlying the practice of criminal psychological profiling.

7.10 Consider the unique characteristics of those found "not criminally responsible by reason of mental disorder."

INTRODUCTION

Some crimes defy explanation. In December 2002, Germans were horrified by a story sweeping the nation about a respectable engineer and software specialist who was alleged to have mutilated and eaten a 43-year-old microchip engineer. As police investigators descended upon the home and property of Armin Meiwes on the outskirts of Kassel, Germany, the gruesome details of ritualistic torture and cannibalism unfolded. Frozen human flesh that had been bagged and labelled by body part was found in a freezer, and human bones were discovered discarded in the gardens around the house.

Using advertisements on the internet such as "Wanted: young, well-built 18–30-year-old for slaughter," Meiwes lured scores of men from around the world to his chat room, where he confessed his cannibalistic tendencies. Some of the chat-room participants agreed to meet with Meiwes; one 27-year-old conference organizer from London, England, allowed Meiwes to chain him to a bed and stick pins in his body, marking out his liver, a kidney, and other organs to be consumed. Yet another, a 34-year-old cook from southern Germany, allowed Meiwes to string him up on meat hooks in a slaughter parlour in his house. Both men decided that the fantasy had gone far enough and did not proceed to the ultimate conclusion.

One man, Bernd Brandes, did not leave, however. A leading microchip designer who lived in a luxury penthouse suite, Brandes sold his car and other valuables and met with Meiwes at his home in March 2001. Details of their meeting were recorded on a videotape made by Meiwes; together the two men planned a grisly ritual and then executed it as they amputated, fried, and ate part of Brandes's body. Meiwes then stabbed Brandes to death. He sliced his flesh into small chunks, which he wrapped and stored in the freezer. He confessed to eating about 20 kilograms of the flesh in the months between the killing and his arrest.

Armin Meiwes was charged with first-degree murder only, since cannibalism is not legally prohibited in Germany. Thousands of printed emails and internet exchanges were presented as evidence in court. Details of Meiwes's life revealed that he had lived alone with his mother until her death. His father had left the family when Meiwes was eight years old, and his mother subsequently married and divorced three times. Psychologist Heinrich Wilmer testified at the trial that Meiwes was neither mentally ill nor motivated by sexual gratification. Rather, he lacked male role models, was incredibly lonely, and made up imaginary friends whom he imagined eating so that they would never go away.[2] The defence argued that Meiwes's victim had volunteered for sacrifice; Meiwes was merely assisting Brandes to fulfill his death wish. Prosecutors, on the other hand, argued that Meiwes premeditated the murder of his victim and did it for his own sexual satisfaction. In one email read at his trial, Meiwes, who became known around the world as the "Cannibal of Rotenburg," wrote that cannibalism should be promoted as a form of development aid. "We could solve the problem of

Armin Meiwes used the internet to lure victims into his cannibalistic ritual. What explains the public's fascination with bizarre killers?

Dpa picture alliance archive/Alamy Stock Photo

over-population and famine at a stroke," he stated. He also told the court that his cannibalism stemmed from an acute sense of loneliness and that his desperate need for a brother led him to consume a male so he would be "bound to me forever."[3] Meiwes was found guilty of manslaughter in January 2004 and received an eight-and-a-half-year sentence. In 2005, an appeal by the prosecution argued that Brandes was not legally capable of agreeing to his killing due to apparent mental challenges and alcohol over-consumption. At the trial, a psychologist testified that Meiwes still had fantasies about consuming human flesh and was a threat to reoffend. The court agreed, and Meiwes was sentenced to life in prison in May 2006.[4]

In 1989, in a very violent incident that has since heightened the public's awareness of violence against women, 14 female students at L'École Polytechnique in Montreal were shot to death by Marc Lepine, an embittered misogynist. Lepine entered a classroom and shouted, "I want the women," and then, "You're all a bunch of feminists, and I hate feminists."[5] After ordering all the men to leave the room, Lepine shot six women dead. Over the next 20 minutes, the 25-year-old Lepine methodically stalked the cafeteria, the classrooms, and the corridors of the school, leaving 8 other women dead and 13 injured. He finally turned the gun on himself. In the three-page suicide note found in his pocket, Lepine blamed feminists for ruining his life. Lepine's actions were explained by Dr. Renée Fugère, forensic psychiatrist at Montreal's Allan Memorial Institute, as those of a delusional man who repeatedly failed to achieve his ambitions in work—and with women. "Lepine probably did not have the capacity to mourn his failed relationships," she said, "so he kept it inside. Those feelings piled up and finally exploded."[6]

7.1 | LEARNING OBJECTIVE

MAJOR PRINCIPLES OF PSYCHOLOGICAL AND PSYCHIATRIC THEORIES

WHAT MOTIVATES PEOPLE TO KILL OR MAIM—OR EVEN TO COMMIT OTHER, LESS serious, offences? How can many killers seem "so normal" before their crimes, giving no hints of the atrocities they are about to commit? For answers to questions such as these, many people turn to psychological theories. Psychologists are the pundits of the modern age of behaviourism, offering explanations rooted in determinants lying within individual actors. Psychological determinants of deviant or criminal behaviour are couched in various terms, including *exploitative personality characteristics*, *poor impulse control*, *emotional arousal*, and *an immature personality*, among others. Before beginning a discussion of psychological theories, however, it

Table 7.1 Types of Psychological and Psychiatric Theories

Theory	Cognitive Theories	Personality Disturbances Theory	Behaviour Theory	Frustration–Aggression Theory	Crime as Adaption	Psychoanalytic Criminology
Period	1930s–present	1930s–present	1940s–present	1940s–present	1970s–present	1920s–present
Theorists	Jean Piaget, Lawrence Kohlberg, Roger C. Shank, and others	Hervey M. Cleckley, Hans J. Eysenck, and others	B.F. Skinner, Gabriel Tarde, Albert Bandura, and others	J. Dollard, Albert Bandura, and others	Seymour L. Halleck, Donald A. Andrews, James Bonta, and others	Sigmund Freud and others
Concepts	Moral development, scripts, cognitive information processing	Personality, psychopath, sociopath, anti-social personality disorder, personality traits, Five Factor Model	Operant behaviour, conditioning, stimulus-response, reward, punishment, social cognition, modelling, disengagement	Frustration, aggression, displacement	Alloplastic and autoplastic adaption, criminogenic needs, criminogenic domains	Psychiatric criminology, id, ego, superego, neurosis, psychosis, sublimation, paranoid schizophrenia

is necessary to provide a brief overview of the terminology used to describe the psychological study of crime and criminality. **Forensic psychology**, one of the fastest-growing subfields of psychology, is the application of the science and profession of psychology to questions and issues relating to law and the legal system.[7] Forensic psychology is sometimes referred to as *criminal psychology*, and forensic psychologists are also called criminal psychologists, correctional psychologists, and police psychologists. Unlike forensic psychologists (who generally hold PhDs), forensic psychiatrists are medical doctors, and **forensic psychiatry** is a medical subspecialty that applies psychiatry to the needs of crime prevention and solution, criminal rehabilitation, and issues of criminal law.[8] See Table 7.1 for an overview of the theories discussed in this chapter.

Most psychological and psychiatric theories of crime causation make the following fundamental assumptions:

- The individual is the primary unit of analysis.

- Personality is the major motivational element within individuals because it is the seat of drives and the source of motives.

- Crimes result from abnormal, dysfunctional, or inappropriate mental processes within the personality.

- Criminal behaviour, although condemned by the social group, may be purposeful for the individual insofar as it addresses certain felt needs. Behaviour can be judged "inappropriate" only when measured against external criteria purporting to establish normality.

- Normality is generally defined by social consensus—that is, what the majority of people in any social group agree is "real," appropriate, or typical.

- Defective, or abnormal, mental processes may have a variety of causes, including a diseased mind, inappropriate learning or improper conditioning, the emulation of inappropriate role models, and adjustment to inner conflicts.

Forensic psychology The application of the science and profession of psychology to questions and issues relating to law and the legal system. Also called *criminal psychology*.

Forensic psychiatry A branch of psychiatry having to do with the study of crime and criminality.

PERSONALITY THEORIES

TWO MAJOR IDEAS CHARACTERIZE PSYCHOLOGICAL THEORIES: **PERSONALITY** AND **behaviourism**. Personality theory builds on the burgeoning area of cognitive science, including personality disturbances, the process of moral development, and diseases of the mind, whereas behaviourism (also known as *behaviour theory*) examines social learning with an emphasis on behavioural **conditioning**. Together, these two areas formed the early foundation of psychological criminology. An examination of personality theories will be followed by an overview of behaviour theory.

COGNITIVE THEORIES

THEORIES OF COGNITION FORM AN AREA OF PERSONALITY THEORY. COGNITIVE APPROACHES are learning theories that examine thought processes and seek to explain how people: (1) learn to solve problems, including those that involve questions of value and morality, and (2) perceive and interpret the social environment. Cognitive theory has a number of branches, including one that focuses on moral and intellectual development and another that examines how people process information.

Moral Development Theory

The first branch of cognitive theory, **moral development theory**, holds that individuals become criminal when they have not successfully completed their intellectual development from child to adult. One of the first comprehensive maps of human psychological development was created by Swiss developmental psychologist Jean Piaget. Piaget believed that human thinking and intellectual processes went through a number of bio-psychological stages of development—something that Piaget saw as a natural extension of evolutionary adaptation. Just as a species adapts to its environment, Piaget believed, individual human beings respond to their environment by developing intellectually. He posited four stages of human intellectual development:[9]

1. The *sensory-motor stage* lasts from birth to age two. During this stage, children are extremely egocentric (or focused on themselves and their personal experiences) and learn about the world through the physical senses and the movement of their bodies.

2. The *preoperational stage* lasts from ages two to seven. During this stage, children are not able to reason well or to use logical thinking, but egocentrism begins to weaken and motor skills are acquired.

3. The *concrete operational stage* runs from ages 7 to 11. In this stage, children start to develop the ability to reason and to think logically, although they are very concrete in their thinking and often require practical aids such as buttons or coins to aid in counting and arithmetic. By the time children reach the end of this stage, they are no longer egocentric and are able to appreciate the needs and feelings of others.

4. The *formal operational stage* lasts from ages 11 to 16 and continues into adulthood. During this stage, the developing adolescent acquires abstract reasoning skills and learns how to think and reason without the need for external aids.

Central to Piaget's perspective on moral development is the idea that, as children grow and learn, they become able to reflect on their own actions—acquiring a sense of the unspoken rules that govern human interaction. According to Piaget, children apply their burgeoning ability to reflect and use it to examine themselves; in the process, they learn right from wrong. Once a child has moved through the four developmental stages, said Piaget, he or she would have moved from moral absolutism (in which the child unquestioningly accepts the dictates of his or her parents or caregivers) to moral relativism (where actions are seen as right or wrong depending on the circumstances in which they are undertaken).

Following Piaget, Lawrence Kohlberg offered an expanded cognitive structural theory of morality in a six-stage typology.[10] In Kohlberg's first stage, people only obey the law because they are afraid of being punished if they don't. In the second stage, self-interest is primary and negotiation develops. In the third stage, the importance of behavioural standards is understood. In the fourth stage, rule following is viewed as a social duty. The fifth stage is the point at which the relativity of law and social contracts are understood. By the sixth and final stage, obedience to the law becomes an obligation that is willingly assumed, and people choose not to violate the law because they value the principle of fairness and believe in interpersonal justice. Those who have evolved to higher stages of moral reasoning are unlikely to commit crimes because they appreciate not only their own needs but the needs and interests of others as well.

Kohlberg argued that a preference for higher levels of moral thinking must be universal in human beings, although not necessarily inborn. He believed that people who have successfully moved through all stages of moral development have the ability to objectively evaluate opinions and either accept them or reject them without irrationally clinging to their own beliefs. Kohlberg posited that people may turn to crime if they are unsuccessful at making the normal transition between developmental stages of moral reasoning.

Research based on Kohlberg's work has demonstrated that offenders are less able to make moral judgments than are non-criminals, even when they have similar backgrounds and experiences. In 2015, for example, researchers associated with the Pathways to Desistance project in the United States found that youths experience protracted maturation, into their mid-20s, of brain systems responsible for self-regulation. Researchers concluded that "youth whose antisocial behavior persisted into early adulthood were found to have lower levels of psychosocial maturity in adolescence and deficits in their development of maturity (i.e., arrested development) compared with other antisocial youth."[11]

Anders Behring Breivik clenches his fist as he arrives in the courtroom for the first day of his trial in Oslo, Norway, April 16, 2012. Breivik, a militant anti-Islamic extremist, was convicted of killing 77 people in Norway and was given a 21-year prison sentence by an Oslo court. Breivik claimed that he acted in self-defence and said that his victims were traitors for embracing multiculturalism. How might moral development theory apply to Breivik?

Hakon Mosvold Larse/Alamy Stock Photo

Cognitive Information-Processing Theory

Cognitive information-processing theory A psychological perspective that involves the study of human perceptions, information processing, and decision making.

Another major area of cognitive theory applicable to criminology is **cognitive information-processing theory (CIP)**. CIP involves the study of human perceptions, information processing, and decision making. Psychological research suggests that people make decisions by engaging in a series of complex thought processes, or steps. In the first step, they encode and interpret the information they are presented with or the experiences they have. In the next stage, they search for an appropriate response; in the third stage, they act on their decision.[12]

Some information-processing theorists believe that violent individuals may be using information incorrectly when making decisions. Violence-prone individuals, for example, may see people as more aggressive or threatening than they actually are. Such a view may result in violence even at the slightest provocation. Supportive research suggests that some people engage in violent attacks on others because they believe that they are actually defending themselves, even in the face of misperceived threat.[13] Because of the way that some people process information, they are unable to recognize the harm they are doing to others.[14]

In the late 1970s, Roger C. Schank and Robert P. Abelson developed script theory in order to explain the understanding process that occurs during a situation or event.[15] **Scripts** refer to generalized knowledge about specific types of situations that is stored in the mind. More formally, Schank and Abelson described a script as "a predetermined, stereotyped sequence of actions that define a well-known situation."

Scripts Generalized knowledge about specific types of situations that is stored in the mind.

People use ready-made scripts in everyday life to anticipate an appropriate sequence of events in a given context. We build scripts in our minds to allow for a number of different roles for those actors (other than ourselves) whose presence is anticipated to play out in the script, and we allow for possible variations in the physical scene and in the progression of events. In this sense, scripts are like stories that we use to structure our expectations of and reactions to circumstances that we expect to typically encounter. Take, for example, the internal script that we might use for restaurant dining. We know that when we arrive at a restaurant we should check with the host or hostess to see if a table is available. We expect that he or she will take us to our table and that a server will arrive soon after we are seated to present us with a menu and to take our drink order. We have similar expectations as to what will occur as our dinner progresses, including the eventual arrival of the bill, and the amount or percentage of a tip to be left at the completion of the evening.

Because most events play out according to the scripts that we have in mind, things typically go smoothly. Sometimes, however, we can be surprised and find ourselves forced to innovate. In our restaurant example, we might unexpectedly be served the wrong meal, or (worse) the server might trip and spill food on us. Unless we are surprised, however, things generally go according to plan and events fit with previous experiences we have had involving the same kind of activity.

According to Helen Gavin and David Hockey, two British criminologists writing in 2010, "scripts are used to guide behaviour because the script provides the holder with a set of expectations about what will happen during the unfolding of an event, thus offering a way of predicting the outcome and aid[ing] the individual to act accordingly."[16] Gavin and Hockey recognize that people develop scripts based on the learning opportunities and experiences that are presented to them within their social environment. The idea is similar to that of role play, whereby children practice for the adult roles they will assume later in life.

The applicability of scripts to criminal behaviour can be seen in the fact that career offenders routinely develop scripts to guide them through criminal activity. Gavin and Hockey say that these particular kinds of scripts "consist of a goal aim, a criminal belief system, a criminally motivated perception, and a self-serving set of distorted cognitions that protect the individual's low self-esteem." Criminals use scripts in their approach to crime commission, much of which becomes routine over time. Consequently, criminal motivations and drives underpin criminal scripts.

In their 2010 study of criminal scripts, Gavin and Hockey detailed the scripts of career offenders and found that they could "be acquired through . . . various relevant psychological processes,"[17] along with other more conservative scripts that most people use in their daily lives. Moreover, they concluded that criminal scripts help to form a criminal identity once they have been internalized.

PERSONALITY DISTURBANCES

7.4 **LEARNING OBJECTIVE**

PSYCHOLOGISTS WORKING IN THE FIRST HALF OF THE 20TH CENTURY ADAPTED THE DISEASE model—a paradigm that had worked so well in the field of medicine—in an effort to cure mental and emotional problems. Consequently, early cognitive perspectives in psychology were couched in terms of mental disease, personality disorder, and **psychopathy**.

Psychologists and psychiatrists today distinguish between the terms *psychopathy* and *psychopathology*. In the psychological literature, psychopathology "refers to any sort of psychological disorder that causes distress either for the individual or for those in the individual's life."[18] Today, depression, **schizophrenia**, attention deficit hyperactivity disorder, alcoholism, and bulimia are all considered forms of psychopathology, or mental disease.

One of the most serious of mental diseases is psychopathy, "a very specific and distinctive type of psychopathology."[19]

Psychopathy A personality disorder characterized by anti-social behaviour and a failure to feel remorse or guilt.

Schizophrenia A serious mental illness that distorts the way a person thinks, feels, and behaves. Primary features of schizophrenia include the inability to distinguish between real and imagined experiences and the inability to think logically.

The Psychopath

Psychopathy is a personality disorder characterized by anti-social behaviour and by a lack of sympathy, empathy, and embarrassment. Psychopaths, many of whom are known as effective manipulators and who clearly understand the motivations of others, are said to dissociate emotionally from their actions and lack empathy or sensitivity toward others.

The concept of psychopathy, called "one of the most durable, resilient and influential of all criminological ideas,"[20] may have evolved from the work of French physician Philippe Pinel (1745–1826), who described a form of "insanity without delirium." The concept is summarized in the words of Nolan D.C. Lewis, who wrote that "the criminal, like other people, has lived a life of instinctive drives, of desires, of wishes, of feelings, but one in which his intellect has apparently functioned less effectually as a brake upon certain trends. His constitutional makeup deviates toward the abnormal, leading him into conflicts with the laws of society and its cultural patterns."[21]

The term *psychopathy* comes from the Greek words *psyche* (meaning "soul" or "mind") and *pathos* ("suffering" or "illness"). The word, which appears to have been coined by the 19th-century German psychiatrist Richard von Krafft-Ebing (1840–1902),[22] made its way into English psychiatric literature through the writings of Polish-born American psychiatrist Bernard Glueck[23] (1884–1972) and William Healy (1869–1963).[24] The **psychopath** has been historically viewed as perversely cruel, often without thought or feeling for his victims.[25]

The concept of a psychopathic personality, which by its very definition is asocial, was fully developed by the neuropsychiatrist Hervey Cleckley in his 1941 book *The Mask of Sanity*[26]—a work that has had considerable impact on the field of

Psychopath An individual who has a personality disorder, especially one manifested in aggressively anti-social behaviour, and who is lacking in empathy.

psychology. Cleckley described the psychopath as a "moral idiot," as one who does not feel empathy with others even though that person may be fully cognizant of what is objectively happening around him or her. The central defining characteristic of a psychopath came to be "poverty of affect" or the inability to accurately imagine how others think and feel, so it becomes possible for a psychopath to inflict pain and engage in acts of cruelty without appreciation for the victim's suffering. In *The Mask of Sanity*, Cleckley described numerous characteristics of the psychopathic personality:

- superficial charm and "good intelligence"
- absence of delusions, hallucinations, or other signs of psychosis
- absence of nervousness or psychoneurotic manifestations
- inability to feel guilt or shame
- unreliability
- chronic lying
- ongoing anti-social behaviour
- poor judgment and inability to learn from experience
- self-centredness and incapacity to love
- unresponsiveness in general interpersonal relations
- impersonal, trivial, and poorly integrated sex life
- failure to follow any life plan

For Cleckley, "psychopathy was defined by a constellation of dysfunctional psychological processes as opposed to specific behavioral manifestations."[27] Even though psychopaths have a seriously flawed personality, they can easily fool others into trusting them—hence the title of Cleckley's book.

According to Cleckley, indicators of psychopathy appear early in life, often in the teenage years, and include lying, fighting, stealing, and vandalism. Even earlier signs may be found, according to some authors, in bed-wetting, cruelty to animals, sleepwalking, and fire-setting.[28] In a recent report prepared for the Correctional Service of Canada, psychopaths were described as "individuals who display impulsiveness, callousness, insincerity, pathological lying and deception, egocentricity, poor judgment, an impersonal sex life, and an unstable life plan."[29]

Cleckley believed that there were two kinds of psychopaths: primary and secondary. In later work, psychologist David Lykken refined those terms, saying that *primary psychopaths* are somehow neurologically different from other people, and that makes them behave the way they do.[30] Hence, primary psychopaths are born with psychopathic personalities, whereas *secondary psychopaths* (sometimes called **sociopaths**) are born with a "normal" personality, but personal experiences (frequently physical and emotional abuse or trauma) when they are young cause them to develop psychopathic characteristics.

One of the most definitive modern measures of psychopathy can be found in the Psychopathy Checklist (PCL), developed by Robert Hare of the University of British Columbia.[31] (The checklist is sometimes called the Hare Psychopathy Checklist.) When used by qualified experts employing information from subject interviews and official records, the checklist produces a series of ratings assessing degree of psychopathy. The checklist uses two kinds of indicators: affective and interpersonal traits (glibness, emotional detachment, egocentricity, superficial charm, and shallow affect) and traits associated with a chronic unstable and anti-social lifestyle (irresponsibility, impulsivity, criminality, and proneness to boredom).[32] Hence, psychopathy has both emotional and behaviour components. A number of studies have demonstrated that

Sociopath An individual who has a personality disorder, especially one manifested in aggressively anti-social behaviour, and who is lacking in empathy. Also called *secondary psychopaths*, sociopaths may have been born "normal," but personal experiences they have in early life cause them to develop psychopathic characteristics.

the presence of callous, unemotional traits in adolescence reliably predicts later anti-social behaviours.[33]

One study of eight Canadian maximum-security male prisoners classified as psychopaths according to the PCL found that the men were not only impaired emotionally but also unable to efficiently process abstract words, perform abstract categorization tasks, understand metaphors, and process emotionally weighted words and speech.[34] During a test on abstract concepts, the men's brains were scanned using functional magnetic resonance imaging (fMRI); scans showed that a section of their brains did not activate as it should have. The researchers concluded that their findings "support the hypothesis that there is an abnormality in the function of the right anterior superior temporal gyrus in psychopathy."[35]

Some have questioned whether psychopaths merely lack empathy or really don't know the difference between right and wrong. Recent research seems to show that the ability to tell right from wrong is something that human beings are born with, that the human brain is hard-wired to make moral distinctions, and that the same distinctions tend to be made across cultures.[36]

Traditionally, psychopathology has been regarded as difficult or impossible to treat. But a recent study of adolescent psychopaths found that "youth with psychopathic features who received intensive treatment" in sanction-based programs that held youth accountable for their actions "had significantly lower rates of violent recidivism and a longer time to re-arrest for violent behavior" than those who received treatment in a typical juvenile correctional facility.[37] In 2007, the United Kingdom launched an unprecedented treatment and research program focused on "Dangerous People with Severe Personality Disorder" (DPSPD).[38] Although not everyone placed in the program had been diagnosed as a psychopath, in order to be eligible for the program participants had to be diagnosed with a severe personality disorder and there had to be a demonstrable link between that disorder and the risk of violent offending.

Trait Theory

In 1964, Hans J. Eysenck, a British psychologist, published *Crime and Personality*, a book in which he explained crime as the result of fundamental personality characteristics, or **traits**, which he believed are largely inherited.[39] Psychological traits are stable personality patterns that tend to endure throughout the life course and across social and cultural contexts. They include behavioural, cognitive, and affective predispositions to respond to a given situation in a particular way. According to trait theory, as an individual grows older or moves from one place to another, his or her personality remains largely intact—defined by the traits that comprise it. Trait theory links personality (and associated traits) to behaviour and holds that it is an individual's personality, combined with her or his intelligence and natural abilities,[40] that determines his or her behaviour in a given situation.[41]

Eysenck believed that the degree to which just three universal supertraits are present in an individual accounts for his or her unique personality. He termed these supertraits (1) introversion/extraversion, (2) neuroticism/emotional stability, and (3) psychoticism. Eysenck thought that people who score high on extraversion, neuroticism, or psychoticism are not easily conditioned or socialized and thus commit more crime in adulthood. Like many other psychologists, he accepted the fact that personality holds steady throughout much of life, but he stressed that it is largely determined by genetics. He argued that what we call *personality* is a reflection of variations in the component operating systems of the major behavioural pathways of the brain.

In support of his idea of the genetic basis of personality, Eysenck pointed to twin studies showing that identical twins display strikingly similar behavioural tendencies, whereas fraternal twins demonstrate far less likelihood of similar behaviours. Eysenck also argued that psychological conditioning occurs more rapidly in some people than in others because of biological differences and that anti-social individuals are difficult to condition (or to socialize) because of underlying genetic characteristics. He believed that up to two-thirds of all "behavioural variance" could be strongly attributed to genetics.[42]

Of Eysenck's three personality dimensions, one in particular—psychoticism—was thought to be closely correlated with criminality at all stages.[43] According to Eysenck, psychoticism is defined by such characteristics as lack of empathy, creativeness, tough-mindedness, and anti-sociability. Extroverts, Eysenck's second personality group that was associated with criminality, are described as carefree, dominant, and venturesome, operating with high levels of energy. "The typical extrovert," Eysenck wrote, "is sociable, likes parties, has many friends, needs to have people to talk to, and does not like reading or studying by himself."[44] Neuroticism, the third of the personality characteristics Eysenck described, is said to be typical of people who are irrational, shy, moody, and emotional.

According to Eysenck, psychotics are the most likely to be criminal because they combine high degrees of emotionalism with similarly high levels of extroversion; individuals with such characteristics are especially difficult to socialize and to train and do not respond well to the external environment. Eysenck cited many studies in which children and others who harboured characteristics of psychoticism performed poorly on conditioning tests designed to measure how quickly they would respond appropriately to external stimuli. Because conscience is fundamentally a conditioned reflex, Eysenck said, an individual who does not take well to conditioning will not fully develop a conscience and will continue to exhibit the asocial behavioural traits of a very young child. In essence, criminality can be seen as a personality type characterized by self-centredness, indifference to the suffering and needs of others, impulsiveness, and low self-control, which, taken together, lead to law-violating behaviour.

Today, trait theories of personality have expanded beyond Eysenck's basic three-trait model to encompass five basic traits: (1) openness to experience, (2) extraversion, (3) conscientiousness, (4) neuroticism, and (5) agreeableness. People are said to possess more or less of any one trait, and the combination of traits and the degree to which they are characteristic of an individual define that person's personality. Psychologists call these traits the *Big Five*, and according to many psychologists, "the Big Five are strongly genetically influenced, and the genetic factor structure of the Big Five appears to be invariant across European, North American, and East Asian samples,"[45] which suggests that personality traits, to a greater or lesser degree, are universally shared by all peoples. Conscientiousness, for example, is related to self-control and is unlikely to be associated with criminality.

BEHAVIOUR THEORY

BEHAVIOUR THEORY, THE SECOND MAIN THRUST OF EARLY PSYCHOLOGICAL THEORIZING, built upon the concept of conditioned behaviour. The idea that behaviour could be "conditioned" or *shaped* was popularized through the work of Russian physiologist Ivan Pavlov (1849–1936), whose work with dogs won the Nobel Prize in Physiology or Medicine in 1904. The dogs, which salivated when food was presented to them, were always fed in the presence of a ringing bell. Soon, Pavlov found, the dogs would salivate as if in preparation for eating when the bell alone was rung, even when no food was present. Hence, salivation, an automatic response to the presence of food, could be conditioned to occur in response to some other stimulus, demonstrating that animal behaviour could be predictably altered via association with external changes arising from the environment surrounding the organism. The kind of conditioning that Pavlov demonstrated, which is the association of a particular response to a conditioned stimulus, is referred to today as *classical conditioning*.

Behavioural Conditioning

Behaviour theory has sometimes been called the "stimulus–response theory of human behaviour." When an individual's behaviour results in rewards or feedback that the individual regards as pleasurable and desirable, that behaviour will likely become more frequent. Under such circumstances, the behaviour in question is reinforced, and the rewards themselves are referred to as *reinforcements*. Conversely, when punishment follows behaviour, chances are that the frequency of that type of behaviour will decrease. The individual's responses are termed **operant behaviour** because a person's behavioural choices effectively operate on the surrounding environment to produce consequences for the individual.

Behaviour theory is often used by parents seeking to control children through a series of **rewards** and **punishments**. Young children may be punished, for example, by having a favourite toy taken away or by the television being turned off. Older children are often told what rules they are expected to obey and what rewards they can anticipate if they adhere to those rules. They also know that punishments will follow if they do not obey the rules. Rewards and punishments have been further divided into four conceptual categories: (1) positive reinforcements, which increase the frequency of approved behaviour by adding something desirable to the situation—as when a "good" child is given a toy; (2) negative reinforcements, which increase the frequency of approved behaviour by removing something distressful from the situation—as when a "good" child is permitted to skip the morning's chores; (3) positive punishments, which decrease the frequency of unwanted behaviour by adding something undesirable to the situation—as when a "bad" child is sent to his room; and (4) negative punishments, which decrease the frequency of unwanted behaviour by removing something desirable from the situation—as when a "bad" child's candy is taken away. According to behaviour theory, it is through the application of rewards and punishments that behaviour is shaped.

Behaviour theory differs from other psychological theories in that the major determinants of behaviour are envisioned as existing in the environment surrounding the individual rather than in the individual. B.F. Skinner (1904–1990), the best-known proponent of behaviour theory, rejected unobservable psychological constructs, focusing instead on patterns of responses to external rewards and stimuli. Skinner did extensive animal research involving behavioural concepts and created programmed instruction, which allows students to work at their own pace and provides immediate rewards for learning accomplishments.

Behaviour theory is important in the study of criminology because much human behaviour is the result of conditioning, and people can be conditioned to respond to situations with either pro-social or anti-social conduct. It's also important because it is the foundation on which social cognition theory (which is discussed in the following section) is built. In fact, teachers and parents often use punishments and rewards in an effort to condition their students and children, respectively, to engage in appropriate or desired behaviour. Consequently, from the perspective of behaviour theory, crime can be explained as the result of inappropriate behavioural conditioning.

Behaviour theory A psychological perspective positing that behaviour that is rewarded will increase in frequency and behaviour that is punished will decrease in frequency.

Operant behaviour Behaviour that affects the environment so as to produce responses or further behavioural cues.

Rewards Desirable behavioural consequences likely to increase the frequency of occurrence of that behaviour.

Punishments Undesirable behavioural consequences likely to decrease the frequency of occurrence of that behaviour.

Modelling theory contends that we learn how to behave by observing others. Do you think this theory can help to explain a link between violent computer games and violent crime?

Paul Sakuma/The Canadian Press

Social Cognition and Role Modelling

One of the earliest attempts to explain crime and deviance as learned behaviour can be found in the work of Gabriel Tarde (1843–1904), a French social theorist of the late 1800s. Tarde discounted the biological theories of Lombroso and others. The basis of any society, Tarde believed, was imitation, the tendency of people to pattern their behaviour after the behaviour of others. Tarde developed a theory of human behaviour that built upon three laws of imitation and suggestion.[46] Tarde's first law held that individuals in close intimate contact with one another tend to imitate each other's behaviour. His second law stated that imitation moves from the top down so that, for example, youngsters tend to emulate those who are older. The third law of imitation is the law of insertion, which says that new acts and behaviours tend to either reinforce or replace old ones. Hence, the music of each generation replaces the music of the one that preceded it, the politics of young people eventually become the politics of the nation, faddish drugs are substituted for traditional ones, and new forms of crime tend to take the place of older ones (e.g., when computer criminals become a more serious threat to financial institutions than bank robbers).

More recently, Albert Bandura developed a comprehensive **social cognition theory** of aggression that depends for its explanatory power on cognitive processes. Bandura believed that reinforcement theory could not account for all types of learning. Although everyone is capable of aggression, Bandura said, "people are not born with . . . repertories of aggressive behavior. They must learn them."[47] Bandura is often referred to as the creator of *social learning theory* in the field of psychology. Because of the central role of cognition in Bandura's learning theory, however, he preferred to call his approach *social cognition theory*. Central to Bandura's theory are the ideas of observation, imitation, and modelling.

The concept of **modelling** acknowledges the fact that people learn how to act through their life experiences, and especially by observing others. Bandura wrote that "most human behavior is learned observationally through modeling: from observing others, one forms an idea of how new behaviors are performed, and on later occasions this coded information serves as a guide for action."[48] In some of his early work, Bandura experimented with children who observed adult role models striking inflatable cartoon characters. When the children were observed after their encounter with adult behaviour, they, too, exhibited similarly aggressive behaviour. Bandura also studied violence on television and concluded that "television is an effective tutor. Both laboratory and controlled field studies in which young children and adolescents are repeatedly shown either violent or nonviolent fare disclose that exposure to film violence shapes the form of aggression and typically increases interpersonal aggressiveness in everyday life."[49] A later study by other researchers showed that even after 10 years, the level of violence that young adults engaged in was directly related to the degree of violent television they had been exposed to as children.[50]

Aggression can be provoked, Bandura suggests, through physical assaults and verbal threats and insults, as well as by thwarting a person's hopes or obstructing his or her goal-seeking behaviour. Deprivation and "adverse reductions in the conditions of life" (a lowered standard of living or the onset of disease, for example) are other potential triggers of aggression. Bandura adds, however, that a human being's ability to foresee the future consequences of present behaviour adds another dimension to the activation of learned patterns of aggression. That is, aggressive behaviour can be perceived as holding future benefits for individuals exhibiting it. In short, it can be seen as a means to a desired end. Bandura also says that individuals sometimes become aggressive because they are rewarded for doing so. The early 20th-century North American concept of a "macho"—virile and masculine—male figure, for example, was often associated with the expectation of substantial reward. Whether or not this perception was accurate, a significant proportion of North American men subscribed to it nonetheless, and for many decades, it served as a guide to daily behaviour.

Another form of reward can flow from aggression. Bandura called it the "reduction of aversive treatment." By this, he meant that simply standing up for oneself can improve the way one is treated by others. For example, standing up to a bully may be the most effective way of dealing with the harassment one might otherwise face. Bandura recognized that everyone has self-regulatory mechanisms that can inhibit the tendency toward aggression. People reward or punish themselves, Bandura said, according to internal standards they have for judging their own behaviour. Thus, aggression may be inhibited in people who, for example, value religious, ethical, or moral standards of conduct, such as compassion, thoughtfulness, and courtesy. Bandura concluded that people who devalue aggression may still engage in it via a process he called *disengagement*. Disengagement may result from (1) "attributing blame to one's victims"; (2) dehumanization through bureaucratization, automation, urbanization, and high social mobility; (3) vindication of aggressive practices by legitimate authorities; and (4) desensitization resulting from repeated exposure to aggression in any of a variety of forms.

How a Bright Kid with Excellent Self-Esteem Slaughtered His Whole Family

An example of aggression that resulted from thwarted goal seeking, and which may have been seen as holding future benefits for the boy involved, occurred in the early 1990s when Gavin Mandin shot and killed his parents and two sisters. Mandin, who was 15 at the time, waited in the family farm-house not far from Edmonton, Alberta, for the rest of his family to return from a shopping trip. When the car pulled into the driveway, Mandin sighted through the scope of his pump-action, .22-calibre rifle and fired through a window and screen in the house. The bullet penetrated his stepfather Maurice's temple as he stepped out of the car, killing him instantly. His mother, Susan, still in the car, looked up as another shot crashed through the car's windshield and entered her brain. Mandin then shot his two sisters, Islay, 12, and Janelle, 10, at point-blank range as they sat in the back seat of the car, first in the head and then with the rifle pressed against their chests. Mandin then drove the car with the bodies in it to an area of thick bush nearby. Using ropes and an all-terrain vehicle, Mandin dragged his stepfather's body further into the bush.

By all accounts, Mandin's home life had been normal enough. Mandin was, reportedly, the "apple of his mother's eye," and she defended him in all circumstances. However, there were signs that Mandin was not as enamoured of his family. Notes found behind Mandin's bed read, "I hate Janelle, I hate Susan, I hate Islay," and "Susan can't make me do anything. I wish she were dead." One particularly disturbing treatise said, "There will come the day when I rule. I will be the leader of the universe. All I love and desire will be mine. I will be the most powerful man on earth. I will have all the world it will be my backyard, all my enemies will die by my hand." During his interrogation by RCMP investigators, Mandin cited many reasons for his actions. He stated that he was made to clean his room, carry groceries into the house, and wash dishes. He disliked going to church services with the family, so he put a lock on his door to keep them from disturbing him. Mandin told RCMP investigator Corporal Ted Lachuk,

Sometimes, like, I will have something important to say to my mother and she will be sitting down and

eating and I will come up to her and say "mom" and she won't do anything and I'll just keep calling her again and again. One time I called her eight or nine times and she didn't even answer. A couple of times I even tapped her on the shoulder and she ignores me and it really makes me angry.

Shortly after being taken into custody, Mandin declared, "I guess I get the house now, eh?" Later he stated that he intended to use a $1000 bond his mother had saved for him as an investment, to become a "zillionaire."

Mandin was denied parole in 2001, largely owing to his lack of remorse for his crime. He underwent many psychological reports while incarcerated, some of which labelled him a psychopath; however, he has never met the criteria of the Hare Psychopathy Checklist. In 2012, Gavin Mandin applied for and was granted full parole; he is living in the community and goes by the name Gavin Ian Maclean. Since he was originally given a life sentence, he will be monitored in the community for the rest of his life.

Discussion Questions

1. Some individuals become aggressive because they are rewarded for doing so. Do you think Gavin Mandin's criminal behaviour can be explained this way?

2. Albert Bandura posited that some who engage in aggressive behaviour justify it by placing blame on their victims. Was this part of Gavin Mandin's rationalization for his actions?

3. Gavin Mandin was tested for psychopathic tendencies. Do you think he fits the profile of a psychopath?

Sources: Based on Jim Demers, "'I Am Gavin' How a Bright Kid with Excellent Self-Esteem Slaughtered His Whole Family," *Alberta Report*, December 6, 1993, pp. 18–22. Ryan Tumilty, "At 20-year mark, one question lingers in Mandin murder case," *St Albert Gazette*, August 10, 2011

Psychiatric criminology A theory that is derived from the medical sciences (including neurology) and that, like other psychological theories, focuses on the individual as the unit of analysis. Psychiatric theories form the basis of psychiatric criminology.

THE PSYCHOANALYTIC PERSPECTIVE—CRIMINAL BEHAVIOUR AS MALADAPTATION

PSYCHIATRIC CRIMINOLOGY (ALSO CALLED *FORENSIC PSYCHIATRY*) ENVISIONS A COMPLEX set of drives and motives operating from hidden recesses deep within the personality to determine behaviour. Perhaps the best-known psychiatrist of all time is Sigmund Freud (1856–1939). Freud coined the term **psychoanalysis** in 1896 and based an entire theory of human behaviour on it. Freud said nothing about criminal behaviour, and it wasn't

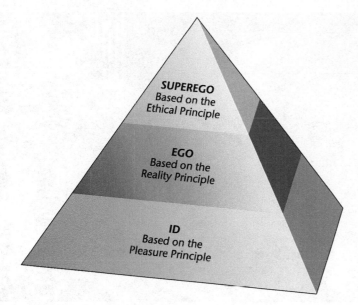

Figure 7.1 The Psychoanalytic Structure of Personality

until later that other psychoanalysts began to apply concepts that Freud had developed to the study of criminal behaviour. From the point of view of **psychoanalysis**, criminal behaviour is maladaptive, or the product of inadequacies in the offender's personality. Significant inadequacies may result in full-blown mental illness, which can be a direct cause of crime. The psychoanalytic perspective encompasses diverse notions, such as personality, **neurosis**, and **psychosis**, and more specific concepts, such as transference, **sublimation**, and repression. **Psychotherapy**, referred to in its early days as the "talking cure" because it relied on patient–therapist communication, is the attempt to relieve patients of their mental disorders through the application of psychoanalytic principles and techniques.

According to Freud, the personality is made up of three components—the id, the ego, and the superego—as shown in Figure 7.1. The **id** is the fundamental aspect of the personality from which drives, wishes, urges, and desires emanate. Freud focused primarily on love, aggression, and sex as fundamental drives in any personality. The id operates according to the pleasure principle, seeking full and immediate gratification of its needs. However, according to Freud, individuals are rarely fully aware of the urges that manifest (occasionally into awareness) from the id because it is a largely unconscious region of the mind. Nonetheless, from the Freudian perspective, each of us carries within our id the prerequisite motivation for criminal behaviour. We are, each one of us, potential murderers, sexual aggressors, and thieves—our drives and urges kept in check only by other controlling aspects of our personalities.

The **ego** is primarily charged with reality testing. Freud's use of the word *ego* should not be confused with popular usage, whereby a person might talk about an "inflated ego" or an "egotistical person." For Freud, the ego was primarily concerned with how objectives might be best accomplished. The ego tends to effect strategies for the individual that maximize pleasure and minimize pain. It lays out the various paths of action that can lead to wish fulfillment. The ego inherently recognizes that it may be necessary to delay gratification to achieve a more fulfilling long-term goal.

The **superego** is much like a moral guide to right and wrong. If properly developed, it evaluates the ego's plans, dismissing some as morally inappropriate while accepting others as ethically viable. When the dictates of the superego are not followed, feelings of guilt may result. The superego is one of the most misunderstood

Psychoanalysis The theory of human psychology founded by Sigmund Freud based on the concepts of the unconscious, resistance, repression, sexuality, and the Oedipus complex.

Neurosis A functional disorder of the mind or of the emotions involving anxiety, phobia, or other abnormal behaviour.

Psychosis A form of mental illness in which sufferers are said to be out of touch with reality.

Sublimation The psychological process whereby one aspect of consciousness comes to be symbolically substituted for another.

Psychotherapy A form of psychiatric treatment based on psychoanalytical principles and techniques.

Id The aspect of the personality from which drives, wishes, urges, and desires emanate. More formally, this division of the psyche is associated with instinctual impulses and demands for immediate satisfaction of primitive needs.

Ego The reality-testing part of the personality, also called the *reality principle*. More formally, this personality component is conscious, most immediately controls behaviour, and is most in touch with external reality.

Superego The moral aspect of the personality, much like the conscience. More formally, this division of the psyche develops by the incorporation of the perceived moral standards of the community, is mainly unconscious, and includes the conscience.

Sigmund Freud (1856–1939) examines a manuscript in the office of his Vienna home circa 1930. How have Freud's theories influenced contemporary criminology?

Bettmann/Getty Images

of Freudian concepts. In addition to elements of conscience, the superego also contains what Freud called the "ego-ideal," which is a symbolic representation of what society values. The ego-ideal differs from the conscience in that it is less forceful in controlling behaviour in the absence of the likelihood of discovery. Although, as previously mentioned, Freud did not directly address crime, he did spend much of his time examining abnormal behaviours, many of which might lead to violations of the criminal law.

The Psychotic Offender

Some seemingly inexplicable forms of criminality may be the result of psychosis. People with psychotic disorders are out of touch with reality in some fundamental way, possibly suffering from hallucinations, delusions, or other breaks with reality. Psychoses may be either organic (resulting from physical damage to, or abnormalities in, the brain) or functional (having no known physical cause). Canadian criminologist Gwynn Nettler said, "Thought disorder is the hallmark of psychosis. People are called crazy when, at some extremity, they cannot 'think straight.'"[51] Nettler identified three characteristics of psychotic individuals: "(1) a grossly distorted conception of reality, (2) moods, and swings of mood, that seem inappropriate to circumstance, and (3) marked inefficiency in getting along with others and caring for oneself."[52]

Psychiatrists today recognize at least nine different types of psychotic disorders, and one important category is schizophrenia. Schizophrenics are characterized by disordered or disjointed thinking, in which the types of logical associations they make are atypical of other people. **Paranoid schizophrenics**, one of the four major subgroups of schizophrenics, also suffer from delusions and hallucinations. Schizophrenia is disorganization of the personality, and in its most extreme form, it may manifest itself in seemingly irrational behaviour as well as hallucinations and delusions.

A recent study of male schizophrenics found that 3 percent started a criminal career, and 13 percent had committed their first violent crime before having any contact with the psychiatric hospital system. Study authors concluded that "the criminality committed [by schizophrenics] before first contact to the psychiatric hospital system is substantial, especially among males with schizophrenia."[53] Many studies

Paranoid schizophrenic A schizophrenic individual who suffers from delusions and hallucinations.

confirm the association between violence and schizophrenia, but recent evidence from a study conducted in Britain suggests that the proportion of violent crime directly attributable to schizophrenia is below 1 percent.[54] When substance abuse is added to the mix, however, the amount of violence associated with schizophrenia increases considerably. Consequently, a 2009 article in the *Journal of the American Medical Association* found that schizophrenics are four to six times as likely as members of the general population to commit a violent crime and noted that current medical guidelines "recommend that violence risk assessment should be conducted for all patients with schizophrenia."[55]

Not all people who are psychotic commit crimes, and many remain law abiding throughout their entire lives. Occasionally, the behaviours of some are difficult to understand, as the story of Vincent Li illustrates[56] (see the Who's Responsible? box in this chapter). Refer to the section of this chapter entitled "Mental Illness and the Law" for an understanding of how our criminal justice system deals with those who are afflicted with a recognized psychosis such as paranoid schizophrenia.

Frustration–Aggression Theory

In his early writings, Freud suggested that aggressive behaviour is a response to frustration and limitations imposed upon a person. The *frustration–aggression thesis* was later developed more fully in the writings of J. Dollard, Albert Bandura, Richard H. Walters, and others. Dollard's frustration–aggression theory held that although frustration can lead to various forms of behaviour—including regression, sublimation, and aggressive fantasy—direct aggression toward others is its most likely consequence.[57] Because everyone suffers frustration at times in life, (beginning with weaning and toilet training), aggression is a natural consequence of living, but that aggression can be manifested in socially acceptable ways (contact sports, military or law enforcement careers, simple verbal attacks) and/or engaged in vicariously by observing others who are acting violently (in movies, on television, in fiction). Dollard applied the psychoanalytical term *displacement* to the type of violence that is vented on something or someone who is not the source of the original frustration and suggested that satisfying one's aggressive urges via observation was a form of "catharsis."

The story of Pierre Lebrun, a former employee of a public transit company, provides an example of the frustration–aggression theory applied to real-life crime. In 1999, the 40-year-old Lebrun entered the maintenance garage at a public bus company in Ottawa and opened fire with a high-powered .30-06-calibre hunting rifle, killing four people and wounding two others before taking his own life. In his suicide note left at his parents' home, Lebrun expressed his anger toward certain former co-workers whom, he claimed, had teased him for a speech impediment. Ironically, none of the men on his "hit list" were victimized. He had been fired by his company several years earlier, but his union had fought the dismissal and won. Lebrun had resigned from the company four months before the killing. It appears he was acting out of the frustrations born of his experiences with his co-workers.[58]

Some psychologists have tried to identify what causes some individuals to displace aggression or to experience it vicariously (through catharsis), while others respond violently and directly toward the immediate source of their frustrations. Andrew F. Henry and James F. Short, Jr., for example, suggested that child-rearing practices are a major determining factor in such a causal nexus.[59] Restrictive parents who both punish and love their children, said Henry and Short, will engender in their children the ability to suppress outward expressions of aggression, but when one parent punishes and the other loves, or when both punish but neither shows love,

Children can be expected to show anger directly and perhaps even immediately because they will not be threatened with the loss of love.

In 1960, Stewart Palmer studied murderers and their siblings to determine the degree of frustration they had been exposed to as children.[60] He found that male murderers had experienced much more frustration than their brothers and that more than twice as many frustrating experiences—ranging from difficult births to serious illnesses, childhood beatings, severe toilet training, and negative school experiences—were reported by the murderers than by their law-abiding siblings.

Crime as Adaption

Some psychiatric perspectives have held that crime is an adaptation to life's stresses. According to Seymour L. Halleck, turning to crime can provide otherwise disenfranchised individuals with a sense of power and purpose.[61] Halleck says that crime can also provide "excellent rationalizations" for perceived inadequacies, especially for those whose lives have been failures when judged against the benchmarks of the wider society. "The criminal is able to say . . . , 'I could have been successful if I had not turned to crime. All my troubles have come to me because I have been bad.'" Thus, crime, according to Halleck, provides "a convenient resource for denying, forgetting or ignoring . . . other inadequacies."[62]

Alloplastic adaptation A form of adjustment that results from changes in the environment surrounding an individual.

Autoplastic adaptation A form of adjustment that results from changes within an individual.

Insofar as the choice of crime reduces stresses that the individual faces by producing changes in the environment (empowerment), it is referred to as an **alloplastic adaptation**. When crime leads to stress reduction as a result of internal changes in beliefs, value systems, and so forth, it is called **autoplastic adaptation**. The offender who is able to deny responsibility for other failures by turning to crime is said to be seeking autoplastic adaptation. Because other forms of behaviour may also meet many of the same needs as does crime, Halleck pointed out, individuals may choose crime only when no reasonable alternatives are available or when criminal behaviour has inherent advantages—as might be the case under instances of economic or social oppression (i.e., individuals who are actively discriminated against may find personal and political significance in violating the laws of the oppressing society).

From Halleck's point of view, crime "has many advantages even when considered independently of the criminal's conscious or unconscious needs for gratification."[63] Even though crime can be immediately rewarding or intensely pleasurable, such a reward is more like a "fringe benefit"; its central significance is that it "is an action which helps one survive with dignity."[64] Halleck explained that "we cannot understand the criminal unless we appreciate that his actions are much more than an effort to find a specific gratification."[65]

Another approach to stress as a causative agent in crime commission suggests that stress may lead to aggression toward others and toward oneself (through self-destructive behaviour, such as suicide, smoking, and abuse of alcohol).[66] This approach measured stress at the societal level, arguing that although the relationship between stress and aggression has been studied at the individual level, "the neglect of social stress as an explanation for society-to-society differences in aggression may be partially due to a lack of an objective means of comparing the stressfulness of life in different societies."[67] Concluding that societal stress levels heighten levels of aggression, adherents of this approach suggested that social policies should be created to reduce the impact of stressful events, such as having to stop work, foreclosing on a mortgage, and dropping out of school.

Finally, we should recognize that perceptions vary and that although criminal behaviour may appear to be a valid choice for some individuals who are seeking viable responses to perceived stresses and oppression, their perceptions may not be wholly accurate.

Criminogenic Needs

In their 1998 book entitled *The Psychology of Criminal Conduct*, Canadians Donald A. Andrews and James Bonta identified major risk factors associated with criminal conduct that they termed **criminogenic needs**.[68] Criminogenic needs, which Andrews and Bonta referred to in later writings as *criminogenic domains*,[69] can be described as dynamic attributes of offenders and their circumstances that are associated with rates of recidivism.[70] Among the "needs" or risk factors that Andrews and Bonta listed are (1) anti-social attitudes, values, and beliefs; (2) anti-social personality, including low self-control; (3) anti-social associates and friends; (4) low levels of social achievement, including a lack of educational, vocational, or financial achievement; (5) family factors, including marital instability, a criminal family, and poor parenting skills; (6) substance abuse; and (7) a lack of pro-social pursuits. Criminogenic needs, because they are dynamic or amenable to change, can be targeted by treatment strategies intended to reduce criminality and recidivism.

In their writings, Andrews and Bonta developed the term *criminogenic domain* to refer to major risk factors for continuing criminality. They identified criminal history as a major criminogenic domain and noted that in combination with anti-social attitudes, criminal associates, and anti-social personality, these represent the "big four" risk factors. Andrews and Bonta were careful, however, not to include criminal history as a criminogenic need because it is a static element unamenable to change.[71]

Later writers have developed an enriched concept of criminogenic needs, suggesting that they are not positive desires that individuals seek to fulfill. Rather, according to Australian criminologists Tony Ward and Claire Stewart, "they can be seen as internal and external obstacles . . . linked to basic need distortion." Unlike our general understanding of needs, Ward and Stewart suggest that criminogenic needs arise in "the absence of the internal and external conditions necessary for a person to lead a fulfilling life."[72] Seen this way, criminogenic needs are not actually needs in themselves; rather, they are psychopathological symptoms or indicators of maladaptive functioning. Hence, offenders see "criminal acts as advantageous [because they are] causally related to socio-emotional deficits."[73] Hence, the fulfillment of criminogenic needs provides a proxy for meeting an individual's otherwise valid needs. So, for example, the need for social achievement can be fulfilled through criminal activity even though the offender does not have the education or skills needed for gainful employment. From the point of view of Ward and Stewart, "criminogenic needs arise from frustrated basic human needs and involve the acquisition of proxy goals and their accompanying dysfunctional beliefs and behavioral strategies." Moreover, they add, criminogenic needs "can be viewed as means to the commission of a crime" because "they represent the social and psychological conditions necessary for a crime to occur."[74]

Criminogenic needs Dynamic attributes (also known as *dynamic risk factors*) of offenders and their circumstances that are associated with rates of recidivism.

POLICY AND TREATMENT IMPLICATIONS OF PSYCHOLOGICAL AND PSYCHIATRIC APPROACHES

7.7 | LEARNING OBJECTIVE

NO DISCUSSION OF SOCIAL POLICY AS IT RELATES TO THE INSIGHTS OF CRIMINAL PSYCHOLOGY would be complete without mention of correctional psychology. **Correctional psychology** is concerned with the diagnosis and classification of offenders, the treatment of correctional populations, and the rehabilitation of inmates and law violators. Various forms of psychological and psychiatric treatments for criminal offenders have been developed based on the theories discussed in this chapter. In 2006, John C. Norcross and colleagues used a panel of 101 experts to generally assess the effectiveness of differing psychological assessments and treatments.[75] Fifty-nine treatments and 30 assessment

Correctional psychology The branch of forensic psychology concerned with the diagnosis and classification of offenders, the treatment of correctional populations, and the rehabilitation of inmates and other law violators.

techniques were evaluated, with the experts scoring each on a scale of 1 (not at all discredited) to 5 (totally discredited).

There are many different psychological and psychiatric treatments available today, including psychotherapy, guided group interaction, behavioural modification, parent training, peer programs, and individual counselling. In *The Psychology of Criminal Conduct*, Andrews and Bonta asked for the objective application of what is understood about the psychology of crime, behaviour, and criminal offenders through the application of readily available high-quality psychological findings. Based on nearly 500 published reports on "controlled evaluations of community and correctional interventions," they concluded that treatment reduces recidivism "to at least a mild degree."[76] Targeting higher-risk cases and using treatments outside of formal correctional settings (such as the offender's family and peers) are elements of the most effective treatment strategies. Along with objective measures of the success of rehabilitation programs and strategies, effective intervention and treatment services based on the use of psychological assessment instruments that have already demonstrated their validity, empirically established risk factors that can be accurately assessed, and accurately measured community crime rates are all ready and waiting to make a practical psychology of criminal conduct available to today's policy-makers. In the words of Andrews and Bonta, "There exists now an empirically defensible general psychology of criminal conduct (PCC) that is of practical value. It should speak to policy advisors, policy makers and legislators who must come to see that human science is not just [a] relic of a positivistic past."[77] They concluded that the major remaining issue, "on which work is only beginning, is how to make use of what works."[78]

Among the other most successful treatments are those that aim to change impulsivity and other offender personality characteristics. One such effective correctional technique is *cognitive behavioural intervention* (CBI). CBI is based on the belief that offenders need to acquire better social skills in order to become more pro-social. Cognitive skill building enables offenders to modify their cognitive processes to control themselves and interact positively with others. According to one source, "the goal of cognitive skills is to teach offenders to manage their own behavior by engaging in processes that develop self-control, making them responsible for and in charge of their actions no matter how stressful the situation. These specific skills include problem solving, social skills training (learned behaviours that enable one to interact with others in ways that elicit positive responses), anger management, and empathy training."[79] CBI programs not only target the offender's environment, behavioural responses, and skill development; they also seek to increase the offender's reasoning skills and problem-solving abilities and expand the offender's empathy toward others.

Another classification instrument commonly used in correctional facilities today is the Minnesota Multiphasic Personality Inventory, better known as the MMPI. Based on results of MMPI inventories, an offender may be assigned to a security level, a correctional program, or a treatment program. Psychological treatment typically takes the form of individual or group counselling, such as psychotherapy, guided group interaction, cognitive therapy, behavioural modification, and various forms of interpersonal therapy. Canadian Paul Gendreau is internationally recognized for his research on techniques for improving the practice of correctional psychology and reducing the risk of criminal reoffending. In 2007, Gendreau was appointed an officer of the Order of Canada in recognition of his service to Canada.

It should be noted that psychopathology has been regarded as notoriously resistant to treatment of any kind. One of the first comprehensive studies of treatments intended for psychopaths, conducted by the NATO Advanced Study Institute, concluded that "no demonstrably effective treatment has been found."[80] However, a more recent survey by Friedrich Lösel, a psychology professor at the University of

Erlangen-Nuremberg (Germany) found that only a small proportion of 500 English psychiatrists shared that viewpoint.[81] Lösel concluded that effective treatment with psychopaths should involve behaviour modification techniques, educational measures, involvement in therapeutic communities, and pharmacological agents.

Assessing Dangerousness

Can past behaviour predict future behaviour? Do former instances of criminality presage additional ones? Are there other identifiable characteristics violent offenders might manifest that could serve as warning signs to criminal justice decision makers faced with the dilemma of whether to release convicted felons? One study found a strong relationship between childhood behavioural difficulties and later problem behaviour: "Early antisocial behavior is the best predictor of later antisocial behavior. It appears that this rule holds even when the antisocial behavior is measured as early as the pre-school period." Using children as young as three years old, researchers were able to predict later delinquency, leading them to conclude that "some antisocial behavioral characteristics may be components of temperament."[82] A 1996 analysis of recidivism studies by Canadians Paul Gendreau, Tracy Little, and Claire Goggin found that criminal history, pre-adult anti-social behaviour, and "criminogenic needs" (measurable antisocial thoughts, values, and behaviour) were all predictors of recidivism.[83]

Prediction requires more than generalities; it necessitates the ability to predict which specific individuals will engage in future violations of criminal law. **Selective incapacitation**, although it is not a crime-prevention policy developed by psychologists, is based on the notion of career criminality predicated on the use of psychological techniques to effectively identify likely offenders and those who are likely to reoffend.[84] Career criminals, also called *habitual offenders*, are people who repeatedly violate the criminal law. Research has shown that only a small percentage of all offenders account for most crimes reported to the police. Some studies have found that as few as 8 percent of all offenders commit as many as 60 percent of serious crimes each year.[85] The strategy of selective incapacitation has been criticized by some authors for yielding a rate of "false positives" of over 60 percent.[86] Potentially violent offenders are not easy to identify, even on the basis of past criminal records, and sentencing individuals to long prison terms simply because they are thought likely to commit crimes in the future would no doubt violate their *Charter* rights.

> **Selective incapacitation** A social policy that seeks to protect society by incarcerating those individuals deemed to be the most dangerous.

Part XXIV of the *Criminal Code of Canada* deals with dangerous and long-term offenders. The Crown Attorney can make an application upon conviction (before sentencing) to have an offender designated as "dangerous." The dangerous offender designation brings with it an indefinite or indeterminate sentence of incarceration and a lengthened period of parole ineligibility. The past decade has seen an increase in the use of the dangerous offender designation to deal with repeat and violent offenders. The 2015 annual report of Public Safety Canada reported 735 offenders designated as dangerous; the majority of these were convicted of offences involving sexual aggression.[87] The *Tackling Violent Crime Act* of 2008 introduced changes to the dangerous offender provisions by putting the onus on an individual who has been convicted of specific violent or sexual crimes three or more times to convince the court why he or she should not be designated a dangerous offender.

Definitions of *dangerousness* are fraught with difficulty because "dangerousness is not an objective quality like obesity or brown eyes, rather it is an ascribed quality like trustworthiness."[88] Dangerousness is not necessarily a personality trait that is stable or easily identifiable, but even if it were, some studies of criminal careers seem to show that involvement in crime decreases with age.[89] One author stated that if "criminality declines more or less uniformly with age, then many offenders will be 'over the hill' by the time they are old enough to be plausible candidates for preventive incarceration."[90]

In recent years, a central focus of correctional psychologists has been on the development of a number of empirical risk assessment and classification tools. Such tools have gone through four generations of development:[91]

1. *First generation:* For most of the 20th century, professional judgment or intuition was the most common method used to predict criminal behaviour. Clinical professionals and correctional psychologists were guided by their own training and experiences, and the lessons they learned were often anecdotal.

2. *Second generation:* Beginning in the 1970s, the assessment of risk began to depend more on actuarial, evidence-based science and less on professional judgment and intuition. Second-generation risk assessments are often referred to as *actuarial risk assessments*, and they consider individual indicators (e.g., a history of substance abuse) that have been demonstrated to increase the risk of reoffending and assign these items quantitative scores.

3. *Third generation:* In the early 1980s, risk-assessment instruments began to take into consideration dynamic risk factors; they are commonly referred to as *risk-need assessments*. Third-generation instruments combine the static predictor variables of the second-generation instruments with measured changes in an offender's circumstances.

4. *Fourth generation:* Beginning in the early 2000s, fourth-generation risk-assessment instruments began to assess a broader range of risk factors along with what are referred to as *responsivity factors*, which many regard as important to treatment. Responsivity factors include reading and cognitive abilities, race, gender, and motivation to change as well as external factors, such as treatment setting and counsellor characteristics.

One of the most commonly used risk assessment instruments in correctional facilities in Canada today is the Level of Service Inventory–Revised (LSI-R). Developed by Andrews and Bonta, the LSI-R scores offenders as low, moderate, or high risk based on 54 items about the offender that are categorized into 10 sublevels: criminal history, education/employment, financial situation, family/marital relationships, accommodation, leisure and recreation, companions, alcohol or drug use, emotional/mental health, and attitudes and orientation.[92] A 2007 study showed "that the total LSI-R score is significantly related to the prediction of future criminal behavior."[93] The higher the total risk score, the study showed, the more likely that the client would reoffend.

Nonetheless, assessing dangerousness is a central issue in criminology and especially in psychological approaches to criminality.[94] Consequently, those who score high on dimensions meant to measure dangerousness are often committed to mental or forensic hospitals or other controlled facilities, even in the absence of overt criminal behaviour.

7.8 | LEARNING OBJECTIVE | CRITIQUE OF PSYCHOLOGICAL AND PSYCHIATRIC THEORIES

CRITICS SAY THAT BY FOCUSING ON THE INDIVIDUAL, PSYCHOLOGICAL AND PSYCHIATRIC theories of criminality do not sufficiently take into account social or environmental conditions that produce crime. In fact, if social conditions are the primary cause of crime, then individual change brought about by psychological or psychiatric interventions will not necessarily reduce levels of criminal offences or lower rates of crime.

Similarly, psychological and psychiatric theories place the locus of control within the individual by positing a sense of moral reasoning. However, effective social control may actually stem from within social and physical arrangements that comprise the environment in which the individual functions. In other words, physical and social barriers to crime (such as the presence of a police officer) may be more effective at preventing crime than the sense of right or wrong that psychological theories find so important. Moreover, "some criminologists have an ideological aversion to locating the blame for criminal behavior on individuals and not on inequities in the social structure."[95] Freudian theory, discussed earlier, has been criticized on several levels. The first and most fundamental criticism of this perspective is its lack of scientific support. Critics point out that Freud's theories are not based on research and that there is no substantial support for his concepts. As such, Freudian theory has been seen as less of a scientific explanation for human behaviour based on sound methodology and more of a belief system, valuable as a tool for literary and philosophical interpretation.[96]

Moreover, some claim that psychiatric theories, as distinguished from psychological ones, are appropriate only for explanations of abnormal cognition and do not apply well to otherwise normal people who turn to crime. In fact, some criminologists point to the fact that criminological predicators such as offence history are more accurate in forecasting future offences than are psychological assessments and diagnosis, even among individuals characterized as mentally ill.[97]

Modelling theory, a more sophisticated form of cognitive theory, has been criticized for lacking comprehensive explanatory power. How, for example, can striking differences in sibling behaviour, when early childhood experiences were likely much the same, be explained? Similarly, why do apparent differences exist between the sexes with regard to degree and type of criminality, irrespective of social background and early learning experiences? More recent versions of modelling theory, sometimes called *cognitive social learning theory*,[98] attempt to account for such differences by hypothesizing that reflection and cognition play a significant role in interpreting what one observes and in determining responses. Hence, few people are likely to behave precisely as others do because they will have their own ideas about what observed behaviour means and about the consequences of imitation.

CRIMINAL PSYCHOLOGICAL PROFILING

7.9 | LEARNING OBJECTIVE

DURING WORLD WAR II, THE U.S. WAR DEPARTMENT RECRUITED PSYCHOLOGISTS AND psychoanalysts in an attempt to predict future moves enemy forces might make; the psychological and psychoanalytical techniques were applied to the study of German leader Adolf Hitler, Italian leader Benito Mussolini, Japanese general and prime minister Hideki Tojo, and other Axis leaders. Such psychological profiling of enemy leaders may have given the Allies the edge in battlefield strategy.

Today, **psychological profiling** (also called *criminal profiling* and *behavioural profiling*) is used to assist criminal investigators seeking to better understand individuals wanted for serious offences. Psychological profiling is built on the idea that behavioural clues left behind at a crime scene may reflect the personality of the offender.

Profilers develop a list of typical offender characteristics and other useful principles by analyzing crime scene and autopsy data, in conjunction with interviews and other studies of past offenders, in the belief that almost any form of conscious behaviour (including behaviour engaged in by the offender during a criminal episode) is symptomatic of an individual's personality. The way a kidnapper approaches victims, the manner of attack used by a killer, and the specific sexual activities of a rapist—all of these might help paint a picture of the offender's motivations, personal characteristics, and likely future behaviour. Sometimes psychological profiles can provide clues as

Psychological profiling The attempt to categorize, understand, and predict the behaviour of certain types of offenders based on behavioural clues they provide; also called *criminal profiling* and *behavioural profiling*.

to what an offender might do following an attack. Some offenders have been arrested, for example, after returning to the crime scene, a behaviour typically predicted by specific behavioural clues left behind, and a remorseful type can be expected to visit the victim's grave, permitting fruitful stakeouts of cemeteries.

Although criminal profiling may not be useful in every case, it can help narrow the search for an offender in repetitive crimes involving one offender, such as serial sexual assault or murder. Knowledge gleaned from profiling can also help in the interrogation of suspects and can be used to identify and protect possible victims before the offender has a chance to strike again.

Profiles have also contributed significantly to the scientific literature in criminology. In a well-known study of lust murderers (men who kill and often mutilate victims during or following a forced sexual episode), Robert R. Hazelwood and John E. Douglas distinguished between the organized non-social and the disorganized asocial types.[99] The organized non-social lust murderer exhibits complete indifference to the interests of society and is completely self-centred, methodical, cunning, and "fully cognizant of the criminality of his act and its impact on society."[100] The disorganized asocial lust murderer was described this way:

> [He] exhibits primary characteristics of societal aversion. This individual prefers his own company to that of others and would be typified as a loner. He experiences difficulty in negotiating interpersonal relationships and consequently feels rejected and lonely. He lacks the cunning of the non-social type and commits the crime in a more frenzied and less methodical manner. The crime is likely to be committed in close proximity to his residence or place of employment, where he feels secure and more at ease.[101]

During the 1980s, the Federal Bureau of Investigation (FBI) in the United States led the movement to develop psychological profiling techniques through its concentration on violent sex offenders and arsonists. Much of that work continues at the FBI's Training Academy in Quantico, Virginia, in the Behavioral Science Unit (BSU), whose official mission continues to focus on serial killers, lust murderers, domestic terrorists, and the like and aims to develop and provide programs of training, research, and consultation in the behavioural and social sciences for the FBI and the law enforcement community. The unit's activities have been popularized by movies and television shows such as *Silence of the Lambs* (1991) and *Criminal Minds*; however, media representations may lead the public to put too much stock in behavioural techniques such as psychological profiling. "It's not the magic bullet of investigations," said retired agent Robert Ressler, "it's simply another tool."[102]

Based on training acquired at the FBI Training Academy, Canadian police officials have developed an automated case linkage system that uses some of the behavioural principles of psychological profiling to identify and track violent serial criminals. Through the pioneering work of Inspector Ron MacKay of the RCMP and Sergeant Greg Johnston of the Ontario Provincial Police (OPP), the **Violent Crime Linkage Analysis System (ViCLAS)** was introduced in 1995. ViCLAS is a centralized computer bank containing details of violent crimes, allowing police to recognize patterns among violent offences. In cases of solved or unsolved homicides and sexual assaults, missing persons, and non-parental abductions, police investigators must respond to over 200 questions covering details of all aspects of an incident, including victimology, modus operandi, forensics, and behavioural information. The information is then forwarded to one of the ViCLAS centres throughout the country, where trained ViCLAS specialists input it and interpret the results. There is a ViCLAS centre in every province except for Prince Edward Island. Seven sites are maintained by the RCMP, and one each maintained by the OPP and the Sûreté du Québec. These sites perform data entry,

Violent Crime Linkage Analysis System (ViCLAS) A centralized computer bank containing details of violent crimes that assists police in recognizing patterns among violent offences and offenders.

conduct quality reviews, and await further processing and/or analysis. The last available data indicates that there were approximately 300 000 cases on the system and over 3200 linkages made.[103]

Most initial operational difficulties have been worked out, and the system has been adopted internationally in countries such as Belgium, Australia, and the United Kingdom. Advocates of ViCLAS believe it is serving to facilitate communication between investigators with the common goal of solving serious serial criminal acts and protecting the public from dangerous repeat offenders. In the words of RCMP inspector Ron MacKay, "The linking of a series of crimes committed by the same offender not only increases investigative efficiency, it also enhances the grounds for multiple charges and dangerous offender status, with resultant indefinite/longer sentences for serial offenders."[104]

Terms like *offender profiling* and *crime-action profiling* are used today to describe the work of profilers. Today's profilers tend to analyze crime-scene data and offender interviews, searching for commonalities that can be used to distinguish between types of offenders. Another term commonly used today is *investigative psychology*, which can be defined as "the scientific discipline of applying, analyzing, or developing psychological principles, theories or empirical findings to aid investigations and the legal process."[105]

Some contemporary psychologists discount the value of profiling. In 2007, a meta-analysis of profiling studies found that "trained profilers did only slightly better than non-profilers at estimating the overall characteristics of offenders from information about their crimes."[106] The studies compared the ability of profilers with non-profilers to gauge an offender's physical characteristics, thinking processes (including motives), and personal habits.[107] Nonetheless, profiling remains highly visible in today's media and continues to be popular with the public.

MENTAL ILLNESS AND THE LAW

UNFORTUNATELY FOR CRIMINOLOGISTS, PSYCHOLOGICAL CONCEPTIONS OF MENTAL ILLNESS, anti-social personality disorder, and even psychopathy are not readily applicable to the criminal justice system, which relies instead on the legal concept of insanity. Insanity, for purposes of the criminal law, is strictly a legal, not a clinical, determination. Seen this way, *insanity* is a term that refers to a type of defence allowable in criminal courts. Although the legal concept of insanity is based on claims of mental illness, it has no precise counterpart in the jargon of contemporary psychologists or psychiatrists, who speak in terms of mental status or, at most, psychosis or personality; as a consequence, legal and psychiatric understandings of mental impairment rarely coincide.

The *Criminal Code of Canada* defines **mental disorder** as a "disease of the mind." Whether a specific condition is a disease of the mind, however, is a question of law. While medical evidence is used to assist a judge in deciding whether the accused suffers a disease of the mind, the Supreme Court of Canada has stated that the protection of public safety must also be considered. The Court has ruled that if the accused suffers from a recurring condition that may continue to present a danger to the public, the accused's condition should be treated as a mental disorder.[108] A number of mental disorders are recognized by the courts as diseases of the mind, including schizophrenia, paranoia, senile dementia, melancholia, various types of epilepsy, and delirium tremens caused by alcohol abuse. Self-induced states caused by alcohol or drugs, and temporary conditions such as hysteria and concussion, are excluded.[109] The burden of proving a claim of "not criminally responsible on account of mental disorder," however, falls upon the defendant. Just as a person is assumed to be innocent at the start of any criminal trial, so too is the person assumed to be sane.

Mental disorder (psychological)   Disease of the mind, including schizophrenia, paranoia, senile dementia, melancholia, various types of epilepsy, and delirium tremens caused by alcohol abuse.

Mental disorder (legal)   A legally established inability to understand right from wrong or to conform one's behaviour to the requirements of the law. Also, a defence allowable in criminal courts.

Tragedy on a Greyhound Bus

On July 30, 2008, at 5:55 p.m., 22-year-old Tim McLean boarded a Greyhound bus in Erickson, Manitoba, bound for Winnipeg. He was returning home from a summer job on the carnival circuit. He took a seat at the back of the bus, several rows behind Vince Li, who had already been travelling on the bus for a day and was headed to Thunder Bay.

The bus stopped between Brandon and Portage la Prairie, where both men got off for a break. Upon reboarding, Vince Li moved to the back of the bus and sat beside Tim McLean. The two men did not exchange any words.

At approximately 8:30 p.m., in an unprovoked attack and for no apparent reason, Vince Li began to repeatedly stab Tim McLean. Despite his efforts to defend himself and get out of his seat, McLean was trapped at the back of the bus, the seats in front of him barring him from escape. He fell to the floor while Li continued to stab him, apparently oblivious to the screams of the other passengers and the bus driver exhorting him to stop. Only after the passengers vacated the bus did Li attempt to escape through the front door, but he was trapped when the bus driver managed to close the door on his arm. Li pulled his arm free and returned to the body of McLean, continuing to defile it with cuts and stabs.

As panicked passengers waited for emergency personnel, Li attempted again to exit the bus, now holding Tim McLean's severed head in one hand, his bloodied buck knife in the other. The quick-thinking bus driver had managed to cut the power to the door and a truck driver who had stopped to help barricaded the door with a snipe bar. Trapped, Li went back to McLean's torso and continued to mutilate it.

Upon their arrival, RCMP officers ordered Vince Li to throw the knife out of the bus window. He refused and continued to cut McLean's body with the knife and a pair of scissors. Witnesses reported seeing Li licking blood from his fingers and placing some of McLean's internal organs and body parts in plastic bags.

After several hours, Li decided to surrender, jumping out a window of the bus. After a scuffle, he was subdued by the RCMP and formally arrested. Charged with second-degree murder, Li appeared in court several months later. At his trial, psychiatrists testified Li was schizophrenic and suffering a major psychotic episode at the time of the killing. Li heard voices from God telling him that McLean, sitting next to him on the bus, was an evil threat that needed to be eliminated, psychiatrists said. Even after the killing, Li believed McLean might come back to life and threaten him. Li was found "not criminally responsible on account of mental disorder" (NCRMD), the judge ruling that he was suffering hallucinations from untreated schizophrenia at the time of the attack. Li was sent to a secure psychiatric facility.

A shocked public reacted to the tragic event, and McLean's mother, Carol deDelley, led a very public crusade to change Canada's laws. Launching a petition, she called on the federal government to enact "Tim's Law," an amendment to the *Criminal Code* that would ensure that those who are found not criminally responsible for crimes on account of a mental disorder are jailed for a minimum period of time.

In May 2013, the Criminal Court Review Board ruled that Vince Li be granted escorted full-day passes as far away as Winnipeg. In 2015, the board ruled that Li could live in a supervised group home, and in 2016 it ruled that he could live independently.

Think about it:

1. Most people with diagnosed mental illness never commit acts of violence. In rare cases such as the one described here, how should perpetrators be dealt with?

2. Do you agree with the legal definition of NCRMD? Should Vince Li have been deemed to be "not responsible" for his violent acts?

3. Do our current laws regarding those deemed NCRMD sufficiently recognize the rights of the victim?

Sources: Based on "Accused in Manitoba Bus Killing Fit to Stand Trial: Court," *CBC News*, October 6, 2008 , Tom Broadbeck, "The Story of Vince Li," March 4, 2009, "Bus Slaying's Grim Anniversary Marked," *CBC News*, July 30, 2009, and Vince Li gets Winnipeg visitation privileges", *CBC News*, May 17, 2013, Steve Lambert, "Vince Li, Ma Who Beheaded Greyhound Passenger, Wins Right to Love Alone", *Huffington Post Canada*, February 26, 2016.

The McNaughten Rule

One of the first instances within Western legal tradition where insanity was accepted as a defence to criminal liability can be found in the British case of Daniel McNaughten (also spelled M'Naughton and M'Naghton). McNaughten was accused of the 1844 killing of Edward Drummond, the secretary of British prime minister Sir Robert Peel. McNaughten had intended to kill Peel, but because he was suffering from mental disorganization, he shot Drummond instead, mistaking him for Peel. At his trial, the defence presented information to show that McNaughten was suffering from delusions, including the belief that Peel's political party was, in some vague way, persecuting him. The court accepted his lawyer's claims, and the defence of insanity was established in Western law. Other jurisdictions were quick to adopt the **McNaughten rule**, as the judge's decision in the case came to be called, which holds that individuals cannot be held criminally responsible for their actions if at the time of the offence either (1) they did not know what they were doing, or (2) they did not know that what they were doing was wrong.

McNaughten rule A standard for judging legal insanity that requires that offenders did not know what they were doing, or if they did, that they did not know it was wrong.

Today, the McNaughten rule is still followed in Canada when mental disorder is at issue in criminal cases. Critics of the McNaughten rule say that, although the notion of intent inherent within it appeals to lawyers, "it is so alien to current concepts of human behavior that it has been vigorously attacked by psychiatrists. An obvious difficulty with the McNaughten rule is that practically everyone, regardless of the degree of his criminal disturbance, knows the nature and quality and rightness or wrongness of what he is doing."[110]

Fitness to Stand Trial and Not Criminally Responsible on Account of Mental Disorder

When the question of mental fitness arises, two standards are assessed. First, is the accused fit to stand trial; that is, does he or she understand the nature of charges against him or her? If a court-ordered psychiatric assessment determines that the accused is unfit to stand trial (UST), then that individual is usually placed in a psychiatric facility or released under community supervision for ongoing treatment. The individual's case is reviewed annually, and the Crown is responsible for bringing it before the courts every two years. If the individual becomes fit to stand trial, he or she may do so at that time.

The second standard of fitness is the accused's mental state at the time of the offence. A finding of **not criminally responsible on account of mental disorder (NCRMD)** acknowledges that the accused committed the offence but finds that the accused suffered from a mental disorder that made him or her incapable of appreciating the nature and quality of his or her actions or that the actions were wrong. When such a verdict of NCRMD is made, a disposition hearing is ordered to assess whether or not the accused poses any threat to the public or to him- or herself. If not, the accused may be released under supervision to the community. Otherwise, the accused may be detained in a secure hospital, under certain conditions.

Not criminally responsible on account of mental disorder (NCRMD) A finding that offenders are responsible for committing the offence that they have committed and, because of their prevailing mental condition, should be sent to a psychiatric hospital for treatment rather than to prison.

The length of time in hospital detention for those deemed to be NCRMD has been a subject of controversy in recent years. The Supreme Court decision *R. v. Swain* resulted in an overhaul of the existing legal insanity criteria and practices, most notably the automatic and indefinite detention for those found legally insane. In that decision, the Court held not only that "the duty of the trial judge to detain is unqualified by any standard whatsoever" but also that "insanity acquitees should be detained no longer than necessary to determine whether they are currently dangerous due to their

Box 7.1 MENTAL DISORDER AS A DEFENCE

The *Criminal Code of Canada* permits the defence of insanity, as follows:

Defence of Mental Disorder	**16.** (1) No person is criminally responsible for an act committed or an omission made while suffering from a mental disorder that rendered the person incapable of appreciating the nature and quality of the act or omission or of knowing that it was wrong.
Presumption	(2) Every person is presumed not to suffer from a mental disorder so as to be exempt from criminal responsibility by virtue of subsection (1), until the contrary is proved on the balance of probabilities.
Burden of Proof	(3) The burden of proof that an accused was suffering from a mental disorder so as to be exempt from criminal responsibility is on the party that raises the issue.

Source: *Criminal Code of Canada*, R.S.C. 1985, c. C-46, s.16 [as amended S.C. 1991, c. 43, s. 2].

insanity."[111] Amendments to the *Criminal Code* passed in 1992 (see Box 7.1) reflect the basic principle of Canadian criminal law that to convict someone of a crime, the state must prove not only a wrongful act but also a guilty mind. In the words of then Minister of Justice Kim Campbell, "The mental disorder provisions of the *Criminal Code* needed to be updated to reflect the evolution of society and the law. These changes will ensure that individuals are not deprived of their *Charter* rights. At the same time, the amendments offer protection of the public from dangerous mentally disordered persons who come into conflict with the law."[112]

Interestingly, other countries use a variety of definitions of legal insanity. In the United States, where the issue falls within the jurisdiction of the individual state, a number of alternatives exist. In addition to the McNaughten rule, the irresistible-impulse test is employed in 18 states and holds that a defendant is not guilty of a criminal offence if the person, by virtue of his or her mental state or psychological condition, was not able to resist committing the action in question. Several U.S. states have adopted the "guilty but mentally ill" (GBMI) standard. A GBMI verdict means that a person can be held responsible for a specific criminal act, even though a degree of mental incompetence may be present in his or her personality. Individuals adjudicated GBMI are found guilty of the criminal offence with which they are charged but, because of their mental condition, are generally sent to psychiatric hospitals for treatment rather than to prison.[113] Other standards include the Durham rule and the Brawner rule.

Provisions for Individuals Found NCRMD   Section 672.38, Part XX.1 of the *Criminal Code of Canada* makes provisions for the treatment of individuals found NCRMD. Procedures for dealing with those found NCRMD stipulate that such a person must attend a disposition hearing, which can either be held by the trial court or be referred to a provincial review board made up of lawyers, psychiatrists, and other appointees, which is the usual course of action. This disposition hearing must be held within 45 days of the NCRMD finding. If the court holds the hearing and makes an order other than an absolute discharge, the review board must review the case within 90 days. The NCRMD person may be present at the disposition, may be represented by counsel, and may cross-examine witnesses. The disposition hearings are public and "may be conducted in as informal a manner as is appropriate in the circumstances."[114] The recommendation of the review board for the treatment of the NCRMD individual is expected to reflect the least intrusive or restrictive option consistent with the

André Dallaire, a diagnosed paranoid schizophrenic, was declared not criminally responsible for attempting to kill Prime Minister Chrétien after breaking into his home. How does the Canadian criminal justice system deal with people such as Dallaire?

Fred Chartrand/The Canadian Press

protection of society. For example, the court or review board might allow someone who committed a theft, who is not dangerous, and who is willing to submit to psychiatric treatment on an outpatient basis to stay at home rather than be sent to a hospital setting. Such a condition would be subject to the supervision of medical staff giving the treatment and to periodic reviews; changes may be effected as required. The review board in such a case would have the authority to revoke this status and order hospitalization should the person's condition deteriorate.

In 1990, proposed amendments to the *Criminal Code* would have introduced a system of "caps" in order to place maximum times for which individuals can be detained under review board dispositions. These revisions were subsequently repealed from the *Criminal Code* without ever having been brought into force. Despite public perception, the defence of mental disorder has not been used successfully in a large number of cases in Canada. Yet some argue that this defence is being used more often since the introduction of the 25-year minimum life sentence for first-degree murder in 1976.[115] The Canadian Department of Justice statistics indicate that the total number of UST and NCRMD cases in 2015 was fewer than 5000, and in that same year, NCRMD cases represented approximately 9 percent of all adult criminal court cases.[116] Some high-profile Canadian cases in which the defence of mental disorder was used successfully include those of André Dallaire, the paranoid schizophrenic who tried unsuccessfully to assassinate then Prime Minister Chrétien; Dorothy Joudrie, who attempted to murder her husband with five blasts from a shotgun in Calgary; and Elizabeth Elliott, who stepped in front of a transport truck on a highway near Perth, Ontario, while carrying her five-year-old daughter. Elliott's schizophrenia and bipolar disorder had caused her to have religious delusions that were responsible for her behaviour.[117]

PSYCHOLOGICAL AND PSYCHIATRIC THEORIES APPLIED

COGNITIVE THEORY

holds that learning processes determine how people learn to solve problems and how they perceive and interpret their social environment. Could it be argued that Armin Meiwes had an underdeveloped sense of morals?

PSYCHOANALYTIC CRIMINOLOGY

holds that criminal behaviour can be explained by considering the role of personality in determining human behaviour. Could Armin Meiwes's behaviour demonstrate an overactive id, which could not be controlled by his superego?

Psychological and psychiatric theories of criminal behaviour emphasize individual propensities and characteristics in the genesis of criminality. Whether the emphasis is on conditioned behaviour, human cognition, or psychoanalytic structure of the human personality, these approaches see the wellsprings of human motivation, desire, and behavioural choice as being firmly rooted in the personality.

Can the bizarre perversions of Armin Meiwes and the murderous actions of Marc Lepine be explained from a psychological and/or psychiatric perspective?

BEHAVIOUR THEORY

holds that criminal behaviour is learned by modelling others whom an individual has the opportunity to observe. Marc Lepine blamed his victims for his personal failures and thereby justified his violent outburst. Can this behaviour be explained using the notion of disengagement?

FRUSTRATION– AGGRESSION THEORY

holds that criminal behaviour is a form of adaptation to reduce stress caused by frustration. Can Marc Lepine's frustration and anger at the female students, who had succeeded in studying engineering at Montreal's L'École Polytechnique when he had not, be explained by frustration–aggression theory?

PERSONALITY DISTURBANCES

holds that criminal behaviour is linked to a complex set of drives and motives operating from the recesses deep within the personality. Did either Armin Meiwes or Marc Lepine exhibit any of the traits characterizing the psychopathic or anti-social personality?

SUMMARY OF LEARNING OBJECTIVES

7.1 Psychological and psychiatric theories of criminal behaviour emphasize individual propensities and characteristics in explaining criminality. Whether the emphasis is on conditioned behaviour, human cognition, or psychoanalytic structure of the human personality, these approaches see the wellsprings of human motivation, desire, and behavioural choice as being firmly rooted in the personality.

7.2 Two major ideas characterized early psychological theories: personality and behaviourism. Personality theory built on the burgeoning area of cognitive science, including personality disturbances and diseases of the mind; behaviourism examined social learning with an emphasis on behavioural conditioning.

7.3 Cognitive theories are learning theories that examine thought processes and seek to explain how people learn to solve problems and how they perceive and interpret their social environment. Cognitive theory has a number of branches, including one that focuses on moral and intellectual development and another that examines how people process information.

7.4 The psychopathic personality, one that is cunning and self-serving but without empathy, offers an explanation for personality found in the unrestrained desires of offenders. The anti-social personality, by contrast, is essentially unsocialized and generally in conflict with society.

7.5 Behaviour theory (or the stimulus–response approach to human behaviour) holds that behaviour is directly determined by the environmental consequences it produces for the individual exhibiting the behaviour. When an individual's behaviour results in rewards or positive feedback, that behaviour will increase in frequency; when punishment follows behaviour, that behaviour will decrease. Modelling theory asserts that people learn how to act by observing others. Once aggressive patterns of behaviour have been thus acquired, aggression can be activated by people experiencing physical assaults or verbal threats and insults, having their hopes thwarted, or having their goal-seeking behaviour obstructed.

7.6 From the point of view of psychoanalysis, criminal behaviour is maladaptive, the product of inadequacies in the offender's personality. The psychoanalytic perspective, advanced by Sigmund Freud in the early 1900s, encompasses diverse notions like personality, neurosis, and psychosis as well as transference, sublimation, and repression.

7.7 Some theorists now consider that psychological criminology can be used for the development of consistent and dependable social policy in the prediction of dangerousness and the rehabilitation of offenders and that selective incapacitation may be a workable policy to prevent future criminality.

7.8 Critics say that by focusing on the individual, psychological and psychiatric theories of criminality do not sufficiently take into account social or environmental conditions that produce crime. In fact, if social conditions are the primary cause of crime, then individual change brought about by psychological or psychiatric interventions will not necessarily reduce levels of criminal offences or lower rates of crime.

7.9 Psychological profiling of criminal offenders, based on the belief that almost any form of conscious behaviour is symptomatic of the individual's personality, is a serious crime-fighting undertaking that may change the nature of localized crime-prevention strategies.

7.10 Psychological and psychiatric conceptions of mental illness, anti-social personality, and even psychopathy are not readily applicable to the criminal justice system, which relies instead on the legal concept of insanity. Although the legal concept of insanity is based on claims of mental illness, it has no precise counterpart in the jargon of contemporary psychologists or psychiatrists.

Questions for Review

1. What are the major principles of psychological and psychiatric perspectives on criminal behaviour?

2. How do personality theories explain criminality?

3. What is moral development theory and how does it explain crime?

4. What are the characteristics of a psychopath? What is the relationship between psychopathy and criminal behaviour?

5. How does the social cognition theory explain how aggressive patterns of behaviour, once acquired, can be activated?

6. How can criminality be seen as a form of adaptive behaviour?

7. What is the role of correctional psychology in current social policy and treatment approaches to criminality?

8. What are the major criticisms of the psychological and psychiatric approaches to criminality?

9. What is the role of criminal profilers?

10. What is the difference between the person diagnosed as a psychopath and the person deemed to be "not criminally responsible on account of mental disorder" (NCRMD)?

Multiple-Choice Questions

1. According to _____ , aggressive and anti-social behaviour is a cognitive process that includes the ideas of observation, imitation, and modelling.
   a. Sigmund Freud
   b. Lawrence Kohlberg
   c. B.F. Skinner
   d. Hervey Cleckley
   e. Albert Bandura

2. When the question of mental fitness arises, two standards are assessed. They are _____.
   a. the accused's remorse and willingness to declare guilt
   b. the severity of the crime and the circumstances surrounding the crime
   c. the number of victims and the extent of their injuries
   d. the accused's fitness to stand trial and mental state at the time of the offence
   e. the accused's history of mental illness and treatment

3. _____ are said to be characterized as effective manipulators who clearly understand the motivations of others, are said to dissociate emotionally from their actions, and lack empathy or sensitivity toward others.
   a. Psychopaths
   b. Persons with asocial personalities
   c. Schizophrenics
   d. Persons with anti-social personalities
   e. Sociopaths

4. Canadians Donald A. Andrews and James Bonta identified major risk factors associated with criminal conduct that they termed _____.
   a. criminogenic needs
   b. anti-social personality disorder
   c. personality traits
   d. cognitive information processing
   e. the Big Five

5. Which of the following statements is not a fundamental assumption of psychological/psychiatric theories of crime causation?

   a. The individual is the primary unit of analysis.

   b. Personality is the major motivational element within individuals because it is the seat of drives and the source of motives.

   c. Crimes result from abnormal, dysfunctional, or inappropriate mental processes within the personality.

   d. Defective, or abnormal, mental processes may have a variety of causes, including a diseased mind, inappropriate learning or improper conditioning, the emulation of inappropriate role models, and adjustment to inner conflicts.

   e. Basic determinants of human behaviour, including criminality, can be passed on from generation to generation.

Multiple Choice Answers: 1e, 2d, 3a, 4a, 5e

Chapter 8
The Meaning of Crime: Social Structure Perspective

Monkey Business Images/Shutterstock

If we would change the amount of crime in the community, we must change the community.

—Frank Tannenbaum[1]

LEARNING OBJECTIVES

After reading this chapter, you should be able to

8.1 Understand the nature of sociological theorizing, and discuss some of the assumptions of the sociological perspective of crime causation.

8.2 Describe the major principles of social structure theories of criminal behaviour.

8.3 Distinguish between the three types of social structure theories discussed in this chapter.

8.4 Identify social policy implications of the theories that reflect the social structure approach.

8.5 Assess the shortcomings of the social structure approach to understanding and preventing criminal behaviour.

INTRODUCTION

In March 1994, police responded to a 911 call reporting a collapsed man on a busy street in Ottawa, Ontario. It soon became apparent that the man had been shot through the chest; he died on the sidewalk before he could be taken to hospital. The incident shocked the nation's capital when details of the case revealed that Nicholas Battersby, a 27-year-old British-born engineer, had been the victim of a so-called drive-by shooting. An employee at a local high-tech firm, Battersby had simply been out for a stroll at 7:30 in the evening when a bullet from a sawed-off .22-calibre rifle shot from within a Jeep hit him in the chest.

After several days of an intensive police manhunt, three local teens, Rubens Henderson, Brian Raymond, and Cory Cyr, were charged with Battersby's murder. All three youths had long records of trouble with the law. Henderson, who had been adopted from a Brazilian orphanage, never really adapted to life in Ottawa. Despite sincere attempts by his mother to provide support, Henderson soon became known as a troublemaker in school. In grade six, he assaulted a student, a teacher, and a vice-principal and was expelled from the school with grades ranging from C to F. He soon acquired a young offender's record, which included break and enter, assault, joyriding in stolen cars, being unlawfully at large, and the use of illicit drugs. His activities brought him into contact with Brian Raymond and Cory Cyr. Raymond was raised by a single mother in a neighbourhood where there was a motorcycle gang clubhouse. Psychologists used words like "dull" and "borderline" when labelling Raymond's language, math, and reasoning skills. Yet he knew how to hot-wire cars and get his hands on all sorts of drugs. Cory Cyr had spent many of his 16 years in group homes. Two days before the Battersby shooting, he had been released from jail after serving a 30-day sentence for assaulting a youth into unconsciousness after losing a Nintendo game to him. In 1996, Rubens Henderson received a life sentence for second-degree murder, while Cory Cyr and Brian Raymond received five- and four-year sentences, respectively, for manslaughter.[2] In 2015, the Parole Board of Canada granted Henderson two unescorted temporary absences during which he stayed for three months at a residential facility. Unescorted absences are considered an important stepping stone toward full parole. While incarcerated, Henderson has completed substance abuse and anger management programs, has finished his high school education, and has gone on 40 escorted temporary absences without incident.[3] In October 2016, Henderson, now 38, was released on day parole and is now living in the community.

The motivation behind the killing of Nicholas Battersby is not entirely clear. There is no doubt that the three youths were intoxicated on drugs and alcohol as they rode around in the stolen Jeep taking random shots at storefronts and people. What is also certain is that all three had socially deprived backgrounds. They lacked educational achievement and the basic skills needed for success in the modern world. Academic failure, and subcultural values that focused on excitement and greed, dictated the direction their lives were to take—and all but ensured their fateful encounter with Nicholas Battersby. At a parole hearing, Rubens Henderson told the board that on the night of the murder he "acted impulsively to please others in the vehicle" who urged him to shoot a pedestrian. At the time, Henderson said, he harboured a lot of anger about his childhood and suffered from low self-esteem and poor emotional control.[4]

SOCIOLOGICAL THEORIES

8.1 | LEARNING OBJECTIVE

THEORIES THAT EXPLAIN CRIME BY REFERENCE TO SOCIAL STRUCTURE ARE ONLY ONE OF three major sociological approaches to crime causation. The other two are social process theories and social conflict approaches (which are described in Chapters 9 and 10).

Although sociological perspectives on crime are diverse, most build upon the following fundamental assumptions:

- Social groups, social institutions, arrangements of society, and social roles all provide the focus for criminological study.
- Group dynamics, group organization, and subgroup relationships form the causal nexus out of which crime develops.
- The structure of society and its relative degree of organization or disorganization are important factors contributing to the prevalence of criminal behaviour.

Sociological theories examine both institutional arrangements within a **social structure** (i.e., interrelationships among society's institutions) and **social processes** (i.e., interactions between and among different social institutions, groups, and individuals) as they affect socialization and have an impact on **social life** (i.e., social interaction).

In contrast to more individualized biological and psychological theories (discussed in Chapters 6 and 7), which have what is called a *micro focus*, sociological approaches utilize a *macro focus*, stressing the type of behaviour likely to be exhibited by group members rather than attempting to predict the behaviour of specific individuals. As noted in Chapter 1, sociological thought has influenced criminological theory construction more significantly than any other perspective during the past half century, due (at least in part) to a widespread concern with social issues, including civil rights, the women's movement, issues of poverty, and the changing influence of many traditional social institutions, such as the family, government, organized religion, and educational systems. Although all sociological perspectives on crime share a common starting point, particular theories give greater or lesser weight to selected components of social life. We can identify three key sociological explanations for crime:

1. *Crime is the result of an individual's location within the structure of society.* This approach focuses on the social and economic conditions of life, including poverty, alienation, social disorganization, weak social control, personal frustration, relative deprivation, differential opportunities, alternative means to success, and deviant subcultures and subcultural values that conflict with conventional values. (These are the primary features of *social structure theories*, which are discussed in this chapter.)

2. *Crime is the end product of various social processes.* This approach stresses inappropriate socialization and social learning as well as interpersonal relationships, strength of the social bond, and personal and group consequences of societal reactions to deviance as they contribute to crime. (These are the primary characteristics of the *social process theories*, which are discussed in Chapter 9.)

3. *Crime is the product of class struggle.* This perspective emphasizes existing power relationships between social groups, ownership of the means of production, and economic and social structures of society as they relate to social class and social control. (These are the primary features of the *social conflict theories*, which are discussed in Chapter 10.)

Sociological theory A perspective that focuses on the nature of the power relationships between social groups and on the influences that various social phenomena bring to bear on the types of behaviours that tend to characterize groups of people.

Social structure The pattern of social organization and the interrelationships among institutions characteristic of a society.

Social process The interaction between and among social institutions, groups, and individuals.

Social life The ongoing (typically) structured interaction—including socialization and social behaviour in general—that occurs between persons in a society.

8.2 | LEARNING OBJECTIVE

MAJOR PRINCIPLES OF THE SOCIAL STRUCTURE PERSPECTIVE

SOCIAL STRUCTURE THEORIES EXPLAIN CRIME BY REFERENCE TO THE ECONOMIC AND social arrangements (or structure) of society. They see the various formal and informal arrangements between social groups (i.e., the structure of society) as the root causes of crime and deviance. Structural theories predict that negative aspects of societal structure—such as disorganization within the family, poverty or income inequality within the economic arrangements of society, and disadvantages due to lack of success in the educational process—produce criminal behaviour.

Although different kinds of social structure theories have been advanced to explain crime, they all have one thing in common: they highlight those arrangements within society that contribute to the low socio-economic status of identifiable groups as significant causes of crime. Social structure theorists view members of socially and economically disadvantaged groups as being more likely to commit crime, and they see economic and social disenfranchisement as fundamental causes of crime. Poverty, lack of education, absence of saleable skills, and subcultural values conducive to crime are all thought to be predicated on the social conditions surrounding early life experiences, and they provide the causal underpinnings of social structure theories.

Environmental influences, socialization, and traditional and accepted patterns of behaviour are all used by social structuralists to portray the offender as a product of his or her social environment, and the immediate social environment is viewed as a consequence of the structure of the society to which the offender belongs. Although criminality is recognized as a form of acquired behaviour, it is depicted as the end result of social injustice, racism, and feelings of disenfranchisement to which existing societal arrangements give rise. Similarly, social structure, insofar as it is unfair and relatively unchangeable, is believed to perpetuate the fundamental conditions that cause crime. Consequently, viewed from a social structure perspective, crime is seen largely as a lower-class phenomenon, while the criminality of the middle and upper classes is generally discounted as less serious, less frequent, and less dangerous.

Social structure theory A theory that explains crime by reference to the economic and social arrangements in society. This type of theory emphasizes relationships among social institutions and describes the types of behaviour that tend to characterize groups of people rather than individuals.

TYPES OF SOCIAL STRUCTURE THEORIES

8.3 | LEARNING OBJECTIVE

THIS CHAPTER DESCRIBES THREE MAJOR TYPES OF SOCIAL STRUCTURE THEORIES: (1) SOCIAL disorganization theory (also called the *ecological approach*), (2) strain theory, and (3) culture conflict theory (see Table 8.1). All have a number of elements in common, and the classification of a theory into a subcategory is often more a matter of which aspects a writer chooses to emphasize than the result of any clear-cut definitional elements inherent in that theory.

Social Disorganization Theory

Social disorganization theory (which depicts social change, social conflict, and lack of social consensus as the root causes of crime and deviance) is closely associated with the ecological school of criminology. *Ecology* is a term borrowed from biology that describes the interrelationships between living organisms and their environment, and social scientists use the term *human ecology* to describe the interrelationship between human beings

Social disorganization theory A perspective on crime and deviance that sees society as a kind of organism and crime and deviance as a kind of disease or social pathology.

Table 8.1 Social Structure Theories			
Theory	**Social Disorganization**	**Strain**	**Culture Conflict**
Period	1920s–1930s	1930s–present	1920s–present
Theorists	Robert Park and others	Robert Merton and others	Thorsten Sellin and others
Concepts	Social ecology, Chicago school, concentric zones, criminology of place	Anomie, goals, means, opportunity structures, reaction formation, general strain theory	Conduct norms, focal concerns, subculture, socialization, subculture of violence

and the physical and cultural environments in which they live.[5] Pioneers in the human ecology movement saw cities as "superorganisms" that incorporated areas adapted to specific groups, including ethnic groups (e.g., "Little Italy," "Chinatown"), which were functional enclaves within a larger organized whole that possessed its own dynamics.

The idea of the community as a functional whole that directly determines the quality of life for its members was developed and explored around the beginning of the 20th century by sociologists like Émile Durkheim (1858–1917).[6] Durkheim believed that crime was a normal part of all societies and that law was a symbol of social solidarity, so an act was "criminal when it offend[ed] strong and defined states of the collective conscience."[7]

Some of the earliest sociologists to study communities were W.I. Thomas and Florian Znaniecki. In *The Polish Peasant in Europe and America*, Thomas and Znaniecki described the problems Polish immigrants faced in the early 1900s when they left their homeland and moved to American cities.[8] The authors noted that crime rates rose among displaced people and hypothesized that the cause was the **social disorganization** that resulted from immigrants' inability to successfully transplant guiding norms and values from their home cultures into the new one.

Social disorganization A condition said to exist when a group is faced with social change, uneven development of culture, maladaptiveness, disharmony, conflict, and lack of consensus.

Social ecology An approach to criminological theorizing that attempts to link the structure and organization of a human community to interactions with its localized environment.

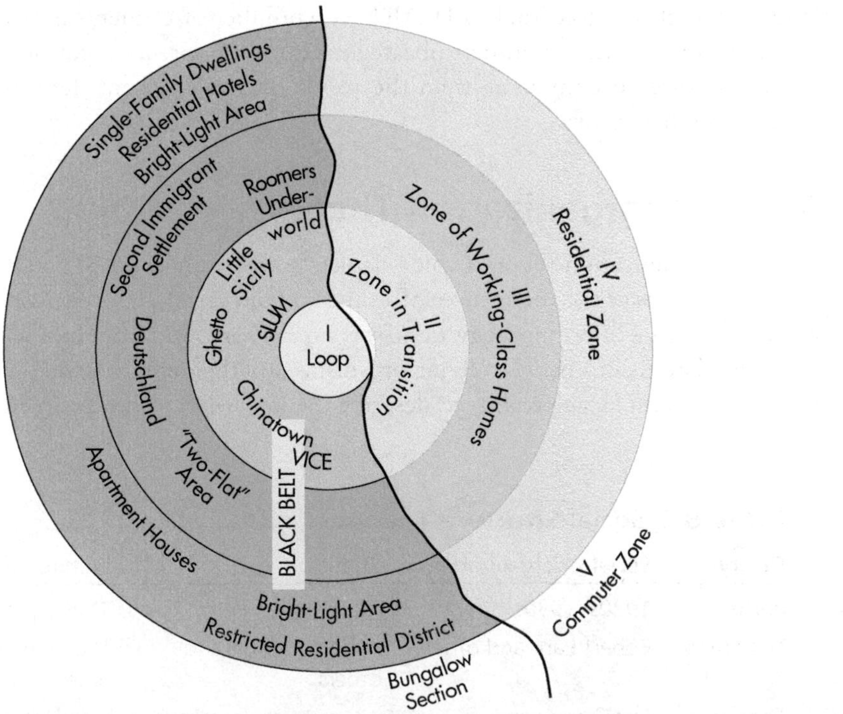

Chicago School   Some of the earliest sociological theories to receive widespread recognition can be found in the writings of Robert Park and Ernest Burgess. In the 1920s and 1930s at the University of Chicago, they developed what became known as **social ecology**, or the ecological school of criminology.[9] With the rapid influx of immigrant populations at the beginning of the 20th century, American cities in particular were caught up in swift social change, and Park and Burgess saw them as an ideal focus for study of social change and disorganization. They viewed cities as having five concentric zones, much like the circles on a target, each with unique characteristics and populations (see Figure 8.1). Park and Burgess referred to the central business zone as

Figure 8.1 Chicago's Concentric Zones

Source: Robert E. Park, Ernest W. Burgess, and R. D. McKenzie, *The City* (Chicago: University of Chicago Press, 1925), p. 55. Copyright © 1969; University of Chicago Press. Reprinted with permission.

Zone I or the "loop," where retail businesses and light manufacturing were located; Zone II, surrounding the city centre, was home to recent immigrant groups and was characterized by deteriorated housing, factories, and abandoned buildings; Zone III contained mostly working-class tenements; Zone IV was occupied by middle-class citizens with single-family homes; and Zone V, the suburbs, was called the "commuter zone." Park and Burgess noticed that residents of inner-city zones tended to migrate to outer zones as their economic positions improved.

Clifford Shaw and Henry McKay, other early advocates of the ecological approach, applied the concentric zone model to the study of juvenile delinquency, conducting empirical studies of arrest rates for juveniles in Chicago during the years 1900–1906, 1917–1923, and 1927–1933. These years were associated with high rates of neighbourhood transition, during which one immigrant group after another moved in rapid succession from the inner city toward the suburbs—a process that was repeated with the arrival of each new wave of immigrants. Shaw and McKay found that rates of offending remained relatively constant over time within zones of transition, and they concluded, therefore, that delinquency was caused by the nature of the environment in which immigrants lived rather than by characteristics of the immigrant groups themselves.[10] Shaw and McKay saw social disorganization as the inability of local communities to solve common problems, and they believed that the degree of disorganization in a community was largely predicated upon the extent of residential mobility and racial heterogeneity present in that community. In effect, as a new immigrant group, like the Polish, replaced an old immigrant group, like the Irish, and became dominant in a particular location, the process of succession was complete.

Because early **ecological theories** focused on selected geographic areas, their methodology came to be known as *area studies*. Because 1920s Chicago served as the model for most of these studies, they became collectively referred to as the **Chicago school of criminology**. Although the applicability of these early studies to other time periods may be questionable, the Chicago school demonstrated the tendency of criminal activity to be associated with urban transitional zones, which were typified by social disorganization, turmoil, lower property values, poverty, and lack of privacy.

The greatest contribution the ecological school made to criminological literature can be found in its claim that society wields a major influence on human behaviour.[11] Ecological theorists of the Chicago school used two sources of information: (1) population statistics and official crime and (2) ethnographic data. Population statistics (demographics), when combined with crime information, provided empirical material that gave scientific weight to ecological investigations; ethnographic information, gathered in the form of life stories (ethnographies), described the lives of city inhabitants. By comparing one set of data with the other—demographics with ethnographies—ecological investigators were able to show that life experiences varied from one location to another and that personal involvement in crime was strongly associated with place of residence.

The work of Canadian Carol La Prairie, which looks at the reality of high crime rates on some First Nations reserves in Canada, is representative of the ecological approach. In one of her studies, La Prairie concluded that those Aboriginal communities that remained "institutionally complete" had significantly lower rates of crime compared with those reserves that experienced rapid change due to economic and cultural pressures.[12] Other studies by La Prairie used the concepts of social ecology to help explain the variation in rates of incarceration of Aboriginal peoples between the eastern and western provinces. In her comparison of two eastern and two western urban centres, La Prairie noted significant differences in the degree of integration of the Aboriginal populations. While the eastern centres showed more social integration of inner-city Aboriginal residents, the western cities had displaced most of the

Ecological theory A type of sociological approach that emphasizes demographics (the characteristics of population groups) and geographics (the mapped location of such groups relative to one another) and sees the social disorganization that characterizes delinquency areas as a major cause of criminality and victimization.

Chicago school of criminology An ecological approach to explaining crime that examines how social disorganization contributes to social pathology.

Aboriginal population to communities outside the city centres. Not surprisingly, the incarceration rate of Aboriginal peoples was significantly higher in the western centres. La Prairie's findings recognized the importance of social organization from a social-ecological point of view. The author also stressed the additional need for efforts to stabilize Aboriginal populations within urban centres through the provision of, for example, decent, affordable housing.[13]

Criminology of Place   Ecological approaches to crime causation have found a modern birth in the **criminology of place** (also called **environmental criminology**), which builds on the contributions of routine activities theory and situational crime prevention (both of which were discussed in Chapter 5). It emphasizes the importance of geographic location and architectural features in terms of prevalence of victimization. Such "hot spots" of crime, including neighbourhoods, specific streets, and even individual houses and businesses, have been identified by recent writers. Lawrence W. Sherman and colleagues, for example, cited a study that revealed that 3 percent of places (addresses and intersections) in Minneapolis produced 50 percent of all calls to the police and noted that crime in Minneapolis, although relatively rare, was geographically concentrated.[14]

Reflecting on the questions first addressed by Shaw and McKay, researcher Rodney Stark asked, "How is it that neighborhoods can remain the site of high crime and deviance rates despite a complete turnover in their populations. There must be something about places as such that sustains crime."[15] Stark developed a *theory of deviant neighbourhoods* consisting of 30 propositions, including the following:[16]

- To the extent that neighbourhoods are dense and poor, homes will be crowded.
- Where homes are more crowded, there will be a greater tendency to congregate outside the home in places and circumstances that raise levels of temptation and opportunity to deviate.
- Where homes are more crowded, there will be lower levels of supervision of children.
- Reduced levels of child supervision will result in poor school achievement, with a consequent reduction in stakes in conformity and an increase in deviant behaviour.
- Poor, dense neighbourhoods tend to be mixed-use neighbourhoods.
- Mixed use increases familiarity with and easy access to places offering the opportunity for deviance.

Central to the criminology of place is the **broken windows thesis**, first advanced in a 1982 article by James Q. Wilson and George Kelling entitled "Broken Windows: The Police and Neighborhood Safety."[17] The thesis holds that physical deterioration and an increase in unrepaired buildings leads to increased concerns for personal safety among area residents.[18] These concerns lead to further decreases in maintenance and repair; to increased delinquency, vandalism, and crime; and to even further deterioration in safety and the physical environment—all resulting in offenders from other neighbourhoods being increasingly attracted by the area's perceived vulnerability. Physical disorder, left unchecked, leads to crime by driving residents indoors and sending a message to would-be offenders that a neighbourhood is out of control.[19] The adoption of this approach to policing in many American, and to a lesser extent, Canadian urban centres resulted in the increase in the use of "order maintenance policing" and a crackdown on quality-of-life offences, such as panhandling, graffiti, jaywalking, public urination, public drinking, and prostitution.

Even within high-crime neighbourhoods and neighbourhoods characterized by urban decay, crimes tend to be concentrated at specific locations, such as street blocks

Criminology of place or environmental criminology A perspective that emphasizes the importance of geographic location and architectural features as they are associated with the prevalence of criminal victimization.

Broken window thesis A perspective on crime that holds that physical deterioration in an area leads to increased concerns for personal safety among area residents and to higher crime rates in that area.

or multiple-family dwellings, and some units within specific apartment buildings are more likely to be the site of criminal occurrences. The criminology of place employs the concept of **defensible space**. The concept was developed by architect Oscar Newman in 1972[20] and means "the range of mechanisms—real and symbolic barriers, strongly defined areas of influence, and improved opportunities for surveillance—that combine to bring an environment under the control of its residents."[21]

Defensible space The range of mechanisms that combine to bring an environment under the control of its residents.

The criminology of place holds that location can be as predictive of criminal activity as lifestyles of victimized individuals or social features of victimized households. (*Place* has been defined by researchers as "a fixed physical environment that can be seen completely and simultaneously, at least on its surface, by one's naked eyes."[22]) Places can be criminogenic because they have certain routine activities associated with them or because they provide the characteristics that facilitate crime commission.

Recognizing the criminology of place, the Peel Regional Police Service (located just west of Toronto) introduced to the Canadian market in the early 1980s a program of **Crime Prevention Through Environmental Design (CPTED)**. It is based on the theory that the proper design and effective use of a physical environment can help reduce the incidence and fear of crime. The CPTED program revolves around three strategies: (1) natural surveillance (keeping potential intruders under observation); (2) natural access control (decreasing the opportunity for crime); and (3) territorial reinforcement (extending a sphere of influence through physical design to develop a sense of ownership by users). In an example cited by Peel Regional Police, a CPTED review of a restaurant recommended the following changes: (1) improvement of sightlines to the outside by removing unnecessary clutter such as bushy plants and promotional material from the take-out window; (2) improvement of sightlines within the restaurant by removing planters that divided the dining room and waiting area; and (3) improvement of lighting by repairing defective ceiling lamps and increasing the number of light fixtures. These changes resulted in a more intimidating and less private target to would-be offenders while also giving staff the ability to better observe potential offenders before a robbery.[23] (See Chapter 11 for an in-depth look at the CPTED model.)

Crime Prevention Through Environmental Design (CPTED) A crime-prevention strategy based on the premise that the design and effective use of the built environment can lead to a reduction in the incidence and fear of crime.

More recent studies of the broken windows thesis have cast doubt on the assertion made by Wilson and Kelling that police intervention into the process that links disorder and crime can be effective in reducing crime.[24] It may be that disorder and crime have common roots and that one is more associated with the other than produced by it.[25] Hence, efforts to target quality-of-life offences in urban areas that are experiencing high levels of social disorganization may not have the desired effect of reducing crime.

London's Metropolitan Police officers view displays from TV cameras around London in the Special Operations Room of their Central Communications Command. Defensible space can be defined in terms of barriers to crime commission and preventive surveillance opportunities. How might such features be enhanced in high-crime areas?

Oli Scarff/Getty Images

Strain Theory

The second type of social structure theory discussed in this chapter is strain theory. *Strain* can be defined as the pressure that individuals feel to reach socially determined goals.[26] The classic statement of **strain theory**—which depicts delinquency as a form of adaptive problem-solving behaviour committed in response to problems involving frustrating and undesirable social environments—was offered in 1938 by Robert K. Merton, who also developed the concept of **anomie** (a French word meaning "normlessness").

Anomie was popularized by Émile Durkheim in his 1897 book, *Suicide*, in which he used the term to explain how a breakdown of predictable social conditions can lead to feelings of personal loss, dissolution, and a lack of a sense of belonging.[27] Merton's use of the term *anomie* was somewhat different and meant a disjunction between socially approved means to success and legitimate goals.[28] Merton maintained that legitimate goals, such as wealth, status, and personal happiness, are generally defined as desirable for everyone. But the widely acceptable means to these goals, such as education, hard work, and financial savings, are not equally available. As a consequence, crime and deviance tend to arise as an alternative means to success when individuals feel the strain of being pressured to succeed in socially approved ways but find that the tools for such success are unavailable to them, and that strain increases as the gulf between the goals and the means available to achieve them widens. Merton's emphasis on the felt strain resulting from the lack of fit between goals and means led to his approach being called strain theory. In Merton's words, "It's not how you play the game, it's whether you win."[29]

Complicating the picture further, Merton maintained that not everyone accepts the legitimacy of socially approved goals. Merton diagrammed possible combinations of goals and means (see Table 8.2). The first row, labelled *conformity*, signifies acceptance of the goals that society holds as legitimate for everyone, with ready availability of the means approved for achieving those goals; the mode of adaptation associated with this combination of goals and means typifies most middle- and upper-class individuals.

Innovation arises when the emphasis on approved goal achievement combines with a lack of opportunity to participate fully in socially acceptable means to success. This form of adaptation is experienced by many lower-class individuals who have been socialized to desire traditional success symbols (expensive cars, large homes, big bank accounts) but who do not have ready access to approved means of acquiring them (educational opportunity).

Innovative behavioural responses, including crime, can be expected to develop when individuals find themselves so deprived. Merton said that "poverty as such, and consequent limitation of opportunity, are not sufficient to induce a conspicuously

Table 8.2 Goals and Means Disjuncture

	GOALS	MEANS
Conformity	+	+
Innovation	+	−
Ritualism	−	+
Retreatism	−	−
Rebellion	±	±

Source: Adapted from Robert K. Merton, "Social Structure and Anomie," *American Sociological Review*, Vol. 3, No. 5 (October 1938), pp. 672–682.

high rate of criminal behavior. Even the often mentioned 'poverty in the midst of plenty' will not necessarily lead to this result."[30] It is when those who find themselves in poverty are pressured to achieve material success and acquire other associated symbols of status that innovation results.

The third row, *ritualism*, refers to the type of behaviour arising when members of society participate in socially desirable means but show little interest in goal achievement. A ritualist may get a good education, work every day in an acceptable occupation, and appear to be leading a solid middle-class lifestyle yet care little for the symbols of success, choosing to live an otherwise independent lifestyle.

Retreatism describes the behaviour of those who reject both the socially approved goals and the means. They may become dropouts, drug abusers, or homeless persons, or participate in alternative lifestyles, such as communal living. Such individuals are often socially and psychologically separate from the larger society around them.

Merton's last category, *rebellion*, describes the actions of a person who wishes to replace socially approved goals and means with some other system. Political radicals, revolutionaries, and anti-establishment agitators may fit into this category. Merton believed that conformity was the most common mode of adaptation prevalent in society, whereas retreatism was least common.

An application of Merton's strain theory was offered by Margaret Beare in her examination of the increased involvement of Canadian Mohawks in the smuggling of cigarettes. High taxes on Canadian cigarettes tempted many smokers to turn to cheaper contraband U.S. cigarettes. In Ontario and Quebec, residents of some Aboriginal communities along the Canada–U.S. border were the main sources of contraband cigarettes. The last time statistics were available, it was believed that almost one-quarter of the cigarettes smoked in Canada were illegal.[31]

General Strain Theory In 1992, strain theory was reformulated by Robert Agnew and others who moulded it into a comprehensive perspective called *general strain theory* (GST).[32] GST sees law-breaking behaviour as a coping mechanism enabling those who engage in it to deal with the socio-emotional problems generated by negative social relations.

According to GST, strain occurs when others do the following: (1) prevent or threaten to prevent an individual from achieving positively valued goals; (2) remove or threaten to remove positively valued stimuli that a person possesses, such as the death of a loved one; or (3) present or threaten to present someone with noxious or negatively valued stimuli, like physical abuse. Agnew explained that strains most likely to cause crime include child abuse and neglect; negative secondary-school experiences; abusive peer relations; chronic unemployment; marital problems; parental rejection; erratic, excessive, and or/harsh supervision or discipline; criminal victimization; homelessness; racial, ethnic, or gender discrimination; and a failure to achieve selected goals. Factors that increase the likelihood of criminal coping include poor conventional coping skills and resources; availability of criminal skills and resources; low levels of conventional social support; routine association with criminal others; personal beliefs and values favourable to crime; frequent exposure to situations where the costs of crime are low; low levels of social control, including weak bonds to conventional others; and lack of investment in conventional institutions. Agnew's strategies for reducing exposure to strains include eliminating strains conducive to crime, altering strains to make them less conducive to crime, removing individuals from exposure to strain, and equipping individuals with the traits and skills needed to avoid strains conducive to crime.

General strain theory expands on traditional strain theory in several ways. First, it significantly expands the focus of strain theory to include all types of negative relations between an individual and others. Second, GST maintains that strain is likely to have a cumulative effect on delinquency after reaching a certain threshold. Third, GST provides a more comprehensive account of the cognitive, behavioural, and emotional adaptations to strain than do traditional strain approaches. Finally, GST more fully describes the wide variety of factors affecting the choice of delinquent adaptations to strain.

Agnew saw the crime-producing effects of strain as cumulative and concluded that whatever form it takes, "strain creates a predisposition for delinquency in those cases in which it is chronic or repetitive."[33] Predispositions may be manifested in the form of negative affective states, meaning emotions such as anger, fear, depression, and disappointment. An analysis by Agnew of other strain theories found that all such theories share at least two central explanatory features.[34] Strain theories, Agnew said, focus "explicitly on negative relationships with others; relationships in which the individual is not treated as he or she wants to be treated," and he argued that "adolescents are pressured into delinquency by the negative affective states—most notably anger and related emotions—that often result from negative relationships."[35]

A 1994 study tested some of the assumptions underlying GST through an analysis of American data.[36] It found partial support for GST and discovered that negative relations with adults, feelings of dissatisfaction with friends and school life, and the experience of stressful events (e.g., family dissolution) were positively related to delinquency, as was living in an unpleasant neighbourhood (one beset by social problems and physical deterioration). When conceived of more broadly as exposure to negative stimuli, the study found general strain to be significantly related to delinquency.

Contrary to Agnew's hypothesis, however, the study found no evidence that the effects of strain were increased when they were experienced for longer periods of time or that they were diminished when adolescents classified that part of their life in which they experienced strain as "unimportant." Consistent with earlier findings, the study also found that feelings of general strain were positively related to later delinquency, regardless of the number of delinquent peers, moral beliefs, self-efficacy, and level of conventional social support.[37] Some support was found for the belief that general strain leads to delinquency by weakening the conventional social bond and strengthening the unconventional bond with delinquent peers.

Culture Conflict Theory

Culture conflict theory A sociological perspective on crime that suggests that the root cause of criminality can be found in a clash of values between variously socialized groups over what is acceptable or proper behaviour.

Conduct norms Shared expectations of a social group relative to personal conduct.

The third type of social structure theory discussed in this chapter is **culture conflict theory**, which suggests that the root cause of criminality can be found in a clash of values between differently socialized groups over what is acceptable or proper behaviour. The culture conflict concept is inherent in ecological criminology (discussed earlier in this chapter) and its belief that zones of transition tend to be in flux and harbour groups of people whose values are often at odds with those in the larger society.

The culture conflict perspective found its clearest expression in the writings of Thorsten Sellin in his 1938 book *Culture Conflict and Crime*, where he stated that the root cause of crime could be found in different values about what is acceptable or proper behaviour.[38] According to Sellin, **conduct norms**, which provide the valuative basis for human behaviour, are acquired early in life through childhood socialization, and it is the clash of norms between variously socialized groups that results in crime. Because crime is a violation of laws established by legislative decree, the criminal event itself, from this point of view, is nothing other than a disagreement over what should be acceptable behaviour.

Sellin described two types of culture conflict. *Primary conflict* arises when a fundamental clash of cultures occurs, as when an immigrant father kills his daughter's lover following an old-world tradition that demands that a family's honour be kept intact.[39]

Secondary conflict occurs, according to Sellin, when smaller cultures within the primary one clash, as when middle-class values (upon which most criminal laws are based) find fault with inner-city or lower-class norms, resulting in the social phenomenon we call *crime*.

Subcultural Theory

Fundamental to the notion of culture conflict is the idea of **subculture**, a collection of values and preferences that is communicated to subcultural participants through a process of socialization. Subcultures differ from the larger culture in that they claim the allegiance of smaller groups of people. For example, the wider North American culture may proclaim that hard work and individuality are valuable, but a particular subculture may espouse the virtues of deer hunting, male bonding, and recreational alcohol consumption. Countercultures, which tend to reject and invert the values of the surrounding culture, and criminal subcultures, which may actively espouse deviant activity, represent extremes. **Subcultural theory** is a sociological perspective that emphasizes the contribution made by variously socialized cultural groups to the phenomenon of crime.

Early writings on subcultures include *The Gang* by Frederic M. Thrasher.[40] Thrasher studied 1313 gangs in Chicago in 1927, and his descriptive work led to a typology in which he described different types of gangs. In 1943, William Foote Whyte, drawing on Thrasher's work, published *Street Corner Society*.[41] Whyte, in describing his three-year study of the Italian slum he called "Cornerville," further developed the subcultural thesis, showing that lower-class residents of a typical slum could achieve success through the opportunities afforded by slum culture, including racketeering and bookmaking.

Focal Concerns

In 1958, Walter B. Miller attempted to detail the values that drive members of lower-class subcultures into delinquent pursuits, describing *lower-class culture* as "a long-established, distinctively patterned tradition with an integrity of its own."[42] According to his article, entitled "Lower Class Culture as a Generating Milieu of Gang Delinquency," a large body of systematically interrelated attitudes, practices, behaviours, and values characteristic of lower-class culture are designed to support and maintain the basic features of the lower-class way of life. In areas where these differ from features of middle-class culture, action oriented to the achievement and maintenance of the lower-class system may violate norms of the middle class and be perceived as deliberately non-conforming. Miller stated, "This does not mean, however, that violation of the middle-class norm is the dominant component of motivation; it is a by-product of action primarily oriented to the lower-class system."

Miller also outlined what he termed the **focal concerns** (key values) of delinquent subcultures: trouble, toughness, smartness, excitement, fate, and autonomy. Miller concluded that subcultural crime and deviance are not the direct consequences of poverty and lack of opportunity but emanate from specific values characteristic of such subcultures. According to Miller, *trouble* is a dominant feature of lower-class culture. Getting into trouble, staying out of trouble, and dealing with trouble when it arises become focal points in the lives of many members of lower-class culture. Miller recognized that getting into trouble is not necessarily valued in and of itself but is seen as an oftentimes necessary means to valued ends.

Like many theorists of the time, Miller was primarily concerned with the criminality of men. The lower-class masculine concern with *toughness* may have been due to many men in the groups he examined being raised in female-headed families and may have reflected an almost obsessive concern with masculinity as a reaction to the perceived threat of over-identification with female role models.

Miller described *smartness* as the "capacity to outsmart, outfox, outwit, dupe, take, [or] con another or others and the concomitant capacity to avoid being outwitted,

Subculture A collection of values and preferences that is communicated to subcultural participants through a process of socialization.

Subcultural theory A sociological perspective that emphasizes the contribution made by variously socialized cultural groups to the phenomenon of crime.

Focal concerns The key values of any culture, especially a delinquent subculture.

taken or duped oneself. . . . In its essence smartness involves the capacity to achieve a valued entity—material goods, personal status—through a maximum use of mental agility and a minimum of physical effort."

Excitement was seen as a search for thrills—often necessary to overcome the boredom inherent in lower-class lifestyles. Fights, gambling, picking up women, and making the rounds were all described as derivative aspects of the lower-class concern with excitement.

Fate is related to the quest for excitement and to the concept of luck or of being lucky. As Miller stated, "Many lower-class persons feel that their lives are subject to a set of forces over which they have relatively little control. These are not supernatural forces or organized religion . . . but relate more to a concept of 'destiny' or man as a pawn. This often implicit world view is associated with a conception of the ultimate futility of directed effort toward a goal."

Autonomy, manifested in statements like "I can take care of myself" or "No one's going to push me around," produces behavioural problems from the perspective of middle-class expectations when it surfaces in work environments, public schools, or other social institutions built on expectations of conformity.

Miller's work on subcultures and their focal concerns was derived almost entirely from his study of African-American inner-city delinquents in the Boston area in the 1950s and may have less relevance to members of lower-class subcultures in other times or in other places.

Violent Subcultures Some subcultures are decidedly violent and are built around violent themes and around values supporting violent activities. In 1967, Franco Ferracuti and Marvin Wolfgang published their seminal work, *The Subculture of Violence: Toward an Integrated Theory of Criminology*,[43] which drew together many of the sociological perspectives previously advanced to explain delinquency and crime. Ferracuti and Wolfgang's main thesis was that violence is a learned form of adaptation to certain problematic life circumstances and that learning to be violent takes place within the context of a subcultural milieu that emphasizes the advantages of violence over other forms of adaptation. Such subcultures are characterized by songs and stories that glorify violence, by gun ownership, and by rituals tending to stress macho models. They are likely to teach that a quick and decisive response to insults is necessary to preserve one's prestige within the group. Subcultural group members have a proclivity for fighting as a means of settling disputes. Subcultures of violence both expect violence from their members and legitimize it when it occurs. In Ferracuti and Wolfgang's words, "The use of violence is not necessarily viewed as illicit conduct, and the users do not have to deal with feelings of guilt about their aggression."[44] In other words, for participants in violent subcultures, violence can be a way of life.

Ferracuti and Wolfgang based their conclusions on an analysis of data that showed substantial differences in the rate of homicides between racial groups in the Philadelphia area—non-Caucasian men had a homicide rate of 41.7 per 100 000, versus only 3.4 for Caucasian men, and non-Caucasian women showed a homicide rate of 9.3, versus 0.4 for Caucasian women. Explaining these findings, Ferracuti and Wolfgang stated,

> Homicide is most prevalent, or the highest rates of homicide occur, among a relatively homogeneous subcultural group in any large urban community. . . . The value system of this group, as we are contending, constitutes a subculture of violence. From a psychological viewpoint, we might hypothesize that the greater the degree of integration of the individual into this subculture, the higher the probability that his behavior will be violent in a variety of situations.[45]

Ferracuti and Wolfgang extend their theory of subcultural violence with the following "corollary propositions":[46]

- No subculture can be totally different from or totally in conflict with the society of which it is a part.

- To establish the existence of a subculture of violence does not require that the actors sharing in these basic value elements express violence in all situations.

- The potential to resort or willingness to resort to violence in a variety of situations emphasizes the penetrating and diffusive character of this culture theme.

- The subcultural ethos of violence may be shared by all ages in a subsociety, but this ethos is most prominent in a limited age group, ranging from late adolescence to middle age.

- The counter-norm is non-violence.

- The development of favourable attitudes toward and the use of violence in a subculture usually involves learned behaviour and a process of differential learning, association, or identification.

- The use of violence in a subculture is not necessarily viewed as illicit conduct, and the users therefore do not have to deal with feelings of guilt about their aggression.

Canadian researchers have commented on geographical distinctions between violent subcultures in different parts of Canada. National homicide rates have consistently shown a distinct east-to-west/south-to-north upward trend over the last several decades. Homicide rates during this period have been lowest in New Brunswick, highest in Manitoba, and two to three times higher in Yukon and Northwest Territories than in Manitoba. The reasons for these persistent regional differences are difficult to pinpoint. While certain elements of Canada's social structure (age, ethnicity, economic well-being) are obvious contributing factors, some researchers suggest that cultural differences among regions of Canada also need to be taken into account. Do the accumulated traditions and shared experiences shaping the values and beliefs of people in different regions contribute to varying levels of violence? Many Canadian researchers believe that this cannot be overlooked.[47]

Violent subcultures produce violent acts. Why are some subcultures "violent" while others are not?

Bob Pardue - SC/Alamy Stock Photo

Regional variations are found in other countries as well. In the United States, for example, a body of criminological literature claims that certain forms of criminal violence are more acceptable in the South than in northern portions of the country.[48] Some writers have also referred to variability in the degree to which interpersonal violence has been accepted in the South over time, whereas others have suggested that violence in the South might be a traditional tool in the service of social order.[49]

The wider culture often recognizes a violent subculture's internal rules, so that when one member of such a subculture kills another, the wider society may take the killing less seriously than if someone outside the subculture had been killed. Franklin Zimring and his associates described what they called "wholesale" and "retail" costs of homicide, in which killings that are perceived to occur within a subculture of violence (when both the victim and the perpetrator are seen as members of a violent subculture) generally result in a less harsh punishment than do killings that occur outside of the subculture.[50] Punishments relate to the perceived seriousness of the offence; if members of the subculture within which a crime occurs accept the offence as part of the landscape, so too will members of the wider culture.

Much of the original research into subcultural theory dates back to the 1950s and 1960s. However, the reality of inner-city gangs and violence, especially in the United States but also in Canada, has brought with it a renewed interest in this approach in recent decades. In his review of the research literature on gangs, Canadian criminologist John Hagan suggested that subcultural theories continue to have a role to play in understanding the serious problems of largely ethnic, urban youth who see themselves as marginalized.[51]

Differential Opportunity Theory   In 1960, Richard Cloward and Lloyd Ohlin published *Delinquency and Opportunity*.[52] Their book, a report on the nature and activities of juvenile gangs, blended the subcultural thesis with ideas derived from strain theory and identified two types of socially structured opportunity for success: legitimate and illegitimate. Legitimate opportunities are generally available to individuals born into middle-class culture, but participants in lower-class subcultures are often denied access to them, so illegitimate opportunities for success are often seen as quite acceptable by participants in so-called illegitimate subcultures.

Illegitimate opportunity structure   A subcultural pathway to success that is disapproved of by the wider society.

Cloward and Ohlin used the term **illegitimate opportunity structure** to describe preexisting subcultural paths to success that are not approved of by the wider culture. Where illegitimate paths to success are not already in place, alienated individuals may undertake a process of ideational evolution through which "a collective delinquent solution" or a "delinquent means of achieving success" may be decided upon by members of a gang. Because the two paths to success—legitimate and illegitimate—differ in their availability to members of society, Cloward and Ohlin's perspective has been termed *differential opportunity*.

According to Cloward and Ohlin, delinquent behaviour may result from the ready availability of illegitimate opportunities with the effective replacement of the norms of the wider culture with expedient and "legitimate" subcultural rules. The authors wrote, "A delinquent subculture is one in which certain forms of delinquent activity are essential requirements for the performance of the dominant roles supported by the subculture."[53] Its most crucial elements are the "prescriptions, norms, or rules of conduct that define the activities required of a full-fledged member."[54] They continued, "A person attributes legitimacy to a system of rules and corresponding models of behavior when he accepts them as binding on his conduct."[55] They concluded, "Delinquents have withdrawn their support from established norms and invested officially forbidden forms of conduct with a claim to legitimacy."[56]

Cloward and Ohlin noted that there are two necessary parts to a delinquent act: "It is behavior that violates basic norms of the society, and, when officially known, it evokes a judgment by agents of criminal justice that such norms have been violated."[57] For Cloward and Ohlin, however, crime and deviance are just as normal as any other form of behaviour supported by group socialization. In their words, "Deviance and conformity generally result from the same kinds of social conditions [and] deviance ordinarily represents a search for solutions to problems of adjustment." In their view, deviance is just as much an effort to conform, albeit to subcultural norms and expectations, as is conformity to the norms of the wider society. They added, however,

> It has been our experience that most persons who participate in delinquent subcultures, if not lone offenders, are fully aware of the difference between right and wrong, between conventional behavior and rule-violating behavior. They may not care about the difference, or they may enjoy flouting the rules of the game, or they may have decided that illegitimate practices get them what they want more efficiently than legitimate practices.[58]

Cloward and Ohlin described three types of delinquent subcultures: (1) criminal subcultures, in which criminal role models are readily available for adoption by those being socialized into the subculture; (2) conflict subcultures, in which participants seek status through violence; and (3) retreatist subcultures, where drug use and withdrawal from the wider society predominate. These delinquent subcultures have at least three identifiable features: "acts of delinquency that reflect subcultural support are likely to recur with great frequency, access to a successful adult criminal career sometimes results from participation in a delinquent subculture, and the delinquent subculture imparts to the conduct of its members a high degree of stability and resistance to control or change."[59]

Cloward and Ohlin divided lower-class youth into four types according to their degree of commitment to middle-class values and/or material achievement. Type I youths desire entry to the middle class through improvement in their economic position. Type II youths desire entry to the middle class but not improvement in their economic position. Type III youths desire wealth but not entry to the middle class and are seen as the most crime prone. Type IV youths are dropouts who retreat from the cultural mainstream through drug and alcohol use (see the Who's Responsible? box).

Cloward and Ohlin had a substantial impact on social policy, resulting in government programs designed to change the structures of legitimate opportunities in poor communities. Programs such as Mobilization for Youth (MFY), Job Corps, and Opportunities for Youth created employment and educational opportunities for deprived youths and were largely based on opportunity theory.

Reaction Formation   Another criminologist whose work is often associated with both strain theory and the subcultural perspective is Albert Cohen, whose work focused primarily on the gang behaviour of delinquent youth. In Cohen's words,

> When we speak of a delinquent subculture, we speak of a way of life that has somehow become traditional among certain groups in American society. These groups are the boys' gangs that flourish most conspicuously in the "delinquency neighborhoods" of our larger American cities. The members of these gangs grow up, some to become law-abiding citizens and others to graduate to more professional and adult forms of criminality, but the delinquent tradition is kept alive by the age-groups that succeed them.[60]

Cohen argued that youths from all backgrounds are generally held accountable to the norms of the wider society through a "middle-class measuring rod" of expectations related to such items as school performance, language proficiency, cleanliness, punctuality, neatness, non-violent behaviour, and allegiance to other similar standards. But he noted that not everyone is prepared, by birth and subsequent socialization, to effectively meet such expectations.

Like Father, Like Son

Reginald Barfield, 22, was arrested for driving under the influence of alcohol and taken to jail. A judge set bail at $500, and his mother came to the jail to post bond for him. She didn't have much money, so she used the services of a bondsman, who charged her a $70 fee and arranged for Reginald's release. As she drove her son home, she began yelling at him, telling him that he had turned out just like his father, who had had a long-standing problem with alcohol.

"You're just like your father," she said. "And if you don't change, you'll end up just like him—dead."

Reginald became angry and blurted out that he drank because that was all he had known as a child.

"What do you mean?" his mother asked.

"Whenever Dad had a problem, or when you two fought," Reginald said, "Dad broke open a bottle and killed the pain. It worked for him. It works for me. So, you're right, I'm just like him. But it's not my fault. I learned it from him. You didn't stop him. And you didn't stop me."

Think about it:

1. Is Reginald right—did he learn his problem behaviour from his father? What other factors might have contributed to his excessive use of alcohol?

2. Might the concept of reaction formation help explain Reginald's behaviour? If so, how?

3. If you were Reginald's mother, to what degree would you hold your son responsible for his problem-drinking behaviour? To what degree would you hold him responsible if you were a judge hearing his case in court?

4. Are questions about responsibility merely exercises in blame shifting? Is blame shifting ever appropriate when assessing criminal responsibility?

Note: This example is a fictionalized one intended to encourage critical thinking.

In an examination of vandalism, Cohen found that "non-utilitarian" delinquency, in which things of value are destroyed rather than stolen or otherwise used for financial gain, is the result of middle-class values being turned upside down.[61] Delinquent youths, often alienated from middle-class values and lifestyles through deprivation and limited opportunities, can achieve status among their subcultural peers through vandalism and other forms of delinquent behaviour.

Children, especially those from deprived backgrounds, turn to delinquency because they experience status-frustration when judged by others according to middle-class standards and goals that they are unable to achieve, Cohen claimed. Because it is nearly impossible for them to succeed in middle-class terms, they also may overcome anxiety through the process of **reaction formation**, in which hostility toward middle-class values develops. (Cohen adapted reaction formation from psychiatric perspectives and used it to mean "the process in which a person openly rejects that which he wants, or aspires to, but cannot obtain or achieve."[62])

Cohen discovered the roots of delinquent subcultures in what he termed the "collective solution to the problem of status."[63] When youths who experience the same kind of alienation from middle-class ideals band together, they achieve a collective and independent solution and create a delinquent subculture. Cohen wrote,

> The delinquent subculture, we suggest, is a way of dealing with the problems of adjustment. . . . These problems are chiefly status problems: certain children are denied status in the respectable society because they cannot meet the criteria of the respectable status system. The delinquent subculture deals with these problems by providing criteria of status that these children can meet.[64]

Cohen's approach is effectively summarized in a theoretical scenario offered by Donald J. Shoemaker, who said that lower-class youths undergo a working-class

Reaction formation The process by which a person openly rejects that which he or she wants or aspires to but cannot obtain or achieve.

socialization that combines lower-class values and habits with middle-class success values.[65] Lower-class youths experience failure in school because they cannot live up to the middle-class norms operative in educational institutions, suffer a consequent loss of self-esteem and increased feelings of rejection, drop out of school and associate with delinquent peers, and experience hostility and resentment toward middle-class standards through reaction formation. Such alienated youths achieve status and a sense of improved self-worth through participation in a gang of like-minded peers. Delinquency and crime are the result.

Code of the Street Work by Elijah Anderson, who studied African-American neighbourhoods along Philadelphia's Germantown Avenue and published the results in his book titled *The Code of the Street*, offered a subcultural ethnography of the social mores operating in some American inner cities today.[66] In *Code*, Anderson detailed aspects of street code that stress a hyper-inflated notion of manhood resting squarely on the idea of respect: "At the heart of the code is the issue of respect, loosely defined as being treated 'right' or being granted one's 'props' (or proper due) or the deference one deserves." In street culture, a man's sense of worth is determined by the respect he commands when in public.

A crucial distinction between both families and individuals in inner-city neighbourhoods like Germantown are expressed by what residents call the "decent family" and the "street family," marking people as either trying to uphold positive values or being oriented toward the street. Street life, Anderson explained, involves displays of physical strength and intellectual prowess meant to demonstrate that "I can take care of myself" and "I can take care of my own." Those who wholeheartedly embrace the street code are proud to live the "thug life," identify with role models like Tupac Shakur and Young Jeezy, and see people and situations as obstacles to be subdued or overcome, learning to outsmart or hustle others while avoiding being hustled themselves. (See the Crime in the News story about gang member John Richardson and Ace Crew.)

CRIME IN THE NEWS

Murder Showed Gang Would Stop at Nothing

On Sept. 6, 1995, John Wartley Richardson walked out of Millhaven penitentiary in Kingston, Ontario. He'd just turned 24, a hardened and violent Ottawa street thug with a previous conviction for robbery. Now, he was free again after serving part of a 30-month prison term for pimping.

National Parole Board file No. 233185C, obtained by the *Citizen*, reveals officials had little doubt Mr. Richardson would strike again. In fact, it took just 50 days.

The crime would be murder. The victim would be Sylvain Leduc.

The file shows Mr. Richardson, now 26, has never held a legitimate job. He's been a pimp and a brute, involved in narcotics and the misery of vulnerable, strung-out young women trapped in Ottawa's street sex trade.

In prison, he was sometimes locked in segregation for "negative behaviour." He showed no remorse for anything. An area woman who helped put him away for procuring was so scared afterwards, the file notes, she had police help her relocate to a new town.

In the fall of 1994, Mr. Richardson was rejected for early parole.

"The board is satisfied that reasonable grounds exist to believe that, if released, you are likely to commit an offence involving violence and directs that you not be released."

But 11 months later, parole officials had little choice but to let him go because of a federal statute that grants all but the most dangerous inmates parole after serving two-thirds of their sentences.

"You remain a high risk to reoffend," officials wrote in his file. "Strict adherence to release conditions (including regularly reporting in to authorities) will be required in order to render that risk manageable."

Mr. Richardson, unmanageable as ever, ignored the conditions. He finally met with authorities Jan. 2, 1996, when heavily armed police in Winnipeg arrested him as an armed-and-dangerous fugitive wanted for the Leduc homicide.

A subsequent parole board document added a grim footnote to the file: "The risk you represent is clearly not

(Continued)

Murder Showed Gang Would Stop at Nothing

manageable and the board orders that your statutory release be revoked."

Yesterday, a judge and jury went further. The jury revoked much of what's left of Mr. Richardson's life by finding him guilty of first-degree murder. Justice Douglas Rutherford then shipped him back to a bleak federal cellblock for life, with no chance of parole for at least 25 years. He also sentenced him to an additional 73 years, to be served concurrently, for various other crimes.

Sylvain Leduc was killed because he innocently strayed into the nasty underworld of urban street gangs, where extreme violence and revenge are rewarded with criminal status and power.

Mr. Leduc, 17, offended a dangerous collection of mostly young, Black men who called themselves Ace Crew and sold $20-hits of crack cocaine on the streets of Lowertown. His death sentence was sealed with one ugly, unfortunate word: he called them "niggers."

Mr. Leduc's timing was particularly bad. In the fall of 1995, the gang's members were feeling threatened on several fronts.

Police, they worried, might be on to them. And at least one of the teenage girls the gang used for drug-running and sex—she was Mr. Leduc's cousin—wanted out, undermining the group's authority and its all-important reputation on the street. As well, rival drug dealers, they suspected, were muscling in on their turf, on their money.

Ace Crew was, at best, disorganized crime. But in late October 1995, it appeared to be losing its grip on even that existence. And that made it potentially lethal.

Enter John Richardson, fresh out of Millhaven. He was a friend of Mark Williams, the then 19-year-old reputed leader of Ace Crew. Mr. Richardson was just the type of crime consultant who could help the outfit rebuild.

If Ace was struggling, perhaps Mr. Richardson and his pal, Kurton Edwards, 28, could teach the gang a thing or two about becoming so bad, so feared, that people would be afraid to walk the streets of Ottawa.

At least that's how it appeared in the hours leading up to the Leduc murder, as Mr. Richardson regaled the group with violent tales about how notorious U.S. Black ghetto gangs ruthlessly maintain their turf. He talked about violence. He talked about retribution. He talked about torture. And he had a gun.

Sylvain Leduc was tortured and killed by members of the Ace Crew gang because he had been disrespectful toward them. Was Sylvain Leduc a victim of a violent subculture?

Ottawa Sun/QMI Agency/Sun Media Corporation

Ace Crew, police believe, has now largely disbanded. Six members and associates have been convicted for various roles in Mr. Leduc's slaying. Another was imprisoned for 11 years for the bold March 1997 shooting of two men inside the crowded Rideau Centre. Five other members and associates, all non-Canadians, have been deported to their native countries because of their criminal activities here.

Discussion Questions

1. What subcultural elements (beliefs, conduct norms, behaviour patterns, etc.) may have contributed to Sylvain Leduc's death?

2. Does the subculture of violence thesis help to explain the behaviour of gang members, such as the named Ace Crew who killed Leduc? If so, how?

3. What explanations, other than a subculture of violence thesis, might be offered to explain the death of Leduc?

Source: Material republished with the express permission of: Ottawa Citizen, a division of Postmedia Network Inc.

Gangs Today   Gangs have become a major source of concern in contemporary North American society, particularly in the United States. Although the writings of investigators such as Cohen, Thrasher, and Cloward and Ohlin focused on the illicit activities of juvenile gangs in inner cities, most gang-related crimes of the period involved vandalism, petty theft, and battles over turf. Today, the ethnic distinctions that gave rise to gang culture in the 1920s through the 1950s are largely forgotten. Italian, Hungarian, Polish, and Jewish immigrants, whose children made up many of the early gangs, have been, for the most part, successfully integrated into modern North American society.

Today's gangs are quite different. Members appear more violent, involved with drugs, and intransigent than those studied by early researchers. Although the United States is the nation with the most gangs (and has the best information about them), Canada is not exempt from them. One of the challenges in determining accurate amounts of gang activity in Canada stems from issues surrounding the definition of *gang* and *gang member*. Law enforcement officials and the media often refer to small groups of offenders as gangs, even though the members of these groups do not see themselves that way. In a comprehensive study of gangs in the Greater Vancouver area, this concern with definition was addressed and distinctions were made between *criminal business organizations, street gangs,* and *wannabe groups.*[67] In a report entitled *Promising Practices for Addressing Youth Involvement in Gangs,* Mark Totten defined gangs as "visible, hardcore groups that come together for profit-driven criminal activity and severe violence. They identify themselves through the adoption of a name, common brands/colours of clothing, and tattoos to demonstrate gang membership to rival gangs."[68] In a later work entitled *Nasty, Brutish and Short. The Lives of Gang Members in Canada,* Totten contended that "gang involvement in Canada exists on a continuum, and there are different types of gangs. The degree of organization in the gang is defined by its structure and hierarchy; its connection to larger, more serious organized crime groups; its sophistication and permanence; the existence of a specific code of conduct or set of formal rules; initiation practices; and the level of integration, cohesion, and solidarity among the gang's members."[69]

Bill C-24, known as the Organized Crime Bill, includes the current legal definition of an organized crime group such as a gang. See Box 8.1 for this definition.

In the most recent *Annual Report on Organized Crime,* the Criminal Intelligence Service of Canada (CISC) reported that street gangs are characterized by their involvement in the street-level trafficking of illicit drugs, such as crack cocaine, methamphetamine, ecstasy, and marijuana. Other activities include street-level prostitution, theft, robbery, fraud, and weapons offences. CISC contended that while some street gangs across Canada work on behalf of other organized crime groups and may engage in

Box 8.1 DEFINITION OF CRIMINAL ORGANIZATION

As stated in the *Criminal Code,* section 467.1(1), a "criminal organization" means a group, however organized, that

- is composed of three or more persons in or outside Canada; and,
- has as one of its main purposes or main activities the facilitation or commission of one or more serious offences, that, if committed, would likely result in the direct or indirect receipt of a material benefit, including a financial benefit, by the group or by any one of the persons who constitute the group.

It does not include a group of persons that form randomly for the immediate commission of a single offence.

In determining whether an individual participates in OR actively contributes to any activity of a criminal organization, the Court may look at the following:

- If they use a name, word, symbol, or other representation that identifies, or is associated with, that criminal organization;
- If they frequently associate with any of the persons who constitute the criminal organization;
- If they receive any benefit from the criminal organization;
- If they repeatedly engage in activities at the instruction of any of the persons who constitute the criminal organization.

Source: *Criminal Code,* http://laws-lois.justice.gc.ca/PDF/C-46.pdf, Section 467.1(1), definition of a "criminal organization", page 506. Department of Justice Canada, 2016. Reproduced with the permission of the Department of Justice Canada, 2017.

more sophisticated crimes, such as drug importation or manufacturing, most street gangs operate with relatively low criminal capabilities and within a defined area of operation. Trends show that street gangs are increasingly using technology to not only conceal their criminal activity, such as credit card fraud, but also to conduct it. Social networking sites are used to advertise and connect with possible recruits. Youth gang member collaboration with established criminal organizations (such as the Hells Angels, Big Circle Boys, and Indian Posse) involves criminal activities such as chemical trafficking, intimidation/extortion, kidnapping, and sophisticated auto theft rings.[70]

According to the most recent statistics available, over 300 street gangs have been identified in Canada, with an estimated 11 000 gang members and associates operating across the country. The gangs are primarily local in scope, with only a limited number having interprovincial and international criminal links. Street gangs are composed primarily of males and almost half are 17 years of age or younger. Gang members are predominantly African-Canadian (25 percent), Aboriginal (22 percent), and Caucasian (18 percent). Over one-third of gangs in Canada are composed of two or more ethno-racial groups (hybrid gangs). Nationally, almost half of Canadian police forces believe that the return of adult or youth gang member inmates to the community has a negative influence on street gangs on the outside, particularly those young males on the periphery and those who are in the process of being tested out for membership.[71]

While street gang-related violence is not a new phenomenon, a recent increase in gang-related violence is being reported and appears to be related to street gang expansion, recruitment, and encroachment on the territory of other criminal groups. The degree of street gang violence differs by region and gang. Violence may be planned—to promote and protect the gang's interests, such as targeting rival gang members or resources—or be spontaneous and opportunistic, resulting in intentional or unintentional harm to the general public from drive-by shootings, street gang cross-fire, and mistaken identities. Street gangs use a wide variety of weapons, including swords, knives, machetes, hammers, screwdrivers, and firearms. Illicit firearms used by street gangs are typically acquired through residential or commercial thefts, or are smuggled into the country from the United States.[72]

Information about gangs in the United States is much more detailed. More than one-third of jurisdictions covered by the 2010 National Youth Gang Survey (NYGS) conducted by the National Gang Center (NGC) reported experiencing gang problems in 2010, the highest annual estimate since before 1999.[73] Overall, an estimated 3500 jurisdictions served by city and county law enforcement agencies reported gang problems. Survey results also indicated that an estimated 756 000 gang members and 29 400 gangs were active in the United States during 2010. The 2010 NYGS confirmed previous findings that gang members are often involved in a variety of serious and violent crimes. Almost half of the law enforcement agencies reporting gang problems are involved in collaborative efforts with other law enforcement and criminal justice agencies to combat youth gangs and the serious and violent crimes they commit.

The National Gang Crime Research Center's Project, Gangfact, provides a profile of gangs and gang members throughout the United States, though its data are older than the data available through the NGC. The most recent Gangfact report, based on data collected by 28 researchers in 17 states, presents much detailed information specific to the United States but shows characteristics similar to the Canadian reality:[74]

- The national average age for joining a gang is 12.8 years.
- Over half who joined gangs have tried to quit.
- More than two-thirds of gangs have written rules for members to follow.

- Over one-half of all gangs hold regular weekly meetings.

- Nearly 30 percent of gangs require their members to pay dues.

- Approximately 55 percent of gang members were recruited by other gang members; the remainder sought out gang membership.

- Most gang members (79 percent) say they would leave the gang if given a second chance in life.

- Four-fifths of gang members report that their gangs sell crack cocaine.

- Most gangs (70 percent) are not racially exclusive and consist of members drawn from a variety of ethnic groups.

- One-third of gang members report that they have been able to conceal their gang membership from their parents.

- Most gangs (83 percent) report having female members, but few allow female members to assume leadership roles.

- Many gang members (40 percent) report knowing male members of their gangs who had raped females.

Contemporary researchers are drawing some new distinctions between gangs and violence. Some years ago, G. David Curry and Irving A. Spergel, in a study of Chicago communities, distinguished between juvenile delinquency and gang-related homicide.[75] They found that communities characterized by high rates of delinquency do not necessarily experience exceptionally high rates of crime or of gang-related homicides, and they concluded that although gang activity may be associated with homicide, "gang homicide rates and delinquency rates are ecologically distinct community problems." Gang-related homicide seems to be well explained by classical theories of social disorganization and is especially prevalent in areas of the city characterized by in-migration and by the "settlement of new immigrant groups." In their study, high rates of juvenile delinquency seemed to correlate more with poverty, which the researchers defined as "social adaptation to chronic deprivation." According to Curry and Spergel, "Social disorganization and poverty rather than criminal organization and conspiracy may better explain the recent growth and spread of youth gangs to many parts of the country. Moreover, community organization and social opportunity in conjunction with suppression, rather than simply suppression and incapacitation, may be more effective policies in dealing with the social problem."[76] In devising strategies to counter gang activity, policy-makers must remember that many gang members are delinquent before they become associated with gangs and that merely suppressing gangs should not replace other youth crime intervention and prevention strategies.[77]

Mark Totten's most recent research, based on in-depth interviews with 519 Canadian gang members, concluded that "gangs are a symptom, not a cause, of social ills."[78] He identified a number of factors correlated with gang membership, including entrenched poverty, school exclusion and unemployment, racism, imploding families, emotional and behavioural disorders, ineffective child welfare and justice systems, and psychological despair and homelessness. A recent study by Margaret Beare and Chris Hogg at York University attempts to understand the environments within which street gangs operate. They conclude that gang membership seldom provides the supportive, family-type environment that entice youth into joining but rather are characterized more by tension, violence, and betrayal, both from rival gangs and from fellow gang members. They conclude that what is needed is a better balance between enforcement spending (gang-and-guns police units) and the allocation of funds into job creation programs, accessible mental health support, adequate and affordable housing, and social service agencies, in addition to policing that is committed to working in support of these communities.[79]

Members of the Manitoba Warriors leave a courthouse in Winnipeg after being sentenced to time already served following their conviction on drug charges. Gangs have become a concern in today's society. What social structure theories might explain the proliferation of gangs and gang-related activity in Canada?

Phil Hossack/Winnipeg Free Press/ The Canadian Press

POLICY IMPLICATIONS OF SOCIAL STRUCTURE THEORIES

THEORETICAL APPROACHES THAT LOOK TO THE SOCIAL STRUCTURE AS THE ROOT CAUSE OF crime point in the direction of social action as a panacea. In the 1930s, for example, Clifford Shaw, in an effort to put his theories into practice and to reduce delinquency in transitional neighbourhoods, established the Chicago Area Project. Shaw analyzed oral histories gathered from neighbourhood citizens to determine that delinquents were essentially normal youngsters who entered into illegal activities at early ages, often through street play, so he worked to increase opportunities for young people to embark on successful work careers.

The Chicago Area Project attempted to reduce social disorganization in slum neighbourhoods through the creation of community committees staffed with local residents rather than professional social workers. The project had three broad objectives: (1) improving the physical appearance of poor neighbourhoods, (2) providing recreational opportunities for youth, and (3) involving project members directly in the lives of troubled youth through school and courtroom mediation. Although no effective assessment programs were established to evaluate the Chicago Area Project during the program's tenure, in 1984 a 50-year review of the program was published that declared the program "effective in reducing rates of juvenile delinquency."[80]

Mobilization for Youth (a programmatic outgrowth of Cloward and Ohlin's theory of differential opportunity) provides a bold example of the treatment implications of social structure theories seeking not only to provide new opportunities but also to change the fundamental arrangements of society through direct social action and thereby address the root causes of crime and deviance. Leaders of Mobilization for Youth decided that "what was needed to overcome formidable barriers to opportunity was not community organization but community action" that attacked entrenched political interests, so the program promoted "boycotts against schools, protests against welfare policies, rent strikes against 'slum landlords,' lawsuits to ensure poor people's rights, and voter registration."[81] A truly unusual government-sponsored program for its time, Mobilization for Youth was eventually disbanded amid protests that its mandate was to reduce delinquency, not to reform urban society or test sociological theories.[82]

A contemporary example of social intervention efforts based on sociological theories is the Youth Violence Project: A Community-Based Violence Prevention Project, introduced in a Vancouver Island school district. It is a community-based initiative designed to address the problem of youth violence and involves teachers, counsellors, parents, students, and representatives from health and social service agencies. Consisting of 13 individual anti-violence initiatives, it is intended to educate and train students and community members in a preventative approach to violence by helping individuals change their behaviour and acquire skills that enable them to use non-violent responses in circumstances where violence might previously have been used.[83]

Mobilization for Youth and the Youth Violence Project both stand as examples of the kinds of programs that theorists who focus on the social structure typically seek to implement. Social programs of this sort are intended to change the cultural conditions and societal arrangements that lead people into crime.

CRITIQUE OF SOCIAL STRUCTURE THEORIES

THE FUNDAMENTAL ASSUMPTION OF SOCIAL STRUCTURE APPROACHES IS THAT SOCIAL injustice, racism, and poverty are the root causes of crime. Hence, the social structure perspective is intimately associated with the first part of this textbook's theme, the social problems approach (described in Chapter 1).

Social structure explanations for criminality that portrayed social inequality and stifled opportunity as fundamental causes of crime were popular during the 1960s. Later, a number of social commentators began to question the nature of the relationship among poverty, apparent social inequities, and crime.[84] Some argued the inverse of the root causes argument: poverty and social inequality are produced by crime, rather than the other way around; disorder, fear, and crime undermine positive social and economic institutions; families, schools, churches, businesses, and other institutions cannot function properly in social settings where crime is a taken-for-granted part of the social landscape. If this proposed inverse relationship is even partially true, then addressing poverty and social inequality as the root causes of crime is an ineffective crime-prevention strategy.

This chapter has identified three types of social structure theory, and each can be critiqued. Some authors have suggested that ecological theories give too much credence to the notion that special location determines crime and delinquency because the nature of any given location changes over time, and evolutions in land-use patterns (such as a movement away from home ownership and toward rental or low-income housing) may seriously affect the nature of a neighbourhood and the concomitant quality of its social organization. Rates of neighbourhood crime and delinquency may be "an artifact of police decision-making practices" and bear little objective relationship to the actual degree of law violation in an area.[85] If police bias (the focus on low-income inner-city areas) exists, it may seriously mislead researchers into categorizing certain areas as high in crime when enforcement decisions made by police administrators merely make them appear that way.

Another critique of the ecological school can be found in its seeming inability to differentiate between the condition of social disorganization and the things such a condition is said to cause. What is the difference between social disorganization and high rates of delinquency? Isn't delinquency a form of the very thing said to cause it? As Stephen Pfohl observed, early ecological writers sometimes used the incidence of delinquency as "both an example of disorganization and something caused by disorganization,"[86] making it difficult to gauge the efficacy of their explanatory approach.

Similarly, those who criticize the ecological approach note that many crimes occur outside of geographic areas characterized by social disorganization. Murder, sexual assault, robbery, incidents of drug use, and assault all occur in affluent, well-established neighbourhoods. White-collar crime, cybercrime, and environmental crime may actually occur *more often* in well-established neighbourhoods. Hence, the ecological approach is clearly not an adequate explanation for all crime or all types of crime.

From a social responsibility perspective, those who criticize strain theory note that Merton's strain theory is probably less applicable to North American society today than it was in the 1930s because in the ensuing decades considerable effort has been made toward improving success opportunities for all, regardless of ethnicity, race, or gender. Travis Hirschi criticized contemporary strain theory for its inability "to locate people suffering from discrepancy" and noted that human beings are naturally optimistic—a fact that "overrides [the] aspiration-expectation disjunction," concluding that "expectations appear to affect delinquency, but they do so regardless of aspirations, and strain notions are neither consistent with nor required by the data."[87]

Culture conflict approaches have been questioned by some criminologists who see them as lacking explanatory power. Canadian criminologist Gwynn Nettler called the notion of violent subcultures tautological, or circular, arguing that saying that people fight because they are violent or that "they are murderous because they live violently" does little to explain their behaviour. Attributing fighting to "other spheres of violence" may be true, but it is fundamentally "uninformative."[88]

The subcultural approach has also been criticized for being racist because many so-called violent subcultures are said to be populated primarily by minorities. Margaret Anderson stated that "the problem with this explanation is that it turns attention away from the relationship of black communities to the larger society and it recreates dominant stereotypes about blacks as violent, aggressive, and fearful. Although it may be true that rates of violence are higher in black communities, this observation does not explain the fact."[89] In sociological jargon, an observed correlation between race and violence does not necessarily provide a workable explanation for the relationship.

According to Nettler, social structure theories suffer from another shortcoming that generally affects most other sociological perspectives on crime causation:

> The conceptual bias of social scientists emphasizes environments—cultures and structures—as the powerful causes of differential conduct. This bias places an intellectual taboo on looking elsewhere for possible causes as, for example, in physiologies. This taboo is . . . strongly applied against the possibility that ethnic groups may have genetically transmitted differential physiologies that have relevance for social behavior.[90]

In other words, social scientists downplay the causative role of non-sociological factors. Many outside of sociology believe that such factors are important, but since sociological theorizing has captured most of the academic attention over the past few decades, the role of other causative factors in the etiology of criminal behaviour stands in danger of being shortchanged.

Some also see the inability of social structure theories to predict which individuals—or what proportion of a given population—will turn to crime as a crucial failure of such perspectives. Although the large majority of persons growing up in inner-city, poverty-ridden areas probably experience an inequitable opportunity structure firsthand, only a relatively small number of those people become criminal. Even if substantially more people living under such conditions become criminal compared to those living in other types of social environments, a large proportion of persons being raised in deviant subcultures and experiencing strain still embrace non-criminal lifestyles. In his book *The Moral Sense*, James Q. Wilson suggested that most people—regardless of socialization experiences and the structural aspects of their social circumstances—may still carry within themselves an inherent sense of fairness and interpersonal morality.[91] If what Wilson suggested is even partially true, then the explanatory power of social structure theories may be limited by human nature itself.

SOCIAL STRUCTURE THEORIES APPLIED

STRAIN

holds that crime is a result of the disjuncture between socially and subculturally sanctioned means and goals.

Did the three youths who killed Nicholas Battersby lack the socially acceptable means (education, saleable skills) to achieve socially acceptable goals?

Crime is a result of the economic and social arrangements in society. When these arrangements are unfair and relatively unchangeable, they perpetuate the fundamental conditions that are conducive to crime, such as poverty, lack of education, absence of saleable skills, social injustice, racism, feelings of disenfranchisement, and subcultural values.

How can the actions of Rubens Henderson, Cory Cyr, and Brian Raymond be explained using the social structure perspective?

CULTURE CONFLICT

holds that crime is a result of a clash of values between variously socialized groups over what is acceptable or proper behaviour.

Were the behaviours of the three youths who were involved in the killing of Nicholas Battersby a result of beliefs in subcultural values of excitement, autonomy, and violence?

SOCIAL DISORGANIZATION

holds that society is a kind of organism and crime and deviance are a kind of disease that is rooted in social conditions.

Were the three youths who killed Nicholas Battersby a product of their individual location in the social structure and of social and economic conditions, including lack of education, lack of employment, and disenfranchisement?

SUMMARY OF LEARNING OBJECTIVES

8.1 Sociological theories explore relationships between and among groups and institutions and envision crime as the result of social processes, as the natural consequence of aspects of social structure, or as the result of economic and class struggle. Sociological theories examine institutional arrangements within society and interactions among individuals, groups, and social institutions that affect socialization and have an impact on social behaviour.

8.2 Although different kinds of social structure theories have been advanced to explain crime, they all have one thing in common: they highlight those arrangements within society that contribute to the low socio-economic status of identifiable groups—poverty, lack of education, absence of marketable skills, and subcultural values—as significant causes of crime and view members of socially and economically disadvantaged groups as being more likely to commit crime.

8.3 Three subtypes of social structure theories can be identified: social disorganization theory, strain theory, and culture conflict theory. Social disorganization theory encompasses social pathology, seeing society as a kind of organism and crime and deviance as a kind of disease (or social pathology), and is often associated with social ecology and the Chicago school of criminology. Strain theory points to a lack of fit between socially approved success goals and availability of socially approved means to achieve those goals; individuals unable to succeed through legitimate means turn to other avenues (crime) that promise economic and social recognition. Culture conflict theory suggests that the root cause of criminality can be found in a clash of values between differently socialized groups over what is acceptable or proper behaviour.

8.4 Because theories of social structure look to the organization of society for their explanatory power, intervention strategies based on them typically seek to alleviate the social conditions thought to produce crime through social programs that increase socially acceptable opportunities for success and meaningful employment.

8.5 Social structure theories are open to criticism. Social structure approaches assume that social inequality, racism, and poverty are the root causes of crime, but some argue the inverse: poverty and social injustices are produced by crime rather than the other way around. If this proposed inverse relationship is even partially true, then addressing poverty and social inequality as the root causes of crime is an ineffective crime-prevention strategy.

Questions for Review

1. What is the nature of sociological theorizing? What are the assumptions upon which sociological perspectives on crime causation rest?

2. What do sociologists mean by the term *social structure*? How might the organization and structure of a society contribute to criminality?

3. What are the three types of social structure theories that this chapter describes? What are the major differences among them?

4. What are the policy implications of the theories discussed in this chapter? What kinds of changes in society and in government policy might be based on the theories discussed here? Would they be likely to bring about a reduction in crime?

5. What are the shortcomings of the social structure approaches to understanding and preventing crime? Can these shortcomings be overcome?

Multiple-Choice Questions

1. One of the three subtypes of social structure theory is _____.
   a. the classical school
   b. rational choice theory
   c. social disorganization theory
   d. reaction formation
   e. code of the street

2. Crime Prevention Through Environmental Design (CPTED) is based on the theoretical principles found within the concept of _____.
   a. broken windows
   b. anomie
   c. defensible space
   d. code of the street
   e. ecological theory

3. Which of the following concepts is not included in Robert Merton's strain theory?
   a. retreatism
   b. autonomy
   c. innovation
   d. conformity
   e. rebellion

4. _____ holds that crime is a result of a clash of values between variously socialized groups over what is acceptable or proper behaviour.
   a. Strain theory
   b. Culture conflict theory
   c. Social disorganization theory
   d. Criminology of place
   e. General strain theory

5. Walter Miller's concept of focal concerns has been echoed in the work of _____.
   a. Robert Merton
   b. Albert Cohen
   c. Thorsten Sellin
   d. Elijah Anderson
   e. Henry McKay

Multiple Choice Answers: 1c, 2c, 3b, 4b, 5d

Chapter 9
The Meaning of Crime: Social Process Perspective

Tomas Zelezny/ctk/AP Images

Children learn to become delinquents by becoming members of groups in which delinquent conduct is already established.

—*Albert K. Cohen*[1]

LEARNING OBJECTIVES

After reading this chapter, you should be able to

9.1 Recognize how the process of social interaction between people contributes to criminal behaviour.

9.2 Understand and distinguish between a number of social process theories.

9.3 Identify social policy initiatives that reflect the social process approach.

9.4 Assess the shortcomings of the social process perspective.

INTRODUCTION

Andrew Leyshon-Hughes continues to live in the centre of controversy. Leyshon-Hughes had been found not guilty by reason of insanity for the brutal sexual assault and stabbing murder of Nancy Eaton many decades ago. Eaton, the great-great-granddaughter of Timothy Eaton, founder of Eaton's department store empire, had befriended Leyshon-Hughes, himself a member of an established Toronto family of lawyers. The murder shocked high society, as did the court's ruling. Leyshon-Hughes's lawyer argued that his client, who was 17 at the time, suffered from brain damage at birth and that only the primitive part of his brain was functioning when he killed Nancy Eaton. Leyshon-Hughes was sentenced to treatment in the Ontario psychiatric hospital system and remained in psychiatric custody for the next 15 years.

In 2001, the community learned that Leyshon-Hughes had been granted a number of privileges, including the right to leave the grounds of the psychiatric hospital to attend college or to socialize. His request for longer, overnight visits to stay with family in northern Ontario and British Columbia had the community asking questions about its safety, especially since, a few years earlier, Leyshon-Hughes had been considered too dangerous to leave hospital grounds.

His psychiatrist believed that Leyshon-Hughes wanted to eventually have a normal life and raise a family. Forensic psychiatrist John Bradford argued that his patient was not a sexual deviant or psychopath, testifying that the risk was manageable: "A manageable risk means that a person is in the community and we have procedures and treatment in place that reduces that level of risk," he said. "I don't think there's ever such a thing as a zero-risk. That's not feasible."[2]

Marlys Edwardh, who had been Leyshon-Hughes's lawyer since he was 17, said that her client was misdiagnosed. Once he was locked up, no one took into consideration that he could be treated and rehabilitated.[3] In 2007, the Ontario mental health review board requested new evidence that medical treatments for Leyshon-Hughes had been as effective as asserted by mental health professionals and raised concerns about the community's safety if he continued to be allowed to have freedom of movement. In a subsequent court ruling, Ontario Superior Court Justice Maria Linhares de Sousa criticized Ontario's review board for abusing Leyshon-Hughes's rights, questioning why the review board wanted to reopen his case "in the face of an obviously successful diagnosis and treatment" that had allowed him to spend most of his time in the community. The judge ordered a new hearing before a different review board panel and awarded Leyshon-Hughes his legal costs.[4]

The ongoing case of Andrew Leyshon-Hughes provides an example of how society's continued reaction to what it identifies as criminal behaviour can change the course of an offender's life and how difficult it is for those labelled as offenders to shed that label. As some would say, while there are plenty of ex-cons, there is no such thing as an "ex–ex-con." Or "once a con, always a con."

MAJOR PRINCIPLES OF THE SOCIAL PROCESS PERSPECTIVE

9.1 | LEARNING OBJECTIVE

THE THEORIES DISCUSSED IN THE FIRST PART OF THIS CHAPTER ARE TYPICALLY CALLED **social process theories**, or *interactionist perspectives*, because they emphasize the process of interaction between individuals and society. Social process theories of crime causation assume that everyone has the potential to violate the law and that criminality is not an innate human characteristic; instead criminal behaviour is learned in interaction with others, and the socialization process occurring as the result of group membership is seen as the primary route through which learning occurs. Among the most

Social process theory A theory that asserts that criminal behaviour is learned in interaction with others and that the socialization processes that occur as a result of group membership are the primary route through which this learning occurs. Also called interactionist theory.

important groups contributing to the process of socialization are family, peers, work groups, and reference groups with which one identifies because they instill values and norms in their members and communicate their acceptable world views and patterns of behaviour.

Social process perspectives hold that the process through which criminality is acquired, deviant self-concepts are established, and criminal behaviour results is active, open-ended, and ongoing throughout a person's life. They suggest that individuals who have weak stakes in conformity are more likely to be influenced by the social processes and experiences that lead to crime and that criminal choices tend to persist because they are reinforced by the reaction of society to those whom it has identified as deviant.

9.2 | LEARNING OBJECTIVE

TYPES OF SOCIAL PROCESS THEORIES

A NUMBER OF THEORIES CAN BE CLASSIFIED UNDER THE SOCIAL PROCESS UMBRELLA: social learning theory, labelling theory, reintegrative shaming, social control theory, and social development theories (see Table 9.1). Social learning theory places primary emphasis upon the role of communication and socialization in the acquisition of learned patterns of criminal behaviour and the values that support that behaviour. Labelling theory points to the special significance of society's response to the criminal and sees the process through which a person becomes defined as criminal, along with society's imposition of the label *criminal*, as a significant contributory factor in future criminality. Reintegrative shaming, an offshoot of labelling theory, emphasizes possible positive outcomes of the labelling process. Social control theory focuses on the strength of the bond people share with institutions and individuals around them, especially as those relationships shape their behaviour. Finally, social development theory integrates theories of human development that examine psychological, biological, familial, interpersonal, cultural, societal, and ecological aspects of that development and places a greater emphasis on changes in offending over time.

Social Learning Theory

Social learning theory A perspective that places primary emphasis on the role of communication and socialization in the acquisition of learned patterns of criminal behaviour and the values that support that behaviour.

Social learning theory says that all behaviour is learned in much the same way and that such learning includes the acquisition of norms, values, and patterns of behaviour conducive to crime, meaning that crime is also learned and that people learn to commit crime from others. Criminal behaviour is a product of the social environment, not an innate characteristic of particular people.

Table 9.1 Social Process Theories

Theory	Social Learning	Labelling	Social Control	Social Development
Period	1930s–present	1960s–1980s, 1990s	1950s–present	1980s–present
Theorists	Edwin Sutherland and others	Edwin M. Lemert and others	Travis Hirschi and others	Sheldon and Eleanor Glueck and others
Concepts	Differential association, neutralization techniques, crime as learned	Tagging, primary and secondary deviance, reintegrative shaming	Social bond, inner and outer containment	Life course, evolutionary ecology, developmental pathways

Differential Association   One of the earliest and most influential forms of social learning theory was advanced by Edwin Sutherland in 1939, who stated that criminality is learned through a process of **differential association** with others who communicate criminal values and who advocate the commission of crimes.[5] He emphasized the role of social learning as an explanation for crime because he believed that many of the concepts popular in the field of criminology at the time—including social pathology, genetic inheritance, biological characteristics, and personality flaws—were inadequate to explain the process by which an otherwise normal individual turns to crime. Sutherland was the first well-known criminologist to suggest that all significant human behaviour is learned behaviour and that crime is not substantively different from any other form of behaviour.

Sutherland's nine principles of differential association were presented in complete form three years before his death in 1950 in the fourth edition of his famous book, *Principles of Criminology:*[6]

1. *Criminal behaviour is learned.* Criminal behaviour is learned in the same manner as learning how to read or write. In other words, criminal behaviour is not seen as an inherent character trait.

2. *Criminal behaviour is learned in interaction with other persons in a process of communication.* The learning of criminal behaviour is very much dependent on the association between individuals. Those who are already criminal serve as "teachers" to others.

3. *The principal part of the learning of criminal behaviour occurs within intimate personal groups.* Individuals are influenced by those closest to them—family members, peers, and friends. Relationships with these individuals will control the way one sees the world. For example, studies have shown that children who grow up in households where parents abuse alcohol tend to develop the attitudes that support such behaviour.[7] The belief that many young people are pressured by peers to commit illegal acts is inherent in this third principle.

4. *When criminal behaviour is learned, the learning includes (a) techniques of committing the crime, which are sometimes very complicated and sometimes very simple, and (b) the specific direction of motives, drives, rationalizations, and attitudes.* Since learning criminal behaviour is like learning any other kind of behaviour, the actual techniques of committing the crime must be taught and learned. Offenders learn from others how to pick locks, get involved in prostitution, obtain and use illicit drugs, or shoplift, for example. In addition to learning the actual techniques of criminal behaviour, offenders also learn the attitudes necessary to justify the behaviour. Some of these justifications are discussed in the Neutralization Techniques section later in this chapter.

5. *The specific direction of motives and drives is learned from definitions of the legal codes as favourable or unfavourable.* There are a variety of attitudes toward both the legal code and notions of right and wrong behaviour. The attitudes toward criminal behaviour held by the significant people in an individual's life have the greatest impact on the attitudes developed by the individual, through differential association.

6. *A person becomes delinquent because of an excess of definitions favourable to law violation over definitions unfavourable to law violation.* Interaction with those people or events that promote a disregard for the law will serve to strengthen and solidify those attitudes in another. For example, if a person spends more time in the company of someone who is constantly stealing from stores than with parents who extol the virtues of honesty and respect for the property of others, then disregard for the law becomes reinforced.

Differential association   The sociological thesis that criminality, like any other form of behaviour, is learned through a process of association with others who communicate criminal values.

7. *Differential associations may vary in frequency, duration, priority, and intensity.* Whether a person learns to disobey the law depends upon the quality of the social interactions experienced. The more often one interacts with a deviant group, the greater the likelihood of learning the behaviour. The length of the interaction also influences the likelihood of learning a given behaviour. Priority has been interpreted to mean the age at which a person first encounters criminality. It is believed that contacts made at an earlier age are likely to have a more significant impact on that person's behaviour than those made later in life. For example, for many youth at a certain stage of development, peer groups take priority over parents and can significantly influence a young person's behaviour.

8. *The process of learning criminal behaviour by association with criminal and anti-criminal patterns involves all the mechanisms involved in any other learning.* Learning criminal behaviour occurs the same way as learning any other behaviour and does not simply involve imitation.

9. *Although criminal behaviour is an expression of general needs and values, it is not explained by those general needs and values because non-criminal behaviour is also an expression of the same needs and values.* The motive for criminal behaviour is not the same as that for non-criminal behaviour. In other words, the desire for a leather jacket in and of itself does not foster criminal behaviour. Why one person will work to earn money to buy the jacket and someone else will steal it is largely determined by the different norms learned through associations with various groups. The learning of deviant norms from deviant groups produces criminal behaviour.

Differential association found considerable acceptance among mid-20th-century theorists because it combined then-prevalent psychological and sociological principles into a coherent perspective on criminality. Crime as a form of learned behaviour became the catchword, and biological and other perspectives were largely abandoned by those involved in the process of theory testing.

Neutralization Techniques
Of particular interest to proponents of differential association is the manner in which various rationalizations are employed by those involved in criminal behaviour. Those who disobey the law are, at least to some degree, participants in the larger culture that surrounds them. How is it, then, that they may choose behavioural alternatives that seemingly negate the norms and values of the larger society? While social learning theorists such as Sutherland contend that criminal behaviour is learned through the mastery of techniques, values, and attitudes needed to commit deviant acts, neutralization theory holds that most offenders learn **techniques of neutralization** to allow them to go against conventional values and attitudes. Gresham Sykes and David Matza introduced this notion in their 1957 article "Techniques of Neutralization."[8] Sykes and Matza suggested that offenders and delinquents are aware of conventional values and understand that their offending is wrong but engage in neutralizing self-talk before offending to mitigate the anticipated shame and guilt associated with violating societal norms.[9] Offenders can overcome feelings of responsibility when involved in crime commission by using five types of justifications:

1. *Denying responsibility.* They point to their backgrounds of poverty, abuse, and lack of opportunity: "The trouble I get into is not my fault" or "They made me do it."

2. *Denying injury.* They explain that everyone does it or that individuals or companies can afford it: "They're so rich, they'll never miss it."

3. *Denying the victim.* They justify the harm done by claiming that the victim deserved the victimization: "I only beat up drunks" or "She had it coming."

Techniques of neutralization Culturally available justifications that can provide criminal offenders with the means to disavow responsibility for their behaviour.

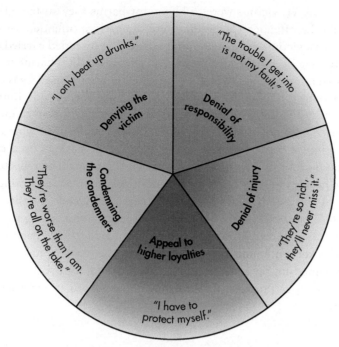

Figure 9.1 Techniques of Neutralization

4. *Condemning the condemners.* They assert that authorities are corrupt or responsible for their own victimization and that society has made them what they are and must now suffer the consequences: "They're worse than I am. They're all on the take" or "If I don't do it to him, he'll do it to me."

5. *Appealing to higher loyalties.* They use the defence of their family honour, gang, girlfriend, or neighbourhood: "I have to protect myself." (See Figure 9.1.)

In the words of Sykes and Matza, "It is our argument that much delinquency is based on what is essentially an unrecognized extension of defenses to crimes, in the form of justifications for deviance that are seen as valid by the delinquent but not by the legal system or society at large."[10]

A few years later, Matza went on to suggest that delinquents tended to drift into crime when available techniques of neutralization combined with weak or ineffective values espoused by the controlling elements in society, stating that the delinquent "drifts between criminal and conventional action,"[11] choosing whichever is the more expedient at the time. By employing techniques of neutralization, delinquents need not be fully alienated from the larger society because these techniques provide an effective way of overcoming feelings of guilt so they can commit crimes. Matza used the phrase "soft determinism" to describe drift, saying that delinquents are neither forced to make choices because of fateful experiences early in life nor entirely free to make choices unencumbered by the realities of their situation.

More recent studies have found that whereas "only a small percentage of adolescents generally approve of violence or express indifference to violence, [a] large percentage of adolescents accept neutralizations justifying the use of violence in particular situations."[12] Studies have found that young people who disapprove of violence but associate with delinquent peers will often use neutralization techniques as justifications for violence in which they personally engage.[13]

A 2003 study by sociologist Lois Presser on remorse and neutralization among violent male offenders, based on interviews with 27 men who had committed serious violent crime, found that the men excused or justified their violent actions through five rationalizations: (1) victims were to blame for harms they sustained that resulted from provoking the offender, (2) victims were themselves offenders or deserving of harm, (3) harm to a victim that was not premeditated or intended carried no blame, (4) the legal sanctioning of an offender negated any harm, and (5) harms to the offender and his family stemming from the crime negated any harms caused by the offender.[14]

In innovative research published in 2008, Orly Turgeman-Goldschmidt of Israel's Bar-Ilan University conducted 54 unstructured, in-depth, face-to-face interviews with malicious Israeli computer vandals (hackers) in order to determine what kinds of neutralization techniques they employed and found that the hackers used neutralization techniques common to other offenders, although their language reflected the cyber-realm.[15] Some hackers were found to be like political criminals, assuming responsibility by means of internal justifications (by attacking al-Qaeda websites or bringing down computers of the Arab news network Al-Jazeera and seeing the activity as a positive contribution to their socio-political environment); these "hacktivists" defined themselves as hackers with political consciences.[16] Other hackers justified illegal hacking as simply being fun, rewarding, or self-fulfilling and argued that anyone or anything affected, such as financial institutions, could afford it and that no one was physically hurt.

Labelling Theory

Another social process perspective is based on the study of societal reactions to deviance. Society's response to known or suspected offenders is important not only because it determines the individual futures of those who are labelled as offenders but also because it may contribute to a heightened incidence of criminality by reducing behavioural options available to labelled offenders.

Tagging An early description of societal reaction to deviance can be found in the work of Frank Tannenbaum, whose 1938 book *Crime and the Community* popularized the term **tagging** to explain what happens to offenders following arrest, conviction, and sentencing. Tannenbaum told his readers that crime was essentially the result of two opposing views—those of the delinquent and those of the community at large:

> This conflict over the situation is one that arises out of a divergence of values. As the problem develops, the situation gradually becomes redefined. The attitude of the community hardens definitely into a demand for suppression. There is a gradual shift from the definition of the specific acts as evil to a definition of the individual as evil, so that all his acts come to be looked upon with suspicion. From the community's point of view, the individual who used to do bad and mischievous things has now become a bad and unredeemable human being. . . . There is a persistent demand for consistency in character. The community cannot deal with people whom it cannot define.[17]

After the process whereby an offender comes to be seen as ultimately and irrevocably bad has been completed, Tannenbaum said, the offender "now lives in a different world. He has been tagged. The process of making the criminal, therefore, is a process of tagging."[18] Once a person has been defined as bad, he or she finds that few legitimate opportunities remain open and that only other people who have been similarly defined by society as bad are available to associate with him or her, and this continued association with negatively defined others leads to continued crime.

Primary and Secondary Deviance Using terminology developed by Edwin M. Lemert, it became fashionable to call an offender's initial acts of deviance **primary deviance** and his or her continued acts of deviance (especially those resulting from

Tagging The process whereby an individual is negatively defined by agencies of justice.

Primary deviance The initial deviance often undertaken to deal with transient problems in living.

forced association with other offenders) **secondary deviance**. Primary deviance may be undertaken to solve some immediate problem or to meet the expectations of one's subcultural group. For example, the robbery of a convenience store by a college student temporarily desperate for tuition money may be the first serious criminal offence ever committed by the student, and he or she may well intend for it to be the last, but if arrest ensues and the student is tagged with the status of a criminal, then secondary deviance may occur as a means of adjustment to the negative status. In Lemert's words, "When a person begins to employ his deviant behaviour or a role based upon it as a means of defense, attack, or adjustment to the overt and covert problems created by the consequent societal reaction to him, his deviation is secondary."[19]

Secondary deviance   The deviant behaviour that results from official labelling and from association with others who have been so labelled.

Secondary deviance is especially important because of the forceful role it plays in causing tagged individuals to internalize the negative labels that have been applied to them and to assume the role of the deviant. According to Lemert, "Objective evidences of this change will be found in the symbolic appurtenances of the new role, in clothes, speech, posture, and mannerisms, which in some cases heighten social visibility, and which in some cases serve as symbolic cues to professionalization."[20]

Labelling   The person most often associated with labelling theory is Howard Becker, who published *Outsiders: Studies in the Sociology of Deviance*, the work in which the perspective of **labelling theory** (the idea that society's response to the criminal and the process through which a person comes to be defined as criminal and labelled "criminal" are significant contributory factors in future criminality) found its fullest development.[21] In *Outsiders*, Becker described the deviant subculture in which jazz musicians live and the process by which an individual becomes a marijuana user, but his primary focus was explaining how a person becomes labelled an outsider, as "a special kind of person, one who cannot be trusted to live by the rules agreed on by the group."[22] The central fact is that society creates both deviance and the deviant person by responding to circumscribed behaviours. In Becker's words,

Labelling theory   An interactionist perspective that sees continued crime as a consequence of limited opportunities for acceptable behaviour that follow from the negative responses of society to those defined as offenders.

> Social groups create deviance by making the rules whose infraction constitutes deviance, and by applying those rules to particular people and labeling them as outsiders. From this point of view, deviance is not a quality of the act the person commits, but rather a consequence of the application by others of rules and sanctions. The deviant is one to whom that label has been successfully applied.[23]

For Becker and other labelling theorists, no act is intrinsically deviant or criminal but must be defined as such by others; becoming deviant involves a sequence of steps that eventually leads to commitment to a deviant identity and participation in a deviant career.

In developing labelling theory, Becker attempted to explain how some rules come to carry the force of law, while others have less weight or apply only within the context of marginal subcultures. His explanation centred on the concept of **moral enterprise**, meaning all the efforts a particular interest group makes to have its sense of propriety embodied in law. "Rules are the products of someone's initiative, and we can think of the people who exhibit such enterprise as moral entrepreneurs."[24] An example of moral enterprise is NORML Canada (the National Organization for the Reform of Marijuana Laws) whose mandate is to "eliminate all civil and criminal penalties for private marijuana use." NORML Canada believes that the current practice of discouraging marijuana use through formal sanctions has been harmful and costly to both society and the individual.[25]

Moral enterprise   The efforts made by an interest group to have its sense of propriety enacted into law.

Moral enterprise is used, Becker claimed, by groups seeking to support their own interests with the weight of law. Often the group that is successful at moral enterprise does not represent a popular point of view. The group is simply more effective than others at maneuvering through the formal bureaucracy that accompanies legislation.

Becker was especially interested in describing deviant careers and the processes by which individuals become members of deviant subcultures and take on the attributes associated with the deviant role. Becker argued that most deviance is likely to be transitory and unlikely to occur again. For example, a youth who shoplifts a candy bar from a convenience store will probably not make a habit out of this behaviour. However, transitory deviance can be effectively stabilized in a person's behavioural repertoire through the labelling process. If that youth is caught and charged by the police, then he or she becomes known as a shoplifter or young offender. Once a person is labelled as deviant, opportunities for conforming behaviour are seriously reduced and behavioural opportunities that remain open are primarily deviant ones; the budding deviant increasingly exhibits deviant behaviour because his or her choices are restricted by society. Successful deviants must acquire the techniques and resources necessary to undertake the deviant act (drug use, bank robbery, breaking and entering) and develop the mindset characteristic of others like them. Near the end of a deviant career, the person labelled a deviant has internalized society's negative label, has assumed a deviant self-concept, and is likely a member of a deviant subgroup (see the Who's Responsible? box). "A drug addict once told me that the moment she felt she was really 'hooked' was when she realized she no longer had any friends who were not drug addicts."[26] In this way, explained Becker, deviance becomes a self-fulfilling prophecy. Labelling, then, is a cause of crime insofar as the actions of society in defining the rule breaker as deviant push the person further in the direction of continued deviance.

WHO'S RESPONSIBLE—THE INDIVIDUAL OR SOCIETY?

Living in Shame

When her son was sent to prison for pedophilia, Sheila was plunged into a world of secrecy and loneliness.

Lance, 21, was convicted last year of sexually assaulting an eight-year-old girl and a ten-year-old boy. He was sentenced to 20 months in jail.

"When I first found out he was charged, I was horrified, and immediately thought, 'What have I done wrong?'" says Sheila, who prefers to be identified only as a Lower Mainland teacher.

"I didn't know what to do. It was a nightmare. And because I didn't know what was going on, I wasn't in any kind of position to offer support to my son—who was terrified."

The experience left Sheila feeling isolated and abandoned. She still hasn't told other members of Lance's family—including her ex-husband—about his crime.

"I was feeling so alone. I mean, who could I talk to about this?

"You have a sense of isolation because you cut off all your friends.

"I was worried that everyone would find out. I was worried it would reflect on me and put my job in jeopardy. I have shared with only a few friends.

"Even some of my friends who do understand . . . their attitude has changed and they stay away. It's like we're all tarred with the same brush.

"People say he's not really a pedophile, and I have to say, 'Yes he is.'"

The system, Sheila says, is just as mystifying to the families of offenders as it is to the victims. For one thing, there are few if any support groups.

"I went to court with my son time after time. I would sit in that courtroom . . . and I was alone."

Lance, she says, was totally unprepared for the prison system.

"When he was taken into jail you would not believe the harassment from staff, and the filthy comments they made.

"This is a first-time offender, a young kid. He was so frightened.

"The day he was pronounced guilty he wrapped piano wire around his top button. He was afraid he'd end up getting raped because of the hatred towards pedophiles."

It was Lance's first conviction. Sheila believes he had never sexually molested children before.

>

But she admits he was a difficult child. Being expelled from kindergarten was only the start.

When she divorced Lance's father, things got worse. The next man she married was an alcoholic.

By the time he reached his teens, Lance was stealing and doing drugs.

Finally, in desperation, Sheila had him placed in a foster home.

"It was the hardest thing I've ever done, signing those papers."

The papers she signed declared that she was legally "abandoning" him. That's the official language of B.C.'s *Family Child Services Act*, but Sheila insists that was never her intention.

Within weeks, Sheila says, Lance was sexually molested by his foster mother.

Within months he was sexually molesting two other kids in the home, resulting in the two charges of sexual assault.

"She (the foster mother) has admitted it to me," says Sheila.

"We have not pressed charges because my son did not want me to go through any more trauma.

"I have a lot of anger toward her (the foster mom). But I have a lot of guilt because I feel that if I hadn't been with an alcoholic husband, I would have been more aware.

"But Lance himself said, 'Mom, I made those choices, I did those things.'"

That admission, and confrontation with his past, came after months of therapy at Stave Lake, a minimum-security institution near Maple Ridge for sex offenders.

Sheila has nothing but praise for the staff and program. Now she does volunteer work with sex offenders, helping them upgrade their education, and with victims, helping them understand offenders.

Lance was released from prison after six months and has moved away from the Lower Mainland.

He lives with a family, Sheila says, which is aware of his conviction, and he is supervised at all times.

She's anxious for him to get back into counselling, but she says his probation officer won't let him because of his living arrangements.

"They want him to move to a family apartment building where there would be no supervision."

Sheila wonders what kind of life Lance will have.

"I look down the road and I really wonder what chance my son has for having a good, wholesome, healthy life—like having a family.

"I just have to turn it over to God."

Think about it:

1. How did the label of "pedophile" affect others associated with Lance? Is there a danger in using such labels?

2. Do you feel any differently about Lance once you know a little about his background and what led him to commit the sexual assaults? Is it possible to separate the offender from the offence?

3. Do you think the names of sexual offenders should be made known to the public? Defend your position.

Source: S. Jiwa and C. Ogilvie, "Living in Shame," *The Province*, February 21, 1993, p. 58. Reprinted with permission from Pacific Newspaper Group.

Contributions of Labelling Theory   Labelling theory contributed a number of unique ideas to the criminological literature:

- Deviance is the result of social processes involving the imposition of definitions rather than the consequence of any quality inherent in human activity itself.

- Deviant individuals achieve their status by virtue of social definition rather than because of inborn traits.

- The reaction of society to deviant behaviour and to actors who engage in such behaviour is the major element in determining the criminality of the person and of the behaviour in question.

- Negative self-images follow from processing by the formal criminal justice system rather than preceding delinquency.

- Labelling by society and handling by the justice system tend to perpetuate crime and delinquency rather than reduce them.

Becker's typology of delinquents—the pure deviant, the falsely accused deviant, and the secret deviant—helped explain the labelling approach. The pure deviant is one who commits norm-breaking behaviour, who is accurately appraised by society, and who is tried, convicted, and sentenced. The falsely accused individual is one who is not guilty but is labelled deviant nonetheless, who experiences the impact of conviction and the experiences that attend prison life, and who is left with a negative self-concept and with group associations practically indistinguishable from those of the true deviant. This person demonstrates the power of social definition—the life of the falsely accused is changed just as thoroughly as is the life of the pure deviant by the process of labelling. The secret deviant violates social norms, but his or her behaviour is not noticed, so negative societal reactions do not follow. A secret deviant again demonstrates the power of societal reaction, but in this case by the very lack of consequences.

Although labelling theory fell into disregard during the late 1970s and early 1980s due to allegations that it was vague and ambiguous, some contemporary criminologists have recast the approach as a developmental theory of structural disadvantage. The theory is now seen as one that points out the cumulative effects over time of official intervention on future life chances and opportunities for approved success. Contemporary proponents of the labelling perspective generally see labelling as only one factor contributing to cumulative disadvantages in life chances. A recent study considered the impact of negative official interventions on young men from the time they were about 13.5 years old until they reached the age of 22. In keeping with what labelling theory would predict, the study found that official intervention during adolescence led to increased criminality in early adulthood because it reduced life chances for educational achievement and successful employment and that poor people were more negatively affected by official processing, probably because they were already disadvantaged along other important social dimensions.[27]

The transition from primary to secondary deviance is outlined in Box 9.1.

Reintegrative Shaming

Reintegrative shaming A form of shaming, imposed as a sanction by the criminal justice system, that is thought to strengthen the moral bond between the offender and the community.

In a contemporary offshoot of labelling theory, John Braithwaite and colleagues at the Australian National University reported initial results of their 1997 studies on **reintegrative shaming**, which describes processes by which a deviant is labelled and sanctioned but then is brought back into a community of conformity through words, gestures, or rituals.[28]

Called RISE (for Reintegrative Shaming Experiments), the project assessed the efficacy of each approach using several criteria: (1) prevalence and frequency of repeat

---

Box 9.1 THE DEVIANCE PROCESS

1. A person commits a deviant/criminal act (if undetected, the act remains primary deviance).

2. Society reacts in a retributive or punitive way.

3. The individual responds by committing more infractions (secondary deviation), which in turn draws additional attention to the criminal. The deviant cycle begins to escalate (e.g., in frequency and/or intensity), a self-fulfilling process.

4. The labelled individual develops more hostility and resentment toward criminal justice agents.

5. Society and the legal system respond by further labelling and stigmatizing the offender.

6. As the individual's options become increasingly restricted, the criminal justice system sees the offender as a problem and the offender sees him- or herself as deviant.

7. The probability for future acts of deviance increases—deviance amplification. Therefore, once labelled and stigmatized, the offender's identity and self-concept evolve around deviance.

General Model of Labelling Process

Primary deviance → information reaction → continuance of deviance → escalation of response (e.g., stereotyping, rejection, alienation of tagged actor) → more delinquency (secondary deviance) → formal intervention → individual begins to see self as delinquent → self-fulfilling process.

Source: J.A. Winterdyk, *Canadian Criminology* (Toronto: Prentice Hall, 2000), p. 241. Reproduced with permission of J.A. Winterdyk.

offending, (2) victim satisfaction with the process, (3) estimated cost savings within the justice process, (4) changes in drinking or drug use behaviour among offenders, and (5) perceptions of procedural justice, fairness, and protection of rights.[29]

At the core of the study is Braithwaite's belief that two different kinds of shame exist. **Stigmatic shaming** is thought to destroy the moral bond between the offender and the community, whereas reintegrative shaming is thought to strengthen the moral bond between the offender and the community. According to Braithwaite and co-author Heather Strang,

> Stigmatic shaming is what American judges employ when they make an offender post a sign on his property saying "a violent felon lives here'" or a bumper sticker on his car saying "I am a drunk driver." Stigmatic shaming sets the offender apart as an outcast—often for the rest of the offender's life. By labeling him or her as someone who cannot be trusted to obey the law, stigmatic shaming says the offender is expected to commit more crimes.[30]

Their alternative to stigmatic humiliation is "to condemn the crime, not the criminal."[31] Through carefully monitored diversionary conferences, Braithwaite and Strang hoped to give offenders the opportunity to rejoin the community as law-abiding citizens, but to earn the right to a fresh start, offenders had to express remorse for their past conduct, apologize to any victims, and repair the harm caused by the crime.

Preliminary results from the RISE study supported the claimed value of reintegrative shaming, but most of these results were measured through interviews with offenders following diversionary conferences and consisted primarily of anecdotal evidence based on the reported feelings of the respondents. These findings showed that offenders were far more likely to feel ashamed of their crimes if handled through conferences rather than through formal court processing and that both offenders and victims reported finding conferences fairer than official court proceedings. See the discussion on the related topic of restorative justice in Chapter 10.

Social Control Theories

Social control theories seek to identify those features of the personality (Chapter 7) and the environment (Chapter 8) that keep people from committing crimes. Social control theories take a step beyond static aspects of the personality and physical features of the environment in order to focus on the *process* through which social integration develops. The extent of a person's integration with positive social institutions and with significant others determines that person's resistance to criminal temptations, and the social control theories focus on the process through which such integration develops. Rather than stressing causal factors in criminal behaviour, social control theories tend to ask why people actually obey rules instead of breaking them.[32]

Containment Theory
In the 1950s, a student of the Chicago school of criminology, Walter C. Reckless, wrote *The Crime Problem*.[33] He tackled head-on the realization that most sociological theories, although conceptually enlightening, offered less-than-perfect predictability, being unable to predict which individuals (even those exposed to various "causes" of crime) would become criminal. Reckless thought that the sociological perspectives prevalent at the time offered only half of a comprehensive theoretical framework, writing that crime was the consequence of both social pressures to become involved in violations of the law and failures to resist such pressures. Reckless called his approach **containment theory** and compared it with a biological immune response, saying that only some people exposed to a disease actually come down with it. Sickness, like crime, results from the failure of control mechanisms, some internal to the person and others external.

Stigmatic shaming A form of shaming, imposed as a sanction by the criminal justice system, that is thought to destroy the moral bond between the offender and the community.

Social control theories The perspectives predicting that when social constraints on anti-social behaviour are weakened or absent, delinquent behaviour emerges. Rather than stressing causative factors in criminal behaviour, social control theory asks why people actually obey rules instead of breaking them.

Containment theory A form of social control theory that suggests a series of both internal and external factors contributes to law-abiding behaviour.

In the case of crime, Reckless wrote that *external containment* consists of "the holding power of the group."[34] Under most circumstances, Reckless said that "the society, the state, the tribe, the village, the family, and other nuclear groups are able to hold the individual within the bounds of the accepted norms and expectations."[35] In addition to setting limits, he saw society as providing individuals with meaningful roles and activities, another important factor of external containment.

Reckless stated that inner containment "represents the ability of the person to follow the expected norms, to direct himself."[36] For Reckless, this ability was enhanced by a positive self-image, a focus on socially approved goals, personal aspirations in line with reality, a tolerance for frustration, and a general adherence to society's norms and values. A person with a positive self-concept can avoid the temptations of crime simply by thinking, "I'm not that kind of person." A focus on approved goals helps keep one on the proverbial straight and narrow path. "Aspirations in line with reality" are simply realistic desires. In other words, if one seriously desires to be the richest person in the world, disappointment will probably result. Even when aspirations are reasonable, however, disappointments will occur—hence the need for a tolerance for frustration. Adherence to the norms and values of the larger society are a basic component of inner containment.

In Figure 9.2 (a diagram of containment theory), "Pushes toward Crime" signifies all the perceived rewards, including financial gain, sexual satisfaction, and higher status, that crime may offer. **Containment** is a stabilizing force that blocks such pushes and pulls from leading the individual into crime.

Reckless believed that inner containment was far more effective than external containment in preventing law violations. "As social relations become more impersonal, as society becomes more diverse and alienated, as people participate more and more for longer periods of time away from a home base, the self becomes more and more important as a controlling agent."[37]

Containment Aspects of the social bond that act as a stabilizing force to prevent individuals from committing crimes and that keep them from engaging in deviance.

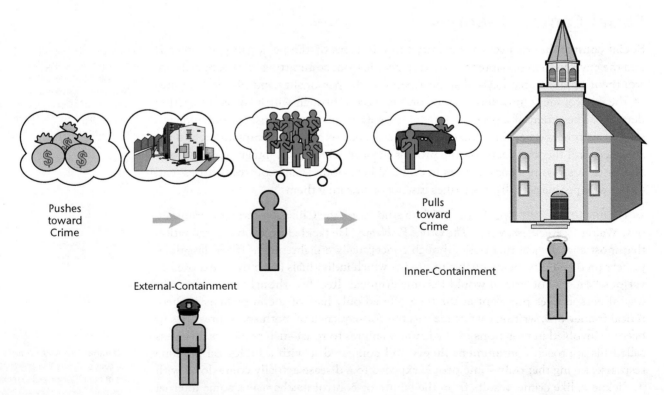

Figure 9.2 A Diagrammatic Representation of Containment Theory

Social Bond Theory   An important form of social control theory was popularized by Travis Hirschi in his 1969 book *Causes of Delinquency*.[38] Hirschi's approach was well received by criminologists and "epitomized social control theorizing for nearly three decades."[39] Hirschi argued that, through successful socialization, a bond forms between individuals and the social group, but when that bond is weakened or broken, deviance and crime may result. Hirschi described four components of the **social bond**: (1) attachment (a person's shared interests with others), (2) commitment (the amount of energy and effort put into activities with others), (3) involvement (the amount of time spent with others in shared activities), and (4) belief (a shared system of values and morals).

Social bond   The link, created through socialization, between individuals and the society of which they are a part.

The first component, attachment, refers to a person's shared interests with others. In his writings, Hirschi cited the psychopath as an example of a kind of person whose attachment to society is nearly non-existent.[40] Other relatively normal individuals may find their attachment to society loosened through "the process of becoming alienated from others, [which] often involves or is based on active interpersonal conflict. Such conflict could easily supply a reservoir of socially derived hostility sufficient to account for the aggressiveness of those whose attachments to others have been weakened."[41] The second component of the social bond—commitment—reflects a person's investment of time and energies into conforming behaviour and the potential loss of rewards that he or she has already gained from that behaviour. In Hirschi's words,

> The idea, then, is that the person invests time, energy, himself, in a certain line of activity—say, getting an education, building up a business, acquiring a reputation for virtue. Whenever he considers deviant behaviour, he must consider the costs of this deviant behaviour, the risk he runs of losing the investment he has made in conventional behaviour.[42]

For such a traditionally successful person, committing a petty theft is stupid because the potential loss far exceeds any possible gains. Recognizing that his approach applies primarily to individuals who have been successfully socialized into conventional society, Hirschi added, "The concept of commitment assumes that the organization of society is such that the interests of most persons would be endangered if they were to engage in criminal acts."[43]

Involvement, the third aspect, means "engrossment in conventional activities"[44] and is similar to Reckless's concept of meaningful roles. In explaining the importance of involvement in determining conformity, Hirschi cited the colloquial saying that "idle hands are the devil's workshop"—time and energy are limited, so if a person is busy at legitimate pursuits, he or she will have little opportunity for crime and deviance.

Belief, the last of his four aspects of the social bond, sets Hirschi's control theory apart from subcultural approaches because "control theory assumes the existence of a common value system within the society or group whose norms are being violated. We not only assume the deviant has believed the rules, [but also] assume he believes the rules even as he violates them."[45] How can a person simultaneously believe it is wrong to commit a crime and still commit it? Hirschi's answer is that "many persons do not have an attitude of respect toward the rules of society."[46] Although they know the rules exist, they basically do not care and invest little of their sense of self in moral standards.

In 1990, Michael R. Gottfredson, in collaboration with Hirschi, proposed a **general theory of crime** based on the concepts advanced earlier in control theory.[47] "Gottfredson and Hirschi's general theory of crime claims to be general, in part, due to its assertion that the operation of a single mechanism, low self-control, accounts for 'all crime, at all times'; acts ranging from vandalism to homicide, from rape to white-collar

General theory of crime   The assertion that the operation of a single mechanism, low self-control, accounts for "all crime, at all time," including acts ranging from vandalism to homicide, from sexual assault to white-collar crime.

crime."[48] Gottfredson and Hirschi defined self-control as the degree to which a person is vulnerable to temptations of the moment.[49] They proposed that self-control is acquired early in life and that low self-control combined with impulsivity is the premier individual-level cause of crime. It develops by the end of childhood and is fostered through parental emotional investment in the child, monitoring the child's behaviour, recognizing deviance when it occurs, and punishing the child.

Gottfredson and Hirschi thought it was important to ask, "What is crime?" Because nearly all crimes are mundane, simple, trivial, easy acts aimed at satisfying desires of the moment, their general theory is built on a classical or rational choice perspective—the belief that crime is a natural consequence of unrestrained human tendencies to seek pleasure and avoid pain. They concluded that crime is little more than a subset of general deviant behaviour and bears little resemblance to the explanations offered in the media, by law enforcement officials, or by most academic thinkers on the subject.

According to Gottfredson and Hirschi, the offender is neither the diabolical genius of fiction nor the ambitious seeker of the "American Dream" often portrayed by other social scientists. Offenders appear to have little control over their own desires, so when personal desires conflict with long-term interests, those who lack self-control often opt for the desires of the moment, thus contravening legal restrictions and becoming involved in crime. Central to Gottfredson and Hirschi's thesis is the belief that a well-developed social bond will result in the creation of effective mechanisms of self-control. "For Gottfredson and Hirschi, self-control is the key concept in the explanation of all forms of crime as well as other types of behaviour. Indeed, they believe that all current differences in rates of crime between groups and categories may be explained by differences in the management of self-control."[50]

One recent Canadian study found that the effect of good parenting on the development of positive self-control was very strong but that the role of factors such as household size and family structure could also make an important difference.[51] Families in which children lived with both biological parents seemed to be best at developing self-control in their children, whereas lower levels of self-control were found in single-parent families and in reconstituted families in which the parents had been divorced and remarried. The researchers concluded that "overall, regardless of family structure, it is evident that a nurturing, accepting family environment is positively associated with self-control."[52]

Social Development Theories

Over the past 25 years, an appreciation for the process of human development (the relationship between the maturing individual and his or her changing environment and to the social processes that relationship entails) has played an increasingly important role in helping us understand criminality.[53] Students of human development recognize that the process of development occurs through reciprocal dynamic interactions that take place between individuals and various aspects of their environment, and the **social development theories** posit that development, which begins at birth (and perhaps even earlier), occurs primarily within a social context. Unlike social learning theory (discussed earlier in this chapter), social development sees socialization as only one feature of that context. If socialization were the primary determinant of criminality, then we might expect that all problem children would become criminals as adults, but since that doesn't happen, there must be other aspects to the development process that social learning theories don't fully cover.

According to the social development perspective, human development simultaneously occurs on many levels—psychological, biological, familial, interpersonal, cultural, societal, and ecological.

Social development theories
An integrated perspective on human development that simultaneously examines many different levels of development—psychological, biological, familial, interpersonal, cultural, societal, and ecological.

cultural, societal, and ecological—so social development theories tend to be integrated theories, or theories combining various points of view. The rest of this chapter looks briefly at the social development perspective.

Most sociological explanations for crime involve the study of groups and the identification of differences among groups of offenders, but social development theories focus more on individual rates of offending and seek to understand both increases and decreases in rates of offending over the individual's lifetime. Social development theories generally employ longitudinal (over time) measurements of delinquency and offending, and they pay special attention to the transitions that people face as they move through the life cycle.

Most theories of social development recognize that a critical transitional period occurs as a person moves from childhood to adulthood, and life course theorists have identified at least seven developmental tasks that adolescents must confront: (1) establishing identity, (2) cultivating symbiotic relationships, (3) defining physical attractiveness, (4) investing in a value system, (5) obtaining an education, (6) separating from family and achieving independence, and (7) obtaining and maintaining gainful employment.[54] Youths are confronted with many obstacles or risks in their attempts to resolve these issues as they work to make a successful transition to adulthood. Figure 9.3 provides a conceptual model of the developmental processes that a maturing youth experiences during adolescence.

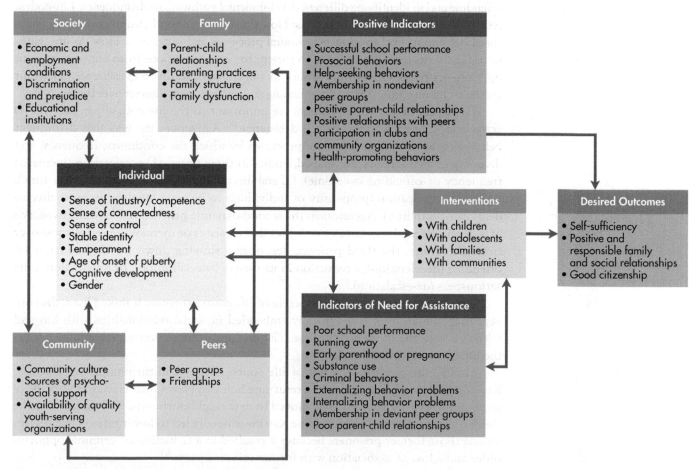

Figure 9.3 A Conceptual Model of Adolescent Development

Source: Family and Youth Services Bureau, *Understanding Youth Development: Promoting Positive Pathways of Growth* (Washington, DC: U.S. Department of Health and Human Services, 2000).

Life Course Perspective Traditional explanations for crime and delinquency often lack a developmental perspective because they generally ignore developmental changes throughout the life course and frequently fail to distinguish between different phases of criminal careers.[55] By contrast, development theories draw attention to the fact that criminal behaviour tends to follow a distinct pattern across the life cycle: Criminality is relatively uncommon during childhood, tends to begin as sporadic instances of delinquency during late adolescence and early adulthood, and then diminishes and sometimes completely disappears from a person's behaviour repertoire by age 30 or 40. Of course, some people never commit crimes or do so only rarely, while others become career criminals and persist in lives of crime.

Life course perspective A perspective that draws attention to the fact that criminal behaviour tends to follow a distinct pattern across the life cycle. Also called life course criminology.

The **life course perspective** (also called *life course criminology*) shifted the traditional focus away from the reasons why people begin offending to questions about what the dimensions of criminal offending are over the entire life course.[56] Life course criminology was given its name in a seminal book written by Robert J. Sampson and John H. Laub in 1993, entitled *Crime in the Making*.[57] Earlier, the concept of life course had been defined as "pathways through the life span involving a sequence of culturally defined, age-graded roles and social transitions enacted over time."[58] Life course theories, which build on social learning and social control principles, recognize that criminal careers may develop as the result of various criminogenic influences that affect individuals over the course of their lives.

Researchers who focus on the life course as it leads to delinquency, crime, and criminal identities are interested both in evaluating the prevalence, frequency, and onset of offending and in identifying different developmental pathways to delinquency. Life course researchers ask a variety of questions: How do early-childhood characteristics (e.g., antisocial behaviour) lead to adult behavioural processes and outcomes? How do life transitions (e.g., shifts in relationships from parents to peers, transitions from same-sex peers to opposite-sex peers, moves from school to work, marriage, divorce) influence behaviour and behavioural choices? How do offending and victimization interact over the life cycle?[59]

Three sets of dynamic concepts are important to the life course perspective: (1) activation, (2) aggravation, and (3) desistance.[60] *Activation*, the way that delinquent behaviours are stimulated and the processes by which the continuity, frequency, and diversity of delinquency are shaped, comes in three types: (1) acceleration (increased frequency of offending over time), (2) stabilization (increased continuity over time), and (3) diversification (propensity of individuals to become involved in more diverse delinquent activities). *Aggravation*, the second dynamic process, refers to the existence of a developmental sequence of activities that escalates or increases in seriousness over time. *Desistance*, the third process, describes a slowing down in the frequency of offending (deceleration), a reduction in its variety (specialization), or a reduction in its seriousness (de-escalation).[61]

Another central organizing principle of life course theories is linked lives, the concept that human lives "are typically embedded in social relationships with kin and friends across the life span";[62] these relationships exercise considerable influence on the life course of most people.

In 2012, in an interesting test of life course theory and turning points, David S. Kirk showed that former prisoners returning home to New Orleans were far less likely to continue lives of crime if they moved to new neighbourhoods. Kirk found that the displacement produced by Hurricane Katrina generally led to lower rates of recidivism among those former prisoners because it resulted in a reduction of criminal opportunities and a loss of association with former criminal peers.[63]

Evolutionary Ecology Because life course theory uses a developmental perspective in the study of criminal careers, life course researchers typically use longitudinal research designs involving **cohort analysis**, which usually begins at birth and traces the development of a population whose members share common characteristics until they reach a certain age. One well-known analysis of a birth cohort, undertaken by Marvin Wolfgang during the 1960s, found that a small nucleus of chronic juvenile offenders accounted for a disproportionately large share of all juvenile arrests.[64] Wolfgang studied males born in Philadelphia in 1945 until they reached age 18 and concluded that a relatively small number of violent offenders were responsible for most of the crimes committed by the cohort—6 percent of cohort members accounted for 52 percent of all arrests. A follow-up study found that the seriousness of offences among the cohort increased in adulthood but that the actual number of offences decreased as the cohort aged.[65] Wolfgang's analysis has since been criticized for its lack of a second cohort, or control group, against which the experiences of the cohort under study could be compared.[66]

The ecological perspective on crime control, pioneered by Lawrence E. Cohen and Richard Machalek, provides a more contemporary example of a life course approach.[67] **Evolutionary ecology** builds on the approach of social ecology while emphasizing developmental pathways encountered early in life. Criminologist Bryan Vila stated that "the evolutionary ecological approach draws attention to the ways people develop over the course of their lives. Experiences and environment early in life, especially those that affect child development and the transmission of biological traits and family management practices across generations, seem particularly important."[68] According to Vila, evolutionary ecology "attempts to explain how people acquire criminality—a predisposition that disproportionately favors criminal behaviour—when and why they express it as crime, how individuals and groups respond to those crimes, and how all these phenomena interact as a dynamic self-reinforcing system that evolves over time."[69]

Developmental Pathways   Researchers have found that manifestations of disruptive behaviours in childhood and adolescence are often age dependent, reflecting a developing capability to display different behaviours with age.[70] One of the most comprehensive studies to date that has attempted to detail life pathways leading to criminality began in 1986. The program, a longitudinal study producing ongoing results, aims to better understand serious delinquency, violence, and drug use by examining how youths develop within the context of family, school, peers, and community.[71] It has compiled data on 4500 youths from three distinct but coordinated projects throughout the United States. Researchers conducted individual face-to-face interviews with inner-city youths considered to be at high risk for involvement in delinquency and drug abuse. Multiple perspectives on each child's development and behaviour were obtained through interviews with the child's primary caretakers and with teachers. In addition to interview data, the studies collected extensive information from official agencies, including police, courts, schools, and social services.[72]

The research found that (1) "the more seriously involved in drugs a youth was, the more seriously that juvenile was involved in delinquency," (2) "greater risks exist for violent offending when a child is physically abused or neglected early in life," (3) students who are not highly committed to school have higher rates of delinquency, (4) "poor family life exacerbates delinquency and drug use," and (5) affiliation with street gangs and illegal gun ownership are both predictive of delinquency. The study also found that "peers who were delinquent or used drugs had a great impact on [other] youth."

Research findings also indicated that positive developmental pathways are fostered when adolescents are able to develop (1) a sense of industry and competency, (2) a

Cohort analysis A social scientific technique that studies a population that shares common characteristics over time. Cohort analysis usually begins at birth and traces the development of cohort members until they reach a certain age.

Evolutionary ecology An approach to understanding crime that draws attention to the ways people develop over the course of their lives.

feeling of connectedness to others and to society, (3) a belief in their ability to control their future, and (4) a stable identity.[73] Competency, connectedness, control, and identity develop through youths' interactions with their community, family, school, and peers. Adolescents who develop these characteristics appear more likely than others to engage in pro-social behaviours, exhibit positive school performance, and be members of non-deviant peer groups.

Perhaps the most significant result of the study is the finding that three separate developmental pathways to delinquency exist:[74]

1. *Authority conflict pathway.* Subjects appear to begin quite young (3 or 4 years of age) on the authority conflict pathway. "The first step," said the study authors, "was stubborn behaviour, followed by defiance around age 11, and authority avoidance—truancy, staying out late at night, or running away."

2. *Covert pathway.* "Minor covert acts such as frequent lying and shoplifting usually [start] around age 10." Delinquents following the covert pathway quickly progress "to acts of property damage, such as fire starting or vandalism, around age 11 or 12, followed by moderate and serious forms of delinquency."

3. *Overt pathway.* The first step on the overt pathway is minor aggression such as "annoying others and bullying—around age 11 or 12." Bullying was found to escalate into "physical fighting and violence as the juvenile progressed along this pathway." The overt pathway eventually leads to violent crimes like sexual assault, robbery, and assault.

Researchers have found that these three different pathways are not necessarily mutually exclusive and can at times converge. Self-report data have shown that simultaneous progression along two or more pathways leads to higher rates of delinquency.[75] Another study that could potentially produce substantially significant results began in 1990.[76] Directors of the project, known as the Project on Human Development in Chicago Neighbourhoods, described their ongoing research as "the major criminologic investigation of this century." The project is actually two studies combined into a single, comprehensive design: One is an intensive study of Chicago's neighbourhoods; is evaluating the social, economic, organizational, political, and cultural components of each neighbourhood; and seeks to identify changes that took place in the neighbourhoods over the study's eight-year data-gathering period. The second study consists of a series of coordinated longitudinal evaluations of 6000 randomly selected children, adolescents, and young adults that looks at the changing circumstances of people's lives and attempts to identify personal characteristics that may lead toward or away from anti-social behaviour. Researchers explore a wide range of variables—from prenatal drug exposure, lead poisoning, and nutrition to adolescent growth patterns, temperament, and self-image—as they try to identify which individuals might be most at risk for crime and delinquency. They also study children's exposure to violence and its consequences and evaluate child care and its impact on early childhood development. A variety of study methodologies are utilized, including self-reports, individualized tests and examinations, direct observation, the examination of existing records, and reports by informants. Researchers hope to provide answers to the following questions: (1) "How and why do anti-social and criminal behaviours originate?" (2) "What causes some individuals to continue those behaviours?" and (3) "How and why do some individuals cease law-violating behaviours while others continue?"

Life course theories, like the one informing the Chicago project, often point to the need for early intervention through nurturant strategies that build self-control through positive socialization. As Vila pointed out, "There are two main types of nurturant strategies: those that improve early life experiences to forestall the development of strategic styles based on criminality, and those that channel child and adolescent development in an effort to improve the match between individuals and their environment."[77]

POLICY IMPLICATIONS OF SOCIAL PROCESS THEORIES

9.3 | LEARNING OBJECTIVE

AS HAS BEEN NOTED THROUGHOUT THIS CHAPTER, BOTH OFFENDERS AND VICTIMS ARE stigmatized through social processes involving the formal and informal imposition of labels. Removal of the stigma would, at least theoretically, restore both to their pre-crime state.

Labelling theory, in particular, cautions against too much intervention, since it is often through contact with various types of rehabilitative programs that individuals become even further labelled. Even well-intentioned programs such as special education programs or support groups for released offenders can serve to label participants as "stupid" or "ex-con." Current restitution and court diversion programs are examples of policy initiatives that recognize the principles of labelling theory. Adult diversion projects or alternative measures for youth are designed to divert the offender away from formal contact with the criminal justice system, thereby avoiding the imposition of a label. For example, a man who is arrested for seeking the services of a prostitute but who has no previous criminal conviction may be ordered to attend "john school." Successful attendance means the offender has no further contact with the criminal justice system and is free of a criminal record. Diversion programs are usually joint initiatives involving the Crown's office and the local police service. Likewise, restitution initiatives are attempts to prevent the stigmatization of the offender. In lieu of the trial and court process, the offender is required to compensate either the victim or the community for the loss or for harm done. Since their inception, diversion programs have been surrounded by controversy. Whether they actually prevent the imposition of a negative label and thereby prevent future criminal activity is open to debate.[78] Social learning perspectives have also had an impact on program initiatives dealing with offenders and those at risk of becoming offenders. Social learning is based on the principle that since criminal behaviour and attitudes can be learned through association with criminal types, conventional values can be learned by interaction with those holding them. Well-known programs such as Night Hoops or After-4 Drop-ins are aimed at "at-risk" youth and provide an opportunity for them to associate with positive role models. Well-known sports figures will often participate and deliver positive messages, telling kids to "stay in school" or "say no to drugs." The Ottawa Police Service runs a youth centre in a neighbourhood once ridden with youth crime and has reported a significant decrease in illegal activity in the area since the centre's opening.

Closely linked to the idea of learned behaviour are the notions of commitment and attachment put forth by social control theorists. Not only do recreation programs run by such organizations as Boys and Girls Clubs and the YM/YWCA promote positive learning; they also help to develop a positive bond between individual participants and the program. Individuals, in turn, will not want to risk losing the privilege of being a member of the program if they break the rules. Similarly, educational programs such as Head Start work to socialize children at the preschool stage to help make their school experiences more enjoyable and thereby decrease the chances of early withdrawal. Social control theorists believe that a strong commitment to school, family, employment, and recreation—assuming these environments are all positive ones—can help decrease an individual's likelihood of succumbing to a criminal lifestyle.

One program emphasizing the development of self-control is the Montreal Preventive Treatment Program, which addresses early-childhood risk factors for gang involvement by targeting boys from poor socio-economic backgrounds who display disruptive behaviour while in kindergarten. The program offers training sessions for parents designed to teach family crisis management, disciplining techniques, and other parenting skills while the boys participate in training sessions emphasizing the development of pro-social skills and self-control. At least one evaluation of the program showed that it was effective at keeping boys from joining gangs.[79]

A contemporary example of social intervention efforts tied to a developmental model is Targeted Outreach, a program operated in the United States by Boys and Girls Clubs of America.[80] Using a wide referral network made up of local schools, police departments, and various youth service agencies, club officials work to end what they call the "inappropriate detention of juveniles."[81] The program's primary goal is to provide a positive, productive alternative to gangs for the youths who are most vulnerable to their influences or are already entrenched in gang activity. Currently, the program recruits at-risk youngsters—many as young as seven years old—and diverts them into activities that are intended to promote a sense of belonging, competence, usefulness, and self-control. A sense of belonging is fostered through clubs that provide familiar settings where each child is accepted. Competence and usefulness are developed through opportunities for meaningful activities that young people in the club program can successfully undertake. Finally, Targeted Outreach provides its youthful participants with a chance to be heard and, consequently, with the opportunity to influence decisions affecting their future. To date, Targeted Outreach has served more than 10 000 at-risk youths. Organizers hope that the program will eventually involve more than 1.5 million youngsters between the ages of 7 and 17.[82]

Life course theories have been widely applied to develop programs aimed at youth in conflict with the law. Most of these programs centre on principles such as strengthening the role of the family in providing guidance and discipline, supporting core social institutions such as schools and community organizations, promoting prevention strategies, and intervening immediately and consistently when delinquent behaviour first occurs. Examples of programs that reflect these principles are found in Chapter 11 in the discussion of nurturant crime-control policies.

9.4 LEARNING OBJECTIVE | CRITIQUE OF SOCIAL PROCESS THEORIES

SOCIAL PROCESS THEORIES SHARE SOME OF THE LIMITATIONS OF SOCIAL STRUCTURE theories, discussed in Chapter 8. Most notable of these is the disregard for biological and/or psychological contributions to criminal behaviour; indeed, all these theories are concerned with the social reality surrounding individuals and their interaction with all or some segments of it. In addition, like social structure theories, the social process perspective fails to fully explain why some individuals who are surrounded by negative environments and poor role models manage to avoid becoming involved in criminal behaviour. How is it that some manage to resist the peer pressure to get involved in deviant activity? How are they able to desist from "learning" from what they see all around them? If socialization is so crucial to an understanding of criminal behaviour, how is it that crime rates fluctuate from region to region in Canada? Are youth in the western provinces, where crime rates are generally higher, socialized differently than those in the eastern parts of the country, where crime rates are generally lower?

A critical examination of the individual theories presented in this chapter confirms these questions. Perhaps the most potent criticism against the concept of differential association, for example, is the claim that the perspective is virtually untestable, because most people experience a multitude of definitions—both favourable and unfavourable to law violation—and it is up to them to interpret what those experiences mean, so classifying experiences as either favourable or unfavourable to crime commission is difficult at best. Other critics suggest that differential association alone is not a sufficient explanation for crime. If it were, then we might expect correctional officers, for example, to become criminals by virtue of their constant and continued association with prison inmates. Similarly, wrongly imprisoned persons might be expected to turn to crime upon release from confinement. Little evidence suggests that either of these scenarios actually occurs. In effect, differential association does not seem to provide for free choice in individual circumstances, nor does it explain why some individuals, even when surrounded by associates who are committed to lives of crime, are still able to hold on to other, non-criminal values.

Although the labelling approach successfully points to the labelling process as a reason for continued deviance and as a cause of stabilization in deviant identities, it does little to explain the origin of crime and deviance, and few studies seem to support the basic tenets of the theory. Critics of labelling have pointed to its "lack of firm empirical support for the notion of secondary deviance" and observed that "many studies have not found that delinquents or criminals have a delinquent or criminal self-image."[83] There is also a lack of empirical support for the claim that contact with the justice system is fundamentally detrimental to the personal lives of criminal perpetrators. Although labelling theory suggests that official processing makes a significant contribution to continued criminality, it is questionable whether offenders untouched by the system would forgo the rewards of future criminality. Rather, it is the "type" of contact with the criminal justice system that many feel influences the future behaviour of an offender.

Like the social structural approaches discussed in Chapter 8, social process and development theories are intimately associated with the social problems approach (described in Chapter 1). For policy-makers, important questions include: What role (if any) does individual choice play in human development? Do people actively select components of the life course? Do they influence their own trajectories? Because so many important life course determinants are set in motion in early childhood and during adolescence, should those who make wrong choices be held accountable?

SOCIAL PROCESS THEORIES APPLIED

SOCIAL LEARNING
holds that all behaviour is learned in much the same way and that crime, like other forms of behaviour, is learned.
Andrew Leyshon-Hughes came from a well-established family. Where might he have learned the deviant behaviour that he exhibited? How might he have justified his behaviour?

Crime is a result of interaction between individuals and society. Criminal behaviour is learned in interaction with others and through the socialization process that occurs as a result of group membership. Among the most important groups contributing to this process of socialization are family, peers, and work groups. These groups instill values and norms in their members and determine what is acceptable and unacceptable. The process through which criminality is learned, deviant self-concepts are established, and criminal behaviour results is active, open-ended, and ongoing throughout a person's life. Criminal choices, once made, tend to persist because they are reinforced by the reaction of society to those whom it has identified as deviant.

How can society's reaction to Andrew Leyshon-Hughes's criminal behaviour be explained using the social process perspective?

SOCIAL DEVELOPMENT
holds that crime is a result of the relationship between the maturing individual and his or her changing environment and of the social processes that relationship entails.
Andrew Leyshon-Hughes's lawyer has argued that her client suffered from brain damage at birth. Is this an example of poor social development?

LABELLING
holds that crime is a result of limited opportunities for acceptable behaviour that follow from the negative responses of society to those defined as offenders. Why has Andrew Leyshon-Hughes been unable to escape from the label of psychopath, despite the efforts of his psychiatrist to deem him well enough to live in the community?

SOCIAL CONTROL
holds that crime is a result of weak or absent social constraints on anti-social behaviour.
Is there evidence that Andrew Leyshon-Hughes lacked strong social bonds? Why might these have been weak or absent?

SUMMARY OF LEARNING OBJECTIVES

9.1 According to social process theories, criminal behaviour is learned in interaction with others. The socialization process occurring as the result of group membership—in families, peer groups, work groups, and reference groups—is seen as the primary route through which learning occurs. Social process theories suggest that individuals who have weak stakes in conformity are more likely to be influenced by the social processes and contingent experiences that lead to crime, and those criminal choices tend to persist because they are reinforced by the reaction of society to those whom it has identified as deviant.

9.2 This examination of the social process perspective looks at several distinct approaches. Social learning theory places primary emphasis upon the role of communication and socialization in the acquisition of learned patterns of criminal behaviour and the values that support that behaviour. Labelling theory points to the special significance of society's response to the criminal and sees society's imposition of the label "criminal" as a significant contributory factor in determining future criminality. Reintegrative shaming emphasizes possible positive outcomes of the labelling process, while social control theory focuses on the strength of the bond people share with institutions and individuals around them, especially as those relationships shape their behaviour. Finally, the social development approach provides an integrated perspective on human development that simultaneously examines many different levels of development—psychological, biological, familial, interpersonal, cultural, societal, and ecological.

9.3 Social process theories suggest that crime-prevention programs should work to enhance self-control and to build pro-social bonds (bonds that strengthen conformity). Labelling theory, in particular, cautions against too much intervention, since it is often through contact with various types of rehabilitative programs that individuals become even further labelled. Even well-intentioned programs, such as special education programs or support groups for released offenders, can serve to label participants. The social development perspective advocates intervention in early delinquent behaviour and responding to serious, violent, and chronic offending.

9.4 Criticisms of social process theories are varied. The social process perspective fails to fully explain why some individuals who are surrounded by negative environments and poor role models manage to avoid becoming involved in criminal behaviour. If socialization is so crucial to an understanding of criminal behaviour, why is it that some manage to resist the peer pressure to get involved in deviant activity and to desist from "learning" from what they see all around them?

Questions for Review

1. How does the process of social interaction contribute to criminal behaviour?

2. Compare and contrast the theories discussed in this chapter, citing differences and similarities between and among them.

3. What kinds of social policy initiatives might be suggested by social process theories? Identify some already in place in Canadian society.

4. Describe the various shortcomings of the social process perspective of criminality.

Multiple-Choice Questions

1. Rather than stressing causative factors in criminal behaviour, social control theory _____
_____.

    a. contends that criminal behaviour is learned through a process of association

    b. holds that an offender is negatively defined by agencies of justice

    c. asks why people actually obey rules instead of breaking them

    d. posits that criminal behaviour is dependent upon the ways in which people develop over their lives

    e. asks what role familial, cultural, interpersonal, and societal realities play in criminal behaviour.

2. According to Sykes and Matza, _____ is used by offenders to disavow their behaviour.

    a. a technique of neutralization

    b. moral enterprise

    c. tagging

    d. labelling

    e. reaction formation

3. Which of the following perspectives draws attention to the fact that criminal behaviour tends to follow a distinct pattern across the life cycle?

    a. reintegrative shaming

    b. life course theory

    c. labelling theory

    d. containment theory

    e. social control theory

4. The social process perspective contends that criminal behaviour _____
_____.

    a. is dependent upon the personality of the individual offender

    b. is learned in interaction with others and through the socialization process

    c. is related to economic and social arrangements in society

    d. is physiologically based and often inherited

    e. is a result of conscious choice.

5. The social process perspective would advocate _____ as a means of preventing criminal behaviour.

    a. the identification of early-childhood risk factors for gang involvement

    b. after-school drop-in programs

    c. adult diversion projects

    d. targeted outreach programs

    e. all of the above

Multiple Choice Answers: 1c, 2a, 3b, 4b, 5a

Chapter 10

The Meaning of Crime: Social Conflict Perspective

Fred Lum/The Globe and Mail/The Canadian Press

HUMAN NEED NOT CORPORATE GREED!

Crime is an opportunity, not a problem. It's an opportunity to find out what's wrong in the relationship that exists in our community.

—*Justice Barry Stuart*[1]

LEARNING OBJECTIVES

After reading this chapter, you should be able to

10.1 Recognize the ways in which power conflict between social groups contributes to crime and criminal activity.

10.2 Understand the distinctions between a number of traditional social conflict theories.

10.3 Identify the distinctions between a number of emerging social conflict theories.

10.4 Identify those policy initiatives that reflect the social conflict approach.

INTRODUCTION

On March 11, 1990, a small Mohawk Aboriginal band erected a barricade along the border of the Mohawk Nation reserve of Kanesatake. The nearby city of Oka, Quebec, was proceeding with plans to enlarge a golf course on 22 hectares of land known as "The Pines" that had been given to the city but was claimed by the Mohawks as a sacred ancestral burial ground. Since the courts had rejected the Mohawks' claim to the land, the band concluded that their only option was to hold a standoff. It lasted 78 days.

Initially, the barricade was guarded mostly by women and children. The standoff intensified, however, as the Mohawks of Kanesatake were joined by Mohawks from other reserves in Canada and the United States, some of whom belonged to a society of heavily armed Mohawk Warriors. The introduction of high-powered firearms and other weapons increased the tension between the Mohawks and authorities, represented largely by the Quebec provincial police force, the Sûreté du Québec (SQ). The city of Oka was successful in obtaining a court order to evict the Mohawks, and on July 11, 1990, about 100 SQ personnel attempted to enforce this injunction on behalf of the municipality. Armed Mohawks were positioned to one side in the woods while police equipped with gas masks and assault rifles advanced on the barricade. An armed conflict erupted, and hundreds of rounds of ammunition were fired from both sides, resulting in the wounding and eventual death of a 31-year-old SQ corporal, Marcel Lemay. The standoff had reached crisis proportions, and each side blamed the other for the death of the police officer.

Thirty kilometres to the south of the Kanesatake reserve, Mohawks from the Kahnawake reserve were outraged by the actions of the police. In a show of support, they blocked off all roads into the reserve. These included two major highways, one of which led to the Mercier Bridge, linking the city of Montreal to the residential neighbourhood of Châteauguay, which forced thousands of commuters to take a two-hour daily detour. Threatening to "bring down the bridge" if there was another police assault at Oka, the Mohawks dug in. Over 100 chiefs from across Canada met at Kahnawake in a show of solidarity.

The crisis captured national attention, and the media transmitted interviews and pictures across the country. As the standoff continued throughout the summer of 1990, both sides in the conflict became more entrenched. Arms and ammunition were smuggled from Native communities in the United States to bolster the Mohawk cause. Mohawk Warriors with monikers such as "Lasagna" and "Noriega" appeared before television cameras in army fatigues, with bandanas covering their faces. Two hundred or so RCMP officers bolstered the 1400 to 1800 SQ forces throughout the duration of the crisis. As the standoff dragged on through the summer, with no progress made toward negotiating a settlement, then prime minister Mulroney called in the Canadian Armed Forces at the request of Quebec premier Bourassa and the provincial government. Approximately 1000 military personnel took over police positions established at Kanesatake and Kahnawake. Numerous violent clashes erupted as each side stood its ground. Canadians witnessed scenes of armoured personnel carriers, barbed-wire barricades, and shouting matches between the two sides as the group of Mohawk Warriors resisted advances by the authorities. Eventually, on September 6, 1990, the Kahnawake Mohawks ended their occupation of the Mercier Bridge. On September 26, after often heated negotiations, the standoff ended when the Mohawk Warriors agreed to lift the barricade. The Oka crisis cost the Canadian people $200 million, including the expense of extra policing and army intervention. The incident at Oka ended relatively peacefully. The golf course has not since been expanded.

On July 11, 2015, dozens of residents and community members marched to commemorate the 25th anniversary of the crisis. John Cree, one of the Mohawks leading

In a standoff at the Kanesatake reserve in Oka, Quebec, a Canadian soldier comes face-to-face with a Mohawk warrior.

Str-Shaney Komulainen/The Canadian Press

the march, reminded the assembled people that the disputed territory remains unceded. Many of the speakers present focused on conciliation and healing. Francine Lemay, the sister of the slain police officer, said the crisis led her to eventually discover the history of the Mohawks and the injustices they have suffered. "People ask, explore, search, regret, act but much still needs to be done concerning recognition and reparation of wrongs," she said.

Kanesatake grand chief Serge Simon and Oka mayor Pascal Quevillon have agreed to jointly fight any development on The Pines. Quevillon said the gesture is "officializing" a reconciliation that has been going on between the town of Oka and its Mohawk neighbours for years.[2]

THE SOCIAL CONFLICT PERSPECTIVE

10.1 | LEARNING OBJECTIVE

SOCIAL CONFLICT THEORIES EMPHASIZE SOCIAL, ECONOMIC, AND POLITICAL REALITIES and place crime within this context. As with social process theories, the **social conflict perspective** focuses on the interaction between groups but views this interaction as one of conflict and maintains that conflict is a fundamental aspect of social life that can never be fully resolved. Various groups within society, defined in terms of their political, economic, or social standing, are seen to compete with one another to promote their own best interests. Crime and criminal activity are the outcome of this struggle. The creation and application of criminal laws is crucial to determining who becomes criminalized; social conflict criminologists see these roles largely filled by that segment of society holding the economic and political power. Formal agencies of social control merely coerce the unempowered and disenfranchised to comply with the rules established by those in power. Laws are a tool of the powerful, useful in keeping others from wresting control over important social institutions. What is considered acceptable and unacceptable behaviour is determined by state-sanctioned laws designed to set boundaries governing such behaviour (see the case of Robert Latimer in the Who's Responsible? box).

Rather than being the result of any consensus or process of dispute resolution, social order rests on the exercise of power through law. Those in power must work ceaselessly to

Social conflict perspective An analytical perspective on social organization that holds that conflict is a fundamental aspect of social life and can never fully be resolved.

remain there, although the structures they impose on society—including the patterns of wealth building that they define as acceptable and the circumstances under which they authorize the exercise of legal power and military might—give them the advantage.

Most social conflict theories of crime causation make the following fundamental assumptions:

- Society is divided by conflict rather than integrated by consensus. Conflict between groups is inevitable and is based on differences held to be socially significant.
- Society is made up of many social groups based on political and economic power. Diversity among groups is also based on distinctions such as social class, gender, and sexual orientation.
- The basic nature of group conflict centres on the exercise of political power. Political power is the key to influence. Differences in social class, and in particular those arrangements within society that maintain class differences, are the focus for criminological study.
- Powerful groups make laws that reflect and protect their interests. Law is a tool of power and furthers the interests of those powerful enough to make the law.
- Crime is an outcome of conflict between those who have power and those who do not.

10.2 | LEARNING OBJECTIVE

TYPES OF SOCIAL CONFLICT THEORIES

VARIOUS THEORIES FOUND UNDER THE RUBRIC OF THE SOCIAL CONFLICT PERSPECTIVE emphasize different root causes of the conflict. This chapter considers a number of these theories, including radical and critical criminology, feminist criminology, the peacemaking model, restorative justice, and the left-realist perspective. Radical criminology is based on Marxist political thought and contends that current inequities in social standing and economic power are the main contributors to the reality of crime. Critical criminology is distinguished from radical criminology by its emphasis on a critique of the relationship between social classes; it is generally viewed as more reactive than the proactive approach taken by the radical criminological outlook. Feminist criminology sees the inequities that exist within society as drawn along gender lines. Peacemaking criminology advocates the reduction of crime through the cooperative efforts of criminal justice agencies and the citizens they serve. Restorative justice and alternative dispute resolution models have their roots in this perspective. Finally, the left-realist perspective moves away from a political-ideological explanation of crime and criminality toward the contention that crime is very "real," especially for marginalized segments of society. Table 10.1 provides an overview of the social conflict theories discussed in this chapter.

Table 10.1 Social Conflict Theories

Theory	Radical Criminology	Left-Realist Criminology	Feminist Criminology	Peacemaking Criminology
Period	1960s–present	1980s–present	1970s–present	1980s–present
Theorists	Karl Marx and others	Walter DeKeseredy and others	Freda Adler and others	Harold Pepinsky and others
Concepts	Social class, bourgeoisie, proletariat	Radical realism, critical realism, street crime, social justice, crime control	Power-control issues, gender socialization, empowerment	Compassionate criminology, restorative justice

Radical Criminology

The social conflict perspective is thoroughly entrenched in **radical criminology,** which is also related to schools of thought referred to as *new, critical,* or *Marxist criminology.* Radical criminology, which appeared on the criminology scene in the 1970s, has its roots in the writings of 19th-century social utopian thinkers. Primary among them is Karl Marx, whose writings on the conflicts inherent in capitalism led to the formulation of communist ideals and the rise of communist societies in the 20th century.

According to Marx, two fundamental social classes exist in any capitalist society: the haves or the **bourgeoisie,** who are capitalists and wealthy owners of the means of production (factories, businesses, land, natural resources), and the have-nots or the **proletariat,** who are relatively uneducated workers without power. Although Marx was German, the terms *proletariat* and *bourgeoisie* were taken from Marx's knowledge of the French language and are in turn derived from Latin. In ancient Rome, for example, that city's lowest class was propertyless, and its members were individually referred to as *proletarius.*

According to Marx, the members of the proletariat, possessing neither capital nor the means of production, must earn their living by selling their labour, and the powerful bourgeoisie oppose the proletariat in an ongoing class struggle. Marx saw such struggle between classes as inevitable to the evolution of any capitalistic society and

Radical criminology A perspective that holds that the causes of crime are rooted in social conditions empowering the wealthy and the politically well organized but disenfranchising the less fortunate.

Bourgeoisie The "haves," or the class of people that owns the means of production, in Marxist theory.

Proletariat The "have-nots," or the working class, in Marxist theory.

WHO'S RESPONSIBLE—THE INDIVIDUAL OR SOCIETY?

"Compassionate Homicide": The Law and Robert Latimer

Robert Latimer, a farmer working a spread in Saskatchewan northwest of Saskatoon, killed his 12-year-old daughter, Tracy, on October 24, 1993. There has never been any doubt about this.

Latimer told police he did it. He said he loved his daughter and could not bear to watch her suffer from a severe form of cerebral palsy. So he placed her in the cab of his Chevy pickup, ran a hose from the exhaust to the cab, climbed into the box of the truck, sat on a tire, and watched her die.

Tracy was a 40-pound quadriplegic, a 12-year-old who functioned at the level of a three-month-old. She had been repeatedly operated on and at the time of her murder was due for more surgery, this time to remove a thigh bone. She could not walk, talk, or feed herself, though she responded to affection and occasionally smiled. Tracy was in constant, excruciating pain yet, for reasons not entirely clear, could not be treated with a painkiller stronger than Tylenol.

On November 4, 1993, Latimer was charged with first-degree murder. A year later, he was convicted of second-degree murder.

End of story?

No.

The issues arising from the Latimer case are momentous. Should courts abide by the letter or the spirit of the law? Would a decision favourable to Latimer legalize euthanasia, mercy killing? Would it put the disabled in danger? Would it mean the end of mandatory minimum sentences for convicted persons?

The killing of Tracy Latimer has been called an act of "compassionate homicide." Others warn that leniency for Latimer, by means of a constitutional exception, would have shown that the disabled are regarded as second-class citizens.

Following his first conviction, the Latimer case became horrendously complex. The Supreme Court ordered a new trial when it was learned that the RCMP, acting on orders from the Crown, had possibly tainted the case by questioning potential jurors on their views on religion, abortion, and mercy killing.

Latimer stood trial again in October 1997. A month later he was convicted, again, of second-degree murder.

The jury recommended he be eligible for parole after a year, even though the minimum sentence for second-degree murder is 25 years with no chance of parole for 10 years.

(Continued)

"Compassionate Homicide": The Law and Robert Latimer

(Automatic minimum sentences for first- and second-degree murder have been mandatory since 1976, as a trade-off for the abolition of capital punishment.)

New legal ground was broken in December 1997, when Justice Ted Noble—trying to distinguish between mercy killing and cold-blooded murder—granted Latimer a constitutional exemption from the minimum sentence for second-degree murder. He explained that, for Latimer, the minimum sentence would constitute "cruel and unusual punishment."

Noble carefully detailed the reasons for his decision, anticipating the controversy it would provoke—and the likelihood it would be appealed. He said the law "recognizes that the moral culpability or the moral blameworthiness of murder can vary from one convicted offender to another." He called Tracy Latimer's murder a "rare act of homicide that was committed for caring and altruistic reasons. That is why for want of a better term this is called compassionate homicide."

Noble also described Latimer's relationship with Tracy as "that of a loving and protective parent" who wanted to end his daughter's suffering. Noble said Latimer "is not a threat to society, nor does he require any rehabilitation."

The Crown argued that Tracy was a relatively cheerful child, and her rights were violated by being killed by her father. According to the Crown brief presented at Latimer's second trial:

"Tracy enjoyed outings, one of which was to the circus, where she smiled when the horses went by. She also responded to visits by her family, smiling and looking happy to see them.

"There is no dispute that through her life, Tracy at times suffered considerable pain. As well, the quality of her life was limited by her severe disability. But the pain she suffered was not unremitting, and her life had value and quality."

Nearly a year later, in November 1998, the Saskatchewan Court of Appeal overturned Noble's ruling, imposing the mandatory minimum sentence: 25 years, with no parole before 10 years.

Then, on January 18, 2001, the Supreme Court of Canada upheld his conviction and life sentence.

His first bid for day parole in December 2007 was denied after a hearing at a Victoria prison. However, that decision was overturned two months later, and Latimer was ultimately released for day parole on March 13, 2008.

At the time of the 2001 Supreme Court ruling, critics worried that a decision soft on Latimer would send a signal to many convicted murderers that they, too, may be victims

Str Kevin Frayer/The Canadian Press

Robert Latimer

of "cruel and unusual punishment" and are eligible for constitutional exceptions to reduce their mandatory minimum sentences.

In February 2010 the National Parole Board approved Latimer's application to continue day parole in British Columbia, where he was working and studying to become an electrician. Latimer was allowed to be at work or school during the day and return to a halfway house five evenings a week. He asked the Parole Board to reverse those conditions so he could spend five days a week at an apartment he rented and two at the halfway house. In November 2010, Latimer was granted full parole. In 2015, the Parole Board of Canada ruled that Latimer can travel freely outside Canada.

An old legal maxim is "Hard cases make bad law." Whether this applies to the case of Robert Latimer remains to be seen.

Think about it:

1. How is it that some people view Robert Latimer as a common criminal while others see him as a hero? How can otherwise law-abiding citizens condone the killing of a child with severe disabilities?

2. What does the debate over euthanasia have to tell us about the role of law in society and about how laws are made and enforced?

3. What other issues can you identify that are officially law violations but that have numerous proponents?

Sources: Based on Martin O'Malley and Owen Wood, "'Compassionate Homicide': The Law and Robert Latimer," *CBC News Online*, December 6, 2012. The Canadian Press, "Robert Latimer Can Travel Freely Outside Canada: National Parole Board", *Huffington Post*, March 3, 2015

believed that the natural outcome of such struggle would be the overthrow of capitalistic social order and the birth of a truly classless, or communist, society.

Central to the perspective of radical criminology is the notion of **social class** (distinctions made between individuals based on characteristics such as race, religion, education, profession, income, wealth, family background, housing, artistic tastes, aspirations, cultural pursuits, child-rearing habits, speech, and accent). Some maintain that "class is nothing but an abbreviation to describe a way of living, thinking, and feeling."[3] Individuals are assigned to classes by others and by themselves on the basis of characteristics that are both ascribed and achieved. Ascribed attributes are those with which a person is born, such as race or gender, while achieved characteristics are acquired through personal effort or chance over the course of one's life and include such things as level of education, income, place of residence, and profession.

Although Marx concerned himself with only two social classes, most social scientists today talk in terms of at least three groups: upper, middle, and lower classes. Some have distinguished among five hierarchically arranged classes (the real upper, semi-upper, limited-success, working, and real lower) while further subdividing classes "horizontally" according to ascribed characteristics such as race and religion.[4]

Within the discipline of criminology, George Vold helped to create the field of radical criminology. In his 1958 work entitled *Theoretical Criminology*, Vold described crime as the product of political conflict between groups, seeing it as a natural expression of the ongoing struggle for power, control, and material well-being.[5] Conflict is "a universal form of interaction," and groups are naturally in conflict as their interests and purposes "overlap, encroach on one another and (tend to) be competitive."[6] Vold's most succinct observation of the role conflict plays in contributing to crime stated: "The whole political process of law making, law breaking, and law enforcement becomes a direct reflection of deep-seated and fundamental conflicts between interest groups. Those who produce legislative majorities win control over the power, and dominate the policies that decide who is likely to be involved in violation of the law."[7]

From Vold's point of view, the body of laws that characterizes any society is a political statement, and crime is a political definition imposed largely upon those whose interests lie outside of that which the powerful, through the law, define as acceptable. Conflict theorists of the early and mid-1900s saw in the concept of social class the rudimentary ingredients of other important concepts, such as authority, power, and conflict. Ralf Dahrendorf wrote that "classes are social conflict groups the determinant of which can be found in the participation in or exclusion from the exercise of authority."[8] For Dahrendorf, conflict was ubiquitous, fundamental, and coextensive: "Not the presence but the absence of conflict is surprising and abnormal, and we have good reason to be suspicious if we find a society or social organization that displays no evidence of conflict."[9]

From Dahrendorf's perspective, power and authority are most at issue between groups and are the cause of class conflicts. It is out of conflict that change—either destructive or constructive—arises. Destructive change brings a lessening of social order, whereas constructive change increases cohesiveness within society.

Another mid-20th-century conflict theorist, Austin Turk, said that in the search for an explanation of criminality, "one is led to investigate the tendency of laws to penalize persons whose behavior is more characteristic of the less powerful than of the more powerful and the extent to which some persons and groups can and do use legal processes and agencies to maintain and enhance their power position vis-à-vis other persons and groups."[10] In his 1969 seminal work, *Criminality and Legal Order*, Turk wrote that in any attempt to explain criminality, "it is more useful to view the social order as mainly a pattern of conflict" rather than to offer explanations for crime based

Social class A distinction made between individuals on the basis of important social characteristics.

on behavioural or psychological approaches.[11] Turk, like most other conflict criminologists, saw the law as a powerful tool in the service of prominent social groups seeking continued control over others and crime as a natural consequence of such intergroup struggle, resulting from the definitions imposed by the laws of the powerful upon the disapproved strivings of the unempowered.

Radical Criminology Today

Contemporary radical criminology holds that the causes of crime are rooted in social conditions that empower the wealthy and the politically well organized but disenfranchise those less fortunate. William J. Chambliss, a well-known spokesperson for radical thinkers, summarized the modern perspective in these words: "What makes the behavior of some criminal is the coercive power of the state to enforce the will of the ruling class."[12]

In 1971, Chambliss, along with Robert T. Seidman, published a critically acclaimed volume entitled *Law, Order, and Power*. Their work represented something of a bridge between earlier conflict theorists and the more radical approach of Marxists. Through its emphasis on social class, class interests, and class conflict, *Law, Order, and Power* presented a Marxist perspective stripped of any overt references to capitalism as the root cause of crime. "The more economically stratified a society becomes, the more it becomes necessary for the dominant groups in the society to enforce through coercion the norms of conduct which guarantee their supremacy."[13] Chambliss and Seidman outlined their position in four propositions:[14]

1. The conditions of one's life affect one's values and norms.

2. Complex societies are composed of groups with widely different life conditions and highly disparate and conflicting sets of norms.

3. The probability of a given group's having its particular normative system embodied in law is not distributed equally but is closely related to the political and economic position of that group.

4. The higher a group's political or economic position, the greater the probability that its views will be reflected in laws.

Chambliss also believed that middle- and upper-class criminals are more apt to escape apprehension and punishment by the criminal justice system, not because they are any smarter or more capable of hiding their crimes than are lower-class offenders but because of a "very rational choice on the part of the legal system to pursue those violators that the community will reward them for pursuing and to ignore those violators who have the capability for causing trouble for the agencies."[15]

By the 1970s, Chambliss's writings assumed a much more Marxist flavour. In a 1975 article, Chambliss once again recognized the huge power gap separating the "haves" from the "have-nots," saying that crime is created by actions of the ruling class, who define as criminal any undertakings and activities contravening their interests yet sometimes violate the criminal law with impunity because it is their own creation.[16] Soon the Marxist flavour of Chambliss's writing had become undeniable: "As capitalist societies industrialize and the gap between the bourgeoisie and the proletariat widens, penal law will expand in an effort to coerce the proletariat into submission."[17] For Chambliss, the economic consequences of crime within a capitalistic society are partially what perpetuate it. Socialist societies, he wrote, should reflect much lower crime rates than capitalist societies because a "less intense class struggle should reduce the forces leading to and the functions of crime."[18]

Although Chambliss provided much of the intellectual bedrock of contemporary radical criminology, that school of thought found its most eloquent expression in the writings of Richard Quinney, who attempted to challenge and change American social life for the better by setting forth in 1974 his six Marxist propositions for an understanding of crime:[19]

1. American society is based on an advanced capitalist economy.

2. The state is organized to serve the interests of the dominant economic class, the capitalist ruling class.

3. Criminal law is an instrument of the state and ruling class to maintain and perpetuate the existing social and economic order.

4. Crime control in capitalist society is accomplished through a variety of institutions and agencies established and administered by a governmental elite, representing ruling-class interests, for the purpose of establishing domestic order.

5. The contradictions of advanced capitalism—the disjunction between existence and essence—require that the subordinate classes remain oppressed by whatever means necessary, especially through the coercion and violence of the legal system.

6. Only with the collapse of capitalist society and the creation of a new society, based on socialist principles, will there be a solution to the crime problem.

Later, Quinney published *Class, State, and Crime*, in which he argued that almost all crimes committed by members of the lower classes are necessary for the survival of individual members of those classes and are actually an attempt by the socially disenfranchised "to exist in a society where *survival* is not assured by other, collective means."[20] He concluded, "Crime is inevitable under capitalist conditions" because crime is "a response to the material conditions of life. Permanent unemployment—and the acceptance of that condition—can result in a form of life where criminality is an appropriate and consistent response."[21] The solution offered by Quinney to the problem of crime was the development of a socialist society. "The *ultimate meaning* of crime in the development of capitalism is the need for a socialist society."[22]

Contemporary radical criminology attributes much of the existing propensity toward criminality to differences in social class, and in particular to those arrangements within society that maintain class differences. Quinney explained, "Classes are an expression of the underlying forces of the capitalist mode of production."[23]

Today's radical criminologies can be divided into two schools: structuralist and instrumentalist. **Structural Marxism** sees capitalism as a self-maintaining system in which the law and the justice system work together to perpetuate the existing system of power relationships. Even the rich are subject to certain laws designed to prevent them from engaging in forms of behaviour that might undermine the system of which they are a part. Laws regulating trade practices and monopolies, for example, regulate the behaviour of the powerful and serve to ensure the survival of the capitalist system. **Instrumental Marxism** sees criminal law and the justice system as tools that the powerful use to control the poor and to keep them disenfranchised. The legal system serves not only to perpetuate the power relationships that exist within society but also to keep control in the hands of those who are already powerful. A popular book by Jeffrey H. Reiman, entitled *The Rich Get Richer and the Poor Get Prison*, is built upon this premise, contending that the criminal justice system is biased against the poor from start to finish and that well-to-do members of society control the criminal justice system from the definition of crime through the process of arrest, trial, and sentencing.[24]

Reiman also claimed that many of the actions taken by well-off people, such as refusal to make workplaces safe, refusal to curtail deadly industrial pollution, promotion of unnecessary surgery, and prescription of unnecessary drugs, should be defined

Structural Marxism A perspective that holds that the structural institutions of society influence the behaviour of individuals and groups by virtue of the type of relationships created.

Instrumental Marxism A perspective that holds that those in power intentionally create laws and social institutions that serve their own interests and that keep others from becoming powerful.

as criminal but are not. This kind of self-serving behaviour creates occupational and environmental hazards for the poor and for those who are less well-off and produces as much death, destruction, and financial loss as the so-called crimes of the poor.

Critical Criminology   Some writers distinguish between critical criminology and radical criminology, claiming that the former is simply a way of critiquing social relationships leading to crime, whereas the latter constitutes a proactive call for a radical change in the social conditions that lead to crime. That is, critical criminology provides a focused critique of current social and economic arrangements as they are related to crime, whereas radical criminology issues a call to action and asks for changes in political and economic systems that are responsible for fostering criminality.

Gresham Sykes explained **critical criminology** this way: "It forces an inquiry into precisely how the normative content of the criminal law is internalized in different segments of society, and how norm-holding is actually related to behavior."[25] Sykes's use of the word *inquiry* reveals the central role of critical inquiry in critical criminology.

A cogent example of the critical perspective in contemporary criminology can be had in the work of Elliott Currie, who claimed that "'market societies'—those in which the pursuit of private gain becomes the dominant organizing principle of social and economic life—are especially likely to breed high levels of violent crime."[26] Market societies are characterized by more than free enterprise and a free-market economy; they are societies in which the striving after personal economic gain runs rampant and becomes the hallmark of social life. The conditions endemic to market societies lead to high crime rates because they undercut and overwhelm more traditional principles that "have historically sustained individuals, families, and communities." North American society, and the United States in particular, is the world's premier market society, and its culture provides "a particularly fertile breeding ground for serious violent crime." According to Currie, seven "profoundly criminogenic and closely intertwined mechanisms" operate in a market society to produce crime:

1. "The progressive destruction of livelihood," which results from the long-term absence of opportunities for stable and rewarding work and is a consequence of the fact that market societies view labour "simply as a cost to be reduced" rather than as an asset with intrinsic value.

2. "The growth of extremes of economic inequality and material deprivation," which causes many children to spend their developmental years in poverty.

3. "The withdrawal of public services and supports, especially for families and children," resulting from the fact that "it is a basic operating principle of market society to keep the public sector small."

4. "The erosion of informal and communal networks of mutual support, supervision, and care," which is brought about by the high mobility of the workforce characteristic of market societies.

5. "The spread of a materialistic, neglectful, and 'hard' culture," which exalts brutal forms of individualized competition.

6. "The unregulated marketing of the technology of violence," which includes ready availability of guns, an emphasis on advancing technologies of destruction (such as the military), and mass-marketed violence on television and in other media.

7. "The weakening of social and political alternatives," which leaves people unable to cope effectively with the forces of the market society, undermines their communities, and destroys valuable interpersonal relationships.

Currie suggested that as more nations emulate the "market society" culture of the United States crime rates throughout the world will rise and that an increasing

Critical criminology   A perspective that holds that crime is the natural product of a capitalist system.

In the fall of 2011, a series of protests swept through downtown Toronto. Known as the Occupy Toronto movement, participants protested against the corrosive power that they claimed major banks and multinational corporations held over the democratic process. They called themselves the "99 percent," referring to their belief that the wealthiest 1 percent of the population controls the Canadian economic and political systems. How would the social conflict perspective interpret the actions of Occupy Toronto?

Torontonian/Alamy Stock Photo

emphasis on punishment and the growth of huge prison systems will consequently characterize most of the world's nations in the 21st century.

Critique of Radical Criminology   Radical criminology has been criticized for its nearly exclusive emphasis on methods of social change at the expense of well-developed theory. As William Pelfrey stated, "It is in the Radical School of Criminology that theory is almost totally disregarded, except as something to criticize, and radical methods are seen as optimum."[27] Radical criminology can also be criticized for failing to recognize what appears to be at least a fair degree of public consensus about the nature of crime—that crime is undesirable and that criminal activity should be controlled. If criminal activity was a true expression of the sentiments of the politically and economically disenfranchised, as some radical criminologists claim, then public opinion might be expected to offer support for at least certain forms of crime, but even the sale of illicit drugs (a type of crime that may provide an alternative path to riches for the otherwise disenfranchised) is frequently condemned by residents of working-class communities.[28]

An effective criticism of Marxist criminology, in particular, centres on the fact that Marxist thinkers appear to confuse issues of personal politics with what could otherwise be social reality, allowing personal values and political leanings to enter the criminological arena and sacrificing their objectivity. Jackson Toby claimed that Marxist and radical thinkers are simply building upon an "old tradition of sentimentality toward those who break social rules."[29] Such sentimentality can be easily discounted when we realize that "color television sets and automobiles are stolen more often than food and blankets."[30]

Marxist criminology has also been refuted by contemporary thinkers who find that it falls short in appreciating the multiplicity of factors that contribute to the problem of crime. Hermann Mannheim critiqued Marxist assumptions by showing how "subsequent developments" have revealed that "Marx was wrong in [his] thinking" in several areas: (1) that "there could be only two classes in a capitalist society," (2) that "class struggle was entirely concerned with the question of private property in the means of production," (3) that "the only way in which fundamental social changes could be effected was by violent social revolution," and (4) that "all conflicts were class conflicts and all social change could be explained in terms of class conflicts."[31]

Mannheim also pointed out that the development of a semiskilled workforce along with the advent of highly skilled and well-educated workers has led to the creation of a multiplicity of classes within contemporary capitalistic societies. The growth of such classes, said Mannheim, effectively spreads the available wealth in those societies where such workers are employed and reduces the likelihood of revolution.

Marxist criminology has suffered a considerable loss of prestige among many would-be followers in the wake of the collapse of the former Soviet Union and its client states in Eastern Europe and other parts of the world. Many would argue that the work of writers such as Quinney and Chambliss presaged the decline of Soviet influence and had already moved Marxist and radical criminology into new areas. The work of Currie and others has since led in a post-Marxist direction while retaining a critical emphasis on the principles out of which radical criminology was fashioned. Today's radical criminologists have largely rescinded calls for revolutionary change and escalated their demands for the eradication of gender, racial, and other inequalities within the criminal justice system; the elimination of prisons; the abolition of capital punishment; and an end to police misconduct.

EMERGING CONFLICT THEORIES

THE RADICAL IDEAS ASSOCIATED WITH MID-20TH-CENTURY MARXIST CRIMINOLOGY contributed to the formation of a number of new and innovative approaches to crime and criminology, such as left-realist criminology, feminist criminology, and peacemaking criminology (including restorative justice). It is to these perspectives that we now turn our attention.

Left-Realist Criminology

Left-realist criminology An approach to criminology based on ideas inherent in the perspectives of left realism.

Left realism A social conflict perspective that insists on a pragmatic assessment of crime and its associated problems.

Left-realist criminology, a natural outgrowth of practical concerns with street crime, the fear of crime, and everyday victimization, approaches criminology based on the ideas of **left realism**, which uses a pragmatic assessment of crime and its problems. Left-realist criminology faults radical-critical criminologists for romanticizing street crime and the criminals who commit it. It does not reject the conflict perspective inherent in radical-critical criminology but shifts the focus to the assessment of crime and the needs of crime victims, seeking to portray crime in terms understandable to those most often affected by it—victims and their families, offenders, and criminal justice personnel. The test insisted upon by realist criminology is not whether a particular perspective on crime control or an explanation of crime causation complies with rigorous academic criteria but whether it speaks meaningfully to those faced with crime on a daily basis. "For realists crime is no less harmful to its victims because of its socially constructed origins."[32]

Left-realist criminology is generally considered synonymous with left realism (also called *radical realism* or *critical realism*) but tends to distance itself from some of the more visionary claims of early radical and Marxist theory.[33] Daniel J. Curran and Claire M. Renzetti portrayed left realism as a natural consequence of increasingly conservative attitudes toward crime and criminals in both Europe and North America: "Though not successful in converting many radicals to the right, this new conservatism did lead a number of radical criminologists to temper their views a bit and to take what some might call a less romanticized look at street crime."[34]

Some authors have credited Walter DeKeseredy[35] with popularizing left-realist notions in North America, and Jock Young[36] has been identified as a major source of left-realist writings in England. Prior to the writings of DeKeseredy and Young, radical criminology, with its emphasis on the crime-inducing consequences of existing power structures, tended to portray the ruling class as the "real criminals" and saw street criminals as social rebels who were acting out of felt deprivation; DeKeseredy and Young were successful in refocusing leftist theories onto the serious consequences of street crime and upon the crimes of the lower classes. Left realists argued that victims of crime are often the poor and disenfranchised who fall prey to criminals with similar backgrounds and saw the criminal justice system and its agents not as pawns of the powerful but rather as institutions that could offer useful services if modifications were made to reduce their use of force and increase their sensitivity toward the public.

A central tenet of left realism is the claim that radical ideas must be translated into realistic social policies if contemporary criminology is to have any practical relevance. Concrete suggestions with respect to community policing models are indicative of the direction left realists are headed. Instead of seeing the police as oppressors working on behalf of the state, left realists recommend that police work with, and answer to, the communities they serve.[37] The major goal of left realism is to achieve "a fair and orderly society" through a practical emphasis on social justice.[38]

Critique of Left-Realist Criminology Left-realist criminology has been criticized for representing more of an ideological emphasis than a theory. As Don C. Gibbons explained, "Left realism can best be described as a general perspective centered on injunctions to 'take crime seriously' and to 'take crime control seriously' rather than as a well-developed criminological perspective."[39] Realist criminologists appear to build upon preexisting theoretical frameworks but rarely offer new propositions or testable hypotheses. They do, however, frequently suggest crime-control approaches that are in keeping with the needs of the victimized. Policies promulgated by left realists understandably include an emphasis on community policing, neighbourhood justice centres, and dispute-resolution mechanisms. Piers Beirne and James W. Messerschmidt summarized the situation this way: "What left realists have essentially accomplished is an attempt to theorize about conventional crime realistically while simultaneously developing a 'radical law and order' program for curbing such behavior."[40]

Feminist Criminology

As some writers have observed, "Women have been virtually invisible in criminological analysis until recently and much theorizing has proceeded as though criminality is restricted to men."[41] Others have put it this way: "Criminological theory assumes a woman is like a man."[42] But beginning in the 1970s, advances in feminist theory were applied to criminology, resulting in what has been called a **feminist criminology** (a model redirecting criminologists' thinking to include gender awareness).

Feminism is a way of seeing the world, not a sexual orientation. To be a feminist is to "combine a female mental perspective with a sensitivity for those social issues that influence primarily women."[43] Central to understanding feminist thought is the realization that feminism views gender in terms of power relationships. According to feminist approaches, men have traditionally held much more power in the patriarchal structure of Western society than women and have excluded women from much decision making in socially significant areas, and sexist attitudes—deeply ingrained notions of male superiority—have perpetuated inequality between the sexes. The consequences of sexism and the unequal gender-based distribution of power have been far-reaching, affecting fundamental aspects of social roles and personal expectations at all levels.

Five strands of feminist thought inform feminist criminology today: liberal feminism, radical feminism, Marxist feminism, socialist feminism, and postmodern feminism. Each of these perspectives argues that conflict in society is based on inequalities focused around issues of gender.

Feminist criminology A corrective model intended to redirect the thinking of mainstream criminologists to include gender awareness.

Liberal feminism A feminist perspective in criminology that sees gender-role socialization as the primary source of women's oppression.

Radical feminism A perspective that sees patriarchy as the cause of women's oppression.

Patriarchy The tradition of male dominance.

Marxist feminism A perspective in feminist criminology that sees the oppression of women as caused by their subordinate class status within capitalist societies.

Socialist feminism A perspective in modern criminology that sees gender oppression as a consequence of the interaction between the economic structure of society and gender-based roles.

Postmodern feminism A perspective in modern criminology that questions the social construction of concepts typically used in discussions of crime and justice.

Liberal feminism sees gender-role socialization as the primary source of women's oppression.[44] Liberal feminists describe a power-based and traditional domination of women's bodies and minds by men throughout history and blame present inequalities on the development within culture and society of "separate and distinct spheres of influence and traditional attitudes about the appropriate role of men and women."[45] Liberal feminists call for elimination of traditional divisions of power and labour between the sexes as a way of eliminating inequality and promoting social harmony.

Radical feminism sees **patriarchy**, or male dominance, as the cause of women's oppression, depicting men as being fundamentally brutish, aggressive, and violent and controlling women through sexuality by taking advantage of both women's biological dependence during childbearing years and their lack of physical strength relative to men. The exploitation of women by men triggers women's deviant behaviour, because young women who are sexually or physically exploited may run away or abuse substances and become criminalized, so the elimination of male domination should reduce crime rates for women and "even precipitate a decrease in male violence against women."[46]

The oppression of women caused by their subordinate working-class status in capitalist societies is the main tenet of **Marxist feminism**. Within capitalist society, women may be drawn into crime commission in an effort to support themselves and their children; men commit violent street crimes more often, whereas women commit property and vice crimes.[47]

Socialist feminism, a fourth perspective, sees gender oppression as a consequence of the interaction between the economic structure of society and gender-based roles. Egalitarian societies would be built around socialist or Marxist principles with the aim of creating a society that is free of gender and class divisions.

The social construction of concepts typically used in any discussion of criminology—including concepts like justice and crime—are questioned by **postmodern feminism**. According to criminologist Amanda Burgess-Proctor, postmodern feminism departs from the other feminist perspectives by questioning the existence of any one "truth," including "women's oppression," and "postmodern feminists reject fixed categories and universal concepts in favor of multiple truths and as such examine the effects of discourse and symbolic representation on claims about knowledge."[48]

Feminist criminology points out the inequities inherent in patriarchal forms of thought. Patriarchy can be defined as a "set of social relations of power in which the male gender appropriates the labour power of women and controls their sexuality."[49] Early works in the field of feminist criminology include *Sisters in Crime* by Freda Adler[50] and *Women and Crime* by Rita J. Simon,[51] both published in 1975. In these books, the authors attempted to explain existing divergences in crime rates between men and women as being due primarily to socialization rather than biology. Women were taught to believe in personal limitations, faced reduced socio-economic opportunities, and, as a result, suffered from lower aspirations. As gender equality increased, these authors said, it could be expected that male and female criminality would take on similar characteristics, but such has not been the case, and the approach of Adler and Simon has not been validated by observations surrounding increased gender equality over the past few decades. One exception, however, comes from Mexico, where the number of women incarcerated for federal crimes grew 400 percent between 2007 and 2012.[52] Most of the crimes for which women are serving time in Mexican federal prisons are drug related, and it may be that that country's crackdown on drug crime over the past several years has had more of an impact on the number of imprisoned women than actual changes in the rate of crime committed by Mexican women.

Another early work, *Women, Crime and Criminology*, was published in 1977 by British sociologist Carol Smart;[53] it sensitized criminologists to sexist traditions within the field. Smart pointed out that men and women perceive and experience the world in different ways. She showed how important it is for women to have a voice in interpreting the behaviour of other women, as opposed to women's behaviour being interpreted from a man's standpoint.

Early feminist theorizing may not have borne the fruit that some researchers anticipated, but it has led to a heightened awareness of gender issues within criminology. Two of the most insightful proponents of the usefulness of applying feminist thinking to criminological analysis, Kathleen Daly and Meda Chesney-Lind, pointed out that "gender differences in crime suggest that crime may not be so normal after all."[54] Traditional understandings about what is typical about crime are derived from the study of men, who commit most crimes. The relative lack of criminality exhibited by women is rarely acknowledged as having criminological significance, which calls into question many traditional assumptions about crime—especially the assumption that crime is somehow a "normal" part of social life. Daly and Chesney-Lind have identified the following five elements of feminist thought that set it apart from other types of social and political thought:[55]

1. Gender is not a natural fact but a complex social, historical, and cultural product that is related to, not simply derived from, biological sex differences and differing reproductive capacities.

2. Gender and gender relations order social life and social institutions in fundamental ways.

3. Gender relations and constructs of masculinity and femininity are not symmetrical but are based on an organizing principle of men's superiority and their socio- and political-economic dominance over women.

4. Systems of knowledge reflect men's views of the natural and social world; the production of knowledge is gendered.

5. Women should be at the centre, not the periphery, of intellectual inquiry; they should not be invisible or treated as appendages to men.

In a more recent analysis of feminist criminology, Susan Caulfield and Nancy Wonders described "five major contributions that have been made by feminist scholarship and practice" to criminological thinking: (1) a focus on gender as a central organizing principle of contemporary life; (2) an awareness of the importance of power in shaping social relationships; (3) a heightened sensitivity to the way in which social context helps shape human relationships; (4) the recognition that social reality must be understood as a process and that the development of research methods must take this into account; and (5) a commitment to social change as a crucial part of feminist scholarship and practice.[56]

John Hagan built upon defining features of power relationships in his book *Structural Criminology*, in which he explained that power relationships existing in the wider society are effectively "brought home" to domestic settings and are reflected in everyday relationships between men, women, and children within the context of family life.[57] Hagan's approach, termed *power-control theory*, suggested that "family class structure shapes the social reproduction of gender relations, and in turn the social distribution of delinquency."[58] In most middle- and upper-middle-class families, said Hagan, a paternalistic model, in which the father works and the mother supervises the children, is the norm. Under the paternalistic model, girls are controlled by both parents— through male domination and by female role modelling. Boys, however, are less closely controlled and are relatively free to deviate from social norms, resulting in higher levels of delinquency among males. In lower-middle- and lower-class families, however, the paternalistic model is frequently absent.

In a work supportive of Hagan's thesis, Evelyn K. Sommers recently conducted a series of four hour-long interviews with 14 female inmates in a Canadian medium-security prison.[59] Focusing on what led to violations of the criminal law, Sommers identified four common themes to explain the criminality of the women she interviewed: (1) economic and financial need, (2) drug involvement, (3) personal anger rooted in sexual and physical abuse or a sense of loss, and (4) fear. Because "need" was identified as the cause of lawbreaking behaviour by the majority of the women interviewed, Sommers concluded that women's criminality is based on two underlying issues: the effort to maintain connection within relationships (such as between mother and child) and a personal quest for empowerment (as single mothers are expected to be independent and capable of providing for themselves and their children).

In a cogent analysis encompassing much of contemporary feminist theory, Daly and Chesney-Lind suggested that feminist thought is more important for the way it informs and challenges existing criminology than for the new theories it offers. Much current feminist thought within criminology emphasizes the need for gender awareness. Theories of crime causation and prevention, it is suggested, must include women, and more research on gender-related issues in the field is badly needed. Daly and Chesney-Lind explained that "criminologists should begin to appreciate that their discipline and its questions are a product of white, economically privileged men's experiences" and that rates of female criminality, which are lower than those of males, may highlight the fact that criminal behaviour is not as "normal" as once thought.[60] Because modern-day criminological perspectives were mostly developed by Caucasian, middle-class men, the perspectives failed to take into consideration women's "ways of knowing."[61] Feminist criminologists Daly and Chesney-Lind asked the question: Given the current situation in theory development, do existing theories of crime causation apply as well to women as they do to men or "do theories of men's crime apply to women?"[62]

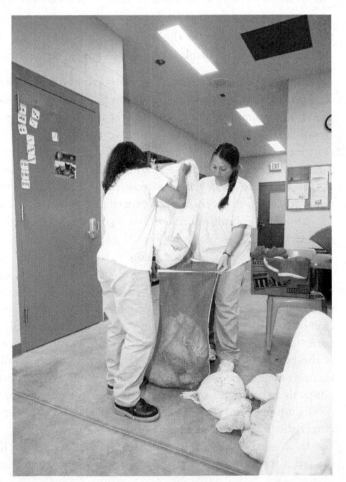

Female inmates at the Edmonton Remand Centre. Feminists claim that much of today's criminology is male centred and that the special needs and interests of women are rarely considered when discussing crimes committed by females. What role does gender play in research on crime and criminality?

Mikael Karlsson/Alamy Stock Photo

Other feminists have analyzed the process by which laws are created and legislation passed and concluded that modern-day statutes frequently represent characteristically masculine modes of thought. Such analysts have concluded that existing criminal laws are overly rational and hierarchically structured, reflecting traditionally male ways of organizing the social world.[63] Until recently, many jurisdictions viewed assault victims differently based on the gendered relationships involved in the offence. *Assault* is defined as an attack by one person upon another, but until the last few decades of the 20th century, domestic violence statutes tended to downplay the seriousness of the attacks involved, giving the impression that because they occurred within the home and the victims were typically women, they weren't as important to the justice system as other forms of assault. Some analysts have suggested that existing laws need to be replaced by, or complemented with, "a system of justice based upon the specifically feminine principles of care, connection, and community."[64]

In the area of social policy, feminist thinkers have pointed to the need for increased controls over men's violence toward women, the creation of alternatives (to supplement the home and traditional family structures) for women facing abuse, and the protection of children. They have also questioned the role of government, culture, and the mass media in promulgating pornography, prostitution, and sexual assault and have generally portrayed ongoing crimes against women as characteristic of continuing traditions in which women are undervalued and controlled. Many radical feminists have suggested the replacement of men with women in positions of power, especially within the justice system and government organizations, while others have noted that such a replacement still would not address needed changes in the structure of the system itself, which is gender-biased due to years of male domination. Centrists, on the other hand, have offered a more balanced approach, believing that individuals of both genders have much to contribute to a workable justice system.[65]

Critique of Feminist Criminology   Some would argue that feminist criminology has yet to live up to its promise because few comprehensive feminist theories of crime were proposed; feminist criminology focused instead on descriptive studies of female involvement in crime.[66] Male violence against women was seen as adding support to the central tenet of feminist criminology (that the relationship between the sexes is primarily characterized by the exercise of power), but that did not make for broad theory building. As one writer explained regarding the current state of feminist criminology, "Feminist theory is a theory in formation."[67]

Feminist criminology has faced criticism from many other directions. Predicted increases in female crime rates have failed to materialize as social opportunities available to both genders have become more balanced, and the gender gap in crime—with males accounting for much more law violation than females—continues to exist. Criminologist Karen Heimer noted that the gender gap is "virtually a truism in criminology. The relationship holds, regardless of whether the data analyzed are arrest rates, victimization incidence reports on characteristics of offenders, or self-reports of criminal behavior. . . . As far as we can tell, males have always been more criminal than females, and gender differences emerge in every society that has been studied systematically."[68] Other critics have pointed to fundamental flaws in feminist thought, asking questions such as, "If men have more power than women, then why are so many more men arrested?"[69]

Some critics have even argued that a feminist criminology is impossible. Daly and Chesney-Lind, for example, agreed that although feminist thought may inform criminology, "a feminist criminology cannot exist because neither feminism nor criminology is a unified set of principles and practices."[70] A criminology built solely on feminist principles is unlikely because neither feminist thought nor criminology meets the strict requirements of formal theory building.

Peacemaking Criminology

Peacemaking criminology
A perspective that holds that crime-control agencies and the citizens they serve should work together to alleviate social problems and human suffering and thus reduce crime.

Throughout much of history, formal agencies of social control—the police, officials of the courts, and corrections personnel—have been seen as pitted against criminal perpetrators and would-be wrongdoers. Crime control has been traditionally depicted in terms of a kind of epic struggle in which diametrically opposed antagonists continuously engage one another but in which only one side can emerge as victorious. Another point of view has come to the fore: **peacemaking criminology** (also called *compassionate criminology*), a form of criminology that has its roots in Christian and Eastern philosophies, advances the notion that crime-control agencies and the citizens they serve should work together to alleviate social problems and human suffering and thus reduce crime.[71] Peacemaking criminology includes the notion of service and suggests that "compassion, wisdom, and love are essential for understanding the suffering of which we are all a part and for practicing a criminology of nonviolence."[72]

Peacemaking criminology was popularized by the works of Harold E. Pepinsky[73] and Richard Quinney.[74] Both Pepinsky and Quinney restated the problem of crime control from one of how to stop crime to one of how to make peace within society and between citizens and criminal justice agencies. Peacemaking criminology draws attention to many issues: (1) perpetuation of violence through the continuation of social policies based on dominant forms of criminological theory; (2) role of education in peacemaking; (3) common-sense theories of crime; (4) crime control as human rights enforcement; and (5) conflict resolution within community settings.[75]

Richard Quinney and John Wildeman summarized well the underpinnings of peacemaking criminology by stating that "a criminology of peacemaking—a nonviolent criminology of compassion and service—seeks to end suffering and thereby eliminate crime."[76]

Other contributors to the peacemaking movement include Bo Lozoff, Michael Braswell, and Clemens Bartollas. In *Inner Corrections*, Lozoff and Braswell claimed that "we are fully aware by now that the criminal justice system in this country is founded on violence. It is a system that assumes that violence can be overcome by violence, evil by evil. Criminal justice at home and warfare abroad are of the same

The principles of restorative justice are reflected in community sentencing conferences such as the one shown here at the Aboriginal Ganootamaage Justice Service Centre in Winnipeg, Manitoba. Do you think this approach is more effective at controlling crime than the adversarial approach? Why or why not?

JoeBryksa/The Canadian Press

principle of violence. This principle sadly dominates much of our criminology."[77] *Inner Corrections* provides meditative techniques and prayers for those seeking to become more compassionate and includes a number of letters from inmates who demonstrate the book's philosophy.

In a work entitled "Correctional Treatment, Peacemaking, and the New Age Movement," Bartollas and Braswell applied New Age principles to correctional treatment:[78] "Most offenders suffered abusive and deprived childhoods. Treatment that focuses on the inner child and such qualities as forgiveness and self-esteem could benefit offenders."[79] In a fundamental sense, peacemaking criminologists exhort their colleagues to transcend personal dichotomies to end the political and ideological divisiveness that separates people.

Restorative Justice

Peacemaking criminology suggests that effective crime prevention can best be achieved by the adoption of a **peace model** based on cooperation rather than on retribution and focused on effective ways of developing a shared consensus on critical issues that have the potential to seriously affect the quality of life. Major issues include crimes like murder and sexual assault but also extend to property rights, rights to the use of new technologies, and the ownership of information; minor issues, including sexual preference, non-violent sexual deviance, gambling, drug use, child-custody claims, and publicly offensive behaviour can be dealt with in ways that require few resources beyond those immediately available in the community.

The concept of **restorative justice** stems from these notions of cooperation and reconciliation rather than from retribution and punishment. Canadian criminologist Ezzat Fattah has been a proponent of alternative forms of justice for several decades. In an article entitled "Restorative and Retributive Justice Models: A Comparison," Fattah critically examined the ineffectiveness of the punishment model.[80] He argued that the punishment model is a costly one, with incarceration being the most expensive sentencing option. Moreover, punishment serves only to treat human beings as a means to an end since it has little positive effect on those being punished. Even though the public and the victim may feel somewhat vindicated by a harsh punitive sentence, punishment does nothing to assist either in the healing process. It is toward the goal of healing that the restorative justice approach reaches.

Restorative justice is defined as an approach to justice that focuses on dealing with the harmful effects of crime by engaging victims, offenders, and the community in a process of reparation and healing. The pain and suffering of victims is central to defining the harm that has resulted from the crime and the manner in which it is to be resolved. The community is active in offering support to victims and in holding offenders accountable for their crimes while giving the offenders the opportunity to make amends.[81]

Whereas the traditional adversarial system of justice defines crime as a violation of rules and a harm to the state, the restorative justice approach views crime as a harm done to the victim and the community. The adversarial system blames and punishes the offender and assumes a win–lose outcome; the restorative justice approach looks to a win–win outcome by focusing on the process of problem solving, including the reintegration of the offender into the community and the preservation of his or her dignity.

Restorative justice models are not new. In Canada, Australia, and the United States, Aboriginal groups have traditionally practised what is commonly referred to as **circle sentencing conferences**, which are based on traditional principles of peacemaking, mediation, and consensus building. Sentencing circles involve participation by the

Peace model An approach to crime control that focuses on effective ways for developing a shared consensus on critical issues that have the potential to seriously affect the quality of life.

Restorative justice A perspective that stresses solutions and restoration rather than imprisonment, punishment, and neglect of victims.

Circle sentencing conferences Groups of community members who actively assist justice authorities by participating in discussions about available sentencing options and plans to reintegrate the offender back into the community.

judge, victim, offender, family or supporters, elders, and other justice and community representatives. Each has input, and the needs of each are considered equally important and worthy of representation. The conference results in sentencing recommendations, which are passed on to the judge with a view to ensuring the protection of the community, healing the victim, and rehabilitating the offender. The judge may accept or reject the recommendations, and community members are responsible for ensuring that the eventual sentence is carried out.

Circle sentencing conferences have been revived in many parts of Canada. Introduced in Yukon, they have become more widely used in other parts of the country, primarily in rural communities. Programs such as the Peigan Nation Youth Traditional Justice Circle on the Peigan Reserve near Lethbridge, Alberta, enable adult and youth criminals to access the circle through pre- or post-charge diversion or even after a guilty plea is entered. The recommendations of the circle are forwarded to the Crown prosecutor, who then endeavours to have the presiding judge incorporate them into the court's final decision. In this way, the circle works in conjunction with the existing criminal justice system. Crown prosecutors screen cases coming through the courts and select those that appear suitable for referral to the circle. It is ultimately the circle's decision whether it wishes to accept any case. Interestingly, in cases where the Crown feels that a sentence of incarceration is warranted, the circle is advised of this at the time of referral. If the circle decides to accept the referral, it will often make a recommendation to the court that will not contradict the Crown's position, thereby ensuring that the court will not have to make a decision contrary to the wishes of the circle.[82]

The principles of restorative justice can be seen in a number of other Canadian criminal justice initiatives. The first **Victim–Offender Reconciliation Program (VORP)** was established by the Mennonite community in Kitchener, Ontario, in 1974, and the model spread rapidly, in various forms; there are now dozens of programs across Canada and hundreds in the United States and throughout Europe.[83] Based on mediation and alternative dispute resolution principles, the VORP involves face-to-face meetings between victim and offender, facilitated by a trained mediator, to discuss the events of the crime and its effects and reach an agreed-upon outcome. The program is usually used with young offenders in the post-charge phase of the criminal justice process or as an alternative measure. The proliferation of community and neighbourhood justice centres has enabled expansion of VORPs and other similar mediation and dispute resolution programs that deal with both criminal and civil cases.

Since the inception of VORPs, restorative-justice principles have been manifest in a number of other criminal justice initiatives. **Family group conferencing** provides a forum for dealing with unanswered questions, emotions, and the victim's right to restitution and reparation resulting from a crime. These conferences involve participation of the victim, the offender, and their family members and supporters. **Community sentencing panels** are composed of volunteers from the community and focus on restorative measures such as restitution, reparation, mediation, and victim involvement. These panels also consider crime prevention by addressing social factors that may contribute to crime. The principles of **community policing**, which emphasize a proactive approach to law enforcement through the establishment of partnerships with the community, can be seen to be compatible with much of the philosophy of restorative justice. The community policing approach has been formally adopted by the Royal Canadian Mounted Police and the Ontario Provincial Police and is practised by most police services across Canada.

The restorative justice philosophy has been embraced and endorsed by all levels of government in Canada as well as by voluntary and community organizations. The federal department Public Safety Canada and the Department of Justice Canada, along

Victim–Offender Reconciliation Program (VORP) A program that gives the offender the opportunity to meet face-to-face with the victim in the presence of a trained mediator in an attempt to reduce the victim's fears while establishing accountability and reparation by the offender for the crime.

Family group conferencing A forum for dealing with unanswered questions, emotions, and the victim's right to restitution and reparation resulting from a crime.

Community sentencing panels Groups composed of volunteers from the community who focus on restorative measures such as restitution, reparation, mediation, and victim involvement.

Community policing A philosophy of policing involving proactive collaboration between the police and the community to prevent and respond to crime and other community problems.

with the Parole Board of Canada and Correctional Service Canada, are exploring the scope of restorative approaches and developing strategies for implementing them.

Restorative Resolutions is a community-based sentencing program that has been operating in Winnipeg, Manitoba, for more than a decade. It is a unique partnership between the John Howard Society of Manitoba and the province of Manitoba's Department of Justice. The high success rate of the program, as demonstrated by its consistently low recidivism rate, can be attributed to a blend of restorative justice principles along with the "what works model" of intervention, providing a viable and more effective alternative to incarceration. Clients must be facing a minimum sentence of six months to be considered. The key to acceptance into the program is a client's willingness to take responsibility for his or her actions by pleading guilty and making a commitment to try to repair the harm done to the victim and the community as a whole. Restorative practices usually take the form of letters of apology to victims, direct restitution paid to victims, and community service work. In terms of intervention, clients often take part in cognitive-behavioural groups that provide them with tools to connect how they think with how they feel, which impacts how they behave and helps them empathize with the victim. Experience demonstrates that clients do make pro-social lifestyle changes more readily after receiving education and support in a group setting. However, the one-to-one work between client and Restorative Resolutions staff also addresses issues related to education and employment, relationships, attitudes, companions, leisure and recreation, addictions, and social patterns. Restorative Resolutions clients are involved in treatment programs, educational upgrading, and/or employment searches. It is always up to the victims to decide how much or even if they want to be involved in the process. Victims who do participate give the program high satisfaction marks and report feeling well served by the program.

One client of the program, reflecting on her experience, stated,

> Going to jail would have been easier for me because I would not have had to be accountable for what I'd done. Restorative Resolutions challenged me to be honest with myself and others for the first time in my life. They forced me to figure out the real reasons why I did what I did, whom I had hurt, what I needed to do to fix it, and most important, how not to fall back into that destructive pattern. My victims now receive money from me on a monthly basis.[84]*

Alternative dispute resolution is another example of the restorative-justice approach and peacemaking perspective. Mediation programs such as dispute resolution centres are characterized by cooperative efforts to reach dispute resolution rather than by the adversarial proceedings characteristic of most Canadian courts. Dispute resolution programs are based on the principle of **participatory justice**, in which all parties to a dispute accept a kind of binding arbitration by neutral parties.

The Ontario Mandatory Mediation Program, operating in a number of centres across Ontario, is designed to help parties involved in civil litigation and estate matters attempt to settle their cases before they get to trial. Under this program, cases are referred to a mediation session early in the litigation process to give parties an opportunity to discuss the issues in dispute. With the assistance of a trained mediator, the parties explore settlement options and may be able to avoid the pre-trial and trial process. The benefits of the program include resolutions that are tailored to the needs of the parties and a greater sense of satisfaction because participants play an active role in resolving their dispute rather than having a solution determined by a judge.

Participatory justice A relatively informal type of justice case processing that makes use of local community resources rather than requiring traditional forms of official intervention.

---

*From Restorative Resolutions, published by The John Howard Society of Manitoba. © 2006.

Table 10.2 Differences between Retributive and Restorative Justice

Retributive Justice	Restorative Justice
Crime is an act against the state, a violation of a law, an abstract idea.	Crime is an act against another person or the community.
The criminal justice system controls crime.	Crime control lies primarily with the community.
Offender accountability is defined as taking punishment.	Offender accountability is defined as assuming responsibility and taking action to repair harm.
Crime is an individual act with individual responsibility.	Crime has both individual and social dimensions of responsibility.
Victims are peripheral to the process of resolving a crime.	Victims are central to the process of resolving a crime.
The offender is defined by deficits.	The offender is defined by the capacity to make reparation.
The emphasis is on adversarial relationships.	The emphasis is on dialogue and negotiation.
Pain is imposed to punish, deter, and prevent.	Restitution is a means of restoring both parties; the goal is reconciliation.
The community is on the sidelines, represented abstractly by the state.	The community is the facilitator in the restorative process.
The response is focused on the offender's past behaviour.	The response is focused on harmful consequences of the offender's behaviour; the emphasis is on the future and on reparation.
There is dependence on criminal justice professionals.	There is direct involvement by both the offender and the victim.

Source: Based on Gordon Bazemore and Mark S. Umbreit, *Balanced and Restorative Justice: Program Summary* (Washington, DC: Office of Juvenile Justice and Delinquency Prevention, 1994), p. 7.

The restorative justice approach has often been criticized for its vagueness of definition and direction. The term "community," for example, is an abstract one and has been used indiscriminately. Not all communities are clearly defined, nor are they all capable of engaging in partnerships that will sustain a restorative-justice approach; for some, involving the community in restorative justice is seen as a quick fix for a crime issue that may require a more traditional approach. Some critics claim that the lack of due process and unclear legal procedures all serve to render the restorative-justice approach ineffective. Concern around disparity of sentencing has been raised, especially if not all accused persons are afforded access to restorative justice programs. Whether or not power imbalances between those in positions of authority and the accused can be rectified to allow for the true implementation of restorative-justice initiatives has been questioned as well. Finally, some critics charge that existing structural and legislative realities restrict or prevent widespread acceptance of the restorative-justice approach. Table 10.2 compares retributive and restorative-justice approaches.

Critique of Peacemaking Criminology

Peacemaking criminology has been criticized as being naïve and utopian and for failing to recognize the realities of crime control and law enforcement, because few victims would expect to gain much during the victimization process from attempting to make peace with their victimizers (although such strategies do occasionally work). Such criticisms may be improperly directed at a level of analysis that peacemaking criminologists have not assumed.

Although it involves work with individual offenders, peacemaking criminology envisions positive change on the societal and institutional levels and does not suggest to victims that they attempt to effect personal changes in offenders.

POLICY IMPLICATIONS OF SOCIAL CONFLICT THEORIES

THE POLICY IMPLICATIONS OF THE SOCIAL CONFLICT THEORY ARE FAIRLY CLEAR: BRING about social change and redistribute the wealth in society and crime rates will fall. At one extreme, radical-Marxist criminologists argue that the only effective way of reducing conflict is through a total dismantling of the existing capitalist state and its replacement by a socialist economic structure. Most radical-critical criminologists of today have come to recognize that this is highly unlikely. As a consequence, such theorists have begun to focus on promoting a gradual transition to socialism and to socialized forms of government activity. These middle-range policy alternatives include "equal justice in the bail system, the abolition of mandatory sentences, prosecution of corporate crimes, increased employment opportunities, and promoting community alternatives to imprisonment."[85] Likewise, programs to reduce prison overcrowding, efforts to highlight injustices within the current system, the elimination of racism and other forms of inequality in the handling of both victims and offenders, growing equality in criminal justice system employment, and the like are all frequently mentioned as mid-range strategies for bringing about a justice system that is more fair and closer to the radical ideal.

At the other extreme are the calls of peacemaking criminologists for a practical application of the principles of conflict resolution. Between these two extremes lie left-realist and feminist criminology, although the solutions they offer vary from the reduction of paternalism to a practical recognition of the consequences of crime to victims.

SOCIAL CONFLICT THEORIES APPLIED

RADICAL CRIMINOLOGY

holds that the causes of crime are rooted in social conditions that empower the wealthy and the politically well organized but disenfranchise those less fortunate. In the Oka crisis, the city of Oka, supported by the army and the police, is considered to be the "haves," while the members of the Mohawk Nation are the "have-nots."

Crime is a result of constant conflict and struggle between groups attempting to promote their own disparate interests. These groups have different amounts of power, and as the groups struggle for power, conflict ensues, which promotes crime. The law is a tool of the powerful, who use it to control the less fortunate.

How can the Oka crisis be explained using the social conflict perspective?

LEFT-REALIST CRIMINOLOGY

holds that crime is a real social problem experienced by the lower classes and that the criminal justice system can be an effective crime-reduction tool through reduced use of force and increased awareness of the plight of the have-nots. Throughout the Oka crisis, the use of force and confrontation by the agents of the justice system represented them as the oppressors working on behalf of the state.

PEACEMAKING CRIMINOLOGY

holds that crime and violence are perpetuated through social policy based on the dominant perspective of crime control, which tends to be based on naïve theories and to disregard human rights. The Oka crisis is an example of disharmony around human rights that serves to perpetuate the naïve theory that First Nations peoples are more crime-prone.

FEMINIST CRIMINOLOGY

holds that the conflict and inequality in society are based on gender. Women are more likely to be victims of crime, and females who commit crime do so for different reasons and are treated differently by the criminal justice system. The crisis in Oka would equate the lack of rights afforded to First Nations peoples as similar to the realities for women.

SUMMARY OF LEARNING OBJECTIVES

10.1 The social conflict perspective focuses on the interaction between groups but views this interaction as one of conflict and maintains that conflict is a fundamental aspect of social life that can never be fully resolved. Various groups within society, defined in terms of their political, economic, or social standing, are seen to compete with one another to promote their own best interests. Crime and criminal activity are the outcome of this struggle.

10.2 Radical criminology holds that the root causes of crime are found in social conditions empowering the wealthy and the politically well organized but disenfranchising the less successful and that law is a tool of the powerful, who use it to control the less fortunate. Various groups within society, defined in terms of their political, economic, or social standing, are seen to complete with one another to promote their own best interests. Crime and criminal activity are the outcome of this struggle.

10.3 Three emerging perspectives offer explanations of crime and criminality: left-realist criminology, feminist criminology, and peacemaking criminology. Left-realist criminology is concerned with street crime, fear of crime, and everyday victimization and embraces radical and Marxist criminology. Feminist criminology believes that sexism and an unequal gender-based distribution of power in our patriarchal society affect both crime and its understanding in the field of criminology. Peacemaking criminology restates the problem of crime control from how to stop crime to how to make peace within society and between citizens and criminal justice agencies.

10.4 Conflict theories hold that social conflict and its manifestations are the root causes of crime, the crime-control implications involve redressing injustices to end the marginalization of the politically and economically disadvantaged.

Questions for Review

1. Does the social conflict perspective hold any significance for contemporary Canadian society? Why or why not?

2. How do the social conflict perspectives discussed in this chapter purport to explain crime and criminality? Use examples of specific theories.

3. Does the radical nature of the social conflict theories fall short in explaining crime in contemporary Canadian society? Why or why not?

4. What are the social policy implications of social conflict theories? Give an example.

Multiple-Choice Questions

1. According to _____, crime is a consequence of conflict between those groups with power who control the laws and those groups without power whose behaviours are defined by the laws.
   - **a.** Karl Marx
   - **b.** William Chambliss
   - **c.** Roscoe Pound
   - **d.** Austin Turk
   - **e.** Richard Quinney

2. Central to the perspective of feminist criminology is the notion of _____.
   - **a.** terrorism
   - **b.** state-organized crime
   - **c.** consensus
   - **d.** social class
   - **e.** gender inequality

3. Which of the following is not a strategy proposed by peacemaking criminologists to bring about a justice system closer to the radical ideal?
   - **a.** increased involvement of the victim in the criminal justice process
   - **b.** increased use of mandatory sentences
   - **c.** increased use of reparation in the sentencing process
   - **d.** increased crime prevention by focusing on cooperation
   - **e.** increased use of a community policing approach to law enforcement

4. _____ criminology believes that in order to reduce crime, we must achieve a fair and orderly society through a practical emphasis on social justice. Crime-control agencies and citizens must work together to alleviate social problems.
   - **a.** Left-realist
   - **b.** Feminist
   - **c.** Realist
   - **d.** Marxist
   - **e.** Peacemaking

5. _____ give the offender the opportunity to meet face-to-face with the victim and involve participation by the judge, victim, offender, family or supporters, elders, and other justice and community representatives.
   - **a.** Sentencing circles
   - **b.** Victim-offender reconciliation programs
   - **c.** Community policing approaches
   - **d.** Power-control circles
   - **e.** Left-realism participation circles

Multiple Choice Answers: 1d, 2e, 3b, 4a, 5b

Chapter 11
Criminology and Social Policy

Jonathan Hayward/The Canadian Press

While the justice system is necessary to hold offenders accountable for their actions, it is only part of the solution to crime. A better solution is to prevent crime in the first place.

—National Crime Prevention Council[1]

LEARNING OBJECTIVES

After reading this chapter, you should be able to

11.1 Understand how crime-prevention and public policy is developed.

11.2 Recognize and understand the various types of crime-prevention philosophies and strategies.

11.3 Relate various crime-prevention strategies to recent Canadian crime-prevention policy initiatives and discuss the strengths and weaknesses of each.

11.4 Consider the impact of an evidence-based crime-prevention approach in Canada.

INTRODUCTION

On June 15, 2016, criminologists Travis W. Hirschi, emeritus professor at the University of Arizona; Cathy Spatz Widom, professor at John Jay College of Criminal Justice; and Per-Olof Wikström, professor at the University of Cambridge, were recognized as the recipients of the 2016 Stockholm Prize in Criminology at the awards ceremony of the International Stockholm Criminology Symposium.

Considered to be one of the most influential criminological theories, Travis Hirschi's social bond theory was based on a study begun in 1965 that gathered data on over 4 000 youth. His theory did not ask why people *do* break the law, but why people *don't* break the law. He proposed that the social bond between youth and positive influences—which he described as attachments, commitments, involvement, and beliefs—is instrumental in a youth's decision to engage in criminal behaviour. Hirschi's theory is discussed in detail in Chapter 9.

Cathy Spatz Widom's research began with a study in 1967 and tracked almost 1 000 children who had been victims of criminal abuse or neglect by responsible adults before the age of 11. Over the next 20 years, she found that while the maltreatment of children increased their adult rates of crime and violence, most maltreated children had no criminal record as adults. Spatz Widom's work extended the work done by Hirschi by concluding that even bad parenting can have good features and that even criminal parents might build strong attachments with their children, which lead children to obey the law.

Finally, Per-Olof Wikström's research offered the most detailed evidence on the dynamic processes by which children negotiate their daily lives between their parents and peers. In a 10-year study of over 700 families, his data included the measurement of adolescent exposure to morally hazardous peers and situations as well as the youths' moral beliefs and propensity to commit crimes. Wikström added major insights into the role parents play in preventing youth crime.

First awarded in 2006, the Stockholm Prize in Criminology recognizes outstanding achievements in criminological research or in the practical implementation of research findings in order to combat crime and promote human rights. It carries a cash award of 1 million Swedish kronor (about US$150 000). Financed by the Jerry Lee Centre of Experimental Criminology in the United States, the Japanese Correctional Association and Hitachi Mirai Foundation in Japan, and the Söderberg Foundations of Sweden, the prize intends to promote

- improved knowledge of causes of crime on an individual and structural level
- more effective and humane public policies for dealing with criminal offenders
- greater knowledge of alternative crime-prevention strategies inside and outside the judicial system
- policies for helping victims of crime
- better ways to reduce the global problem of illegal or abusive practices that may occur in the administration of justice

Past recipients include John Braithwaite of Australia National University and Friedrich Lösel of Cambridge University (2006) for their work on reintegrative shaming (see Chapter 9) and their systematic reviews of empirical evidence on the effectiveness of correctional treatment. The 2007 prize was awarded to Alfred Blumstein of Carnegie Mellon University in Pittsburgh and Terrie E. Moffitt of the University of London and Duke University, North Carolina, for their discoveries about the development of criminal behaviour over the life course of individuals (see Chapter 9). In 2011, John Laub of the U.S. National Institute of Justice and Robert Sampson of Harvard

University received the award for their research into explanations of why and how criminals stop offending (see Chapter 9). Joan Petersilia from Stanford University and Daniel S. Nagin from Carnegie Mellon University were the 2014 recipients, recognized for their research that has helped to reshape the use of prison and community corrections based on evidence of what works and what doesn't.[2]

In Chapter 1, we made reference to the importance of the link between objective findings of well-conducted criminological research and the development of effective social policy. The Stockholm Prize in Criminology is a recent recognition that this link is indeed being made. This chapter will examine a number of Canadian public policies related to crime prevention and consider the current call to continue to create crime-prevention policies based on scientific research and evaluation. We will begin with an outline of current crime-prevention directions.

CRIME PREVENTION AND PUBLIC POLICY

11.1 **LEARNING OBJECTIVE**

SOME UNDERSTANDING OF HOW PUBLIC POLICY—ESPECIALLY CRIME-PREVENTION POLICY—IS created is essential to the study of criminology. Before we consider a number of current public policies in the criminal justice area, a definition of the term *public policy* is in order. **Public policy**, also called *social policy*, can be defined as "those standing directives, formulated by public organizations, on behalf of the public good"[3] or "a course of action that government takes in an effort to solve a problem or to achieve an end."[4] Other definitions contend that public policy is an expression of meaning: "A policy statement in the criminal justice system constitutes a declaration of social value, and it is upon the basis of the declared value that subsequent decisions are shaped."[5] Social values, in turn, are defined as ideals, customs, or institutions that society regards either positively (such as freedom) or negatively (such as cruelty). There are various types of public policy. Descriptors such as "social," "fiscal," "housing," "health," and "economic" can all be attached to the word *policy*. Generally, policy dealing with issues of crime and its prevention and control fall under the rubric of social policy, which can be defined as policy "concerned with the betterment of social life, the amelioration of social ills, and the allocation of public money to accomplish that end."[6]

Public policy Government-formulated directives made on behalf of the public good to solve a problem or achieve an end.

Analysts of public policy have observed that policies undergo five stages in their development:[7]

1. identification of the problem
2. agenda setting or the prioritization of problems
3. policy formation
4. program implementation
5. program evaluation and reassessment

The outline in Box 11.1 illustrates this process by examining legislation introduced to address the public's concern with violent youth crime.

The issue of criminal justice policymaking in Canada is a concentrated interest for the field of criminology, yet there is debate within Canadian criminology circles as to the impact of criminological research on the development of public crime policy. As John Ekstedt and Curt Griffiths have noted,

> Public policy making in areas of critical social awareness has taken on the atmosphere of political "campaigns" with all the attention to the marketing of ideas, the testing of public reaction, and the selling of policy positions normally associated with an election process. Governments seek to promote policies that can contribute to the common good without resulting in political disruption.[8]

Box 11.1 STAGES OF CRIMINAL JUSTICE POLICY IN CANADA

Identification of a problem

Increase in reported incidence of violent crime by youth.

Agenda setting/Prioritization of the problem

Interested groups respond and a critical mass of attention is established. Responses come from:

government bureaucracy: (collects and reports data on youth crime, shifts or increases resources from another social problem, provides/enforces sanctions to fight youth crime)

media: (reports on incidences of youth violent crime, focuses public attention/sensationalizes the reality of violent youth crime, provides editorial insight on the reasons for and how to combat youth crime)

political: (manages perceived threat to political stability as public demands political response, maintains balance in designation of resources to government services, uses media to respond to issue by pledging to address the matter of youth crime)

Policy formation

Government announces and implements a major initiative to combat youth violent crime. Resources (money and personnel) are committed, a program is described, legal changes to powers of arrest/criminal sanctions are initiated.

Program implementation

As pressure from the public and the media continue and/or mount and threaten political stability, the bureaucracy responsible implements the program to tackle youth violent crime. Procedures for implementation of the program include:

laws/regulations: changes are made to the criminal law (increased sanctions) and regulations (*Youth Criminal Justice Act*)

enforcement: additional police and correctional/aftercare resources/personnel are committed

Program evaluation and reassessment

Research, data gathering, and analysis continues. Effectiveness of the program to meet objectives and cost perspectives is determined.

Sources: Nancy E. Marion, *A History of Federal Crime Control Initiatives, 1960–1993* (Westport: Praeger, 1994), p. 3. For a more detailed analysis of the process by which crime control policies are created, see Paul Rock, "The Opening Stages of Criminal Justice Policy Making," *British Journal of Criminology*, vol. 35, no. 1 (Winter 1995) and *Canadian Criminology: Perspectives on Crime and Criminality*, Second Edition by Jackson/Griffiths, 1995. Reprinted with permission of Nelson, a division of Thomson Learning

---

Others have made the comment, "As all criminologists know, criminality is decided as much by legal and political authorities, and by their strategies of criminalization, enforcement, and control, as by criminals themselves."[9] Yet others have argued that Canadian political scientists pay more attention to criminal justice issues than is commonly believed. Troy Riddell argued, for example, that political scientists are well positioned to study how the policy process influences the formation of criminal justice policy.[10]

The emphasis on evidence-based crime-prevention policymaking continues to grow. This growth was initially fostered by a number of developments, including a movement toward an evidence-based approach in other disciplines, such as medicine and education, and large-scale government- and foundation-sponsored reviews of "what works" in crime prevention. We will take a closer look at the status of evidence-based crime prevention at the end of this chapter.

11.2 | LEARNING OBJECTIVE

CRIME-PREVENTION PHILOSOPHIES

TODAY'S POLICY RESPONSE TO CRIME HAS TWO PRONGS. ONE PRONG DEFINES CRIME AS AN issue of individual responsibility. The other sees crime and criminal behaviour as resulting from poor social conditions and dysfunctional social structures. In Chapter 1, the first prong was termed the *social responsibility perspective*, and the second approach was called the *social problems perspective*.

Each of these perspectives sees the root causes of crime very differently and dictates a different approach to its resolution. Our American neighbours, for example, appear to have embraced the social responsibility perspective, which is clearly reflected in their current criminal justice policies. Since 1980, the United States has been "waging a war" on crime, criminals, and, most recently, terror, resulting in such legislation as the *Comprehensive Crime Control Act* (1984), the *Omnibus Anti-Drug Abuse Act* (1988), the *Violent Crime Control and Law Enforcement Act* (1994), and the *USA PATRIOT Act* (2001). All of these pieces of legislation have introduced harsher penalties and increased law enforcement powers. Currently, policies at both the state and federal levels are becoming increasingly focused on strict enforcement of existing laws and on strict punishments.[11] Americans continue to push their political representatives for the creation of conservative policy tools to deal with crime and the fear it engenders. At recent count, there were some 2.22 million people incarcerated in the United States, or roughly 698 per 100 000 population (see Figure 11.1). In fact, the United States now imprisons more people per capita than any other country in the Western world.

Number of inmates per 100 000 population

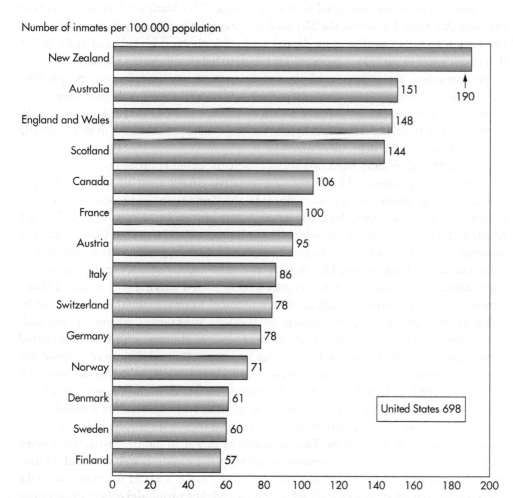

Figure 11.1 Canada's Incarceration Rate Is High Relative to Most Western European Countries

Canada's incarceration rate is higher than the rates in most Western European countries but much lower than the United States, where the most recent incarceration rate was 698 per 100 000 general population. Based on the most up-to-date information available from the International Centre for Prison Studies, Canada's incarceration rate was 106 per 100 000. When ranked from highest to lowest, Canada's prison population rate was 141 of 222 countries.

Source: Public Safety Canada Portfolio Corrections Statistics Committee, *Correction and Conditional Release Statistical Overview: Annual Report* 2015 (Ottawa: Public Works and Government Services Canada, 2016.

By way of contrast, the history of criminal justice policymaking in Canada is largely based on the social problems perspective. Traditionally, the federal government and others have decried the "get tough" approach to crime prevention as being purely reactive and failing to address the underlying causes of crime and criminality. Decades of crime-prevention policymaking have reflected the sentiments of a former federal minister of justice:

> We do not think for a moment that violent crime is going to be resolved in this society by tinkering with statutes or changing Acts. The fact of the matter is that the criminal justice system itself is not going to end violent crime. It only deals with the consequences of the underlying social problems. It is crime prevention that must have at least the equal focus of the House of Commons.[12]

By addressing social problems and the need for improvements in the social infrastructure, the social problems perspective takes a *proactive* rather than *reactive* approach to the reality of crime. Within this context, Canadian crime policy initiatives overall have stressed strategies designed to prevent crime. The National Crime Prevention Strategy (formerly known as the National Strategy on Community Safety and Crime Prevention and discussed in more detail later in this chapter) is anchored in the belief that crime prevention is best promoted through social development and that "in order to prevent crime, action must take place at the community level. It is the people who live, work and play in a community who best understand their area's resources, problems, needs and capacities."[13] The Who's Responsible box presents the case of a fictitious, yet typical, offender and emphasizes the importance of investing in young people at the early stages of a delinquent lifestyle.

Recently, a shift away from this social problems–based approach to crime prevention has been apparent. The former Conservative government of Stephen Harper introduced legislation that appeared closer to the "get tough" approach to crime and criminality. In 2006, the federal government introduced legislation designed to get tough with high-risk and sex offenders. The reforms targeted *Criminal Code* provisions governing dangerous offenders, to make it easier for Crown prosecutors to obtain dangerous offender designations. The *Tackling Violent Crime Act* of 2008 increased mandatory minimum sentences for gun crimes and impaired driving and required those convicted of three serious sexual or violent offences to prove why they should not be jailed indefinitely. In 2012, the passage of the *Safe Streets and Communities Act* (Bill C-10) increased penalties for sexual offences against children and for drug-related crimes, increased the use of adult sentences for youth, limited the use of judicial discretion in issuing conditional sentences, and extended the ineligibility period for criminal pardons. (Bill C-10 will be discussed in more detail later in this chapter.) Bill C-51, the *Anti-Terrorism Act*, was passed into law in 2015 and significantly expanded the power of the Canadian Security Intelligence Service to disrupt threats rather than just collect information about them. This includes the power to interfere with travel plans and transactions of suspected terrorists and to disrupt radical websites and Twitter accounts. Changes to the *Criminal Code of Canada* make it easier for police to make preventative arrests and make it illegal to "encourag[e] or promot[e] others to carry out a terrorist threat." The act also eases the transfer of confidential information between federal agencies, such as Passport Canada and the Canadian Revenue Agency.

We are currently at a crossroads regarding the direction of crime-prevention policy. The current Liberal government has vowed to revisit a number of these new pieces of legislation. In a mandate letter from Prime Minister Justin Trudeau to the justice minister, Trudeau called for an overhaul of the measures brought in by the Conservatives: "You should conduct a review of the changes in our criminal justice system and sentencing reforms over the past decade with a mandate to assess the changes, ensure that we are increasing the safety of our communities, getting value for money, addressing gaps and ensuring that current provisions are aligned with the objectives of the criminal justice system."[14] Recent Supreme Court decisions found two sentencing changes introduced in the *Safe Streets and Communities Act* to be unconstitutional: it ruled that a person who is denied bail because of prior convictions cannot be ineligible to receive credit for time served before sentencing and that the newly introduced mandatory minimum sentence of one year in prison for a drug offence violates the *Charter of Rights and Freedoms*. Commitments to repeal the problematic elements of Bill C-51 and introduce new legislation that better balances our collective security with our rights and freedoms has yet to occur.[15]

WHO'S RESPONSIBLE?—THE INDIVIDUAL OR SOCIETY?

Tyler's Troubled Life: The Story of One Young Man's Path Towards a Life of Crime

Studies have shown that the majority of Canadians engage in some form of delinquent behaviour during adolescence. Most people eventually outgrow these behaviours and go on to become responsible, productive members of society. However, a small portion of the population continues to commit crimes into adulthood.

Research tells us that certain characteristics increase a person's likelihood of becoming entrenched in crime. These characteristics are called risk factors. Researchers have identified a number of risk factors that have been shown to predict criminal offending later in life, such as early behavioural problems and family conflict.

Not all individuals exposed to these factors become involved in crime. However, the more risk factors an individual presents, the greater the probability that he or she will become involved in crime. Fortunately, the identification of risk factors related to criminal offending allows us to develop and target effective interventions to reduce an individual's overall risk of becoming involved in crime.

The following story is fictional and does not depict any real persons or events.

Introducing Tyler . . .

Meet Tyler, a teen on a troubled path towards a life of crime. Tyler had a challenging childhood with a negative family life environment. As a teenager, Tyler rebels against his parents, seems to be perpetually moody and experiences conflicts with his peers. However, unlike the majority of Canadian youth, Tyler continues on a criminal path and eventually ends up in federal prison.

This is Tyler's story.

Tyler's Story
Age 0-2 years

In her last year of high school, Tyler's mother became pregnant. Wanting to keep the baby, but afraid of her parents' disapproval, she moved in with her boyfriend (Tyler's father) and his friends. To support the family, she quit school and began working part-time as a waitress at a local restaurant.

■ Risk Factor: young mother (17 years or younger)

Tyler's father was an unemployed high school dropout with a long history of property crimes. He was known in the neighbourhood for buying and selling stolen electronics, like laptops, TVs and DVDs.

■ Risk Factor: criminal family members

Child and Family Services first began investigating Tyler's living situation after a neighbour called the police to report suspicious activity at the house. When the police arrived, they discovered a large amount of stolen goods, and arrested Tyler's father and his friends. Tyler's father was sentenced to nine months in jail, leaving Tyler's mother to support their son on her own. Tyler's mother could not afford to rent the house with what she made as a waitress, so they had to move to a small apartment in a community housing complex.

■ Police Call for Service per call: $1,142

■ Child Services Per Investigation: $11,261

Although the investigation showed no evidence that Tyler was being physically maltreated, social service workers were concerned about the family's lifestyle and its impact on the child. As

(Continued)

Tyler's Troubled Life: The Story of One Young Man's Path Towards a Life of Crime

such, social services placed custody conditions on Tyler's mother that required her to avoid contact with individuals with a criminal record. In addition, the family had to submit to unscheduled home visits conducted by Children's Aid Society workers.

- Risk Factor: broken home/family transitions (parental separation)
- Child Services Home Visits per family: $8,002
- Risk Factor: family contact with child welfare agency

Age 3-5 years

By the time Tyler was three, he was already displaying problematic behaviour. He had no friends at daycare because he was physically aggressive towards other children, hitting and biting them when they took his toys. Tyler had a loud and hostile demeanour that made other children afraid of him. Following complaints from other parents, the staff eventually asked Tyler's mother to remove him from the daycare. As a result, Tyler had to stay with a neighbour while his mother was at work.

- Risk Factor: early conduct problems
- Risk Factor: aggressive behaviour

When Tyler's father was released from prison, he resumed living with his girlfriend (Tyler's mother) and son in the subsidized housing community. Because Tyler was no longer welcome at the daycare, he stayed at home with his father while his mother went to work.

- Risk Factor: social disadvantage

When left alone with his father, Tyler was ignored while his father watched TV. Tyler often went hours without food. After a few weeks, Tyler began acting out in his mother's absence, breaking his toys and other items around the house.

- Risk Factor: poor parental monitoring
- Risk Factor: poor child-rearing methods

Tyler's father rarely even noticed the behaviour unless it interrupted his TV programs, at which point he would yell and hit Tyler repeatedly.

- Risk Factor: authoritarian parenting

On one occasion, Tyler accidently broke the television remote. His father became furious, grabbed Tyler and threw him against the wall, breaking his arm. Tyler was still crying when his mother came home. After seeing him in pain, she took him

to the emergency room, but would not explain to the doctor what had happened to her son's arm. The ER doctor became suspicious and called Child and Family Services to investigate.

- Risk Factor: low parental empathy
- Emergency Room Visit: $402
- Child Services Investigation: $11,261

Child and Family Services investigated Tyler's situation and recommended that Tyler be removed from his parents' care. The case ended up in Family Court when Tyler's parents refused to comply with the custody order. A Family Court judge determined that Tyler was not safe with his parents, and so Tyler was immediately taken into the custody of the Children's Aid Society. Tyler was five years old when he was first placed into the foster care system.

- Child Custody Hearing: $45,000
- Risk Factor: involvement with alternative care (foster care)
- Foster Care: $886 per month for children aged 11 & under

Age 6-10 years

Over the next five years, Tyler lived in three foster homes with three different foster families. Each new placement meant a new school and new classmates. Tyler had an increasingly difficult time adjusting with each subsequent move. He also became increasingly aggressive, both physically and verbally, with his new foster family, often shoving them around and screaming obscenities.

- Risk Factor: broken home/family transitions (frequent moves)
- Risk Factor: hyperactivity
- Risk Factor: adjustment problems
- Risk Factor: attention problems

In school, Tyler struggled to keep up with his peers. It was his first grade teacher who first recognized that Tyler was having problems, and suggested that his foster parents take him to see a psychologist to have him tested for a learning disability. Tyler was diagnosed with a learning disability and Attention Deficit Hyperactivity Disorder (ADHD) at the age of seven and placed in a special education classroom at school. He was then referred to a child psychiatrist who prescribed medication for his hyperactivity. Despite the positive effects of the medication, Tyler's current foster family could no longer cope with his disruptive, violent behaviour.

(Continued)

Tyler's Troubled Life: The Story of One Young Man's Path Towards a Life of Crime

- Risk Factor: poor academic achievement
- Psychological Assessment: $2,609
- Special Education: $9,602 per year
- Initial Psychiatric Assessment: $310
- ADHD Medication: $1,328 per year

At age eight, Tyler was sent to live with a fourth foster family. The repeated disruptions in his life made it hard for Tyler to make friends in his neighbourhood and at his school. It was also difficult for Tyler to maintain his daily medication schedule, and he would often miss doses. This resulted in more frequent episodes of irritability and disruptive behaviour.

- Psychiatric Follow-Up: $1,987 for 12 one-hour appointments
- Risk Factor: poor peer relations (peer rejection)
- Risk Factor: antisocial behaviour

Child and Family Services kept monitoring Tyler during his time in foster care and encouraged his new foster parents to continue taking Tyler to the psychiatrist. However, Tyler began to refuse to attend the appointments after some children at school found out that he was seeing a "shrink" because he was "crazy". Tyler was teased constantly at school because of his learning disability and often reacted violently. He became repeatedly involved in physical fights at school and had regular visits to the principal's office. After one particularly bad schoolyard fight, Tyler was suspended by the principal. Tyler refused to take responsibility for the fight, saying that the other boy "deserved what he got".

Age 11-14 years

By the age of 12, Tyler had established a reputation with his classmates and teachers for having a violent temper. In seventh grade, he became friends with a group of boys who were known as troublemakers in the neighbourhood. These boys would steal from the local convenience store and vandalize school property. They told Tyler that to prove himself, he would have to steal a bike from the high school next door and ride it around the neighbourhood. Tyler completed the challenge and officially became "one of the guys".

Tyler hung out with his friends in the park every day after school and on weekends. The boys would smoke cigarettes they had stolen from their parents. Tyler's foster parents didn't smoke, so instead he stole money from them to buy cigarettes from his friends. On a number of occasions, Tyler's foster parents confronted him about the missing money, but Tyler lied to them

and said he knew nothing about it. He even blamed it on his younger foster siblings, saying he saw them take the money.

- Risk Factor: antisocial peer associates
- Foster Care: $886 per month for children aged 11 & under; $1,003 per month for children aged 12+

In grade nine, Tyler and his friends began experimenting with alcohol and marijuana. Soon after, the boys began breaking into neighbours' houses and stealing items they could sell to buy drugs and alcohol. These thefts were what prompted Tyler's first encounter with the police, when a neighbour reported seeing Tyler leaving the scene of a break-and-enter across the street. Tyler and two of his friends were charged with break-and-enter, theft under $5,000 and property damage, and were required to report to youth court. Because this was Tyler's first recorded offence, the youth court judge ordered Tyler to provide a written apology to the victims, and pay restitution for the damages he caused and the property he stole.

- Risk Factor: alcohol/substance abuse
- Break-and-Enter: $3,208
- Theft under $5,000: $1,739
- Damage to Property: $948
- Police Call for Service: $1,142
- Initial Police Contact: $1,912
- Arrest of Juvenile: $1,262
- Youth Court Appearance: $1,275
- Police Attendance at Court: $239

However, Tyler did not comply with the order to repay the victims. One of the victims reported Tyler's refusal to pay to the court and Tyler was brought before a youth court judge a second time for not complying with the first judge's order. This time, Tyler was sentenced to 90 days probation, including the completion of 50 hours of community service. This sentence marked the beginning of Tyler's chronic involvement with the justice system.

- Youth Court Appearance: $1,275
- Probation Supervision (90 Days): $523
- Community Service Supervision: $1,934

Age 15-17 years

At school, Tyler and his friends rarely attended their classes. When they did show up, they were loud and obnoxious,

(Continued)

Tyler's Troubled Life: The Story of One Young Man's Path Towards a Life of Crime

disrespectful to the teacher and picked fights with their classmates. As a result, Tyler was suspended numerous times. The only times Tyler wasn't a disruption to his class was when he was suspended from school or when he came to class hungover and just sat with his head down on his desk.

- Risk Factor: poor regard for school (truancy)
- Risk Factor: psychosocial immaturity
- Risk Factor: poor regard for school (suspension)

By the time he was 16, Tyler had begun drinking almost daily. He and his friends attended all the high school parties and often drank until they passed out. Just before he turned 17, Tyler dropped out of school. Instead of going to class, he and his friends would hang around the neighbourhood park to drink and get high on drugs.

At one house party, Tyler became severely intoxicated and ended up in a vicious fight with another partygoer. Tyler punched his opponent in the face and broke his nose. When someone at the party called for an ambulance, Tyler and his friends tried to flee the scene. However, when the police arrived with the ambulance, the partygoers who witnessed the fight were able to provide the police with a description of Tyler and his friends. Tyler didn't get too far before he was picked up by the police and charged with assault.

Tyler appeared in youth court the next morning and pled not-guilty to the assault charge, claiming he had no recollection of the fight. He also suggested that the other youth at the party were trying to frame him. The judge did not believe Tyler's story and sentenced him to six months probation for the assault, including a condition to abide by the curfew set by his current foster parents.

Immediately after Tyler returned home, he got into an argument with his foster mother about his new curfew. He became furious at her and pushed her so hard that she fell down the stairs. Tyler's foster father called the police and Tyler was arrested for a second assault. This time, Tyler was sentenced to six months in a secure youth custody facility.

- Risk Factor: alcohol and/or drug use
- Foster Care: $1,003 per month for children age 12+
- Assault: $2,115
- Police Call for Service: $1,142
- Initial Police Contact: $1,912
- Ambulance Transportation: $558

- Emergency Room Visit: $402
- Arrest of Juvenile: $1,262
- Youth Court Appearance: $1,275
- Probation Supervision (6 months): $1,046
- Police Attendance at Court: $239
- Assault: $2,115
- Police Call for Service: $1,142
- Initial Police Contact: $1,912
- Ambulance Transportation: $558
- Emergency Room Visit: $402
- Arrest of Juvenile: $1,262
- Youth Court Appearance: $1,275
- Police Attendance at Court: $239
- Youth Custody Facility (6 months): $45,000

During his time in custody, Tyler made friends with a few of the other boys in the facility. Most of the boys were also charged with property offences, drug offences and minor assaults, and had life stories similar to Tyler's. Tyler became particularly close friends with his roommate Ryan, an experienced drug dealer, who told Tyler about how much money he was making dealing cocaine. As Tyler's only source of income was social assistance, he knew that it would be difficult, without a high school diploma, to find a job that would pay as much as dealing drugs.

- Risk Factor: antisocial peers associates
- Social Assistance for High School Drop Out: $681 per month
- Risk Factor: availability of drugs

Tyler was determined not to return to foster care, so when the two boys were released from the custody facility, they stayed together at another friend's apartment. Tyler eventually became Ryan's "business partner," and the two teens supplied cocaine to much of the neighbourhood. Tyler had only been working with Ryan for a few months when their apartment was raided by the police. Both Tyler and Ryan were arrested for possession and intent to traffic a controlled substance.

- Initial Police Contact: $1,912
- Arrest of Adult: $1,149
- Drug Offence/Investigation: $3,452
- Risk Factor: criminal history

(Continued)

Tyler's Troubled Life: The Story of One Young Man's Path Towards a Life of Crime

Age 18+ years

By the time he was 18, Tyler had been arrested and charged on five separate occasions. However, this time was different. This time, Tyler was taken to adult court to face drug charges. He received an 18-month sentence for possession with intent to traffic and was sent to an adult facility to serve his time. This was but the first of many times that Tyler would be sent to jail.

■ Adult Court Appearance: $2,810

■ Police Attendance at Court: $239

■ Provincial Custody (18 months): $107,541

Tyler was arrested again in his early twenties for common assault and drug possession and was sentenced to two years less a day in provincial custody. While serving his sentence, Tyler would often participate in inmate activities to pass the time. During a routine game of basketball, Tyler became enraged over a hard foul and assaulted a fellow inmate, causing serious injury. For his actions, Tyler was handed an additional year's sentence to be served consecutively. Upon his release, Tyler returned to his old neighbourhood, met up with old acquaintances and returned to dealing drugs and stealing to make money. Occasionally, Tyler would move in with a girl he just met if he needed a place to stay. This was the case with Katie.

■ Initial Police Contact: $1,912

■ Arrest of Adult: $1,149

■ Adult Court Appearance: $2,810

■ Police Attendance at Court: $239

■ Assault: $2,115

■ Drug Offence: $3,452

■ Assault on Inmate: $2,115

■ Emergency Room Visit: $402

■ Provincial Custody (~ 3 years): $218,069

■ Drug Offence: $3,452

■ Theft under $5,000: $1,739

A few months into their relationship, Katie found out she was pregnant. Although Tyler was excited, the responsibility of a child terrified him. Katie insisted that Tyler give up drugs and find a stable job to support them. Money became a source of stress for both Katie and Tyler. As the due date grew closer, the two began fighting more and more.

■ Risk Factor: relationship difficulties

One night during a heated argument, Tyler lost his temper and attacked Katie with a knife from their kitchen and threatened to kill her. A neighbour heard Katie scream and called the police. Tyler was arrested and charged with aggravated assault, assault causing bodily harm, assault with a weapon and uttering threats.

■ Police Call for Service: $1,142

■ Initial Police Contact: $1,912

■ Arrest of Adult: $1,149

■ Ambulance Transportation: $558

■ Emergency Room Visit: $402

Fortunately, both Katie and the baby survived the assault. Once the baby was born, Katie moved out of town and obtained a restraining order against Tyler. Tyler never saw either of them again.

■ Aggravated Assault: $85,795

■ Adult Court Appearance: $2,810

■ Police Attendance at Court: $239

■ Federal Prison (Medium-Security): $552,592

Tyler was found guilty of all charges. He was sentenced to a total of five years in federal custody and ordered to complete mandatory anger management training and substance abuse programs.

■ Anger Management Training: $1,923

■ Substance Abuse Program: $6,502

Today, at the age of 30, Tyler has already spent more than 10 years of his life in custody.

■ Grand Total: $1,403,476

Think about it:

1. Identify and explain examples of crime-prevention initiatives which might address the risk factors identified in the story of Tyler's life. Do you think one approach more desirable than another? If so, why?

2. How would a deterrent approach to crime prevention manifest itself in the ways in which society would deal with a person like Tyler?

3. Does Canadian society have an obligation to support youth like Tyler and incur the costs of doing so? Why or why not?

Source: *From* "Who's Responsible? – The Individual or Society?", Tyler's Troubled Life, *The story of one young man's path towards a life of crime.* Copyright © by Minister of Public Works and Government Services Canada. https://www.publicsafety.gc.ca/cnt/rsrcs/pblctns/2016-r005/2016-r005-en.pdf

Types of Crime-Prevention Strategies

The range of effective crime-prevention alternatives available to today's policy-makers can be classified into three types of strategies. These three strategies differ in terms of strategic focus.[16] That is, they are distinguishable from one another "by whether they attempt to block opportunities for crime, alter the outcome of conscious or unconscious decision making that precedes a criminal act, or alter the broad strategic style with which people approach many aspects of their lives."[17] The three strategies are

1. nurturant strategies
2. protection/avoidance strategies
3. deterrence strategies

Nurturant strategy A crime-prevention strategy that attempts to forestall development of criminality by improving early life experiences and channelling child and adolescent development into desirable directions.

Nurturant strategies "attempt to forestall development of criminality by improving early life experiences and channelling child and adolescent development" into desirable directions. They "focus on prevention of criminality rather than its remediation or control."[18] Nurturant strategies include increased infant and maternal health care, child care for low-income families, training in parenting skills, enhanced public education, and stay-in-school programs.

Protection/avoidance strategy A crime-prevention strategy that attempts to reduce criminal opportunities by changing people's routine activities, increasing guardianship, or incapacitating convicted offenders.

Protection/avoidance strategies "attempt to reduce criminal opportunities by changing people's routine activities, increasing guardianship, or incapacitating convicted offenders."[19] Incapacitating convicted offenders through incarceration or the use of electronic monitoring would be considered examples of protection/avoidance strategies. Target hardening or opportunity reduction through the use of architectural design, crime-prevention programs such as neighbourhood watch, and increased policing also fit into this category.

Deterrence strategy A crime-prevention strategy that attempts to diminish motivation for crime by increasing the perceived certainty, severity, or celerity of penalties.

Deterrence strategies "attempt to diminish motivation for crime by increasing the perceived certainty, severity, or celerity of penalties."[20] New and tougher laws, quicker trial-court processing, harsher punishments, and faster imposition of sentences are all deterrence strategies.

A comprehensive crime-prevention strategy, according to some criminologists, would be "a balanced mix of protection/avoidance, deterrence, and nurturant

Aboriginal sweat lodges within Canadian correctional facilities allow Aboriginal inmates to continue to practise traditional customs. What type of crime-prevention strategy does this represent?

Judy Waytiuk/Alamy Stock Photo

strategies."[21] Achieving the most effective balance in a politically sensitive world, however, is a difficult undertaking. In Canada, many crime-prevention initiatives continue to emphasize the nurturant approach. Influential political constituencies, however, have increased the pressure for crime-prevention measures that have protection/avoidance and deterrence strategies as their focus.

CURRENT CRIME-PREVENTION INITIATIVES

11.3 | LEARNING OBJECTIVE

The National Crime Prevention Strategy

OVER THE PAST TWO DECADES, THE CANADIAN FEDERAL AND PROVINCIAL GOVERNMENTS have been paying greater attention to crime and community safety, allocating resources to understanding and addressing risk factors associated with crime and victimization. In the 1990s, parliamentary committee reports called for a more concerted, national approach to crime prevention. In 1994, the federal government introduced the National Strategy on Community Safety and Crime Prevention, now known as the **National Crime Prevention Strategy (NCPS)**.[22] The broad vision of the strategy was to encourage federal and provincial cooperation and the inclusion of citizens at the local level in a national crime-prevention initiative. The specific objectives of the National Strategy are as follows:

National Crime Prevention Strategy (NCPS) A federal crime-prevention initiative designed to create safer communities by supporting community-based crime-prevention efforts, enhancing communities' knowledge and experience with respect to crime prevention, and fostering partnerships and collaboration.

- to promote the integrated action of key governmental and non-governmental partners to reduce crime and victimization

- to assist communities in developing and implementing community-based solutions to problems that contribute to crime and victimization, particularly as they affect children, youth, women, and Aboriginal people

- to increase public awareness of and support for effective approaches to crime prevention

Referred to as "crime prevention through social development," this initiative is emblematic of a nurturant strategy.

Phase I of the National Crime Prevention Strategy set the groundwork for its national implementation. The creation of the National Crime Prevention Council, with the mission to "develop strategies to empower individuals and their communities to improve their safety, security and well-being,"[23] resulted in the identification of children and youth as the immediate focus for a national crime-prevention policy. The council concluded that the failure of Canadians to invest in the social development of children and youth has had serious implications in the areas of criminal activity and victimization. It stated that what is needed in Canada is "a comprehensive approach to systemic crime prevention through social development" to best address "the combination of social, systemic, personal, and situational factors which place children and youth at risk and contribute to crime."

Phase II of the National Strategy was launched in 1998 with a mandate to "provide national leadership on effective and cost-efficient ways to both prevent and reduce crime by addressing known risk factors in high-risk populations and places."[24] To achieve its mission, the National Crime Prevention Centre (NCPC) was created. With a mission to "provide national leadership on effective and cost-efficient ways to both prevent and reduce crime by addressing known-risk factors in high risk populations and places,"[25] the NCPC develops policies, gathers and disseminates knowledge to Canadian communities, and cooperates with the provinces and territories to manage funding programs that support community crime-prevention projects through time-limited grants and contributions.

The NCPS identified various risk factors for engaging in crime, including (1) individual-related factors (impulsiveness, alienation, early aggressiveness, early use of substances), (2) family-related factors (parent or family member involved in crime, addictions or substance abuse, family violence), (3) peer-related factors (deviant or criminalized friends, friends who are gang members, little social commitment), (4) school-related factors (poor school performance, low attachment to school, dropping out of school, exclusion or suspension from school), and (5) community-related factors (availability of firearms or drugs, weak or poor social networks).

The initiative focuses on groups identified as being most at risk of offending, categorized as (1) children aged 6–11 (to prevent their initiation to criminal activity), (2) young people aged 12–17 (to reduce pressures brought about by known risk factors), (3) young adults aged 18–24 (particularly those who have a history of offending), and (4) offenders who have completed sentences and have been released to the community (to prevent or reduce recidivism). In all four of these groups, a particular emphasis has been placed on Aboriginal populations.

Currently, the NCPS consists of four funding programs:

- The Communities at Risk: Security Infrastructure Program provides time-limited funding to enhance the security infrastructure of communities that are targeted by hate-motivated crime.

- The Crime Prevention Action Fund provides time-limited grant and contribution funding that supports evidence-based crime-prevention initiatives in communities.

- The Northern and Aboriginal Crime Prevention Fund supports the adaptation, development, and implementation of innovative and promising culturally sensitive crime-prevention practices that address known risk and protective factors to reduce offending among at-risk children and youth and high-risk offenders in communities; the dissemination of knowledge and the development of tools and resources for Aboriginal and northern populations; and capacity building as a means to explore ways to develop or implement culturally sensitive crime-prevention practices among Aboriginal and northern populations.

- The Youth Gang Prevention Fund provides time-limited grant and contribution funding for initiatives in communities where youth gangs are an existing or emerging threat and supports initiatives that clearly target youth in gangs or at greatest risk of joining gangs.

In recent years, the National Crime Prevention Strategy has been at a crossroads. Despite public announcements of an annual budget of $41 million annually to crime-prevention programs, some reports indicate that about $28 million in promised spending for the strategy was allowed to lapse between 2012 and 2015 and that the amount of unspent money rose each year, to more than 30 percent of the 2014–2015 budget, or about $12 million.[26] Time will tell if the current Liberal government will reinvest full funding in the NCPS.

Box 11.2 highlights three recent crime-prevention projects from across Canada that have received funding.

Crime Prevention Through Environmental Design

Crime Prevention Through Environmental Design (CPTED) A crime-prevention strategy based on the premise that the proper design and effective use of the built environment can lead to a reduction in the incidence and fear of crime.

Indicative of the protection/avoidance approach to crime prevention is the notion of **Crime Prevention Through Environmental Design (CPTED)**. C. Ray Jeffery's work entitled *Crime Prevention Through Environmental Design* introduced the concept to North America.[27] CPTED is based on the concept of *defensible space*, which holds that crime can be prevented through proper residential and commercial architectural design and the layout of the physical environment. The concept was introduced to Canada in the early 1980s by the Peel Regional Police Service and has since been endorsed by a great number of police services throughout the country (including the RCMP), many of whom have trained CPTED officers.

Box 11.2 CANADIAN CRIME-PREVENTION PROJECTS

Youth Gang Prevention, Aboriginal Crime Prevention—WrapEd

WrapEd is a comprehensive, team-based approach that involves individualized care plans and a variety of formal and informal community services and supports to address specific risk factors and builds on the strengths and resiliency of youth participants and their families in Edmonton, Alberta. Implemented in 2013 for a five-year period, the program will reach 180 youth, primarily from Aboriginal and refugee communities, between the ages of 12 and 17 who are most at risk of involvement with guns and/or gangs. Key activities of the project include youth outreach and engagement, youth assessment, systems navigation, and advocacy and trauma counselling. Family supports are also in place to assist families with issues related to youth, including family counselling, conflict resolution, and parent education programs.

Youth Gang Prevention—Taking Action Against Gangs Scarborough (TAAGS)

The Agincourt Community Services Association (ASCA) runs this youth gang prevention project. In response to increasing youth violence in Scarborough, Ontario, the goal of Taking Action Against Gangs Scarborough (TAAGS) is to reduce serious physical violence, drug dealing, and gang-related criminal activities. Funded from 2013 to 2018, TAAGS focuses on youth aged 12 to 18 who are associated with gangs, trying to leave gangs, or at risk of joining a gang. The program expects to reach 160 youth per year. The key

components of TAAGS are to provide participants with constant on-call support, intensive supervision, educational support, referrals to partner agencies for job training and employment opportunities, pro-social activities, and therapeutic support. Families and caregivers of the youth will also be involved in the program.

General Crime Prevention, Youth—Prévencité

The goal of Prévencité is to provide assistance and support services to youth aged 16 to 19 in Montreal, Quebec, who present multiple risk factors, including behavioural problems, drug and other substance abuse, poor academic performance, and delinquent peers. Some 100 participants aged 16 to 19, selected because of their behavioural problems, will benefit from the full program of resiliency groups, volunteering, and outdoor activities. During weekly resiliency group sessions held at school during school hours, the youth in the program talk about violence and substance abuse prevention, anger management, and healthy peer and family relationships. Participants learn how to set and achieve goals and to develop empathy by caring for others and working with mistreated or abandoned animals or in a group kitchen. Participants also lead awareness activities for younger children as well as taking part in outdoor activities offered after school and during the summer.

Source: Adapted from Public Safety Canada, "Crime Prevention Projects," http://www.publicsafety.gc.ca/cnt/cntrng-crm/crm-prvntn/crm-prvntn-prjcts-en.aspx [Accessed August 6, 2016].

The concept of CPTED has been widely incorporated into crime-prevention plans at the national and municipal levels. The RCMP provides a general overview of CPTED for professionals who work in urban development and related areas.[28] Local governmental crime-prevention plans in an increasing number of cities, including Toronto, Edmonton, Vancouver, Kingston, and Mississauga, include CPTED concepts in building codes and zoning bylaws, as do the mandates of numerous police services, such as the Peel Regional Police Service in Ontario. Box 11.3 illustrates examples of CPTED principles in practice.

Traditional "target hardening" crime-prevention approaches have employed physical or artificial barriers, such as locks, alarms, fences, and gates, to deny access to a crime target. The CPTED model recognizes that these traditional methods tend to place constraints on use, access, and enjoyment of the "hardened" environment. As an alternative, CPTED focuses on *natural surveillance* (keeping potential intruders under observation), *natural access control* (decreasing the opportunity for crime), and *territorial reinforcement* (creating or extending the sphere of influence through physical design to develop a sense of ownership). Further, the CPTED model insists upon an assessment of the physical environment to be protected. The designated purpose of the space; the social, cultural, legal, or physical definitions that suggest desired and acceptable behaviours for it; and the appropriateness of the design in the productive use of the space are included in this assessment.[29] The CPTED Ontario identified the

Box 11.3 CPTED PRINCIPLES IN PRACTICE

Natural Surveillance

Natural surveillance is a design strategy based on the premise that a person inclined to engage in criminality will be less likely to act on impulse if he or she can be seen. Natural surveillance is commonly associated with the establishment of clear sightlines.

Natural Access Control

Natural access control is based on the premise that a person who is confronted with a clearly defined and/or strategically developed boundary will typically show it some deference by respecting the way it guides and influences their movement as they transition from public through private space.

Source: Based on CPTED Ontario, "What Is CPTED?" http://cptedontario.ca/mission/what-is-cpted/

following CPTED tactics that support the core principles of natural surveillance, natural access control, and territorial reinforcement:[30]

Natural surveillance applications include:

■ orienting driveways and paths toward natural forms of surveillance, such as building entrances and windows

■ increasing visual permeability of vulnerable areas, such as building entrances, stairwells, playgrounds, and so on, through the strategic use of windows, fencing material, and landscaping

■ trimming back overgrown landscaping

■ strategically lighting pathways and other potentially problematic areas where opportunities for natural surveillance exist

■ developing uses for the environment that are capable of strategically generating activity, including the establishment of sidewalk patios, seating areas, and other amenities

Natural access control applications include:

■ providing clear border definition of controlled space

- limiting uncontrolled and/or unobserved access onto properties, buildings, and private space
- adding dense or thorny landscaping as a natural barrier to reinforce fences and discourage unwanted entry
- using space to provide natural barriers to conflicting activities

Territorial reinforcement applications include:

- creating clearly marked transitional zones as persons move from public to semi-public and private space using paving patterns, symbolic barriers or markers, signs, and other visual cues
- providing amenities in the communal area that encourage activity and use
- avoiding the creation of no-man's-land by ensuring that all space is assigned a clear and preferably active purpose
- developing visitor-reporting procedures for larger-scale entities that regularly receive people
- conducting timely maintenance

Advocates of CPTED stress that it should be considered only part of a comprehensive approach to crime prevention. Modifications to the physical environment will be

Dick Hemingway

Nurturant crime-prevention strategies are largely aimed at improving the social conditions and experiences of youth such as these living in Toronto's Regent Park housing development prior to its redevelopment. Do you think the focus on preventing crime through social development is an effective crime-prevention approach?

Andrew Francis Wallace/Toronto Star/Getty Images

effective only if they complement community policing efforts and social programs that address some of the root causes of crime. One of CPTED's most ardent supporters, Greg Saville, insisted that there must be a balance struck between the physical aspects of CPTED, such as access control and natural surveillance, with psycho-social crime-prevention strategies, such as community building, neighbourhood accords, school programs, and community policing. In keeping with this sentiment, the 2016 CPTED Ontario's annual conference will examine and celebrate the transformative power of "community revitalization" and focus on the transformation of Toronto's Regent Park neighbourhood from an at-risk community into a successful mixed-income, mixed-use neighbourhood, with rental buildings, market condominium buildings, town homes, commercial space, community facilities, active parks, and open space.[31]

Safe Streets and Communities Act

Over the last decade, the federal government of Canada has promoted a series of "tackling community crime bills" to address the issue of public safety. Included in this series is an intended National Anti-Drug Strategy, a comprehensive review of the *Youth Criminal Justice Act*, the introduction of the *Tackling Violent Crime Act*, and, most recently, the *Safe Streets and Communities Act*.

The **Safe Streets and Communities Act**, which came into force in March 2012, is an example of a deterrence strategy, or an attempt to diminish crime by making penalties more severe. Passed as Bill C-10, the *Safe Streets and Communities Act*, the act legislates increased penalties and a number of "get tough" approaches to sentencing. A change in the Canadian federal government in 2015 has resulted in a re-examination of a number of the elements of this act. Prime Minister Justin Trudeau said the government's approach to criminal justice is to protect public safety while respecting rights and noted that mandatory minimums are appropriate in some conditions and for certain crimes, such as murder.[32] The repealed sections of the *Safe Streets and Communities Act* are highlighted in Box 11.4.

Highlights of the *Safe Streets and Communities Act* include the following:

1. **Increased penalties and mandatory sentences of incarceration**

   New mandatory minimum penalties have been created for seven existing offences related to child exploitation, including prohibiting anyone from providing sexually explicit material to a child or from using any means of telecommunications, including the internet, to agree to or make arrangements with another person for the purpose of committing a sexual offence against a child.

   New mandatory minimum penalties have been introduced for serious drug offences, when such offences are carried out for organized crime purposes or if they involve targeting youth. Mandatory minimum penalties have also been increased for nine existing offences related to child exploitation.

   The maximum penalty for the production of drugs has been increased. Sentencing provisions for violent and repeat offenders have been strengthened and barriers to custody reduced for these same offenders. All young offenders under 18 given a conditional sentence are to serve it in a youth facility.

2. **Changes to court discretion**

   The discretion of judges, the Crown, and police officers has been limited by some of the provisions of the *Safe Streets and Communities Act*. Pretrial detention rules have been amended to help ensure that, when necessary, violent and repeat young offenders are kept off the streets while awaiting trial. In addition, the act requires the Crown to consider seeking adult sentences for youth convicted of the most serious violent crimes (murder, attempted murder, manslaughter, and aggravated sexual assault), while provinces and territories maintain the discretion to set the age at which this requirement would apply.

Box 11.4 RECENT REPEALS OF *SAFE STREETS AND COMMUNITIES ACT*

In 2016, the Supreme Court of Canada ruled that two "tough on crime" measures brought in by the previous Conservative government with the *Safe Streets and Communities Act* are unconstitutional.

The first case involved Joseph Ryan Lloyd, a man with drug addictions in Vancouver's Downtown Eastside who was convicted of trafficking in drugs in 2013 with less than 10 grams of heroin, crack cocaine, and crystal methamphetamine. The court ruled 6–3 that a mandatory minimum sentence of one year in prison for this drug offence constituted "cruel and unusual punishment" and thereby violated the *Charter of Rights and Freedoms*. "If Parliament hopes to maintain mandatory minimum sentences for offences that cast a wide net, it should consider narrowing their reach so that they only catch offenders that merit that mandatory minimum sentence," the court decision read. "In the alternative, Parliament could provide for judicial discretion to allow for a lesser sentence where the mandatory minimum would be grossly disproportionate and would constitute cruel and unusual punishment." The dissenting view argued that the law as drafted was narrow enough and that it did not amount to cruel and unusual punishment.

In the second case, the Supreme Court unanimously ruled that a person who is denied bail prior to trial should be able to receive credit for time served before sentencing. Before the changes brought in by the *Safe Streets and Communities Act*, the *Criminal Code of Canada* allowed a person who is denied bail to receive 1.5 to 3 days of credit for each day spent in custody before trial. This practice is meant to recognize what are often harsh conditions in pretrial incarceration, also known as remand jail. This "hard time" is often served in overcrowded conditions with a lack of access to treatment or programs. *The Safe Streets and Communities Act* had removed this enhanced credit eligibility for those denied bail.

This Supreme Court case involved Sean Summers, who was convicted of manslaughter in the shaking death of his infant daughter. The Crown and defence agreed to a sentence of between 8 and 10 years' imprisonment. The trial judge handed down a sentence of six years and eight months after taking into account the 10.5 months in pretrial custody that Summers spent before pleading guilty, granting a credit of 1.5 years to 1. The Supreme Court upheld the initial ruling, thereby deeming unconstitutional the removal of the enhanced credit eligibility. "A rule that results in longer sentences for offenders who do not obtain bail, compared to otherwise identical offenders does not result in 'similar . . . sentences imposed on similar offenders for similar offences committed in similar circumstances'," said the ruling.

Sources: Based on EN1 Kathleen Harris, "Supreme Court strikes down 2 Conservative sentencing reforms, *CBC News*, April 15, 2016, and Sean Fine, "Supreme Court strikes down Tories tough-on-crime laws", *The Globe and Mail*, April 15, 2016.

Courts are now required to consider lifting the publication ban on the names of young offenders who are convicted of "violent offences" when youth sentences are given, and police are required to keep records when informal measures are used in order to make it easier to identify patterns of reoffending. Finally, the list of offences for which a conditional sentence is not a sentencing option is expanded.

3. **Changes to offender accountability**

The *Safe Streets and Communities Act* requires the Parole Board to consider the seriousness of the offender's offence in its decision making and authorizes police to arrest an offender who appears to be breaking his or her release conditions without the need for a warrant. It extends the ineligibility periods for an application for a pardon to 5 years from 3 years for a summary conviction offence and to 10 years from 5 years for an indictable offence and makes those convicted of a sexual offence in relation to a minor or those convicted of more than three offences unable to apply for a pardon. Finally, a number of additional factors must now be considered before an offender can be granted a transfer back to Canada, including whether he or she will endanger public safety, continue to engage in criminal activity, or endanger the safety of any child.

Detractors of the *Safe Streets and Communities Act* have been many. Groups like the Canadian Bar Association, the Canadian Centre for Policy Alternatives, and the Canadian Civil Liberties Association argue that the act ignores decades of research and experience that show that what actually reduces crime is the focus on child poverty, provision of services for the mentally ill, diversion of young offenders from the adult justice system, and rehabilitation of prisoners to assist with their reintegration into society. Others argue that the increased punishments outlined in the act eclipse the crimes. The elimination of the use of conditional sentences for more than the most serious crimes will result in more offenders being given sentences of incarceration. "Is roughly $100 000 per year to incarcerate someone a good use of taxpayers' money?" they ask. With mandatory minimum prison sentences replacing conditional sentences, people in remote, rural, and northern communities will be moved far from their families to serve time. Aboriginals currently represent up to 80 percent of inmates in institutions in the Prairie provinces, and the direction of the *Safe Streets and Communities Act* will not reverse this trend.

The changes to the treatment of young offenders mean that more youth will spend months in custodial centres before trial. Experience has shown that at-risk youth learn or reinforce criminal behaviour in custodial centres; only when diverted to community options are they more likely to be reformed.

Finally, longer and harsher sentences will increase the strains on a justice system already at the breaking point. Courts and Crown prosecutors' offices are currently overwhelmed, legal aid plans are at the breaking point, and police services don't have the resources to do their jobs properly. Critics argue that the *Safe Streets and Communities Act* addresses none of these problems and will serve to make these realities much worse.

11.4 LEARNING OBJECTIVE CAN WE SOLVE THE PROBLEM OF CRIME?

IN 1956, EUROPEAN WRITER HERMANUS BIANCHI EMPHASIZED WHAT HE SAW AS THE difference between criminology and what he termed *Kriminalpolitik*, meaning the political handling of crime or a criminology-based social policy.[33] Criminology, according to Bianchi, should be considered a "metascience" or "a science of wider scope (than that of criminal law, jurisprudence, criminal justice, or corrections) whose terminology can be used to clarify the conceptions of its subdisciplines. Far from being a mere auxiliary to the criminal law, it is therefore superior to it."[34] Bianchi believed that if criminology were to remain pure, it could not afford to sully its hands, so to speak, with political concerns.

Today, the image esteemed by criminologists and the expectations they hold for their discipline are quite different than in Bianchi's time. Many criminologists expect to work hand-in-hand with politicians and policy-makers forging crime-prevention agendas based on scientific knowledge and criminological theorizing and would say that this change in attitude represents a maturation of the discipline of criminology.

Whether effective crime-prevention policies can ever be implemented, however, is an unanswered question. Central to this discussion is the political nature of crime prevention in this country. Creating, selecting, and implementing new crime-prevention programs and expanding and/or discontinuing existing programs involves many considerations. Government priorities such as health care, environmental protection, and defence spending compete for resources. Opinion polls are used to indicate issues of concern to the Canadian public and often play a more prominent role in determining how to implement or continue crime-prevention programs than evidence-based research on what actually works to prevent crime.

Within the field of criminology and crime-prevention policy creation, a more concentrated focus on evidence-based crime prevention is emerging with an appeal that the best available evidence be considered in decisions around crime-prevention approaches. The introduction to a report prepared for the National Crime Prevention Centre entitled *Evidence-Based Crime Prevention: Scientific Basis, Trends, Results and Implications for*

Canada reads: "Crime prevention should be rational and should be based on the best possible evidence. One would expect decision-makers to weigh heavily any available evidence on what works. How can a program that has produced no discernable evidence of effectiveness in numerous evaluations be considered for implementation?"[35] It goes on to pose these key questions:

- What is the scientific foundation of the evidence-based model? How is the evidence-based model applicable to crime prevention?

- Is there an institutional foundation for evidence-based crime prevention? What are some of the key developments in evidence-based crime prevention in selected Western countries?

- What is the state of science on what works to prevent crime?

- What are the main challenges of evidence-based crime prevention?

- What are some of the key implications of other countries' evidence-based crime prevention for Canada, specifically for its National Crime Prevention Strategy and National Crime Prevention Centre?

The report makes a strong case for the use of valid facts and evidence and the methods used to locate, appraise, and synthesize the evidence, namely experimental (randomized and non-randomized) and quasi-experimental research designs. (See Chapter 1 for an overview of research design.) It goes on to identify four approaches that have been recognized to be effective. These include the following:

1. Family-based prevention programs: home visitation, day care/preschool, parent training (with younger children), home/community parent training (with older children), and multisystemic therapy

2. Community-based prevention programs: gang member intervention programs focused on reducing cohesion among youth gangs and individual gang members, community-based mentoring, and after-school recreation

3. School-based prevention programs: school and discipline management, interventions to establish norms or expectations for behaviour and self-control, or social competency instruction using cognitive-behavioural instruction methods

4. Place-focused prevention: nuisance abatement, closed-circuit television surveillance cameras, and improved street lighting

The trend toward evidence-based crime prevention has entered into various components of the criminal justice system, most notably the police. The Canadian Society of Evidence Based Policing (CAN-SEBP) was formed in April 2015. An association of police practitioners, academic researchers, public policy-makers, and others, the CAN-SEBP's mission is to foster the creation and mobilization of quality research in order to make evidence-based approaches a cornerstone of policing in Canada. It identifies its three goals as: (1) the increased use of best available research evidence to solve policing problems, (2) the production of new research evidence by police practitioners and researchers, and (3) the communication of research evidence to police practitioners and the public.[36]

A Canadian system of new crime-prevention programs incorporating high quality evaluation designs is needed in order to create a foundation for evidence-based crime prevention now and in the long run. These new crime-prevention programs should be selected so that they contribute to scientific evidence presently deemed insufficient, such as in the area of promising practices, or as part of a program of replications to test effective practices with different populations and in different regions of the country. As part of the original research design, experiments and quasi-experiments should include large samples, long follow-up periods, follow-up interviews, and provision for an economic analysis. Funding decisions need to be guided by evidence on what works best.[37]

SUMMARY OF LEARNING OBJECTIVES

11.1 Policies dealing with issues of crime and its prevention and control fall under social policy. Policies undergo five stages in their development: identification of the problem; agenda setting, or the prioritization of problems; policy formation; program implementation; and program evaluation and reassessment.

11.2 Most crime-prevention strategies can be described as nurturant, protection/avoidant, or deterrent in nature. Nurturant approaches focus on improving early life experiences and child and adolescent development as the way to effectively prevent crime. Protection/avoidant strategies seek to reduce criminal opportunities by changing routine patterns, increasing guardianship, or incapacitating offenders. Deterrent strategies attempt to reduce motivation for crime by increasing certainty and severity of penalties.

11.3 Examples of all three crime-prevention strategies exist in Canada. The nurturant approach is exemplified in the National Crime Prevention Strategy; examples of the protection/avoidant approach are found in the Crime Prevention Through Environmental Design initiatives across the country; and the *Safe Streets and Communities Act* embodies the notions of increased certainty and severity of penalties as a means of controlling crime.

11.4 Crime prevention is a matter of public policy. Efforts to reduce crime will only be strengthened through the incorporation of high-quality evaluation designs that are supported by evidence-based program design.

Questions for Review

1. What are the typical stages in the development of public policy? Does criminal justice policymaking in Canada follow these stages? Why or why not?

2. What are the three types of crime-prevention strategies described in this chapter? Which comes closest to your own philosophy? Why?

3. Provide one recent Canadian example for each of the three crime-prevention strategies outlined in this chapter. Outline one strength and one weakness for each of the three crime-prevention strategies.

4. Funding decisions about crime-prevention policies and programs must be "guided by evidence on what works best." Do you agree? Why or why not?

Multiple-Choice Questions

1. Which of the following is an example of a protection/avoidance strategy?
   a. decreasing the age at which one is considered a young offender
   b. developing an anger-management program for indigenous youth
   c. reducing the number of entry and exit points on a neighbourhood block
   d. creating clear sight lines or natural surveillance
   e. introducing a parenting skills group for men

2. The first stage of public policy development is _____.
   a. policy formation
   b. program evaluation and reassessment
   c. identification of the problem
   d. agenda setting or the prioritization of problems
   e. program implementation

3. A crime-prevention strategy that attempts to forestall development of criminality by improving early life experiences and channelling child and adolescent development into desirable directions is known as a _____.

   a. protection/avoidance strategy

   b. nurturant strategy

   c. safe streets strategy

   d. deterrence strategy

   e. target-hardening strategy

4. Which of the following is *not* a specific objective of the National Crime Prevention Strategy?

   a. to assist communities in developing and implementing community-based solutions to problems that contribute to crime and victimization

   b. to promote the integrated action of key governmental and non-governmental partners to reduce crime and victimization

   c. to increase sentences of incarceration for firearms-related offences

   d. to increase public awareness of and support for effective approaches to crime prevention

   e. to focus on children, youth, women, and Aboriginal people in community-based solutions to crime and criminality

5. Which of the following have been recognized to be effective evidence-based crime-prevention approaches?

   a. family-based prevention programs

   b. community-based prevention programs

   c. school-based prevention programs

   d. place-focused prevention programs

   e. all of the above

Multiple Choice Answers: 1a, 2c, 3b, 4c, 5e

Chapter 12
The Globalization of Crime

Rexfeatures/AP Images

Technology, international trade and the unprecedented movement of people and businesses around the world have resulted in increasingly porous borders. This brings the benefits of globalization but also provides for new opportunities for exploitation by criminals. Globalization has created new vulnerabilities to old threats.

—*Eileen Skinnider*[1]

LEARNING OBJECTIVES

After reading this chapter, you should be able to

12.1 Explain globalization and understand its impact on contemporary transnational criminal activity.

12.2 Recognize the global and transnational nature of emerging crime trends.

12.3 Realize the role of technology in emerging crime trends and its use in the fight against these trends.

INTRODUCTION

In November 2014, Europol's European Cybercrime Centre (EC3) and enforcement agents in 16 other countries took down over 400 "dark market" websites. The sites, all of which were using Tor hidden service ".onion" addresses, were offering a range of illegal goods and services for sale, including drugs and sexual services. Some even offered murder for hire and women and children as "slaves."[2] The Tor network is a special component of the internet that is designed to conceal the locations of individuals and machines using it. An official commented on the enforcement action, saying, "It is a plain fact that criminals use advanced technology to commit their crimes and conceal evidence—and they hide behind international borders so they can stymie law enforcement. . . . But the global law enforcement community has innovated and collaborated to disrupt these 'dark market' websites, no matter how sophisticated or far-flung they have become."[3]

GLOBALIZATION

12.1 LEARNING OBJECTIVE

GLOBALIZATION, THE INCREASINGLY INTERNATIONAL CHARACTER OF SOCIAL LIFE IS relevant to understanding emerging forms of criminality that are having an impact on much of society, including technology, commerce, communication, and crime. **Globalization**, which can be defined as a process of social homogenization by which the experiences of everyday life, marked by the diffusion of commodities and ideas, can foster a standardization of cultural expressions around the world.[4] The impact of the increasing integration of previously isolated events is an important aspect of globalization, and the idea of globalization encompasses the increasing interconnectedness of people, ideas, and things on a worldwide scale. Globalization, occurring in communications, economics, science, education, and business, involves the progressive erosion of the influence of nation-states and the rise in influence of global decision makers at both public and private levels. Some have used the term *globalization of knowledge* to describe the increase in understanding that results from a sharing of information between cultures. The globalization of knowledge is beginning to play a significant role in both the process of theory formation within criminology and the development of Canadian crime control policies. According to some, "Globalization will make it increasingly difficult for nation-states to ignore the criminal justice information of other countries."[5]

Globalization A process of social homogenization by which the experiences of everyday life, marked by the diffusion of commodities and ideas, can foster a standardization of cultural expressions around the world.

TRANSNATIONAL CRIMES

12.2 LEARNING OBJECTIVE

GLOBALIZATION IS MAKING IT IMPOSSIBLE FOR POLICY-MAKERS TO IGNORE CRIMINAL activity in other parts of the world, especially where that crime is perpetrated by transnational criminal and terrorist organizations. **Transnational crime** has emerged as one of the most pressing challenges of the early 21st century and refers to any unlawful activity undertaken and supported by organized groups operating across national boundaries. The growing globalization of crime has required the coordination of law enforcement efforts in different parts of the world and the expansion of domestic enforcement activities internationally. Transnational crimes range from relatively simple fraudulent email and phishing schemes to the more dangerous and threatening illegal trafficking in human beings, human organs, and illicit drugs. It includes the activities of multinational drug cartels, the support of terrorist groups by criminal organizations seeking armed protection, and well-funded and sophisticated efforts by organized criminal groups looking to overthrow the ruling regime in regions with others sympathetic to their operations.

Transnational crime An unlawful activity undertaken and supported by organized groups operating across national boundaries.

In 2004, the United Nations (UN) made the issue of organized crime one of its priorities for the 21st century and ratified the *United Nations Convention against Transnational Organized Crime and the Protocols*.[6] As a signatory to the UN Convention and its protocols, Canada is a world partner in the effort to seek ways to prevent and control transnational organized crime. The Criminal Intelligence Service Canada (CISC) is an organization that provides the facilities to unite the criminal intelligence units of Canadian law enforcement agencies in the fight against organized crime and other serious crime in Canada. CISC provides an overview of selected global trends and highlights some of the threats and opportunities that have the potential to develop within specific criminal markets. CISC contends that transnational criminal activity is a growing problem in Canada and that technological advances over the past 20 years have made national borders irrelevant to telecommunications and financial transactions and have enabled the globalization of criminal activity.

Although statistics vary, CISC reports that there appear to be anywhere from 5 to 18 active transnational criminal organizations represented in Canada. This includes Asian triads, Colombian cartels, Italian Mafia groups (the most influential being the Sicilian Mafia), Russian/Eastern European *mafiyas*, Nigerian crime groups, and major outlaw motorcycle gangs. Whereas crime syndicates of the past were involved in illegal street-level activities, such as drug trafficking, prostitution, illegal gambling, loan sharking, and extortion, CISC reports that today's organized crime syndicates have become quasi-corporate in their activities and are now involved in arms dealing, large-scale insurance and financial fraud, environmental crime, the trafficking and smuggling of humans, money laundering, bank fraud, and gasoline tax fraud.[7]

Human Smuggling and Trafficking

Trafficking in persons and human smuggling are two of the fastest-growing areas of international criminal activity today. There are important distinctions between the two. The *United Nations Convention against Transnational Organized Crime* defines **human smuggling** as the "procurement for financial or other material benefit of illegal entry of a person into a State of which the person is not a national or resident."[8] In other words, *human smuggling* refers to illegal immigration in which an agent is paid to help a person cross a border clandestinely.[9] Human smuggling may be conducted to obtain financial or other benefits for the smuggler, although sometimes people smuggle others to reunite their families. Human smuggling generally occurs with the consent of the people being smuggled, who often pay for the services. Once in the country they've paid to enter, they usually are no longer in contact with the smuggler. The vast majority of people who are assisted in illegally entering Canada are smuggled rather than trafficked.

In contrast to smuggling, **trafficking in persons (TIP)** can be compared to a modern-day form of slavery. Trafficking involves the exploitation of unwilling people through force, coercion, threat, or deception and includes human rights abuses such as debt bondage, deprivation of liberty, or lack of control over freedom and labour. Trafficking is often undertaken for purposes of sexual exploitation or labour exploitation.

Trafficking involves the delivery of persons to individuals or organizations who have paid for their delivery and the repayment of those debts to the traffickers by the trafficked persons, usually through prostitution or forced labour.[10] Practically speaking, it is sometimes difficult to distinguish between a smuggling case and a trafficking case because trafficking often includes an element of smuggling (i.e., the illegal crossing of a national border). Some trafficking victims are unaware of their eventual fate; they

Human smuggling A type of illegal immigration in which an agent is paid to help a person cross a border clandestinely.

Trafficking in persons (TIP) The exploitation of unwilling or unwitting people through force, coercion, threat, or deception.

may believe they are being smuggled when they are really being trafficked. This happens, for example, when women believe they are agreeing to work in legitimate industries for decent wages, part of which they may have agreed to pay to the trafficker who smuggled them, when in fact they are being trafficked for sexual exploitation. They didn't know that upon arrival the traffickers would keep them in bondage, subject them to physical force or sexual violence, force them to work in the sex trade, and take most or all of their income. Table 12.1 draws some important distinctions between human trafficking and smuggling.

Reports estimate that there are hundreds of thousands of TIP victims in the world each year. At least 152 different nationalities were trafficked and detected in 124 different countries between 2010 and 2012.[11]

Women account for 49 percent of all trafficking victims detected globally; men comprise 18 percent. Children make up 33 percent of all victims detected globally—21 percent are girls, 12 percent are boys.[12] Although human trafficking is often an international crime that involves the crossing of borders, it is important to note that human trafficking victims can be trafficked within their own countries and communities. Traffickers can move victims between locations within the same country and often sell them to other trafficking organizations. The International Labor Organization (ILO), the UN agency charged with addressing labour standards, employment, and social protection issues, estimates that 12.3 million people live in conditions of forced labour, bonded labour, forced child labour, and sexual servitude throughout the world today.[13] Other estimates range as high as 27 million. Worldwide, however, fewer than 10 000 prosecutions for human trafficking occurred in 2013.[14]

According to the United Nations, human smuggling and trafficking have become a worldwide industry affecting millions of people and involving billions of dollars.

Table 12.1 Differences between Human Trafficking and Smuggling

Trafficking	Smuggling
Must contain an element of force, fraud, or coercion (actual, perceived, or implied) unless the victim in under 18 years of age and is involved in commercial sex acts.	The person being smuggled is generally cooperating.
Forced labour and/or exploitation.	No forced labour or other exploitation.
Persons trafficked are victims.	Persons smuggled are violating the law. They are not victims.
Enslaved, subjected to limited movement or isolation, or had documents confiscated.	Persons are free to leave, change jobs, etc.
Need not involve the actual movement of the victim.	Facilitates the illegal entry of person(s) from one country into another.
No requirement to cross an international border.	Smuggling always crosses an international border.
Person must be involved in labour/services or commercial sex acts (i.e., must be "working").	Person must only be in the country or attempting entry illegally.

Note: This table is meant to be conceptual and is not intended to provide precise legal distinctions between trafficking and smuggling.

Source: Adapted from U.S. Department of State, Bureau for International Narcotics and Law Enforcement Affairs, Human Smuggling and Trafficking Center, *Fact Sheet: Distinctions Between Human Smuggling and Trafficking*, April 2006, http://www.state.gov/documents/organization/90541.pdf [Accessed August 10, 2016].

Many of the routes used by smugglers—from Mexico and Central America to the United States, from West Asia through Greece and Turkey to Western Europe, and within East and Southeast Asia—have become well established and are widely known. The UN has attributed the flourishing smuggling routes to weak legislation, lax border controls, corrupt officials, and organized crime's power and influence. While there are significant differences between human smuggling and TIP, the underlying conditions that give rise to both are similar: extreme poverty, lack of economic opportunity, civil unrest, and political uncertainty.

A comprehensive report released in 2014 by the United Nations Office on Drugs and Crime (UNODC) entitled *Global Report on Trafficking in Persons* identified countries of origin, transit, and destination as they pertain to the trafficking of human beings. The report noted that Canada ranks high in terms of a destination country; however, the scope of these criminal activities in Canada remains a small percentage of the international (or even the North American) criminal market. Canada is largely a destination and a transit country for women who are trafficked for the purposes of sexual exploitation. Most arrive from Asia, Latin America, Russia, and Eastern Europe.[15] According to the latest strategic intelligence assessment on human trafficking produced by the RCMP,

> Human trafficking may as likely be orchestrated by transnational organized criminal networks as it may be coordinated by a few family-based opportunists with little formal structure. It is also a borderless crime that victimizes vulnerable persons regardless of their nationality. Human trafficking is a crime that thrives in stigmatized facets of the work force, like the sex trade and illegal labour, and hides in the privacy of homes and businesses.[16]

Based on various reports, the RCMP estimates that anywhere between 1500 and 2200 persons are trafficked from Canada into the United States each year.[17]

Trafficking in human beings is a global issue, and illegal migrants and trafficking victims have become another commodity in a larger arena of criminal commerce involving other commodities, such as narcotic drugs, firearms or other weapons, and money laundering, all of which generate illicit revenues or seek to reduce risks for traffickers. To date, the lack of systematic research in this area means that reliable data on

A poster designed by the RCMP to raise public awareness about the growing issue of human trafficking. How does this type of criminal activity represent the globalization of crime?

© 2013 HER MAJESTY THE QUEEN IN RIGHT OF CANADA as represented by the Royal Canadian Mounted Police

the trafficking of human beings that would allow comparative analyses and the design of preventative measures are limited. The relatively low risks associated with trafficking and the potential for substantial profits have, in some cases, induced criminals to become involved as an alternative to other, riskier criminal pursuits. Furthermore, victims are intimidated by traffickers, both in destination countries, where they fear deportation or prosecution for offences such as prostitution or illegal immigration, and in their countries of origin, where they are often vulnerable to retaliation or revictimization. As a result, many are reluctant to cooperate with criminal justice authorities, making detection and prosecution difficult. Supporting and protecting victims are critical elements in the fight against trafficking to increase victims' willingness to cooperate with authorities and as a necessary means of rehabilitation.

The adoption of the UNODC's *Protocol to Prevent, Suppress, and Punish Trafficking in Persons, Especially Women and Children* has initiated the cooperation of all signing countries to work together to produce and share greater information on the trafficking of humans, to enact domestic laws making human trafficking an offence, to ensure that such legislation applies to victims of all ages and both sexes, and to implement measures to provide for the physical, psychological, and social recovery of victims. More recently, the UNODC has launched a human trafficking case law database that aims at assisting judges and prosecutors by making available details of real cases with examples of how the respective national laws can be used to prosecute trafficking in persons. Since very little is currently known internationally about the cases where prosecutions have been carried out, the case law database serves to provide immediate public access to officially documented instances of this crime and contains details on victims' and perpetrators' nationalities, trafficking routes, verdicts, and other information related to prosecuted cases from across the world.[18]

Human Trafficking and the Law   In Canada, trafficking in humans wasn't recognized as an offence until November 2001, when Bill C-11 amended the former *Immigration Act* to include fines of up to $1 million and life imprisonment for the trafficking of people. The new *Immigration and Refugee Protection Act (IRPA)* was proclaimed in June 2002. In 2005, the *Criminal Code of Canada* was amended, creating three additional offences to cover all forms of trafficking. Section 279 includes the prohibition of trafficking in persons, defined as the recruitment, transport, transfer, receipt, concealment, or harbouring of a person, or the exercise of control, direction, or influence over the movements of a person for the purpose of exploitation. It also prohibits a person from benefiting economically from trafficking, as well as prohibiting the withholding or destroying of identity, immigration, or travel documents to facilitate trafficking in persons.

Even with the appropriate legislation in place, it is difficult to lay charges for human trafficking as these are not regular criminal cases. The low number of human trafficking charges in Canada speaks in large part to the very covert nature of these crimes, the reluctance of victims to come forward, and the complexity of human trafficking investigations that often span multiple international jurisdictions. In 2004, the RCMP established a new human trafficking unit to provide guidance and analytical support for domestic investigations across Canada and to mount joint investigations with foreign law enforcement agencies. The unit shares information with the Canadian Security and Intelligence Service (CSIS) and works to coordinate domestic efforts of individual police services across the country and to link these efforts to the protocols, investigative standards, and training in the international arena. Within its Immigration and Passport Branch, the RCMP has created the Human Trafficking National Coordination Centre, which oversees six regional immigration and passport sections, employing about 160 officers who are mandated to investigate immigration and human trafficking offences.[19]

TECHNOLOGY AND CRIME

TECHNOLOGY AND CRIME HAVE ALWAYS BEEN CLOSELY LINKED. THE CON ARTIST WHO uses a telephone in a financial scam, the robber who uses a firearm and drives a getaway car, even the murderer who wields a knife—all employ at least rudimentary forms of technology in the crimes they commit. Early forms of technology, including the telegraph, the telephone, and the automobile, were embraced by agents of law enforcement as soon as they became available. Evidence derived from fingerprint and ballistics analysis is routinely employed by prosecutors, and emerging technologies promise to keep criminologists and law enforcement agents in step with high-tech offenders.

As technology advances, it facilitates new forms of behaviour, so we can be certain that tomorrow's crimes will differ from those of today. Personal crimes of violence and traditional property crimes will continue to occur, but advancing technology will create new and as yet unimaginable opportunities for criminals positioned to take advantage of it and of the power it will afford. The very nature of this criminal activity makes it a global concern and transnational in scope—indeed, technology is one of the easiest ways to organize and undertake unlawful activity that transcends national borders.

A frightening preview of such possibilities was seen during the collapse of the Soviet Union when the resulting social disorganization made the acquisition of fissionable materials, stolen from Soviet stockpiles, simple for even relatively small outlaw organizations. In what is a nightmare for authorities throughout the world, Middle Eastern terrorist groups are making forceful efforts to acquire former Soviet nuclear weapons and the raw materials necessary to manufacture their own bombs, and some evidence suggests that nuclear weapons parts may have already been sold to wealthy international drug cartels and organized criminal groups, who could hoard them to use as bargaining chips against possible government prosecution.

More recently, Canada's chief information officer identified that a "highly sophisticated Chinese state-sponsored actor" had managed to hack into the computer systems at Canada's National Research Council. This was not the first time the Canadian government had fallen victim to a cyberattack that seems to have originated in China, but it was the first time the Canadian government has unequivocally blamed China for the attack.[20]

Cybercrime Any crime that involves a computer as the object of the crime or as the tool used to commit a material component of the offence.

The realities of today's digital world have led to a relatively new form of crime, called *cybercrime*, and to new laws intended to combat it. Simply put, **cybercrime**, or *computer crime*, refers to any crime that involves the use of computers or the manipulation of digital data and is generally defined as "a criminal offence involving a computer as the object of the crime, or the tool used to commit a material component of the offence."[21] Many argue that only those crimes that employ computer technology as central to their commission and that could not be committed without it may properly be called *cybercrimes*. However, the Canadian Police College recognizes two broad categories of cybercrime—one in which the computer is the *tool* of the crime and one in which the computer is the *object* of the crime.

Types of criminal behaviour in which the computer is the *tool* of the crime include traditional crimes that are now being perpetrated more widely through the use of the internet. They include child pornography, child luring, criminal harassment, cyberbullying, fraud, theft of intellectual property and information, and the sale of humans, illegal goods, and substances. (For a more in-depth look at cyberbullying, see the Crime in the News box.)

The second category of cybercrime, in which the computer is the *object* of the crime, speaks to crimes that are related more specifically to computer technology. This category includes such activities as hacking or unauthorized use of computer

Table 12.2 Categories of Cybercrime

Internal Cybercrimes (Malware)	Support of Criminal Enterprises
Trojan horses	Databases to support drug distribution
Logic bombs	Databases to support loan-sharking
Trapdoors	Databases to support illegal gambling
Viruses	Databases to keep records of illegal client transactions
	Electronic money laundering
	Communications in furtherance of criminal conspiracies
Internet and Telecommunications Crimes	
Phone phreaking	**Computer-Manipulation Crimes (aka Computer Fraud)**
Hacking	Embezzlement
Denial of service attacks	Electronic fund transfer fraud
Illegal websites	Other fraud/phishing
Dissemination of illegal material (e.g., child pornography)	Extortion threats/electronic terrorism
Misuse of telephone systems	**Hardware, Software, and Information Theft**
Theft of telecommunications services	Software piracy (warez)
Illegal eavesdropping	Theft of computers
Illegal internet-based gambling	Theft of microprocessor chips
	Theft of trade secrets and proprietary information
	Identify theft

systems, defacing of websites, and the creation and malicious dissemination of computer viruses.[22]

The FBI in the United States recognizes five types of computer crime: (1) internal computer crimes, such as viruses; (2) internet and telecommunications crimes, such as illegal hacking; (3) support of criminal enterprises, such as databases supporting drug distribution; (4) computer manipulation crimes, including embezzlement; and (5) hardware, software, and information theft.[23] (See Table 12.2 for a more detailed breakdown of the categories of computer crimes as defined by the FBI.)

Computers as Tools of Crime

Information is vital to the success of any endeavour, and certain forms of information hold nearly incalculable value for those who possess them. Patents on new products, pharmaceutical formulations, corporate strategies, and the financial resources of corporations all represent competitive and corporate trade secrets. Government databases, if infiltrated, can offer terrorists easy paths to destruction and mayhem.

Some cybercriminals intend simply to destroy or alter data without otherwise accessing or copying the information. Disgruntled employees, mischievous computer **hackers**, business competitors, and others may have varied degrees of interest in destroying a company's records or computer capabilities.

High-tech criminals seeking illegitimate access to computerized information take a number of routes. One is the path of direct access, wherein office workers

Hacker A person who uses computers for exploration and exploitation.

Cyberbullying Creating Difficult Questions for Legal System

Victims' advocates calling for new cyberbullying laws, but pinning down broad term difficult

When B.C. native Amanda Todd took her own life in 2012 after being harassed online, a video she released detailing her experience caused widespread concern and raised questions as to how police handle the online world.

Her tragedy shared similarities with another one that raised public outcry. Rehtaeh Parsons of Nova Scotia attempted suicide after being cyberbullied and died soon afterward in 2013, prompting demands for a substantive response to cyberbullying.

Politicians have tried to respond, but their efforts have run into roadblocks and conflict has arisen over how to tackle cyberbullying without breaching people's freedom of expression. Such was the case when Nova Scotia's Cyber-Safety Act—the first law in Canada aimed at cyberbullying—was struck down in December 2015 by the Supreme Court of Nova Scotia for infringing on the Canadian Charter of Rights and Freedoms.

The definition of the cyberbullying in the act was called a "colossal failure" in the ruling because it covered too many forms of expression beyond what was intended.

Halifax-based privacy lawyer David Fraser, who made the charter challenge against the act, said the difficulty of pushing forward cyberbullying law is keeping the definition precise. "The main challenge is actually defining what cyberbullying is because cyberbullying covers a huge range of behaviours," said Fraser.

What should cyberbullying mean?

Nova Scotia's Cyber-Safety Act was created in the weeks following Parsons's death and allowed victims to apply for protection orders to place restrictions on cyberbullies. But the broad definition of cyberbullying in the act garnered it immediate opposition and was eventually grounds for striking the law down.

Cara Zwibel, a director at the Canadian Civil Liberties Association, opposed the act for its infringements on Canadian freedoms. She said lawmakers need to be more focused about cyberbullying by thinking specifically of what harms they seek to address and by "coming up with a relatively clear and a relatively narrow definition of what constitutes bullying."

Fraser said more experts need to be consulted to determine a clear definition of cyberbullying, something that did not happen when the act was originally drafted.

Despite the problems associated with the Cyber-Safety Act, there are those who would like to see parts of it imitated elsewhere. Kendra Milne, director of law reform for West Coast LEAF—a group that advocates for law reform in support of women's rights—agreed the Nova Scotia law was too broad. But she added the law's protection orders could work well and other provinces should try to adopt similar laws with better definitions of cyberbullying.

Criminal harassment on Twitter

With new laws not forthcoming for many aspects of cyberbullying, courts have relied on extending the boundries of older laws.

One such instance was in the Ontario trial of Gregory Alan Elliott, who was found not guilty of criminally harassing online feminists Stephanie Guthrie and Heather Reilly on Twitter on January 22, 2016. The ruling said that the threshold of criminal harassment—an objectively reasonable fear for one's safety—had not been met in the case.

A recent CBC investigation also highlighted the limitations of criminal harassment. While the RCMP recommended the charge against B.C. native Patrick Fox, who aims to 'destroy' his ex-wife Desiree Capuano with a revenge website, the Crown opted not to proceed. A spokesperson for the Crown said they couldn't conclude the threshold for criminal harassment was being met, in part because Capuano lives in Arizona. Fraser said the definition of criminal harassment could be examined by lawmakers to better address online behaviour.

"I do think that maybe we need to be thinking about tweaking the [criminal] harassment [law]," he said. "Maybe there should be something relating to seriously psychological injury or harm or intimidation."

Milne disagrees with the idea, saying she thinks the court has underlying biases and assumptions about reasonable fear that need to change more than criminal harassment law itself.

"The problem is understanding what is likely or when it is reasonable for someone to be fearful for themselves," said Milne. "It's more a matter of shifting stereotypes and assumptions in the legal system and in society at large about what that means when people can and do reasonably feel fearful."

Beyond legal measures

Beyond Canada, lawmakers are also trying to find legal means to handle cyberbullying.

On February 10, 2016, game developer Zoe Quinn decided to drop her U.S. lawsuit against ex-boyfriend Eron Gjoni, a case stemming from him allegedly leading online harassment against her. In an online statement, she said she no longer wanted to gamble on what precedent would be established in her case, which was held in a Boston municipal court.

>

or corporate spies, planted as seemingly innocuous employees, use otherwise legitimate work-related entry to a company's computer resources to acquire wanted information.

Another path of illegal access, called *computer trespass*, involves remote access to targeted machines. Anyone equipped with a computer and internet access has potential access to numerous computer systems. Many such systems have few, if any, security procedures in place (see the following Who's Responsible? box). Similarly, electromagnetic field decoders can scan radio frequency emanations generated by all types of computers. Keystroke activity, internal chip-processed computations, and disk reads, for example, can be detected and interpreted at a distance by such sophisticated devices. Computers secured against such passively invasive practices are rarely found in the commercial marketplace, although the military has adopted them for many applications. Within the last decade, wireless networking has heightened fears of data theft, and cell phones, handheld devices, and other forms of radio communication offer opportunities for data interception.

In 1988, the first criminal prosecution of a person accused of creating a computer virus took place. According to Richard Baker, author of the respected *Computer Security Handbook*, "The greatest threat to your computers and data comes from inside your company, not outside. The person most likely to invade your computer is not a gawky youngster in some other part of the country but an employee who is currently on your payroll."[24]

Software piracy, or the unauthorized and illegal copying of software programs, is also rampant. According to the Business Software Alliance, global losses from software piracy (known as "warez" in the computer underground) totalled nearly $52.2 billion in 2015; however, cyberattacks cost business over $400 billion in the same year. The Alliance found that 39 percent of all personal computer software installed in 2013 was pirated and contends that a strong connection exists between cyberattacks and the use of illegitimate or unlicensed software.[25]

Software piracy The unauthorized and illegal copying of software programs.

One of the earliest forms of cybercrime was committed by **phone phreaks**, who use special dial-up access codes and other restricted technical information to avoid long-distance charges. Some are able to place calls from pay phones, while others fool telephone equipment into billing other callers. "Many organizations discover they have been victims of telephone fraud only after their telephone bill arrives in a carton instead of an envelope."[26]

Phone phreak A person who uses switched, dialled-access telephone services for exploration and exploitation.

Another form of phone phreaking has emerged that involves the electronic theft of cellular telephone numbers and access codes. Thieves armed with simple mail-order scanners and low-end computers can "literally grab a caller's phone number and identification number out of the air."[27] According to some experts, "Those numbers are [then] used to program computer chips, which are placed inside other cellular phones—or 'clones'—so the long-distance calls appear on the victim's bill."[28]

Developments in Voice-over Internet Protocol (VoIP) technology have made the theft of telecommunications services less lucrative but have also opened the door to

Criminal Activity or Performing a Good Deed?

His second academic year had barely begun in September 2008 when Mansour Moufid withdrew from his math program at Carleton University in Ottawa amid controversy surrounding his involvement in an attempt to expose the weaknesses of the university's security system.

In a 16-page report sent to university administrators and students under the pseudonym "Kasper Holmberg," Moufid showed that he had accessed the campus card accounts of 32 students. His letter indicated that, while he could have accessed student emails, course registrations, library records, and personal financial information, as well as any money students put on their cards, he did not, stating that he was only interested in encouraging the university to improve its security.

Cited for violation of the school's Student Rights and Responsibilities Policy, the university administration imposed six sanctions on Moufid, including paying $608 for the cost of 32 new student cards; paying $2160 for the cost of extra security staff for the residence buildings due to the unknown risk caused by the breach of the campus card system; seven hours of community service per week at a local food bank; and the completion of an ethics course. It was made very clear that if Moufid violated the university's student policy again, he would face expulsion.

The controversy about the situation and what ultimately resulted in Moufid's withdrawal from Carleton University was the university's requirement that he write a letter of apology to all 32 students, the university, and the university community, admitting that he had lied about alerting the university before distributing his report. Moufid refused, insisting that he had mailed a copy of his report to Carleton's Information Privacy Officer and its Information Coordinator two weeks before he sent it to the affected students and campus media. In his statement of defence, Mr. Moufid indicated that he never had any intention of harming his fellow students or Carleton University in any way, and that his ultimate goal was to see security improved.

"To be clear: I did not create any security problem, but simply revealed it; I did not alter or destroy any data although I could have; I did not take any advantage of any student, either financially or otherwise, although I could have; I was acting in good faith, with the interests of the student body—of which I am a part of—in mind," read a portion of his statement.

In addition to being submitted to the university's discipline, Mr. Moufid was also charged under the *Criminal Code* with mischief to data and unauthorized use of a computer. Both charges carry a maximum prison sentence of 10 years. Mr. Moufid said he was surprised by the severity of the charges. "Ten years in prison? That's like the Mafia or something."

Think about it:

1. Was Mansour Moufid, as he claimed, doing a service by showing weaknesses in the university's security infrastructure?

2. Might there have been better ways for Moufid to make his point? Would these ways have been as effective as the computer mischief in which he engaged? Why or why not?

Source: Based on "Hacker Quits School to Avoid Punishment," Ottawa Citizen, September 28, 2008, and Karen Pinchin, "All Charges Against Carleton Hacker Dropped," *Maclean's On Campus*, July 27, 2009.

---

new kinds of crime. The rapid growth of VoIP communications services makes surveillance and wiretapping difficult and is thought to facilitate "drug trafficking, organized crime, and terrorism."[29] Legislators in some countries are considering changes to VoIP regulations to require telecommunications providers to build "back doors" into VoIP networks that would allow for court-ordered wiretaps to be successfully enforced.

Phishing An internet-based scam to steal valuable information, such as credit card numbers, social insurance numbers, user IDs, and passwords.

Another form of technology fraud is **phishing**, a scam that uses official-looking email to steal valuable information, such as credit card numbers, social insurance numbers, user IDs, and passwords from victims. The emails appear to come from a user's bank, credit card company, retail store, or internet service provider (ISP) and generally inform the recipients that some vital information in their account urgently needs to be updated. Those who respond are provided with an official-looking online form into which they can enter their private financial information. Once the information is submitted, it enters the phisher's database.

The Anti-Phishing Working Group (APWG), a coalition of banks and ISPs, estimated that a typical phishing scheme reaches up to 1 million email inboxes. The watchdog group has identified more than 38 000 different phishing websites.[30] Some observers have noted that in addition to losses suffered by individuals and institutions, phishing has the potential to threaten the viability of ecommerce and to call into question the safety of all Web-based financial transactions.[31] Although servers that run those sites can be anywhere in the world, the APWG found that more than 5 percent of them are located in the United States. Reports indicated that Canada ranked second worldwide after the United States for hosted phishing sites. See Box 12.1 for some suggestions on protecting yourself from identity theft.

Box 12.1 IDENTITY THEFT: WHAT IT IS AND WHAT YOU CAN DO ABOUT IT

Identity theft is the unauthorized collection and use of personal information, usually for criminal purposes. Name, date of birth, address, credit card, social insurance number, and other personal identification numbers can be used to open credit card and bank accounts; redirect mail; establish cellular phone service; rent vehicles, equipment, or accommodation; and even secure employment. Victims can be left with the bills, charges, bad cheques, and taxes. In 2010, Bill S-4 became law in Canada, making it illegal to possess another person's identity information for criminal purposes. Section 402 of the *Criminal Code of Canada* addresses identity theft.

Every year, thousands of Canadians are victims of identity theft. While recent developments in telecommunications and computer processing make it easier for companies and consumers to reach each other, they can also scatter your personal information more widely, making life easier for criminals. In 2011, 17 002 victims of identity fraud reported a combined loss of over $13 million (see Figure 12.1).

Prevention is the best way to deal with identity theft:

■ Identity theft can occur over the internet or telephone, or via fax or regular mail. Therefore, be particularly wary of unsolicited emails, telephone calls, or mail attempting to extract personal or financial information from you.

■ Ask yourself if you really need all the identity documents you carry in your wallet or purse. Remove any you don't need and keep them in a secure place instead.

■ Periodically check your credit reports and bank and credit card statements and report any irregularities promptly to the relevant financial institution and to the credit bureaus.

■ During transactions, it's safer to swipe your cards yourself than it is to allow a cashier to do it for you. If you must hand over your card, never lose sight of it.

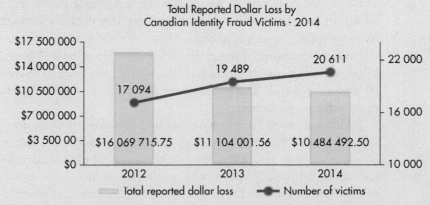

Figure 12.1 Total Reported Dollar Loss by Canadian Identity Fraud Victims, 2014

Source: Canadian Anti-Fraud Centre, *Annual Statistical Report 2014*, http://www.antifraudcentre-centreantifraude.ca/reports-rapports/2014/ann-ann-eng.htm#a1 [Accessed August 10, 2016].

(Continued)

- Always shield your personal identification number when using an ATM or a PIN pad.

- Memorize all personal identification numbers for payment cards and telephone calling cards. Never write them on the cards.

- Familiarize yourself with billing cycles for your credit and debit cards.

- Trash bins are a goldmine for identity thieves. Make sure you shred personal and financial documents before putting them in the garbage.

- When you change your address, make sure you notify the post office and all relevant financial institutions (your bank and credit card companies).

Sources: From Canadian Anti-Fraud Centre, *Annual Statistical Report 2014*, and "Identity Theft and Identity Fraud," Royal Canadian Mounted Police website, December 4, 2015.

Computers as Objects of Crime

Not all cybercrime is committed for financial gain. Some types of cybercrime, including the creation and transmission of destructive computer viruses, "worms," spyware, and other malicious forms of programming code (often called *malware*) might better be classified as "criminal mischief." These types of activities are typically associated with young, technologically sophisticated males seeking a kind of clandestine recognition from their computer-savvy peers. Computer crimes committed by youthful idealistic offenders may represent a new form of juvenile delinquency—one aimed at expressing dissatisfaction with the status quo.

Computer viruses have shown signs of becoming effective terrorist-like tools in the hands of young, disaffected "technonerds" intent on attacking or destroying existing social institutions. A **computer virus** is simply a computer program that is designed to secretly invade computer systems either to modify the way in which they operate or to alter the information they store.[32] Other types of destructive programs are logic bombs, worms, and Trojan horse routines. Distinctions among these programs are based on the way in which they infect targeted machines or the way they behave once they have managed to find their way into a computer. Not all malware is created by disaffected programmers. In 2014, computer security company Symantec announced the discovery of what it called the "world's most sophisticated computer malware."[33] The software code, named Reign, is a highly sophisticated worm designed to provide backdoor access to computers that it infects. It is virtually undetectable and can modify its own code or simply disappear from infected systems in order to avoid discovery. Cybersecurity experts suspect that it was developed by a Western intelligence agency to target foreign governments and that it may have been in operation for years before its discovery. Figure 12.2 provides an overview of some of the most damaging computer viruses of all time.

Although many hardware devices and software products now on the market offer some degree of virus protection to individual and commercial users, new viruses are constantly being created that may soon have the ability to circumvent all security procedures now in place. The only fully effective technique for avoiding viral contamination is the complete and total isolation of computer equipment, a strategy as unlikely to be maintained as it is to be implemented. Once certain forms of malicious software code have successfully invaded a computer, they can take over the machine and use it to send out additional copies of themselves or send spam and other information (including the legitimate user's personal information) to various places on the internet.

Computer virus A set of computer instructions that propagates copies or versions of itself into computer programs or data when it is executed.

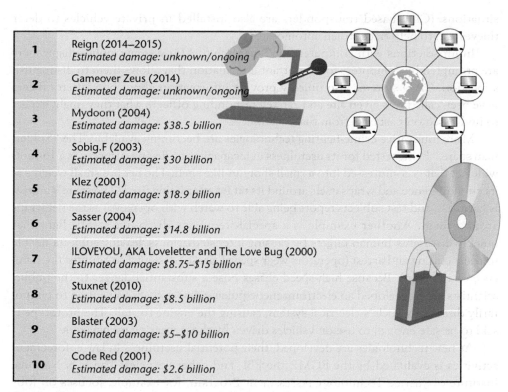

1	Reign (2014–2015) *Estimated damage: unknown/ongoing*
2	Gameover Zeus (2014) *Estimated damage: unknown/ongoing*
3	Mydoom (2004) *Estimated damage: $38.5 billion*
4	Sobig.F (2003) *Estimated damage: $30 billion*
5	Klez (2001) *Estimated damage: $18.9 billion*
6	Sasser (2004) *Estimated damage: $14.8 billion*
7	ILOVEYOU, AKA Loveletter and The Love Bug (2000) *Estimated damage: $8.75–$15 billion*
8	Stuxnet (2010) *Estimated damage: $8.5 billion*
9	Blaster (2003) *Estimated damage: $5–$10 billion*
10	Code Red (2001) *Estimated damage: $2.6 billion*

Figure 12.2 The Ten Most Damaging Computer Viruses and Worms of All Time

Sources: Magazine, "Top Ten Most-Destructive Computer Viruses," , "Computer Invaders," , "The Most Damage Causing Computer Viruses Revealed.

Technology in the Fight against Crime

Technology is a double-edged sword: it arms evildoers with potent new weapons of crime commission, yet it provides police agencies and criminal justice personnel with powerful tools useful in the battle against crime. Criminally useful or evasive technologies and law enforcement capabilities commonly leapfrog one another. Consider traffic radar, which has gone from early always-on units through trigger-operated radar devices to today's sophisticated laser-based speed-measuring apparatus—each change being an attempt by enforcement agencies to keep a step ahead of increasingly sophisticated radar-detection devices marketed to drivers. Radar-jamming devices and laser jammers are also now used by people apparently intent on breaking speed-limit laws. Not to be outdone, suppliers to law enforcement agencies have created radar-detector detectors, which are used by authorities in jurisdictions where radar detectors have been outlawed.[34]

Other potent technologies in law enforcement today are computer databases of known offenders (including public access to sex-offender databases), machine-based expert systems, cellular communications, video surveillance (often combined with face-recognition technology), electronic eavesdropping, DNA analysis, and less-lethal weapons. Transponder-based automated vehicle location (AVL) systems now use patrol car–based transmitters in tandem with orbiting global positioning satellites (GPS) to pinpoint locations of police vehicles so that dispatchers can better allocate available resources on a given shift and substantially reduce police response times in crisis situations. (Chip-based transponders are also installed in private vehicles to deter thieves and to help trace stolen automobiles.)

In jurisdictions with computer-aided dispatch (CAD) systems, police dispatchers are prompted by computers for important information that allows them to distinguish a location. CAD systems also quickly provide information about how often officers have been called to a given site and can tell responding officers what they might expect to find based on past calls from that location.

More innovative crime-fighting technologies are becoming available. The "Spider-man snare," being tested for its usefulness in incapacitating fleeing suspects, is a 16-foot-wide net that is compressed into a small shotgun-like shell. The net has small weights at its circumference and wraps itself around its target after being fired. The snare's impact is harmless, and test subjects report being able to watch with open eyes as the net wraps around them. Another example is a special-frequency disco-like strobe light that quickly disorients human targets by causing intense dizziness, leaving subjects unable to resist cuffing and arrest (operators wear special glasses designed to counter the influence of the light). Because high-speed chases pose a substantial danger to the public, scientists have developed an electromagnetic pulsing device that can be used to temporarily disable a vehicle's electrical system, causing the engine to stall. The prototype is said to be safe enough to use on vehicles driven by those wearing pacemakers.

As new technologies are developed, their potential usefulness in law enforcement activities is evaluated by the RCMP, the FBI, and other agencies. The U.S. National Institute of Justice Technology Assessment Program, for example, focuses on four areas of advancing technology: protective equipment, such as bullet-proof vests and other body armour; forensic sciences, including advances in DNA technology; transportation and weapons, such as electronic stun guns and other less-lethal weapons; and communications and electronics, including computer security and electronic eavesdropping.

Computers also connect people. The internet contains a large number of law-oriented and law enforcement–oriented newsgroups and provides access to the United Nations and worldwide crime data through its link to the United Nations Criminal Justice Information Network. Other computer services provide access to security information and to software useful in law enforcement administration. Innovative computer technologies facilitate the work of enforcement agents. Among them are automated fingerprint identification systems, or AFISs; computerized crime-scene simulations and reenactments; expert systems; and online clearinghouses containing data on criminal activity and offenders. AFISs allow investigators to complete in a matter of minutes what would otherwise consume weeks or months of work manually matching a suspect's fingerprints against stored records. AFIS computers are able to compare and eliminate from consideration many thousands of fingerprints per second, sometimes leading to the identification of a suspect in a short time. Once crime-related information or profiles of criminal offenders have been generated, they are typically stored in a database and often made accessible to law enforcement agencies at other sites. The RCMP's Violent Crime Linkage Analysis System (ViCLAS) is used internationally (and is described in more detail in Chapter 7). Other specialized database programs now track inner-city gang activity and gang membership, contain information on known sexual predators, and describe missing children.

The automated measurement of human traits and identifiers, such as face, finger, and iris recognition, is now a widespread practice among law enforcement agencies and others. These biometric technologies are used for two main purposes: to identify individuals in a database and to support identity assurance, meaning that a user of a system is who he or she claims to be. See Box 12.2 for a more detailed look at a new use for biometric technologies in Canada.

Biometrics, which identifies a person by measuring unique characteristics such as fingerprints, will also free consumers from the need to memorize a myriad of characters.

In the not-too-distant future, your bank will be able to prevent fraud by learning how you type, your car will unlock when it senses the electrical activity of your heart and the security system at your office will recognize your facial features.

That's according to experts in the field of biometrics, which identifies a person by measuring unique characteristics such as their fingerprints, their retinas or their voice. But these types of distinctive identification authentication processes offer more than the promise of a higher degree of security than traditional passwords. Biometrics will also free consumers from the need to memorize a myriad of characters—a convenience that will appeal to anyone who needs to access a secure computer or network regularly.

"People are having to jump through more and more hoops to create a secure authentication," says Karl Martin, the CEO of Nymi, a Toronto-based startup that created a wristband that can identify its wearer based on their electrocardiogram, or the electrical activity of their heart. "How many times a day do you have to prove who you are, whether it be through a password or a biometric or other means?"

Banks—and the financial services industry, more broadly—have been one of the quickest adopters of biometrics technology, given their strong need for security and identity verification, says Bianca Lopes, director of strategy at BioConnect. "They're inherently wired and regulated to protect the customer with things like know-your-client and anti-money laundering rules," says Lopes, whose company helps businesses integrate biometrics technologies across various channels.

The Royal Bank is currently testing out technologies such as iris scanning, face recognition, speech recognition and fingerprint scans—and is expecting to roll out the features to customers in 2017. Martin says Nymi has completed successful pilot projects alongside RBC and TD Bank to test out how its wristband can be used to verify purchases, while MasterCard recently launched a service that allows users to verify their identities with their smartphones by taking a selfie or using a fingerprint scanner.

Notably, it's the popularity of the fingerprint scanner on Apple iPhones that's made consumers more comfortable and familiar with biometrics, says Dennis Gamiello, vice-president of identity solutions at MasterCard. "Fortunately, Apple and some of the other digital players that have introduced (biometric) capabilities are in some ways helping train the consumers for us."

Biometrics can also identify users based on how they behave—for instance, their typing patterns or the way that they swipe across the screen on a mobile device. In the

Nymi has completed successful pilot projects alongside RBC and TD Bank to test out how its wristband can be used to verify purchases.

Chris Young/The Canadian Press

future, behavioural biometrics could even be used to detect if a fraudster has somehow gained access to your bank account, Lopes adds.

While identity verification is important, the capabilities of biometrics go beyond that function, notes Martin. The technology can also be used to create personalized environments—by setting the thermostat to your preferred temperature, for example—at your home, the office or a commercial space. "We're looking at how can identity be used to create completely personalized experiences," says Martin, pointing to cars as an example. "You may have a shared vehicle but you have preferences in terms of the seat height and position and the steering wheel and entertainment and all of those things."

Experts concede that while biometrics can beef up security, improve convenience and create personalized environments, for some users the technologies may evoke scenes from the popular science fiction film "Minority Report"—a Tom Cruise mystery-thriller, which features a future of nearly boundless technological advancements designed to protect its citizenry. "There will be consumers who get creeped out," says Krista Jones, head of work and learning at the MaRS Discovery District.

Ultimately, though, the technology gives consumers a greater guarantee that their private information will be kept safe, she adds. "We have an opportunity to craft this in such a way that the privacy of the consumer is at the heart of this."

Recently, the U.S. Department of Justice's National Law Enforcement and Corrections Technology Center (NLECTC) began testing a high-power compact microwave source designed for vehicle immobilization.[35] The microwave beam emitted by the device can interfere with an automobile's computer circuitry, effectively shutting down a car's engine from up to 10 metres away. As the technology is improved, the device will likely become operable over longer distances, and it may soon become a routine tool in police work.

Automated monitoring of network traffic is an area of considerable interest to law enforcement officials. One network "sniffer" created by the FBI called DCS–1000 (previously known as "Carnivore") was a diagnostic tool intended to assist in criminal investigations by monitoring and capturing large amounts of internet traffic. DCS–1000 was to be installed by FBI agents in ISP data centres as necessary to monitor the electronic communications of individuals suspected of federal crimes, such as terrorism. The Carnivore/DCS–1000 initiative was later retitled **DCS–3000**, and its focus was changed to intercepting suspect personal communications delivered via wireless services.[36] More recent versions, DCS–5000 and DCS–6000, are used with wiretaps and text messages.

DCS–3000 An FBI-developed network diagnostic tool that is capable of assisting in criminal investigations by monitoring and capturing large amounts of internet traffic.

As privacy activist Edward Snowden showed the world in 2013, information is a precious commodity. Nations that can effectively manage valuable information and make it accessible to their citizens will receive enhanced productivity and greater wealth as a reward. Moving information safely and securely is also important; today, a large part of that responsibility falls to the internet. The internet provides amazing and constantly growing capabilities. Unfortunately, as the internet has grown, it has been targeted by hackers and computer criminals, some of whom have introduced rogue computer programs into the network's machines.

Cybercrime and the Law   The borderless reality of the internet allows for crimes to be committed through a number of different countries. Challenges to the prevention and control of cybercrime are that a criminal can commit a crime from any country in the world, target victims all over the world, hide his or her identity by using computer systems located in many different countries, and store evidence in remote locations. Given this transnational reality of cybercrime, initiatives for combatting and preventing computer-based crime largely rely on international cooperation. The Council of Europe *Convention on Cybercrime*, signed by Canada and 29 other nations, is the first international treaty on crimes that are committed via the internet and that involve the use of computer networks. Critics of the convention contend that the treaty fails to provide meaningful privacy and civil liberties protections and that its scope is too broad and covers much more than computer-related crimes. Moreover, they argue, the treaty lacks a "dual criminality" provision, under which an activity must be considered a crime in both countries before one nation can demand cooperation from another.[37] In 2005, Canada signed the *Additional Protocol to the Convention on Cybercrime*, which addresses material and acts of a racist or xenophobic nature committed through computer networks.

One of the challenges within Canada in the battle against cybercrime is the difficulty of applying existing legislation to criminal activities that involve new technologies. Amendments to the *Criminal Code of Canada* have addressed theft of telecommunications services, possession of a device to obtain computer services, computer fraud, and mischief in relation to data, among criminal acts. In many instances, revisions to legislation ensure that existing offences are defined in such a way as to address the new technological aspects of the crime. For example, revisions to legislation making the possession of child pornography illegal have now made it also illegal to download and view child pornography online.[38]

In addition, the Canadian government launched Canada's Cyber Security Strategy in 2010, designed to enhance the protection from cyberthreats for Canadian governments, industries, and families. The strategy is built on three pillars: (1) securing government systems—putting in place the necessary structures, tools, and personnel to meet the government's obligations for cybersecurity; (2) partnering to secure vital cybersystems outside the federal government—supporting initiatives and strengthening Canada's cyber-resiliency, including that of its critical infrastructure sectors, in cooperation with provincial/territorial governments and the private sector; and (3) helping Canadians to be secure online—assisting Canadians in getting the information they need to protect themselves and their families online. Since 2010, $245 million has been spent on defending government computer networks, safeguarding critical infrastructure, and educating the public, and another $142 million has been committed to tackle cyberthreats, particularly against critical infrastructure.[39]

But leaders in Canada's policing, IT, and cybersecurity sectors say the federal strategy is focused primarily on national security threats and does little to combat the dramatic growth in email scams, online extortion, and breaches at corporate computer networks. Canada has no central agency to track cyberattacks and scams, and no federal legislation exists requiring companies to disclose security breaches or theft of data. The federal government does maintain a Spam Reporting Centre and an Anti-Fraud Centre where individuals and companies can report incidents of cybersecurity breaches, but there is concern that neither is equipped to handle the marked increase in cyberscams and malware. The RCMP has a dedicated cybercrime unit; however, it is unclear whether that will help local police services given the RCMP's mandate to probe crimes that are national in scope.

In 2015, the Canadian Association of Chiefs of Police issued a report calling for more coordination and information sharing between police and industry and recommended the creation of a national cybersecurity centre involving government, industry, and all major police forces to help investigate and warn the public about new and emerging cyberthreats. According to Calgary chief of police Roger Chaffin, "Canadian policing in its current format is ill-suited to address crime on a global basis. Nothing really brings it to light more than cybercrime, because your threat actor could be next door to you, or across the world from you. And the ability and the agility to respond to that is going to challenge our model."[40]

SUMMARY OF LEARNING OBJECTIVES

12.1 *Globalization* refers to the increasing integration of previously isolated events in all areas of life and to its effects on people throughout the world. Globalization makes it impossible for Canadian policy-makers to ignore criminal activity in other parts of the world.

12.2 Transnational crime refers to unlawful activity undertaken and supported by organized criminal groups operating across national boundaries whose activities include fraudulent email and phishing schemes, drug running, sex tourism, illegal trafficking in human beings and human organs, and international trade in weapons of mass destruction.

12.3 Technology and criminology have always been closely linked—as technology advances, it facilitates new forms of criminal behaviour. High-technology offences can dramatically change our understanding of crime. Some forms of high-tech crime, committed without regard for national borders or even the need for physical travel, hold dangers never before imagined. High technology provides new criminal opportunities by making available to perpetrators new tools and advanced techniques useful in the commission of crime, and by contributing to the development of items of value, such as computer codes, that did not previously exist. Technology in law enforcement today involves computer databases of known offenders, expert systems, cellular communications, video surveillance and face-recognition technology, electronic eavesdropping, DNA analysis, and less-lethal weapons.

Questions for Review

1. What is globalization? How does it affect criminal activity in today's world?

2. Do you believe that transnational crimes will eventually surpass the abilities of enforcement agencies to prevent or solve them? Why?

3. What are the differences between cybercrime and traditional forms of criminal activity? How does technology provide new criminal opportunities? What new technologies are being used in today's fight against crime?

Multiple-Choice Questions

1. One of the challenges within Canada in the battle against cybercrime is _____.
   a. a lack of police resources
   b. the difficulty of applying existing legislation to criminal activities that involve new technologies
   c. a lack of understanding of the issue by the government
   d. a lack of understanding of the issue by Canadians
   e. the inability of security measures to keep up with the cybercriminals

2. Which of the following is not included in the description of human smuggling?
   a. an element of force, fraud, or coercion (actual, perceived, or implied)
   b. forced labour and/or exploitation
   c. person must be involved in labour/services or commercial sex acts (i.e., must be "working")
   d. facilitates the illegal entry of person(s) from one country into another
   e. person is enslaved, subjected to limited movement or isolation, or had documents confiscated

3. Any crime that involves a computer as the object of the crime or as the tool used to commit a material component of the offence is known as _____.

    a. computer crime

    b. malware

    c. information theft

    d. computer fraud

    e. cybercrime information theft

4. A _____ is a person who uses computers for exploration and exploitation.

    a. phone phreak

    b. software pirate

    c. technonerd

    d. hacker

    e. phisher

5. _____ is defined as an unlawful activity undertaken and supported by organized groups operating across national boundaries.

    a. Globalization

    b. Human trafficking

    c. Human smuggling

    d. Organized crime

    e. Transnational crime

Multiple Choice Answers: 1b, 2d, 3e, 4d, 5e

Notes

Chapter 1

1. Thomas Gabor, *Everybody Does It! Crime by the Public* (Toronto: University of Toronto Press, 1994), p. 307.
2. Sarah Bibel, "'CSI: Crime Scene Investigation' Is the Most-Watched Show in the World," *TV by the Numbers*, June 14, 2012, http://tvbythenumbers.zap2it.com/2012/06/14/csi-crime-scene-investigation-is-the-most-watched-show-in-the-world-2/138212/ [Accessed July 22, 2016].
3. From the standpoint of the law, the proper word is *conduct* rather than *behaviour*, because the term *conduct* implies intentional and wilful activity, whereas *behaviour* refers to any human activity—even unintended and unconscious actions.
4. Paul W. Tappan, "Who Is the Criminal?" in Gilbert Geis and Robert F. Meier, eds., *White Collar Crime* (New York: Free Press, 1947), p. 277.
5. Edwin Sutherland, *Principles of Criminology*, 4th ed. (New York: J.B. Lippincott, 1947).
6. "The Fight for the Right to Die," *CBC News*, June 15, 2012, http://www.cbc.ca/news/canada/story/2012/06/15/f-assisted-suicide.html [Accessed July 25, 2016].
7. John F. Galliher, *Criminology: Human Rights, Criminal Law, and Crime* (Upper Saddle River, NJ: Prentice Hall, 1989), p. 2.
8. C.D. Shearing, "Criminologists Must Broaden Their Field of Study beyond Crime and Criminals," in R. Boostrom, ed., *Enduring Issues in Criminology* (San Diego, CA: Greenhaven, 1995).
9. Ezzat Fattah, *Introduction to Criminology* (Burnaby, BC: School of Criminology, Simon Fraser University, 1989).
10. Hermann Mannheim, *Comparative Criminology* (Boston: Houghton Mifflin, 1965).
11. Ron Claassen, *Restorative Justice: Fundamental Principles*, Centre for Peacekeeping and Conflict Studies, Fresno Pacific College, http://peace.fresno.edu/docs/rjprinc.html [Accessed July 25, 2016].
12. H. Schwendinger and J. Schwendinger, "Defenders of Order or Guardians of Human Rights?" in I. Taylor, P. Walton, and J. Young, eds., *Critical Criminology* (London: Routledge and Kegan Paul, 1975).
13. Ibid.
14. Jeffrey H. Reiman, *The Rich Get Richer and the Poor Get Prison*, 4th ed. (Boston: Allyn & Bacon, 1997), p. 49.
15. Fattah, *Introduction to Criminology*.
16. Matthew B. Robinson, "Defining 'Crime,'" http://www.appstate.edu/~robinsnmb/smokeharms.htm [Accessed November 4, 2006].
17. Piers Beirne and James W. Messerschmidt, *Criminology* (San Diego, CA: Harcourt Brace Jovanovich, 1991), p. 20.
18. See this site maintained by the Canadian Automobile Association (CAA) for an overview of each province's legislation: http://distracteddriving.caa.ca/education/distracted-driving-laws-in-canada.php [Accessed July 25, 2016].
19. Raymond J. Michalowski, "Perspectives and Paradigm: Structuring Criminological Thought," in Robert F. Meier, ed., *Theory in Criminology* (Beverly Hills, CA: Sage, 1977), pp. 17–39.
20. Ibid.
21. Ibid.
22. Piers Beirne, *Inventing Criminology* (Albany: State University of New York Press, 1993).
23. See also Paul Topinard, *Anthropology* (London: Chapman and Hall, 1984).
24. Joseph F. Sheley, *Criminology: A Contemporary Handbook* (Belmont, CA: Wadsworth, 1991), p. xxiii.
25. Edwin H. Sutherland, *Criminology* (Philadelphia: Lippincott, 1924), p. 11.
26. Edwin H. Sutherland, *Principles of Criminology* (Chicago: University of Chicago Press, 1934).
27. Edwin H. Sutherland and Donald R. Cressey, *Criminology*, 9th ed. (Philadelphia: Lippincott, 1974), p. 3.
28. Gennaro F. Vito and Ronald M. Holmes, *Criminology: Theory, Research, and Policy* (Belmont, CA: Wadsworth, 1994), p. 3.
29. Clemens Bartollas and Simon Dinitz, *Introduction to Criminology: Order and Disorder* (New York: Harper & Row, 1989), p. 548.
30. Marvin E. Wolfgang and Franco Ferracuti, *The Subculture of Violence: Towards an Integrated Theory in Criminology* (London: Tavistock, 1967).
31. European Society of Criminology, Constitution, Section 1(d), http://www.esc-eurocrim.org/index.php/the-esc/constitution [Accessed July 26, 2016].
32. Jack P. Gibbs, "The State of Criminological Theory," *Criminology*, vol. 25, no. 4 (November 1987), pp. 822–823.
33. Piers Beirne and Colin Sumner, "Editorial Statement," *Theoretical Criminology*, vol. 1, no. 1 (February 1997), pp. 5–141. Available through Sage Publications, Thousand Oaks, CA.
34. There are, however, those who deny that criminology deserves the name *discipline*. See, for example, Don C. Gibbons, *Talking about Crime and Criminals: Problems and Issues in Theory Development in Criminology* (Englewood Cliffs, NJ: Prentice Hall, 1994), p. 3.
35. Gibbons, *Talking about Crime and Criminals*, p. 4.
36. Sutherland, *Principles of Criminology*.
37. Don M. Gottfredson, "Criminological Theories: The Truth as Told by Mark Twain," in William S. Laufer and Freda Adler, eds., *Advances in Criminological Theory*, vol. 1 (New Brunswick, NJ: Transaction, 1989), p. 1.
38. Gregg Barak, *Integrating Criminologies* (Boston: Allyn & Bacon, 1998), p. 5.
39. Don G. Gibbons, "Talking about Crime: Observations on the Prospects for Causal Theory in Criminology," *Criminal Justice Research Bulletin*, vol. 7, no. 6 (Huntsville, TX: Sam Houston State University, 1992).
40. Ibid.
41. *The American Heritage Dictionary*, CD-ROM (Boston: Houghton Mifflin, 1992).
42. *The American Heritage Dictionary of the English Language*, 3rd ed. (Boston: Houghton Mifflin, 1996).
43. This list is not meant to be exclusive. There are many other journals in the field, too many to list here.
44. Statistics Canada reported in 2006 that there were three private security personnel (102 000) for every two police officers (68 000). See G. Li, "Private Security and Public Policing in Canada, 2006," *Juristat*, vol. 28, no. 10 (Ottawa: Minister of Industry, 2009). In 2013, the numbers reported were more than 140 000 licensed private security guards compared with about 70 000 active public police officers. See "Surge in Private Security Raises Concerns Over Rights" *CBC News*, January 16, 2013, http://www.cbc.ca/news/canada/surge-in-private-security-raises-concerns-over-rights-1.1335730 [Accessed July 26, 2016].

45. Hermann Mannheim, *Comparative Criminology* (Boston: Houghton Mifflin, 1967), p. 20.

46. Details for this story come from Paul Stokes, "Extra Police Put on the Beat for Full Moon," *The Telegraph*, June 7, 2006, http://www.telegraph.co.uk/news/uknews/1553751/ Extra-police-put-on-the-beat-for-full-moon.html [Accessed February 1, 2017].

47. Gottfredson, "Criminology Theories," p. 3.

48. Kenneth R. Hoover, *The Elements of Social Scientific Thinking*, 5th ed. (New York: St. Martin's Press, 1992), p. 34.

49. Todd Clear, "Policy and Evidence: The Challenge to the American Society of Criminology—2009 Presidential Address to the American Society of Criminology," *Criminology*, vol. 48, no. 1 (2010), p. 6.

50. Susette M. Talarico, *Criminal Justice Research: Approaches, Problems and Policy* (Cincinnati, OH: Anderson, 1980), p. 3.

51. Ibid.

52. For a good review of secondary research, see J.H. Laub, R.J. Sampson, and K. Kiger, "Assessing the Potential of Secondary Data Analysis: A New Look at the Gluecks' Unraveling Juvenile Delinquency Data," in Kimberly L. Kempf, ed., *Measurement Issues in Criminology* (New York: Springer-Verlag, 1990), pp. 241–257; and Robert J. Sampson and John H. Laub, *Crime in the Making* (Cambridge, MA: Harvard University Press, 1993).

53. Sampson and Laub, *Crime in the Making*, p. 3.

54. According to Denise C. Gottfredson, "Midnight basketball programs are not likely to reduce crime." Gottfredson cites research (J.G. Ross et al., "The Effectiveness of an After-School Program for Primary Grade Latchkey Students on Precursors of Substance Abuse," *Journal of Community Psychology*, OSAP Special Issue [1992], pp. 22–38) showing that such programs may actually increase the risk for delinquency by increasing risk-taking and impulsiveness. See Denise C. Gottfredson, "School-Based Crime Prevention," in Lawrence W. Sherman et al., eds., *Preventing Crime: What Works, What Doesn't, What's Promising* (Washington, DC: National Institute of Justice, 1998).

55. Frank E. Hagan, *Research Methods in Criminal Justice and Criminology*, 6th ed. (New York: Allyn & Bacon, 2003).

56. Canadian Centre for Justice Statistics, *The Juristat Reader: A Statistical Overview of the Criminal Justice System* (Toronto: Thompson Educational Publishing, 1999), p. v.

57. As with almost anything else, qualitative data can be assigned to categories and the categories numbered. Hence qualitative data can be quantified, although the worth of such effort is subject to debate.

58. Patrick J. Desroches, *Behind the Bars—Experiences in Crime* (Toronto: Canadian Scholars' Press, 1996), pp. 27–28.

59. Hagan, *Research Methods in Criminal Justice and Criminology*.

60. Ibid.

61. Faye S. Taxman, "Research and Relevance: Lessons from the Past, Thoughts for the Future," *Criminology and Public Policy*, vol. 3, no. 2 (March 2004), p. 170.

62. Julian Leigh, "Mandatory Arrest Laws Can Reduce Domestic Violence," in Tamara L. Roleff, ed., *Domestic Violence: Opposing Viewpoints* (San Diego, CA: Greenhaven Press, 2000).

63. Kevin D. Haggerty, "Displaced Expertise: Three Constraints on the Policy Relevance of Criminological Thought," *Theoretical Criminology*, vol. 8, no. 2 (2004), pp. 211–231.

64. Scot Wortley and Rosemary Gartner, "Highlights of a Criminological Career: Anthony Doob and the State of Evaluation Research in Canada," *Canadian Journal of Criminology and Criminal Justice*, vol. 55, no. 4, (October 2013), pp. 577–594.

65. Ibid.

66. The Campaign for an Effective Crime Policy, *The Impact of Three Strikes and You're Out Laws: What Have We Learned?* (Washington, DC: CECP, 1997).

67. Fox Butterfield, no headline, *New York Times News Service Online*, April 16, 1997.

68. Sherman et al., *Preventing Crime: What Works, What Doesn't, What's Promising*.

69. Mennonite Central Committee, "Harsher Penalties Not Answer to Canada's Crime Problem," *Mennonite Central Committee News Service*, October 26, 1994, http://www. faslink.org/crime1.htm [Accessed February 1, 2017].

70. Carol La Prairie, "The Impact of Aboriginal Justice Research on Policy: A Marginal Past and an Even More Uncertain Future," *Canadian Journal of Criminology*, vol. 41, no. 2 (April 1999), p. 249.

71. Ibid., p. 250.

72. Kimberley N. Varinos and Voula Marinos, "Three Decades of Public Attitudes Research on Crime and Punishment in Canada," *Canadian Journal of Criminology and Criminal Justice*, vol. 54, no. 4 (October 2013), pp. 549–562.

73. Julian V. Roberts, *Fear of Crime and Attitudes to Criminal Justice: A Review of Recent Trends, 2001–02*. Report for the Ministry of the Solicitor General (Ottawa: Public Works and Government Services Canada, 2001), pp. 24–26.

74. Angus Reid Strategies, *Canadians Endorse Federal Government's Anti-Crime Proposals*, June 26, 2009, http://www.angus-reid. com/polls/40374/canadians-endorse-federal-governments-anti-crime-proposals/ [Accessed November 24, 2012].

75. Jake Edmiston, "Canada's Inexplicable Anxiety over Violent Crime," *National Post*, August 4, 2012, http://news. nationalpost.com/news/canada/canadas-inexplicable-anxiety-over-violent-crime [Accessed July 29, 2016].

76. Karin Stein, *Public Perception of Crime and Justice in Canada: A Review of Opinion Polls* (Ottawa: Department of Justice Canada, 2001), p. x.

77. For an especially good discussion of this issue, see Theodore Sasson, *Crime Talk: How Citizens Construct a Social Problem* (Hawthorne, NY: Aldine de Gruyter, 1995).

78. Dan Gardner, *Risk: The Science and Politics of Fear* (Toronto: McClelland & Stewart, 2008).

79. Public Safety Canada, *Supporting the Successful Implementation of the National Crime Prevention Strategy*, http://www.publicsafety.gc.ca/cnt/rsrcs/pblctns/spprtng-mplmtn/index-en.aspx [Accessed July 29, 2016].

80. Frank Schmalleger, *Criminology Today: An Integrative Introduction* (Upper Saddle River, NJ: Prentice Hall, 2017), p. 17.

81. For a good overview of this issue, see Wesley G. Skogan, ed., *Reactions to Crime and Violence: The Annals of the American Academy of Political and Social Science* (Thousand Oaks, CA: SAGE, 1995).

82. For an excellent discussion of crime as a social event, see Leslie W. Kennedy and Vincent F. Sacco, *Crime Counts: A Criminal Event Analysis* (Toronto: Nelson Canada, 1996).

83. For a good discussion of the social construction of crime, see Leslie T. Wilkins, "On Crime and Its Social Construction: Observations on the Social Construction of Crime," *Social Pathology*, vol. 1, no. 1 (January 1995), pp. 1–11.

84. For a parallel approach, see Terance D. Miethe and Robert F. Meier, *Crime and Its Social Context: Toward an Integrated Theory of Offenders, Victims, and Situations* (Albany: State University of New York Press, 1995).

85. Joan McCord, "Family Relationships, Juvenile Delinquency, and Adult Criminality," *Criminology*, vol. 29, no. 3 (August 1991), pp. 397–417.

86. Elizabeth Candle and Sarnoff A. Mednick, "Perinatal Complications Predict Violent Offending," *Criminology*, vol. 29, no. 3 (August 1991), pp. 519–529.

87. Carol W. Kohfeld and John Sprague, "Demography, Police Behavior, and Deterrence," *Criminology*, vol. 28, no. 1 (February 1990), pp. 111–136.

88. Leslie W. Kennedy and David R. Forde, "Routine Activities and Crime: An Analysis of Victimization in Canada," *Criminology*, vol. 28, no. 1 (February 1990), pp. 137–152.

89. William G. Doerner, "The Impact of Medical Resources on Criminally Induced Lethality: A Further Examination," *Criminology*, vol. 26, no. 1 (February 1988), pp. 171–177.

90. Ibid., p. 177.

91. James F. Gilsinan, "They Is Clowning Tough: 911 and the Social Construction of Reality," *Criminology*, vol. 27, no. 2 (May 1989), pp. 329–344.

92. See, for example, T.D. Miethe and R.F. Meier, *Crime and Its Social Context: Toward an Integrated Theory of Offenders, Victims, and Situations* (New York: SUNY Press, 1994).

93. For a good discussion of the historical development of criminology, see Leon Radzinowicz, *In Search of Criminology* (Cambridge, MA: Harvard University Press, 1962).

94. Diana Fishbein, as quoted in W. Wayt Gibbs, "Trends in Behavioral Science: Seeking the Criminal Element," *Scientific American*, vol. 272, no. 3 (1995), pp. 100–107.

Chapter 2

1. F. Schmalleger, D. MacAlister, P.F. McKenna, and J. Winterdyk, *Canadian Criminal Justice Today: An Introductory Text for the Twenty-First Century* (Toronto: Prentice Hall Allyn & Bacon Canada, 2000), p. 29.

2. This section adapted from CBC News, "'Black Widow' Charged with Attempted Murder," *CBC News*, October 2, 2012, http://www.cbc.ca/news/canada/nova-scotia/story/2012/10/02/ns-black-widow-charged.html [Accessed July 3, 2016]; *The Canadian Press*, "Man Who Wed Black Widow Says Marriage Unregistered," *CBC News*, October 18, 2012, http://www.cbc.ca/news/canada/nova-scotia/story/2012/10/18/ns-black-widow-marriage-weeks.html [Accessed July 3, 2016]; "Trial for 'Internet Black Widow' Set for June," *CBC News*, December 3, 2012, http://www.cbc.ca/news/canada/nova-scotia/story/2012/12/03/ns-black-widow-trial-june.html [Accessed July 3, 2016]; "'Internet Black Widow' Melissa Ann Shepard Case Put Over in Halifax Court," *CBC News*, http://www.cbc.ca/news/canada/nova-scotia/melissa-ann-shepard-due-in-halifax-court", http://www.cbc.ca/news/canada/nova-scotia/melissa-ann-shepard-due-in-halifax-court-1.3663191 [Accessed July 8, 2016].

3. A number of contemporary criminologists continue to study the effect of weather on crime. See, for example, Ellen G. Cohn, "The Effect of Weather and Temporal Variations on Calls for Police Service," *American Journal of Police*, vol. 15, no. 1 (1996), pp. 23–43; Ellen G. Cohn, "The Prediction of Police Calls for Service: The Influence of Weather and Temporal Variables on Rape and Domestic Violence," *Environmental Psychology*, vol. 13 (1993), pp. 71–83; Ellen G. Cohn, "Weather and Crime," *British Journal of Criminology*, vol. 30, no. 1 (1990), pp. 51–64; and Derral Cheatwood, "Is There a Season for Homicide?" *Criminology*, vol. 26, no. 2 (May 1988), pp. 287–306.

4. B.J. Ennis and T.R. Litwack, "Psychiatry and the Presumption of Expertise: Flipping Coins in the Classroom," *California Law Review*, vol. 62 (1974), pp. 693–725.

5. Canadian Centre for Justice Statistics, *The Juristat Reader. A Statistical Overview of the Canadian Justice System* (Toronto: Thompson Educational Publishing, 1999), p. v.

6. R.A. Silverman, J.T. Teevan, and V.F. Sacco, eds., *Crime in Canadian Society* (Toronto: Harcourt Brace, 1996), pp. 62–63.

7. Statistics Canada, Uniform Crime Reporting Survey: Detailed Information, http://www23.statcan.gc.ca/imdb/p2SV.pl?Function=getSurvey&SDDS=3302 [Accessed July 3, 2016].

8. Ibid.

9. Jillian Boyce, "Police-Reported Crime Statistics in Canada, 2014," *Juristat*, vol. 34, no. 1 (Ottawa: Minister of Industry, 2015).

10. Ibid.

11. K. AuCoin, "Children and Youth as Victims of Violent Crime," *Juristat*, vol. 25, no. 1 (Ottawa: Minister of Industry, 2005).

12. Solicitor General of Canada, "Victims of Crime," *Canadian Urban Victimization Survey* (Ottawa: Solicitor General of Canada, 1983).

13. J. Short and F. Nye, "Extent of Unrecorded Juvenile Delinquency: Tentative Conclusions," *Journal of Criminal Law, Criminology and Police Science*, vol. 49 (1958), pp. 296–302.

14. J. Latimer, S. Kleinknecht, K. Hung, and T. Gabor, *The Correlates of Self-Reported Delinquency: An Analysis of the National Longitudinal Survey of Children and Youth* (Ottawa: Research and Statistics Division, Department of Justice Canada, 2003).

15. For an overview of the reliability of self-report studies, see M.J. Hindelang, T. Hirschi, and J.G. Weis, *Measuring Delinquency* (Beverly Hills, CA: SAGE, 1981).

16. For an excellent overview of the social dimensions of crime, see John Hagan and Ruth D. Peterson, *Crime and Inequality* (Stanford, CA: Stanford University Press, 1995); and James W. Messerschmidt, *Crime as Structured Action: Gender, Race, Class and Crime in the Making* (Thousand Oaks, CA: SAGE, 1997).

17. D.A. Andrews and J. Bonta, *The Psychology of Criminal Conduct* (Cincinnati, OH: Anderson Publishing, 1989).

18. V.P. Bunge, H. Johnson, and T. Baldé, "Exploring Crime Patterns in Canada," *Crime and Research Justice Research Paper Series*, Cat. no. 85-561-MIE (Ottawa: Minister of Industry, 2005).

19. Ibid.

20. Marc Ouimet, "Explaining the American and Canadian Crime 'Drop' in the 1990s," *Canadian Journal of Criminology*, vol. 45, no. 2 (2002), pp. 33–50.

21. Samuel Perreault, "Criminal Victimization in Canada, 2014," *Juristat*, vol. 35, no. 1 (Ottawa: Minister of Industry, 2015).

22. Lucie Ogrodnik, "Child and Youth Victims of Police-Reported Violent Crime, 2008," *Canadian Centre for Justice Statistics Profile Series* (Ottawa: Minister of Industry, 2010).

23. Stephen E. Brown, Finn-Aage Esbensen, and Gilbert Geis, *Criminology: Explaining Crime and Its Context*, 2nd ed. (Cincinnati, OH: Anderson, 1996), p. 198.

24. Tina Hotton Mahony, "Women and the Criminal Justice System," *Women in Canada: A Gender-Based Statistical Report*, Cat. no. 89-503-X (Ottawa: Minister of Industry, April 2011).

25. Nicole Bermbach, "Putting Increase in Female Crime Rates in Context," *Pathways: The Elizabeth Fry Society of Calgary*, vol. 1, no. 5 (September/October 2012), http://www.elizabethfrycalgary.ca/files/pdf/Newsletter_Vol-1_Iss-5_2012-SeptemberOctober.pdf [Accessed December 29, 2012].

26. Elizabeth Cormack, "Women and Crime," in R. Linden, ed., *Criminology: A Canadian Perspective* (Toronto: Harcourt Brace Canada, 1996), pp. 139–175.

27. Leanne Fiftal Alarid, James W. Marquart, Velmer S. Burton, Jr., Francis T. Cullen, and Steven J. Cuvelier, "Women's Roles in Serious Offenses: A Study of Adult Felons," *Justice Quarterly*, vol. 13, no. 3 (September 1996), pp. 432–454.

28. Bermbach, "Putting Increase in Female Crime Rates in Context."

29. Perreault, "Criminal Victimization in Canada, 2014."

30. Statistics Canada, *Violence Against Women Survey: Survey Highlights* (Ottawa: Minister of Industry, 1993).

31. Public Safety Canada Portfolio Corrections Statistics Committee, *Corrections and Conditional Release Statistical*

Overview: Annual Report 2015 (Ottawa: Public Works and Government Services Canada, 2016).

32. P. Havemann, K. Couse, L. Foster, and R. Matonovich, *Law and Order for Canada's Indigenous People* (Regina: Prairie Justice Research, School of Human Justice, University of Regina, 1985); John Hagan, "Criminal Justice in Rural and Urban Communities," *Social Forces*, vol. 55, no. 3 (1977), pp. 597–612; and D.F. Wayne and T.F. Hartnagel, "Race and Plea Negotiation," *Canadian Journal of Sociology*, vol. 1, no. 2 (1975), pp. 147–155.

33. Nancy Macdonald, "Canada's Prisons Are the New Residential Schools," *Maclean's*, February 18, 2016, http://www.macleans.ca/news/canada/canadas-prisons-are-the-new-residential-schools/ [Accessed July 8, 2016].

34. J.H. Hylton, "The Native Offender in Saskatchewan," *Canadian Journal of Criminology*, vol. 24, no. 2 (1982), pp. 121–131; and Carol La Prairie, "Aboriginal Crime and Justice," *Canadian Journal of Criminology*, vol. 34 (1992), pp. 281–297.

35. Carol La Prairie, "Aboriginal Over-representation in the Criminal Justice System: A Tale of Nine Cities," *Canadian Journal of Criminology*, vol. 44, no. 2 (2002), pp. 181–208.

36. Havemann et al., *Law and Order for Canada's Indigenous People*.

37. John Hagan, "Criminal Justice and Native People," *Canadian Review of Sociology and Anthropology*, Special Issue (August 1974), pp. 220–236.

38. Jillian Boyce, "Victimization of Aboriginal People in Canada, 2014, 2014," *Juristat*, vol. 36, no. 1 (Ottawa: Minister of Industry, 2016).

39. For a good review of the issues involved, see John Hagan, *Structural Criminology* (New Brunswick, NJ: Rutgers University Press, 1989).

40. Charles R. Tittle, Wayne Villemez, and Douglas Smith, "The Myth of Social Class and Criminality: An Empirical Assessment of the Empirical Evidence," *American Sociological Review*, vol. 43, no. 5 (1978), pp. 643–656; see also Charles R. Tittle, "Social Class and Criminality," *Social Forces*, vol. 56, no. 2 (1977), pp. 474–502.

41. John Braithwaite, "The Myth of Social Class and Criminality Reconsidered," *American Sociological Review*, vol. 46, no. 1 (1981), pp. 36–57.

42. Margaret Farnworth, Terence P. Thornberry, and Marvin D. Krohn, "Measurement in the Study of Class and Delinquency: Integrating Theory and Research," *Journal of Research in Crime and Delinquency*, vol. 31, no. 1 (1994), pp. 32–61.

43. J. Hagan and B. McCarthy, "Street Life and Delinquency," *British Journal of Sociology*, vol. 43, no. 4 (1992), pp. 533–561.

44. J. Savoie, "Youth Self-Reported Delinquency, Toronto, 2006," *Juristat*, vol. 27, no. 5 (Ottawa: Minister of Industry, 2007).

45. Latimer et al., *The Correlates of Self-Reported Delinquency*.

46. Bunge, Johnston, and Baldé, "Exploring Crime Patterns in Canada."

47. D.P. Farrington, "Early Predictors of Adolescent Aggression and Adult Violence," *Violence and Victims*, vol. 4, no. 2 (1989), pp. 79–100; and M.W. Lipsey and J.H. Derzon, "Predictors of Violent or Serious Delinquency in Adolescence and Early Adulthood," in R. Loeber and D.P. Farrington, eds., *Serious and Violent Juvenile Offenders: Risk Factors and Successful Interventions* (Thousand Oaks, CA: SAGE, 1998).

48. C.R. Tittle and R.F. Meier, "Specifying the SES/Delinquency Relationship by Characteristics of Contexts," *Journal of Research on Crime and Delinquency*, vol. 28, no. 4 (1991), pp. 430–455; and P.H. Wilkström and R. Loeber, "Do Disadvantaged Neighbourhoods Cause Well-Adjusted Children to Become Adolescent Delinquents? A Study of Male Juvenile Serious Offending, Individual Risk and Protective Factors, and Neighborhood Context," *Criminology*, vol. 38, no. 4 (2000), pp. 1109–1142.

49. Perreault, "Criminal Victimization in Canada, 2014."

Chapter 3

1. Anthony Doob, quoted in "Crime Rate Continues to Drop Across Canada," *National Post*, August 25, 2011, http://news.nationalpost.com/2011/07/21/crime-rate-down-across-canada/ [Accessed December 1, 2012].

2. From Patrick Fox denied bail in criminal harassment case by Natalie Clancy and Yvette Brend, Published by CBC News, © 2016. Used by permission of CBC news.

3. Jillian Boyce, "Police-Reported Crime Statistics in Canada, 2014," *Juristat*, vol. 34, no. 1 (Ottawa: Minister of Industry, 2015).

4. "Teenager Gets Nine Years in Dagenais Murders," *CBC News*, http://www.cbc.ca/news/canada/ottawa/teenager-gets-nine-years-in-dagenais-murders-1.379959 [Accessed July 15, 2016].

5. Bureau of Justice Statistics, *Report to the Nation on Crime and Justice* (Washington, DC: U.S. Government Printing Office, 1988), p. 4.

6. Frank Schmalleger, *Criminology Today: An Integrated Introduction* (Upper Saddle River, NJ: Prentice Hall, 1999), p. 63.

7. Bureau of Justice Statistics, *Report to the Nation on Crime and Justice*, p. 4.

8. Detailed information about homicide in Canada is from Zoran Miladinovic and Leah Mulligan, "Homicide in Canada, 2014," *Juristat*, vol. 35, no. 1 (Ottawa: Minister of Industry, November 25, 2015).

9. Federal Bureau of Investigation, *Crime in the United States, 2014* (Washington, DC: U.S. Department of Justice, 2011), https://www.fbi.gov/about-us/cjis/ucr/crime-in-the-u.s/2014/crime-in-the-u.s.-2014 [Accessed July 15, 2016].

10. Jens Manuel Krogstad, "Gun Homicide Steady after Decline in '90s; Suicide Rate Edges Up," *Pew Research Centre*, October 21, 2015, http://www.pewresearch.org/fact-tank/2015/10/21/gun-homicides-steady-after-decline-in-90s-suicide-rate-edges-up/.

11. See Elizabeth Cormack, "Women and Crime," in Rick Linden, ed., *Criminology: A Canadian Perspective* (Toronto: Harcourt Brace Canada, 1996), pp. 139–175.

12. Boyce, "Police-Reported Crime Statistics in Canada, 2014."

13. Samuel Perreault, "Criminal Victimization in Canada, 2014," *Juristat*, vol. 35, no. 1 (Ottawa: Minister of Industry, 2015).

14. Boyce, "Police-Reported Crime Statistics in Canada, 2014."

15. Martha R. Burt, "Cultural Myths and Supports for Rape," *Journal of Personality and Social Psychology*, vol. 38 (1980), pp. 217–230.

16. For example, see Mary P. Koss et al., "Nonstranger Sexual Aggression: A Discriminant Analysis of the Psychological Characteristics of Undetected Offenders," *Sex Roles*, vol. 12 (1985), pp. 981–992.

17. Martha R. Burt, "Rape Myths," in Andrea Parrot and Laurie Bechhofer, eds., *Acquaintance Rape: The Hidden Crime* (New York: John Wiley & Sons, 1991).

18. Boyce, "Police-Reported Crime Statistics in Canada, 2014."

19. Shelly Milligan, "Criminal Harassment in Canada, 2009," *Juristat*, Cat no. 85-005-X (Ottawa: Minister of Industry, March 2011). Reproduced and distributed on an "as is" basis with the permission of Statistics Canada.

20. Boyce, "Police-Reported Crime Statistics in Canada, 2014."

21. The most recent data are from 1999. See Karen Hackett, "Criminal Harassment," *Juristat*, vol. 20, no. 11 (Ottawa: Minister of Industry, 2000).

22. Milligan, "Criminal Harassment in Canada, 2009."
23. Mia Dauvergne, "Police-Reported Robbery in Canada, 2009," *Juristat*, vol. 35, no. 1 (Ottawa: Minister of Industry, March 2010).
24. Mary Allen, "Police-Reported Hate Crime in Canada, 2013," Juristat, vol. 30, no. 2 (Ottawa: Ministry of Industry, March 2015). Reproduced and distributed on an "as is" basis with the permission of Statistics Canada.
25. Ibid.
26. Peter Hum, "Compassion for a Child Killer," *Ottawa Citizen*, December 28, 1999, p. B1.
27. D. Finkelhor, R.K. Ormrod, H.A. Turner, and M.A. Holt, "Pathways to Poly-Victimization," *Child Maltreatment*, vol. 14, no. 4 (2009), pp. 316–329.
28. Cathy S. Widom, "The Intergenerational Transmission of Violence," in Neil Warner and Marvin Wolfgang, eds., *Pathways to Criminal Violence* (Newbury Park, CA: SAGE, 1989).
29. Orest Fedorowycz, "Breaking and Entering in Canada—2002," *Juristat*, vol. 24, no. 5 (Ottawa: Minister of Industry, July 2004).
30. R. Barnhorst and S. Barnhorst, *Criminal Law and the Canadian Criminal Code* (Toronto: McGraw-Hill Ryerson, 2009), p. 303.
31. Mia Dauvergne, "Motor Vehicle Theft in Canada, 2007," *Juristat*, vol. 28, no. 10 (Ottawa: Minister of Industry, 2008).
32. Boyce, "Police-Reported Crime Statistics in Canada, 2014."
33. Dauvergne, "Motor Vehicle Theft in Canada, 2007."
34. Royal Canadian Mounted Police, *National Identity Crime Strategy*, http://www.rcmp-grc.gc.ca/pubs/cc-dc/strat/index-eng.htm [Accessed July 17, 2016].
35. Ibid.
36. *Bank of Canada Review Supplement*, June 2011, http://www.bankofcanada.ca/wp-content/uploads/2011/06/spencer.pdf [Accessed July 18, 2016].
37. Alison Crawford, "Counterfeiters Perplexed by Canada's Plastic Money," *CBC News*, January 14, 2016, http://www.cbc.ca/news/politics/counterfeiters-perplexed-by-canada-s-plastic-money-1.3401839 [Accessed July 18, 2016].
38. *Brian M. Willis and Barry S. Levy*, "Child Prostitution: Global Health Burden, Research Needs, and Interventions," National Institutes of Health, *2002*, http://citeseerx.ist.psu.edu/viewdoc/download?doi=10.1.1.399.7703&rep=rep1&type=pdf *[Accessed September 25, 2016]*.
39. Adam Cotter, Jacob Greenland, and Maisie Karam, "Drug-Related Offences in Canada, 2013," *Juristat*, vol. 35, no. 1 (Ottawa: Minister of Industry, 2015).
40. Ibid.
41. Boyce, "Police-Reported Crime Statistics in Canada, 2014."
42. Cotter, Greenland, and Karam, "Drug-Related Offences in Canada, 2013."
43. Joanna Smith, "Marijuana Legislation Coming to Canada Next Spring," The Star.com, April 20, 2016, https://www.thestar.com/news/canada/2016/04/20/marijuana-legislation-coming-to-canada-next-spring.html [Accessed July 22, 2016].
44. Rina Egbo, "Memorializing the Victims of Terrorism," *Research and Statistics Division, Department of Justice* (Government of Canada, 2009), http://www.justice.gc.ca/eng/rp-pr/cj-jp/victim/rr09_6/index.html [Accessed July 22, 2016].

Chapter 4

1. Sue O'Sullivan, *Remarks to Senate Standing Committee on Legal and Constitutional Affairs*, March 26, 2015, http://www.victimsfirst.gc.ca/vv/sub-pre/20150326.html [Accessed January 8, 2016].
2. G. Dimmock and J. Rupert, "Student Dies Trying to Stop Bar Fight," *Ottawa Citizen*, December 24, 1998, http://andymoffitt.org/newspapers/ottawacitizen/dec241998/2130553_modified.html [Accessed February 1, 2017].
3. Material republished with the express permission of: Ottawa Citizen, a division of Postmedia Network Inc.
4. Ibid
5. Karola Dillenburger, "A Behavior Analytic Perspective on Victimology," *International Journal of Behavioral Consultation and Therapy*, vol. 3, no. 3 (2007), pp. 433–448.
6. John P.J. Dussich, "The Challenges of Victimology: Past, Present and Future," 144th International Senior Seminar, Visiting Experts' Papers, Resource Material Series, No. 81.
7. Hans von Hentig, *The Criminal and His Victim: Studies in the Socio-biology of Crime* (New York: Archon Books, 1948).
8. Michael Hindelang, Michael R. Gottfredson, and James Garofalo, *Victims of Personal Crime: An Empirical Foundation for a Theory of Personal Victimization* (Cambridge, MA: Ballinger, 1978).
9. L.W. Kennedy and D.R. Forde, "Routine Activities and Crime: An Analysis of Victimization in Canada," *Criminology*, vol. 28, no. 1 (1990), pp. 137–152.
10. Fernando Miro, "Routine Activity Theory," in J. Mitchell Miller, ed., *The Encyclopedia of Theoretical Criminology* (Maiden, MA: Blackwell Publishing, 2014), p. 5.
11. Lawrence E. Cohen and Marcus Felson, "Social Change and Crime Rate Trends: A Routine Activity Approach," *American Sociological Review*, vol. 44, no. 4 (August 1979), pp. 588–608.
12. Marcus Felson, "Routine Activities and Crime Prevention in the Developing Metropolis," *Criminology*, vol. 25, no. 4 (1987), pp. 911–931.
13. The study defined *socio-emotional problems* as "the experience of one or more of the following: feelings of moderate to severe distress; significant problems with work or school, such as trouble with a boss, coworkers, or peers; or significant problems with family members or friends, including more arguments than before the victimization, an inability to trust, or not feeling as close after the victimization."
14. Ezzat Fattah, "Victimology Today: Recent and Applied Developments." Paper presented at the 112 International Training Course, Tokyo, 2000, http://www.unafei.or.jp/english/pdf/RS_No56/No56_09VE_Fattah2.pdf [Accessed January 8, 2016].
15. Samuel Perreault, "Criminal Victimization in Canada, 2014," *Juristat*, vol. 33, no. 1 (Ottawa: Minister of Industry, 2015).
16. Rodney Stark, "Deviant Places: A Theory of the Ecology of Crime," *Criminology*, vol. 25, no. 4 (1987), pp. 893–909.
17. Rosa Casarez-Levison, "An Empirical Investigation of the Coping Strategies Used by Victims of Crime: Victimization Redefined," in Emilio Viano, ed., *Critical Issues in Victimology: International Perspectives* (New York: Springer, 1992).
18. Morton Bard and Dawn Sangrey, *The Crime Victim's Book*, 2nd ed. (New York: Brunner/Mazel, 1986).
19. Elisabeth Kübler-Ross, *On Death and Dying* (New York: Macmillan, 1969).
20. For an excellent review of many of these studies, see Alan Young, *The Role of the Victim in the Criminal Process: A Literature Review—1989 to 1999*, Victims of Crime Research Series (Ottawa: Department of Justice, 2001), pp. 57–59.

21. A. Karmen, *Crime Victims: An Introduction to Victimology*, 4th ed. (Belmont, CA: Wadsworth/Thomson Learning, 2001).

22. D. Kilpatrick and R. Otto, "Constitutionally Guaranteed Participation in Criminal Proceedings for Victims: Potential Effects on Psychological Functioning," *Wayne Law Review*, vol. 37, no. 7 (1987), p. 27.

23. See D. Hall, "Victims' Voices in Criminal Court: The Need for Restraint," *American Criminal Law Review*, vol. 28 (1991); J. Acker, "Social Sciences and the Criminal Law: Victims of Crime—Plight vs. Rights," *Criminal Law Bulletin*, vol. 28 (1992); and R. Black, "Forgotten Penological Purposes: A Critique of Victim Participation in Sentencing," *American Journal of Jurisprudence*, vol. 39 (1994).

24. Herbert Packer, *The Limits of the Criminal Process* (Stanford, CA: Stanford University Press, 1968).

25. Kent Roach, *Due Process and Victims' Rights: The New Law and Politics of Criminal Justice* (Toronto: University of Toronto Press, 1999).

26. V.F. Sacco and H. Johnson, *Patterns of Criminal Victimization in Canada* (Ottawa: Statistics Canada, 1990); and M. Baril, S. LaFlamme-Cusson, and S. Beauchemin, *Working Paper No. 12. Crime Victims Compensation: An Assessment of the Quebec IVAC Program* (Ottawa: Policy Planning and Development Branch, Department of Justice, 1984).

27. André Marin, *Investigation into the Treatment of Victims by the Criminal Injuries Compensation Board. "Adding Insult to Injury"* (Toronto: Ombudsman of Ontario, 2007).

28. Fattah, "Victimology Today," p. 61.

29. I. Waller, "Victims, Safer Communities and Sentencing," *Canadian Journal of Criminology*, vol. 32, no. 2 (1990), pp. 461–469.

30. For more information about the role of the National Office for Victims, visit http://www.publicsafety.gc.ca/cnt/cntrng-crm/crrctns/ntnl-ffc-vctms-en.aspx [Accessed March 12, 2016].

31. For a detailed look at the Office of the Federal Ombudsman for Victims of Crime, see http://www.victimsfirst.gc.ca/ [Accessed March 11, 2016].

32. Visit the website for the Policy Centre for Victim Issues at http://www.justice.gc.ca/eng/cj-jp/victims-victimes/ [Accessed March 11, 2016].

33. Mary Allen, "Victim Services in Canada, 2011/2012," *Juristat*, vol. 34, no. 1 (Ottawa: Minister of Industry, 2014).

34. J. Sauvé, "Victim Services in Canada, 2007/2008," *Juristat*, vol. 29, no. 4 (Ottawa: Minister of Industry, 2009).

35. Joseph Moylan, *Victim Services and Canadian Police Agencies—A Source Book* (Ottawa: Canadian Association of Chiefs of Police and Solicitor General of Canada, 1990). See also the overview of victim services by province on the Office of the Federal Ombudsman for Victims of Crime website at http://www.victimsfirst.gc.ca/serv/vsc-svc.html [Accessed January 31, 2016].

36. W. Jamieson and R.R. Ross, "An Evaluation of the Victim/Witness Assistance Programme, Ministry of the Attorney General of Ontario," *Canadian Journal of Program Evaluation*, vol. 6, no. 1 (1991), pp. 83–96. See also the Victim Witness Assistance website at https://www.attorneygeneral.jus.gov.on.ca/english/service_standards/service_standards_victim_services.php [Accessed January 24, 2016].

37. A. Hatch Cunningham and C.T. Griffiths, *Canadian Criminal Justice: A Primer* (Toronto: Harcourt Brace Canada, 1997), p. 79.

38. Dean Beeby, "Canadians Have Little Confidence in Justice System: Study," *Canadian Press*, February 17, 2014, http://www.huffingtonpost.ca/2014/02/18/canada-justice-system-prison-poll_n_4801426.html [Accessed February 2, 2016].

39. Ezzat Fatah, "Victims and Victimology: The Facts and the Rhetoric," *International Review of Victimology*, vol. 1 (1989), p. 43.

40. R. Elias, *Victims Still: The Political Manipulation of Crime Victims* (Thousand Oaks, CA: SAGE, 1993), p. 26.

41. Irvin Waller, *Less Law, More Order* (Westport, CT: Praeger, 2006).

42. Sue O'Sullivan, *Strengthening the Canadian Victims Bill of Rights*, Office of the Federal Ombudsman for the Victims of Crime, http://www.victimsfirst.gc.ca/vv/vbra-cdv.html [Accessed February 2, 2016].

43. From Victimology program receives $200,000 in research funding over three years. Used by permission of Victim Justice Network. http://www.victimjusticenetwork.ca/resource/534-victimology-program-receives-200-000-in-research-funding-over-three-years

Chapter 5

1. Cesare Beccaria, *Essay on Crimes and Punishments*, translated by Henry Paolucci (New York: Bobbs-Merrill, 1963); first printed 1764.

2. Pete Williams and Halimah Abdullah, "FBI San Bernardino Shooters Radicalized Before They Met," *NBC News*, December 9, 2015, http://www.nbcnews.com/storyline/san-bernardino-shooting/fbi-san-bernardino-shooters-radicalized-they-met-n476971 [Accessed March 4, 2016].

3. Danny Lewis, "What the All Writs Act of 1798 Has to Do with the iPhone," *Smithsonian.com*. http://www.smithsonianmag.com/smart-news/what-all-writs-act-1789-has-do-iphone-180958188/?no-ist [Accessed March 4, 2016].

4. From Why Brooklyn judge's All Writs Act decision is huge win for Apple Alison Frankel, © 2016. Used by permission of Reuters.

5. William Graham Sumner, *Folkways* (New York: Dover, 1906).

6. Marvin Wolfgang, "The Key Reporter," *Phi Beta Kappa*, vol. 52, no. 1.

7. Roman influence in England had ended by 442 AD, according to Crane Brinton, John B. Christopher, and Robert L. Wolff, *A History of Civilization*, 3rd ed., vol. 1 (Englewood Cliffs, NJ: Prentice Hall, 1967), p. 180.

8. Howard Abadinsky, *Law and Justice* (Chicago: Nelson-Hall, 1988), p. 6.

9. Edward McNall Burns, *Western Civilization*, 7th ed. (New York: W.W. Norton, 1969), p. 339.

10. Ibid.

11. Brinton, Christopher, and Wolff, *A History of Civilization*, p. 274.

12. Referred to in official transcripts as Rudolf Franz Ferdinand Hoess.

13. International Military Tribunal, "One Hundred and Eighth Day, Monday, 4/15/1946, Part 03," in *Trial of the Major War Criminals before the International Military Tribunal*, Volume XI. Proceedings: 4/8/1946–4/17/1946 (Nuremberg: IMT, 1943), pp. 398–400.

14. The quotations attributed to Beccaria in this section are from Cesare Beccaria, *Essay on Crimes and Punishments* (Livorno, Italy: Tipografia Coltellini, 1764).

15. The quotations attributed to Bentham in this section are from Jeremy Bentham, *An Introduction to the Principles of Morals and Legislation* (Oxford: Clarendon Press, 1907); reprint of the 1823 edition, first printed 1780.

16. R. Martinson, "What Works? Questions and Answers about Prison Reform," *Public Interest*, vol. 35 (1974).

17. James Q. Wilson, *Thinking about Crime* (New York: Basic Books, 1975).

18. David Fogel, *We Are the Living Proof: The Justice Model of Corrections* (Cincinnati, OH: Anderson, 1975), p. 18.

19. Conrad P. Rutkowski, "Fogel's 'Justice Model': Stop Trying to Reform. Punish, but Treat All Alike," *Illinois Issues*, February 1976.

20. Ronald V. Clarke and Derek B. Cornish, eds., *Crime Control in Britain: A Review of Police and Research* (Albany: State University of New York Press, 1983).

21. Felton M. Earls and Albert J. Reiss, *Breaking the Cycle: Predicting and Preventing Crime* (Washington, DC: National Institute of Justice, 1994), p. 49.

22. Lawrence E. Cohen and Marcus Felson, "Social Change and Crime Rate Trends: A Routine Activity Approach," *American Sociological Review*, vol. 44, no. 4 (August 1979), pp. 588–608. Also, see Marcus Felson and L.E. Cohen, "Human Ecology and Crime: A Routine Activity Approach," *Human Ecology*, vol. 8, no. 4 (1980), pp. 389–406; Marcus Felson, "Linking Criminal Choices, Routine Activities, Informal Control, and Criminal Outcomes," in Derek B. Cornish and Ronald V. Clarke, eds., *The Reasoning Criminal: Rational Choice Perspectives on Offending* (New York: Springer-Verlag, 1986), pp. 119–128; and Ronald V. Clarke and Marcus Felson, eds., *Advances in Criminological Theory: Routine Activity and Rational Choice* (New Brunswick, NJ: Transaction, 1993).

23. Cohen and Felson, "Social Change and Crime Rate Trends," p. 595.

24. For a test of routine activities theory as an explanation for victimization in the workplace, see John D. Wooldredge, Francis T. Cullen, and Edward J. Latessa, "Victimization in the Workplace: A Test of Routine Activities Theory," *Justice Quarterly*, vol. 9, no. 2 (June 1992), pp. 325–335.

25. Marcus Felson, *Crime and Everyday Life: Insight and Implications for Society* (Thousand Oaks, CA: Pine Forge Press, 1994).

26. Gary LaFree and Christopher Birkbeck, "The Neglected Situation: A Cross-National Study of the Situational Characteristics of Crime," *Criminology*, vol. 29, no. 1 (February 1991), p. 75.

27. Ronald V. Clarke and Derek B. Cornish, eds., *Crime Control in Britain: A Review of Police and Research* (Albany: State University of New York Press, 1983), p. 8.

28. See Derek B. Cornish and Ronald V. Clarke, "Understanding Crime Displacement: An Application of Rational Choice Theory," *Criminology*, vol. 25, no. 4 (November 1987), p. 933.

29. See Tomislav V. Kovandzic, Lynne M. Vieraitis, and Denise Paquette Boots, "Does the Death Penalty Save Lives? New Evidence from State Panel Data, 1977 to 2006," *Criminology and Public Policy*, vol. 8, no. 4 (2009), pp. 803–843.

30. Werner Einstadter and Stuart Henry, *Criminological Theory: An Analysis of Its Underlying Assumptions* (Fort Worth, TX: Harcourt Brace, 1995), p. 70.

31. Daniel J. Curran and Claire M. Renzetti, *Theories of Crime* (Boston: Allyn & Bacon, 1994), p. 18.

32. The quotations attributed to Weisburd in this section are from David Weisburd, "Reorienting Crime Prevention Research and Policy: From the Causes of Criminality to the Context of Crime," *NIJ Research Report* (Washington, DC: NIJ, June 1997).

33. See P.J. Brantingham and P.L. Brantingham, "Situational Crime Prevention in Practice," *Canadian Journal of Criminology* (January 1990), pp. 17–40; and R.V. Clarke, "Situational Crime Prevention: Achievements and Challenges," in M. Tonry and D. Farrington, eds., *Building a Safer Society: Strategic Approaches to Crime Prevention, Crime and Justice: A Review of Research*, vol. 19 (Chicago: University of Chicago Press, 1995).

34. Quotations in this paragraph and the next are taken from Weisburd, "Reorienting Crime Prevention Research and Policy."

35. See, for example, J.E. Eck and D. Weisburd, eds., *Crime and Place: Crime Prevention Studies*, vol. 4 (Monsey, NY: Willow Tree Press, 1995).

36. M. Lyn Exum, "The Application and Robustness of the Rational Choice Perspective in the Study of Angry Intentions to Aggress," *Criminology*, vol. 40, no. 4 (2002), p. 933, citing Allen E. Liska and Stephen F. Messner, *Perspectives on Crime and Deviance*, 3rd ed. (Upper Saddle River, NJ: Prentice Hall, 1999).

37. Dolf Zillman, *Hostility and Aggression* (Hillsdale, NJ: Lawrence Erlbaum Associates, 1979), p. 279.

38. David Lee and Justin McCrary, "Crime, Punishment, and Myopia," NBER Working Paper No. W11491 (Cambridge, MA: National Bureau of Economic Research, 2005), http://ssrn.com/abstract=762770 [Accessed March 12, 2016].

39. Ibid.

40. Kenneth D. Tunnell, "Choosing Crime: Close Your Eyes and Take Your Chances," *Justice Quarterly*, vol. 7 (1990), pp. 673–690.

41. See R. Barr and K. Pease, "Crime Placement, Displacement and Deflection," in M. Tonry and N. Morris, eds., *Crime and Justice: A Review of Research*, vol. 12 (Chicago: University of Chicago Press, 1990).

42. For a good summation of target hardening, see Ronald V. Clarke, *Situational Crime Prevention* (New York: Harrow and Heston, 1992).

43. For a good summation of studies on displacement, see R. Hesseling, "Displacement: A Review of the Empirical Literature," in R.V. Clarke, ed., *Crime Prevention Studies*, vol. 3 (Monsey, NY: Willow Tree Press, 1994).

44. For a good overview of the challenges in defining recidivism and determining rates of recidivism, see T. Nouwens, L. Motiuk, and R. Boe, "So You Want to Know the Recidivism Rate," *Forum on Correctional Research*, vol. 5, no. 3 (1993), pp. 22–26.

45. J. Bonta, T. Rugge, and M. Dauvergne, *The Reconviction Rate of Federal Offenders 2003–2004* (Ottawa: Solicitor General of Canada, 2003).

46. See, for example, W.C. Bailey, "Deterrence and the Death Penalty for Murders in Utah: A Time Series Analysis," *Journal of Contemporary Law*, vol. 5, no. 1 (1978), pp. 1–20; and "An Analysis of the Deterrent Effect of the Death Penalty for Murders in California," *Southern California Law Review*, vol. 52, no. 3 (1979), pp. 743–764.

47. See, for example, B.E. Forst, "The Deterrent Effect of Capital Punishment: A Cross-State Analysis of the 1960s," *Minnesota Law Review*, vol. 61 (1977), pp. 743–764.

48. Kovandzic, Vieraitis, and Boots, "Does the Death Penalty Save Lives?" p. 803.

49. Correctional Services Program, "Adult Correctional Statistics in Canada, 2013–2014," *Juristat*, vol. 35, no. 1 (Ottawa: Minster of Industry, April 22, 2015).

50. E. Ann Carson, *Prisoners in 2013* (Washington, DC: Bureau of Justice Statistics, 2014).

51. Marvin Wolfgang, Thorsten Sellin, and Robert Figlio, *Delinquency in a Birth Cohort* (Chicago: University of Chicago Press, 1972).

52. Randy Martin, Robert J. Mutchnick, and W. Timothy Austin, *Criminological Thought: Pioneers Past and Present* (New York: Macmillan, 1990), p. 17.

53. Ibid., p. 18.

Chapter 6

1. Anthony Walsh, "Biological Theories of Criminal Behavior," in Richard A. Wright and J. Mitchell Miller, eds., *Encyclopedia of Criminology*, vol. 1 (New York: Routledge, 2005), p. 106.

2. Megan Visscher, "How Food Can Cut Crime," *Ode Magazine*, February 9, 2010, http://www.care2.com/greenliving/how-food-can-cut-crime.html?page=4 [Accessed June 5, 2016).

3. C.B. Gesch, S.M. Hammond, S.E. Hampson, A. Eves, and M.J. Crowder, "Influence of Supplementary Vitamins, Minerals and Essential Fatty Acids on the Antisocial Behavior of Young Adult Prisoners: Randomized, Placebo-Controlled Trial," *British Journal of Psychiatry*, vol. 181 (July 2002), pp. 22–28.

4. Visscher, "How Food Can Cut Crime."

5. C. Ray Jeffery, "Biological Perspectives," *Journal of Criminal Justice Education*, vol. 4, no. 2 (Fall 1993), pp. 292–293.

6. Anthony Walsh, "Biological Theories of Criminal Behavior," in Richard A. Wright and J. Mitchell Miller, eds., *Encyclopedia of Criminology*, vol. 1 (New York: Routledge, 2005), p. 106.

7. See K.L. Henwood and N.F. Pidgeon, "Qualitative Research and Psychological Theorising," *British Journal of Psychology*, vol. 83 (1992), pp. 97–111.

8. Cesare Lombroso, "Introduction," in Gina Lombroso-Ferrero, ed., *Criminal Man According to the Classification of Cesare Lombroso* (1911; reprint, Montclair, NJ: Patterson Smith, 1972), p. xiv.

9. See Robert Fletcher, "The New School of Criminal Anthropology," *The American Anthropologist*, vol. 4, no. 3 (July 1891), pp. 201–236.

10. Lombroso, "Introduction," in Lombroso-Ferrero, *Criminal Man According to the Classification of Cesare Lombroso*, p. xv.

11. Charles Darwin, *Descent of Man: And Selection in Relation to Sex*, rev. ed. (London: John Murray, 1874), p. 137.

12. The English-language version appeared in 1895 as Cesare Lombroso, *The Female Offender* (New York: D. Appleton & Co., 1895).

13. Marvin Wolfgang, "Cesare Lombroso," in Hermann Mannheim, ed., *Pioneers in Criminology*, 2nd ed. (Montclair, NJ: Patterson Smith, 1972), p. 254.

14. Charles Goring, *The English Convict: A Statistical Study* (London: His Majesty's Stationary Office, 1913). Reprinted in 1972 by Patterson Smith, Montclair, NJ, p. 15.

15. Ibid.

16. Earnest A. Hooton, *Crime and the Man* (Cambridge, MA: Harvard University Press, 1939). Reprinted in 1972 by Greenwood Press, Westport, CT.

17. Earnest A. Hooton, *The American Criminal: An Anthropological Study* (Cambridge, MA: Harvard University Press, 1939).

18. Nichole Hahn Rafter, "Criminal Anthropology in the United States," *Criminology*, vol. 30, no. 4 (1992), p. 525.

19. L. Arseneault et al., "Minor Physical Anomalies and Family Adversity as Risk Factors for Violent Delinquency in Adolescence," *American Journal of Psychiatry*, vol. 157, no. 6 (June 2000), pp. 917–923.

20. William H. Sheldon, *Varieties of Delinquent Youth* (New York: Harper & Brothers, 1949).

21. Ibid.

22. Richard Louis Dugdale, *The Jukes: A Study in Crime, Pauperism, Disease, and Heredity*, 3rd ed. (New York: G.P. Putnam's Sons, 1895).

23. Arthur H. Estabrook, *The Jukes in 1915* (Washington, DC: Carnegie Institute of Washington, 1916).

24. Henry Herbert Goddard, *The Kallikak Family: A Study in the Heredity of Feeblemindedness* (New York: Macmillan, 1912).

25. See Nicole Hahn Rafter, *Creating Born Criminals* (Urbana: University of Illinois Press, 1997).

26. T.L. Chapman, "The Early Eugenics Movement in Western Canada," *Alberta History*, vol. 25 (1977), pp. 9–17. See also A. McLaren, "The Creation of a Haven for Human Thoroughbreds," *Canadian Historical Review*, vol. 67 (1986), pp. 264–268.

27. P.A. Jacobs, M. Brunton, and M. Melville, "Aggressive Behavior, Mental Subnormality, and the XXY Male," *Nature*, vol. 208 (1965), p. 1351.

28. Biologists often define *karyotype* as "a photomicrograph of metaphase chromosomes in a standard array." The process of karyotyping typically involves drawing a small sample of blood.

29. Anthony Walsh, *Biology and Criminology: The Biosocial Synthesis* (New York: Routledge, 2009), p. 268.

30. See David A. Jones, *History of Criminology: A Philosophical Perspective* (Westport, CT: Greenwood Press, 1986), p. 124.

31. As reported by S.A. Mednick and J. Volavka, "Biology and Crime," in N. Morris and M. Tonry, eds., *Crime and Justice: An Annual Review of Research*, vol. 2 (Chicago: University of Chicago Press, 1980), pp. 85–158; and D.A. Andrews and James Bonta, *The Psychology of Criminal Conduct* (Cincinnati, OH: Anderson, 1994), pp. 126–127.

32. T. Sarbin and J. Miller, "Demonism Revisited: The XYY Chromosomal Anomaly," *Issues in Criminology*, vol. 5 (1970), p. 199.

33. Johannes Lange, *Verbrechen als Schicksal* (Leipzig, Germany: Georg Thieme, 1929).

34. Karl O. Christiansen, "A Preliminary Study of Criminality among Twins," in Sarnoff Mednick and Karl Christiansen, eds., *Biosocial Bases of Criminal Behavior* (New York: Gardner Press, 1977).

35. Peter McGuffin and Anita Thapar, "Genetic Basis of Bad Behaviour in Adolescents," *Lancet*, vol. 350 (August 9, 1997), pp. 411–412.

36. Wendy Slutske et al., "Modeling Genetic and Environmental Influences in the Etiology of Conduct Disorder: A Study of 2,682 Adult Twin Pairs," *Journal of Abnormal Psychology*, vol. 106, no. 2 (1997), pp. 266–279.

37. Louise Arseneault et al., "Strong Genetic Effects on Cross-Situational Antisocial Behaviour among 5-Year-Old Children According to Mothers, Teachers, Examiner-Observers, and Twins' Self-Reports," *Journal of Child Psychology and Psychiatry*, vol. 44, no. 6 (September 2003), pp. 832–848.

38. Ibid.

39. Mary Kugler, "What Are Genes, DNA and Chromosomes?" About.com, http://rarediseases.about.com/od/geneticdisorders/a/genesbasics.htm [Accessed June 5, 2016].

40. Ibid.

41. James Watson and Francis Crick, "Molecular Structure of Nucleic Acids: A Structure for Deoxyribose Nucleic Acid," *Nature*, vol. 171 (April 1953), p. 737.

42. Johns Hopkins Medicine, "Scientific Team Sequences 1092 Human Genomes to Determine Standard Range of Human Genetic Variation," http://www.hopkinsmedicine.org/news/media/releases/1092_human_genomes_sequenced [Accessed June 5, 2016].

43. Much of the information and some of the wording in this section come from the National Human Genome Research Institute's Web page, http://www.nhgri.nih.gov/HGP [Accessed June 5, 2016].

44. Geoffrey Cowley and Carol Hallin, "The Genetics of Bad Behavior: A Study Links Violence to Heredity," *Newsweek*, November 1, 1993, p. 57.

45. Ibid.

46. Quoted in Tim Friend, "Violence Linked to Gene Defect: Pleasure Deficit May Be the Spark," *USA Today*, May 9, 1996. See the original research at Kenneth Blum et al., "Reward Deficiency Syndrome," *American Scientist*, vol. 84 (March/April 1996), pp. 132–145, http://www.jstor.org/stable/29775633?seq=1#page_scan_tab_contents [Accessed June 5, 2016].

47. See, for example, M. Rutter, H. Giller, and A. Hagell, *Antisocial Behavior by Young People* (Cambridge, UK: Cambridge University Press, 1998).

48. Avshalom Caspi et al., "Role of Genotype in the Cycle of Violence in Maltreated Children," *Science*, vol. 298, no. 2 (August 2002), p. 851.

49. For more information on the Dunedin Multidisciplinary Health and Development Study, see T. E. Moffitt et al., *Sex Differences in Antisocial Behavior: Conduct Disorder, Delinquency and Violence in the Dunedin Longitudinal Study* (Cambridge, UK: Cambridge University Press, 2001). Visit the Dunedin Multidisciplinary Health and Development Research Unit at http://healthsci.otago.ac.nz/dsm/dmhdru.

50. Ibid.

51. A. E. Baum et al., "A Genome-Wide Association Study Implicates Diacylglycerol Kinase Eta (DGKH) and Several Other Genes in the Etiology of Bipolar Disorder," *Molecular Psychiatry*, http://www.ncbi.nlm.nih.gov/pubmed/17486107 [Accessed June 5, 2016].

52. National Institute on Drug Abuse, "Genetics of Addiction: A Research Update from the National Institute on Drug Abuse," https://www.drugabuse.gov/sites/default/files/genetics.pdf [Accessed June 5, 2016].

53. Nathalie M.G. Fontaine, Eamon J.P. McCory, et al., "Predictors and Outcomes of Joint Trajectories of Callous–Unemotional Traits and Conduct Problems in Childhood," *Journal of Abnormal Psychology*, vol. 123, no. 3 (August 2011), pp. 740–741.

54. Twins Early Development Study, "TEDS," https://www.teds.ac.uk/ [Accessed June 5, 2016].

55. Danielle Boisvert, John Paul Wright, Valerie Knopik, and Jamie Vaske, "A Twin Study of Sex Differences in Self-Control," *Justice Quarterly*, vol. 30, no. 3 (2013), pp. 529–559.

56. D. Hill and W. Sargent, "A Case of Matricide," *Lancet*, vol. 244 (1943), pp. 526–527.

57. William Dufty, *Sugar Blues* (Pandor, PA: Chilton, 1975).

58. Nanci Hellmich, "Sweets May Not Be Culprit in Hyper Kids," *USA Today*, February 3, 1994, p. 1A (reporting on a study reported in the *New England Journal of Medicine*).

59. Ibid.

60. See, for example, C. Hawley and R.E. Buckley, "Food Dyes and Hyperkinetic Children," *Academy Therapy*, vol. 10 (1974), pp. 27–32; and Alexander Schauss, *Diet, Crime and Delinquency* (Berkeley, CA: Parker House, 1980).

61. "Special Report: Measuring Your Life with Coffee Spoons," *Tufts University Diet and Nutrition Letter*, vol. 2, no. 2 (April 1984), pp. 3–6.

62. See, for example, "Special Report: Does What You Eat Affect Your Mood and Actions?" *Tufts University Diet and Nutrition Letter*, vol. 2, no. 12 (February 1985), pp. 4–6.

63. See *Tufts University Diet and Nutrition Newsletter*, vol. 2, no. 11 (January 1985), p. 2; and "Special Report: Why Sugar Continues to Concern Nutritionists," *Tufts University Diet and Nutrition Letter*, vol. 3, no. 3 (May 1985), pp. 3–6.

64. A. Hoffer, "Children with Learning and Behavioral Disorders," *Journal of Orthomolecular Psychiatry*, vol. 5 (1976), p. 229.

65. S.J. Schoenthaler and D. Bier, "The Effect of Vitamin-Mineral Supplementation on Juvenile Delinquency among American Schoolchildren: A Randomized, Double-Blind Placebo-Controlled Trial," *Journal of Alternative Complementary Medicine*, vol. 6, no. 1 (February 2000), pp. 31–35.

66. I.B. Helland, L. Smith, K. Saarem, O.D. Saugstad, and C.A. Drevon, "Maternal Supplements with Very-Long-Chain Omega-3 Fatty Acids during Pregnancy and Lactation Augments Children's IQ at 4 Years of Age," *Pediatrics*, vol. 111, no. 1 (January 2003), pp. 39–44.

67. C. Iribarren, J.H. Markovitz, D.R. Jacobs, Jr., P.J. Schreiner, M. Daviglus, and J.R. Hibbeln, "Dietary Intake of Omega-3, Omega-6 Fatty Acids and Fish: Relationship with Hostility in Young Adults—The CARDIA Study," *European Journal of Clinical Nutrition*, vol. 50, no. 1 (January 2004), pp. 24–31.

68. David Benton, "The Impact of Diet on Anti-social, Violent and Criminal Behaviour," *Neuroscience and Biobehavioral Reviews*, vol. 31 (2007), pp. 752–774.

69. Roger D. Masters, Brian Hone, and Anil Doshi, "Environmental Pollution, Neurotoxicity, and Criminal Violence," in J. Rose, ed., *Environmental Toxicology* (London and New York: Gordon and Breach, 1997), pp. 13–48.

70. Peter Montague, "Toxics and Violent Crime," *Rachel's Environment and Health Weekly*, no. 551 (June 19, 1997).

71. See, for example, Rick Nevin, "How Lead Exposure Relates to Temporal Changes in IQ, Violent Crime, and Unwed Pregnancy," *Environmental Research*, vol. 83, no. 1 (May 2000), pp. 1–22.

72. Alison Motluck, "Pollution May Lead to a Life of Crime," *New Scientist*, vol. 154, no. 2084 (May 31, 1997), p. 4.

73. L. Goldschmidt, N.L. Day, and G.A. Richardson, "Effects of Prenatal Marijuana Exposure on Child Behavior Problems at Age 10," *Neurotoxicology and Teratology*, vol. 22, no. 3 (May/June 2000), pp. 325–336.

74. David Fergusson, Lianne Woodward, and L. John Horwood, "Maternal Smoking during Pregnancy and Psychiatric Adjustment in Late Adolescence," *Archives of General Psychiatry*, vol. 55 (August 1998), pp. 721–727.

75. Jacob F. Orlebeke, Dirk L. Knol, and Frank C. Verhulst, "Increase in Child Behavior Problems Resulting from Maternal Smoking during Pregnancy," *Archives of Environmental Health*, vol. 52, no. 4 (July/August 1997), pp. 317–321.

76. Travis C. Pratt, Jean Marie McGloin, and Noelle E. Fearn, "Maternal Cigarette Smoking during Pregnancy and Criminal/Deviant Behavior: A Meta-Analysis," *International Journal of Offender Therapy and Comparative Criminology*, vol. 50, no. 6 (2006), pp. 672–690.

77. Ann Pytkowicz Streissguth et al., "Fetal Alcohol Syndrome in Adolescents and Adults," *Journal of the American Medical Association*, vol. 265, no. 15 (April 17, 1991).

78. Tresa M. Roebuck, Sarah N. Mattson, and Edward P. Riley, "Behavioral and Psychosocial Profiles of Alcohol-Exposed Children," *Alcoholism: Clinical and Experimental Research*, vol. 23, no. 6 (June 1999), pp. 1070–1076.

79. See, for example, R.T. Rada, D.R. Laws, and R. Kellner, "Plasma Testosterone Levels in the Rapist," *Psychomatic Medicine*, vol. 38 (1976), pp. 257–268.

80. "The Insanity of Steroid Abuse," *Newsweek*, May 23, 1988, p. 75.

81. Dan Olweus, Mattsson Ake, Daisy Schalling, and Hans Low, "Testosterone, Aggression, Physical and Personality Dimensions in Normal Adolescent Males," *Psychosomatic Medicine*, vol. 42 (1980), pp. 253–269.

82. Richard Udry, "Biosocial Models of Adolescent Problem Behaviors," *Social Biology*, vol. 37 (1990), pp. 1–10.

83. Dan Olweus, "Testosterone and Adrenaline: Aggressive Antisocial Behavior in Normal Adolescent Males," in Sarnoff A. Mednick, Terrie E. Moffitt, and Susan A. Stack, eds., *The Causes of Crime: New Biological Approaches* (Cambridge, UK: Cambridge University Press, 1987), pp. 263–282.

84. Alan Booth and D. Wayne Osgood, "The Influence of Testosterone on Deviance in Adulthood: Assessing and Explaining the Relationship," *Criminology*, vol. 31, no. 1 (1993), p. 93.

85. Richard Udry, Luther Talbert, and Naomi Morris, "Biosocial Foundations for Adolescent Female Sexuality," *Demography*, vol. 23 (1986), pp. 217–227.

86. James M. Dabbs, Jr., and Marian F. Hargrove, "Age, Testosterone, and Behavior among Female Prison Inmates," *Psychosomatic Medicine*, vol. 59 (1997), pp. 447–480.

87. A. Maras et al., "Association of Testosterone and Dihydrotestosterone with Externalizing Behavior in Adolescent Boys and Girls," *Psychoneuroendocrinology*, vol. 28, no. 7 (October 2003), pp. 932–940.

88. Paul C. Bernhardt, "Influences of Serotonin and Testosterone in Aggressions and Dominance: Convergence with Social Psychology," *Current Directions in Psychological Science*, vol. 6. no. 2 (1997), pp. 44–48.

89. Anastasia Toufexis, "Seeking the Roots of Violence," *Time*, April 19, 1993, pp. 52–54.

90. Terrie E. Moffitt et al., "Whole Blood Serotonin Relates to Violence in an Epidemiological Study," *Biological Psychiatry*, vol. 43, no. 6 (1998), pp. 446–457.

91. H. Soderstrom, K. Blennow, A.K. Sjodin, and A. Forsman, "New Evidence for an Association between the CSF HVA:5–HIAA Ratio and Psychopathic Traits," *Journal of Neurology, Neurosurgery and Psychiatry*, vol. 74 (2003), pp. 918–921.

92. See E.G. Stalenheim, L. von Knorring, and L. Wide, "Serum Levels of Thyroid Hormones as Biological Markers in a Swedish Forensic Psychiatric Population," *Biological Psychiatry*, vol. 43, no. 10 (1998), pp. 755–761; and P.O. Alm et al., "Criminality and Psychopathy as Related to Thyroid Activity in Former Juvenile Delinquents," *Acta Psychiatrica Scandinavica*, vol. 94, no. 2 (1996), pp. 112–117.

93. Stalenheim, von Knorring, and Wide, "Serum Levels of Thyroid Hormones as Biological Markers in a Swedish Forensic Psychiatric Population."

94. Based on Psychophysiology of Aggression, Psychopathy, and Conduct Problems: A Meta-Analysis by Michale F. Lorber, Heart Rate Level and Antisocial Behavior in Children and Adolescents: A Meta-Analysis by Jame Ortiz and Adrian Raine

95. Arthur Fisher, "A New Synthesis Comes of Age," *Mosaic*, vol. 22, no. 1 (Spring 1991), pp. 2–9.

96. The quotations attributed to Wilson in this section are from Edward O. Wilson, *Sociobiology: The New Synthesis* (Cambridge, MA: The Belknap Press of Harvard University Press, 1975).

97. Konrad Lorenz, *On Aggression* (New York: Harcourt, Brace & World, 1966).

98. Ibid., p. 23.

99. Ibid., p. 38.

100. Ibid., p. 249.

101. Ibid., p. 225.

102. Edward O. Wilson, *Sociobiology: The New Synthesis*.

103. Research by Martin Daly and Margo Wilson of McMaster University in Hamilton, Ontario, as reported in Arthur Fisher, "A New Synthesis II: How Different Are Humans?" *Mosaic*, vol. 22, no. 1 (Spring 1991), p. 14.

104. Arthur Fisher, "A New Synthesis II: How Different Are Humans?" *Mosaic*, vol. 22, no. 1 (Spring 1991), p. 11.

105. John H. Beckstrom, *Evolutionary Jurisprudence: Prospects and Limitations on the Youth of Modern Darwinism throughout the Legal Process* (Urbana: University of Illinois Press, 1989).

106. John Madison Memory, "Sociobiology and the Metamorphoses of Criminology: 1978–2000," unpublished manuscript.

107. Gail S. Anderson, *Biological Influences on Criminal Behavior* (Boca Raton, FL: CRC Press, 2006).

108. James Q. Wilson and Richard J. Herrnstein, *Crime and Human Nature* (New York: Simon & Schuster, 1985).

109. Quoted in Karen J. Winkler, "Criminals Are Born as Well as Made, Authors of Controversial Book Assert," *Chronicle of Higher Education*, January 16, 1986, p. 5.

110. Wilson and Herrnstein, *Crime and Human Nature*.

111. Winkler, "Criminals Are Born as Well as Made," p. 8.

112. Anthony Walsh, *Biosocial Criminology: Introduction and Integration* (Cincinnati, OH: Anderson, 2002), p. vii.

113. Anthony Walsh, "Biological Theories of Criminal Behavior," in Richard A. Wright and J. Mitchell Miller, eds., *Encyclopedia of Criminology*, vol. 1 (New York: Routledge, 2005), p. 106.

114. Ibid.

115. Ibid.

116. Diana Fishbein, *Biobehavioral Perspectives in Criminology* (Belmont, CA: Wadsworth, 2001), p. 3.

117. C. Ray Jeffery, "Biological Perspectives," *Journal of Criminal Justice Education*, vol. 4, no. 2 (Fall 1993), p. 300.

118. Kevin Beaver, "Foreword," in Anthony Walsh, ed., *Feminist Criminology through a Biosocial Lens* (Durham, NC: Carolina Academic Press, 2011), p. 11.

119. F. Schmalleger and R. Volk, *Canadian Criminology Today. Theories and Applications* (Toronto: Pearson Canada, 2014), p. 158.

120. Diana Kendall, Jane L. Murray, and Rick Linden, *Sociology in Our Times: The Essentials* (Toronto: ITP Nelson, 2008).

121. Freda Adler, *Sisters in Crime: The Rise of the New Female Criminal* (New York: McGraw-Hill, 1975).

122. T. Bernard, J. Snipes, and A. Gerould, *Vold's Theoretical Criminology* (New York: Oxford University Press, 2010), cited in Anthony Walsh, ed., *Feminist Criminology through a Biosocial Lens* (Durham, NC: Carolina Academic Press, 2011), p. xi.

123. Anthony Walsh, ed., *Feminist Criminology through a Biosocial Lens* (Durham, NC: Carolina Academic Press, 2011), p. 22.

124. Ibid.

125. Laura Klappenbach, "Sexual Selection," About.com [Accessed June 5, 2016].

126. I. Silverman, J. Choi, and M. Peters, "The Hunter-Gatherer Theory of Sex Differences in Spatial Abilities: Data from 40 Countries," *Archives of Sexual Behavior*, vol. 36 (2007), pp. 261–268.

127. A. Walsh and L. Ellis, *Criminology: An Interdisciplinary Approach* (Thousand Oaks, CA: SAGE, 2007).

128. Walsh, ed., *Feminist Criminology*, p. 125.

129. Jerome H. Barkow, Leda Cosmides, and John Tooby, eds., *The Adapted Mind: Evolutionary Psychology and the Generation of Culture* (New York: Oxford University Press, 1992).

130. Steven Pinker, *The Blank Slate: The Modern Denial of Human Nature* (New York: Viking, 2002).

131. Lee Ellis and Anthony Walsh, "Gene-Based Evolutionary Theories in Criminology," *Criminology*, vol. 35, no. 2 (1997), pp. 229–230.

132. Elizabeth Englander, *Understanding Violence*, 3rd ed. (Mahwah, NJ: Lawrence Erlbaum Associates, 2007).

133. Lee Ellis, "Theory Explaining the Biological Correlates of Criminality," *European Journal of Criminology*, vol. 2, no. 3 (2005), pp. 287–314.

134. Julian Roberts and T. Gabor, "Lombrosian Wine in a New Bottle: Research on Crime and Race," *Canadian Journal of Criminology*, vol. 32, pp. 291–313.

135. Ibid., p. 309.

136. Toufexis, "Seeking the Roots of Violence," p. 53.

Chapter 7

1. D.A. Andrews and James Bonta, *The Psychology of Criminal Conduct* (Cincinnati, OH: Anderson, 1998), p. 93.

2. "Manslaughter Verdict for Cannibal," *BBC News*, January 30, 2004, http://news.bbc.co.uk/2/hi/europe/3443293.stm [Accessed October 21, 2102].

3. K. Connolly, "Cannibal Filmed Himself Killing and Eating His 'Willing' Victim," *The Telegraph*, December 4, 2003, http://www.telegraph.co.uk/news/worldnews/europe/germany/1448497/Cannibal-filmed-himself-killing-and-eating-his-willing-victim.html [Accessed October 21, 2012].

4. "German Cannibal Guilty of Murder," *BBC News*, May 6, 2006, http://news.bbc.co.uk/2/hi/europe/4752797.stm [Accessed October 21, 2012].

5. Barry Came, "Montreal Massacre," *Maclean's*, December 18, 1989, p. 14.

6. Bruce Wallace, "The Making of a Mass Killer," *Maclean's*, December 18, 1989, p. 22.

7. Canadian Psychological Association, Criminal Justice Section, http://www.cpa.ca/aboutcpa/cpasections/criminaljusticepsychology/criminaljusticesectionexecutive [Accessed July 1, 2016].

8. Canadian Academy of Psychiatry and the Law, http://www.capl-acpd.org/ [Accessed July 1, 2016].

9. Jean Piaget, *The Moral Judgment of the Child* (London: Kegan Paul, Trench, Trübner & Co., 1932). See also J. Piaget, *The Child's Construction of Reality* (London: Routledge and Kegan Paul, 1955).

10. Lawrence Kohlberg, *Stages in the Development of Moral Thought and Action* (New York: Holt, Rinehart and Winston, 1969).

11. Sergio Herzog, "Moral Judgment, Crime Seriousness, and the Relations between Them: An Exploratory Study," *Crime and Delinquency*, December 27, 2012.

12. K. Dodge, "A Social Information Processing Model of Social Competence in Children," *Minnesota Symposium in Child Psychology*, vol. 8 (1986), pp. 77–125.

13. J. Lochman, Self and Peer Perceptions of Attributional Biases of Aggressive and Non-aggressive Boys in Dyadic Interactions," *Journal of Consulting and Clinical Psychology*, vol. 55 (1987), pp. 404–410.

14. Calvin Langton and W. Marshall. "Contagion in Rapists: Theoretical Patterns by Typological Breakdown," *Aggression and Violent Behaviour*, vol. 6 (2001), pp. 499–518.

15. R.C. Schank and R.P. Abelson, *Scripts, Plans, Goals and Understanding, an Inquiry into Human Knowledge Structures* (Hillsdale, NJ: Lawrence Erlbaum, 1977).

16. Helen Gavin and David Hockey, "Criminal Careers and Cognitive Scripts: An Investigation into Criminal Versatility," *The Qualitative Report*, vol. 15, no. 2 (March 2010), pp. 389–410.

17. Ibid.

18. Laurence Steinberg, "The Juvenile Psychopath: Fads, Fictions, and Facts," *National Institute of Justice Perspectives on Crime and Justice: 2001 Lecture Series*, vol. V (Washington, DC: NIJ, 2002), pp. 35–64.

19. Ibid.

20. Nicole Hahn Rafter, "Psychopathy and the Evolution of Criminological Knowledge," *Theoretical Criminology*, vol. 1, no. 2 (May 1997), p. 236.

21. Nolan D.C. Lewis, "Foreword," in David Abrahamsen, *Crime and the Human Mind* (New York: Columbia University Press, 1944; reprint, Montclair, NJ: Patterson Smith, 1969), p. vii.

22. As noted by Nicole Hahn Rafter in "Psychopathy and the Evolution of Criminological Knowledge." See Richard von Krafft-Ebing, *Psychopathia Sexualis* (New York: Stein and Day, 1965), reprint of the original 1886 edition; and *Text-Book of Insanity* (Philadelphia: F.A. Davis Company, 1904), first German edition, 1879.

23. Bernard H. Glueck, *Studies in Forensic Psychiatry* (Boston: Little, Brown, 1916).

24. William Healy, *The Individual Delinquent* (Boston: Little, Brown, 1915).

25. Early writings about the psychopath personality focused almost exclusively on men, and most psychiatrists appeared to believe that very few women (if any) possessed such traits.

26. Hervey M. Cleckley, *The Mask of Sanity*, 4th ed. (St. Louis, MO: C.V. Mosby, 1964).

27. Quoted in Joseph P. Newman and Chad A. Brinkley, "Psychopathy: Rediscovering Cleckley's Construct," *Psychopathology Research*, vol. 9, no. 1 (1998).

28. Gwynn Nettler, *Killing One Another* (Cincinnati, OH: Anderson, 1982), p. 179.

29. Ralph Serin, "Can Criminal Psychopaths Be Identified?" *Correctional Service of Canada*, October 22, 1999.

30. David T. Lykken, *The Antisocial Personalities* (Hillsdale, NJ: Lawrence Erlbaum, 1995).

31. Robert D. Hare, "Checklist for the Assessment of Psychopathy in Criminal Populations," in M.H. Ben-Aron, S.J. Hucker, and C.D. Webster, eds., *Clinical Criminology* (Toronto: University of Toronto, Clarke Institute of Psychiatry, 1985), pp. 157–167.

32. Adapted from Laurence Steinberg, "The Juvenile Psychopath: Fads, Fictions, and Facts," *National Institute of Justice Perspectives on Crime and Justice: 2001 Lecture Series*, vol. 5 (Washington, DC: NIJ, 2002), pp. 35–64.

33. Robert J. McMahon, Katie Witkiewitz, Julie S. Kotler, and The Conduct Problems Prevention Research Group, "Predictive Validity of Callous-Unemotional Traits Measured in Early Adolescence with Respect to Multiple Antisocial Outcomes," *Journal of Abnormal Psychology*, vol. 119 (2010), pp. 752–763.

34. Kent A. Kiehl, Andra M. Smith, Adrianna Mendrek, Bruce B. Forster, Robert D. Hare, and Peter F. Liddle, "Temporal Lobe Abnormalities in Semantic Processing by Criminal Psychopaths as Revealed by Functional Magnetic Resonance Imaging," *Psychiatry Research: Neuroimaging*, vol. 130 (2004), pp. 27–42.

35. Ibid.

36. Ivan Semeniuk, "How We Tell Right from Wrong: An Interview with Marc Hauser," *New Scientist*, March 3, 2007, p. 44.

37. Michael Caldwell et al., "Treatment Response of Adolescent Offenders with Psychopathy Features: A 2-Year Follow-Up," *Criminal Justice and Behavior*, vol. 33, no. 5 (2006), pp. 571–576.

38. Peter Aldhous, "Violent, Antisocial, Past Redemption?" *New Scientist*, April 14, 2007, pp. 8–9.

39. Hans J. Eysenck, *Crime and Personality* (Boston: Houghton Mifflin, 1964).

40. Intelligence may also be seen as an ability. See, for example, Colin G. DeYoung, "Intelligence and Personality," in R. J. Sternberg and S. B. Kaufman, eds., *The Cambridge Handbook of Intelligence* (New York: Cambridge University Press, 2011), p. 2.

41. Some early personality theorists considered intelligence to be part of personality. See, for example, R. B. Cattell, *Personality* (New York: McGraw-Hill, 1950); and J.P. Guilford, *Personality* (New York: McGraw-Hill, 1959).

42. Ibid., p. 92.

43. Hans J. Eysenck, "Personality and Criminality: A Dispositional Analysis," in William S. Laufer and Freda Adler, eds., *Advances in Criminology Theory*, vol. 1 (New Brunswick, NJ: Transaction, 1989), p. 90.

44. Eysenck, *Crime and Personality*, pp. 35–36.

45. Colin G. DeYoung, "Intelligence and Personality," in R.J. Sternberg and S. B. Kaufman, eds., *The Cambridge Handbook of Intelligence* (New York: Cambridge University Press, 2011), pp. 711–737.

46. Gabriel Tarde, *The Laws of Imitation*, translated by E.C. Parsons (1890; reprint, Gloucester, MA: Peter Smith, 1962).

47. Albert Bandura, "The Social Learning Perspective: Mechanisms of Aggression," in Hans Toch, ed., *Psychology of Crime and Criminal Justice* (Prospect Heights, IL: Waveland, 1979), p. 198.

48. Albert Bandura, *Social Learning Theory* (Englewood Cliffs, NJ: Prentice Hall, 1977).

49. Ibid., p. 199.

50. M.M. Lefkowitz et al., "Television Violence and Child Aggression: A Follow-up Study," in G.A. Comstock and E.A. Rubinstein, eds., *Television and Social Behavior*, vol. 3 (Washington, DC: U.S. Government Printing Office, 1972), pp. 35–135.

51. Nettler, *Killing One Another*, p. 159.

52. Ibid., p. 155.

53. Runa Munkner, Soeren Haastrup, Torben Joergensen, and Peter Kramp, "The Temporal Relationship between Schizophrenia and Crime," *Social Psychiatry and Psychiatric Epidemiology*, vol. 38, no. 7 (July 2003), pp. 347–353.

54. Elizabeth Walsh, Alec Buchanan, and Thomas Fahy, "Violence and Schizophrenia: Examining the Evidence," *The British Journal of Psychiatry*, vol. 180 (2002), pp. 490–495.54.

55. Seena Fazel, Niklas Långström, Anders Hjern, Martin Grann, and Paul Lichtenstein, "Schizophrenia, Substance Abuse, and Violent Crime," *Journal of the American Medical Association*, vol. 301, no. 19 (2009), pp. 2016–2023.

56. "40-Year-Old Suspect Held in Gruesome Manitoba Bus Killing," *CBC News*, July 31, 2008, http://www.cbc.ca/news/canada/manitoba/40-year-old-suspect-held-in-gruesome-manitoba-bus-killing-1.705008 [Accessed July 1, 2016]; "Vince Li Not Criminally Responsible for Beheading," *CTV News*, March 5, 2009, http://www.ctv.ca/servlet/ArticleNews/story/CTVNews/20090304/bus_verdict_090305/20090305/ [Accessed July 1, 2016].

57. J. Dollard, L. Doob, N. Miller, O. Mowrer, and R. Sears, *Frustration and Aggression* (New Haven, CT: Yale University Press, 1939).

58. Maria Bohuslawsky, "Troubled Killer Was Once Fired," *Ottawa Citizen*, April 7, 1999, p. C1.

59. Andrew F. Henry and James F. Short, Jr., *Suicide and Homicide: Economic, Sociological, and Psychological Aspects of Aggression* (Glencoe, IL: Free Press, 1954).

60. Stewart Palmer, *A Study of Murder* (New York: Crowell, 1960).

61. Seymour L. Halleck, *Psychiatry and the Dilemmas of Crime: A Study of Causes, Punishment and Treatment* (Berkeley: University of California Press, 1971).

62. Ibid., p. 78.

63. Ibid., p. 80.

64. Ibid.

65. Ibid.

66. Arnold S. Linsky, Ronet Bachman, and Murray A. Straus, *Stress, Culture, and Aggression* (New Haven, CT: Yale University Press, 1995).

67. Ibid., p. 7.

68. D.A. Andrews and James Bonta, *The Psychology of Criminal Conduct* (Cincinnati, OH: Anderson, 1998).

69. D. A. Andrews and J. Bonta, "Rehabilitating Criminal Justice Policy and Practice," *Psychology, Public Policy, and Law*, vol. 16, no. 1 (2010), pp. 39–55.

70. Adapted from Tony Ward and Claire Stewart, "Criminogenic Needs and Human Needs: A Theoretical Model," *Psychology, Crime and Law*, vol. 9, no. 2 (2003), pp. 125–143.

71. Andrews and Bonta, "Rehabilitating Criminal Justice Policy and Practice," p. 46.

72. Ward and Stewart, p. 128.

73. Ibid.

74. Ibid, p. 182.

75. John C. Norcross, Gerald P. Koocher, and Ariele Garofalo, "Discredited Psychological Treatments and Tests: A Delphi Poll," *Professional Psychology: Research and Practice*, vol. 37, no. 5 (2006), pp. 515–522.

76. For one of the first and still definitive works in the area of selective incapacitation, see Peter Greenwood and Allan Abrahamsen, *Selective Incapacitation* (Santa Monica, CA: Rand, 1982).

77. M.A. Peterson, H.B. Braiker, and S.M. Polich, *Who Commits Crimes?* (Cambridge, MA: Oelgeschlager, Gunn & Hain, 1981).

78. Jeremy Travis, "But They All Come Back," papers from the Executive Session on Sentencing and Corrections, No. 7 (Washington, DC: National Institute of Justice, 2000).

79. North Carolina Department of Public Safety, Cognitive Behavioral Interventions (CBI): Standard Operating Procedures (December 2001).

80. Friedrich Losel, *Treatment and Management of Psychopaths*. Paper presented at the NATO Advanced Study Institute on Psychopathy, November 1996, Alvor, Portugal.

81. Friedrich Losel, "Treatment and Management of Psychopaths," *NATO ASI Series*, vol. 88 (1998), pp. 303–354.

82. Jennifer L. White, Terrie E. Moffitt, Felton Earls, Lee Robins, and Phil A. Silva, "How Early Can We Tell? Predictors of Childhood Conduct Disorder and Adolescent Delinquency," *Criminology*, vol. 28, no. 4 (1990), pp. 507–528.

83. Paul Gendreau, Tracy Little, and Claire Goggin, "A Meta-Analysis of the Predictors of Adult Offender Recidivism: What Works!" *Criminology*, vol. 34, no. 4 (November 1996), pp. 575–607.

84. For one of the first and still definitive works in the area of selective incapacitation, see Peter Greenwood and Allan Abrahamsen, *Selective Incapacitation* (Santa Monica, CA: Rand Corporation, 1982).

85. M.A. Peterson, H.B. Braiker, and S.M. Polich, *Who Commits Crimes?* (Cambridge, MA: Oelgeschlager, Gunn and Hain, 1981).

86. J. Monahan, *Predicting Violent Behavior: An Assessment of Clinical Techniques* (Beverly Hills, CA: SAGE, 1981).

87. Public Safety Canada, *Corrections and Conditional Release Statistical Overview: Annual Report, 2015* (Ottawa: Public Works and Government Services Canada, 2016).

88. Jill Peay, "Dangerousness—Ascription or Description," in M.P. Feldman, ed., *Developments in the Study of Criminal Behavior, vol. 2, Violence* (New York: John Wiley & Sons, 1982), p. 211, citing N. Walker, "Dangerous People," *International Journal of Law and Psychiatry*, vol. 1 (1978), pp. 37–50.

89. See, for example, Michael Gottfredson and Travis Hirschi, *A General Theory of Crime* (Stanford, CA: Stanford University Press, 1990); and Travis Hirschi and Michael Gottfredson, "Age and the Explanation of Crime," *American Journal of Sociology*, vol. 89 (1983), pp. 552–584.

90. David F. Greenberg, "Modeling Criminal Careers," *Criminology*, vol. 29, no. 1 (1991), p. 39.

91. James L. Johnson et al., "The Construction and Validation of the Federal Post Conviction Risk Assessment (PCRA)," *Federal Probation* (September 2011), http://www.fjc.gov/public/pdf.nsf/lookup/NSPI201220.pdf/$file/NSPI201220.pdf [Accessed July 1, 2016].

92. Tracy L. Fass, "The LSI-R and the COMPAS: Validation Data on Two Risk-Needs Tools," *Criminal Justice and Behavior*, July 8, 2008, http://citeseerx.ist.psu.edu/viewdoc/summary?doi=10.1.1.622.4810 [Accessed July 1, 2016].

93. Christopher T. Lowenkamp and Kristin Bechtel, "Predictive Validity of the LSI-R on a Sample of Offenders Drawn from the Records of the Iowa Department of Corrections Data Management System," *Federal Probation*, vol. 71, no. 3 (December 2007), pp. 25–29.

94. See, for example, Michael Gottfredson and Travis Hirschi, *A General Theory of Crime* (Stanford, CA: Stanford University Press, 1990); and Travis Hirschi and Michael Gottfredson, "Age and the Explanation of Crime," *American Journal of Sociology*, vol. 89 (1983), pp. 552–584.

95. David P. Farrington et al., "Advancing Knowledge about the Onset of Delinquency and Crime," in B.B. Lahey and A.E. Kazdin, eds., *Advances in Clinical Child Psychology*, vol. 13 (New York: Plenum, 1990), pp. 283–342.

96. Paul C. Vitz, "The Use and Abuse of Freud," a review of *Freudian Fraud: The Malignant Effect of Freud's Theory on American Thought and Culture* by E. Fuller Torrey (Leadership U., 1993), p. 52.

97. J. Bonta, M. Law, and R. K. Hanson, "The Prediction of Criminal and Violent Recidivism among Mentally Disordered Offenders: A Meta-Analysis," *Psychological Bulletin*, vol. 123 (1998), pp. 123–142.

98. Cathy Spatz Widom and Hans Toch, "The Contribution of Psychology to Criminal Justice Education," *Journal of Criminal Justice Education*, vol. 4, no. 2 (Fall 1993), p. 253.

99. Robert R. Hazelwood and John E. Douglas, "The Lust Murderer," *FBI Law Enforcement Bulletin* (Washington, DC: U.S. Department of Justice, April 1980).

100. Ibid.

101. Ibid.

102. Anastasia Toufexis, "Mind Games with Monsters," *Time*, May 6, 1991, pp. 68–69.

103. "Violent Crime Linkage System (ViCLAS)," RCMP website, http://www.rcmp-grc.gc.ca/to-ot/cpcmec-ccpede/bs-sc/viclas-salvac-eng.htm [Accessed June 29, 2016].

104. Ibid.

105. International Academy of Investigative Psychology, http://www.ia-ip.org/ip/what-is-ip.html [Accessed July 1, 2016].

106. Scott O. Lilienfeld, Steven Jay Lynn, John Ruscio, and Barry L. Beyerstein, *50 Great Myths of Popular Psychology* (Malden, MA: Wiley-Blackwell, 2010), p. 215.

107. B. Snook, J. Eastwood, P. Gendreau, C. Goggin, and R. M. Cullen, "Taking Stock of Criminal Profiling: A Narrative Review and Meta-Analysis," *Criminal Justice and Behavior*, vol. 34 (2007), pp. 437–453.

108. *R. v. Parks* (1992), 75 C.C.C. (3d) 287 (S.C.C.).

109. R. Barnhorst and S. Barnhorst, *Criminal Law and the Canadian Criminal Code* (Toronto: McGraw-Hill Ryerson, 2009), p. 59.

110. Halleck, *Psychiatry and the Dilemmas of Crime*, p. 213.

111. *R. v. Swain* (1991), 63 C.C.C. (3d) 481 (S.C.C.).

112. Minister of Justice and Attorney General of Canada, *Justice Communiqué*, January 30, 1992, p. 2.

113. F. Schmalleger, *Criminology Today: An Integrated Introduction* (Upper Saddle River, NJ: Prentice-Hall, 2012), pp. 141–142.

114. *Martin's Annual Criminal Code* (Aurora, ON: Canada Law Book, 2007), s. 672.5(2).

115. M.A. Jackson and C.T. Griffiths, *Canadian Criminology: Perspectives on Crime and Criminality* (Toronto: Harcourt Brace and Co., 1995), p. 73.

116. Jeff Latimer and Austin Lawrence, *The Review Board Systems in Canada: An Overview of Results from the Mentally Disordered Accused Data Collection Study*, (Ottawa: Department of Justice Canada, Research and Statistics Division, January 2006) and Zoran Miladinovic And Jennifer Lukassen, "Verdicts of Not Criminally Responsible on Account of Mental Disorder in Adult Criminal Courts, 2005/2006 – 2011/2012," *Juristat* (Ottawa: Minister of Industry, 2014).

117. Pauline Tam, *Ottawa Citizen*, October 29, 1996, p. C3.

Chapter 8

1. Frank Tannenbaum, *Crime and the Community* (Boston: Ginn and Company, 1938), p. 25.

2. P. Tam, "Driver in Battersby Killing Sent to Adult Jail," *Ottawa Citizen*, November 8, 1996, p. D1; and M. Blanchfield, "Crossed Paths," *Ottawa Citizen*, February 17, 1996, p. B2.

3. Andrew Duffy, "Notorious Elgin Street murderer wins temporary prison pass" *Ottawa Citizen*, December 4, 2015, http://ottawacitizen.com/news/local-news/notorious-elgin-street-murderer-wins-temporary-prison-pass [Accessed February 13, 2016].

4. Ibid.

5. See Anthony Walsh, *Biosocial Criminology: Introduction and Integration* (Cincinnati, OH: Anderson, 2002).

6. Emile Durkheim, *The Division of Labor in Society*, translated by George Simpson (New York: Free Press, 1947). Originally published in 1893.

7. Ibid., p. 80.

8. W.I. Thomas and Florian Znaniecki, *The Polish Peasant in Europe and America* (Boston: Gorham, 1920).

9. Robert Park and Ernest Burgess, *The City* (Chicago: University of Chicago Press, 1925).

10. Clifford R. Shaw et al., *Delinquency Areas* (Chicago: University of Chicago Press, 1929).

11. David Matza, *Becoming Deviant* (Englewood Cliffs, NJ: Prentice Hall, 1969).

12. C.P. La Prairie, "Community Types, Crime and Police Services on Canadian Indian Reserves," *Journal of Research in Crime and Delinquency*, vol. 25 (1987), pp. 375–391.

13. C.P. La Prairie, "Seen but Not Heard: Native People in the Inner City," in *City-By-City Differences: Inner Cities and the Criminal Justice System, Report 2, Aboriginal Justice Directorate* (Ottawa: Department of Justice, 1994).

14. Lawrence W. Sherman, Patrick R. Gartin, and Michael E. Buerger, "Hot Spots of Predatory Crime: Routine Activities and the Criminology of Place," *Criminology*, vol. 27, no. 1 (1989), pp. 27–55.

15. Rodney Stark, "Deviant Places: A Theory of the Ecology of Crime," *Criminology*, vol. 25, no. 4 (1987), p. 893.
16. Ibid., pp. 895–899.
17. James Q. Wilson and George L. Kelling, "Broken Windows: The Police and Neighborhood Safety," *Atlantic Monthly*, March 1982, http://www.theatlantic.com/politics/crime/windows.htm [Accessed February 15, 2010].
18. Ibid.
19. David Thacher, "Order Maintenance Reconsidered: Moving beyond Strong Causal Reasoning," *Journal of Criminal Law and Criminology*, vol. 94, no. 2 (2004), pp. 381–414.
20. Sherman, Gartin, and Buerger, "Hot Spots of Predatory Crime," p. 31.
21. Oscar Newman, *Architectural Design for Crime Prevention* (Washington, DC: U.S. Department of Justice, 1973). See also Oscar Newman, *Defensible Space* (New York: Macmillan, 1972); and Oscar Newman, *Creating Defensible Space* (Washington, DC: Office of Housing and Urban Development, 1996).
22. Oscar Newman, *Defensible Space: Crime Prevention Through Urban Design* (New York: Macmillan, 1972), p. 3. See also Ralph B. Taylor and Adele V. Harrell, *Physical Environment and Crime* (Washington, DC: National Institute of Justice, May 1996).
23. "Crime Prevention Through Environmental Design," Peel Regional Police website, 2012, http://www.peelpolice.on.ca/en/crimeprevention/crimepreventionthroughenvironmentaldesign.asp [Accessed May 6, 2012].
24. Bernard E. Harcourt, *Illusion of Order: The False Promise of Broken Windows Policing* (Cambridge, MA: Harvard University Press, 2001).
25. Robert J. Sampson and Stephen W. Radenbush, "Systematic Social Observation of Public Spaces: A New Look at Disorder in Urban Neighborhoods," *American Journal of Sociology*, vol. 105 (1999), p. 603.
26. Thomas M. Arvanites and Robert H. Defina, "Business Cycles and Street Crime," *Criminology*, vol. 44, no. 1 (2006), pp. 141.
27. Émile Durkheim, *Suicide: A Study in Sociology* (New York: Free Press, 1897). Reprinted and translated in 1951.
28. Robert K. Merton, "Social Structure and Anomie," *American Sociological Review*, vol. 3 (October 1938), pp. 672–682; and Robert K. Merton, *Social Theory and Social Structure*, rev. ed. (New York: Free Press, 1957).
29. Robert K. Merton, *Social Theory and Social Structure* (New York: Glencoe, 1957), p. 190.
30. Merton, "Social Structure and Anomie," p. 681.
31. M. Beare, *Criminal Conspiracies: Organized Crime in Canada* (Toronto: McClelland & Stewart, 1996); and Criminal Intelligence Service of Canada, *2008 Report on Organized Crime*, 2008, http://www.cisc.gc.ca/annual_reports/annual_report_2008/frontpage_2008_e.html [Accessed May 7, 2012].
32. Robert Agnew, "Foundation for a General Strain Theory of Crime and Delinquency," *Criminology*, vol. 30, no. 1 (1992), pp. 47–87.
33. Ibid.
34. Ibid.
35. Ibid.
36. Raymond Paternoster and Paul Mazerolle, "General Strain Theory and Delinquency: A Replication and Extension," *Journal of Research in Crime and Delinquency*, vol. 31, no. 3 (1994), pp. 235–263.
37. Robert Agnew and Helene Raskin White, "An Empirical Test of General Strain Theory," *Criminology*, vol. 30, no. 4 (1992), pp. 475–499.
38. Thorsten Sellin, *Culture Conflict and Crime* (New York: Social Science Research Council, 1938).
39. Ibid., p. 68.
40. Frederick M. Thrasher, *The Gang* (Chicago: University of Chicago Press, 1927).
41. William F. Whyte, *Street Corner Society: The Social Structure of an Italian Slum* (Chicago: University of Chicago Press, 1943).
42. The quotations attributed to Miller in this section are from Walter Miller, "Lower Class Culture as a Generating Milieu of Gang Delinquency," *Journal of Social Issues*, vol. 14, no. 3 (1958), pp. 5–19.
43. Franco Ferracuti and Marvin Wolfgang, *The Subculture of Violence: Toward an Integrated Theory of Criminology* (London: Tavistock, 1967).
44. Ibid.
45. Ibid., p. 151.
46. Ibid.
47. Jeffrey I. Ross, *Violence in Canada: Sociopolitical Perspectives* (Toronto: Oxford University Press, 1995), pp. 195–196.
48. For an excellent review of the literature, see F. Frederick Hawley, "The Southern Violence Construct: A Skeleton in the Criminological Closet." Paper presented at the annual meeting of the American Society of Criminology, 1988.
49. Bertram Wyatt-Brown, *Southern Honor: Ethics and Behavior in the Old South* (Oxford: Oxford University Press, 1983).
50. Franklin Zimring et al., "Punishing Homicide in Philadelphia: Perspectives on the Death Penalty," *University of Chicago Law Review*, vol. 43 (1976), pp. 227–252.
51. John Hagan, "Structural and Cultural Disinvestment and the New Ethnographies of Poverty and Culture," *Contemporary Sociology*, vol. 22, no. 3 (1993), pp. 327–331.
52. Richard A. Cloward and Lloyd E. Ohlin, *Delinquency and Opportunity: A Theory of Delinquent Gangs* (Glencoe, IL: Free Press, 1960).
53. Ibid., p. 7.
54. Ibid., p. 13.
55. Ibid., p. 16.
56. Ibid., p. 19.
57. Ibid., p. 3.
58. Ibid., p. 37.
59. Ibid., pp. 12–13.
60. Albert H. Cohen, *Delinquent Boys: The Culture of the Gang* (Glencoe, IL: Free Press, 1955).
61. Ibid., p. 13.
62. Donald J. Shoemaker, *Theories of Delinquency: An Examination of Explanations of Delinquent Behavior* (New York: Oxford University Press, 1984), p. 102, citing Cohen.
63. Cohen, *Delinquent Boys*, p. 76.
64. Ibid., p. 121.
65. Shoemaker, *Theories of Delinquency*, p. 105.
66. Elijah Anderson, *The Code of the Street: Decency, Violence, and the Moral Life of the Inner City* (New York: W.W. Norton, 1990).
67. Robert M. Gordon, "Criminal Business Organizations, Street Gangs and 'Wanna Be' Groups: A Vancouver Perspective," *Canadian Journal of Criminology*, vol. 42, no. 1 (January 2000), pp. 39–60.
68. Mark Totten, *Promising Practices for Addressing Youth Involvement in Gangs*, April 2008, http://www2.gov.bc.ca/assets/gov/public-safety-and-emergency-services/crime-prevention/community-crime-prevention/publications/totten-report.pdf [Accessed October 8, 2016].
69. Mark Totten, *Nasty, Brutish and Short. The Lives of Gang Members in Canada* (Toronto: James Lorimer and Company Ltd, 2012), p. 29.
70. Criminal Intelligence Service of Canada, *2010 Annual Report on Organized Crime*, May 2010, http://publications.gc.ca/collections/collection_2010/grc-rcmp/PS61-1-2010-eng.pdf [Accessed March 12, 2016].

71. Mark Totten, *Promising Practices for Addressing Youth Involvement in Gangs*, April 2008, http://www.gangprevention.ca/partners/resources/promising-practices-addressing-youth-involvement-gangs-report [Accessed March 12, 2016].

72. Criminal Intelligence Service Canada, *2009 Annual Report on Organized Crime*, May 2009, http://publications.gc.ca/collections/collection_2009/sp-ps/PS61-1-2009E.pdf [Accessed March 12, 2016].

73. Arlen Egley, Jr. and James C. Howell, *Highlights of the 2010 National Youth Gang Survey* (Washington, DC: Office of Juvenile Justice and Delinquency Prevention, 2012).

74. National Gang Crime Research Center, *Achieving Justice and Reversing the Problem of Gang Crime and Gang Violence in America Today: Preliminary Results of the Project Gangfact Study* (Chicago: National Gang Crime Research Center, 1996).

75. G. David Curry and Irving A. Spergel, "Gang Homicide, Delinquency, and Community," *Criminology*, vol. 26, no. 3 (1988), pp. 381–405.

76. Ibid., p. 401.

77. Cited in Mary H. Glazier, a review of J. Mitchell Miller and Jeffrey P. Rush, eds., *Gangs: A Criminal Justice Approach* (Cincinnati, OH: Anderson, 1996), in *The Criminologist* (July/April 1996), p. 29.

78. Totten, *Nasty, Brutish and Short*, p. 241.

79. Margaret E. Beare and Chris Hogg, "Listening In . . . to Gang Culture," *Canadian Journal of Criminology and Criminal Justice*, vol. 55, no. 3 (July 2013), pp. 421–453.

80. Steven Schlossman et al., *Delinquency Prevention in South Chicago: A Fifty-Year Assessment of the Chicago Area Project* (Santa Monica, CA: Rand Corporation, 1984).

81. J. Robert Lilly, Francis T. Cullen, and Richard A. Ball, *Criminological Theory: Context and Consequences* (Newbury Park, CA: SAGE, 1989), p. 80.

82. Lamar T. Empey, *American Delinquency: Its Meaning and Construction* (Homewood, IL: Dorsey, 1982), p. 243.

83. Sibylle Artz, *Sex, Power and the Violent School Girl* (Toronto: Trifolium Books, 1998), p. 24.

84. See, for example, George L. Kelling, "Crime Control, the Police, and Culture Wars: Broken Windows and Cultural Pluralism," in *National Institute of Justice, Perspectives on Crime and Justice: 1997–1998 Lecture Series* (Washington, DC: National Institute of Justice, 1998).

85. Robert J. Bursik, "Social Disorganization and Theories of Crime and Delinquency: Problems and Prospects," *Criminology*, vol. 26, no. 4 (1988), p. 519.

86. Stephen J. Pfohl, *Images of Deviance and Social Control* (New York: McGraw-Hill, 1985), p. 167.

87. Travis Hirschi, review of Delbert S. Elliott, David Huizinga, and Suzanne S. Ageton, "Explaining Delinquency and Drug Use," in *Criminology*, vol. 25, no. 1 (February 1987), p. 195.

88. Gwynn Nettler, *Killing One Another* (Cincinnati, OH: Anderson, 1982), p. 67.

89. Margaret Anderson, "Review Essay: Rape Theories, Myths, and Social Change," *Contemporary Crises*, vol. 5 (1983), p. 237.

90. Nettler, *Killing One Another*, p. 54.

91. James Q. Wilson, *The Moral Sense* (New York: The Free Press, 1993).

Chapter 9

1. Albert K. Cohen, *Delinquent Boys: The Culture of the Gang* (Glencoe, IL: Free Press, 1995), p. 11.

2. From Killer seeks family visits, published by CBC, © 2001. Used by permission of CBC News.

3. "Freedom Weighed for Killer of Heiress," *CBC News*, February 13, 2001, http://www.cbc.ca/news/story/2001/02/13/ott_eatonkiller010213.html [Accessed February 19, 2010].

4. Kirk Makin, "Court Rules Rights of Eaton's Killer Were Abused," *Globe and Mail*, June 29, 2007, http://www.theglobeandmail.com/news/national/court-rules-rights-of-eatons-killer-were-abused/article688733/ [Accessed March 15, 2016].

5. Edwin Sutherland, *Principles of Criminology* (New York: Lippincott, 1939).

6. Edwin H. Sutherland and Donald R. Cressey, *Criminology* (New York: Lippincott, 1978).

7. S. Brown, V. Creamer, and B. Stetson, "Adolescent Alcohol Expectancies in Relation to Personal and Parental Drinking Patterns," *Journal of Abnormal Psychology*, vol. 96 (1987), pp. 117–121.

8. Gresham Sykes and David Matza, "Techniques of Neutralization: A Theory of Delinquency," *American Sociological Review*, vol. 22 (December 1957), pp. 664–670.

9. See Volkan Topalli, "When Being Good Is Bad: An Expansion of Neutralization Theory," *Criminology*, vol. 43 (2005), p. 797.

10. Ibid., pp. 664–670.

11. Charles R. Tittle, *Control Balance: Toward a General Theory of Deviance* (Boulder, CO: Westview Press, 1995).

12. Robert Agnew, "The Techniques of Neutralization and Violence," *Criminology*, vol. 32, no. 4 (1994), pp. 555–580.

13. Ibid.

14. Lois Presser, "Remorse and Neutralization among Violent Male Offenders," *Justice Quarterly*, vol. 20, no. 4 (2003), pp. 801–825.

15. Orly Turgeman-Goldschmidt, "The Rhetoric of Hackers' Neutralizations," in Frank Schmalleger and Michale Pittaro, eds., *Crimes of the Internet* (Upper Saddle River, NJ: Prentice Hall, 2008).

16. See, for example, Dorothy E. Denning, "Activism, Hacktivism, and Cyberterrorism: The Internet as a Tool for Influencing Foreign Policy," *Computer Security Journal*, vol. 16 (2000), pp. 15–35; and Tim Jordan and Paul Taylor, *Hacktivism and Cyberwars: Rebels with a Cause?* (New York: Routledge, 2004).

17. Frank Tannenbaum, *Crime and the Community* (New York: Atheneum Press, 1938), pp. 17–18.

18. Ibid., p. 19.

19. Edwin M. Lemert, *Social Pathology: A Systematic Approach to the Theory of Sociopathic Behavior* (New York: McGraw-Hill, 1951), p. 76.

20. Ibid.

21. Howard Becker, *Outsiders: Studies in the Sociology of Deviance* (New York: Free Press, 1963).

22. Ibid., p. 1.

23. Ibid., p. 9.

24. Ibid., p. 147.

25. NORML Canada, http://norml.ca/project/mandate/ [Accessed March 19, 2016].

26. Becker, *Outsiders*, pp. 37–38.

27. Jon Gunnar Bernburg and Marvin D. Krohn, "Labeling, Life Chances, and Adult Crime: The Direct and Indirect Effects of Official Intervention in Adolescence on Crime in Early Adulthood," *Criminology*, vol. 41, no. 4 (2003), pp. 1287–1318.

28. A number of papers have been released in the Reintegrative Shaming Experiments (RISE) series to date: Lawrence W. Sherman and Heather Strang, *The Right Kind of Shame for Crime Prevention* (Canberra: Australian National University, 1997); Heather Strang and Lawrence W. Sherman, *The Victim's Perspective* (Canberra: Australian National University, 1997); Lawrence W. Sherman and Geoffrey C. Barnes, *Restorative Justice and Offenders' Respect for the Law*

(Canberra: Australian National University, 1997); Lawrence W. Sherman and Heather Strang, *Restorative Justice and Deterring Crime* (Canberra: Australian National University, 1997); and Nathan Harris and Jamie B. Burton, *The Reliability of Observed Reintegrative Shaming, Shame, Defiance and Other Key Concepts in Diversionary Conferences* (Canberra: Australian National University, 1997).

29. *RISE Working Papers: Introduction* (Canberra: Australian National University, 1997).

30. Cited in Lawrence W. Sherman and Heather Strang, *The Right Kind of Shame for Crime Prevention* (Canberra: Australian National University, 1997).

31. Ibid.

32. For a good overview of social control approaches, see George S. Bridges and Martha Myers, eds., *Inequality, Crime, and Social Control* (Boulder, CO: Westview Press, 1994).

33. Walter C. Reckless, *The Crime Problem*, 4th ed. (New York: Appleton-Century-Crofts, 1967).

34. Ibid., p. 470.

35. Ibid.

36. Ibid., p. 475.

37. Ibid.

38. Travis Hirschi, *Causes of Delinquency* (Berkeley: University of California Press, 1969).

39. Charles R. Tittle, "Theoretical Developments in Criminology," in National Institute of Justice, ed., *The Nature of Crime: Continuity and Change*, vol. 1 of *Criminal Justice 2000* (Washington, DC: National Institute of Justice, 2000), p. 65.

40. Hirschi, *Causes of Delinquency*.

41. Ibid.

42. Ibid.

43. Ibid.

44. Ibid.

45. Ibid.

46. Ibid.

47. Michael Gottfredson and Travis Hirschi, *A General Theory of Crime* (Stanford, CA: Stanford University Press, 1990).

48. Teresa C. LaGrange and Robert A. Silverman, "Low Self-Control and Opportunity: Testing the General Theory of Crime as an Explanation for Gender Differences in Delinquency," *Criminology*, vol. 37, no. 1 (1999), p. 41.

49. Gottfredson and Hirschi, *A General Theory of Crime*.

50. Werner Einstadter and Stuart Henry, *Criminological Theory: An Analysis of Its Underlying Assumptions* (Fort Worth, TX: Harcourt Brace, 1995), p. 189.

51. Kelli Phythian, Carl Keane, and Catherine Krull, "Family Structure and Parental Behavior: Identifying the Sources of Adolescent Self-Control," *Western Criminology Review*, vol. 9, no. 2 (2008), pp. 73–87.

52. Ibid., p. 73.

53. For some influential writings of the period, see K.F. Riegel, "Toward a Dialectical Theory of Development," *Human Development*, vol. 18 (1975), pp. 50–64; and U. Bronfenbrenner, *The Ecology of Human Development* (Cambridge, MA: Harvard University Press, 1979).

54. R.M. Lerner, "Early Adolescence: Towards an Agenda for the Integration of Research, Policy and Intervention," in R.M. Lerner, ed., *Early Adolescence: Perspectives on Research, Policy, and Intervention* (Hillsdale, NJ: Erlbaum, 1993), pp. 1–13.

55. See T.P. Thornberry, *Developmental Theories of Crime and Delinquency* (Piscataway, NJ: Transaction, 1997).

56. A. Blumstein et al., eds., *Criminal Careers and Career Criminals* (Washington, DC: National Academy Press, 1986).

57. Robert J. Sampson and John H. Laub, *Crime in the Making: Pathways and Turning Points through the Life Course* (Cambridge, MA: Harvard University Press, 1993).

58. G. H. Elder, Jr., "Perspectives on the Life-Course," in G. H. Elder, Jr., ed., *Life-Course Dynamics* (Ithaca, NY: Cornell University Press, 1985).

59. Philip W. Harris, Wayne N. Welsh, and Frank Butler, "A Century of Juvenile Justice," in *Criminal Justice 2000*, vol. 1 (Washington, DC: National Institute of Justice, 2000).

60. Marc LeBlanc and Rolf Loeber, "Developmental Criminology Updated," in Michael Tonry, ed., *Crime and Justice: A Review of Research*, vol. 23 (Chicago: University of Chicago Press, 1998).

61. Adapted from Harris, Welsh, and Butler, "A Century of Juvenile Justice," p. 379.

62. Glen H. Elder, Jr., "Time, Human Agency, and Social Change: Perspectives on the Life Course," *Social Psychology Quarterly*, vol. 57, no. 1 (1994), pp. 4–15.

63. David S. Kirk, "Residential Change as a Turning Point in the Life Course of Crime: Desistance or Temporary Cessation?" *Criminology*, vol. 50, no. 2 (2012), p. 1.

64. Marvin Wolfgang, Robert Figlio, and Thorsten Sellin, *Delinquency in a Birth Cohort* (Chicago: University of Chicago Press, 1972).

65. Marvin Wolfgang, Terence Thornberry, and Robert Figlio, *From Boy to Man, From Delinquency to Crime* (Chicago: University of Chicago Press, 1987).

66. Steven P. Lab, "Analyzing Change in Crime and Delinquency Rates: The Case for Cohort Analysis," *Criminal Justice Research Bulletin*, vol. 3, no. 10 (Huntsville, TX: Sam Houston State University, 1988), p. 2.

67. Lawrence E. Cohen and Richard Machalek, "A General Theory of Expropriative Crime: An Evolutionary Ecological Approach," *American Journal of Sociology*, vol. 94, no. 3 (1988), pp. 465–501; and Lawrence E. Cohen and Richard Machalek, "The Normalcy of Crime: From Durkheim to Evolutionary Ecology," *Rationality and Society*, vol. 6 (1994), pp. 286–308.

68. Bryan Vila, "Human Nature and Crime Control: Improving the Feasibility of Nurturant Strategies," *Politics and the Life Sciences* (March 1997), pp. 3–21.

69. Ibid.

70. Barbara Tatem Kelley et al., *Developmental Pathways in Boys' Disruptive and Delinquent Behavior* (Washington, DC: Office of Juvenile Justice and Delinquency Prevention, December 1997).

71. See Stuart Greenbaum, "Drugs, Delinquency, and Other Data," in *Juvenile Justice*, vol. 2, no. 1 (Spring/Summer 1994), pp. 2–8.

72. Adapted from Katharine Browning et al., "Causes and Correlates of Delinquency Program," OJJDP Fact Sheet (Washington, DC: U.S. Department of Justice, April 1999).

73. Family and Youth Services Bureau, *Understanding Youth Development: Promoting Positive Pathways of Growth*.

74. For another interesting analysis, see Robert J. Sampson and John H. Laub, *Crime in the Making* (Cambridge, MA: Harvard University Press, 1993).

75. Kelley et al., *Developmental Pathways in Boys' Disruptive and Delinquent Behavior*, p. 14.

76. See Felton J. Earls and Albert J. Reiss, *Breaking the Cycle: Predicting and Preventing Crime* (Washington, DC: National Institute of Justice, 1994).

77. Vila, "Human Nature and Crime Control," p. 10.

78. C.T. Griffiths and S. Verdun-Jones, *Canadian Criminal Justice* (Toronto: Harcourt Brace Canada, 1994), p. 559.

79. See R.E. Tremblay et al., "From Childhood Physical Aggression to Adolescent Maladjustment: The Montreal Prevention Experiment," in R.D. Peters and R.J. McMahon, eds., *Preventing Childhood Disorders, Substance Abuse, and Delinquency* (Thousand Oaks, CA: SAGE, 1996), pp. 268–298.

80. Robert W. Sweet, Jr., "Preserving Families to Prevent Delinquency," *Office of Juvenile Justice and Delinquency Prevention Model Programs, 1990* (Washington, DC: U.S. Department of Justice, April 1992).

81. Ibid.

82. Frank Schmalleger, *Criminology Today: An Integrative Introduction* (Upper Saddle River, NJ: Pearson Education, 2009), p. 336.

83. Randy Martin, Robert J. Mutchnick, and W. Timothy Austin, *Criminological Thought: Pioneers Past and Present* (New York: Macmillan, 1990), p. 368.

Chapter 10

1. *Communities and the Challenge of Conflict: Perspectives on Restorative Justice* [Monograph]. Law Commission of Canada, 2000.

2. Morgan Lowry, "First Nations Groups Mark 25 Years Since Oka Crisis," *Canadian Press*, July 11, 2015, http://www.ctvnews.ca/canada/first-nations-groups-mark-25-years-since-oka-crisis-1.2464631 [Accessed March 25, 2016].

3. Richard Quinney, *Class, State, and Class: On the Theory and Practice of Criminal Justice* (New York: David McKay, 1977), p. 145.

4. Vance Packard, *The Status Seekers* (London: Harmondsworth, 1961).

5. George B. Vold, *Theoretical Criminology* (New York: Oxford University Press, 1958).

6. Ibid., p. 205.

7. Ibid., pp. 208–209.

8. Ralf Dahrendorf, *Class and Class Conflict in Industrial Society* (Stanford, CA: Stanford University Press, 1959).

9. Ralf Dahrendorf, "Out of Utopia: Toward a Reorientation of Sociological Analysis," *American Journal of Sociology*, vol. 64 (1958), pp. 115–127.

10. Austin Turk, *Criminality and Legal Order* (Chicago: Rand McNally, 1969), p. vii.

11. Ibid.

12. William J. Chambliss, "Toward a Political Economy of Crime," in C. Reasons and R. Rich, eds., *The Sociology of Law* (Toronto: Butterworth, 1978), p. 193.

13. William Chambliss and Robert T. Seidman, *Law, Order, and Power* (Reading, MA: Addison-Wesley, 1971), p. 33.

14. Adapted from Chambliss and Seidman, *Law, Order, and Power*, pp. 473–474.

15. William J. Chambliss, *Crime and the Legal Process* (New York: McGraw-Hill, 1969), p. 88.

16. William J. Chambliss, "Toward a Political Economy of Crime," *Theory and Society*, vol. 2 (1975), pp. 152–153.

17. Ibid.

18. Ibid., p. 152.

19. Richard Quinney, *Critique of the Legal Order: Crime Control in Capitalist Society* (Boston: Little, Brown, 1974), p. 16.

20. Quinney, *Class, State, and Class*, p. 58.

21. Ibid.

22. Ibid., p. 61.

23. Ibid., p. 65.

24. Jeffrey H. Reiman, *The Rich Get Richer and the Poor Get Prison: Ideology, Class and Criminal Justice* (Boston: Allyn & Bacon, 2000).

25. Gresham M. Sykes, "Critical Criminology," *Journal of Criminal Law and Criminology*, vol. 65 (1974), pp. 206–213.

26. Elliott Currie, "Market, Crime, and Community," *Theoretical Criminology*, vol. 1, no. 2 (May 1997), pp. 147–172.

27. William V. Pelfrey, *The Evolution of Criminology* (Cincinnati, OH: Anderson, 1980), p. 86.

28. For a good overview of critiques of radical criminology, see J.F. Galliher, "Life and Death of Liberal Criminology," *Contemporary Crisis*, vol. 2, no. 3 (July 1978), pp. 245–263.

29. Jackson Toby, "The New Criminology Is the Old Sentimentality," *Criminology*, vol. 16 (1979), pp. 516–526.

30. Ibid.

31. Hermann Mannheim, *Comparative Criminology* (Boston: Houghton Mifflin, 1965), p. 445.

32. Werner Einstadter and Stuart Henry, *Criminological Theory: An Analysis of Its Underlying Assumptions* (Fort Worth, TX: Harcourt Brace, 1995), p. 233.

33. For an excellent review of critical realism in a Canadian context, see John Lowman and Brian D. MacLean, eds., *Realist Criminology: Crime Control and Policing in the 1990s* (Toronto: University of Toronto Press, 1994).

34. Daniel J. Curran and Claire M. Renzetti, *Theories of Crime* (Boston: Allyn & Bacon, 1994), p. 283.

35. See M.D. Schwartz and W.S. DeKeseredy, "Left Realist Criminology: Strengths, Weaknesses, and the Feminist Critique," *Crime, Law, and Social Change*, vol. 15, no. 1 (January 1991), pp. 51–72; W.S. DeKeseredy and B.D. MacLean, "Exploring the Gender, Race, and Class Dimensions of Victimization: A Left Realist Critique of the Canadian Urban Victimization Survey," *International Journal of Offender Therapy and Comparative Criminology*, vol. 35, no. 2 (Summer 1991), pp. 143–161; and W.S. DeKeseredy and M.D. Schwartz, "British and U.S. Left Realism: A Critical Comparison," *International Journal of Offender Therapy and Comparative Criminology*, vol. 35, no. 3 (Fall 1991), pp. 248–262.

36. See Jock Young, "The Failure of Criminology: The Need for a Radical Realism," in R. Matthews and J. Young, eds., *Confronting Crime* (Beverly Hills, CA: SAGE, 1986), pp. 4–30; Jock Young, "The Tasks of a Realist Criminology," *Contemporary Crisis*, vol. 11, no. 4 (1987), pp. 337–356; and "Radical Criminology in Britain: The Emergence of a Competing Paradigm," *British Journal of Criminology*, vol. 28 (1988), pp. 159–183.

37. D. Brown and R. Hogg, "Essentialism, Radical Criminology, and Left Realism," *Australian and New Zealand Journal of Criminology*, vol. 25 (1992), pp. 195–230.

38. Roger Matthews and Jock Young, "Reflections on Realism," in Jock Young and Roger Matthews, eds., *Rethinking Criminology: The Realist Debate* (Newbury Park, CA: SAGE, 1992).

39. Don C. Gibbons, *Talking about Crime and Criminals: Problems and Issues in Theory Development in Criminology* (Englewood Cliffs, NJ: Prentice Hall, 1994), p. 170.

40. Piers Beirne and James W. Messerschmidt, *Criminology* (New York: Harcourt Brace Jovanovich, 1991), p. 501.

41. Gibbons, *Talking about Crime and Criminals*, p. 165, citing Loraine Gelsthorpe and Alison Morris, "Feminism and Criminology in Britain," *British Journal of Criminology* (Spring 1988), pp. 93–110.

42. Sally S. Simpson, "Feminist Theory, Crime and Justice," *Criminology*, vol. 27, no. 4 (1989), p. 605.

43. Roslyn Muraskin and Ted Alleman, eds., *It's a Crime: Women and Justice* (Upper Saddle River, NJ: Prentice Hall, 1993), p. 1.

44. As stated in Amanda Burgess-Proctor, "Intersections of Race, Class, Gender, and Crime: Future Directions for Feminist Criminology," *Feminist Criminology*, vol. 1, no. 27 (2006), p. 29.

45. Carol Pateman, "Feminist Critiques of the Public/Private Dichotomy," in Anne Phillips, ed., *Feminism and Equality* (Oxford, UK: Blackwell, 1987).

46. F.P. Williams III and M.D. McShane, *Criminological Theory* (Upper Saddle River, NJ: Prentice Hall, 1994), p. 238.

47. Ibid.

48. Burgess-Proctor, "Intersections of Race, Class, Gender, and Crime," p. 29.

49. James W. Messerschmidt, *Capitalism, Patriarchy, and Crime: Toward a Socialist Feminist Criminology* (Totowa, NJ: Rowman and Littlefield, 1986).

50. Freda Adler, *Sisters in Crime: The Rise of the New Female Criminal* (New York: McGraw-Hill, 1975).

51. Rita James Simon, *Women and Crime* (Lanham, MD: Rowman & Littlefield, 1975).

52. Damien Cave, "Mexico's Drug War, Feminized," *New York Times*, August 13, 2011.

53. Carol Smart, *Women, Crime and Criminology: A Feminist Critique* (London: Routledge, 1977).

54. Kathleen Daly and Meda Chesney-Lind, "Feminism and Criminology," *Justice Quarterly*, vol. 5, no. 5 (December 1988), pp. 497–535.

55. The following list is adapted from Daly and Chesney-Lind, "Feminism and Criminology," pp. 497–535.

56. Susan Caulfield and Nancy Wonders, "Gender and Justice: Feminist Contributions to Criminology," in Gregg Barak, ed., *Varieties of Criminology: Readings from a Dynamic Discipline* (Westport, CT: Praeger, 1994), pp. 213–229.

57. John Hagan, *Structural Criminology* (New Brunswick, NJ: Rutgers University Press, 1989), p. 130.

58. Ibid.

59. Evelyn K. Sommers, *Voices from Within: Women Who Have Broken the Law* (Toronto: University of Toronto Press, 1995).

60. Daly and Chesney-Lind, "Feminism and Criminology," p. 506.

61. Ibid.

62. Ibid.

63. For an intriguing analysis of how existing laws tend to criminalize women and their reproductive activities, see Susan O. Reed, "The Criminalization of Pregnancy: Drugs, Alcohol, and AIDS," in Muraskin and Alleman, eds., *It's a Crime*, pp. 92–117; and Drew Humphries, "Mothers and Children, Drugs and Crack: Reactions to Maternal Drug Dependency," in Muraskin and Alleman, eds., *It's a Crime*, pp. 131–145.

64. Dawn H. Currie, "Feminist Encounters with Postmodernism: Exploring the Impasse of the Debates on Patriarchy and Law," *Canadian Journal of Women and the Law*, vol. 5, no. 1 (1992), p. 10.

65. For an excellent overview of feminist theory in criminology, and for a comprehensive review of research regarding female offenders, see Joanne Belknap, *The Invisible Woman: Gender Crime and Justice* (Belmont, CA: Wadsworth, 1996).

66. Such studies are still ongoing and continue to add to the descriptive literature of feminist criminology. See, for example, Deborah R. Baskin and Ira Sommers, "Female Initiation into Violent Street Crime," *Justice Quarterly*, vol. 10, no. 4 (December 1993), pp. 559–583; Scott Decker, Richard Wright, Allison Redfern, and Dietrich Smith, "A Woman's Place Is in the Home: Females and Residential Burglary," *Justice Quarterly*, vol. 10, no. 1 (March 1993), pp. 143–162; and Jill L. Rosenbaum, "The Female Delinquent: Another Look at the Role of the Family," in Muraskin and Alleman, eds., *It's a Crime*, pp. 399–420.

67. Ronald L. Akers, *Criminological Theories: Introduction and Evaluation* (Los Angeles, CA: Roxbury, 1994), p. 39.

68. Karen Heimer, "Changes in the Gender Gap in Crime and Women's Economic Marginalization," in *The Nature of Crime: Continuity and Change*, vol. 1 of *Criminal Justice 2000* (Washington, DC: National Institute of Justice, 2000), p. 428.

69. Daly and Chesney-Lind, "Feminism and Criminology," p. 512.

70. Cited in Allison Morris, *Women, Crime and Criminal Justice* (New York: Blackwell, 1987).

71. For examples of how this might be accomplished, see F.H. Knopp, "Community Solutions to Sexual Violence: Feminist/Abolitionist Perspectives," in Harold E. Pepinsky and Richard Quinney, eds., *Criminology as Peacemaking* (Bloomington: Indiana University Press, 1991), pp. 181–193; and S. Caringella-MacDonald and D. Humphries, "Sexual Assault, Women, and the Community: Organizing to Prevent Sexual Violence," in Pepinsky and Quinney, eds., *Criminology as Peacemaking*, pp. 98–113.

72. Richard Quinney, "Life of Crime: Criminology and Public Policy as Peacemaking," *Journal of Crime and Justice*, vol. 16, no. 2 (1993), pp. 3–9.

73. See, for example, Harold E. Pepinsky, "This Can't Be Peace: A Pessimist Looks at Punishment," in W.B. Groves and G. Newman, eds., *Punishment and Privilege* (Albany, NY: Harrow and Heston, 1986); Harold E. Pepinsky, "Violence as Unresponsiveness: Toward a New Conception of Crime," *Justice Quarterly*, vol. 5 (1988), pp. 539–563; and Pepinsky and Quinney, eds., *Criminology as Peacemaking*.

74. See, for example, Richard Quinney, "Crime, Suffering, Service: Toward a Criminology of Peacemaking," *Quest*, vol. 1 (1988), pp. 66–75; Richard Quinney, "The Theory and Practice of Peacemaking in the Development of Radical Criminology," *Critical Criminologist*, vol. 1, no. 5 (1989), p. 5; and Richard Quinney and John Wildeman, *The Problem of Crime: A Peace and Social Justice Perspective*, 3rd ed. (Mayfield, CA: Mountain View Press, 1991), originally published as *The Problem of Crime: A Critical Introduction to Criminology* (New York: Bantam, 1977).

75. All these themes are addressed, for example, in Pepinsky and Quinney, eds., *Criminology as Peacemaking*.

76. Richard Quinney and John Wildeman, *The Problem of Crime: A Critical Introduction to Criminology* (New York: Harper & Row, 1977), pp. vii–viii.

77. Bo Lozoff and Michael Braswell, *Inner Corrections: Finding Peace and Peace Making* (Cincinnati, OH: Anderson, 1989).

78. Clemmons Bartollas and Michael Braswell, "Correctional Treatment, Peacemaking, and the New Age Movement," *Journal of Crime and Justice*, vol. 16, no. 2 (1993), pp. 43–58.

79. Ibid.

80. E.A. Fattah, "Restorative and Retributive Justice Models: A Comparison," in H.H. Kuhne, ed., *Festschrift fur Koichi Miyazawa* (Baden-Baden, DE: Nomos Verlagsgesllschaft, 1995).

81. J. Bonta, S. Wallace-Capretta, and J. Rooney, *Restorative Justice: An Evaluation of the Restorative Justice Project*, User Report 1998–05 (Ottawa: Solicitor General Canada, 1998). See also *Restorative Justice in Canada: A Consultation Paper*, Department of Justice Canada, May 2000.

82. Robin Dann, *Restorative Justice Initiatives in South Eastern Alberta* (unpublished paper, 2000). See also Heino Lilles, Territorial Judge, Whitehorse, Yukon, *Circle Sentencing: Part of the Restorative Justice Continuum*, Plenary Speaker, August 9, 2002, Third International Conference on Conferencing, August 8–10, 2002, Minneapolis, Minnesota.

83. Bonta et al., *Restorative Justice*.

84. "Restorative Resolutions," The John Howard Society of Manitoba website, 2006, http://www.johnhoward.mb.ca/pages/home.php [Accessed January 24, 2012].

85. Michael J. Lynch and W. Byron Groves, *A Primer in Radical Criminology*, 2nd ed. (Albany, NY: Harrow and Heston, 1989), p. 128.

Chapter 11

1. National Crime Prevention Council (NCPC), "Working Together for Safer Communities," National Crime Prevention Strategy (Ottawa: NCPC, 1997).
2. "The Stockholm Criminology Symposium," Stockholm University website, http://www.su.se/english/about/prizes-awards/the-stockholm-prize-in-criminology [Accessed August 1, 2016].
3. John Ekstedt, "Canadian Justice Policy," in Margaret A. Jackson and Curt T. Griffiths, eds., Canadian Criminology: Perspectives on Crime and Criminality (Toronto: Harcourt Brace Canada, 1995), p. 311.
4. James E. Anderson, Public Policymaking: An Introduction (Boston: Houghton Mifflin, 1990).
5. Ekstedt, "Canadian Justice Policy," p. 308.
6. Ibid., p. 312.
7. Nancy E. Marion, A History of Federal Crime Control Initiatives, 1960–1993 (Westport, CT: Praeger, 1994), p. 3. For a more detailed analysis of the process by which crime-control policies are created, see Paul Rock, "The Opening Stages of Criminal Justice Policy Making," British Journal of Criminology, vol. 35, no. 1 (Winter 1995).
8. Ekstedt, "Canadian Justice Policy," p. 308.
9. Jeff Ferrell, "Criminological Verstehen: Inside the Immediacy of Crime," Justice Quarterly, vol. 14, no. 1 (1997), p. 16.
10. Troy Q. Riddell, "What Can Political Science Contribute to the Study of Criminal Justice in Canada?" Canadian Journal of Criminology and Criminal Justice, vol. 52, no. 3 (June 2010), p. 321.
11. For an excellent discussion of the policies associated with law, punishment, and social control, see Thomas G. Blomberg and Stanley Cohen, eds., Punishment and Social Control: Essays in Honor of Sheldon L. Messinger (Hawthorne, NY: Aldine de Gruyter, 1995).
12. From an address to the Standing Committee on Justice and the Solicitor General, 1993.
13. Department of Justice Canada, The National Strategy on Community Safety and Crime Prevention: Building Safer Communities, http://www.acsacaah.ca/Portals/0/Member/PDF/en/documents/nationalstrat.pdf [Accessed April 7, 2012].
14. Kathleen Harris, "Supreme Court Strikes Down 2 Conservative Sentencing Reforms," CBC News, April 15, 2016, http://www.cbc.ca/news/politics/supreme-court-sentencing-mandatory-minumums-1.3537150 [Accessed August 1, 2016].
15. Liberal Party of Canada website, https://www.liberal.ca/realchange/bill-c-51/ [Accessed August 1, 2106].
16. Bryan Vila, "A General Paradigm for Understanding Criminal Behavior: Extending Evolutionary Ecological Theory," Criminology, vol. 32, no. 3 (August 1994), pp. 311–359.
17. Bryan Vila, "Could We Break the Crime Control Paradox?" Paper presented at the annual meeting of the American Society of Criminology, Miami, Florida, November 1994 [abstract].
18. Bryan Vila, "Human Nature and Crime Control: Improving the Feasibility of Nurturant Strategies," Politics and the Life Sciences, March 1997, p. 10.
19. Ibid., pp. 3–21.
20. Vila, "A General Paradigm."
21. Vila, "Human Nature and Crime Control," p. 11.
22. Information for this section has been obtained from Public Safety Canada website, http://www.publicsafety.gc.ca/cnt/cntrng-crm/crm-prvntn/index-en.aspx [Accessed August 4, 2016].
23. Dean Beeby, "Harper Government Withholds Millions Targeted for Crime Prevention," CBC News, October 16, 2015, http://www.cbc.ca/news/politics/harper-government-withholds-millions-budgeted-for-crime-prevention-1.3272773 [Accessed August 7, 2016].
24. C. Ray Jeffery, Crime Control Through Environmental Design (Beverley Hills, CA: SAGE, 1971).
25. Royal Canadian Mounted Police, Crime Control Through Environmental Design, March 16, 2011, http://www.rcmp-grc.gc.ca/pubs/ccaps-spcca/safecomm-seccollect-eng.htm [Accessed April 7, 2012].
26. Peel Regional Police, Fact Sheet: Crime Prevention Through Environmental Design, May 2008, http://www.peelpolice.on.ca/en/crimeprevention/resources/cpted.pdf [Accessed August 7, 2016].
27. CPTED Ontario, "What Is CPTED?" http://cptedontario.ca/mission/what-is-cpted/ [Accessed August 7, 2016].
28. CPTED Ontario, 2016 CPTED Ontario Conference, http://cptedontario.ca/2016-conference/ [Accessed August 7, 2016].
29. Harris, "Supreme Court Strikes Down 2 Conservative Sentencing Reforms."
30. H. Bianchi, Position and Subject-Matter of Criminology (Amsterdam: North Holland Pub., 1956).
31. Hermann Mannheim, Comparative Criminology (New York: Houghton Mifflin, 1965), p. 18.
32. Brandon C. Welsh, "Evidence-Based Crime Prevention: Scientific Basis, Trends, Results and Implications for Canada," Research Report, National Crime Prevention Centre.
33. Public Safety Canada, June 2007, https://www.publicsafety.gc.ca/cnt/rsrcs/pblctns/vdnc-prvntn/vdnc-prvntn-eng.pdf [Accessed August 7, 2016].
34. Canadian Society of Evidence Based Policing, http://www.can-sebp.net/ [Accessed August 7, 2016].
35. Brandon C. Welsh, "Evidence-Based Crime Prevention: Scientific Basis, Trends, Results and Implications for Canada."

Chapter 12

1. Eileen Skinnider, "Some Recent Criminal Justice Reforms in Canada—Examples of Responding to Global and Domestic Pressures." Paper presented at The Canada China Procuratorate Reform Cooperation Programme Lecture Series, Xi'an, and Lanzhou, China, August 2005 and The 1st Session of the International Forum on Contemporary Criminal Law, Criminal Law Reform in the Era of Globalization International Community's Experience and Its Inspiration to China, Beijing, China, August 2005.
2. Europol, "Global Action against Dark Markets on Tor Network," November 7, 2014, https://www.europol.europa.eu/content/global-action-against-dark-markets-tor-network [Accessed August 10, 2016].
3. U.S. Dept. of Justice, press release, "More than 400 Onion Addresses, Including Dozens of 'Dark Market' Sites, Targeted as Part of Global Enforcement Action on Tor Network," November 7, 2014.
4. Frank Schmalleger, Criminology Today: An Integrative Introduction (Upper Saddle River, NJ: Pearson Education, 2017), p. 410.
5. Ibid.
6. United Nations Office on Drugs and Crime, United Nations Convention against Transnational Organized Crime and the Protocols Thereto, 2004, http://www.unodc.org/documents/treaties/UNTOC/Publications/TOC%20Convention/TOCebook-e.pdf [Accessed August 10, 2016].

7. Criminal Intelligence Service Canada, *2009 Report on Organized Crime*, http://publications.gc.ca/collections/collection_2009/sp-ps/PS61-1-2009E.pdf [Accessed August 10, 2016].

8. United Nations Office on Drugs and Crime (UNODC), "Migrant Smuggling," 2004, http://www.unodc.org/unodc/en/human-trafficking/smuggling-of-migrants.html [Accessed August 10, 2016].

9. Raimo Väyrynen, "Illegal Immigration, Human Trafficking, and Organized Crime," United Nations University/World Institute for Development Economics Research, Discussion Paper No. 2003/72 (October 2003), p. 16.

10. Kristiina Kangaspunta, "Mapping the Inhuman Trade: Preliminary Findings of the Database on Trafficking in Human Beings," *Forum on Crime and Society*, vol. 3, nos. 1 and 2 (2003), p. 83.

11. United Nations Office on Drugs and Crime (UNDOC), *Global Report on Trafficking in Persons 2014*, http://www.unodc.org/documents/data-and-analysis/glotip/GLOTIP_2014_full_report.pdf [Accessed August 10, 2016].

12. Ibid.

13. Ibid.

14. U.S. Department of State, *Trafficking in Persons Report* (Washington, DC: State Department, 2014), p. 45.

15. United Nations Office on Drugs and Crime (UNODC), *Global Report on Trafficking in Persons, 2012*, p. 3, http://www.unodc.org/documents/data-and-analysis/glotip/Trafficking_in_Persons_2012_web.pdf [Accessed August 10, 2016].

16. RCMP Criminal Intelligence, *Human Trafficking in Canada*, March 2012, p. 44, http://publications.gc.ca/collections/collection_2011/grc-rcmp/PS64-78-2010-eng.pdf [Accessed August 10, 2016].

17. RCMP, *Gazette*, vol. 66, no. 3 (2004).

18. UNODC, *Global Report on Trafficking in Persons, 2012*, p. 91.

19. RCMP, *Gazette*, vol. 66, no. 2 (2004).

20. Rosemary Barton, "Chinese Cyberattack Hits Canada's National Research Council," *CBC News*, July 29, 2014, http://www.cbc.ca/news/politics/chinese-cyberattack-hits-canada-s-national-research-council-1.2721241 [Accessed August 10, 2016].

21. From Canadian Centre for Justice Statistics, Cyber-Crime: Issues, Data Sources, and Feasibility of Collecting Police-Reported Statistics by Melanie Kowalski, published by Statistics of Canada. © 2002.

22. Ibid.

23. Catherine H. Conley and J. Thomas McEwen, "Computer Crime," *NIJ Reports* (January/February 1990).

24. Richard H. Baker, *The Computer Security Handbook* (Blue Ridge Summit, PA: TAB Books, 1985).

25. Business Software Alliance, "BSA Global Software Survey, 2016," http://globalstudy.bsa.org/2016/ [Accessed August 10, 2016].

26. Stephen R. Purdy, "Protecting Your Telephone Systems against Dial Tone Thieves," *Infosecurity News*, July/August, 1993, p. 43.

27. Paul Keegan, "High Tech Pirates Collecting Phone Calls," *USA Today*, September 23, 1994, p. 4A.

28. Ibid.

29. Fraser Lovatt, "U.S. Department of Justice: VoIP Fosters Crime, Drugs and Terrorism," *Digital-Lifestyles.info*, June 18, 2004, http://digital-lifestyles.info/2004/06/18/us-department-of-justice-voip-fosters-crime-drugs-and-terrorism/ [Accessed January 1, 2013].

30. The Anti-Phishing Working Group, *Phishing Activity Trends*, April 2007, http://www.antiphishing.org/reports/apwg_report_april_2007.pdf [Accessed August 10, 2016].

31. The Anti-Phishing Working Group, *Global Phishing Survey: Trends and Domain Name Use in 1H 2012*, http://docs.apwg.org/reports/APWG_Global_Phishing_Report_1H_2014.pdf [Accessed August 10, 2016].

32. Donn B. Parker, *Computer Crime: Criminal Justice Resource Manual* (Washington, DC: National Institute of Justice, 1989).

33. Sam Jones and Hannah Kuchler, "World's Most Advanced Hacking Spyware Let Loose," *Financial Times*, November 23, 2014.

34. For insight into how security techniques often lag behind the abilities of criminal perpetrators in the high-technology arena, see James A. Fagin, "Computer Crime: A Technology Gap," *International Journal of Comparative and Applied Criminal Justice*, vol. 15, nos. 1 and 2 (Spring/Fall 1991), pp. 285–297.

35. Eureka Aerospace, "High-Power Compact Microwave Source for Vehicle Immobilization: Final Report," U.S. Department of Justice, National Institute of Justice, April 20, 2006, https://www.ncjrs.gov/pdffiles1/nij/grants/236756.pdf [Accessed August 10, 2016].

36. The Liberty Coalition, "Carnivore/DCS–1000," http://www.libertycoalition.net/backgrounders/carnivore-dcs-1000 [Accessed June 17, 2007].

37. "The Council of Europe's Convention on Cyber-Crime," Electronic Privacy Information Center, 2005, http://www.epic.org/privacy/intl/ccc.html [Accessed August 10, 2016].

38. Kowalski, *Cyber-Crime*.

39. Dave Seglins and Lynn Burgess, "Canada 'Failing' in Fight against Cybercrime, Hacking," *CBC News*, November 24, 2015, http://www.cbc.ca/news/technology/canada-cybercrime-hacking-seglins-1.3312153 [Accessed August 10, 2016].

40. Ibid.

Glossary

Alloplastic adaptation A form of adjustment that results from changes in the environment surrounding an individual.

Anomie A social condition in which norms are uncertain or lacking.

Applied research Research based on scientific inquiry that is designed and carried out with practical application in mind.

Assault The intentional or threatened application of force on another person without consent. The categories of assault include level 1—assault or common assault; level 2—assault that involves the use of a weapon or that causes bodily harm; and level 3—assault that results in wounding or endangering the life of the victim.

Atavism A term used by Cesare Lombroso to suggest that criminals are physiological throwbacks to earlier stages of human evolution.

Autoplastic adaptation A form of adjustment that results from changes within an individual.

Behaviour theory A psychological perspective positing that behaviour that is rewarded will increase in frequency and behaviour that is punished will decrease in frequency.

Behaviourism A psychological perspective that stresses observable behaviour and disregards unobservable events that occur in the mind.

Biological theory A theory that maintains that the basic determinants of human behaviour, including criminality, are constitutionally or physiologically based and often inherited.

Biosocial criminology A theoretical perspective that sees the interaction between biology and the physical and social environments as key to understanding human behaviour, including criminality.

Born criminal An individual who is born with a genetic predilection toward criminality.

Bourgeoisie The "haves," or the class of people that owns the means of production, in Marxist theory.

Breaking and entering The unlawful entry of a place to commit an indictable offence.

Broken window thesis A perspective on crime that holds that physical deterioration in an area leads to increased concerns for personal safety among area residents and to higher crime rates in that area.

Canadian Victims Bill of Rights Federal legislation establishing statutory rights to information, protection, participation, and *to seek restitution* for victims of crime.

Capable guardian One who effectively discourages crime; effective deterrents to criminal activity.

Capital punishment The legal imposition of a sentence of death upon a convicted offender.

Case study An investigation into an individual case.

Chicago school of criminology An ecological approach to explaining crime that examines how social disorganization contributes to social pathology.

Circle sentencing conferences Groups of community members who actively assist justice authorities by participating in discussions about available sentencing options and plans to reintegrate the offender back into the community.

Classical school A criminological perspective of the late 18th and early 19th centuries that had its roots in the Enlightenment and held that men and women are rational beings, that crime is the result of the exercise of free will, and that punishment can be effective in reducing the incidence of crime to the degree that it negates the pleasure to be derived from crime commission.

Cognitive information-processing theory A psychological perspective that involves the study of human perceptions, information processing, and decision making.

Cohort analysis A social scientific technique that studies a population that shares common characteristics over time. Cohort analysis usually begins at birth and traces the development of cohort members until they reach a certain age.

Common law Law originating from usage and custom rather than from written statutes. The term refers to non-statutory customs, traditions, and precedents that help guide judicial decision making.

Community policing A philosophy of policing involving proactive collaboration between the police and the community to prevent and respond to crime and other community problems.

Community sentencing panels Groups composed of volunteers from the community who focus on restorative measures such as restitution, reparation, mediation, and victim involvement.

Computer virus A set of computer instructions that propagates copies or versions of itself into computer programs or data when it is executed.

Conditioning A psychological principle that holds that the frequency of any behaviour can be increased or decreased through reward, punishment, or association with other stimuli.

Conduct norms Shared expectations of a social group relative to personal conduct.

Conflict perspective An analytical approach to social organization that holds that conflict is a fundamental aspect of social life and can never be fully resolved.

Confounding effect A rival explanation, or competing hypothesis, that is a threat to the internal or external validity of a research design.

Consensus perspective An analytical perspective on social organization that holds that laws should be enacted to criminalize given forms of behaviour when members of society generally agree that such laws are necessary.

Constitutional theories Theories that explain criminality by reference to offenders' body types, inheritance, genetics, or external observable physical characteristics.

Containment Aspects of the social bond that act as a stabilizing force to prevent individuals from committing crimes and that keep them from engaging in deviance.

Containment theory A form of social control theory that suggests a series of both internal and external factors contributes to law-abiding behaviour.

Controlled experiment An experiment that attempts to hold conditions (other than the intentionally introduced experimental intervention) constant.

Correctional psychology The branch of forensic psychology concerned with the diagnosis and classification of offenders, the treatment of correctional populations, and the rehabilitation of inmates and other law violators.

Correlation A causal, complementary, or reciprocal relationship between two measurable variables.

Counterfeiting Any unauthorized reproduction of a thing with the intention that it be accepted as genuine. It can thus refer to anything that is capable of reproduction, including things that are subjects of rights of private property. It also includes the reproduction of documents for identification, such as passports, or any paper that represents value (e.g., stamps, travellers' cheques, or negotiable instruments).

Crime Human conduct in violation of the criminal laws of the federal government or a provincial or local jurisdiction that has the power to make such laws.

Crime Prevention Through Environmental Design (CPTED) A crime-prevention strategy based on the premise that the proper design and effective use of the built environment can lead to a reduction in the incidence and fear of crime.

Crime rate Crime per capita based on the number of recorded crimes calculated per 100 000 population.

Criminal anthropology The scientific study of the relationship between human physical characteristics and criminality.

Criminal behaviour Human behaviour, both intentional and negligent, that violates criminal law. It may include a failure to act when there is a legal obligation to do so.

Criminal harassment Also known as *stalking*, the repeated following, watching, or communicating with a person or someone known to the person in a way that causes that person to fear for his or her safety or for the safety of someone known to him or her.

Criminal justice The scientific study of crime, the criminal law, and components of the criminal justice system, including the police, courts, and corrections.

Criminal justice system The various agencies of justice, especially police, courts, and corrections, whose goal it is to apprehend, convict, sanction, and rehabilitate law violators.

Criminalist A specialist in the collection and examination of the physical evidence of crime.

Criminality A behavioural predisposition that disproportionately favours criminal activity.

Criminalize To make illegal.

Criminaloid A term used by Cesare Lombroso to describe occasional criminals who were pulled into criminality primarily by environmental influences.

Criminogenic needs Dynamic attributes (also known as *dynamic risk factors*) of offenders and their circumstances that are associated with rates of recidivism.

Criminologist One who is trained in the field of criminology; also, one who studies crime, criminals, and criminal behaviour.

Criminology An interdisciplinary profession built around the scientific study of crime and criminal behaviour, including their forms, causes, legal aspects, prevention, and control.

Criminology of place or environmental criminology A perspective that emphasizes the importance of geographic location and architectural features as they are associated with the prevalence of criminal victimization.

Critical criminology A perspective that holds that crime is the natural product of a capitalist system.

Culture conflict theory A sociological perspective on crime that suggests that the root cause of criminality can be found in a clash of values between variously socialized groups over what is acceptable or proper behaviour.

Cybercrime Any crime that involves a computer as the object of the crime or as the tool used to commit a material component of the offence.

Data confidentiality The ethical requirement of social scientific research to protect the confidentiality of individual research participants while preserving justified research access to the information participants provide.

DCS–3000 An FBI-developed network diagnostic tool that is capable of assisting in criminal investigations by monitoring and capturing large amounts of internet traffic.

Defensible space The range of mechanisms that combine to bring an environment under the control of its residents.

Demographics The characteristics of population groups, usually expressed in statistical form.

Determinate sentencing A criminal punishment strategy that mandates a specified and fixed amount of time to be served for every offence category. Under the strategy, for example, all offenders convicted of the same degree of robbery would be sentenced to the same length of time behind bars.

Deterrence The prevention of crime.

Deterrence strategy A crime-prevention strategy that attempts to diminish motivation for crime by increasing the perceived certainty, severity, or celerity of penalties.

Deviant behaviour Human activity that violates social norms.

Deviant places theory A spatially oriented theory of victimization that suggests that victimization occurs most frequently in socially disorganized, high-crime areas and that people become victims as a result of their exposure to such areas.

Differential association The sociological thesis that criminality, like any other form of behaviour, is learned through a process of association with others who communicate criminal values.

Displacement A shift of criminal activity from one spatial location to another.

Dizygotic (DZ) twin A twin who develops from a separate ovum and who carries the genetic material shared by siblings.

Ecological theory A type of sociological approach that emphasizes demographics (the characteristics of population groups) and geographics (the mapped location of such groups relative to one another) and sees the social disorganization that characterizes delinquency areas as a major cause of criminality and victimization.

Ectomorph A body type described as thin and fragile, with long, slender, poorly muscled extremities and delicate bones.

Ego   The reality-testing part of the personality, also called the *reality principle*. More formally, this personality component is conscious, most immediately controls behaviour, and is most in touch with external reality.

Endomorph   A body type described as soft and round or overweight.

Eugenic criminology   A perspective that holds that the root causes of criminality are passed from generation to generation in the form of "bad genes."

Eugenics   The study of hereditary improvement by genetic control.

Evidence-based criminology   A form of contemporary criminology that uses rigorous social scientific techniques, especially randomized, controlled experiments and the systematic review of research results.

Evolutionary ecology   An approach to understanding crime that draws attention to the ways people develop over the course of their lives.

Family group conferencing   A forum for dealing with unanswered questions, emotions, and the victim's right to restitution and reparation resulting from a crime.

Feminist criminology   A corrective model intended to redirect the thinking of mainstream criminologists to include gender awareness.

First-degree murder   Culpable homicide that is planned and deliberate.

Focal concerns   The key values of any culture, especially a delinquent subculture.

Folkways   Time-honoured customs. Although folkways carry the force of tradition, their violation is unlikely to threaten the survival of the group.

Forensic psychiatry   A branch of psychiatry having to do with the study of crime and criminality.

Forensic psychology   The application of the science and profession of psychology to questions and issues relating to law and the legal system. Also called *criminal psychology*.

General deterrence   A goal of criminal sentencing that seeks to prevent others from committing crimes similar to the one for which a particular offender is being sentenced.

General theory   A theory that attempts to explain all (or at least most) forms of criminal conduct through a single overarching approach.

General theory of crime   The assertion that the operation of a single mechanism, low self-control, accounts for "all crime, at all time," including acts ranging from vandalism to homicide, from sexual assault to white-collar crime.

Genetic determinism   The belief that genes are the major determining factor in human behaviour.

Globalization   A process of social homogenization by which the experiences of everyday life, marked by the diffusion of commodities and ideas, can foster a standardization of cultural expressions around the world.

Hacker   A person who uses computers for exploration and exploitation.

Hard determinism   The belief that crime results from forces beyond the control of the individual.

Hate crime   A criminal act directed toward a person or group because of race, national or ethnic origin, religion, language, colour, sex, age, sexual orientation, or mental or physical disability. Also referred to as *hate-motivated crime*, or *bias crime*.

Hedonistic calculus or utilitarianism   The belief, first proposed by Jeremy Bentham, that behaviour holds value to any individual undertaking it according to the amount of pleasure or pain that it can be expected to produce for that person.

Homicide   When a person, directly or indirectly, by any means, causes the death of a human being. Homicide can be culpable or non-culpable.

Human genome   A complete copy of the entire set of human gene instructions.

Human smuggling   A type of illegal immigration in which an agent is paid to help a person cross a border clandestinely.

Hypoglycemia   A medical condition characterized by low blood sugar.

Id   The aspect of the personality from which drives, wishes, urges, and desires emanate. More formally, this division of the psyche is associated with instinctual impulses and demands for immediate satisfaction of primitive needs.

Identity fraud   Fraudulently personating another person, living or dead, with intent to gain advantage for themselves or another person, to obtain any property or an interest in any property, to cause disadvantage to the person being personated or another person, to avoid arrest or prosecution, or to obstruct, pervert, or defeat the course of justice.

Identity theft   Knowingly obtaining or possessing another person's identity information with the intent of using the information to commit an indictable offence that includes fraud, deceit, or falsehood as an element of the offence.

Illegitimate opportunity structure   A subcultural pathway to success that is disapproved of by the wider society.

Incapacitation   The use of imprisonment or other means to reduce the likelihood that an offender will be capable of committing future offences.

Infanticide   When a female considered disturbed from the effects of giving birth causes the death of her newborn child (under one year old).).

Informed consent   The ethical requirement of social scientific research that research subjects be informed as to the nature of the research about to be conducted, their anticipated role in it, and the uses to which the data they provide will be put.

Instrumental Marxism   A perspective that holds that those in power intentionally create laws and social institutions that serve their own interests and that keep others from becoming powerful.

Integrated theory   An explanatory perspective that merges (or attempts to merge) concepts drawn from different sources.

Italian school of criminology   A perspective on criminology developed in the late 1800s that held that criminals can be identified by physical features and are throwbacks to earlier stages of human evolution.

Juke family   A well-known "criminal family" studied by Richard L. Dugdale.

Just deserts model   The notion that criminal offenders deserve the punishment they receive at the hands of the law and that punishments should be appropriate to the type and severity of the crime committed.

Kallikak family   A well-known "criminal family" studied by Henry H. Goddard.

Labelling theory An interactionist perspective that sees continued crime as a consequence of limited opportunities for acceptable behaviour that follow from the negative responses of society to those defined as offenders.

Left realism A social conflict perspective that insists on a pragmatic assessment of crime and its associated problems.

Left-realist criminology An approach to criminology based on ideas inherent in the perspectives of left realism.

Liberal feminism A feminist perspective in criminology that sees gender-role socialization as the primary source of women's oppression.

Life course perspective A perspective that draws attention to the fact that criminal behaviour tends to follow a distinct pattern across the life cycle. Also called life course criminology.

Mala in se An act that is thought to be wrong in and of itself.

Mala prohibita An act that is wrong only because it is prohibited.

Manslaughter All non-intentional homicide.

Marxist feminism A perspective in feminist criminology that sees the oppression of women as caused by their subordinate class status within capitalist societies.

Mass murder The illegal killing of four or more victims at one location, within one event.

McNaughten rule A standard for judging legal insanity that requires that offenders did not know what they were doing, or if they did, that they did not know it was wrong.

Mental disorder (legal) A legally established inability to understand right from wrong or to conform one's behaviour to the requirements of the law. Also, a defence allowable in criminal courts.

Mental disorder (psychological) Disease of the mind, including schizophrenia, paranoia, senile dementia, melancholia, various types of epilepsy, and delirium tremens caused by alcohol abuse.

Mesomorph A body type described as athletic and muscular.

Monozygotic (MZ) twin A twin who develops from the same egg and who carries virtually the same genetic material.

Moral enterprise The efforts made by an interest group to have its sense of propriety enacted into law.

Mores Behavioural proscriptions covering potentially serious violations of a group's values. Examples might include strictures against murder, sexual assault, and robbery.

Motivated offender The population of potential criminal offenders in a given area.

Motor vehicle theft The taking of a vehicle without the owner's authorization. A motor vehicle is defined as a car, truck, van, bus, recreational vehicle, semi-trailer truck, motorcycle, construction machinery, agricultural machinery, or other land-based motor vehicle (such as a go-kart, snowmobile, all-terrain vehicle, or dune buggy).

Murder When a person intentionally causes the death of another human being or intends to cause bodily harm likely to result in death.

National Crime Prevention Strategy (NCPS) A federal crime-prevention initiative designed to create safer communities by supporting community-based crime-prevention efforts, enhancing communities' knowledge and experience with respect to crime prevention, and fostering partnerships and collaboration.

Natural law The philosophical perspective that certain immutable laws are fundamental to human nature and can be readily ascertained through reason. Human-made laws, in contrast, are said to derive from human experience and history—both of which are subject to continual change.

Natural rights Rights that, according to natural law theorists, individuals retain in the face of government action and interests.

Neoclassical criminology A contemporary version of classical criminology that emphasizes deterrence and retribution, with reduced emphasis on rehabilitation.

Neurosis A functional disorder of the mind or of the emotions involving anxiety, phobia, or other abnormal behaviour.

Not criminally responsible on account of mental disorder (NCRMD) A finding that offenders are responsible for committing the offence that they have committed and, because of their prevailing mental condition, should be sent to a psychiatric hospital for treatment rather than to prison.

Nurturant strategy A crime-prevention strategy that attempts to forestall development of criminality by improving early life experiences and channelling child and adolescent development into desirable directions.

Operant behaviour Behaviour that affects the environment so as to produce responses or further behavioural cues.

Paradigm An example, model, or theory.

Paranoid schizophrenic A schizophrenic individual who suffers from delusions and hallucinations.

Participant observation A strategy in data gathering in which the researcher observes a group by participating, to varying degrees, in the activities of the group.

Participatory justice A relatively informal type of justice case processing that makes use of local community resources rather than requiring traditional forms of official intervention.

Patriarchy The tradition of male dominance.

Peace model An approach to crime control that focuses on effective ways for developing a shared consensus on critical issues that have the potential to seriously affect the quality of life.

Peacemaking criminology A perspective that holds that crime-control agencies and the citizens they serve should work together to alleviate social problems and human suffering and thus reduce crime.

Personality The characteristic patterns of thoughts, feelings, and behaviours that make a person unique and that tend to remain stable over time. Personality influences an individual's thoughts, behaviours, and emotions.

Phishing An internet-based scam to steal valuable information, such as credit card numbers, social insurance numbers, user IDs, and passwords.

Phone phreak A person who uses switched, dialled-access telephone services for exploration and exploitation.

Phrenology The study of the shape of the head to determine anatomical correlates of human behaviour.

Pluralist perspective An analytical approach to social organization that holds that a multiplicity of values and beliefs exists in any complex society but that most social actors agree on the usefulness of law as a formal means of dispute resolution.

Positivism The application of scientific techniques to the study of crime and criminals.

Postmodern feminism A perspective in modern criminology that questions the social construction of concepts typically used in discussions of crime and justice.

Primary deviance The initial deviance often undertaken to deal with transient problems in living.

Primary research Research characterized by original and direct investigation.

Proletariat The "have-nots," or the working class, in Marxist theory.

Prostitution Most commonly used to refer to the illegal activities of publicly communicating with another person for the purposes of buying or selling sexual services, material benefit from sexual services, or advertising sexual services.

Protection/avoidance strategy A crime-prevention strategy that attempts to reduce criminal opportunities by changing people's routine activities, increasing guardianship, or incapacitating convicted offenders.

Psychiatric criminology A theory that is derived from the medical sciences (including neurology) and that, like other psychological theories, focuses on the individual as the unit of analysis. Psychiatric theories form the basis of psychiatric criminology.

Psychoanalysis The theory of human psychology founded by Sigmund Freud based on the concepts of the unconscious, resistance, repression, sexuality, and the Oedipus complex.

Psychological profiling The attempt to categorize, understand, and predict the behaviour of certain types of offenders based on behavioural clues they provide; also called *criminal profiling* and *behavioural profiling*.

Psychopath An individual who has a personality disorder, especially one manifested in aggressively anti-social behaviour, and who is lacking in empathy.

Psychopathy A personality disorder characterized by anti-social behaviour and a failure to feel remorse or guilt.

Psychosis A form of mental illness in which sufferers are said to be out of touch with reality.

Psychotherapy A form of psychiatric treatment based on psychoanalytical principles and techniques.

Public policy Government-formulated directives made on behalf of the public good to solve a problem or achieve an end.

Punishments Undesirable behavioural consequences likely to decrease the frequency of occurrence of that behaviour.

Pure research Research undertaken simply for the sake of advancing scientific knowledge.

Qualitative method A research technique that produces subjective results, or results that are difficult to quantify.

Quantitative method A research technique that produces measurable results.

Quasi-experimental design An approach to research that, although less powerful than an experimental design, is deemed worthy of use when better designs are not feasible.

Radical criminology A perspective that holds that the causes of crime are rooted in social conditions empowering the wealthy and the politically well organized but disenfranchising the less fortunate.

Radical feminism A perspective that sees patriarchy as the cause of women's oppression.

Rape myth A false assumption about sexual assault, such as "When a woman says no, she really means yes."

Rational choice theory A perspective holding that criminality is the result of conscious choice and predicting that individuals choose to commit crime when the benefits outweigh the costs of disobeying the law.

Reaction formation The process by which a person openly rejects that which he or she wants or aspires to but cannot obtain or achieve.

Recidivism The repetition of criminal behaviour.

Recidivism rate The percentage of convicted offenders who have been released from prison and who are later rearrested for a new crime.

Reintegrative shaming A form of shaming, imposed as a sanction by the criminal justice system, that is thought to strengthen the moral bond between the offender and the community.

Research The use of standardized, systematic procedures in the search for knowledge.

Research design The logic and structure inherent in an approach to data gathering.

Restitution A criminal sanction, in particular the payment of compensation by the offender to the victim.

Restorative justice A perspective that stresses solutions and restoration rather than imprisonment, punishment, and neglect of victims.

Retribution The act of taking revenge upon a criminal perpetrator.

Rewards Desirable behavioural consequences likely to increase the frequency of occurrence of that behaviour.

Robbery The unlawful taking or attempted taking of property that is in the immediate possession of another by threatened or actual use of force or violence.

Routine activities theory A theory that examines the interaction of motivated offenders, capable guardians, and suitable targets as an explanation for crime, and which suggests that an individual's everyday activities contribute significantly to the likelihood of his or her criminal victimization.

Routine activities theory or lifestyle theory A brand of rational choice theory posited by Lawrence Cohen and Marcus Felson that suggests that lifestyles contribute significantly to both the volume and the type of crime found in any society.

Safe Streets and Communities Act Canadian legislation that introduces changes to the *Criminal Code of Canada*, including increased penalties for sexual offences against children and for drug crimes, denial of release for violent and repeat young offenders, adult sentences for and the publication of the names of youths convicted of the most serious crimes, and the reduction of judicial discretion in sentencing for crimes involving serious personal injury, which carry a maximum prison term of 14 years or more.

Schizophrenia A serious mental illness that distorts the way a person thinks, feels, and behaves. Primary features of schizophrenia include the inability to distinguish between real and imagined experiences and the inability to think logically.

Scripts Generalized knowledge about specific types of situations that is stored in the mind.

Secondary analysis The reanalysis of existing data.

Secondary deviance The deviant behaviour that results from official labelling and from association with others who have been so labelled.

Secondary research Research based on new evaluations of existing information collected by other researchers.

Secondary victimization Social injuries that occur not as a direct result of a criminal act but through the response of social institutions and individuals to the victim.

Second-degree murder All murder that is not first-degree murder.

Selective incapacitation A social policy that seeks to protect society by incarcerating those individuals deemed to be the most dangerous.

Self-report A research investigation of subjects in order to record and report their behaviours.

Serial murder Culpable homicide that involves the killing of several victims in three or more separate events.

Serotonin A neurotransmitter that is commonly found in the pineal gland, the digestive tract and intestines, the central nervous system, and the blood platelets.

Sexual assault An assault committed in circumstances of a sexual nature such that the sexual integrity of the victim is violated. The categories of sexual assault include level 1—assault that violates the sexual integrity of a person; level 2—sexual assault that involves a weapon, bodily harm, or threats to cause bodily harm to a person; and level 3—sexual assault that wounds, maims, disfigures, or endangers the life of another person.

Situational choice theory A brand of rational choice theory that views criminal behaviour "as a function of choices and decisions made within a context of situational constraints and opportunities."

Situational crime prevention A social policy approach that looks to develop greater understanding of crime and more effective crime-prevention strategies through concern with the physical, organizational, and social environments that make crime possible.

Social bond The link, created through socialization, between individuals and the society of which they are a part.

Social class A distinction made between individuals on the basis of important social characteristics.

Social conflict perspective An analytical perspective on social organization that holds that conflict is a fundamental aspect of social life and can never fully be resolved.

Social contract The Enlightenment-era concept that human beings abandon their natural state of individual freedom to join together and form society. In the process of forming a social contract, individuals surrender some freedoms to society as a whole, and government, once formed, is obligated to assume responsibilities toward its citizens and to provide for their protection and welfare.

Social control theories The perspectives predicting that when social constraints on anti-social behaviour are weakened or absent, delinquent behaviour emerges. Rather than stressing causative factors in criminal behaviour, social control theory asks why people actually obey rules instead of breaking them.

Social development theories An integrated perspective on human development that simultaneously examines many different levels of development—psychological, biological, familial, interpersonal, cultural, societal, and ecological.

Social disorganization A condition said to exist when a group is faced with social change, uneven development of culture, maladaptiveness, disharmony, conflict, and lack of consensus.

Social disorganization theory A perspective on crime and deviance that sees society as a kind of organism and crime and deviance as a kind of disease or social pathology.

Social ecology An approach to criminological theorizing that attempts to link the structure and organization of a human community to interactions with its localized environment.

Social learning theory A perspective that places primary emphasis on the role of communication and socialization in the acquisition of learned patterns of criminal behaviour and the values that support that behaviour.

Social life The ongoing (typically) structured interaction—including socialization and social behaviour in general—that occurs between persons in a society.

Social policy A government initiative, program, or plan intended to address problems in society.

Social problems perspective The belief that crime is a manifestation of underlying social problems such as poverty, discrimination, pervasive family violence, inadequate socialization practices, and the breakdown of traditional social institutions.

Social process The interaction between and among social institutions, groups, and individuals.

Social process theory A theory that asserts that criminal behaviour is learned in interaction with others and that the socialization processes that occur as a result of group membership are the primary route through which this learning occurs. Also called interactionist theory.

Social relativity The notion that social events are differently interpreted according to the cultural experiences and personal interests of the initiator, the observer, or the recipient of that behaviour.

Social responsibility perspective The belief that individuals are fundamentally responsible for their own behaviour and that they choose crime over other, more law-abiding, courses of action.

Social structure The pattern of social organization and the interrelationships among institutions characteristic of a society.

Social structure theory A theory that explains crime by reference to the economic and social arrangements in society. This type of theory emphasizes relationships among social institutions and describes the types of behaviour that tend to characterize groups of people rather than individuals.

Socialist feminism A perspective in modern criminology that sees gender oppression as a consequence of the interaction between the economic structure of society and gender-based roles.

Socialization The lifelong process of social experience whereby individuals acquire the cultural patterns of their society.

Sociobiology The systematic study of the biological basis of all social behaviour.

Sociological theory A perspective that focuses on the nature of the power relationships between social groups and on the influences that various social phenomena bring to bear on the types of behaviours that tend to characterize groups of people.

Sociopath An individual who has a personality disorder, especially one manifested in aggressively anti-social behaviour, and who is lacking in empathy. Also called *secondary psychopaths*, sociopaths may have been born "normal," but personal experiences they have in early life cause them to develop psychopathic characteristics.

Soft determinism The belief that human behaviour is the result of choices and decisions made within a context of situational constraints and opportunities.

Software piracy The unauthorized and illegal copying of software programs.

Somatotyping The classification of human beings into types according to body build and other physical characteristics.

Specific deterrence A goal of criminal sentencing that seeks to prevent a particular offender from engaging in repeat criminality.

Statistical school A criminological perspective with roots in the early 19th century that seeks to uncover correlations between crime rates and other types of demographic data.

Statute A formal written enactment of a legislative body.

Statutory law Law in the form of statutes or formal written strictures made by a legislature or governing body with the power to make law.

Stigmatic shaming A form of shaming, imposed as a sanction by the criminal justice system, that is thought to destroy the moral bond between the offender and the community.

Stigmatized neighbourhoods Residential areas with bad reputations that hold little attraction for those who can afford to live elsewhere.

Strain theory A sociological approach that posits a disjuncture between socially and subculturally sanctioned means and goals as the cause of criminal behaviour.

Structural Marxism A perspective that holds that the structural institutions of society influence the behaviour of individuals and groups by virtue of the type of relationships created.

Subcultural theory A sociological perspective that emphasizes the contribution made by variously socialized cultural groups to the phenomenon of crime.

Subculture A collection of values and preferences that is communicated to subcultural participants through a process of socialization.

Sublimation The psychological process whereby one aspect of consciousness comes to be symbolically substituted for another.

Suitable target Something or someone of value to offenders in a criminal offence.

Superego The moral aspect of the personality, much like the conscience. More formally, this division of the psyche develops by the incorporation of the perceived moral standards of the community, is mainly unconscious, and includes the conscience.

Supermale A male individual displaying the XYY chromosome structure.

Survey research Research using a social science data-gathering technique that involves the use of questionnaires.

Tagging The process whereby an individual is negatively defined by agencies of justice.

Target hardening The reduction in criminal opportunity for a particular location, generally through the use of physical barriers, architectural design, and enhanced security measures.

Techniques of neutralization Culturally available justifications that can provide criminal offenders with the means to disavow responsibility for their behaviour.

Terrorism An act committed in whole or in part for a political, religious, or ideological purpose, objective, or cause with the intention of intimidating the public with regard to its security, including its economic security, or compelling a person, a government, or a domestic or an international organization to do or to refrain from doing any act.

Testosterone The primary male sex hormone. It is produced in the testes, and its function is to control secondary sex characteristics and sexual drive.

The Enlightenment A social movement that arose during the 17th and 18th centuries and built upon ideas such as empiricism, rationality, free will, humanism, and natural law.

Theft The act of dishonestly taking property belonging to another person with the intention of depriving its owner of it either permanently or temporarily.

Theory A series of interrelated propositions that attempt to describe, explain, predict, and ultimately control some class of events. A theory gains explanatory power from inherent logical consistency and is "tested" by how well it describes and predicts reality.

Trafficking in persons (TIP) The exploitation of unwilling or unwitting people through force, coercion, threat, or deception.

Transnational crime An unlawful activity undertaken and supported by organized groups operating across national boundaries.

Tribalism The attitudes and behaviour that results from strong feelings of identification with one's own social group.

Truth in sentencing A collection of different but related public policy stances on sentencing of those convicted of crimes in the justice system.

Twelve Tables Early Roman laws written circa 450 BCE that regulated family, religious, and economic life.

Typologies of crime Classifications of crime are useful in identifying patterns of criminal activity and motivations for criminal behaviour.

Variable A concept that can undergo measurable changes.

Victim impact statement A written document that describes the losses, suffering, and trauma experienced by the crime victim or by the victim's survivors. Judges are expected to consider these effects in arriving at an appropriate sentence for the offender.

Victim precipitation Any contribution made by the victim to the criminal event, especially one that led to its initiation.

Victim surcharge A mandatory, judicial imposition of a monetary fine administered in addition to a criminal sentence and used to finance victim services.

Victim/Witness Assistance Program A program in Ontario that counsels victims, orients them to the justice process, and provides a variety of other services, such as transportation to court, child care during court appearances, and referrals to social service agencies.

Victimization Survey First conducted as the Canadian Urban Victimization Survey in 1981 by Statistics Canada and then every five years since 1988 as part of the General Social Survey. It provides data on surveyed households reporting that they had been affected by crime.

Victim–Offender Reconciliation Program (VORP) A program that gives the offender the opportunity to meet face-to-face with the victim in the presence of a trained mediator in an attempt to reduce the victim's fears while establishing accountability and reparation by the offender for the crime.

Victimogenesis The contribution to victimization made by the background of a victim.

Victimologist One who studies victims and the process of criminal victimization.

Victimology The scientific study of crime victims and the victimization process.

Violent Crime Linkage Analysis System (ViCLAS) A centralized computer bank containing details of violent crimes that assists police in recognizing patterns among violent offences and offenders.

Name Index

Subject Index

A

Aboriginal peoples
  circle sentencing conferences, 282, 283–284
  ecological theory regarding, 217–218
  justice initiatives for, 28
  offender profile of, 65
  Oka crisis, 266–267
  over-representation in criminal justice system, 63–65, 64f
  sweat lodges, 300
  victimization of, 65
abortion, 128
activation, 256
An Act Respecting Victims of Crime-Victims' Bill of Rights, 109
adaptation, crime as, 196
Adding Insult to Injury report, 108
Additional Protocol to the Convention on Cybercrime, 328
administrative law, 4b
adolescent development, 255f
Aftermath of Murder: Survivor Stories, 113b
age, criminal behaviour and, 59–61, 60f, 61b
Age of Reason, 126–128
aggravation, 256
Aggregate Uniform Crime Reporting Survey, 47–49
aggression
  biological roots of, 167–168
  social cognition theory of, 191
  stress and, 196
alcohol, prenatal exposure, 164
alloplastic adaptation., 196
All Writs Act of 1789, 122
Andrew Moffitt Memorial Scholarship, 101
Annual Report on Organized Crime, 231
anomie, 220
Anti-Fraud Centre, 329
Anti-Phishing Working Group (APWG),, 323
Anti-Terrorism Act, 296, 297
applied research, 20
arrests, 34
assault, 82, 281
Assessing Violence Against Women: A Statistical Profile, 55
assisted suicide, 4–5
atavism, 152, 153, 154–155
attachment, 253
Australian and New Zealand Journal of Criminology, 16

authority conflict pathway to delinquency, 258
automated fingerprint identification system (AFIS), 326
automated vehicle location (AVL) systems, 325
autonomy, 224
autoplastic adaptation, 196

B

Bank of Canada polymer series, 91–93, 92b
behavioural conditioning, 189
behaviourism, 182
behaviour theory
  behavioural conditioning, 189
  classical conditioning, 188–189
  defined, 189
  social conditioning/role modelling, 190–191
belief, 253
Big Five trait model, 188
Bill C-10. *See Safe Streets and Communities Act*
Bill C-24, 231
Bill C-25, 142
Bill C-32, 109
Bill C-36, 93
Bill C-393, 101
Bill C-51, 296, 297
Bill S-7, 96
biological theories
  applied, 175
  biological roots of aggression, 167–168
  biosocial criminology, 170–172
  body chemistry, 161–167
  constitutional theories, 155–156
  criminal families, 156–157
  critique of, 173–174
  defined, 150
  environmental pollution, 163–164
  genetics, 151–161
  hormones, 164–167
  Human Genome Project, 159–161
  ingested substances/nutrition, 161–163
  introduction, 149–150
  Italian school, 152–155
  major principles of, 150–151, 150t
  physical features, 151–152
  policy implications of, 173
  twin studies, 158–159
  XYY supermale, 157–158
biometrics, 327b
biosocial criminology, 170–172
The Blank Slate: The Modern Denial of Human Nature (Pinker), 173

body chemistry, criminal behaviour and, 161–167
born criminals (atavism), 152, 153, 154–155
bourgeoisie, 269
breaking and entering, 86–87, 87f
British Journal of Criminology, 16
British Journal of Psychiatry, 149
broken windows thesis, 218
Business Software Alliance, 321

C

Canada, social problems perspective and, 296
Canada's Prisons Are the New Residential Schools (Maclean's), 63–65
Canadian Centre for Justice Statistics (CCJS), 24, 46, 46b
Canadian Charter of Rights and Freedoms, 5, 93, 126, 143, 297, 320
Canadian Crime Prevention Through Environmental Design model (CPTED), 45
Canadian Journal of Criminology and Criminal Justice, 16
Canadian Journal of Law and Society, 16
Canadian Journal of Women and the Law, Criminology, 16
Canadian Resource Centre for Victims of Crime, 102
Canadian Society of Evidence Based Policing (CAN-SEBP), 309
Canadian Statement of Basic Principles of Justice for Victims of Crime, 109
Canadian Urban Victimization Survey (CUVS), 51
Canadian Victims Bill of Rights, 109, 110b, 118
cannabis
  decriminalization of, 95–96
  prenatal exposure, 163
cannibalism, 179–180
capable guardians, 103
capital punishment, 139–140
Carter v. Canada, 5, 5f
case studies, 23
causes, of crime, 32–36, 33f
Causes of Delinquency (Hirschi), 253
Chicago Area Project, 234
Chicago school of criminology, 216–218, 216f
child abuse
  adult violence and, 160–161
  defining/recording, 51
  sexual violations, 79
child pornography, 79